USING
J2SE 7.0

FOURTH
EDITION

DATA STRUCTURES & OTHER OBJECTS

Using Java™

MICHAEL MAIN

University of Colorado at Boulder

Boston Columbus Indianapolis New York San Francisco Upper Saddle River
Amsterdam Cape Town Dubai London Madrid Milan Munich Paris Montreal Toronto
Delhi Mexico City Sao Paulo Sydney Hong Kong Seoul Singapore Taipei Tokyo

Editorial Director: Marcia Horton
Editor in Chief: Michael Hirsch
Acquisitions Editor: Tracy Dunkelberger
Editorial Assistants: Stephanie Sellinger/Emma Snider
Director of Marketing: Patrice Jones
Marketing Manager: Yezan Alayan
Marketing Coordinator: Kathryn Ferranti
Vice President, Production: Vince O'Brien
Managing Editor: Jeff Holcomb
Associate Managing Editor: Robert Engelhardt

Manufacturing Manage: Nick Sklitsis
Operations Specialist: Lisa McDowell
Creative Director: Jayne Conte
Cover Designer: Bruce Kenselaar
Manager, Rights and Permissions: Karen Sanatar
Cover Art: © Shutterstock/Ford Prefect
Media Editor: Dan Sandin
Printer/Binder: RR Donnelley, Harrisonburg
Cover Printer: RR Donnelley, Harrisonburg

Credits and acknowledgments borrowed from other sources and reproduced, with permission, in this textbook appear on the appropriate page within text.

Java is a trademark of the Oracle Corporation, 500 Oracle Parkway, Redwood Shores, CA 94065.

Many of the designations by manufacturers and sellers to distinguish their products are claimed as trademarks. Where those designations appear in this book, and the publisher was aware of a trademark claim, the designations have been printed in initial caps or all caps.

Library of Congress Cataloging-in-Publication Data

Main, M. (Michael)
    Data structures & other objects using Java : using J2SE 7.0 / Michael
Main.-- 4th ed.
        p. cm.
    Includes bibliographic references and index.
    ISBN 978-0-13-257624-6 (alk. paper)
    1. Java (Computer program language) 2. Data structures (Computer
science)
    I. Title. II. Title: Data structures and other objects using Java.

QA76.73.J38M33 2012
005.13'3--dc23

2011037942

www.pearsonhighered.com

ISBN-10: 0-13-257624-4
ISBN-13: 978-0-13257624-6

5 2020

Preface

Java provides programmers with an immediately attractive forum. With Java and the World Wide Web, a programmer's work can have quick global distribution with appealing graphics and a marvelous capability for feedback, modification, software reuse, and growth. Certainly, Java's other qualities have also contributed to its rapid adoption: the capability to implement clean, object-oriented designs; the familiarity of Java's syntactic constructs; the good collection of ready-to-use features in the Java Class Libraries. But it's the winsome ways of the World Wide Web that have pulled Java to the front for both experienced programmers and the newcomer entering a first-year computer science course.

With that said, it's satisfying to see that the core of the first-year courses remains solid even as courses start using Java. The proven methods of representing and using data structures remain vital to beginning programmers in a data structures course, even as the curriculum is shifting to accommodate an object-oriented approach.

This book is written for just such an evolving data structures course, with the students' programming carried out in Java. The text's emphasis is on the *specification*, *design*, *implementation*, and *use* of the basic data types that are normally covered in a second-semester, object-oriented course. There is wide coverage of important programming techniques in recursion, searching, and sorting. The text also provides coverage of big-O time analysis of algorithms, an optional appendix on writing an interactive applet to test an implementation of a data structure, using Javadoc to specify precondition/postcondition contracts, and a new introduction to the increasingly important topic of concurrency.

The text assumes that the student has already had an introductory computer science and programming class, but we do include coverage of those topics (such as the Java Object type and a precise description of parameter passing) that are not always covered completely in a first course. The rest of this preface discusses ways that this material can be covered, starting with a brief review of how contemporary topics from earlier editions are intermixed with new material from the new Java 2 Standard Edition 7.0.

New to the Fourth Edition

This edition retains contemporary topics from earlier editions that define a coherent approach to the implementation and use of data structures in Java. These topics, listed below, have been updated to align with the latest software engineering practices suggested by the designers and implementors of Java 2 Standard Edition 7.0. The most important of these topics are listed here:

- **Better input/output support** (Chapter 1 and Appendix B) continues in this edition, including formatted output (with the `System.out.printf` method) and the input of primitive values (with the `java.util.Scanner` class). Our earlier input and output classes (`EasyReader` and `Format-Writer`) are still available online at www.cs.colorado.edu/~main/edu/colorado/io.

- **Earlier integration of the Java Class Libraries** begins in Chapter 2 of this edition. Although the emphasis of this textbook remains on the underlying design and implementation of classic data structures, we've found it increasingly important to give students significant exposure to the elements of class libraries. We begin this process in Section 2.5 with the easy-to-use `BigInteger` class. Chapters 3 to 5 give more examples that use the Java Class Libraries, including `Arrays`, `HashSet`, `ArrayList`, `LinkedList`, `ListIterator`, and others.

- **A modified approach to generic collection classes** occurs in Chapter 5 of this edition. Starting with J2SE 5.0, generic methods and generic classes allowed libraries to depend on an unspecified underlying data type (that we'll call E). Originally, collection classes were often implemented with arrays in which the component type was an unspecified generic type (i.e., a private member variable of type E[ ]).

  Over the years, it was recognized that the E[ ] practice had a potential pitfall: We could use a typecast to pretend that we had that kind of array, but at run time, the program really had an array of Java objects (i.e., a private member variable of type `Object[ ]`, which by design contains only E objects). Within the generic class itself, this type mismatch did not cause a problem (because generic types are not checked at run time). But if the generic class provides the array to an outside application, then the possibility of a runtime type error existed.

  The solution, eloquently written about by Neal Gafter, is for the generic class to use an array of Java objects (rather than an array of type E[ ]) along with specific programming practices (described in Chapter 5) that ensure that unchecked typecasts cannot lead to runtime type errors. Starting in Chapter 5 and continuing throughout the rest of the textbook, we now use this new approach for all of our generic classes.

- **Variable arity methods** (Chapter 3) allow a method to have a variable number of arguments. Generic classes have special considerations for variable arity methods that are newly discussed in Chapter 5 of this edition.

- **Enhanced for-loops** (Chapters 3 and 5) were introduced in the previous edition of this textbook. They allow easy iteration through the elements of an array, through a collection of elements that has implemented the `Iterable` interface, or through the elements of an enum type.

- **Autoboxing and auto-unboxing** of primitive values (Chapter 5) continue to be used in this edition to allow the storage and retrieval of primitive data values (such as an `int`) in Java's generic collections (such as the `Vector`).

- **Java's priority queue** (Chapter 7) has been added as a new topic in the fourth edition.

- **The binary search and sort methods from the Java Class Libraries** have a new presentation in Chapters 11 (searching) and 12 (sorting).

- **The important new topic of concurrency** is introduced through a concurrent sort in Chapter 12. The approach uses the `RecursiveAction` and `ForkJoinPool` classes from Java2SE 7, which provides an extremely clean introduction with very few distractions for the first-year student.

- **Covariant return types** allow the return type of an overridden inherited method to be any descendant class of the original return type. We use this idea for clone methods throughout the text, thereby avoiding a typecast with each use of a clone method and increasing type security. The larger use of the technique is postponed until the chapter on inheritance (Chapter 13).

- **Enum types** (Chapter 13) provide a convenient way to define a new data type whose objects may take on a small set of discrete values.

Beyond these new, coherent language features, the fourth edition of this text presents the same foundational data structures material as the earlier editions. In particular, the data structures curriculum emphasizes the ability to specify, design, and analyze data structures independently of any particular language, as well as the ability to implement new data structures and use existing data structures in any modern language. You'll see this approach in the first four chapters as students review Java and then go on to study and implement the most fundamental data structures (bags and sequence classes) using both arrays and linked-list techniques that are easily applied to any high-level language.

Chapter 5 is a bit of a departure, bringing forward several Java-specific techniques that are particularly relevant to data structures: how to build generic collection classes based on Java's new generic types, using Java interfaces and the API classes, and building and using Java iterators. Although much of the subse-

new material on Java interfaces and the API classes

quent material can be taught without these Java features, this is a natural time for students to learn them.

Later chapters focus on particular data structures (stacks, queues, trees, hash tables, graphs) or programming techniques (recursion, sorting techniques, inheritance). The introduction of recursion is delayed until just before the study of trees. This allows us to introduce recursion with some simple but meaningful examples that do more than just tail recursion. This avoids the mistaken first impression that some students get of recursion being some kind of magic loop. After the first simple examples (including one new example for this edition), students see significant examples involving two recursive calls in common situations with binary trees.

new projects for trees and other areas

Trees are particularly emphasized in this text, with Chapter 10 taking the students through two meaningful examples of data structures that use balanced trees (the heap project and the B-tree project). Additional projects for trees and other areas have also been added online at `http://cssupport.pearsoncmg.com.`.

Other new Java features have been carried over from the third edition of the text as needed: the use of assertions to check preconditions, a more complete coverage of inheritance, a new example of an abstract class to build classes that play two-player strategy games such as Othello or Connect Four, an introduction to new classes of the Java API (now in the generic form of `ArrayList`, `Vector`, `HashMap`, and `Hashtable`), and new features of Javadoc.

All these new bells and whistles of Java are convenient, and students need to be up-to-date—but it's the approaches to designing, specifying, documenting, implementing, using, and analyzing the data structures that will have the most enduring effect on your students.

The Five Steps for Each Data Type

The book's core consists of the well-known data types: *sets*, *bags* (or *multisets*), *sequential lists*, *stacks*, *queues*, *tables*, and *graphs*. There are also additional supplemental data types, such as a priority queue. Some of the types are approached in multiple ways, such as the bag class that is first implemented by storing the elements in an array and is later reimplemented using a binary search tree. Each of the data types is introduced following a pattern of five steps.

Step 1: Understand the Data Type Abstractly. At this level, a student gains an understanding of the data type and its operations through concepts and pictures. For example, a student can visualize a stack and its operations of pushing and popping elements. Simple applications are understood and can be carried out by hand, such as using a stack to reverse the order of letters in a word.

Step 2: Write a Specification of the Data Type as a Java Class. In this step, the student sees and learns how to write a specification for a Java class that can implement the data type. The specification, written using the Javadoc tool, includes headings for the constructors, public methods, and sometimes other public features (such as restrictions tied to memory limitations). The heading of each method is presented along with a precondition/postcondition contract that completely specifies the behavior of the method. At this level, it's important for the students to realize that the specification is not tied to any particular choice of implementation techniques. In fact, this same specification may be used several times for several different implementations of the same data type.

Step 3: Use the Data Type. With the specification in place, students can write small applications or applets to show the data type in use. These applications are based solely on the data type's specification because we still have not tied down the implementation.

Step 4: Select Appropriate Data Structures and Proceed to Design and Implement the Data Type. With a good abstract understanding of the data type, we can select an appropriate data structure, such as an array, a linked list of nodes, or a binary tree of nodes. For many of our data types, a first design and implementation will select a simple approach, such as an array. Later, we will redesign and reimplement the same data type with a more complicated underlying structure.

Because we are using Java classes, an implementation of a data type will have the selected data structures (arrays, references to other objects, etc.) as private instance variables of the class. In my own teaching, I stress the necessity for a clear understanding of the rules that relate the private instance variables to the abstract notion of the data type. I require each student to write these rules in clear English sentences that are called the *invariant of the abstract data type*. Once the invariant is written, students can proceed to implementing various methods. The invariant helps in writing correct methods because of two facts: (a) Each method (except the constructors) knows that the invariant is true when the method begins its work; and (b) each method is responsible for ensuring that the invariant is again true when the method finishes.

Step 5: Analyze the Implementation. Each implementation can be analyzed for correctness, flexibility, and time analysis of the operations (using big-*O* notation). Students have a particularly strong opportunity for these analyses when the same data type has been implemented in several different ways.

Where Will the Students Be at the End of the Course?

At the end of our course, students understand the data types inside out. They know how to use the data types and how to implement them in several ways. They know the practical effects of the different implementation choices. The students can reason about efficiency with a big-*O* analysis and can argue for the correctness of their implementations by referring to the invariant of the ADT.

the data types in this book are cut-down versions of the Java Class Libraries

One of the lasting effects of the course is the specification, design, and implementation experience. The improved ability to reason about programs is also important. But perhaps most important of all is the exposure to classes that are easily used in many situations. The students no longer have to write everything from scratch. We tell our students that someday they will be thinking about a problem, and they will suddenly realize that a large chunk of the work can be done with a bag, a stack, a queue, or some such. And this large chunk of work is work that they won't have to do. Instead, they will pull out the bag or stack or queue that they wrote this semester—using it with no modifications. Or, more likely, they will use the familiar data type from a library of standard data types, such as the proposed *Java Class Libraries*. In fact, the behavior of some data types in this text is a cut-down version of the JCL, so when students take the step to the real JCL, they will be on familiar ground—from the standpoint of how to use the class and also having a knowledge of the considerations that went into building the class.

Other Foundational Topics

Throughout the course, we also lay a foundation for other aspects of "real programming," with coverage of the following topics beyond the basic data structures material.

Object-Oriented Programming. The foundations of object-oriented programming are laid by giving students a strong understanding of Java classes. The important aspects of classes are covered early: the notion of a method, the separation into private and public members, the purpose of constructors, and a small exposure to cloning and testing for equality. This is primarily covered in Chapter 2, some of which can be skipped by students with a good exposure to Java classes in the CS1 course.

Further aspects of classes are introduced when the classes first use dynamic arrays (Chapter 3). At this point, the need for a more sophisticated clone method is explained. Teaching this OOP method with the first use of dynamic memory has the effect of giving the students a concrete picture of how an instance variable is used as a reference to a dynamic object such as an array.

Conceptually, the largest innovation of OOP is the software reuse that occurs via inheritance. There are certainly opportunities for introducing inheritance right from the start of a data structures course (such as implementing a set class as a descendant of a bag class). However, an early introduction may also result in students juggling too many new concepts at once, resulting in a weaker understanding of the fundamental data structures. Therefore, in my own course, I introduce inheritance at the end as a vision of things to come. But the introduction to inheritance (Sections 13.1 and 13.2) could be covered as soon as classes are understood. With this in mind, some instructors may wish to cover Chapter 13 earlier, just before stacks and queues, so that stacks and queues can be derived from another class.

Another alternative is to identify students who already know the basics of classes. These students can carry out an inheritance project (such as the ecosystem of Section 13.3), while the rest of the students first learn about classes.

Java Objects. The Java `Object` type lies at the base of all the other Java types—or at least almost all the other types. The eight primitive types are not Java objects, and for many students, the CS1 work has been primarily with the eight primitive types. Because of this, the first few data structures are collections of primitive values, such as a bag of integers or a sequence of double numbers.

Iterators. Iterators are an important part of the Java Class Libraries, allowing a programmer to easily step through the elements in a collection class. The `Iteratable` interface is introduced in Chapter 5. Throughout the rest of the text, iterators are not directly used, although they provide a good opportunity for programming projects, such as using a stack to implement an iterator for a binary search tree (Chapter 9).

Recursion. First-semester courses often introduce students to recursion. But many of the first-semester examples are tail recursion, where the final act of the method is the recursive call. This may have given students a misleading impression that recursion is nothing more than a loop. Because of this, I prefer to avoid early use of tail recursion in a second-semester course.

So, in our second-semester course, we emphasize recursive solutions that use more than tail recursion. The recursion chapter provides four examples along these lines. Two of the examples—generating random fractals and traversing a maze—are big hits with the students. The fractal example runs as a graphical applet, and although the maze example is text based, an adventurous student can convert it to a graphical applet. These recursion examples (Chapter 8) appear just before trees (Chapter 9) since it is within recursive tree algorithms that recursion becomes vital. However, instructors who desire more emphasis on recursion can move that topic forward, even before Chapter 2.

In a course that has time for advanced tree projects (Chapter 10), we analyze the recursive tree algorithms, explaining the importance of keeping the trees balanced—both to improve worst-case performance and to avoid potential execution stack overflow.

Searching and Sorting. Chapters 11 and 12 provide fundamental coverage of searching and sorting algorithms. The searching chapter reviews binary search of an ordered array, which many students will have seen before. Hash tables are also introduced in the search chapter by implementing a version of the JCL hash table and also a second hash table that uses chaining instead of open addressing. The sorting chapter reviews simple quadratic sorting methods, but the majority of the chapter focuses on faster algorithms: the recursive merge sort (with worst-case time of $O(n \log n)$), Tony Hoare's recursive quicksort (with average-time $O(n \log n)$), and the tree-based heapsort (with worst-case time of $O(n \log n)$).

Advanced Projects, Including Concurrency

The text offers good opportunities for optional projects that can be undertaken by a more advanced class or by students with a stronger background in a large class. Particular advanced projects include the following:

- Interactive applet-based test programs for any of the data structures (outlined in Appendix I).
- Implementing an iterator for the sequence class (see Chapter 5 Programming Projects).
- Writing a deep clone method for a collection class (see Chapter 5 Programming Projects).
- Writing an applet version of an application program (such as the maze traversal in Section 8.2 or the ecosystem in Section 13.3).
- Using a stack to build an iterator for the binary search tree (see Chapter 9 Programming Projects).
- A priority queue implemented as an array of ordinary queues (Section 7.4) or implemented using a heap (Section 10.1).
- A set class implemented with B-trees (Section 10.2). I have made a particular effort on this project to provide sufficient information for students to implement the class without need of another text. Advanced students have successfully completed this project as independent work.
- Projects to support concurrent sorting in the final section of Chapter 12.
- An inheritance project, such as the ecosystem of Section 13.3.
- A graph class and associated graph algorithms in Chapter 14. This is another case in which advanced students may do work on their own.

Java Language Versions

All the source code in the book has been tested to work correctly with Java 2 Standard Edition Version 7.0, including new features such as generics and new concurrency support. Information on all of the Java products from Sun Microsystems is available at http://java.sun.com/products/index.html.

Flexibility of Topic Ordering

This book was written to give instructors latitude in reordering the material to meet the specific background of students or to add early emphasis to selected topics. The dependencies among the chapters are shown on the next page. A line joining two boxes indicates that the upper box should be covered before the lower box.

Here are some suggested orderings of the material:

Typical Course. Start with Chapters 1–9, skipping parts of Chapter 2 if the students have a prior background in Java classes. Most chapters can be covered in a week, but you may want more time for Chapter 4 (linked lists), Chapter 8 (recursion), or Chapter 9 (trees). Typically, I cover the material in 13 weeks,

Chapter Dependencies

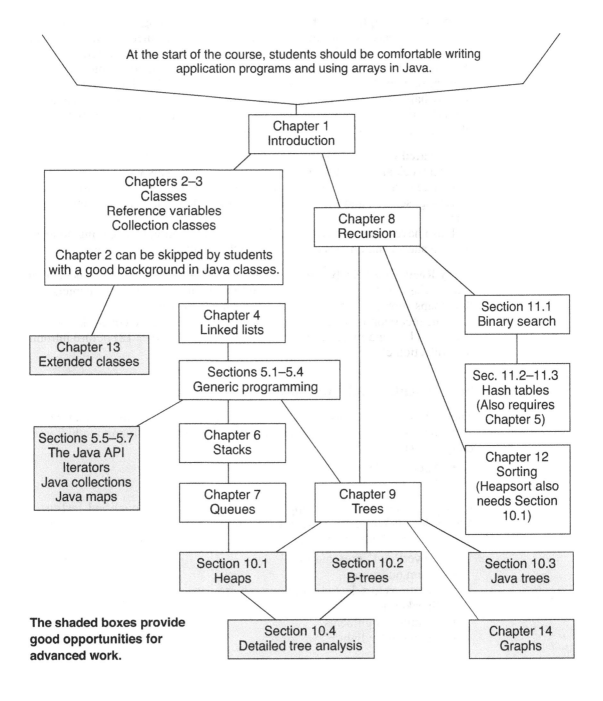

At the start of the course, students should be comfortable writing application programs and using arrays in Java.

Chapter 1
Introduction

Chapters 2–3
Classes
Reference variables
Collection classes

Chapter 2 can be skipped by students with a good background in Java classes.

Chapter 8
Recursion

Section 11.1
Binary search

Chapter 4
Linked lists

Chapter 13
Extended classes

Sections 5.1–5.4
Generic programming

Sec. 11.2–11.3
Hash tables
(Also requires Chapter 5)

Sections 5.5–5.7
The Java API
Iterators
Java collections
Java maps

Chapter 6
Stacks

Chapter 12
Sorting
(Heapsort also needs Section 10.1)

Chapter 7
Queues

Chapter 9
Trees

Section 10.1
Heaps

Section 10.2
B-trees

Section 10.3
Java trees

The shaded boxes provide good opportunities for advanced work.

Section 10.4
Detailed tree analysis

Chapter 14
Graphs

including time for exams and extra time for linked lists and trees. Remaining weeks can be spent on a tree project from Chapter 10 or on binary search (Section 11.1) and sorting (Chapter 12).

Heavy OOP Emphasis. If students will cover sorting and searching elsewhere, then there is time for a heavier emphasis on object-oriented programming. The first three chapters are covered in detail, and then derived classes (Section 13.1) are introduced. At this point, students can do an interesting OOP project, perhaps based on the ecosystem of Section 13.3. The basic data structures (Chapters 4–7) are then covered, with the queue implemented as a derived class (Section 13.4). Finish up with recursion (Chapter 8) and trees (Chapter 9), placing special emphasis on recursive methods.

Accelerated Course. Assign the first three chapters as independent reading in the first week and start with Chapter 4 (linked lists). This will leave two to three extra weeks at the end of the term so that students can spend more time on searching, sorting, and the advanced topics (shaded in the chapter dependencies list).

I also have taught the course with further acceleration by spending no lecture time on stacks and queues (but assigning those chapters as reading).

Early Recursion / Early Sorting. One to three weeks may be spent at the start of class on recursive thinking. The first reading will then be Chapters 1 and 8, perhaps supplemented by additional recursive projects.

If the recursion is covered early, you may also proceed to cover binary search (Section 11.1) and most of the sorting algorithms (Chapter 12) before introducing collection classes.

Supplements Via the Internet

The following materials are available to all readers of this text at cssupport.pearsoncmg.com (or alternatively at www.cs.colorado.edu/~main/dsoj.html):

- Source code
- Errata

In addition, the following supplements are available to qualified instructors. Visit Addison-Wesley's Instructor Resource Center (www.aw.com/irc) or contact your local Addison-Wesley representative for access to these:

- PowerPoint® presentations
- Exam questions
- Solutions to selected programming projects
- Speaker notes
- Sample assignments
- Suggested syllabi

Acknowledgments

This book grew from joint work with Walter Savitch, who continues to be an ever-present and enthusiastic supporter, colleague, and friend. My students from the University of Colorado at Boulder serve to provide inspiration and joy at every turn, particularly the spring seminars in Natural Computing and Ideas in Computing. During the past few years, the book has also been extensively reviewed by J.D. Baker, Philip Barry, Arthur Crummer, Herbert Dershem, Greg Dobbins, Zoran Duric, Dan Grecu, Scott Grissom, Bob Holloway, Rod Howell, Danny Krizanc, Ran Libeskind-Hadas, Meiliu Lu, Catherine Matthews, Robert Moll, Robert Pastel, Don Slater, Ryan Stansifer, Deborah Trytten, and John Wegis. I thank these colleagues for their excellent critique and their encouragement.

At Addison-Wesley, I thank Tracy Dunkelberger, Michael Hirsch, Bob Engelhardt, and Stephanie Sellinger, who have provided continual support and knowledgeable advice.

I also thank my friends and colleagues who have given me daily encouragement and friendship during the writing of this fourth edition: Andrzej Ehrenfeucht, Marga Powell, Grzegorz Rozenberg, and Allison Thompson-Brown, and always my family: Janet, Tim, Hannah, Michelle, and Paul.

Michael Main (main@colorado.edu)
Boulder, Colorado

Chapter List

Contents

CHAPTER 3 COLLECTION CLASSES   103

CHAPTER 5 GENERIC PROGRAMMING   251

Chapter 6 STACKS   315

CHAPTER 9 TREES 453

CHAPTER 10 TREE PROJECTS   520

CHAPTER 13 SOFTWARE REUSE WITH EXTENDED CLASSES 675

CHAPTER 14 GRAPHS   728

APPENDIXES

CHAPTER 1

The Phases of Software Development

LEARNING OBJECTIVES

When you complete Chapter 1, you will be able to ...

- use Javadoc to write a method's complete specification, including a precondition/postcondition contract.
- recognize quadratic, linear, and logarithmic runtime behavior in simple algorithms, and write big-O expressions to describe this behavior.
- create and recognize test data that is appropriate for a problem, including testing boundary conditions and fully exercising code.

CHAPTER CONTENTS

The Phases of Software Development

*Chapter the first which explains how, why, when, and where
there was ever any problem in the first place*

NOEL LANGLEY
The Land of Green Ginger

This chapter illustrates the phases of software development. These phases occur for all software, including the small programs you'll see in this first chapter. In subsequent chapters, you'll go beyond these small programs, applying the phases of software development to organized collections of data. These organized collections of data are called **data structures**, and the main topics of this book revolve around proven techniques for representing and manipulating such data structures.

Data Structure

A **data structure** is a collection of data, organized so that items can be stored and retrieved by some fixed techniques. For example, a Java array is a simple data structure that allows individual items to be stored and retrieved based on an index ([0], [1], [2], ...) that is assigned to each item.

Throughout this book, you will be presented with many forms of data structures with organizations that are motivated by considerations such as ease of use or speed of inserting and removing items from the structure.

Years from now, you may be a software engineer writing large systems in a specialized area, perhaps artificial intelligence or computational biology. Such futuristic applications will be exciting and stimulating, and within your work you will still see the data structures that you learn and practice now. You will still be following the same phases of software development that you learned when designing and implementing your first programs. Here is a typical list of the software development phases:

The Phases of Software Development

- Specification of the task
- Design of a solution
- Implementation (coding) of the solution
- Analysis of the solution
- Testing and debugging
- Maintenance and evolution of the system
- Obsolescence

You don't need to memorize this list; throughout the book, your practice of these phases will achieve far better familiarity than mere memorization. Also, memorizing an "official list" is misleading because it suggests that there is a single sequence of discrete steps that always occur one after another. In practice, the phases blur into each other. For instance, the analysis of a solution's efficiency may occur hand in hand with the design, before any coding, or low-level design decisions may be postponed until the implementation phase. Also, the phases might not occur one after another. Typically, there is back and forth travel between the phases.

Most work in software development does not depend on any particular programming language. Specification, design, and analysis can all be carried out with few or no ties to a particular programming language. Nevertheless, when we get down to implementation details, we do need to decide on one particular programming language. The language we use in this book is **Java**™, and the particular version we use is Java Standard Edition 7.

What You Should Know About Java Before Starting This Text

The Java language was conceived by a group of programmers at Sun Microsystems™ in 1991. The group, led by James Gosling, had an initial design called Oak that was motivated by a desire for a single language in which programs could be developed and easily moved from one machine to another. Over the next four years, many Sun programmers contributed to the project, and Gosling's Oak evolved into the Java language. Java's goal of easily moving programs between machines was met by introducing an intermediate form called **byte codes**. To run a Java program, the program is first translated into byte codes; the byte codes are then given to a machine that runs a controlling program called the **Java Runtime Environment (JRE)**. Because the JRE is freely available for a wide variety of machines, Java programs can be moved from one machine to another. Because the JRE controls all Java programs, there is an added level of security that comes from avoiding potential problems from running unknown programs.

the origin of Java

In addition to the original goals of program transportability and security, the designers of Java also incorporated ideas from other modern programming languages. Most notably, Java supports **object-oriented programming (OOP)** in a manner that was partly taken from the C++ programming language. OOP is a programming approach that encourages strategies of information hiding and component reuse. In this book, you will be introduced to these important OOP principles to use in your designs and implementations.

this book gives an introduction to OOP principles for information hiding and component reuse

All of the programs in this book have been developed and tested with Sun's **Java Development Kit (JDK 7)**, but many other Java programming environments may be successfully used with this text. You should be comfortable writing, compiling, and running short Java application programs in your environment. You should know how to use the Java primitive types (the number types, char, and boolean), and you should be able to use arrays.

The rest of this chapter will prepare you to tackle the topic of data structures in Java. Section 1.1 focuses on a technique for specifying program behavior, and you'll also see some hints about design and implementation. Section 1.2 illustrates a particular kind of analysis: the running time analysis of a program. Section 1.3 provides some techniques for testing and debugging Java programs.

1.1 SPECIFICATION, DESIGN, IMPLEMENTATION

One begins with a list of difficult design decisions which are likely to change. Each module is then designed to hide such a decision from the others.

D. L. PARNAS
"On the Criteria to Be Used in Decomposing Systems into Modules"

you should already know how to write, compile, and run short Java programs in some programming environment

As an example of software development in action, let's examine the specification, design, and implementation for a particular problem. The **specification** is a precise description of the problem; the **design** phase consists of formulating the steps (or **algorithm**) to solve the problem; and the **implementation** is the actual Java code to carry out the design.

```
TEMPERATURE CONVERSION
----------------------

Celsius     Fahrenheit
-50.00C
-40.00C     The equivalent
-30.00C     Fahrenheit
-20.00C     temperatures will be
-10.00C     computed and
  0.00C     displayed on this side
 10.00C     of the table.
 20.00C
 30.00C
 40.00C
 50.00C
----------------------
```

The problem we have in mind is to display a table for converting Celsius temperatures to Fahrenheit, similar to the table shown here. For a small problem, a sample of the desired output is a reasonable specification. Such a sample is *precise,* leaving no doubt as to what the program must accomplish. The next step is to design a solution.

An **algorithm** is a procedure or sequence of directions for solving a problem. For example, an algorithm for the temperature problem will tell how to produce the conversion table. An algorithm can be expressed in many different ways, such as in English, in a mixture of English and mathematical notation, or in a mixture of English with a programming language. This mixture of English and a programming language is called **pseudocode**. Using pseudocode allows us to avoid programming language details that may obscure a simple solution, but at the same time we can use Java code (or another language) when the code is clear. Keep in mind that the reason for pseudocode is to improve *clarity.*

Algorithm

An **algorithm** is a procedure or sequence of instructions for solving a problem. Any algorithm may be expressed in many different ways: in English, in a particular programming language, or (most commonly) in a mixture of English and programming called **pseudocode**.

We'll use pseudocode to design a solution for the temperature problem, and we'll also use the important design technique of decomposing the problem, which we'll discuss now.

Design Technique: Decomposing the Problem

Key Design Concept

Break down a task into a few subtasks; then decompose each subtask into smaller subtasks.

A good technique for designing an algorithm is to break down the problem at hand into a few subtasks, then decompose each subtask into smaller subtasks, then replace the smaller subtasks with even smaller subtasks, and so forth. Eventually the subtasks become so small that they are trivial to implement in Java or whatever language you are using. When the algorithm is translated into Java code, each subtask is implemented as a separate Java method. In other programming languages, methods are called "functions" or "procedures," but it all boils down to the same thing: The large problem is decomposed into subtasks, and subtasks are implemented as separate pieces of your program.

For example, the temperature problem has at least two good subtasks: converting a temperature from Celsius degrees to Fahrenheit and printing a number with a specified accuracy (such as rounding to the nearest hundredth). Using these two subproblems, the first draft of our pseudocode might look like this:

1. Display the labels at the top of the table.
2. For each line in the table (using variables `celsius` and `fahrenheit`):
   2a. Set `celsius` equal to the next Celsius temperature of the table.
   <u>2b</u>. `fahrenheit` = the `celsius` temperature converted to Fahrenheit.
   <u>2c</u>. Print one line of the output table with each temperature rounded to the nearest hundredth and labeled (by the letter C or F).
3. Print the line of dashes at the bottom of the table.

what makes a good decomposition?

The underlined steps (2b and 2c) are the major subtasks. But aren't there other ways to decompose the problem into subtasks? What are the aspects of a good decomposition? One primary guideline is that the subtasks should help you produce short pseudocode—no more than a page of succinct description to solve the entire problem and ideally much less than a page. In your first designs, you can also keep in mind two considerations for selecting good subtasks: the potential for code reuse and the possibility of future changes to the program. Let's see how our subtasks embody these considerations.

the printf method

Step 2c is a form of a common task: printing some information with a specified format. This task is so common that newer versions of Java have included a method, `System.out.printf`, that can be used by any program that produces formatted output. We'll discuss and use this function when we implement Step 2c.

code reuse

The `printf` method is an example of **code reuse**, in which a single method can be used by many programs for similar tasks. In addition to Java's many packages of reusable methods, programmers often produce packages of their own Java methods that are intended to be reused over and over with many different application programs.

easily modified code

Decomposing problems also produces a good final program in the sense that the program is easy to understand, and subsequent maintenance and modifications are relatively easy. For example, our temperature program might later be modified to convert to Kelvin degrees instead of Fahrenheit. Since the conversion task is performed by a separate Java method, most of the modification will be confined to this one method. Easily modified code is vital since real-world studies show that a large proportion of programmers' time is spent maintaining and modifying existing programs.

For a problem decomposition to produce easily modified code, the Java methods you write need to be genuinely separated from one another. An analogy can help explain the notion of "genuinely separated." Suppose you are moving a bag of gold coins to a safe hiding place. If the bag is too heavy to carry, you might divide the coins into three smaller bags and carry the bags one by one. Unless you are a character in a comedy, you would not try to carry all three bags at once. That would defeat the purpose of dividing the coins into three groups. This strategy works only if you carry the bags one at a time. Something similar happens in problem decomposition. If you divide your programming task into three subtasks and solve these subtasks by writing three Java methods, you have traded one hard problem for three easier problems. Your total job has become easier—provided that you design the methods separately. When you are working on one method, you should not worry about how the other methods perform their jobs. But the methods do interact. So when you are designing one method, you need to know something about what the other methods do. The trick is to know *only as much as you need but no more*. This is called **information hiding**. One technique for information hiding involves specifying your methods' behavior using *preconditions* and *postconditions*, which we discuss next.

How to Write a Specification for a Java Method

When you implement a method in Java, you give complete instructions for how the method performs its computation. However, when you are *using a method* in your pseudocode or writing other Java code, you only need to think about *what the method does*. You need not think about *how the method* does its work. For example, suppose you are writing the temperature-conversion program and you are told that the following method is available for you to use:

```java
// Convert a Celsius temperature c to Fahrenheit degrees.
public static double celsiusToFahrenheit(double c)
```

signature of a method

This information about the method is called its *signature*. A **signature** includes the method name (`celsiusToFahrenheit`), its parameter list (`double c`), its return type (a `double` number), and any modifiers (`public` and `static`).

In your program, you might have a `double` variable called `celsius` that contains a Celsius temperature. Knowing this description, you can confidently write the following statement to convert the temperature to Fahrenheit degrees, storing the result in a `double` variable called `fahrenheit`:

```java
fahrenheit = celsiusToFahrenheit(celsius);
```

When you use the celsiusToFahrenheit method, you do not need to know the details of how the method carries out its work. You need to know *what* the method does, but you do not need to know *how* the task is accomplished.

When we pretend that we do not know how a method is implemented, we are using a form of information hiding called **procedural abstraction**. This simplifies your reasoning by abstracting away irrelevant details (that is, by hiding them). When programming in Java, it might make more sense to call it "method abstraction" since you are abstracting away irrelevant details about how a method works. However, computer scientists use the term *procedure* for any sequence of instructions, so they also use the term *procedural abstraction*. Procedural abstraction can be a powerful tool. It simplifies your reasoning by allowing you to consider methods one at a time rather than all together. *procedural abstraction*

To make procedural abstraction work for us, we need some techniques for documenting what a method does without indicating how the method works. We could just write a short comment as we did for celsiusToFahrenheit. However, the short comment is a bit incomplete; for instance, the comment doesn't indicate what happens if the parameter c is smaller than the lowest Celsius temperature (−273.15°C, also called **absolute zero**). For better completeness and consistency, we will follow a fixed format that is guaranteed to provide the same kind of information about any method you may write. The format has five parts, which are illustrated below and on the next page for the celsiusToFahrenheit method.

♦ **celsiusToFahrenheit**
```
public static double celsiusToFahrenheit(double c)
```
Convert a temperature from Celsius degrees to Fahrenheit degrees.

Parameters:
c – a temperature in Celsius degrees

Precondition:
c >= -273.15.

Returns:
the temperature c converted to Fahrenheit degrees

Throws: IllegalArgumentException
Indicates that c is less than the smallest Celsius temperature (−273.15).

This documentation is called the method's **specification**. Let's look at the five parts of this specification.

1. Short Introduction. The specification's first few lines are a brief introduction. The introduction includes the method's name, the complete heading (public static double celsiusToFahrenheit(double c)), and a short description of the action that the method performs.

2. Parameter Description. The specification's second part is a list of the method's parameters. We have one parameter, c, which is a temperature in Celsius degrees.

3. Precondition.   A **precondition** is a condition that is supposed to be true when a method is called. The method is not guaranteed to work correctly unless the precondition is true. Our method requires that the Celsius temperature c be no less than the smallest valid Celsius temperature (−273.15°C).

4. The Returns Condition or Postcondition.   A **returns** condition specifies the meaning of a method's return value. We used a returns condition for celsiusToFahrenheit, specifying that the method "returns the temperature c converted to Fahrenheit degrees." More complex methods may have additional effects beyond a single return value. For example, a method may print values or alter its parameters. To describe such effects, a general *postcondition* can be provided instead of just a returns condition. A **postcondition** is a complete statement describing what will be true when a method finishes. If the precondition was true when the method was called, then the method will complete and the postcondition will be true when the method completes. The connection between a precondition and a postcondition is given here:

A Method's Precondition and Postcondition

A **precondition** is a statement giving the condition that is supposed to be true when a method is called. The method is not guaranteed to perform as it should unless the precondition is true.

A **postcondition** is a statement describing what will be true when a method call is completed. If the method is correct and the precondition was true when the method was called, then the method will complete and the postcondition will be true when the method's computation is completed.

For small methods that merely return a calculated value, the specification provides a precondition and a returns condition. For more complex methods, the specification provides a precondition and a general postcondition.

programming teams   Preconditions and postconditions are even more important when a group of programmers work together. In team situations, one programmer often does not know how a function written by another programmer works. In fact, sharing knowledge about how a function works can be counterproductive. Instead, the precondition and postcondition provide all the interaction that's needed. In effect, the precondition/postcondition pair forms a contract between the programmer who uses a function and the programmer who writes that function. To aid the explanation of this "contract," we'll give these two programmers names. Judy is the head of a programming team that is writing a large piece of software.

Jervis is one of her programmers, who writes various functions for Judy to use in large programs. If Judy and Jervis were lawyers, the contract might look like the scroll shown in the margin. As a programmer, the contract tells them precisely what the function does. It states that if Judy makes sure that the precondition is met when the function is called, then Jervis ensures that the function returns with the postcondition satisfied.

Before long, we will provide both the specification and the implementation of the celsiusToFahrenheit method. But keep in mind that we need only the specification in order to know how to use the method.

the precondition/ postcondition contract

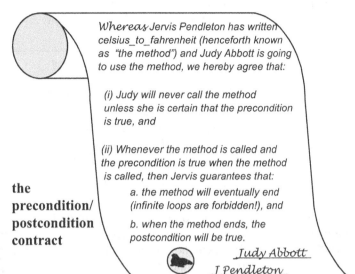

Whereas Jervis Pendleton has written *celsius_to_fahrenheit* (henceforth known as "the method") and Judy Abbott is going to use the method, we hereby agree that:

(i) Judy will never call the method unless she is certain that the precondition is true, and

(ii) Whenever the method is called and the precondition is true when the method is called, then Jervis guarantees that:

    a. the method will eventually end (infinite loops are forbidden!), and

    b. when the method ends, the postcondition will be true.

Judy Abbott

J Pendleton

5. The Throws List. It is always the responsibility of the programmer who *uses* a method to ensure that the precondition is valid. Calling a method without ensuring a valid precondition is a programming error. Once the precondition fails, the method's behavior is unpredictable—the method *could* do anything at all. Nonetheless, the person who writes a method should make every effort to avoid the more unpleasant behaviors, even if the method is called incorrectly. As part of this effort, the first action of a method is often to check that its precondition has been satisfied. If the precondition fails, then the method *throws an exception*. You may have used exceptions in your previous programming, or maybe not. In either case, the next programming tip describes the exact meaning of *throwing an exception* to indicate that a precondition has failed.

PROGRAMMING TIP 🎧

THROW AN EXCEPTION TO INDICATE A FAILED PRECONDITION

It is a programming error to call a method when the precondition is invalid. For example, celsiusToFahrenheit should not be called with an argument that is below -273.15. Despite this warning, some programmer may try celsiusToFahrenheit(-9001) or celsiusToFahrenheit(-273.16). In such a case, our celsiusToFahrenheit method will detect that the precondition has been violated, immediately halt its own work, and pass a "message" to the calling program to indicate that an illegal argument has occurred. Such messages for programming errors are called **exceptions**. The act of halting your own work and passing a message to the calling program is known as **throwing an exception**.

how to throw an exception

The Java syntax for throwing an exception is simple. You begin with the keyword throw and follow this pattern:

throw new _____ ("_____");

This is the type of exception we are throwing. To begin with, all of our exceptions will be the type IllegalArgumentException, which is provided as part of the Java language. This type of exception tells a programmer that one of the method's arguments violated a precondition.

This is an error message that will be passed as part of the exception. The message should describe the error in a way that will help the programmer fix the programming error.

what happens when an exception is thrown?

When an exception is thrown in a method, the method stops its computation. A new "exception object" is created, incorporating the indicated error message. The exception, along with its error message, is passed up to the method or program that made the illegal call in the first place. At that point, where the illegal call was made, there is a Java mechanism to "catch" the exception, try to fix the error, and continue with the program's computation. You can read about exception catching in Appendix C. However, exceptions that arise from precondition violations should never be caught because they indicate programming errors that must be fixed. When an exception is not caught, the program halts, printing the error message along with a list of the method calls that led to the exception. This error message can help the programmer fix the programming error.

Now you know the meaning of the specification's "throws list." It is a list of all the exceptions that the method can throw, along with a description of what causes each exception. Certain kinds of exceptions must also be listed in a method's implementation, after the parameter list, but an IllegalArgument-Exception is listed only in the method's specification.

Temperature Conversion: Implementation

Our specification and design are now in place. The subtasks are small enough to implement, though during the implementation you may need to finish small design tasks such as finding the conversion formula. In particular, we can now implement the temperature program as a Java application program with two methods:

- a main method that follows the pseudocode from page 5. This main method prints the temperature conversion table using the method celsiusToFahrenheit to carry out some of its work.

- the celsiusToFahrenheit method.

The Java application program with these two methods appears in Figure 1.1. The program produces the output from our initial specification on page 4.

A few features of the implementation might be new to you, so we will discuss these in some programming tips after the figure.

FIGURE 1.1 Specification and Implementation for the Temperature Conversion Application

Class TemperatureConversion

❖ **public class TemperatureConversion**
   The TemperatureConversion Java application prints a table converting Celsius to Fahrenheit degrees.

Specification

♦ **main**
   public static void main(String[ ] args)
   The main method prints a Celsius-to-Fahrenheit conversion table. The String arguments (args) are not used in this implementation. The bounds of the table range from –50C to +50C in 10-degree increments.

♦ **celsiusToFahrenheit**
   public static double celsiusToFahrenheit(double c)
   Convert a temperature from Celsius degrees to Fahrenheit degrees.
   Parameters:
      c – a temperature in Celsius degrees
   Precondition:
      c >= -273.15.
   Returns:
      the temperature c converted to Fahrenheit degrees
   Throws: IllegalArgumentException
      Indicates that c is less than the smallest Celsius temperature (–273.15).

> *These specifications were automatically produced by the Javadoc tool. Appendix H describes how to use Javadoc to produce similar information.*

(continued)

(FIGURE 1.1 continued)

Java Application Program

The actual implementation includes
Javadoc comments that are omitted here
but are listed in Appendix H. The
comments allow Javadoc to produce
nicely formatted information
automatically. See Appendix H to read
about using Javadoc for your programs.

```
// File: TemperatureConversion.java from
// www.cs.colorado.edu/~main/applications/
// A Java application to print a
// temperature conversion table.
// Additional Javadoc information is available on page 11 or at
// http://www.cs.colorado.edu/~main/docs/TemperatureConversion.html.

public class TemperatureConversion
{
    public static void main(String[ ] args)
    {
        // Declare values that control the table's bounds.
        final double TABLE_BEGIN = -50.0; // The table's first Celsius temperature
        final double TABLE_END   =  50.0; // The table's final Celsius temperature
        final double TABLE_STEP  =  10.0; // Increment between temperatures in table

        double celsius;                    // A Celsius temperature
        double fahrenheit;                 // The equivalent Fahrenheit temperature

        System.out.println("TEMPERATURE CONVERSION");
        System.out.println("----------------------");
        System.out.println("Celsius      Fahrenheit");
        for (celsius = TABLE_BEGIN; celsius <= TABLE_END; celsius += TABLE_STEP)
        {   // The for-loop has set celsius equal to the next Celsius temperature of the table.
            fahrenheit = celsiusToFahrenheit(celsius);
            System.out.printf("%6.2fC", celsius);
            System.out.printf("%14.2fF\n", fahrenheit);
        }
        System.out.println("----------------------");
    }

    public static double celsiusToFahrenheit(double c)
    {
        final double MINIMUM_CELSIUS = -273.15;
        if (c < MINIMUM_CELSIUS)
            throw new IllegalArgumentException("Argument " + c + " is too small.");
        return (9.0/5.0) * c + 32;
    }
}
```

USE JAVADOC TO WRITE SPECIFICATIONS

The specification at the start of Figure 1.1 was produced in an interesting way. Most of it was automatically produced from the Java code by a tool called **Javadoc**. With a web browser, you can access this specification over the Internet at: http://www.cs.colorado.edu/~main/docs/TemperatureConversion.html.

the Javadoc tool automatically produces nicely formatted information about a class

To use Javadoc, the .java file that you write needs special **Javadoc comments**. These necessary comments are not listed in Figure 1.1, but Appendix H is a short manual on how to write these comments. Before you go on to Chapter 2, you should read through the appendix and be prepared to produce Javadoc comments for your own programs.

USE FINAL VARIABLES TO IMPROVE CLARITY

The method implementation in Figure 1.1 has a local variable declared this way:

```
final double MINIMUM_CELSIUS = -273.15;
```

This is a declaration of a double variable called MINIMUM_CELSIUS, which is given an initial value of −273.15. The keyword final, appearing before the declaration, makes MINIMUM_CELSIUS more than just an ordinary declaration. It is a **final variable**, which means that its value will never be changed while the program is running. A common programming style is to use all capital letters for the names of final variables. This makes it easy to determine which variables are final and which may have their values changed.

There are several advantages to defining MINIMUM_CELSIUS as a final variable rather than using the constant −273.15 directly in the program. Using the name MINIMUM_CELSIUS makes the comparison (c < MINIMUM_CELSIUS) easy to understand; it's clear that we are testing whether c is below the minimum valid Celsius temperature. If we used the direct comparison (c < −273.15) instead, a person reading our program would have to stop to remember that −273.15 is "absolute zero," the smallest Celsius temperature.

To increase clarity, some programmers declare all constants as final variables. This is a good rule, particularly if the same constant appears in several different places in the program or if you plan to later compile the program with a different value for the constant. However, well-known formulas may be more easily recognized in their original form. For example, the conversion from Celsius to Fahrenheit is recognizable as $F = \frac{9}{5}C + 32$. Thus, Figure 1.1 uses this statement:

```
return (9.0/5.0) * c + 32;
```

This return statement is clearer and less error prone than a version that uses final variables for the constants $\frac{9}{5}$ and 32.

Advice: Use final variables instead of constants. Make exceptions when constants are clearer or less error prone. When in doubt, write both solutions and interview several colleagues to decide which is clearer.

🛈 PROGRAMMING TIP

MAKE EXCEPTION MESSAGES INFORMATIVE

If the `celsiusToFahrenheit` method detects that its parameter, `c`, is too small, then it throws an `IllegalArgumentException`. The message in the exception is:

```
"Argument " + c + " is too small."
```

The parameter, `c`, is part of the message. If a programmer attempts to call `celsiusToFahrenheit(-300)`, the message will be "Argument –300 is too small."

🛈 PROGRAMMING TIP

FORMAT OUTPUT WITH SYSTEM.OUT.PRINTF

Our pseudocode for the temperature problem includes a step to print the Celsius and Fahrenheit temperatures rounded to a specified accuracy. Java has a method, `System.out.printf`, that we can use to print formatted output such as rounded numbers. The method, which is based on a similar function in the C language, always has a "format string" as its first argument. The format string tells how subsequent arguments should be printed to `System.out` (which is usually the computer monitor). For example, you could create an appropriate format string and print two numbers called age and height:

```
System.out.println( format string , age, height);
```

Two things can appear in a format string:

1. Most ordinary characters are just printed as they appear in the format string. For example, if the character F appears in the format string, then this will usually just print an F. Some sequences of characters are special, such as \n (which moves down to start the next new line). The complete list of special characters is in Appendix B.

2. Parts of the format string that begin with the % character are called **format specifiers**. Each format specifier indicates how the next item should be printed. Some of the common format specifiers are shown here:

Format specifier	Causes the next item to be printed as ...
%d	... a decimal (base 10) whole number
%f	... a floating point number with six digits after the decimal point
%g	... a floating point number using scientific notation for large exponents
%s	... a string

The format specifiers have several additional options that are described in Appendix B. For our program, we used a format specifier of the form %6.2f, which means that we want to print a floating point number using six total spaces, two of which are after the decimal point. Within these six spaces, the number will be rounded to two decimal points and right justified. For example, the number 42.129 will print these six characters (the first of which is a blank space):

	4	2	.	1	3

In the format specifier %6.2f, the number 6 is the **field width**, and the number 2 is the **precision**.

As an example, System.out.println("%14.2fF\n", fahrenheit) prints the value of the fahrenheit variable using a field width of 14 and a precision of 2. After printing this number, the character F and a new line will appear.

Self-Test Exercises for Section 1.1

Each section of this book finishes with a few self-test exercises. Answers to these exercises are given at the end of each chapter. The first exercise refers to a method that Judy has written for *you* to use. Here is the specification:

♦ **dateCheck**

```
public static int dateCheck(int year, int month, int day)
```
Compute how long until a given date will occur.

Parameters:
year – the year for a given date
month – the month for a given date (using 1 for Jan, 2 for Feb, etc.)
day – the day of the month for the given date

Precondition:
The three arguments are a legal year, month, and day of the month in the years 1900 to 2099.

Returns:
If the given date has been reached on or before today, the return value is zero. Otherwise, the return value is the number of days until the given date returns.

Throws: IllegalArgumentException
Indicates the arguments are not a legal date in the years 1900 to 2099.

1. Suppose you call the method dateCheck(2013, 7, 29). What is the return value if today is July 22, 2013? What if today is July 30, 2013? What about February 1, 2014?

2. Can you use dateCheck even if you don't know how it is implemented?

3. Suppose that boodle is a double variable. Write two statements that will print boodle to System.out in the following format: $ 42,567.19
The whole dollars part of the output can contain up to nine characters (including the comma), so this example has three spaces before the six characters of 42,567. The fractional part has just two digits. Appendix B describes the format string that you'll need in order to have the number include a comma separator between the thousands and hundreds.

4. Consider a method with this heading:

   ```
   public static void printSqrt(double x)
   ```

   The method prints the square root of x to the standard output. Write a reasonable specification for this method and compare your answer to the solution at the end of the chapter. The specification should forbid a negative argument.

5. Consider a method with this heading:

   ```
   public static double sphereVolume(double radius)
   ```

   The method computes and returns the volume of a sphere with the given radius. Write a reasonable specification for this method and compare your answer to the solution at the end of the chapter. The specification should require a positive radius.

6. Write an if-statement to throw an IllegalArgumentException when x is less than zero. (Assume that x is a double variable.)

7. When can a final variable be used?

8. How was the specification produced at the start of Figure 1.1?

9. What are the components of a Java signature?

10. Write a Java statement that will print two variables called age and height. The age should be printed as a whole number using 10 output spaces; the height should be printed using 12 output spaces and three decimal digits. Label each part of the output as "Age" and "Height". Use Appendix B if necessary.

1.2   RUNNING TIME ANALYSIS

Time analysis consists of reasoning about an algorithm's speed. *Does the algorithm work fast enough for my needs? How much longer does the algorithm take when the input gets larger? Which of several different algorithms is fastest?* These questions can be asked at any stage of software development. Some analysis of an algorithm is useful before any implementation is done to avoid the wasted work of implementing inappropriately slow solutions. Further analysis can be carried out during or after an implementation. This section discusses time analysis, starting with an example that involves no implementation in the usual sense.

The Stair-Counting Problem

Suppose you and your friend Judy are standing at the top of the Eiffel Tower. As you gaze out over the French landscape, Judy turns to you and says, "I wonder how many steps there are to the bottom?" You, of course, are the ever-accommodating host, so you reply, "I'm not sure ... but I'll find out." We'll look at three techniques that you could use and analyze the time requirements of each.

Technique 1: Walk Down and Keep a Tally. In the first technique, Judy gives you a pen and a sheet of paper. "I'll be back in a moment," you say as you dash down the stairs. Each time you take a step down, you make a mark on the sheet of paper. When you reach the bottom, you run back up, show Judy the piece of paper, and say, "There are this many steps."

Technique 2: Walk Down, but Let Judy Keep the Tally. In the second technique, Judy is unwilling to let her pen or paper out of her sight. But you are undaunted. Once more you say, "I'll be back in a moment," and you set off down the stairs. But this time you stop after one step, lay your hat on the step, and run back to Judy. "Make a mark on the piece of paper!" you exclaim. Then you run back to your hat, pick it up, take one more step, and lay the hat down on the second step. Then back up to Judy: "Make another mark on the piece of paper!" you say. You run back down the two stairs, pick up your hat, move to the third step, and lay down the hat. Then back up the stairs to Judy: "Make another mark!" you tell her. This continues until your hat reaches the bottom, and you speed back up the steps one more time. "One more mark, please." At this point, you grab Judy's piece of paper and say, "There are this many steps."

Technique 3: Jervis to the Rescue. In the third technique, you don't walk down the stairs at all. Instead, you spot your friend Jervis by the staircase, holding the sign shown here. The translation is *There are 2689 steps in this stairway (really!)*. So you take the paper and pen from Judy, write the number 2689, and hand the paper back to her, saying, "There are this many steps."

This is a silly example, but even so, it does illustrate the issues that arise when performing a time analysis for an algorithm or program. The first issue is deciding exactly how you will measure the time spent carrying out the work or executing the program. At first glance, the answer seems easy: For each of the three stair-counting techniques, just measure the actual time it takes to carry out the work. You could do this with a stopwatch. But there are some drawbacks to measuring actual time. Actual time can depend on various irrelevant details, such as whether you or somebody else carried out the work. The actual elapsed time may vary from person to person, depending on how fast each person can run the stairs. Even if we decide that *you* are the runner, the time may vary depending on other factors such as the weather, what you had for breakfast, and what other things are on your mind.

decide what operations to count

So, instead of measuring the actual elapsed time, we count certain operations that occur while carrying out the work. In this example, we will count two kinds of operations:

1. Each time you walk up or down one step, that is one operation.
2. Each time you or Judy marks a symbol on the paper, that is also one operation.

Of course, each of these operations takes a certain amount of time, and making a mark may take a different amount of time than taking a step. But this doesn't concern us because we won't measure the actual time taken by the operations. Instead, we will ask: *How many operations are needed for each of the three techniques?*

For the first technique, you take 2689 steps down, another 2689 steps up, and you also make 2689 marks on the paper, for a total of 3×2689 operations—that is 8067 total operations.

For the second technique, there are also 2689 marks made on Judy's paper, but the total number of operations is much greater. You start by going down one step and back up one step. Then down two and up two. Then down three and up three, and so forth. The total number of operations taken is shown below.

Downward steps $= 3,616,705$ (which is $1 + 2 + \dots + 2689$)

Upward steps $= 3,616,705$

Marks made $= 2689$

Total operations $=$ Downward steps
                        $+$ Upward steps
                        $+$ Marks made
                    $= 7,236,099$

The third technique is the quickest of all: Only four marks are made on the paper (that is, we're counting one "mark" for each digit of 2689), and there is no going up and down stairs. The number of operations used by each of the techniques is summarized here:

Technique 1   8067 operations
Technique 2   7,236,099 operations
Technique 3   4 operations

Doing a time analysis for a program is similar to the analysis of the stair-counting techniques. For a time analysis of a program, usually we do not measure the actual time taken to run the program, because the number of seconds can depend on too many extraneous factors—such as the speed of the processor and whether the processor is busy with other tasks. Instead, the analysis counts the number of operations required. There is no precise definition of what constitutes an **operation**, although an operation should satisfy your intuition of a "small step." An operation can be as simple as the execution of a single program statement. Or we could use a finer notion of operation that counts each arithmetic operation (addition, multiplication, etc.) and each assignment to a variable as a separate operation.

For most programs, the number of operations depends on the program's input. *dependence on input size* For example, a program that sorts a list of numbers is quicker with a short list than with a long list. In the stairway example, we can view the Eiffel Tower as the input to the problem. In other words, the three different techniques all work on the Eiffel Tower, but the techniques also work on Toronto's CN Tower or on the stairway to the top of the Statue of Liberty or on any other stairway.

When a time analysis depends on the size of the input, then the time can be given as an expression, where part of the expression is the input's size. The time expressions for our three stair-counting techniques are:

Technique 1 $3n$

Technique 2 $n + 2 (1 + 2 + ... + n)$

Technique 3   The number of digits in the number n

The expressions in this list give the number of operations performed by each technique when the stairway has n steps.

The expression for the second technique is not easy to interpret. It needs to be simplified to become a formula that we can easily compare to other formulas. So let's simplify it. We start with the following subexpression:

$$(1 + 2 + ... + n)$$

There is a trick that will enable us to find a simplified form for this expression. *simplification of the time analysis for Technique 2* The trick is to *compute twice the amount of the expression and then divide the result by 2*. Unless you've seen this trick before, it sounds crazy. But it works fine. The trick is illustrated in Figure 1.2. Let's go through the computation of that figure step by step.

We write the expression $(1 + 2 + ... + n)$ twice and add the two expressions. But as you can see in Figure 1.2, we also use another trick: When we write the expression twice, *we write the second expression backward*. After we write down the expression twice, we see the following:

$$(1 + 2 + ... + n)$$
$$+(n + ... + 2 + 1)$$

We want the sum of the numbers on these two lines. That will give us twice the value of $(1 + 2 + ... + n)$, and we can then divide by 2 to get the correct value of the subexpression $(1 + 2 + ... + n)$.

Now, rather than proceeding in the most obvious way, we instead add pairs of numbers from the first and second lines. We add the 1 and the n to get $n + 1$. Then we add the 2 and the $n - 1$ to again get $n + 1$. We continue until we reach the last pair consisting of an n from the top line and a 1 from the bottom line. All the pairs add up to the same amount, namely $n + 1$. Now that is handy! We get n numbers, and all the numbers are the same, namely $n + 1$. So the total of all the numbers on the preceding two lines is:

$$n(n + 1)$$

The value of twice the expression is n multiplied by $n + 1$. We are now essentially done. The number we computed is twice the quantity we want. So, to obtain our simplified formula, we only need to divide by 2. The final simplification is thus:

$$(1 + 2 + \ldots + n) = \frac{n(n + 1)}{2}$$

We will use this simplified formula to rewrite the Technique 2 time expression, but you'll also find that the formula occurs in many other situations. The simplification for the Technique 2 expression is as follows:

Number of operations for Technique 2

$$= n + 2(1 + 2 + \ldots + n)$$

$$= n + 2\left(\frac{n(n + 1)}{2}\right) \quad \textit{Plug in the formula for } (1 + 2 + \ldots + n)$$

$$= n + n(n + 1) \qquad \textit{Cancel the 2s}$$

$$= n + n^2 + n \qquad \textit{Multiply out}$$

$$= n^2 + 2n \qquad \textit{Combine terms}$$

So, Technique 2 requires $n^2 + 2n$ operations.

FIGURE 1.2   Deriving a Handy Formula

$(1 + 2 + \ldots + n)$ can be computed by first computing the sum of twice $(1 + 2 + \ldots + n)$, as shown here:

$$
\begin{array}{ccccccccc}
 & 1 & + & 2 & + \ldots + & (n - 1) & + & n \\
+ & n & + & (n - 1) & + \ldots + & 2 & + & 1 \\
\hline
 & (n + 1) & + & (n + 1) & + \ldots + & (n + 1) & + & (n + 1)
\end{array}
$$

The sum is $n(n + 1)$, so $(1 + 2 + \ldots + n)$ is half this amount:

$$(1 + 2 + \ldots + n) = \frac{n(n + 1)}{2}$$

The number of operations for Technique 3 is just the number of digits in the integer *n* when written down in the usual way. The usual way of writing down numbers is called **base 10 notation**. As it turns out, the number of digits in a number *n*, when written in base 10 notation, is approximately equal to another mathematical quantity known as the **base 10 logarithm** of *n*. The notation for the base 10 logarithm of *n* is written:

simplification of time analysis for Technique 3

$$\log_{10} n$$

The base 10 logarithm does not always give a whole number. For example, the actual base 10 logarithm of 2689 is about 3.43 rather than 4. If we want the actual number of digits in an integer *n*, we need to carry out some rounding. In particular, the exact number of digits in a positive integer *n* is obtained by rounding $\log_{10} n$ downward to the next whole number and then adding 1. The notation for rounding down and adding 1 is obtained by adding some symbols to the logarithm notation as follows:

base 10 notation and base 10 logarithms

$$\lfloor \log_{10} n \rfloor + 1$$

This is all fine if you already know about logarithms, but what if some of this is new to you? For now, you can simply define the notation to mean *the number of digits in the base 10 numeral for n*. You can do this because if others use any of the other accepted definitions for this formula, they will get the same answers that you do. You will be right! (And they will also be right.) In Section 10.3 of this book, we will show that the various definitions of the logarithm function are all equivalent. For now, we will not worry about all that detail. We have larger issues to discuss first. The table of the number of operations for each technique can now be expressed concisely as shown here:

Technique 1	$3n$
Technique 2	$n^2 + 2n$
Technique 3	$\lfloor \log_{10} n \rfloor + 1$

Big-*O* Notation

The time analyses we gave for the three stair-counting techniques were precise. They computed the exact number of operations for each technique. But such precision is not always needed. Often it is enough to know in a rough manner how the number of operations is affected by the input size. In the stair example, we started by thinking about a particular tower, the Eiffel Tower, with a particular number of steps. We expressed our formulas for the operations in terms of *n*, which stood for the number of steps in the tower. Now suppose we apply our various stair-counting techniques to a tower with 10 times as many steps as the Eiffel Tower. If *n* is the number of steps in the Eiffel Tower, then this taller tower will have $10n$ steps. The number of operations needed for Technique 1 on the taller tower increases tenfold (from $3n$ to $3 \times (10n) = 30n$); the time for Technique 2 increases approximately 100-fold (from about n^2 to about $(10n)^2 = 100n^2$); and Technique 3 increases by only one operation (from the number of digits in n to the number of digits in $10n$, or to be very concrete, from the four digits in 2689 to the five digits in 26,890). We can express this kind of information in a format called **big-O notation**. The symbol O in this notation is the letter O, so big-O is pronounced "big Oh."

We will describe three common examples of the big-O notation. In these examples, we use the notion of "the largest term in a formula." Intuitively, this is the term with the largest exponent on n or the term that grows the fastest as n itself becomes larger. For now, this intuitive notion of "largest term" is enough.

quadratic time
$O(n^2)$

Quadratic Time. If the largest term in a formula is no more than a constant times n^2, then the algorithm is said to be "**big-O of n^2**," written $O(n^2)$, and the algorithm is called **quadratic**. In a quadratic algorithm, doubling the input size makes the number of operations increase approximately fourfold (or less). For a concrete example, consider Technique 2, requiring $n^2 + 2n$ operations. A 100-step tower requires 10,200 operations (that is, $100^2 + 2 \times 100$). Doubling the tower to 200 steps increases the time approximately fourfold, to 40,400 operations (that is, $200^2 + 2 \times 200$).

linear time $O(n)$

Linear Time. If the largest term in the formula is a constant times n, then the algorithm is said to be "**big-O of n**," written $O(n)$, and the algorithm is called **linear**. In a linear algorithm, doubling the input size makes the time increase approximately twofold (or less). For example, a formula of $3n + 7$ is linear, so $3 \times 200 + 7$ is about twice $3 \times 100 + 7$.

logarithmic time
$O(\log n)$

Logarithmic Time. If the largest term in the formula is a constant times a logarithm of n, then the algorithm is "**big-O of the logarithm of n**," written $O(\log n)$, and the algorithm is called **logarithmic**. (The base of the logarithm may be base 10 or possibly another base. We'll talk about the other bases in Section 10.3.) In a logarithmic algorithm, doubling the input size will make the time increase by no more than a fixed number of new operations, such as one more operation or two more operations—or in general by c more operations, where c is a fixed constant. For example, Technique 3 for stair counting has a logarithmic time formula. And doubling the size of a tower (perhaps from 500 stairs to 1000 stairs) never requires more than one extra operation.

Using big-O notation, we can express the time requirements of our three stair-counting techniques as follows:

Technique 1	$O(n)$
Technique 2	$O(n^2)$
Technique 3	$O(\log n)$

FIGURE 1.3 Number of Operations for Three Techniques

Number of stairs (n)	Logarithmic $O(\log n)$ Technique 3, with $\lfloor \log_{10} n \rfloor + 1$ operations	Linear $O(n)$ Technique 1, with $3n$ operations	Quadratic $O(n^2)$ Technique 2, with $n^2 + 2n$ operations
10	2	30	120
100	3	300	10,200
1000	4	3000	1,002,000
10,000	5	30,000	100,020,000

When a time analysis is expressed with big-O, the result is called the **order** of the algorithm. We want to reinforce one important point: Multiplicative constants are ignored in the big-O notation. For example, both $2n$ and $42n$ are linear formulas, so both are expressed as $O(n)$, ignoring the multiplicative constants 2 and 42. As you can see, this means that a big-O analysis loses some information about relative times. Nevertheless, a big-O analysis does provide some useful information for comparing algorithms. The stair example illustrates the most important kind of information provided by the order of an algorithm.

order of an algorithm

> The order of an algorithm generally is more important than the speed of the processor.

For example, using the quadratic technique (Technique 2), the fastest stair climber in the world is still unlikely to do better than a slowpoke—provided that the slowpoke uses one of the faster techniques. In an application such as sorting a list, a quadratic algorithm can be impractically slow on even moderately sized lists, regardless of the processor speed. To see this, notice the comparisons showing actual numbers for our three stair-counting techniques, which are shown in Figure 1.3.

Time Analysis of Java Methods

The principles of the stair-climbing example can be applied to counting the number of operations required by code written in a high-level language such as Java. As an example, consider the method implemented in Figure 1.4. The method searches through an array of numbers to determine whether a particular number occurs.

FIGURE 1.4   Specification and Implementation of a `search` Method

Specification

♦ **search**

```
public static boolean search(double[ ] data, double target)
```
Search an array for a specified number.

Notice that there is no precondition.

Parameters:

data – an array of double numbers in no particular order
target – a specific number that we are searching for

Returns:

`true` (to indicate that `target` occurs somewhere in the array)
or `false` (to indicate that `target` does not occur in the array)

Implementation

```
public static boolean search(double[ ] data, double target)
{
    int i;

    for (i = 0; i < data.length; i++)
    {  // Check whether the target is at data[i].
        if (data[i] == target)
            return true;
    }

    // The loop finished without finding the target.
    return false;
}
```

Examples:

Suppose that the data array has the five numbers {2, 14, 6, 8, 10}. Then `search(data, 10)` *returns true, but* `search(data, 42)` *returns false.*

As with the stair-climbing example, the first step of the time analysis is to decide precisely what we will count as a single operation. For Java, a good choice is to count the total number of Java operations (such as an assignment, an arithmetic operation, or the < comparison). If a method calls other methods, we would also need to count the operations that are carried out in the other methods.

for our first analysis, the number that we are searching for does not occur in the array

With this in mind, let's do a first analysis of the `search` method for the case in which the array's length is a non-negative integer n and (just to be difficult) the number that we are searching for does not occur in the array. How many operations does the `search` method carry out in all? Our analysis has three parts:

1. When the for-loop starts, there are two operations: an assignment to initialize the variable i to 0 and an execution of the test to determine whether i is less than `data.length`.

2. We then execute the body of the loop, and because the number that we are searching for does not occur, we will execute this body *n* times. How many operations occur during each execution of the loop body? We could count this number, but let's just say that each execution of the loop body requires *k* operations, where *k* is some number around 3 or 4 (including the work at the end of the loop where i is incremented and the termination test is executed). If necessary, we'll figure out *k* later, but for now it is enough to know that we execute the loop body *n* times and each execution takes *k* operations, for a total of *kn* operations.

3. After the loop finishes, there is one more operation (a return statement).

The total number of operations is now $kn + 3$. The +3 is from the two operations before the loop and the one operation after the loop. Regardless of how big *k* is, this formula is always linear time. So, in the case where the sought-after number does not occur, the search method takes linear time. In fact, this is a frequent pattern that we summarize here:

Frequent Linear Pattern

A loop that does a fixed amount of operations *n* times requires $O(n)$ time.

Later you will see additional patterns, resulting in quadratic, logarithmic, and other times. In fact, in Chapter 11 you will rewrite the search method in a way that uses an array that is sorted from smallest to largest but requires only logarithmic time.

Worst-Case, Average-Case, and Best-Case Analyses

The search method has another important feature: For any particular array size *n*, the number of required operations can differ depending on the exact parameter values. For example, with *n* equal to 100, the target could be 27, and the very first array element could also be 27—so the loop body executes just one time. On the other hand, maybe the number 27 doesn't occur until data[99] and the loop body executes the maximum number of times (*n* times). In other words, for any fixed *n*, different possible parameter values result in a different number of operations. When this occurs, we usually count the *maximum* number of required operations for inputs of a given size. Counting the maximum number of operations is called the **worst-case** analysis. In fact, the worst case for the *worst-case* search method occurs when the sought-after number is not in the array, which *analysis* is the reason why we used the "not in array" situation in our previous analysis.

During a worst-case time analysis, you may sometimes find yourself unable to provide an exact count of the number of operations. If the analysis is a worst-case analysis, you may estimate the number of operations, always making your estimate on the high side. In other words, the actual number of operations must be guaranteed to be less than the estimate that you use in the analysis.

In Chapter 11, when we begin the study of searching and sorting, you'll see two other kinds of time analysis: **average-case** analysis, which determines the average number of operations required for a given *n*, and **best-case** analysis, which determines the fewest number of operations required for a given *n*.

Self-Test Exercises for Section 1.2

11. Write code for a method that computes the sum of all the numbers in an integer array. If the array's length is zero, the sum should also be zero. Do a big-*O* time analysis of your method.

12. Each of the following are formulas for the number of operations in some algorithm. Express each formula in big-*O* notation.

    a. $n^2 + 5n$ e. $5n + 3n^2$
    b. $3n^2 + 5n$ f. The number of digits in $2n$
    c. $(n + 7)(n - 2)$ g. The number of times that *n* can be
    d. $100n + 5$ divided by 10 before dropping below 1.0

13. Determine which of the following formulas is $O(n)$:

    a. $16n^3$ c. $\lfloor n^2/2 \rfloor$
    b. $n^2 + n + 2$ d. $10n + 25$

14. What is meant by *worst-case analysis*?

15. What is the worst-case big-*O* analysis of the following code fragment?
    ```
    k = 0;
    for (i = 0; i < n; ++i) {
        for (j = i; j < n; ++j) {
            k += n;
        }
    }
    ```

16. List the following formulas in order of running time analysis, from greatest to least time requirements, assuming that *n* is very large:
    $n^2 + 1$; 50 log *n*; 1,000,000; $10n + 10,000$.

1.3   TESTING AND DEBUGGING

Always do right. This will gratify some people, and astonish the rest.

MARK TWAIN
To the Young People's Society, February 16, 1901

program testing **Program testing** occurs when you run a program and observe its behavior. Each time you execute a program using some input, you are testing to see how the program works for that particular input. The topic of this section is the construction of test inputs that are likely to discover errors.

Choosing Test Data

To serve as good test data, your test inputs need two properties.

Properties of Good Test Data

1. You must know what output a correct program should produce for each test input.
2. The test inputs should include those inputs that are most likely to cause errors.

Do not take the first property lightly; you must choose test data for which you know the correct output. Just because a program compiles, runs, and produces output that looks about right does not mean the program is correct. If the correct answer is 3278 and the program outputs 3277, then something is wrong. How do you know the correct answer is 3278? The most obvious way to find the correct output value is to work it out with pencil and paper using some method other than that used by the program. To aid this, you might choose test data for which it is easy to calculate the correct answer, perhaps by using smaller input values or by using input values for which the answer is well known.

Boundary Values

We will focus on two approaches for finding test data that are most likely to cause errors. The first approach is based on identifying and testing inputs called *boundary values*, which are particularly apt to cause errors. A **boundary value** of a problem is an input that is one step away from a different kind of behavior. For example, recall the dateCheck method from the first self-test exercise on page 15. It has the following precondition:

> **Precondition:**
> The three arguments are a legal year, month, and day of the month in the years 1900 to 2099.

Two boundary values for dateCheck are January 1, 1900 (since one step below this date is illegal) and December 31, 2099 (since one step above this date is illegal). If we expect the method to behave differently for "leap days," we should try days such as February 28, 2000 (just before a leap day); February 29, 2000 (a leap day); and March 1, 2000 (just after a leap day).

Frequently zero has special behavior, so it is a good idea to consider zero to be a boundary value whenever it is a legal input. For example, consider the search method from Figure 1.4 on page 24. This method should be tested with a data array that contains no elements (data.length is 0). For example:

test zero as a boundary value

```
double[ ] EMPTY = new double[0]; // An array with no elements

// Searching the EMPTY array should always return false.
if (search(EMPTY, 0))
    System.out.println("Wrong answer for an empty array.");
else
    System.out.println("Right answer for an empty array.");
```

test 1 and −1 as boundary values

The numbers 1 and −1 also have special behavior in many situations, so they should be tested as boundary values whenever they are legal input. For example, the search method should be tested with an array that contains just one element (data.length is 1). In fact, it should be tested twice with a one-element array: once when the target is equal to the element and once when the target is different from the element.

boundary values are "one step away from different behavior"

In general, there is no precise definition of a boundary value, but you should develop an intuitive feel for finding inputs that are "one step away from different behavior."

Test Boundary Values

If you cannot test all possible inputs, at least test the boundary values. For example, if legal inputs range from zero to one million, be sure to test input 0 and input 1000000. It is a good idea also to consider 0, 1, and −1 to be boundary values whenever they are legal input.

Fully Exercising Code

The second widely used testing technique requires intimate knowledge of how a program has been implemented. The technique, called **fully exercising code**, is stated with two rules:

Fully Exercising Code

1. Make sure that each line of your code is executed at least once by some of your test data. Make sure that this rare situation is included among your set of test data.

2. If there is part of your code that is sometimes skipped altogether, make sure there is at least one test input that actually does skip this part of your code. For example, there might be a loop where the body is sometimes executed zero times. Make sure that there is a test input that causes the loop body to be executed zero times.

---

profiler

Some Java programming environments have a software tool called a **profiler** to help fully exercise code. A typical profiler will generate a listing indicating how many times each method was called, so you can easily check that each method has been executed at least once. Some profilers offer more complete information, telling how often each individual statement of your program was executed. This can help you spot parts of your program that were not tested.

Keep in mind that fully exercised code may still have bugs. Code that has been fully exercised has had each line of code tested at least once, but one test does not guarantee that there are no errors.

PITFALL

AVOID IMPULSIVE CHANGES

Finding a test input that causes an error is only half the problem of testing and debugging. After an erroneous test input is found, you still must determine exactly why the "bug" occurs and then "debug the program." When you have found an error, there is an impulse to dive right in and start changing code. It is tempting to look for suspicious parts of your code and change these suspects to something "that might work better."

Avoid the temptation.

Impulsively changing suspicious code almost always makes matters worse. Instead, you must discover exactly why a test case is failing and limit your changes to corrections of known errors. Once you have corrected a known error, all test cases should be rerun.

Using a Debugger

Tracking down the reason why a test case is failing can be difficult. For large programs, tracking down errors is nearly impossible without the help of a software tool called a **debugger**. A debugger executes your code one line at a time, or it may execute your code until a certain condition arises. Using a debugger, you can specify what conditions should cause the program execution to pause. You can also keep a continuous watch on the location of the program execution and on the values of specified variables.

Assert Statements

> *An early advocate of using assertions in programming was none other than Alan Turing himself. On 24 June 1950 at a conference in Cambridge, he gave a short talk entitled* Checking a Large Routine, *which explains the idea with great clarity: "How can one check a large routine in the sense that it's right? In order that the man who checks may not have too difficult a task, the programmer should make a number of definite assertions which can be checked individually, and from which the correctness of the whole program easily follows."*

C.A.R. HOARE
1980 Turing Award Lecture

Assert statements (also called **assertions**) are boolean expressions that can be checked for validity while a program is running. They were introduced in Java 2, Version 1.4. Assertions can assist in debugging and maintaining programs by documenting conditions that the programmer intends to be valid at particular locations in the program. When a program is running, invalid assertions can be automatically flagged by the Java Runtime Environment, allowing a programmer to spot potential problems as early as possible.

The statement uses the new keyword `assert`, usually following the pattern shown here:

assert ＿＿＿＿＿＿＿＿＿＿＿＿ : "＿＿＿＿＿＿＿＿＿＿＿＿";

This is a boolean expression that we want to make sure is true at this point in the program.   *This is an error message that will be generated if the boolean expression is false.*

When an assert statement is reached, the boolean expression is tested. If the expression is true, then no action is taken: the program merely continues executing. But if the expression is false, then an exception called `AssertionError` is thrown. When an `AssertionError` occurs, the method where the failure occurred will stop its computation and usually the program will stop, printing the indicated error message along with an indication of the line number where the `AssertionError` occurred.

For example, consider the `maxOf3` method in Figure 1.5. The computation finds the largest of three numbers; it could be done in many different ways, such as the if-statements we have written, or perhaps we could make use of the two-argument `max` method from `java.lang.math`. But however the computation is carried out, it's an easy matter to use assertions to check the validity of the answer with the highlighted assertions at the bottom of the figure.

Notice that the error message (which follows the colon in each assertion) does not need to be on the same line as the assertion's boolean expression. Together, the two assertions verify that the answer was computed correctly—or, if there was an error, the program will stop and print an error message to guide the programmer's debugging effort. This particular example uses the "or" operation (`||`) to ensure that the answer is one of the three original parameters, and it uses the "and" operation (`&&`) to ensure that the answer is not smaller than any of the parameters.

Turning Assert Statements On and Off

By using assertions at key points (particularly for postconditions), a programmer finds programming errors at an early point when the errors are often easier to correct. However, once a program is ready to release for public use, Java environments permit assertion checking to be turned on or off as needed.

When a program is run with Java, assertions are *not* normally checked. During debugging, however, a programmer can turn on assertion checking by using the -enableassertions option (or -ea) for the Java runtime system. For example:

```
java -ea TemperatureConversion
```

There are other options that permit the programmer to turn assertions on or off in specific locations, but the general -ea option is sufficient to start.

FIGURE 1.5   Two Examples of Assertions

Specification

♦ **maxOf3**

    public static int maxOf3(int a, int b, int c)
    Returns the largest of three int values.

Parameters:
    a, b, c – any int numbers

Returns:
    The return value is the largest of the three arguments a, b, and c.

Implementation

```
public static int maxOf3(int a, int b, int c)
{
    int answer;

    // Set answer to the largest of a, b, and c:
    answer = a;          // Initially set answer to a
    if (b > answer)      // Maybe change the answer to b
        answer = b;
    if (c > answer)      // Maybe change the answer to c
        answer = c;

    // Check that the computation did what we expected:
    assert (answer == a) || (answer == b) || (answer == c)
        : "maxOf3 answer is not equal to one of the arguments";
    assert (answer >= a) && (answer >= b) && (answer >= c)
        : "maxOf3 answer is not equal to the largest argument";

    return answer;
}
```

⊕ PROGRAMMING TIP

USE A SEPARATE METHOD FOR COMPLEX ASSERTIONS

Some assertions can be implemented with a small boolean expression, such as the two assertions in maxOf3. But when the necessary checking becomes more complex, you should write a separate private method (or several methods) that carry out the checking. The method should return a boolean value that can be used in the assertion, as shown in Figure 1.6. Notice that the boolean methods are private (there is no public keyword), which means they can be used only within the class in which they appear.

FIGURE 1.6   The maxOfArray Method Together with Methods to Implement Assertions

Specification

♦ **maxOfArray**

```
public static int maxOfArray(int[ ])
```
   Returns the largest value in an array.

Parameters:
   a – a non-empty array (the length must not be zero)

Precondition:
   a.length > 0.

Returns:
   The return value is the largest value in the array a.

Throws: ArrayIndexOutOfBounds
   Indicates that the array length is zero.

Implementation

```
// This private method checks to make sure that the specified value is contained somewhere
// in the array a. The return value is true if the value is found; otherwise, the return value
// is false.
static boolean contains(int[ ] a, int value)
{
   int i;

   for (i = 0; i < a.length; i++)
   {
      if (a[i] == value)
         return true;
   }

   // The loop finished without finding the specified value, so we return false:
   return false;
}
```
(continued)

(FIGURE 1.6 continued)

```
//  This private method checks to make sure that the specified value is greater than or equal to
//  every element in the array a. In this case, the method returns true. On the other hand, if the
//  specified value is less than some element in the array, then the method returns false.
static boolean greaterOrEqual(int[ ] a, int value)
{
    int i;

    for (i = 0; i < a.length; i++)
    {
        if (a[i] > value)
            return false;
    }

    //  The loop finished without finding an array element that exceeds the value,
    //  so we can return true:
    return true;
}

public static int maxOfArray(int[ ] a)
{
    int answer;
    int i;

    //  Set answer to the largest value in the array.
    answer = a[0];          //  Initially set answer to the first element.
    for (i = 1; i < a.length; i++)
    {
        if (a[i] > answer)   //  Maybe change the answer to a[i].
            answer = a[i];
    }

    //  Check that the computation did what we expected:
    assert contains(a, answer)
        : "maxOfArray answer is not equal in the array";
    assert greaterOrEqual(a, answer)
        : "maxOfArray answer is less than an array element";

    return answer;
}
```

◑ PITFALL

AVOID USING ASSERTIONS TO CHECK PRECONDITIONS

Because assertions can be turned on and off, most programmers will not use assertions to check preconditions in public methods. Why not? The problem is that public methods may be used by other programmers. Of course, it is the responsibility of that other programmer to ensure that the precondition is valid. Still, if an invalid precondition is detected, it is best to throw an exception that cannot be turned off. Therefore, the designers of the assert statement suggest that assert statements should not be used to check preconditions in public methods.

Static Checking Tools

Static checking refers to program verification that can be carried out before a program is running. The Java compiler does certain kinds of static checking, such as checking that some data types are correct. (You cannot assign a `String` value to a `char` variable.) Other tools are available to do more extensive static checking, including verification of certain kinds of assertions. One such tool is the *Extended Static Checker for Java (ESC/Java)*, developed at the Compaq Systems Research Center and first shown to me by a colleague, Jim Royer, from Syracuse University. The tool is described in more detail at `http://www.eecs.umich.edu/~bchandra/courses/papers/Flanagan_ESC.pdf`.

Self-Test Exercises for Section 1.3

17. Suppose you write a program that accepts as input any integer in the range −20 through 20 and then outputs the number of digits in the input integer. What boundary values should you use as test inputs?
18. Suppose you write a program that accepts a single line as input and then outputs a message telling whether or not the line contains the letter A and whether or not it contains more than three A's. What is a good set of test inputs?
19. What does it mean to "fully exercise" code?
20. Suppose you have written a method with two double-number parameters: x and `epsilon`. The precondition requires that both parameters be actual numbers (rather than special values, such as "infinity"). The return value from the function is a number z so that z*z*z is no more than `epsilon` away from x. Don't worry about exactly how you've written this method; just assume that you wrote it. For this exercise, write an assertion that can be added at the end of the method to check that the return value is correct. Assume that the method has not altered x and `epsilon`, and use `java.math.abs` to compute an absolute value.
21. Why are assertions not usually used to check preconditions of public methods?

CHAPTER SUMMARY

- The first step in producing a program is to write down a precise description of what the program is supposed to do.

- Pseudocode is a mixture of Java (or some other programming language) and English (or some other natural language). Pseudocode is used to express algorithms so that you are not distracted by details about Java syntax.

- One good method for specifying what a method is supposed to do is to provide a *precondition* and *postcondition* for the method. These form a contract between the programmer who uses the method and the programmer who writes the method.

- *Time analysis* is an analysis of how many operations an algorithm requires. Often, it is sufficient to express a time analysis in big-*O* notation, which is the *order* of an algorithm. The order analysis is often enough to compare algorithms and estimate how running time is affected by changing input size.

- Three important examples of big-*O* analyses are *linear* (i.e., $O(n)$), *quadratic* (i.e., $O(n^2)$), and *logarithmic* (i.e., $O(\log n)$).

- An important testing technique is to identify and test *boundary values*. These are values that lie on a boundary between different kinds of behavior for your program.

- A second testing technique is to ensure that test cases are *fully exercising* the code. A software tool called a *profiler* can aid in fully exercising code.

- During debugging, you should discover exactly why a test case is failing and limit your changes to corrections of known errors. Once you have corrected a known error, all test cases should be rerun. Use a software tool called a *debugger* to help track down exactly why an error occurs.

- Assertions can assist in debugging and maintaining programs by documenting conditions that the programmer intends to be valid at particular locations in the program.

? Solutions to Self-Test Exercises

1. The method returns 7 on July 22, 2013. On both July 30, 2013, and February 1, 2014, the method returns 0 (since July 29, 2013, has already passed).

2. Yes. To use a method, all you need to know is the specification.

3. `System.out.printf("$%,12.2f",boodle);`

4. **printSqrt**
    ```
    public static void
    printSqrt(double x)
    ```
    Prints the square root of a number.
    Parameter:
    x – any non-negative double number
    Precondition:
    `x >= 0.`
    Postcondition:
    The positive square root of x has been printed to standard output.
    Throws: `IllegalArgumentException`
    Indicates that x is negative.

5. **sphereVolume**
    ```
    public static double
    sphereVolume(double radius)
    ```
    Compute the volume of a sphere.
    Parameter:
    radius – any positive double number
    Precondition:
    `radius > 0.`
    Returns:
    the volume of a sphere with the specified radius
    Throws: `IllegalArgumentException`
    Indicates that radius is negative.

6. ```
   if (x < 0)
       throw new IllegalArgumentException
       ("x is negative: " + x);
   ```

7. A `final` variable is given an initial value when it is declared, and this value will never change while the program is running.

8. Most of the specification was automatically produced using the Javadoc tool described in Appendix H.

9. The method name, the parameter list, the return type, and any modifiers.

10. ```
    System.out.println(
        "Age %10d Height %12.3f",
        age,
        height
    );
    ```

11. Here is a specification for the method, along with an implementation:
    sum
    ```
    public static int sum(int[ ] a)
    ```
    Compute the sum of the numbers in an array.
    Parameter:
    a – an array whose numbers are to be summed
    Returns:
    the sum of the numbers in the array (which is zero if the array has no elements)
    ```
    public static int sum(int[ ] a)
    {
      int answer, i;

      answer = 0;
      for (i = 0; i < a.length; i++)
        answer += a[i];
      return answer;
    }
    ```
    Our solution uses answer += a[i], which causes the current value of a[i] to be added to what's already in answer.

For a time analysis, let *n* be the array size. There are two assignment operations (i = 0 and answer = 0). The < test is executed $n + 1$ times. (The first *n* times it is true, and the final time, with i equal to *n*, it is false.) The ++ and += operations are each executed *n* times, and an array subscript (a[i]) is taken *n* times. The entire code is $O(n)$.

12. Part (d) is linear (i.e., $O(n)$); parts (f) and (g) are logarithmic (i.e., $O(\log n)$); all of the others are quadratic (i.e., $O(n^2)$).

13. The only $O(n)$ formula is (d).

14. Worst-case analysis counts the maximum required number of operations for a function. If the exact count of the number of operations cannot be determined, the number of operations may be estimated, provided that the estimate is guaranteed to be higher than the actual number of operations.

15. This is a nested loop in which the number of times the inner loop executes is one more than the value of the outer loop index. The inner loop statements execute $n + (n - 1) + \ldots + 2 + 1$ times. This sum is $n(n + 1)/2$ and gives $O(n^2)$.

16. $n^2 + 1$; $10n + 10{,}000$; $50 \log n$; 1,000,000.

17. As always, 0, 1, and −1 are boundary values. In this problem, −20 (smallest value) and 20 (largest value) are also boundary values. Also 9 and 10 (the number changes from a single digit to two digits) and −9 and −10. (By the way, this particular problem is small enough that it would be reasonable to test *all* legal inputs rather than just testing the boundary values.)

18. You should include an empty line (with no characters before the carriage return) and lines with 0, 1, 2, and 3 A's. Also include a line with 4 A's (the smallest case with more than three) and a line with more than 4 A's. For the lines with 1 or more A's, include lines that have only the A's and also include lines that have A's together with other characters. Also test the case in which all the A's appear at the front or the back of the line.

19. See the box "Fully Exercising Code" on page 28.

20.
```
assert
  (java.math.abs(x-z*z*z) < epsilon)
  : "Incorrect z value";
```

21. If an invalid precondition is detected, it is best to throw an exception that cannot be turned off.

CHAPTER **2**

Java Classes and Information Hiding

Java Classes and Information Hiding

*The happiest way to deal with a man is never to tell him
anything he does not need to know.*

ROBERT A. HEINLEIN
Time Enough for Love

Object-oriented programming (**OOP**) is an approach to programming in which data occurs in tidy packages called *objects*. Manipulation of
an object happens with functions called *methods,* which are part and parcel of
their objects. The Java mechanism to create objects and methods is called a
class. The keyword class at the start of each Java application program indicates that the program is itself a class with its own methods to carry out tasks.

This chapter moves you beyond small Java application programs. Your goal
is to be able to write general-purpose classes that can be used by many different
programs. Each general-purpose class will capture a certain functionality, and an
application programmer can look through the available classes to select those
that are useful for the job at hand.

For example, consider a programmer who is writing an application to simulate
a Martian lander as it goes from orbit to the surface of Mars. This programmer
could use classes to simulate the various mechanical components of the lander—
the throttle that controls fuel flow, the rocket engine, and so on. If such classes
are readily available in a package of "mechanical component classes," then the
programmer could select and use the appropriate classes. Typically, one
programming team designs and implements such classes, and other programmers
use the classes. The programmers who use the classes must be provided with a
specification of how the classes work, but they need no knowledge of how the
classes are *implemented*.

The separation of specification from implementation is an example of *information hiding*, which was presented as a cornerstone of program design in
Chapter 1. Such a strong emphasis on information hiding is partly motivated by
mathematical research into how programmers can improve their reasoning about
data types that are used in programs. These mathematical data types are called
abstract data types, or ADTs—and therefore, programmers sometimes use the
term "**ADT**" to refer to a class that is presented to other programmers with information hiding. This chapter presents two examples of such classes. The examples
illustrate the features of Java classes, with emphasis on information hiding. By
the end of this chapter, you will be able to implement your own classes in Java.
Other programmers could *use* one of your classes without knowing the details of
how you implemented the class.

*ADTs
emphasize the
specification
rather than the
implementation*

2.1 CLASSES AND THEIR MEMBERS

A class is a new kind of data type. Each object of a class includes various *data*, such as integers, characters, and so on. In addition, a class has the ability to include two other kinds of items: *constructors* and *methods*. Constructors are designed to provide initial values to the class's data; methods are designed to manipulate the data. Taken together, the data, constructors, and methods of a class are called the class **members**.

But this abstract discussion does not really tell you what a class *is*. We need some examples. As you read the first example, concentrate on learning the techniques for implementing a class. Also notice how you use a class that was written by another programmer, without knowing details of the class's implementation.

PROGRAMMING EXAMPLE: **The Throttle Class**

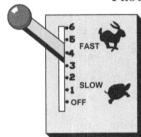

Our first example of a class is a new data type to store and manipulate the status of a mechanical throttle. An object of this new class holds information about one throttle, as shown in the picture. The throttle is a lever that can be moved to control fuel flow. The throttle we have in mind has a single shutoff point (where there is no fuel flow) and a sequence of several on positions where the fuel is flowing at progressively higher rates. At the topmost position, the fuel flow is fully on. At the intermediate positions, the fuel flow is proportional to the location of the lever. For example, with six possible positions and the lever in the fourth position, the fuel flows at $\frac{4}{6}$ of its maximum rate.

A constructor is designed to provide initial values to a class's data. The throttle constructor permits a program to create a new throttle with a specified number of "on positions" above the shutoff point. For instance, a throttle for a lawn mower could specify six positions, whereas a throttle for a Martian lander could specify 1000 positions. The throttle's lever is initially placed at the shutoff point.

Once a throttle has been initialized, there are two methods to shift the throttle's lever: One of the methods shifts the lever by a given amount, and the other method returns the lever to the shutoff position. We also have two methods to examine the status of a throttle. The first of these methods returns the amount of fuel currently flowing, expressed as a proportion of the maximum flow. For example, this method will return approximately 0.667 when a six-position throttle is in its fourth position. The other method returns a true or false value, telling whether the throttle is currently on (that is, whether the lever is above the shutoff point). Thus, the throttle has one constructor and four methods:

one throttle constructor and four throttle methods

- A constructor to create a new throttle with one shutoff point and a specified number of on positions (the lever starts at the shutoff point)
- A method that returns the fuel flow, expressed as a proportion of the maximum flow
- A method to tell us whether the throttle is currently on
- A method to shift a throttle's lever by a given amount
- A method to set the throttle's lever back to the shutoff point

Defining a New Class

We're ready to define a new Java class called `Throttle`. The new class includes data (to store information about the throttle) plus the constructor and methods previously listed. Once the `Throttle` class is defined, a programmer can create objects of type `Throttle` and manipulate those objects with the methods.

Here's an outline of the `Throttle` class definition:

```
public class Throttle
{
    private int top;       // The topmost position of the lever
    private int position;  // The current position of the lever

    This part of the class definition provides the implementations
    of the constructor and methods.

}
```

declaring the
Throttle class

This class definition defines a new data type called `Throttle`. The definition starts with the **class head**, which consists of the Java keywords `public class` followed by the name of the new class. The keyword `public` is necessary before the `class` because we want to allow all other programmers (the "public") to use the new class. The name of the class can be any legal identifier. We chose the name `Throttle`. We always use a capital letter for the first character of names of new classes. This isn't required by Java, but it's a common programming style, making it easy to identify class names.

The rest of the class definition, between the two brackets, is a list of all the components of the class. These components are called **members** of the class, and they come in three varieties: instance variables, constructors, and methods.

three varieties of
class members
appear in the
class definition

Instance Variables

The first kind of member is a variable declaration. These variables are called **instance variables** (or sometimes "member variables"). The `Throttle` class has two instance variables:

```
private int top;       // The topmost position of the lever
private int position;  // The current position of the lever
```

Each instance variable stores some piece of information about the status of an object. For example, consider a throttle with six possible positions where the lever is in the fourth position. This throttle would have `top=6` and `position=4`.

The keyword `private` occurs in front of each of our instance variables. This keyword means that programmers who use the new class have no way to read or assign values directly to the private instance variables. It is possible to have public instance variables that can be accessed directly, but public instance variables tend to reveal too much information about how a class is implemented, violating the principle of information hiding. Therefore, our examples will use private instance variables. Other programmers must access the private instance variables through the constructors and methods provided with the class.

Constructors

The second kind of member is a constructor. (Technically, a constructor is not a member, but the reason is a small concern that we'll see in Chapter 13, and most programmers do think of constructors as members.) A constructor is a method that is responsible for initializing the instance variables. For example, our constructor creates a throttle with a specified number of on positions above the shutoff position. This constructor sets the instance variable top to a specified number and sets position to zero (so that initially the throttle is shut off).

For the most part, implementing a constructor is no different than your past work (such as implementing a method for a Java application). The primary difference is that a constructor has access to the class's instance variables, and it is responsible for initializing these variables. Thus, a throttle constructor must provide initial values to top and position. Before you implement the throttle constructor, you must know several rules that make constructors special:

- Before any constructor begins its work, all instance variables are assigned Java "default values." For example, the Java default value for any number variable is zero.

- If an instance variable has an initialization value with its declaration, the initialization value replaces the default value. For example, suppose we have this instance variable:

  ```
  int jackie = 42;
  ```

  The instance variable jackie is first given its default value of zero; then the zero is replaced by the initialization value of 42.

- The name of a constructor must be the same as the name of the class. In our example, the name of the constructor is Throttle. This seems strange: Normally we *avoid* using the same name for two different things. But it is a requirement of Java that the constructor use the same name as the class.

- A constructor is not really a method, and therefore it does not have *any* return value. Because of this, you must *not* write void (or any other return type) at the front of the constructor's head. The compiler knows that every constructor has no return value, but a compiler error occurs if you actually write void at the front of the constructor's head.

With these rules, we can write the throttle's constructor as shown here (with its specification following the format from Section 1.1):

♦ **Constructor for the Throttle**
```
public Throttle(int size)
```
Construct a Throttle with a specified number of on positions.

Parameter:
   size – the number of on positions for this new Throttle
Precondition:
   size > 0
Postcondition:
   This Throttle has been initialized with the specified number of on
   positions above the shutoff point, and it is currently shut off.
Throws: IllegalArgumentException
   Indicates that size is not positive.

```java
public Throttle(int size)
{
   if (size <= 0)
      throw new IllegalArgumentException("Size <= 0: " + size);
   top = size;
   // No assignment needed for position -- it gets the default value of zero.
}
```

This constructor sets top according to the parameter, size. It does not explicitly
set position, but the comment in the implementation indicates that we did not
just forget about position; the default value of zero is its correct initial value.
The implementation is preceded by the keyword public to make it available to
all programmers.

The throttle has just one constructor, and so just one way of setting the initial
values of the instance variables. Some classes may have many different constructors that set initial values in different ways. If there are several constructors, then
each constructor must have a distinct sequence of parameters to distinguish it
from the other constructors.

*a class can have
many different
constructors*

No-Arguments Constructors

Some classes have a constructor with no parameters, called a **no-arguments**
constructor. In effect, a no-arguments constructor does not need any extra
information to set the initial values of the instance variables.

If you write a class with no constructors at all, then Java automatically provides a no-arguments constructor that initializes each instance variable to its
initialization value (if there is one) or to its default value (if there is no specified
initialization value). There is one situation in which Java does not provide an
automatic no-arguments constructor, and you'll see this situation when you write
subclasses in Chapter 13.

Methods

The third kind of class member is a method. A method does computations that
access the class's instance variables. Classes tend to have two kinds of methods:

1. An **accessor method** gives information about an object without altering the object. In the case of the throttle, an accessor method can return information about the status of a throttle, but it must not change the position of the lever.

2. A **modification method** can change the status of an object. For a throttle, a modification method can shift the lever up or down.

Each class method is designed for a specific manipulation of an object—in our case, the manipulation of a throttle. To carry out the manipulations, each of the throttle methods has access to the throttle's instance variables, top and position. The methods can examine top and position to determine the current status of the throttle, or top and position can be changed to alter the status of the throttle. Let's look at the details of the implementations of the throttle methods, beginning with the accessor methods.

Accessor Methods

Accessor methods provide information about an object without changing the object. Accessor methods are often short, just returning the value of an instance variable or performing a computation with a couple of instance variables. The first of the throttle accessor methods computes the current flow as a proportion of the maximum flow. The specification and implementation are:

♦ **getFlow**

    public double getFlow( )

Get the current flow of this Throttle.

Returns:

the current flow rate (always in the range [0.0 ... 1.0]) as a proportion of the maximum flow

```
public double getFlow( )
{
    return (double) position / (double) top;
}
```

accessor methods often have no parameters

Accessor methods often have no parameters, no precondition, and only a simple return condition in the specification. How does an accessor method manage with no parameters? It needs no parameters because all of the necessary information is available in the instance variables.

 PROGRAMMING TIP

FOUR REASONS TO IMPLEMENT ACCESSOR METHODS

Many classes could be written without accessor methods by making the instance variables public instead of private. For example, the getFlow method would not be needed if position and top were public instance variables (because a programmer could then use those variables directly). However, providing private instance variables and accessor methods does a better job of information hiding, accomplishing these things:

1. A programmer who uses the throttle need not worry about how it is implemented. (It's always good to have fewer details to worry about.)
2. Using accessor methods allows us to later change the implementation of the throttle, perhaps adding a new member variable that always keeps track of the current flow. Programs that use the throttle will still work correctly after we make such changes, provided we have one set of accessor methods whose implementations do not change.
3. When a class implements an accessor method, that method can be thoroughly tested, increasing reliability. Without accessor methods, each program that uses the class is prone to the same potential errors. For example, one potential error in the getFlow method is a division error that we'll describe in a moment.
4. The pattern of "private data, public methods" forbids other programmers from using our instance variables in unintended ways (such as setting position to a negative value).

Java provides many classes for programmers to use. If you read the specifications for these classes (called the **Application Programmers Interface**, or **API**), you'll see the prevalence of accessor methods in professionally written classes.

PITFALL

INTEGER DIVISION THROWS AWAY THE FRACTIONAL PART

The getFlow implementation computes and returns a fractional value. For example, if position is 4 and top is 6, then getFlow returns approximately 0.667. To get a fractional result in the answer, the integer numbers position and top cannot simply be divided using the expression position/top because this would result in an integer division ($\frac{4}{6}$ results in the quotient 0, discarding any remainder). Instead, we must force Java to compute a fractional division by changing the integer values to double values. For example, the expression (double) position is a "cast" that changes the integer value of position to a double value to use in the division.

The throttle's second accessor method returns a true or false value indicating whether the fuel flow is on. Here is this method with its specification:

♦ **isOn**
  public boolean isOn( )
  Check whether this Throttle is on.
  Returns:
    If this Throttle's flow is above zero, then the return value is true; otherwise, the return value is false.

```
public boolean isOn( )
{
    return (position > 0);
}
```

ⓘ PROGRAMMING TIP

USE THE BOOLEAN TYPE FOR TRUE OR FALSE VALUES

Java's basic boolean type may be relatively unfamiliar. You should use the boolean type for any true or false value, such as the return value of the isOn method. The return statement for a boolean method can be any boolean expression, for example, a comparison such as (position > 0). In this example, if position is greater than zero, then the comparison is true, and isOn returns true. On the other hand, if position is equal to zero, then the comparison is false and isOn returns false.

The name "boolean" is derived from the name of George Boole, a 19th-century mathematician who developed the foundations of a formal calculus of logical values. Boole was a self-educated scholar with limited formal training. He began his teaching career at the age of 16 as an elementary school teacher and eventually took a position as professor at Queen's College in Cork. As a dedicated teacher, he died at the age of only 49—the result of pneumonia brought on by a two-mile trek through the rain to lecture to his students.

Modification Methods

There are two more throttle methods. These two are **modification methods**, which means they are capable of changing the values of the instance variables. Here is the first modification method:

♦ **shutOff**
```
public void shutOff( )
```
Turn off this Throttle.

Postcondition:
This Throttle's flow has been shut off.

```
public void shutOff( )
{
    position = 0;
}
```

modification methods are usually void

Modification methods are usually void, meaning there is no return value. In the specification of a modification method, the method's work is fully described in the postcondition.

The throttle's shutOff method has no parameters. This method doesn't need parameters, because it just moves the throttle's position down to zero, shutting off the flow. However, most modification methods do have parameters. For example, consider a throttle method to shift the throttle's lever by a specified amount. This shift method has one integer parameter called amount. If amount is positive, then the throttle's lever is moved up by that amount (but never beyond the topmost position). A negative amount causes the lever to move down (but never below zero). Here are the specification and implementation:

♦ **shift**
> ```
> public void shift(int amount)
> ```
> Move this Throttle's position up or down.
>
> **Parameter:**
>> amount – the amount to move the position up or down (a positive amount moves the position up; a negative amount moves it down)
>
> **Postcondition:**
>> This Throttle's position has been moved by the specified amount. If the result is more than the topmost position, then the position stays at the topmost position. If the result is less than the zero position, then the position stays at the zero position.

```
public void shift(int amount)
{
    if (amount > top - position)
        // Adding amount would put the position above the top.
        position = top;
    else if (position + amount < 0)
        // Adding amount would put the position below zero.
        position = 0;
    else
        // Adding amount puts position in the range [0...top].
        position += amount;
}
```

This might be the first time you've seen the += operator. Its effect is to take the value on the right side (such as amount) and add it to what's already in the variable on the left (such as position). This sum is then stored back in the variable on the left side of +=.

The shift method requires care to ensure that the position does not go above the topmost position nor below zero. For example, the first test in the method checks whether (amount > top - position). If so, then adding amount to position would push the position over top. In this case, we simply set position to top.

It is tempting to write the test (amount > top - position) in a slightly different way, like this:

```
if (position + amount > top)
    // Adding amount would put the position above the top.
    position = top;
```

This seems okay at first glance, but there is a potential problem: What happens if both `position` and `amount` are large integers, such as 2,000,000,000? The subexpression `position + amount` should be 4,000,000,000, but Java tries to temporarily store the subexpression as a Java integer, which is limited to the range −2,147,483,648 to 2,147,483,647. The result is an **arithmetic overflow**, which is defined as trying to compute or store a number that is beyond the legal range of the data type. When an arithmetic overflow occurs, the program might stop with an error message, or it might continue computing with wrong data.

We avoided the arithmetic overflow by rearranging the first test to avoid the troublesome subexpression. The test we use is:

```
if (amount > top - position)
    // Adding amount would put the position above the top.
    position = top;
```

This test uses the subexpression `top - position`. Because `top` is never negative and `position` is in the range `[0...top]`, the subexpression `top - position` is always a valid integer in the range `[0...top]`.

What about the second test in the method? In the second test, we use the subexpression `position + amount`, but at this point, `position + amount` can no longer cause an arithmetic overflow. Do you see why? If `position + amount` is bigger than `top`, then the first test would have been `true`, and the second test is never reached. Therefore, by the time we reach the second test, the subexpression `position + amount` is guaranteed to be in the range `[amount...top]`, and arithmetic overflow cannot occur.

 **PITFALL**

POTENTIAL ARITHMETIC OVERFLOWS

Check arithmetic expressions for potential arithmetic overflow. The limitations for Java variables and subexpressions are given in Appendix A. Often you can rewrite an expression to avoid overflow, or you can use `long` variables (with a range from −9,223,372,036,854,775,808 to 9,223,372,036,854,775,807). If overflow cannot be avoided altogether, then include a note in the documentation to describe the situation that causes overflow.

Complete Definition of Throttle.java

the name of the Java file must match the name of the class

We have completed the `Throttle` class implementation and can now put the complete definition in a file called `Throttle.java`, as shown in Figure 2.1. The name of the file must be `Throttle.java` since the class is named `Throttle`.

FIGURE 2.1	Specification and Implementation for the `Throttle` Class

Class Throttle

❖ **public class Throttle**
A `Throttle` object simulates a throttle that is controlling fuel flow.

Specification

◆ **Constructor for the Throttle**
    `public Throttle(int size)`
    Construct a `Throttle` with a specified number of on positions.
    Parameter:
        `size` – the number of on positions for this new `Throttle`
    Precondition:
        `size > 0`
    Postcondition:
        This `Throttle` has been initialized with the specified number of on positions above the shutoff point, and it is currently shut off.
    Throws: `IllegalArgumentException`
    Indicates that `size` is not positive.

◆ **getFlow**
    `public double getFlow( )`
    Get the current flow of this `Throttle`.
    Returns:
        the current flow rate (always in the range [0.0 ... 1.0]) as a proportion of the maximum flow

◆ **isOn**
    `public boolean isOn( )`
    Check whether this `Throttle` is on.
    Returns:
        If this `Throttle`'s flow is above zero, then the return value is `true`; otherwise, the return value is `false`.

◆ **shift**
    `public void shift(int amount)`
    Move this `Throttle`'s position up or down.
    Parameter:
        `amount` – the amount to move the position up or down (a positive amount moves the position up; a negative amount moves it down)
    Postcondition:
        This `Throttle`'s position has been moved by the specified amount. If the result is more than the topmost position, then the position stays at the topmost position. If the result is less than the zero position, then the position stays at the zero position.

(continued)

(FIGURE 2.1 continued)

◆ **shutOff**

```
public void shutOff( )
```
Turn off this Throttle.

Postcondition:
This Throttle has been shut off.

Implementation

```java
//  File: Throttle.java

public class Throttle
{
    private int top;        //  The topmost position of the throttle
    private int position;  //  The current position of the throttle

    public Throttle(int size)
    {
        if (size <= 0)
            throw new IllegalArgumentException("Size <= 0: " + size);
        top = size;
        //  No assignment needed for position -- it gets the default value of zero.
    }

    public double getFlow( )
    {
        return (double) position / (double) top;
    }

    public boolean isOn( )
    {
        return (getFlow( ) > 0);
    }

    public void shift(int amount)
    {
        if (amount > top - position) //  Adding amount makes position too big.
            position = top;
        else if (position + amount < 0) //  Adding amount makes position below zero.
            position = 0;
        else //  Adding amount puts position in the range [0 ... top].
            position += amount;
    }

    public void shutOff( )
    {
        position = 0;
    }
}
```

Methods May Activate Other Methods

The throttle's isOn method in Figure 2.1 has one change from the original implementation. The change is highlighted here:

```
public boolean isOn( )
{
    return (getFlow( ) > 0);
}
```

In this implementation, we have checked whether the flow is on by calling the getFlow method rather than by looking directly at the position instance variable. Both implementations work: Using position directly probably executes quicker, but you could argue that using getFlow makes the method's intent clearer. Anyway, the real purpose of this change is just to illustrate that one method can call another to carry out a subtask. In this example, the isOn method calls getFlow. An OOP programmer usually would use slightly different terminology, saying that the isOn method **activated** the flow method. **Activating a method** is nothing more than OOP jargon for "calling a method."

Self-Test Exercises for Section 2.1

1. Describe the three kinds of class members we have used. In this section, which kinds of members were public and which were private?
2. We talked about accessor methods and modification methods. Which kind of method often has a void return type? Why?
3. Write a new throttle constructor with no arguments. The constructor sets the top position to 1 and sets the current position to off.
4. Write another throttle constructor with two arguments: the total number of positions for the throttle, and its initial position.
5. Describe the difference between a modification method and an accessor method.
6. Add a new throttle method that will return true when the current flow is more than half of the maximum flow. The body of your implementation should activate the getFlow method.
7. Design and implement a class called Clock. A Clock object holds one instance of a time such as 9:48 P.M. Have at least these public methods:

   - A no-arguments constructor that initializes the time to midnight (see page 43 for the discussion of a no-arguments constructor)
   - A method to explicitly assign a given time (you will have to give some thought to appropriate arguments for this method)
   - Methods to retrieve information: the current hour, the current minute, and a boolean method that returns true if the time is at or before noon
   - A method to advance the time forward by a given number of minutes (which could be negative to move the clock backward or positive to move the clock forward)

8. Suppose you implement a class, but you do not write a constructor. What kind of constructor does Java usually provide automatically?

2.2   USING A CLASS

programs can create new objects of a class

How do you use a new class such as Throttle? Within any program, you can create new throttles and refer to these throttles by names that you define. We will illustrate the syntax for creating and using these objects with an example.

Creating and Using Objects

Suppose a program needs a new throttle with 100 positions above the shutoff. Within the program, we want to refer to the throttle by the name control. The Java syntax has these parts:

```
Throttle control = new Throttle(100);
```

The first part of this statement—Throttle control—declares a new variable called control. The control variable is capable of referring to a throttle. The second part of the statement—new Throttle(100)—creates a new throttle and initializes control to refer to this new throttle. A new throttle that is created in this way is called a Throttle **object**.

There are a few points to notice about the syntax for creating a new Throttle object: new is a keyword to create a new object; Throttle is the data type of the new object; and (100) is the list of arguments for the constructor of the new object. We are creating a new throttle and 100 is the argument for the constructor, so the new throttle will have 100 positions above the shutoff.

using a no-arguments constructor

If the class has a no-arguments constructor, then the syntax for creating an object is the same, except that the list of arguments is empty. For example, suppose that Thermometer is a class with a no-arguments constructor. Then we could write this:

```
Thermometer t = new Thermometer( );
```

Once an object is created, we can refer to that object by the name we declared. For example, suppose we have created a throttle called control and we want to shift the lever up to its third notch. We do this by calling the shift method:

```
control.shift(3);
```

Calling a method always involves these four pieces:

1. Start with a reference to the object you are manipulating. In this example, we want to manipulate control, so we begin with "control". Remember

that you cannot just call a method; you must always indicate which object is being manipulated.

2. Next, place a single period.

3. Next, write the name of the method. In our example, we call the `shift` method, so we write "control.shift"—which you can pronounce "control *dot* shift."

4. Finally, list the parameters for the method call. In our example, `shift` requires one parameter, which is the amount (3) that we are shifting the throttle. Thus, the entire statement is `control.shift(3);`

how to use a method

Our example called the `shift` method. As you've seen before, OOP programmers like their own terminology, and they would say that we **activated** the `shift` method. In the rest of the text, we'll try to use "activate" rather than "call." (This will keep us on the good side of OOP programmers.)

As another example, here is a sequence of several statements to set a throttle to a certain point and then print the throttle's flow:

```
final int SIZE = 8;   // The size of the Throttle
final int SPOT = 3;   // Where to move the Throttle's lever

Throttle small = new Throttle(SIZE);

small.shift(SPOT);
System.out.print("My small throttle is now at position ");
System.out.println(SPOT + " out of " + SIZE + ".");
System.out.println("The flow is now: " + small.getFlow( ));
```

Notice how the return value of `small.getFlow` is used directly in the output statement. As with any other method, the return value of an accessor method can be used as part of an output statement or other expression. The output from this code is:

```
My small throttle is now at position 3 out of 8.
The flow is now: 0.375
```

A Program with Several Throttle Objects

A single program can have many throttle objects. For example, the following code will declare two throttle objects, shifting each throttle to a different point:

```
Throttle tiny = new Throttle(4);
Throttle huge = new Throttle(10000);

tiny.shift(2);
huge.shift(2500);
```

Here's an important concept to keep in mind:

When a program has several objects of the same class, each object has its own copies of the class's instance variables.

In the preceding example, `tiny` has its own instance variables (`top` will be 4 and `position` will be 2); `huge` also has its own instance variables (`top` will be 10,000 and `position` will be 2500). When we activate a method such as `tiny.shift`, the method uses the instance variables from `tiny`; when we activate `huge.shift`, the method uses the instance variables from `huge`.

The variables in our examples—`control`, `small`, `tiny`, `huge`—are called **reference variables** because they are used to *refer* to objects (in our case, throttles). There are several differences between a reference variable (used by Java for all classes) and an ordinary variable (used by Java for the primitive data types of `int`, `char`, and so on). Let's look at these differences, beginning with a special value called `null` that is used only with reference variables.

Null References

The creation of a new object can be separated from the declaration of a variable. For example, the following two statements can occur far apart in a program:

```
Throttle control;
...
control = new Throttle(100);
```

Once both statements finish, `control` refers to a newly created throttle with 100 positions. But what is the status of `control` between the statements? At that point, `control` does not yet refer to any throttle because we haven't yet created a throttle. In this situation, we can assign a special value to `control`, indicating that `control` does not yet refer to anything. The value is called the **null reference**, written with the keyword `null` in Java. So we could change the example to this:

```
Throttle control = null;
...
control = new Throttle(100);
```

In this area, `control` does not refer to anything.

Null Reference

Sometimes a reference variable does not refer to anything. This is a **null reference**, and the value of the variable is called **null**.

Sometimes a program finishes using an object. In this case, the program may explicitly set a reference variable to `null`, as shown here:

```
Throttle control = new Throttle(100);

// Various statements that use the Throttle appear next...
...
// Now we are done with the control Throttle, so we can set the reference to null.
control = null;
```

Once a reference variable is no longer needed, it can be set to `null`, which allows Java to economize on certain resources (such as the memory used by a throttle).

PITFALL

NULLPOINTEREXCEPTION

When a variable such as `control` becomes `null`, it no longer refers to any throttle. If `control` is `null`, then it is a programming error to activate a method such as `control.shift`. The result is an exception called `NullPointer-Exception`.

Assignment Statements with Reference Variables

The usual assignment statement can be used with reference variables. For example, we might have two `Throttle` variables `t1` and `t2`, and an assignment such as `t2 = t1` is permitted. But what is the effect of the assignment? For starters, if `t1` is `null`, then the assignment `t2 = t1` also makes `t2` `null`. Here is a more complicated case in which `t1` is not `null`:

```
Throttle t1;
Throttle t2;

t1 = new Throttle(100);
t1.shift(25);
t2 = t1;
```

The effect of the assignment `t2 = t1` is somewhat different than assignments for integers or other primitive data types. The effect of `t2 = t1` is to "make `t2` refer to the same object that `t1` is already referring to." In other words, we have two reference variables (`t1` and `t2`), but we created only one throttle (with one new statement). This one throttle has 100 positions and is currently in the 25th position. After the assignment statement, both `t1` and `t2` refer to this one throttle.

To explore this example in more detail, let's start with the two declarations:

```
Throttle t1;
Throttle t2;
```

We now have two variables, t1 and t2. If these variables are declared in a method, then they don't yet have an initial value (not even null). We can draw this situation with a question mark for each value:

Throttle t1 ?   Throttle t2 ?

The next two statements are:

```
t1 = new Throttle(100);
t1.shift(25);
```

These statements create a new throttle for t1 to refer to and shift the throttle's position to 25. We will draw a separate box for the throttle and indicate its instance variables (top at 100 and position at 25). To show that t1 refers to this throttle, we draw an arrow from the t1 box to the throttle:

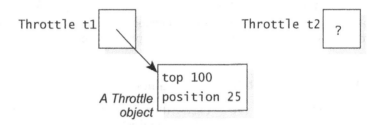

At this point, we can execute the assignment:

```
t2 = t1;
```

After the assignment, t2 will refer to the same object that t1 refers to:

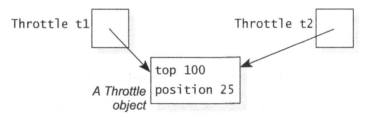

There are now two references to the same throttle, which can cause some surprising results. For example, suppose we shift t2 down five notches and then print the flow of t1, like this:

```
t2.shift(-5);
System.out.println("Flow of t1 is: " + t1.getFlow( ));
```

What flow rate is printed? The t1 throttle was set to position 25 out of 100, and we never *directly* altered its position. But t2.shift(-5) moves the throttle's position down to 20. Since t1 refers to this same throttle, t1.getFlow now returns 20/100, and the output statement prints "Flow of t1 is: 0.2". Here's the entire code that we executed and the final situation drawn as a picture:

```
Throttle t1;
Throttle t2;

t1 = new Throttle(100);
t1.shift(25);
t2 = t1;
t2.shift(-5);
```

Throttle t1

Throttle t2

A Throttle object

```
top 100
position 20
```

Assignment Statements with Reference Variables

If t1 and t2 are reference variables, then the assignment t2 = t1 is allowed.

If t1 is null, then the assignment makes t2 null also.

If t1 is not null, then the assignment changes t2 so that it refers to the same object that t1 already refers to. At this point, changes can be made to that one object through either t1 or t2.

The situation of an assignment statement contrasts with a program that actually creates two separate throttles for t1 and t2. For example, two separate throttles can be created with each throttle in the 25th position out of 100:

```
Throttle t1;
Throttle t2;

t1 = new Throttle(100);
t1.shift(25);
t2 = new Throttle(100);
t2.shift(25);
```

With this example, we have two separate throttles, as shown on the next page.

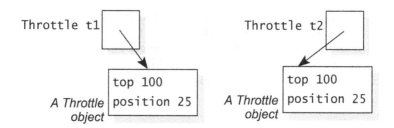

Changes that are now made to one throttle will not affect the other, because there are two completely separate throttles.

Clones

A programmer sometimes needs to make an exact copy of an existing object. The copy must be just like the existing object, but separate. Subsequent changes to the copy should not alter the original, nor should subsequent changes to the original alter the copy. A separate copy such as this is called a **clone**.

An assignment operation t2 = t1 does not create a clone, and in fact the Throttle class does not permit the easy creation of clones. But many other classes have a special method called clone for just this purpose. Writing a useful clone method has some requirements that may not be evident just now, so we will postpone a complete discussion until Section 2.4.

Testing for Equality

A test for equality (t1 == t2) can be carried out with reference variables. The equality test (t1 == t2) is true if both t1 and t2 are null or if they both refer to the exact same object (not two different objects that happen to have the same values for their instance variables). An inequality test (t1 != t2) can also be carried out. The result of an inequality test is always the opposite of an equality test. Let's look at two examples.

The first example creates just one throttle; t1 and t2 both refer to this throttle, as shown in the following picture:

```
Throttle t1;
Throttle t2;

t1 = new Throttle(100);
t1.shift(25);
t2 = t1;
```

Throttle t1

Throttle t2

A Throttle object

top 100
position 25

At this point in the computation, (t1 == t2) is true. Both reference variables refer to the same object.

On the other hand, consider this code, which creates two separate throttles:

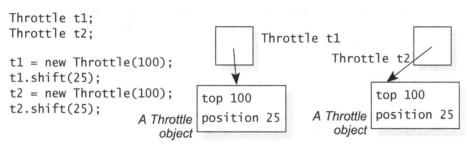

```
Throttle t1;
Throttle t2;

t1 = new Throttle(100);
t1.shift(25);
t2 = new Throttle(100);
t2.shift(25);
```

After this computation, (t1 == t2) is false. The two throttles have the same value (with top at 100 and position at 25), but the equality test returns false because they are two separate throttles.

Test for Equality with Reference Variables

For reference variables t1 and t2, the test (t1 == t2) is true if both references are null or if t1 and t2 refer to the exact same object (not two different objects that happen to have the same values for their instance variables).

Terminology Controversy: "The Throttle That t Refers To"

A declaration such as `Throttle t = new Throttle(42)` declares a reference variable t and makes it refer to a newly created throttle. We can then talk about "the throttle that t refers to." This is the correct terminology, but sometimes a programmer's thinking is clarified by shortening the terminology and saying things like "the throttle t is at position 4" rather than "the throttle that t refers to is at position 4."

Which is right? In general, use the longer terminology when there may be several different variables referring to the same throttle. Otherwise, use the shorter phrase "the throttle t," but somewhere, deep in your mind, remember that you are shortening things for convenience.

Self-Test Exercises for Section 2.2

9. Write some Java code that creates a new throttle with six positions, shifts the throttle halfway up (to the third position), and prints the current flow.

10. A method declares a Throttle variable called control, but there is not yet a throttle. What value should be assigned to control?

11. Suppose control is a null reference. What happens if a program tries to activate control.shift?

12. Suppose that t1 and t2 are throttle variables and that t1 is null but t2 refers to a valid throttle. Which of these statements will cause an error?

    ```
    t1 = t2;    t2 = t1;    t1.shift(2);
    ```

13. This question tests your understanding of assignment statements with reference variables. What is the output of this code?

    ```
    Throttle t1;
    Throttle t2;
    t1 = new Throttle(100);
    t2 = t1;
    t1.shift(40);
    t2.shift(2);
    System.out.println(t1.getFlow( ));
    ```

14. Consider the code from the preceding question. At the end of the computation, is (t1 == t2) true or false?

15. Write some code that will make t1 and t2 refer to two different throttles with 100 positions each. Both throttles are shifted up to position 42. At the end of your code, is (t1 == t2) true or false?

16. Suppose you have a class called Thermometer. The class has a no-arguments constructor that sets the thermometer's temperature to zero Celsius. There are two modification methods (setCelsius and set-Fahrenheit) to change the temperature by a specified amount. (One method has a parameter in Celsius degrees, and the other has a parameter in Fahrenheit.) There are two accessor methods to get the current temperature (getCelsius and getFahrenheit). A thermometer keeps track of only one temperature, but it can be accessed in either Celsius or Fahrenheit. Write code to create a thermometer, add 10 degrees Celsius to it, and then print the Fahrenheit temperature.

2.3 PACKAGES

You now know enough to write a Java application program that uses a throttle. The Throttle class would be in one file (Throttle.java from Figure 2.1 on page 50), and the program that uses the Throttle class would be in a separate file. However, there's one more level of organization called a Java **package**, which we discuss in this section. The package makes it easy to group together related classes, with each class remaining in a separate .java file.

Declaring a Package

The first step in declaring a package of related classes is to decide on a name for the package. For example, perhaps we are declaring a bunch of Java classes to simulate various real-world devices, such as a throttle. A good short name for the package would be the simulations package. But there's a problem with good short names: Other programmers might decide to use the same good short name for their packages, resulting in the same name for two or more different packages.

The solution is to include your Internet domain name as part of the package name. For example, at the University of Colorado, the Internet domain name is colorado.edu. Therefore, instead of using the package name simulations, I will use the longer package name edu.colorado.simulations. (Package names may include a "dot" as part of the name.) Many programmers follow this convention, using the Internet domain name in reverse. The only likely conflicts are with other programmers at your own Internet domain, and those conflicts can be prevented by internal cooperation.

use your Internet domain name

Once you have decided on a package name, a *package declaration* must be made at the top of each .java file of the package. The **package declaration** consists of the keyword package followed by the package name and a semicolon. For example, the start of Throttle.java must include this package declaration:

```
package edu.colorado.simulations;
```

The revised Throttle.java, with a package declaration, is shown in Figure 2.2. Some Java development environments require you to create a directory structure for your classes to match the structure of package names. For example, suppose you are doing your code development in your own directory called classes, and you want to use the edu.colorado.simulations package. You would follow these steps:

- Make sure your Java development environment can find and run any classes in your classes directory. The exact method of setting this up varies from one environment to another, but a typical approach is to define a system CLASSPATH variable to include your own classes directory.
- Underneath the classes directory, create a subdirectory called edu.
- Underneath edu, create a subdirectory called colorado.
- Underneath colorado, create a subdirectory called simulations.
- All the .java and .class files for the package must be placed in the simulations subdirectory.

If the edu.colorado.simulations package has other classes, then their files are also placed in the simulations subdirectory, and the package declaration is placed at the start of each .java file.

FIGURE 2.2 Defining Throttle.java as Part of the edu.colorado.simulations Package

Implementation

```
// File: Throttle.java from the package edu.colorado.simulations
// Documentation is in Figure 2.1 on page 49 or from the Throttle link in
// http://www.cs.colorado.edu/~main/docs/.

package edu.colorado.simulations;  ◄─────────  the package
                                               declaration
```

(continued)

(FIGURE 2.2 continued)

```java
public class Throttle
{
    private int top;        // The topmost position of the throttle
    private int position;   // The current position of the throttle

    public Throttle(int size)
    {
        if (size <= 0)
            throw new IllegalArgumentException("Size <= 0: " + size);
        top = size;
        // No assignment needed for position -- it gets the default value of zero.
    }

    public double getFlow( )
    {
        return (double) position / (double) top;
    }

    public boolean isOn( )
    {
        return (getFlow( ) > 0);
    }

    public void shift(int amount)
    {
        if (amount > top - position)
            // Adding amount would put the position above the top.
            position = top;
        else if (position + amount < 0)
            // Adding amount would put the position below zero.
            position = 0;
        else
            // Adding amount puts position in the range [0 ... top].
            position += amount;
    }

    public void shutOff( )
    {
        position = 0;
    }
}
```

The Import Statement to Use a Package

Once a package is set up and in the correct directory, the package's `.java` files can be compiled to create the various `.class` files. Then any other code you write can use part or all of the package. To use another package, a `.java` file places an import statement after its own package statement but before anything else. An **import statement for an entire package** has the keyword `import` followed by the package name plus ".*" and a semicolon. For example, we can import the entire `edu.colorado.simulations` package with the import statement:

a program can use an entire package or just parts of a package

```
import edu.colorado.simulations.*;
```

If only a few classes from a package are needed, then each class can be imported separately. For example, this statement imports only the `Throttle` class from the `edu.colorado.simulations` package:

```
import edu.colorado.simulations.Throttle;
```

After this import statement, the `Throttle` class can be used. For example, a program can declare a variable:

```
Throttle control;
```

A sample program using our throttle appears in Figure 2.3. The program creates a new throttle, shifts the throttle fully on, and then steps the throttle back down to the shutoff position.

The JCL Packages

The Java language comes with many useful packages called the **Java Class Libraries (JCL)**. Any programmer can use various parts of the JCL by including an appropriate import statement. In fact, one of the packages, `java.lang`, is so useful that it is automatically imported into every Java program. Some parts of the JCL are described in Section 2.5 and Appendix D.

More about Public, Private, and Package Access

As you have seen, the `Throttle` class uses private instance variables (to keep track of the current status of a throttle) and public methods (to access and manipulate a throttle). The keywords `public` and `private` are called the **access modifiers** because they control access to the class members.

What happens if you declare a member with no access modifier—neither `public` nor `private`? In this case, the member can be accessed only by other classes in the same package. This kind of access is called **default access** (because there is no explicit access modifier); some programmers call it **package access**,

---

FIGURE 2.3 Implementation of the `Throttle` Demonstration Program with an Import Statement

Java Application Program

```java
// FILE: ThrottleDemonstration.java
// This small demonstration program shows how to use the Throttle class
// from the edu.colorado.simulations package.

import edu.colorado.simulations.Throttle;

public class ThrottleDemonstration
{
    public static void main(String[ ] args)
    {
        final int SIZE = 8;   // The size of the demonstration Throttle

        Throttle small = new Throttle(SIZE);

        System.out.println("I am now shifting a Throttle fully on, and then I");
        System.out.println("will shift it back to the shutoff position.");

        small.shift(SIZE);
        while (small.isOn( ))
        {
            System.out.printf("The flow is now %5.3f\n", small.getFlow( ));
            small.shift(-1);
        }

        System.out.println("The flow is now off");
    }
}
```

the import statement

the printf method from page 14

Output from the Application

```
I am now shifting a Throttle fully on, and then I
will shift it back to the shutoff position.
The flow is now 1.000
The flow is now 0.875
The flow is now 0.750
The flow is now 0.625
The flow is now 0.500
The flow is now 0.375
The flow is now 0.250
The flow is now 0.125
The flow is now off
```

which is a nice descriptive name. We won't use package access much, because we prefer the pattern of private instance variables with public methods.

One other kind of access—protected access—will be discussed later when we cover derived classes and inheritance.

Self-Test Exercises for Section 2.3

17. Suppose you are writing a package of classes for a company that has the Internet domain knafn.com. The classes in the package perform various statistical functions. Select a good name for the package.

18. Describe the directory structure that must be set up for the files of the package in the preceding question.

19. Write the package declaration that will appear at the top of every Java file for the package of the previous two questions.

20. Write the import statement that must be present to use the package from the previous questions.

21. Suppose you need only one class (called Averager) from the package of the previous questions. Rewrite the import statement to import only this one package.

22. What import statement is needed to use the java.lang package?

23. Describe public access, private access, and package access. What keywords are needed to obtain each kind of access for a method?

2.4   PARAMETERS, EQUALS METHODS, AND CLONES

Every programmer requires an unshakable understanding of methods and their parameters. This section illustrates these issues and other issues that arise in Java, such as how to test whether two objects are equal to each other and how to make a copy of an object. The examples use a new class called Location, which will be placed in a package called edu.colorado.geometry.

The purpose of a Location object is to store the coordinates of a single point on a plane, as in the picture shown here. The location p in the picture lies at coordinates $x = -1.0$ and $y = 0.8$. For future reference, you should know that Java has a similar class called Point in the java.awt package. But Java's Point class is limited to integer coordinates and used primarily to describe points on a computer's screen. I thought about using the same name, Point, for the example class of this section, but I decided against it because a program might want to use both classes. It's not legal to import two different classes with the same names (though you can use a full type name such as java.awt.Point without an import statement).

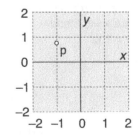

FIGURE 2.4 Three Locations in a Plane

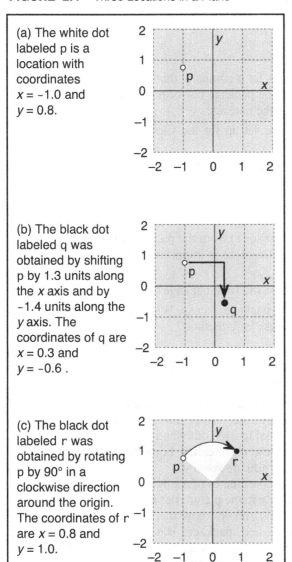

(a) The white dot labeled p is a location with coordinates x = -1.0 and y = 0.8.

(b) The black dot labeled q was obtained by shifting p by 1.3 units along the x axis and by -1.4 units along the y axis. The coordinates of q are x = 0.3 and y = -0.6 .

(c) The black dot labeled r was obtained by rotating p by 90° in a clockwise direction around the origin. The coordinates of r are x = 0.8 and y = 1.0.

The Location Class

Figure 2.4 shows several sample locations. We'll use these sample locations to describe the Location constructor and methods.

- There is a constructor to initialize a location. The constructor's parameters provide the initial coordinates. For example, the location p in Figure 2.4(a) can be constructed with this statement:
  Location p = new Location(-1, 0.8);

- There is a modification method to shift a location by given amounts along the x and y axes, as shown in Figure 2.4(b).

- There is a modification method to rotate a location by 90° in a clockwise direction around the origin, as shown in Figure 2.4(c).

- There are two accessor methods that allow us to retrieve the current x and y coordinates of a location.

- There are a couple of methods to perform computations such as the distance between two locations. These are *static* methods—we'll discuss the importance of the static property in a moment.

- There are three methods called clone, equals, and toString. These methods have special importance for Java classes. The clone method allows a programmer to make an exact copy of an object. The equals method tests whether two different objects are identical. The toString method generates a string that represents an object. Special considerations for implementing these three methods are discussed next.

The Location class is small, yet it forms the basis for an actual data type that is used in graphics programs and other applications. All the methods and the constructor are listed in the specification of Figure 2.5. The figure also shows one way to implement the class. After you've looked through the figure, we'll discuss that implementation.

FIGURE 2.5	Specification and Implementation for the Location Class

Class Location

❖ **public class Location from the package edu.colorado.geometry**
A Location object keeps track of a location on a two-dimensional plane.

Specification

◆ **Constructor for the Location**
> public Location(double xInitial, double yInitial)
Construct a Location with specified coordinates.

> **Parameters:**
> xInitial – the initial *x* coordinate of this Location
> yInitial – the initial *y* coordinate of this Location

> **Postcondition:**
> This Location has been initialized at the given coordinates.

◆ **clone**
> public Location clone( )
Generate a copy of this Location.

> **Returns:**
> The return value is a copy of this Location. Subsequent changes to the copy will not affect the original, nor vice versa. Note that the return value must be typecast to a Location before it can be used.

◆ **distance**
> public static double distance(Location p1, Location p2)
Compute the distance between two Locations.

> **Parameters:**
> p1 – the first Location
> p2 – the second Location

> **Returns:**
> the distance between p1 and p2

> **Note:**
> The answer is Double.POSITIVE_INFINITY if the distance calculation overflows. The answer is Double.NaN if either Location is null.

(continued)

(FIGURE 2.5 continued)

♦ **equals**

```
public boolean equals(Object obj)
```
Compare this Location to another object for equality.

Parameter:
obj – an object with which this Location is compared

Returns:
A return value of true indicates that obj refers to a Location object with the same value as this Location. Otherwise, the return value is false.

Note:
If obj is null or is not a Location object, then the answer is false.

♦ **getX** and **getY**

```
public double getX( )     –and–     public double getY( )
```
Get the *x* or *y* coordinate of this Location.

Returns:
the *x* or *y* coordinate of this Location

♦ **midpoint**

```
public static Location midpoint(Location p1, Location p2)
```
Generates and returns a Location halfway between two others.

Parameters:
p1 – the first Location
p2 – the second Location

Returns:
a Location that is halfway between p1 and p2

Note:
The answer is null if either p1 or p2 is null.

♦ **rotate90**

```
public void rotate90( )
```
Rotate this Location 90° in a clockwise direction.

Postcondition:
This Location has been rotated clockwise 90° around the origin.

♦ **shift**

```
public void shift(double xAmount, double yAmount)
```
Move this Location by given amounts along the *x* and *y* axes.

Postcondition:
This Location has been moved by the given amounts along the two axes.

Note:
The shift may cause a coordinate to go above Double.MAX_VALUE or below –Double.MAX_VALUE. In these cases, subsequent calls of getX or getY will return Double.POSITIVE_INFINITY or Double.NEGATIVE_INFINITY.

(continued)

(FIGURE 2.5 continued)

♦ **toString**

```
public String toString( )
```
Generate a string representation of this Location.

Returns:
a string representation of this Location

Implementation

```java
//  File: Location.java from the package edu.colorado.geometry
//  Documentation is available on pages 67-68 or from the Location link in
//  http://www.cs.colorado.edu/~main/docs/.

package edu.colorado.geometry;

public class Location implements Cloneable
{
    private double x; // The x coordinate of the Location
    private double y; // The y coordinate of the Location

    public Location(double xInitial, double yInitial)
    {
        x = xInitial;
        y = yInitial;
    }

    public Location clone( )
    {   // Clone a Location object.
        Location answer;

        try
        {
            answer = (Location) super.clone( );
        }
        catch (CloneNotSupportedException e)
        {   // This exception should not occur. But if it does, it would indicate a programming
            // error that made super.clone unavailable. The most common cause would be
            // forgetting the "implements Cloneable" clause at the start of the class.
            throw new RuntimeException
            ("This class does not implement Cloneable.");
        }

        return answer;
    }
```

*the meaning of
"implements Cloneable"
and the clone method are
discussed on page 81*

(continued)

(FIGURE 2.5 continued)

```
public static double distance(Location p1, Location p2)
{
    double a, b, c_squared;

    // Check whether one of the Locations is null.
    if ((p1 == null) || (p2 == null))
        return Double.NaN;

    // Calculate differences in x and y coordinates.
    a = p1.x - p2.x;
    b = p1.y - p2.y;

    // Use Pythagorean Theorem to calculate the square of the distance
    // between the Locations.
    c_squared = a*a + b*b;

    return Math.sqrt(c_squared);
}
```

the meaning of a static method is discussed on page 72

the Java constant Double.NaN is discussed on page 74

```
public boolean equals(Object obj)
{
    if (obj instanceof Location)
    {
        Location candidate = (Location) obj;
        return (candidate.x == x) && (candidate.y == y);
    }
    else
        return false;
}
```

the equals method is discussed on page 77

```
public double getX( )
{
    return x;
}
```

```
public double getY( )
{
    return y;
}
```

(continued)

(FIGURE 2.5 continued)

```java
public static Location midpoint(Location p1, Location p2)
{
   double xMid, yMid;

   // Check whether one of the Locations is null.
   if ((p1 == null)  ||  (p2 == null))
      return null;

   // Compute the x and y midpoints.
   xMid = (p1.x/2) + (p2.x/2);
   yMid = (p1.y/2) + (p2.y/2);

   // Create a new Location and return it.
   Location answer = new Location(xMid, yMid);
   return answer;
}

public void rotate90( )
{
   double xNew;
   double yNew;

   // For a 90-degree clockwise rotation, the new x is the original y
   // and the new y is -1 times the original x.
   xNew = y;
   yNew = -x;
   x = xNew;
   y = yNew;
}

public void shift(double xAmount, double yAmount)
{
   x += xAmount;
   y += yAmount;
}

public String toString( )
{
   return "(x=" + x + "  y=" + y + ")";
}

}
```

Static Methods

The implementation of the Location class has several features that may be new to you. Some of the features are in a method called distance, with this specification:

♦ **distance**

```
public static double distance(Location p1, Location p2)
```
Compute the distance between two Locations.

Parameters:
p1 – the first Location
p2 – the second Location

Returns:
the distance between p1 and p2

FIGURE 2.6   The Distance Between Locations

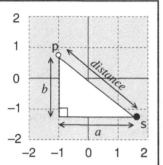

The distance between p and s can be computed with the Pythagorean Theorem.

Horizontal distance: $a = 2.7$

Vertical distance: $b = 2.0$

Distance between the locations =

$$\sqrt{a^2 + b^2} = \sqrt{2.7^2 + 2.0^2} = \text{about } 3.36$$

For example, consider the locations p and s in Figure 2.6. Along a straight line, the distance between these two locations is about 3.36. We can create these two locations and print the distance between them as follows:

```
Location p = new Location(-1, 0.8);
Location s = new Location(1.7, -1.2);

double d = Location.distance(p, s);
System.out.println(d);
```

This code prints the distance between the two locations—a little bit more than 3.36.

The distance method is modified by an extra keyword: static. The static keyword means that the method is not activated by any one object. In other words, we do not write p.distance or s.distance. Instead we write Location.distance.

Because the distance method is not activated by any one object, the method does not have direct access to the instance variables of a location that activates the method. Within the distance implementation, we cannot write simply x or y (the instance variables). Instead, the implementation must carry out its computation based on the arguments it's given. For example, if we activate Location.distance(p, s), then the distance method works with its two arguments p and s. These two arguments are both Location objects. Let's examine exactly what happens when an argument is an object rather than a primitive value such as an integer.

Parameters That Are Objects

What happens when Location.distance(p, s) is activated? For example, suppose we have the two declarations shown previously for p and s. After these declarations, we have these two separate locations:

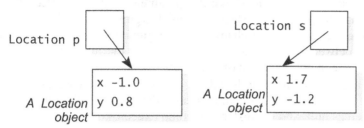

Now we can activate the method Location.distance(p, s), which has an implementation that starts like this:

```
public static distance(Location p1, Location p2)
{
    . . .
```

The names used within the method (p1 and p2) are usually called **parameters** to distinguish them from the values that are passsed in (p and s). On the other hand, the values that are passed in (p and s) are called the **arguments**. The first step of any method activation is to use the *arguments* to provide initial values for the *parameters*. Here's the important fact you need to know about parameters that are objects:

"parameters" versus "arguments"

> When a parameter is an object, such as a Location, then the parameter is initialized so that it refers to the same object that the actual argument refers to.

In our example, Location.distance(p, s), the parameters p1 and p2 are initialized to refer to the two locations we created, like this:

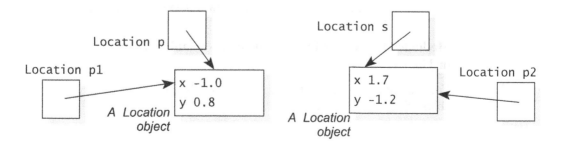

Within the body of the distance method we can access p1 and p2. For example, we can access p1.x to obtain the *x* coordinate of the first parameter. This kind of access is okay in a static method. The only forbidden expression is a direct x or y (without a qualifier such as p1).

be careful about changing the value of a parameter

Some care is needed in accessing a parameter that is an object. For instance, any change to p1.x will affect the actual argument p.x. We don't want the distance method to make changes to its arguments; it should just compute the distance between the two locations and return the answer. This computation occurs in the implementation of distance on page 70.

The implementation also handles a couple of special cases. One special case is when an argument is null. In this case, the corresponding parameter will be initialized as null, and the distance method executes this code:

```
// Check whether one of the Locations is null.
if ((p1 == null) || (p2 == null))
    return Double.NaN;
```

the "not-a-number" constant

If either parameter is null, then the method returns a Java constant named Double.NaN. This is a constant that a program uses to indicate that a double value is "not a number."

Another special case for the distance method is the possibility of a numerical overflow. The numbers obtained during a computation may go above the largest double number or below the smallest double number. These numbers are pretty large, but the possibility of overflow still exists. When an arithmetic expression with double numbers goes beyond the legal range, Java assigns a special constant to the answer. The constant is named Double.POSITIVE_INFINITY if it is too large (above about 1.7^{308}), and it is named Double.NEGATIVE_INFINITY if it is too small (below about -1.7^{308}). Of course, these constants are not really "infinity." They are merely indications to the programmer that a computation has overflowed. In the distance method, we indicate the possibility of overflow with the following comment:

the "infinity" constant

> **Note:**
> The answer is Double.POSITIVE_INFINITY if the distance calculation overflows. The answer is Double.NaN if either Location is null.

Methods May Access Private Instance Variables of Objects in Their Own Class

You may have noticed that the distance method used the x and y instance variables of p1 and p2 directly, for example:

```
a = p1.x - p2.x;
```

Is this allowed? After all, x and y are private instance variables. The answer is yes: A method may access private instance variables of an object as long as the method is declared as part of the same class as the object. In this example, distance is a member function of the Location class, and both p1 and p2 are Location objects. Therefore, the distance method may access the private instance variables of p1 and p2.

The Return Value of a Method May Be an Object

The return value of a method may also be an object, such as a Location object. For example, the Location class has this static method that creates and returns a new location that is halfway between two other locations. The method's specification and implementation are:

♦ **midpoint**
>   public static Location midpoint(Location p1, Location p2)
>   Generates and returns a Location halfway between two others.
>
>   **Parameters:**
>   p1 – the first Location
>   p2 – the second Location
>
>   **Returns:**
>   a Location that is halfway between p1 and p2
>
>   **Note:**
>   The answer is null if either Location is null.

```
public static Location midpoint(Location p1, Location p2)
{
    double xMid, yMid;

    // Check whether one of the Locations is null.
    if ((p1 == null)  ||  (p2 == null))
        return null;

    // Compute the x and y midpoints.
    xMid = (p1.x/2) + (p2.x/2);
    yMid = (p1.y/2) + (p2.y/2);

    // Create a new Location and return it.
    Location answer = new Location(xMid, yMid);
    return answer;
}
```

The method creates a new location using the local variable answer and then returns this location. Often the return value is stored in a local variable such as answer, but not always. For example, we could have eliminated answer by combining the last two statements in our implementation to a single statement:

```
      return new Location(xMid, yMid);
```

Either way—with or without the local variable—is fine.

Here's an example to show how the static midpoint method is used. The method creates two locations and then computes their midpoint:

```
Location low = new Location(0, 0);
Location high = new Location(1000, 5280);
Location medium = Location.midpoint(low, high);
```

In this example, the answer from the midpoint method is stored in a variable called medium. After the three statements, we have three locations:

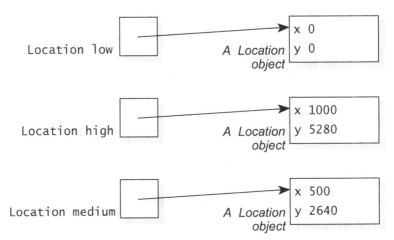

ⓘ PROGRAMMING TIP

HOW TO CHOOSE THE NAMES OF METHODS

Accessor methods: The name of a boolean accessor method will usually begin with "is" followed by an adjective (such as "isOn"). Methods that convert to another kind of data start with "to" (such as "toString"). Other accessor methods start with "get" or some other verb followed by a noun that describes the return value (such as "getFlow").

Modification methods: A modification method can be named by a descriptive verb (such as "shift") or or a short verb phrase (such as "shutOff").

Static methods that return a value: Try to use a noun that describes the return object (such as "distance" or "midpoint").

Rules like these make it easier to determine the purpose of a method.

Java's Object Type

One of the `Location` methods is an accessor method called `equals` with this heading:

```
public boolean equals(Object obj)
```

An accessor method with this name has a special meaning in Java. Before we discuss that meaning, you need to know a bit about the parameter type `Object`. In Java, `Object` is a kind of "super data type" that encompasses all data except the eight primitive types. So a primitive variable (`byte`, `short`, `int`, `long`, `char`, `float`, `double`, or `boolean`) is *not* an `Object`, but everything else is. A `String` is an `Object`, a `Location` is an `Object`, and even an array is an `Object`.

Using and Implementing an equals Method

As your programming expertise progresses, you'll learn a lot about Java's `Object` type, but to start, you need just a few common patterns that use `Object`. For example, many classes implement an `equals` method with the heading we have seen. An `equals` method has one argument: an `Object` called `obj`. The method should return `true` if `obj` has the same value as the object that activated the method. Otherwise, the method returns `false`. Here is an example to show how the `equals` method works for the `Location` class:

```
Location p = new Location(10, 2); // Declare p at coordinates (10,2)
Location s = new Location(10, 0); // Declare s at coordinates (10,0)
```

After these two declarations, we have two separate locations:

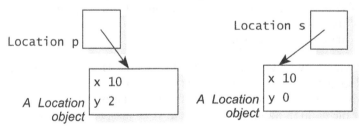

In this example, p and s refer to two separate objects with different values (their *y* coordinates are different), so both `p.equals(s)` and `s.equals(p)` are `false`.

Here's a slightly different example:

```
Location p = new Location(10, 2); // Declare p at coordinates (10,2)
Location s = new Location(10, 0); // Declare s at coordinates (10,0)
s.shift(0, 2);                    // Move s to (10,2)
```

We have the same two declarations, but afterward we shift the *y* coordinate of s so that the two separate locations have identical values, like this:

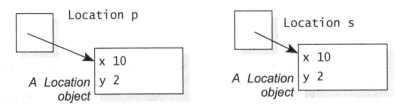

Now p and s refer to identical locations, so both p.equals(s) and s.equals(p) are true. However, the test (p == s) is still false. Remember that (p == s) returns true only if p and s refer to the exact same location (as opposed to two separate locations that happen to contain identical values).

a location can be compared to any object

The argument to the equals method can be any object, not just a location. For example, we can try to compare a location with a string, like this:

```
Location p = new Location(10, 2);
System.out.println(p.equals("10, 2")); // Prints false.
```

This example prints false; a Location object is not equal to the string "10, 2", even if they are similar. You can also test to see whether a location is equal to null:

```
Location p = new Location(10, 2);
System.out.println(p.equals(null)); // Prints false.
```

The location is not null, so the result of p.equals(null) is false. Be careful with the last example: The argument to p.equals may be null and the answer will be false. However, when p itself is null, it is a programming error to activate any method of p. Trying to activate p.equals when p is null results in a NullPointerException (see page 55).

implementing an equals method

Now you know how to use an equals method. How do you write an equals method so that it returns true when its argument has the same value as the object that activates the method? A typical implementation follows an outline that is used for the equals method of the Location class, as shown here:

```
public boolean equals(Object obj)
{
    if ( obj is actually a Location )
    {
        Figure out whether the location that obj refers to has the same
        value as the location that activated this method. Return true if
        they are the same; otherwise, return false.
    }
    else
        return false;
}
```

The method starts by determining whether obj actually refers to a Location object. In pseudocode, we wrote this as "obj is actually a Location." In Java, this is accomplished with the test (obj instanceof Location). This test uses the keyword instanceof, which is a boolean operator. On the left of the operator is a variable such as obj. On the right of the operator is a class name such as Location.

the instanceof operator

The test returns true if it is valid to convert the object (obj) to the given data type (Location). In our example, suppose that obj does not refer to a valid Location. It might be some other type of object, or perhaps it is simply null. In either case, we go to the else-statement and return false.

On the other hand, suppose that (obj instanceof Location) is true, so the code enters the first part of the if-statement. Then obj does refer to a Location object. We need to determine whether the x and y coordinates of obj are the same as the location that activated the method. Unfortunately, we can't just look at obj.x and obj.y, because the compiler thinks of obj as a bare object with no x and y instance variables. The solution is an expression (Location) obj. This expression is called a *typecast*, as if we were pouring obj into a casting mold that creates a Location object. The expression can be used to initialize a Location reference variable, like this:

```
Location candidate = (Location) obj;
```

The **typecast**, on the right side of the declaration, consists of the new data type (Location) in parentheses, followed by the reference variable that is being cast. After this declaration, candidate is a reference variable that refers to the same object that obj refers to. However, the compiler *does* know that candidate refers to a Location object, so we can look at candidate.x and candidate.y to see if they are the same as the x and y coordinates of the object that activated the equals method. The complete implementation looks like this:

typecasts

```
public boolean equals(Object obj)
{
    if (obj instanceof Location)
    {
        Location candidate = (Location) obj;
        return (candidate.x == x) && (candidate.y == y);
    }
    else
        return false;
}
```

The implementation has the return statement:

```
return (candidate.x == x) && (candidate.y == y);
```

The boolean expression in this return statement is true if candidate.x and candidate.y are the same as the instance variables x and y. As with any method, these instance variables come from the object that activated the method. For future reference, the details of using a typecast are given in Figure 2.7.

PITFALL

CLASSCASTEXCEPTION

Suppose you have a variable such as obj, which is an Object. You can try a typecast to use the object as if it were another type. For example, we used the typecast `Location candidate = (Location) obj`.

What happens when obj doesn't actually refer to a Location object? The result is a runtime exception called ClassCastException. To avoid this, you must ensure that a typecast is valid before trying to execute the cast. For example, the instanceof operator can validate the actual type of an object before a typecast.

Every Class Has an equals Method

You may write a class without an equals method, but Java automatically provides an equals method anyway. The equals method that Java provides is actually taken from the Object class, and it works exactly like the == operator. In other words, it returns true only when the two objects are the exact same

FIGURE 2.7 Typecasts

A Simple Pattern for Typecasting an Object

A common situation in Java programming is a variable or other expression that is an Object, but the program needs to treat the Object as a specific data type such as Location. The problem is that when a variable is declared as an Object, that variable cannot be used immediately as if it were a Location (or some other type). For example, consider the parameter obj in the equals method of the Location class:

```
public boolean equals(Object obj)
```

Within the implementation of the equals method, we need to treat obj as a Location rather than a mere Object. The solution has two parts: (1) Check that obj does indeed refer to a valid Location, and (2) declare a new variable of type Location and initialize this new variable to refer to the same object that obj refers to, like this:

```
public boolean equals(Object obj)          ← The parameter, obj, is an Object.
{
    if (obj instanceof Location)            ← Use the instanceof operator to check that
    {                                          obj is a valid Location.
        Location candidate = (Location) obj;
        ...                                 ← After this declaration, candidate refers to
                                               the Location object that obj also refers to.
```

The expression `(Location) obj`, used in the declaration of candidate, is a typecast to tell the compiler that obj may be used as a Location.

---

object—but it returns `false` for two separate objects that happen to have the same values for their instance variables.

Using and Implementing a clone Method

Another feature of our `Location` class is a method with this heading:

```
public Location clone( )
```

The purpose of a `clone` method is to create a copy of an object. The copy is separate from the original so that subsequent changes to the copy won't alter the original, nor will subsequent changes to the original alter the copy. Here's an example of using the `clone` method for the `Location` class:

```
Location p = new Location(10, 2);   // Declare p at (10,2)
Location s = p.clone( );            // Initialize as a copy of p
```

The expression `p.clone( )` activates the `clone` method for p. The method creates and returns an exact copy of p, which we use to initialize the new location s. After these two declarations, we have two separate locations, as shown in this picture:

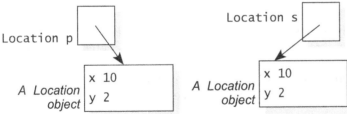

As you can see, s and p have the same values for their instance variables, but the two objects are separate. Changes to p will not affect s, nor will changes to s affect p.

PITFALL

OLDER JAVA CODE REQUIRES A TYPECAST FOR CLONES

Prior to Java 5.0, the data type of the return value of the `clone` method was always an `Object` and not a specific type such as `Location`. Because of this requirement, the `clone` return value could not be used directly in older versions of Java. For example, we could not write a declaration:

```
Location s = p.clone( );
```

Instead, we must apply a typecast to the `clone` return value, converting it to a `Location` before we use it to initialize the new variable s, like this:

```
    //  Typecast required for older Java compilers:
    |      Location s = (Location) p.clone( );
```

Cloning is considerably different from using an assignment statement. For example, consider this code that does not make a clone:

```
Location p = new Location(10, 2); // Declare p at coordinates (10,2).
Location s = p;                    // Declare s and make it refer
                                   // to the same object that p
                                   // refers to.
```

After these two declarations, we have just one location, and both variables refer to this location:

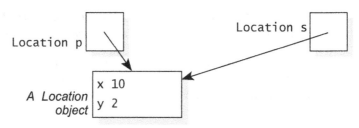

This is the situation with an ordinary assignment. Subsequent changes to the object that p refers to will affect the object that s refers to because there is only one object.

implementing a clone method

You now know how to use a clone method. How do you implement such a method? You should follow a three-step pattern:

1. Modify the Class Head. You must add the words "implements Cloneable" in the class head, as shown here for the Location class:

```
public class Location implements Cloneable
```

The modification informs the Java compiler that you plan to implement certain features that are specified elsewhere in a format called an *interface*. The full meaning of interfaces will be discussed in Chapter 5. At the moment, it is enough to know that implements Cloneable is necessary when you implement a clone method.

2. Use super.clone to Make a Copy. The implementation of a clone method should begin by making a copy of the object that activated the method. The best way to make the copy is to start with this pattern from the Location class:

```
public Location clone( )
{ // Clone a Location object.
   Location answer;

   try
   {
      answer = (Location) super.clone( );
   }
   catch (CloneNotSupportedException e)
   {
      throw new RuntimeException
      ("This class does not implement Cloneable.");
   }
   . . .
```

In an actual implementation, you would use the name of your own class (rather than Location), but otherwise you should follow this pattern exactly.

It's useful to know what's happening in this pattern. The pattern starts by declaring a local Location variable called answer. We then have this block:

```
try
{
   answer = (Location) super.clone( );
}
```

This is an example of a *try block*. If you plan on extensive use of Java exceptions, you should read all about try blocks in Appendix C. But for your first try block, all you need to know is that the code in the try block is executed, and the try block will be able to handle some of the possible exceptions that may arise in the code. In this example, the try block has just one assignment statement: `answer = (Location) super.clone( )`. The right side of the assignment activates a method called super.clone( ). This is actually the clone method from Java's Object type. It checks that the Location class specifies that it "implements Cloneable" and then correctly makes a copy of the location, assigning the result to the local variable answer.

After the try block is a sequence of one or more *catch blocks*. Each catch block can catch and handle an exception that may arise in the try block. Our example has just one catch block:

```
catch (CloneNotSupportedException e)
{
   throw new RuntimeException
   ("This class does not implement Cloneable.");
}
```

This catch block will handle a CloneNotSupportedException. This exception is thrown by the clone method from Java's Object type when a programmer tries to call super.clone( ) without including the implements Cloneable clause as part of the class definition. The best solution is to throw a new RuntimeException, which is the general exception used to indicate a programmer error. In Chapter 13 (page 722), we'll see that the try/catch block isn't always needed, but until we deal with the Chapter 13 topics (extended classes) in detail, we'll always use the format just shown.

After the try and catch blocks, the local variable answer refers to an exact copy of the location that activated the clone method, and we can move to the third part of the clone implementation.

3. Make Necessary Modifications and Return.   The answer is present, and it refers to an exact copy of the object that activated the clone method. Sometimes further modifications must be made to the copy before returning. You'll see the reasons for such modifications in Chapter 3. However, the Location clone needs no modifications, so the end of the clone method consists of just the return statement: return answer.

The complete clone implementation for the Location class looks like this, including an indication of the likely cause of the CloneNotSupportedException:

```java
public Location clone( )
{   // Clone a Location object.
    Location answer;

    try
    {
        answer = (Location) super.clone( );
    }
    catch (CloneNotSupportedException e)
    {   // This exception should not occur. But if it does, it would indicate a
        // programming error that made super.clone unavailable. The
        // most common cause would be forgetting the
        // "implements Cloneable" clause at the start of the class.
        throw new RuntimeException
        ("This class does not implement Cloneable.");
    }

    return answer;
}
```

The method returns the local variable, answer, which is a Location object. This is allowed, even though the return type of the clone method is Object. A Java Object can be anything except the eight primitive types. It might be better if the actual return type of the clone method was Location rather than Object. Using Location for the return type would be more accurate and would make the clone method easier to use (without having to apply a typecast to every usage). Unfortunately, the improvement is not allowed: The return type of the clone method must be Object.

ALWAYS USE SUPER.CLONE FOR YOUR CLONE METHODS

Perhaps you thought of a simpler way to create a clone. Instead of using super.clone and the try/catch blocks, you could write this code:

```
Location answer = new Location(x, y);
return answer;
```

You could combine these into one statement: `return new Location(x, y)`. This creates and returns a new location, using the instance variables x and y to initialize the new location. These instance variables come from the location that activated the clone method, so answer will indeed be a copy of that location. This is a nice direct approach, but the direct approach will encounter problems when we start building new classes that are based on existing classes (see Chapter 13). Therefore, it is better to use the pattern with super.clone and a try/catch block.

PROGRAMMING TIP

WHEN TO THROW A RUNTIME EXCEPTION

A RuntimeException is thrown to indicate a programming error. For example, the clone method from Java's Object type is not supposed to be called by an object unless that object's class has implemented the Cloneable interface. If we detect that the exception has been thrown by the Object clone method, then the programmer probably forgot to include the "implements Cloneable" clause.

When you throw a RuntimeException, include a message with your best guess about the programming error.

A Demonstration Program for the Location Class

As one last example, let's look at a program that creates two locations called still and mobile (see Figure 2.8). Both are initially placed at $x = -2$ and $y = -1.5$, as shown in Figure 2.8(a). To be more precise, the still location is placed at this spot, and then mobile is initialized as a clone of the still location. Because the mobile location is a clone, later changes to one location will not affect the other.

The program prints some information about both locations, and then the mobile location undergoes two 90° rotations, as shown in Figure 2.8(b). The information about the locations is then printed a second time.

FIGURE 2.8 Two 90° Rotations

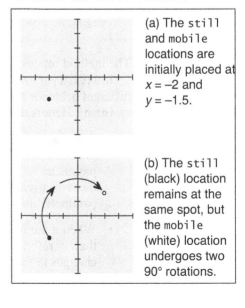

(a) The still and mobile locations are initially placed at $x = -2$ and $y = -1.5$.

(b) The still (black) location remains at the same spot, but the mobile (white) location undergoes two 90° rotations.

The complete program is shown in Figure 2.9 on page 87. Pay particular attention to the specifiedRotation method, which illustrates some important principles about what happens when a parameter is changed within a method. We'll look at those principles in a moment, but first let's look at the complete output from the program:

```
The still location is at:  (x=-2.0 y=-1.5)
The mobile location is at: (x=-2.0 y=-1.5)
Distance between them:  0.0
These two locations have equal coordinates.

I will rotate one location by two 90-degree turns.
The still location is at:  (x=-2.0 y=-1.5)
The mobile location is at: (x=2.0 y=1.5)
Distance between them:  5.0
These two locations have different coordinates.
```

What Happens When a Parameter Is Changed Within a Method?

Let's examine the program's specifiedRotation method to see exactly what happens when a parameter is changed within a method. Here is the method's implementation:

```java
// Rotate a Location p by a number of 90-degree clockwise rotations.
public static void specifiedRotation(Location p, int n)
{
    while (n > 0)
    {
        p.rotate90( );
        n--;
    }
}
```

The method rotates the location p by n 90° clockwise rotations.

In Java, a parameter that is a reference variable (such as the Location p) has different behavior from a parameter that is one of the eight primitive types (such as int n). Here is the difference:

- When a parameter is one of the eight primitive types, the actual argument provides an initial value for that parameter. To be more precise, the parameter is implemented as a local variable of the method, and the argument is used to initialize this variable. Changes that are made to the parameter *do not* affect the actual argument.

- When a parameter is a reference variable, the parameter is initialized so that it refers to the same object as the actual argument. Subsequent changes to this object *do* affect the actual argument's object.

FIGURE 2.9   A Demonstration Program for the Location Class

Java Application Program

```java
// FILE: LocationDemonstration.java
// This small demonstration program shows how to use the Location class
// from the edu.colorado.geometry package.

import edu.colorado.geometry.Location;

public class LocationDemonstration
{
    public static void main(String[ ] args)
    {
        final double STILL_X = -2.0;
        final double STILL_Y = -1.5;
        final int ROTATIONS = 2;

        Location still = new Location(STILL_X, STILL_Y);
        Location mobile = still.clone( );
        printData(still, mobile);

        System.out.println("I will rotate one location by two 90-degree turns.");
        specifiedRotation(mobile, ROTATIONS);
        printData(still, mobile);
    }

    // Rotate a Location p by a specified number of 90-degree clockwise rotations.
    public static void specifiedRotation(Location p, int n)
    {
        while (n > 0)
        {
            p.rotate90( );
            n--;
        }
    }

    // Print some information about two locations: s (a "still" location) and m (a "mobile" location).
    public static void printData(Location s, Location m)
    {
        System.out.println("The still location is at:  " + s.toString( ));
        System.out.println("The mobile location is at: " + m.toString( ));
        System.out.println("Distance between them:  " + Location.distance(s, m));
        if (s.equals(m))
            System.out.println("These two locations have equal coordinates.");
        else
            System.out.println("These two locations have different coordinates.");
        System.out.println( );
    }
}
```

For example, suppose that we have initialized a location called mobile at the coordinates $x = -2$ and $y = -1.5$. Suppose we also have an integer variable called rotations with a value of 2:

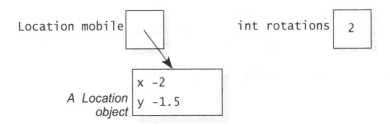

Now suppose the program activates specifiedRotation(mobile, rotations). The method's first parameter, p, is initialized to refer to the same location that mobile refers to. The method's second parameter, n, is initialized with the value 2 (from the rotations argument). So, when the method begins its work, the situation looks like this:

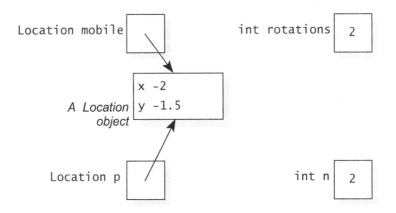

The method now executes its loop:

```
while (n > 0)
{
    p.rotate90( );
    n--;
}
```

The first iteration of the loop rotates the location by 90° and decreases n to 1. The second iteration does another rotation of the location and decreases n to 0. Now the loop ends with these variable values:

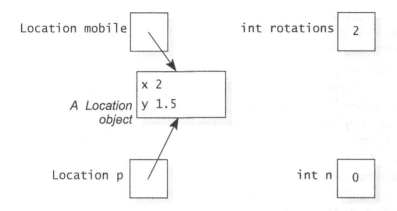

Notice the difference between the two kinds of parameters. The integer parameter n has changed to zero without affecting the actual argument rotations. On the other hand, rotating the location p has changed the object that mobile refers to. When the method returns, the parameters p and n disappear, leaving this situation:

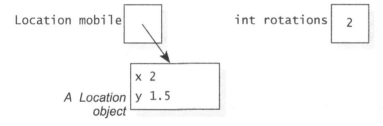

Java Parameters

The eight primitive types (byte, short, int, long, char, float, double, or boolean): The parameter is initialized with the value of the argument. Subsequent changes to the parameter do not affect the argument.

Reference variables: When a parameter is a reference variable, the parameter is initialized so that it refers to the same object as the actual argument. Subsequent changes to this object do affect the actual argument's object.

Self-Test Exercises for Section 2.4

24. Write some code that declares two locations: one at the origin and the other at the coordinates $x = 1$ and $y = 1$. Print the distance between the two locations, and then create a third location that is at the midpoint between the first two locations.

25. The location's `distance` method is a static method. What effect does this have on how the method is used? What effect does this have on how the method is implemented?

26. What is the purpose of the Java constant `Double.NaN`?

27. What is the result when you add two `double` numbers and the answer is larger than the largest possible `double` number?

28. In the `midpoint` method, we used the expression $(p1.x/2) + (p2.x/2)$. Can you think of a reason why this expression is better than $(p1.x + p2.x)/2$?

29. Implement an `equals` method for the `Throttle` class from Section 2.1.

30. If you don't implement an `equals` method for a class, then Java automatically provides one. What does the automatic `equals` method do?

31. Implement a `clone` method for the `Throttle` class from Section 2.1.

32. When should a program throw a `RuntimeException`?

33. Suppose a method has an `int` parameter called x, and the body of the method changes x to zero. When the method is activated, what happens to the argument that corresponds to x?

34. Suppose a method has a `Location` parameter called x, and the body of the method activates `x.rotate90( )`. When the method is activated, what happens to the argument that corresponds to x?

2.5   THE JAVA CLASS LIBRARIES

As a computer scientist, it's important for you to understand how to build and test your own classes, but frequently you'll find that a suitable class has already been built for you to use in an application. There's no need for you to write everything from scratch! In Java, a variety of container classes called the **Java Class Libraries** are available for all programs. This section provides an introduction to one of these classes: the `BigInteger` class.

Each `BigInteger` object holds information about an integer, but unlike an ordinary Java `int`, there is no limit to the size of a `BigInteger`. A `BigInteger` object could be a small integer (perhaps 0, 1, 2, or even a negative number), but it could be much larger than any Java `int`, such as the large number in this output:

```
The value of 42 factorial is
1405006117752879898543142606244511569936384000000000.
```

The `BigInteger` data type is a class that has some interesting private instance variables to hold the information about a potentially large integer. But in order for you to *use* a `BigInteger` object in your program, you don't need to know those private details. All you need to know is the information that the designers of the `BigInteger` class provide about the public member functions, part of which is shown in Figure 2.10.

| FIGURE 2.10 | Part of the Specification for the BigInteger Class |

Class BigInteger

❖ **public class BigInteger from the package java.math**
A BigInteger object provides an immutable arbitrary precision integer.

Partial Specification

(taken partly from `http://download.oracle.com/javase/6/docs/api/java/math/BigInteger.html`)

◆ **One of the Constructors for the BigInteger**
    public Location(String val)
    Translate the decimal String representation of a base 10 integer into a BigInteger.

   Parameter:
    xInitial – a string that contains a base 10 integer of any size

   Postcondition:
    This BigInteger has been initialized to the specified value from val.

◆ **add**
    public BigInteger add(BigInteger val)
    Add this BigInteger to another.

   Returns:
    The return value is this BigInteger + val.

◆ **equals**
    public boolean equals(Object obj)
    Compare this BigInteger to another object for equality.

   Parameter:
    obj – an object with which this BigInteger is compared

   Returns:
    A return value of true indicates that obj refers to a BigInteger object with the same value
    as this BigInteger. Otherwise, the return value is false.

   Note:
    If obj is null or is not a BigInteger object, then the return value is false.

◆ **multiply**
    public BigInteger multiply(BigInteger val)
    Multiply this BigInteger times another.

   Returns:
    The return value is this BigInteger * val.

Here's a short example that uses three BigInteger objects to compute and print the value of 42 factorial (i.e., 1 × 2 × 3 × 4 × ... up to 42):

```java
import java.math.BigInteger;

public class BigIntegerDemonstration
{
    public static void main(String[ ] args)
    {
        // Note: Sample must be >= 2 for this demonstration.
        BigInteger sample = new BigInteger("42");
        BigInteger answer = new BigInteger("1");
        BigInteger factor = new BigInteger("1");

        // Compute the factorial of sample:
        do
        {
            factor = factor.add(BigInteger.ONE);
            answer = answer.multiply(factor);
        } while (!factor.equals(sample));

        System.out.println("The value of " + sample);
        System.out.println(" factorial is " + answer + ".");
    }
}
```

In addition to the methods that were documented in Figure 2.10, the sample program also uses a constant, BigInteger.ONE, that is provided as part of the class.

CHAPTER SUMMARY

- In Java, object-oriented programming (OOP) is supported by implementing *classes*. Each class defines a collection of data, called its *instance variables*. In addition, a class has the ability to include two other items: *constructors* and *methods*. Constructors are designed to provide initial values to the class's data; methods are designed to manipulate the data. Taken together, the instance variables, constructors, and methods of a class are called the class *members*.

- We generally use *private instance variables* and *public methods*. This approach supports information hiding by forbidding data components of a class to be directly accessed outside of the class.

- A new class can be implemented in a Java package that is provided to other programmers to use. The package includes documentation to tell programmers what the new class does without revealing the details of how the new class is implemented.

- A program uses a class by creating new objects of that class and activating these objects' methods through *reference variables*.
- When a method is activated, each of its parameters is initialized. If a parameter is one of the eight primitive types, then the parameter is initialized by the value of the argument, and subsequent changes to the parameter do not affect the actual argument. On the other hand, when a parameter is a reference variable, the parameter is initialized so that it refers to the same object as the actual argument. Subsequent changes to this object do affect the actual argument's object.
- Java programmers must understand how these items work for classes:
  — the assignment operator (x = y)
  — the equality test (x == y)
  — a clone method to create a copy of an object
  — an equals method to test whether two separate objects are equal to each other
- Java provides many prebuilt classes—the Java Class Libraries—for all programmers to use.

Solutions to Self-Test Exercises ?

1. We have used *private* instance variables, *public* constructors, and *public* methods.

2. Accessor methods are not usually void, because they use the return value to provide some information about the current state of the object. Modification methods are often void because they change the object but do not return information.

3. In this solution, the assignment to position is not really needed, since position will be given its default value of zero before the constructor executes. However, including the assignment makes it clear that we intended for position to start at zero:

```java
public Throttle( )
{
    top = 1;
    position = 0;
}
```

4. Notice that our solution (shown at the top of the next column) has the preconditions that 0 < size and 0 <= initial <= size.

```java
public Throttle(int size, int initial)
{
    if (size <= 0)
        throw new
        IllegalArgumentException
        ("Size <= 0:" + size);
    if (initial < 0)
        throw new
        IllegalArgumentException
        ("Initial < 0:" + initial);
    if (initial > size)
        throw new
        IllegalArgumentException
        ("Initial too big:" + initial);
    top = size;
    position = initial;
}
```

5. An accessor method makes no changes to the object's instance variables.

6. The method implementation is:
```java
public boolean isAboveHalf( )
{
    return (getFlow( ) > 0.5);
}
```

7. You'll find part of a solution in Figure 13.1 on page 677.

8. Java usually provides a no-arguments constructor that sets each instance variable to its initialization value (if there is one) or to its default value (if there is no initialization value).

9. The program should include the following statements:
```
Throttle exercise = new Throttle(6);
exercise.shift(3);
System.out.println
   (exercise.getFlow( ));
```

10. The control should be assigned the value of null. By the way, if it is an instance variable of a class, then it is initialized to null.

11. A NullPointerException is thrown.

12. t1.shift(2) will cause an error because you cannot activate methods when t1 is null. The other two statements are fine.

13. Both t1 and t2 refer to the same throttle, which has been shifted up 42 positions. So the output is 0.42.

14. At the end of the code, (t1 == t2) is true since there is only one throttle that both variables refer to.

15. Here is the code (and at the end, t1 == t2 is false since there are two separate throttles):
```
Throttle t1;
Throttle t2;
t1 = new Throttle(100);
t2 = new Throttle(100);
t1.shift(42);
t2.shift(42);
```

16.
```
Thermometer t = new Thermometer( );
t.addCelsius(10);
System.out.println
   (t.getFahrenheit( ));
```

17. com.knafn.statistics

18. Underneath your classes directory, create a subdirectory com. Underneath com create a subdirectory knafn. Underneath knafn create a subdirectory statistics. Your package is placed in the statistics subdirectory.

19. package com.knafn.statistics;

20. import com.knafn.statistics.*;

21. import
   com.knafn.statistics.Averager;

22. Java automatically imports java.lang; no explicit import statement is needed.

23. Public access is obtained with the keyword public, and it allows access by any program. Private access is obtained with the keyword private, and it allows access only by the methods of the class. Package access is obtained with no keyword, and it allows access within the package but not elsewhere.

24. Here is the code:
```
Location p1 = new Location(0, 0);
Location p2 = new Location(1, 1);
System.out.println
   (Location.distance(p1, p2));
Location p3 =
   Location.midpoint(p1, p2);
```

25. A static method is not activated by any one object. Instead, the class name is placed in front of the method to activate it. For example, the distance between two locations p1 and p2 is computed by:
```
Location.distance(p1, p2);
```
Within the implementation of a static method, we cannot directly refer to the instance variables.

26. The constant Double.NaN is used when there is no valid number to store in a double variable ("not a number").

27. The result is the constant
Double.POSITIVE_INFINITY.

28. The alternative (p1.x + p2.x)/2 has a subexpression p1.x + p2.x that could result in an overflow.

29. Here is the implementation for the throttle:
```
public boolean equals(Object obj)
{
    if (obj instanceof Throttle)
    {
      Throttle candidate = (Throttle) obj;
      return
         (candidate.top==top)
         &&
         (candidate.position==position);
    }
    else
      return false;
}
```

30. The automatic `equals` method returns `true` only when the two objects are the exact same object (as opposed to two separate objects that have the same value).

31. The solution is the same as the Location clone on page 69, but change the Location type to Throttle.

32. A `RuntimeException` indicates a programming error. When you throw a `RuntimeException`, you should provide an indication of the most likely cause of the error.

33. The argument remains unchanged.

34. The object that the argument refers to has been rotated 90°.

PROGRAMMING PROJECTS

1 Specify, design, and implement a class that can be used in a program that simulates a combination lock. The lock has a circular knob with the numbers 0 through 39 marked on the edge, and it has a three-number combination, which we'll call *x, y, z*. To open the lock, you must turn the knob clockwise at least one entire revolution, stopping with *x* at the top; then you turn the knob counterclockwise, stopping the *second* time that *y* appears at the top; finally, you turn the knob clockwise again, stopping the next time that *z* appears at the top. At this point, you may open the lock.

Your Lock class should have a constructor that initializes the three-number combination. Also provide methods:
(a) To alter the lock's combination to a new three-number combination
(b) To turn the knob in a given direction until a specified number appears at the top
(c) To close the lock
(d) To attempt to open the lock
(e) To inquire about the status of the lock (open or shut)
(f) To tell what number is currently at the top

2 Specify, design, and implement a class called Statistician. After a statistician is initialized, it can be given a sequence of double numbers. Each number in the sequence is given to the statistician by activating a method called nextNumber. For example, we can declare a statistician called s and then give it the sequence of numbers 1.1, −2.4, 0.8, as shown here:

```
Statistician s = new Statistician( );
s.nextNumber(1.1);
s.nextNumber(-2.4);
s.nextNumber(0.8);
```

After a sequence has been given to a statistician, there are various methods to obtain information about the sequence. Include methods that will provide the length of the sequence, the last number of the sequence, the sum of all the numbers in the sequence, the arithmetic mean of the numbers (i.e., the sum of the numbers divided by the length of the sequence), the smallest number in the sequence, and the largest number in the sequence. Notice that the length and sum methods can be called at any time, even if there are no numbers in the sequence. In this case of an "empty" sequence, both length and sum will be zero. The other methods should return `Double.NaN` if they are called for an empty sequence.

Notes: Do not try to store the entire sequence (because you don't know how long this sequence will be). Instead, just store the necessary information about the sequence: What is the sequence length; what is the sum of the numbers in the sequence; and what are the last, smallest, and largest numbers? Each of these pieces of information can be stored in a private instance variable that is updated whenever `nextNumber` is activated.

3 Write a new static method to allow you to "add" two statisticians from the previous project. If `s1` and `s2` are two statisticians, then the result of adding them should be a new statistician that behaves as if it had all of the numbers of `s1` followed by all of the numbers of `s2`.

4 Specify, design, and implement a class that can be used to keep track of the position of a location in three-dimensional space. For example, consider this location:

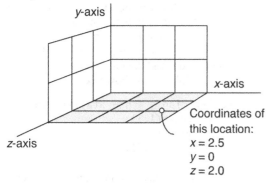

y-axis

x-axis

z-axis

Coordinates of this location:
$x = 2.5$
$y = 0$
$z = 2.0$

The location shown in the picture has three coordinates: $x = 2.5$, $y = 0$, and $z = 2.0$. Include methods to set a location to a specified point, to shift a location a given amount along one of the axes, and to retrieve the coordinates of a location. Also provide methods that will rotate the location by a specified angle around a specified axis.

To compute these rotations, you will need a bit of trigonometry. Suppose you have a location with co-

ordinates *x, y,* and *z.* After rotating this location by an angle θ, the location will have new coordinates, which we'll call x', y', and z'. The equations for the new coordinates use the `java.lang` methods `Math.sin` and `Math.cos`, as shown here:

After a θ rotation around the *x*-axis:

$$x' = x$$
$$y' = y \cos(\theta) - z \sin(\theta)$$
$$z' = y \sin(\theta) + z \cos(\theta)$$

After a θ rotation around the *y*-axis:

$$x' = x \cos(\theta) + z \sin(\theta)$$
$$y' = y$$
$$z' = -x \sin(\theta) + z \cos(\theta)$$

After a θ rotation around the *z*-axis:

$$x' = x \cos(\theta) - y \sin(\theta)$$
$$y' = x \sin(\theta) + y \cos(\theta)$$
$$z' = z$$

5 In three-dimensional space, a line segment is defined by its two endpoints. Specify, design, and implement a class for a line segment. The class should have two private instance variables that are 3D locations from the previous project.

6 Specify, design, and implement a class for a card in a deck of playing cards. The class should contain methods for setting and retrieving the suit and rank of a card.

7 Specify, design, and implement a class that can be used to hold information about a musical note. A programmer should be able to set and retrieve the length of the note and the value of the note. The length of a note may be a sixteenth note, eighth note, quarter note, half note, or whole note. A value is specified by indicating how far the note lies above or below the A note that orchestras use in tuning. In counting "how far," you should include both the white and black notes on a piano. For example, the note numbers for the octave beginning at middle C are shown at the top of the next page.

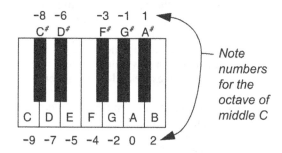

Note numbers for the octave of middle C

The constructor should set a note to a middle C quarter note. Include methods to set a note to a specified length and value. Write methods to retrieve information about a note, including methods to tell you the letter of the note (A, B, C, etc.), whether the note is natural or sharp (i.e., white or black on the piano), and the frequency of the note in hertz. To calculate the frequency, use the formula $440 \times 2^{n/12}$, where n is the note number. Feel free to include other useful methods.

8 — A one-variable **quadratic expression** is an arithmetic expression of the form $ax^2 + bx + c$, where a, b, and c are some fixed numbers (called the **coefficients**) and x is a variable that can take on different values. Specify, design, and implement a class that can store information about a quadratic expression. The constructor should set all three coefficients to zero, and another method should allow you to change these coefficients. There should be accessor methods to retrieve the current values of the coefficients. There should also be a method to allow you to "evaluate" the quadratic expression at a particular value of x (i.e., the method has one parameter x and returns the value of the expression $ax^2 + bx + c$).

Also write the following static methods to perform these indicated operations:

```
public static Quadratic sum(
    Quadratic q1,
    Quadratic q2
)
// Postcondition: The return value is the
// quadratic expression obtained by adding
// q1 and q2. For example, the c coefficient
// of the return value is the sum of q1's c
// coefficient and q2's c coefficient.

public static Quadratic scale(
    double r,
    Quadratic q
)
// Postcondition: The return value is the
// quadratic expression obtained by
// multiplying each of q's
// coefficients by the number r.
```

Notice that the first argument of the `scale` method is a double number (rather than a quadratic expression). For example, this allows the method activation `Quadratic.scale(3.14, q)` where q is a quadratic expression.

9 — This project is a continuation of the previous project. For a quadratic expression such as $ax^2 + bx + c$, a **real root** is any double number x such that $ax^2 + bx + c = 0$. For example, the quadratic expression $2x^2 + 8x + 6$ has one of its real roots at $x = -3$ because substituting $x = -3$ in the formula $2x^2 + 8x + 6$ yields the value:

$$2 \times (-3^2) + 8 \times (-3) + 6 = 0$$

There are six rules for finding the real roots of a quadratic expression:

(1) If a, b, and c are all zero, then every value of x is a real root.

(2) If a and b are zero but c is nonzero, then there are no real roots.

(3) If a is zero and b is nonzero, then the only real root is $x = -c/b$.

(4) If a is nonzero and $b^2 < 4ac$, then there are no real roots.

(5) If a is nonzero and $b^2 = 4ac$, then there is one real root, $x = -b/2a$.

(6) If a is nonzero and $b^2 > 4ac$, then there are two real roots:

$$x = \frac{-b - \sqrt{b^2 - 4ac}}{2a}$$

$$x = \frac{-b + \sqrt{b^2 - 4ac}}{2a}$$

Write a new method that returns the number of real roots of a quadratic expression. This answer could be 0, 1, 2, or infinity. In the case of an infinite number of real roots, have the method return 3. (Yes, we know that 3 is not infinity, but for this purpose it is close enough!) Write two other methods that calculate and return the real roots of a quadratic expression. The precondition for both methods is that the expression has at least one real root. If there are two real roots, then one of the methods returns the smaller of the two roots, and the other method returns the larger of the two roots. If every value of x is a real root, then both methods should return zero.

10 Specify, design, and implement a class that can be used to simulate a lunar lander, which is a small spaceship that transports astronauts from lunar orbit to the surface of the moon. When a lunar lander is constructed, the following items should be initialized as follows:

(1) Current fuel flow rate as a fraction of the maximum fuel flow (initially zero)

(2) Vertical speed of the lander (initially zero meters/sec)

(3) Altitude of the lander (specified as a parameter of the constructor)

(4) Amount of fuel (specified as a parameter of the constructor)

(5) Mass of the lander when it has no fuel (specified as a parameter of the constructor)

(6) Maximum fuel consumption rate (specified as a parameter of the constructor)

(7) Maximum thrust of the lander's engine (specified as a parameter of the constructor)

Don't worry about other properties (such as horizontal speed).

The lander has accessor methods that allow a program to retrieve the current values of any of the preceding seven items. There are only two modification methods, described next.

The first modification method changes the current fuel flow rate to a new value ranging from 0.0 to 1.0. This value is expressed as a fraction of the maximum fuel flow.

The second modification method simulates the passage of a small amount of time. This time, called t, is expressed in seconds and will typically be a small value such as 0.1 seconds. The method will update the first four values in the preceding list to reflect the passage of t seconds. To implement this method, you will require a few physics formulas, listed below. These formulas are only approximate because some of the lander's values are changing during the simulated time period. But if the time span is kept short, these formulas will suffice.

Fuel flow rate: Normally, the fuel flow rate does not change during the passage of a small amount of time. But there is one exception: If the fuel flow rate is greater than zero and the amount of fuel left is zero, then you should reset the fuel flow rate to zero (because there is no fuel to flow).

Velocity change: During t seconds, the velocity of the lander changes by approximately this amount (measured in meters/sec):

$$t \times \left(\frac{f}{m} - 1.62 \right)$$

The value m is the total mass of the lander, measured in kilograms (i.e., the mass of a lander with no fuel plus the mass of any remaining fuel). The value f is the thrust of the lander's engine, measured in newtons. You can calculate f as the current fuel flow rate times the maximum thrust of the lander. The number -1.62 is the downward acceleration from gravity on the moon.

Altitude change: During t seconds, the altitude of the lander changes by $t \times v$ meters, where v is the vertical velocity of the lander (measured in meters/sec with negative values downward).

Change in remaining fuel: During t seconds, the amount of remaining fuel is reduced by $t \times r \times c$ kilograms. The value of r is the current fuel flow rate, and c is the maximum fuel consumption (measured in kilograms per second).

We suggest that you calculate the changes to the four items in the order just listed. After all the changes have been made, there are two further adjustments. First, if the altitude has dropped below zero, then reset both altitude and velocity to zero (indicating that the ship has landed). Second, if the total amount of remaining fuel drops below zero, then reset this amount to zero (indicating that we have run out of fuel).

| 11 | In this project, you will design and implement a class that can generate a sequence of **pseudorandom** integers, which is a sequence that appears random in many ways. The approach uses the **linear congruence method**, explained below. The linear congruence method starts with a number called the **seed**. In addition to the seed, three other numbers are used in the linear congruence method: the **multiplier**, the **increment**, and the **modulus**. The formula for generating a sequence of pseudorandom numbers is quite simple. The first number is:

```
(multiplier * seed + increment) % modulus
```

This formula uses the Java % operator, which computes the remainder from an integer division.

Each time a new random number is computed, the value of the seed is changed to that new number. For example, we could implement a pseudorandom number generator with multiplier = 40, increment = 3641, and modulus = 729. If we choose the seed to be 1, then the sequence of numbers will proceed this way:

First number
= (multiplier * seed + increment) % modulus
= (40 * 1 + 3641) % 729
= 36
and 36 becomes the new seed.

Next number
= (multiplier * seed + increment) % modulus
= (40 * 36 + 3641) % 729
= 707
and 707 becomes the new seed.

These particular values for multiplier, increment, and modulus happen to be good choices. The pattern

generated will not repeat until 729 different numbers have been produced. Other choices for the constants might not be so good.

For this project, design and implement a class that can generate a pseudorandom sequence in the manner described. The initial seed, multiplier, increment, and modulus should all be parameters of the constructor. There should also be a method to permit the seed to be changed and a method to generate and return the next number in the pseudorandom sequence.

| 12 | Add a new method to the random number class of the previous project. The new method generates the next pseudorandom number but does not return the number directly. Instead, the method returns this number divided by the modulus. (You will have to cast the modulus to a double number before carrying out the division; otherwise, the division will be an integer division, throwing away the remainder.)

The return value from this new member function is a pseudorandom double number in the range [0..1). (The square bracket, "[", indicates that the range does include 0, but the rounded parenthesis, ")", indicates that the range goes up to 1, without actually including 1.)

| 13 | Run some experiments to determine the distribution of numbers returned by the new pseudorandom method from the previous project. Recall that this method returns a double number in the range [0..1). Divide this range into 10 intervals and call the method one million times, producing a table such as this:

Range	Number of Occurrences
[0.0..0.1)	99889
[0.1..0.2)	100309
[0.2..0.3)	100070
[0.3..0.4)	99940
[0.4..0.5)	99584
[0.5..0.6)	100028
[0.6..0.7)	99669
[0.7..0.8)	100100
[0.8..0.9)	100107
[0.9..1.0)	100304

Run your experiment for different values of the multiplier, increment, and modulus. With good choices for the constants, you will end up with about 10% of the numbers in each interval. A pseudorandom number generator with this equal-interval behavior is called **uniformly distributed**.

14 This project is a continuation of the previous project. Many applications require pseudorandom number sequences that are *not* uniformly distributed. For example, a program that simulates the birth of babies can use random numbers for the birth weights of the newborns. But these birth weights should have a **Gaussian distribution**. In a Gaussian distribution, numbers form a bell-shaped curve in which values are more likely to fall in intervals near the center of the overall distribution. The exact probabilities of falling in a particular interval can be computed by knowing two numbers: (1) a number called the *variance*, which indicates how widely spread the distribution appears, and (2) the center of the overall distribution, called the *median*. For this kind of distribution, the median is equal to the arithmetic average (the *mean*) and equal to the most frequent value (the *mode*).

Generating a pseudorandom number sequence with an exact Gaussian distribution can be difficult, but there is a good way to approximate a Gaussian distribution using uniformly distributed random numbers in the range [0..1). The approach is to generate three pseudorandom numbers r_1, r_2, and r_3, each of which is in the range [0..1). These numbers are then combined to produce the next number in the Gaussian sequence. The formula to combine the numbers is:

Next number in the Gaussian sequence
$$= \text{median} + (2 \times (r_1 + r_2 + r_3) - 3) \times \text{variance}$$

Add a new method to the random number class, which can be used to produce a sequence of pseudorandom numbers with a Gaussian distribution.

15 Implement the `Thermometer` class from Self-Test Exercise 16 on page 60. Make sure that the methods to alter the temperature do not allow the temperature to drop below absolute zero (−273.16°C). Also include these extra methods:

1. Two accessor methods that return the maximum temperature that the thermometer has ever recorded (with the return value in either Celsius or Fahrenheit degrees)

2. Two accessor methods that return the minimum temperature ever recorded

3. A modification method to reset the maximum and minimum counters

4. A boolean method that returns true if the temperature is at or below 0°C

16 Write a class for rational numbers. Each object in the class should have two integer values that define the rational number: the numerator and the denominator. For example, the fraction $\frac{5}{6}$ would have a numerator of 5 and a denominator of 6. Include a constructor with two arguments that can be used to set the numerator and denominator (forbidding zero in the denominator). Also provide a no-arguments constructor that has zero for the numerator and 1 for the denominator.

Include a method that prints a rational number to `System.out` in a normal form (so that the denominator is as small as possible). Note that the numerator or denominator (or both) may contain a minus sign, but when a rational number is printed, the denominator should never include a minus sign. So if the numerator is 1 and the denominator is -2, then the printing method should print -1/2.

Include a function to normalize the values stored so that, after normalization, the denominator is positive and as small as possible. For example, after normalization, 4/-8 would be represented as -1/2.

Write static methods for the usual arithmetic operators to provide addition, subtraction, multiplication, and division of two rational numbers. Write static boolean methods to provide the usual comparison operations to allow comparison of two rational numbers.

Hints: Two rational numbers *a/b* and *c/d* are equal if *a**d equals *c**b. For positive rational numbers, *a/b* is less than *c/d* provided that *a**d is less than *c**b.

17 Write a class to keep track of a balance in a bank account with a varying annual interest rate. The constructor will set both the bal- and the annual interest rate to some initial values (and you should also implement a no-arguments constructor that sets both the balance and the interest rate to zero).

The class should have methods to change or retrieve the current balance or interest rate. There should also be methods to make a deposit (add to the balance) or a withdrawal (subtract from the balance).

Finally, there should be a method that adds interest to the balance at the current interest rate. This function should have a parameter indicating how many years' worth of interest are to be added. (For example, 0.5 years indicates that the account should have six months' interest added.)

Use the class as part of an interactive program that allows the user to determine how long an initial balance will take to grow to a given value. The program should allow the user to specify the initial balance, the interest rate, and whether there are additional yearly deposits.

Your class should have methods to set and retrieve all four instance variables. Also include a modification method that will change all four instance variables to reflect the passage of a small amount of time t (measured in seconds). When t is small, the equations for the new values of x, y, vx, and vy are given by:

new value of $x = x + vx*t$
new value of $y = y + vy*t$
new value of $vx = vx + ax*t$
new value of $vy = vy + ay*t$.

The numbers ax and ay are the current accelerations from gravity along the x- and y-axes, determined by:

$$ax = -G*M*x/d^3$$
$$ay = -G*M*y/d^3$$

G = gravitational constant in N-m^2/sec^2
  $= 6.67 \times 10^{-11}$

M = mass of the Earth in kilograms
  $= 5.97 \times 10^{24}$

d = distance of the satellite from center of Earth
  $= \sqrt{x^2 + y^2}$

18 This project requires a little understanding of velocity and gravity, but don't let that scare you away! It's actually an easy project. The assignment is to write a class in which each object represents a satellite in orbit around the Earth's equator. Each object has four instance variables.

Two variables store the current x and y positions of the satellite in a coordinate system with the origin at the center of the Earth. The plane formed by the x- and y-axes comes out through the equator, with the positive x-axis passing through the equator at the Greenwich prime meridian. The positive y-axis is 90 degrees away from that, at the 90°W meridian, and all measurements are in meters. The drawing in the next column shows a possible location of the satellite as viewed from far above the South Pole.

Two other variables (vx and vy) store the current velocity of the satellite in the x and y directions. These measurements are in meters per second. The values can be positive (which means that the satellite is moving toward the positive direction of the axis) or negative (which means that the satellite is moving toward the negative axis).

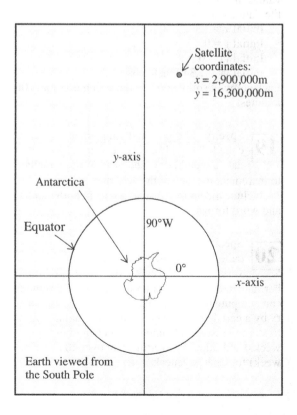

Satellite coordinates:
$x = 2,900,000$m
$y = 16,300,000$m

y-axis

Antarctica

Equator

90°W

0°

x-axis

Earth viewed from the South Pole

Include accessor methods to retrieve the current values of *ax, ay, d,* and the satellite's current altitude above the surface of the Earth (the value of *d* minus the equatorial radius of the Earth, which is about 12,756,300 meters).

Include a boolean method that determines whether the satellite has crashed into the Earth. For the method that simulates the passage of a small amount of time, there should be a check to see whether the satellite has crashed into the surface of the Earth. If so, the method should set both velocities to zero and not change the *x* and *y* locations. Of course, all of this ignores many factors (such as air resistance when the satellite approaches the Earth's atmosphere).

Use your satellite class in a small application program that allows the user to set the initial values of *x, y, vx,* and *vy.* The program then simulates the satellite's flight by repeatedly calling the simulation method with *t* = 1. The program's output consists of a list of the *x, y, vx,* and *vy* values printed once every 60 simulated seconds (with the total amount of time simulated being specified by the user).

You can run your program using some actual values that are similar to Canada's Alouette I satellite, launched in 1962:

Initial *x* = 7,392,000 meters
Initial *y* = 0
Initial *vx* = 0
Initial *vy* = 7,349 meters/sec

Each complete orbit should take a bit more than 106 minutes.

19 Specify, design, and implement a class called Date. Use integers to represent a date's month, day, and year. Write a method to increment the date to the next day.

Include methods to display a date in both number and word format.

20 Specify, design, and implement a class called Employee. The class has instance variables for the employee's name, ID number, and salary based on an hourly wage. Methods can compute the yearly salary and increase the salary by a certain percentage. Add additional members to store the paycheck amount (calculated every two weeks) and calculate overtime (for over 40 hours per week) for each paycheck.

21 Write a class for complex numbers. A complex number has the form *a* + *bi*, where *a* and *b* are real numbers and *i* is the square root of −1. We refer to *a* as the real part and *b* as the imaginary part of the number. The class should have two instance variables to represent the real and imaginary numbers; the constructor takes two arguments to set these members. Discuss and implement other appropriate methods for this class.

22 Write a class called fueler that can keep track of the fuel and mileage of a vehicle.

Include private instance variables to track the amount of fuel that the vehicle has consumed and the distance that the vehicle has traveled. You may choose whatever units you like (for example, fuel could be measured in U.S. gallons, Imperial gallons, or liters), but be sure to document your choices at the point where you declare the variables.

The class should have a constructor that initializes these variables to zero. Include a method that can later reset both variables to zero. There are two different modification methods to add a given amount to the total distance driven (one has a miles parameter, and the other has a kilometers parameter); similarly, there are three methods to add a given amount to the total fuel consumed (with different units for the amount of fuel).

The class has two accessor methods to retrieve the total distance driven (in miles or km), three methods for the fuel consumed (in U.S. gallons, Imperial gallons, or liters), and four for the fuel mileage (in U.S. mpg, Imperial mpg, km per liters, or liters per 100 km).

CHAPTER 3

Collection Classes

Collection Classes

(I am large, I contain multitudes.)

WALT WHITMAN
"Song of Myself"

The Throttle and Location classes in Chapter 2 are good examples of abstract data types (ADTs), but their applicability is limited to a few specialized programs. This chapter begins the presentation of several ADTs with broad applicability to programs large and small. The ADTs in this chapter—bags and sequences—are small, but they provide the basis for more complex ADTs such as Java's ArrayList class.

an ADT in which each object contains a collection of elements

The ADTs in this chapter are examples of **collection classes**. Intuitively, a collection class is a class in which each object contains a collection of elements. For example, one program might keep track of a collection of integers, perhaps the collection of test scores for a group of students. Another program, perhaps a cryptography program, can use a collection of characters.

There are many different ways to implement a collection class; the simplest approach utilizes an array, so this chapter begins with a quick review of Java arrays before approaching actual collection classes.

3.1   A REVIEW OF JAVA ARRAYS

An array is a sequence with a certain number of components. We draw arrays with each component in a separate box. For example, here's an array of the four integers 7, 22, 19, and 56:

7	22	19	56

Each component of an array can be accessed through an index. In Java, the indexes are written with square brackets, beginning with [0], [1], ... The array shown has four components, so the indexes are [0] through [3]:

7	22	19	56
[0]	[1]	[2]	[3]

In these examples, each component is an integer, but arrays can be built for any fixed data type: arrays of double numbers, arrays of boolean values, and even arrays in which the components are objects from a new class that you write yourself.

An array is declared like any other variable, except that a pair of square brackets is placed after the name of the data type. For example, a program can declare an array of integers like this:

```
int[ ] scores;
```

The name of this array is `scores`. The components of this array are integers, but as we have mentioned, the components can be any fixed type. For example, an array of double numbers would use `double[ ]` instead of `int[ ]`.

An array variable, such as `scores`, is capable of referring to an array of any size. In fact, an array variable is a reference variable, just like the reference variables we have used for other objects, and arrays are created with the same new operator that allocates other objects. For example, we can write these statements:

```
int[ ] scores;
scores = new int[4];
```

The number `[4]`, occurring with the new operator, indicates that we want a new array with four components. Once both statements finish, `scores` refers to an array with four integer components:

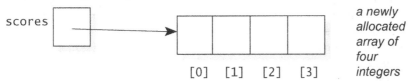

This is an accurate picture, showing how `scores` refers to a new array of four integers, but the picture has some clutter that we can usually omit. Here is a simpler picture that we'll usually use to show that `scores` refers to an array of four integers:

```
        ┌───┬───┬───┬───┐
        │   │   │   │   │
scores  └───┴───┴───┴───┘
        [0]  [1]  [2]  [3]
```

Both pictures mean the same thing. The first picture is a more accurate depiction of what Java actually does; the second is a kind of shorthand that is typical of what programmers draw to illustrate an array.

An array can also be declared and allocated with a single statement, such as:

```
int [ ] scores = new int[4];
```

providing initial values for an array

An array declared like this will initially be filled with Java's default values (for example, zeros for any number type). Instead of specifying an actual size with the new operator, another alternative is to provide a list of initial values. For example, these statements will create an array called b that contains the three values 10, 20, and 30:

```
int[ ] b = new int[ ] { 10, 20, 30 };
```

Once an array has been allocated, individual components can be selected using the square bracket notation with an index. For example, with scores allocated as shown, we can set the array's [2] component to 42 with the assignment scores[2] = 42. The result is shown here:

		42	

scores

[0] [1] [2] [3]

PITFALL

EXCEPTIONS THAT ARISE FROM ARRAYS

Two kinds of exceptions commonly arise from programming errors with arrays. One problem is trying to use an array variable before the array has been allocated. For example, suppose we declare int[ ] scores, but we forget to use the new operator to create an array for scores to refer to. At this point, scores is actually a reference variable, just like the reference variables we discussed for other kinds of objects on page 54. But merely declaring a reference variable doesn't allocate an array, and it is a programming error to try to access a component such as scores[2]. A program that tries to access a component of a nonexistent array may throw a NullPointerException (if the reference is null), or there may be a compile-time error (if the variable is an uninitialized local variable).

Another common programming error is trying to access an array outside of its bounds. For example, suppose that scores refers to an array with four components. The indexes are [0] through [3], so it is an error to use an index that is too small (such as scores[-1]) or too large (such as scores[4]). A program that tries to use these indexes will throw an ArrayIndexOutOfBoundsException.

The Length of an Array

Every array has an instance variable called length, which tells the number of components in the array. For example, consider scores = new int[4]. After this allocation, scores.length is 4. Notice that length is not a method, so the syntax is merely scores.length (with no argument list). By the way, if an array variable is the null reference, you cannot ask for its length. (Trying to do so results in a NullPointerException or a compile-time error.)

Assignment Statements with Arrays

A program can use an assignment statement to make two array variables refer to the same array. Here is some example code:

```
int[ ] scores = new int[ ] {7, 22, 19, 56};
int[ ] exams;
exams = scores;
```

After these statements, scores refers to an array containing the four integers: 7, 22, 19, and 56. The assignment statement, exams = scores, causes exams to refer to the exact same array. Here is an accurate drawing of the situation:

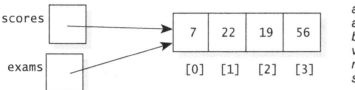

after the assignment, both array variables refer to the same array

Here's a shorthand drawing of the same situation to show that scores and exams refer to the same array:

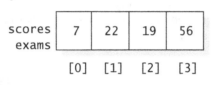

after the assignment, both array variables refer to the same array

In this example, there is only one array, and both array variables refer to this one array. Any change to the array will affect both scores and exams. For example, after the preceding statements, we might assign exams[2] = 42. The situation after the assignment to exams[2] is shown here:

scores exams	7	22	42	56
	[0]	[1]	[2]	[3]

the [2] component has been changed to 42

At this point, both exams[2] and scores[2] are 42.

Clones of Arrays

In Chapter 2, you saw how to use a clone method to create a completely separate copy of an object. Every Java array comes equipped with a clone method to create a copy of the array. Just like the other clones you've seen, changes to the original array don't affect the clone, and changes to the clone don't affect the original array. Here's an example:

```
int[ ] scores = new int[] {7, 22, 19, 56};
int[ ] exams;
exams = scores.clone( );
```

The final statement in this example uses scores.clone( ) to create a copy of the scores array.

Remember that in older versions of Java, the data type of the return value of any clone method was always Java's Object data type. Because of this, older code could not use the clone return value directly. For example, we could not write an assignment:

```
exams = scores.clone( );
```

Instead, older code must apply a typecast to the clone return value, converting it to an integer array before we assign it to exams, like this:

```
exams = (int[ ]) scores.clone( );
```

The expression (int[ ]) tells the compiler to treat the return value of the clone method as an integer array.

After the assignment statement, exams refers to a new array that is an exact copy of the scores array:

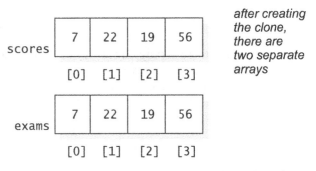

after creating the clone, there are two separate arrays

There are now two separate arrays. Changes to one array do not affect the other. For example, after the preceding statements, we might assign exams[2] = 42. The situation after the assignment to exams[2] is shown here:

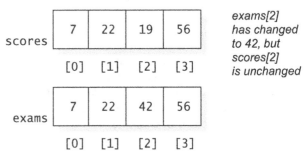

exams[2] has changed to 42, but scores[2] is unchanged

At this point, exams[2] is 42, but scores[2] is unchanged.

The Arrays Utility Class

In Java, a **utility class** is a class that provides methods that are intended to help you manipulate objects from some other class. Generally, these utility methods are static methods of the utility class, meaning that they can be used without being activated by any one particular object (see page 72). One of Java's utility classes is the Arrays utility from java.util.Arrays. It contains several dozen useful static methods for manipulating arrays. We'll look at three of these methods now, and others will be examined in later chapters.

The first method, called Arrays.copyOf, provides an alternative way to make a clone of an array. Here is an example:

copyOf

```
int[ ] scores = new int[] {7, 22, 19, 56};
int[ ] exams = Array.copyOf(scores, 4);
```

The copyOf method has two arguments: an array to copy (such as scores) and the number of elements to copy (which is 4 in our example). So, after these statements, exams is a copy of the scores array:

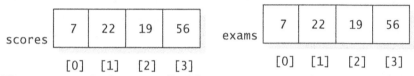

We are not required to copy all of the array. For example, consider the assignment exams = Arrays.copyOf(scores, 2), which results in this situation:

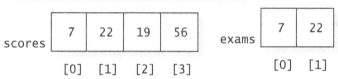

The number of items to copy may also be longer than the original array, such as exams = Arrays.copyOf(scores, 5). In this case, the extra elements of the new array are filled with Java default values (which are zeros for numbers).

Notice that we always call Arrays.copyOf rather than scores.copyOf. That's because copyOf is a static method of the Arrays class. It is not activated by any single object; instead, the object to copy (such as scores) is passed as an argument to the copyOf method.

A second static method, called Arrays.copyRange, allows you to copy a section of one array into a newly created array. For example:

```
int[ ] scores = new int[] {7, 22, 19, 56};
int[ ] exams = Array.copyOfRange(scores, 1, 3);
```

The argument 1 indicates the first index of scores to copy into exams; the argument 3 indicates the index that is just *after* the last element to copy. So, in this case, the elements scores[1] and scores[2] are copied into the new array (but scores[3] is not copied), as shown on the top of the next page.

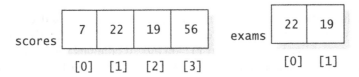

The third method is `Arrays.fill`, which fills a given array with a specified value. For example, `Arrays.fill(exams, 100)` fills every element of the exams array with the number 100. Note that `Arrays.fill` is a static void method that works on an existing array rather than creating a new array. This leads to our next topic: how arrays behave when they are passed as parameters to a method.

Array Parameters

An array can be a parameter to a method. Let's look at an example method with an array as a parameter. This is our own simple version of the `Arrays.fill` method, but it works only with integer arrays and it always fills the array with our favorite number, 42.

◆ **put42s**

```
public static void put42s(int[ ] data)
```
Put 42 in every component of an array.

Parameter:
　data – an array of integers

Postcondition:
　All components of data have been set to 42.

```
public static void put42s(int[ ] data)
{
    int i;
    for (i = 0; i < data.length; i++)
        data[i] = 42;
}
```

Perhaps this is a silly example (when was the last time you really wanted to put 42 in every component of an array?), but it is a good way to show how an array works as a parameter. Notice how the array parameter is indicated by placing array brackets after the parameter name. In the `put42s` example, the array is called `data`, so the parameter list is `(int[ ] data)`.

When a method is activated with an array parameter, the parameter is initialized to refer to the same array that the actual argument refers to. Therefore, if the method changes the components of the array, the changes do affect the actual argument. For example, this code activates the `put42s` method:

```
int[ ] example = new int[7];
put42s(example);
```

After these statements, all seven components of the `example` array contain 42.

Array Parameters

When a parameter is an array, then the parameter is initialized to refer to the same array that the actual argument refers to. Therefore, if the method changes the components of the array, the changes do affect the actual argument.

ENHANCED FOR-LOOPS FOR ARRAYS

There are several new versions of for-loops that you might not have seen before. One version allows a program to step through every element of an array in order. Of course, we can do this with an integer variable that simply steps through each index, such as this method that computes the sum of all elements in an integer array (from Self-Test Exercise 11 on page 26):

```java
public static int sum(int[ ] a)
{
   int answer, i;

   answer = 0;
   for (i = 0; i < a.length; i++)
      answer += a[i];
   return answer;
}
```

The new version of the for-loop uses a control variable that is declared in the parentheses following the keyword for. In the following example, we rewrite the sum method to access the elements of the array a, and we use the name item for the control variable. The body of the loop will be executed once with item set equal to a[0], then with item set to a[1], and so on, through all the items of the array:

```java
public static int sum(int[ ] a)
{
   int answer;

   answer = 0;
   for (int item : a)
      answer += item;
   return answer;
}
```

As with any loop, the work of the loop might be cut short by a return statement that is executed inside the loop. For example, here is another example of a method to determine whether a particular element appears in a double array:

```java
public static boolean search(double[ ] data, double target)
{
    for (double item : data)
    {   // Check whether item is the target.
        if (item == target)
            return true;
    }

    // The loop finished without finding the target.
    return false;
}
```

This form of the for-loop is called **iterating over an array**. The general format is given here, although you can use any variable name instead of item:

```java
for ( data type of the array elements  item :   name of the array )
{
    // Do something with item.
    // The first time through the loop, item will be set equal to the
    // [0] element of the array; the second time through the loop, item will
    // be set equal to the [1] element of the array, and so on.
    ...
}
```

Self-Test Exercises for Section 3.1

1. Suppose I have int b = new int[42]. What are the highest and lowest legal array indexes for b?

2. Write code that follows these steps: (1) Declare an integer array variable called b; (2) allocate a new array of 1000 integers for b to refer to; and (3) place the numbers 1 through 1000 in the array.

3. Redo the preceding exercise with only five elements instead of 1000. Your solution should be just a single Java statement.

4. Write a Java expression that will indicate how many elements are in the array b (from the previous exercise).

5. Consider the following statements:
   ```java
   int[ ] p = new int[100];
   int[ ] s = p;
   ```
   Which of the following statements will change the last value of p to 75? (There may be more than one correct answer.)
   ```java
   p[99] = 75;              p[100] = 75;
   s[99] = 75;              s[100] = 75;
   ```

6. Repeat the previous exercise using these two initial statements:
   ```
   int[ ] p = new int[100];
   int[ ] s = p.clone( );
   ```

7. What is the output from this code?
   ```
   int[ ] a, b;
   a = new int[10];
   a[5] = 0;
   b = a;
   a[5] = 42;
   System.out(b[5]);
   ```

8. What is the output from this code?
   ```
   int[ ] a, b;
   a = new int[10];
   a[5] = 0;
   b = a.clone( );
   a[5] = 42;
   System.out(b[5]);
   ```

9. What kind of exception will be thrown by these statements?
   ```
   int[ ] b;
   b[0] = 12;
   ```

10. Suppose an array is passed as a parameter to a method, and the method changes the first component of the array to 42. What effect does this have on the actual argument back in the calling program?

11. Write a method that copies n elements from the front of one integer array to the front of another. The two arrays and the number n are all arguments to the method. Include a precondition/postcondition contract as part of your implementation.

12. Write a Java method called zero_some with one parameter x that is an array of double numbers. The method changes x[0], x[2], x[4], ... , all to zero. If you activate zero_some(a) for an actual array a of length 6, which components of a will be changed to zero?

13. Use the new form of the for-loop to write a method that counts how many times a certain target appears in an integer array.

3.2   AN ADT FOR A BAG OF INTEGERS

This section provides an example of the design and implementation of a collection class. In this first example, the collection class will use an array to store its collection of elements (but later we will see other ways to store collections).

The example collection class is called a *bag of integers*. To describe the bag data type, think about an actual bag—a grocery bag or a garbage bag—and imagine writing integers on slips of paper and putting them in the bag. A **bag of integers** is similar to this imaginary bag: It's a container that holds a collection of integers that we place into it. A bag of integers can be used by any program that needs to store a collection of integers for its own use. For example, later we will write a program that keeps track of the ages of your family's members. If you have a large family with 10 people, the program keeps track of 10 ages—and these ages are kept in a bag of integers.

The Bag ADT—Specification

We've given an intuitive description of a bag of integers. We will implement this bag as a class called `IntArrayBag`, in which the integers are stored in an array. We'll use a three-part name for a collection: "Int" specifies the type of the elements in the bag; "Array" indicates the mechanism for storing the elements; and "Bag" indicates the kind of collection. For a precise specification of the `IntArrayBag` class, we must describe each of the public methods to manipulate an `IntArrayBag` object.

In Chapter 5, we'll see how to implement more general collections that can be used for any kind of data (not just integers), but the `IntArrayBag` is a good place to start.

The Constructors. The `IntArrayBag` class has two constructors to initialize a new, empty bag. One constructor has a parameter, as shown in this heading:

```
public IntArrayBag(initialCapacity)
```

The parameter, `initialCapacity`, is the initial capacity of the bag—the number of elements that the bag can hold. Once this capacity is reached, more elements can still be added and the capacity will automatically increase in a manner that you'll see in a moment.

The other constructor has no parameters, and it constructs a bag with an initial capacity of 10.

The add Method. This is a modification method that places a new integer, called `element`, into a bag. Here is the heading:

```
public void add(int element)
```

As an example, here are some statements for a bag called `firstBag`:

```
IntArrayBag firstBag = new IntArrayBag( );
firstBag.add(8);
firstBag.add(4);        After these statements, firstBag
firstBag.add(8);        contains two 8s and a 4.
```

After these statements are executed, `firstBag` contains three integers: the number 4 and two copies of the number 8. Notice that a bag can contain many copies of the same integer, such as in this example, which has two copies of 8.

The addMany Method.   This method is similar to the add method, except it has a strange new syntax in the heading:

```
public void addMany(int... elements)
```

The ellipsis after the data type (int...) means that the method can be called with any number of integer arguments. For example, any of these statements are permitted with a bag called firstBag:

```
firstBag.addMany(8,4,4); // Add one 8 and two 4s to the bag.
firstBag.addMany(1,2,3,4,5,6,7,8,9,10); // Add 1 through 10.
firstBag.addMany(5);      // Just like firstBag.add(5);
```

The method adds each of its arguments to the bag. This kind of method has a   *variable arity*
variable number of parameters. Mathematicians use the term **arity** for the number of arguments, so programmers say this is a **variable arity method**. A variable arity may be used only with the final (rightmost) parameter of a method. We'll also need to see how the implementation accesses the many parameters, but that can wait until the implementation stage.

The addAll Method.   This method allows us to insert the contents of one bag into the existing contents of another bag. The method has this heading:

```
public void addAll(IntArrayBag addend)
```

We use the name addend for the parameter, meaning "something to be added." As an example, suppose we create two bags called helter and skelter, and we then want to add all the contents of skelter to helter:

```
IntArrayBag helter = new IntArrayBag( );
IntArrayBag skelter = new IntArrayBag( );
helter.add(8);                    This adds the contents of
skelter.add(4);                   skelter to what's
skelter.add(8);                   already in helter.
helter.addAll(skelter);
```

After these statements, helter contains one 4 and two 8s.

The remove Method.   The heading for this modification method is:

```
public boolean remove(int target)
```

Provided that target is actually in the bag, the method removes one copy of target and returns true to indicate that something has been removed. If target isn't in the bag, then the method just returns false.

The size Method.   This accessor method returns the count of how many integers are in a bag. The heading is:

```
public int size( )
```

For example, suppose firstBag contains one copy of the number 4 and two copies of the number 8. Then firstBag.size( ) returns 3.

The countOccurrences Method. This is an accessor method that determines how many copies of a *particular* number are in a bag. The heading is:

```
public int countOccurrences(int target)
```

The return value of countOccurrences(n) is the number of occurrences of n in a bag. For example, if firstBag contains the number 4 and two copies of the number 8, then we will have these values:

```
System.out.println(firstBag.countOccurrences(1));   ← Prints 0
System.out.println(firstBag.countOccurrences(4));   ← Prints 1
System.out.println(firstBag.countOccurrences(8));   ← Prints 2
```

The union Method. The **union** of two bags is a new, larger bag that contains all the numbers in the first bag and all the numbers in the second bag:

The union of   and   is

We will implement union with a static method that has two parameters:

```
public static IntArrayBag union(IntArrayBag b1, IntArrayBag b2)
```

The union method computes the union of b1 and b2. For example:

```
IntArrayBag part1 = new IntArrayBag( );
IntArrayBag part2 = new IntArrayBag( );

part1.add(8);
part1.add(9);
part2.add(4);
part2.add(8);

IntArrayBag total = IntArrayBag.union(part1, part2);
```

This computes the union of the two bags, putting the result in a third bag.

After these statements, total contains one 4, two 8s, and one 9.

The union method is similar to addAll, but the usage is different. The addAll method is an ordinary method that is activated by a bag (for example, helter.addAll(skelter), which adds the contents of skelter to helter). On the other hand, union is a static method with two arguments. As a static method, union is not activated by any one bag. Instead, the activation of IntArrayBag.union(part1, part2) creates and returns a new bag that includes the contents of both part1 and part2.

The clone Method. As part of our specification, we require that bag objects can be copied with a clone method. For example:

b now contains a 42

```
IntArrayBag b = new IntArrayBag( );
b.add(42);
IntArrayBag c = b.clone( );
```

c is initialized as a clone of b

At this point, because we are only specifying which operations can manipulate a bag, we don't need to say anything more about the clone method.

Three Methods That Deal with Capacity. Each bag has a current **capacity**, which is the number of elements the bag can hold without having to request more memory. Once the capacity is reached, more elements can still be added by using the add method. In this case, the add method itself will increase the capacity as needed. In fact, our implementation of add will double the capacity whenever the bag becomes full.

With this in mind, you might wonder why a programmer needs to worry about the capacity at all. For example, why does the constructor require the programmer to specify an initial capacity? Couldn't we always use the constructor that has an initial capacity of 10 and have the add method increase capacity as more and more elements are added? Yes, this approach will always work correctly. But if there are many elements, then many of the activations of add would need to increase the capacity. This could be inefficient. To avoid repeatedly increasing the capacity, a programmer provides an initial guess at the needed capacity for the constructor.

For example, suppose a programmer expects no more than 1000 elements for a bag named kilosack. The bag is declared this way, with an initial capacity of 1000:

```
IntArrayBag kilosack = new IntArrayBag(1000);
```

After this declaration, the programmer can place 1000 elements in the bag without worrying about the capacity. Later, the programmer can add more elements to the bag, maybe even more than 1000. If there are more than 1000 elements, then add increases the capacity as needed.

There are three methods that allow a programmer to manipulate a bag's capacity after the bag is in use. The methods have these headers:

```
public int getCapacity( )
public void ensureCapacity(int minimumCapacity)
public void trimToSize( )
```

The first method, getCapacity, just returns the current capacity of the bag. The second method, ensureCapacity, increases the capacity to a specified minimum amount. For example, to ensure that a bag called bigboy has a capacity of at least 10,000, we would activate bigboy.ensureCapacity(10000).

The third method, trimToSize, reduces the capacity of a bag to its current size. For example, suppose that bigboy has a current capacity of 10,000, but it contains only 42 elements, and we are not planning to add any more. Then we can reduce the current capacity to 42 with the activation bigboy.trimToSize(). Trimming the capacity is never required, but doing so can reduce the memory used by a program.

That's all the methods, and we're almost ready to write the methods' specifications. But first there are some limitations to discuss.

OutOfMemoryError and Other Limitations for Collection Classes

Our plan is to store a bag's elements in an array and to increase the capacity of the array as needed. The memory for any array comes from a location called the program's **heap** (also called the **free store**). In fact, the memory for all Java objects comes from the heap.

what happens when the heap runs out of memory?

If a heap has insufficient memory for a new object or array, then the result is a Java exception called OutOfMemoryError. This exception is thrown automatically by an unsuccessful "new" operation. For example, if there is insufficient memory for a new Throttle object, then Throttle t = new Throttle( ) throws an OutOfMemoryError. Experienced programmers may monitor the size of the heap and the amount that is still unused. Our programs won't attempt such monitoring, but our specification for any collection class will always mention that the maximum capacity is limited by the amount of free memory. To aid more experienced programmers, the specification will also indicate precisely which methods have the possibility of throwing an OutOfMemoryError. (Any method that uses the "new" operation could throw this exception.)

collection classes may be limited by the maximum value of an integer

Many collection classes have another limitation that is tied to the maximum value of an integer. In particular, our bag stores the elements in an array, and every array has integers for its indexes. Java integers are limited to no more than 2,147,483,647, which is also written as Integer.MAX_VALUE. An attempt to create an array with a size beyond Integer.MAX_VALUE results in an arithmetic overflow during the calculation of the size of the array. Such an overflow usually produces an array size that Java's runtime system sees as negative. This is because Java represents integers so that the "next" number after Integer.MAX_VALUE is actually the smallest negative number.

Programmers often ignore the array-size overflow problem (since today's machines generally have an OutOfMemoryError before Integer.MAX_VALUE is approached). We won't provide special code to handle this problem, but we won't totally ignore the problem either. Instead, our documentation will indicate precisely which methods have the potential for an array-size overflow. We'll also add a note to advise that large bags should probably use a different implementation method anyway because many of the array-based algorithms are slow for large bags ($O(n)$, where n is the number of elements in the bag).

The IntArrayBag Class—Specification

We now know enough about the IntArrayBag to write a specification, as shown in Figure 3.1. It is part of a package named edu.colorado.collections.

FIGURE 3.1	Specification for the `IntArrayBag` Class

Class IntArrayBag

❖ **public class IntArrayBag from the package edu.colorado.collections**
An `IntArrayBag` is a collection of `int` numbers.

Limitations:

(1) The capacity of one of these bags can change after it's created, but the maximum capacity is limited by the amount of free memory on the machine. The constructor, add, clone, and union will result in an `OutOfMemoryError` when free memory is exhausted.

(2) A bag's capacity cannot exceed the largest integer, 2,147,483,647 (`Integer.MAX_VALUE`). Any attempt to create a larger capacity results in failure due to an arithmetic overflow.

(3) Because of the slow linear algorithms of this class, large bags will have poor performance.

Specification

◆ **Constructor for the IntArrayBag**
`public IntArrayBag( )`
Initialize an empty bag with an initial capacity of 10. Note that the add method works efficiently (without needing more memory) until this capacity is reached.

Postcondition:
This bag is empty and has an initial capacity of 10.

Throws: `OutOfMemoryError`
Indicates insufficient memory for `new int[10]`.

◆ **Second Constructor for the IntArrayBag**
`public IntArrayBag(int initialCapacity)`
Initialize an empty bag with a specified initial capacity.

Parameter:
`initialCapacity` – the initial capacity of this bag

Precondition:
`initialCapacity` is non-negative.

Postcondition:
This bag is empty and has the specified initial capacity.

Throws: `IllegalArgumentException`
Indicates that `initialCapacity` is negative.

Throws: `OutOfMemoryError`
Indicates insufficient memory for allocating the bag.

(continued)

(FIGURE 3.1 continued)

♦ add

```
public void add(int element)
```
Add a new element to this bag. If this new element would take this bag beyond its current capacity, then the capacity is increased before adding the new element.

Parameter:

element – the new element that is being added

Postcondition:

A new copy of the element has been added to this bag.

Throws: `OutOfMemoryError`

Indicates insufficient memory for increasing the capacity.

Note:

Creating a bag with capacity beyond `Integer.MAX_VALUE` causes arithmetic overflow.

♦ addAll

```
public void addAll(IntArrayBag addend)
```
Add the contents of another bag to this bag.

Parameter:

addend – a bag whose contents will be added to this bag

Precondition:

The parameter, addend, is not null.

Postcondition:

The elements from addend have been added to this bag.

Throws: `NullPointerException`

Indicates that addend is null.

Throws: `OutOfMemoryError`

Indicates insufficient memory to increase the size of this bag.

Note:

Creating a bag with capacity beyond `Integer.MAX_VALUE` causes arithmetic overflow.

♦ addMany

```
public void addMany(int... elements)
```
Add a variable number of new elements to this bag. If these new elements would take this bag beyond its current capacity, then the capacity is increased before adding the new elements.

Parameter:

elements – a variable number of new elements that are all being added

Postcondition:

New copies of all the elements have been added to this bag.

Throws: `OutOfMemoryError`

Indicates insufficient memory for increasing the capacity.

Note:

Creating a bag with capacity beyond `Integer.MAX_VALUE` causes arithmetic overflow.

(continued)

(FIGURE 3.1 continued)

♦ **clone**

```
public IntArrayBag clone( )
```
Generate a copy of this bag.

Returns:

The return value is a copy of this bag. Subsequent changes to the copy will not affect the original, nor vice versa. The return value must be typecast to an `IntArrayBag` before it is used.

Throws: `OutOfMemoryError`

Indicates insufficient memory for creating the clone.

♦ **countOccurrences**

```
public int countOccurrences(int target)
```
Accessor method to count the number of occurrences of a particular element in this bag.

Parameter:

`target` – the element that needs to be counted

Returns:

the number of times that `target` occurs in this bag

♦ **ensureCapacity**

```
public void ensureCapacity(int minimumCapacity)
```
Change the current capacity of this bag.

Parameter:

`minimumCapacity` – the new capacity for this bag

Postcondition:

This bag's capacity has been changed to at least `minimumCapacity`. If the capacity was already at or greater than `minimumCapacity`, then the capacity is left unchanged.

Throws: `OutOfMemoryError`

Indicates insufficient memory for `new int[minimumCapacity]`.

♦ **getCapacity**

```
public int getCapacity( )
```
Accessor method to determine the current capacity of this bag. The add method works efficiently (without needing more memory) until this capacity is reached.

Returns:

the current capacity of this bag

♦ **remove**

```
public boolean remove(int target)
```
Remove one copy of a specified element from this bag.

Parameter:

`target` – the element to remove from this bag

Postcondition:

If `target` was found in this bag, then one copy of `target` has been removed and the method returns `true`. Otherwise, this bag remains unchanged, and the method returns `false`.

(continued)

(FIGURE 3.1 continued)

♦ **size**
```
public int size( )
```
Accessor method to determine the number of elements in this bag.

Returns:
the number of elements in this bag

♦ **trimToSize**
```
public void trimToSize( )
```
Reduce the current capacity of this bag to its actual size (i.e., the number of elements it contains).

Postcondition:
This bag's capacity has been changed to its current size.

Throws: `OutOfMemoryError`
Indicates insufficient memory for altering the capacity.

♦ **union**
```
public static IntArrayBag union(IntArrayBag b1, IntArrayBag b2)
```
Create a new bag that contains all the elements from two other bags.

Parameters:
b1 – the first of two bags
b2 – the second of two bags

Precondition:
Neither b1 nor b2 is null.

Returns:
a new bag that is the union of b1 and b2

Throws: `NullPointerException`
Indicates that one of the arguments is null.

Throws: `OutOfMemoryError`
Indicates insufficient memory for the new bag.

Note:
Creating a bag with capacity beyond `Integer.MAX_VALUE` causes arithmetic overflow.

The IntArrayBag Class—Demonstration Program

With the specification in hand, we can write a program that uses a bag. We don't need to know what the instance variables of a bag are, and we don't need to know how the methods are implemented. As an example, a demonstration program appears in Figure 3.2. The program asks a user about the ages of family members. The user enters the ages, followed by a negative number to indicate the end of the input. (Using a special value to end a list is a common technique; this value is called a **sentinel value**.) A typical dialogue with the program looks like this:

```
Type the ages of your family members.
Type a negative number at the end and press return.
5    19    47    -1
Type those ages again. Press return after each age.
Age: 19
Yes, I've got that age and will remove it.
Age: 36
No, that age does not occur!
Age: 5
Yes, I've got that age and will remove it.
Age: 47
Yes, I've got that age and will remove it.
May your family live long and prosper.
```

The program puts the ages in a bag and then asks the user to type the ages again. The program's interaction with the user is handled through a new Java class called `java.util.Scanner`, which contains various simple input methods. The class is fully described in Appendix B, but for this program, all that's needed is a single Scanner called `stdin`, which is attached to standard input (`System.in`).

the Scanner class from Appendix B allows simple kinds of input

Once `stdin` is set up, an integer can be read with `stdin.nextInt` (which simply reads an integer input). You might find the Scanner class useful for your own demonstration programs.

As for the `IntArrayBag` class itself, we still don't know how the implementation will work, but we're getting there.

FIGURE 3.2   Demonstration Program for the Bag Class

Java Application Program

```java
// FILE: BagDemonstration.java
// This small demonstration program shows how to use the IntArrayBag class.

import edu.colorado.collections.IntArrayBag;
import java.util.Scanner;
```

The Scanner class is described in Appendix B.

```java
class BagDemonstration
{
    private static Scanner stdin = new Scanner(System.in);

    public static void main(String[ ] args)
    {
        IntArrayBag ages = new IntArrayBag( );
        getAges(ages);
        checkAges(ages);
        System.out.println("May your family live long and prosper.");
    }
```

(continued)

(FIGURE 3.2 continued)

```
public static void getAges(IntArrayBag ages)
// The getAges method prompts the user to type in the ages of family members. These
// ages are read and placed in the ages bag, stopping when the user types a negative
// number. This demonstration does not worry about the possibility of running out
// of memory (therefore, an OutOfMemoryError is possible).
{
    int userInput; // An age from the user's family

    System.out.println("Type the ages of your family members.");
    System.out.println("Type a negative number at the end and press return.");
    userInput = stdin.nextInt( );
    while (userInput >= 0)
    {
        ages.add(userInput);
        userInput = stdin.nextInt( );
    }
}

public static void checkAges(IntArrayBag ages)
// The checkAges method prompts the user to type in the ages of family members once
// again. Each age is removed from the ages bag when it is typed, stopping when the bag
// is empty.
public static void checkAges(IntArrayBag ages)
{
    int userInput; // An age from the user's family

    System.out.print("Type those ages again. ");
    System.out.println("Press return after each age.");
    while (ages.size( ) > 0)
    {
        System.print("Next age: ");
        userInput = stdin.nextInt( );
        if (ages.countOccurrences(userInput) == 0)
            System.out.println("No, that age does not occur!");
        else
        {
            System.out.println("Yes, I've got that age and will remove it.");
            ages.remove(userInput);
        }
    }
}
}
```

The IntArrayBag Class—Design

There are several ways to design the IntArrayBag class. For now, we'll keep things simple and design a somewhat inefficient data structure using an array. Later, the data structure will be redesigned several times for more efficiency.

We start the design by thinking about the data structure—the actual configuration of private instance variables used to implement the class. The primary structure for our design is an array that stores the elements of a bag. Or, to be more precise, we use the *beginning* part of a large array. Such an array is called a **partially filled array**. For example, if the bag contains the integer 4 and two copies of 8, then the first part of the array could look this way:

use the beginning part of an array

Components of the partially filled array contain the elements of the bag.

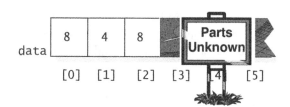

This array, called data, will be one of the private instance variables of the IntArrayBag class. The length of the array will be determined by the current capacity, but as the picture indicates, when we are using the array to store a bag with just three elements, we don't care what appears beyond the first three components. Starting at index 3, the array might contain all zeros, or it might contain garbage or our favorite number—it really doesn't matter.

Because part of the array can contain garbage, the IntArrayBag class must keep track of one other item: *How much of the array is currently being used?* For example, in the preceding picture, we are using only the first three components of the array because the bag contains three elements. The amount of the array being used can be as small as zero (an empty bag) or as large as the current capacity. The amount increases as elements are added to the bag, and it decreases as elements are removed. In any case, we will keep track of the amount in a private instance variable called manyItems. With this approach, there are two instance variables for a bag:

the bag's instance variables

```
public class IntArrayBag implements Cloneable
{
    private int[ ] data;     // An array to store elements
    private int manyItems;   // How much of the array is used

    ‖ The public methods will be given in a moment.
}
```

Notice that we are planning to implement a clone method; therefore, we indicate "implements Cloneable" at the start of the class definition.

The Invariant of an ADT

We've defined the bag data structure, and we have an intuitive idea of how the structure will be used to represent a bag of elements. But as an aid in implementing the class, we should also write down an explicit statement of how the data structure is used to represent a bag. In the case of the bag, we need to state how the instance variables of the class are used to represent a bag of elements. There are two rules for our bag implementation:

rules that dictate how the instance variables are used to represent a value

1. The number of elements in the bag is stored in the instance variable `manyItems`, which is no more than `data.length`.

2. For an empty bag, we do not care what is stored in any of `data`; for a non-empty bag, the elements of the bag are stored in `data[0]` through `data[manyItems-1]`, and we don't care what is stored in the rest of `data`.

The rules that dictate how the instance variables of a class represent a value (such as a bag of elements) are called the **invariant of the ADT**. The knowledge of these rules is essential to the correct implementation of the ADT's methods. With the exception of the constructors, each method depends on the invariant being valid when the method is activated. And each method, including the constructors, has the responsibility of ensuring that the invariant is valid when the method finishes. In some sense, the invariant of an ADT is a condition that is an *implicit* part of every method's postcondition. And (except for the constructors) it is also an implicit part of every method's precondition. The invariant is not usually written as an *explicit* part of the precondition and postcondition because the programmer who uses the ADT does not need to know about these conditions. But to the implementor of the ADT, the invariant is indispensable. In other words, the invariant is a critical part of the implementation of an ADT, but it has no effect on the way the ADT is used.

Key Design Concept

The invariant is a critical part of an ADT's implementation.

The Invariant of an ADT

When you design a new class, always make an explicit statement of the rules that dictate how the instance variables are used. These rules are called the **invariant of the ADT**. All of the methods (except the constructors) can count on the invariant being valid when the method is called. Each method also has the responsibility of ensuring that the invariant is valid when the method finishes.

Once the invariant of an ADT is stated, the implementation of the methods is relatively simple because there is no interaction between the methods—except for their cooperation in keeping the invariant valid. We'll look at these implementations one at a time, starting with the constructors.

The IntArrayBag ADT—Implementation

The Constructor. Every constructor has one primary job: to set up the instance variables correctly. In the case of the bag, the constructor must set up the instance variables so that they represent an empty bag with a current capacity given by the parameter `initialCapacity`. The bag has two instance variables, so its constructor will include two assignment statements, shown in this implementation of one of the constructors:

```
public IntArrayBag(int initialCapacity)
{
    if (initialCapacity < 0)
        throw new IllegalArgumentException
        ("initialCapacity is negative: " + initialCapacity);
    manyItems = 0;
    data = new int[initialCapacity];
}
```

The if-statement at the start checks the constructor's precondition. The first assignment statement, `manyItems = 0`, simply sets manyItems to zero, indicating that the bag does not yet have any elements. The second assignment statement, `data = new int[initialCapacity]`, is more interesting. This statement allocates an array of the right capacity (`initialCapacity`) and makes data refer to the new array. For example, suppose that `initialCapacity` is 6. After the two assignment statements, the instance variables look like this:

implementing the constructor

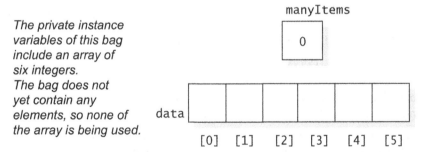

The private instance variables of this bag include an array of six integers. The bag does not yet contain any elements, so none of the array is being used.

Later, the program could add many elements to this bag, maybe even more than six. If there are more than six elements, then the bag's methods will increase the array's capacity as needed.

The other constructor is similar, except it always provides an initial capacity of 10.

The add Method. The add method checks whether there is room to add a new element. If not, the array capacity is increased before proceeding. (The new capacity is twice the old capacity plus 1. The extra +1 deals with the case in which the original size was zero.) The attempt to increase the array capacity may lead to an OutOfMemoryError or an arithmetic overflow, as discussed on page 118. But usually these errors do not occur, and we can place the new element in the next available location of the array. What is the index of the next available location? For example, if manyItems is 3, then data[0], data[1], and data[2] are already occupied, and the next location is data[3]. In general, the next available location will be data[manyItems]. We can place the new element in data[manyItems], as shown in this implementation:

implementing add

```
public void add(int element)
{
    if (manyItems == data.length)
    {
        // Double the capacity and add 1; this works even if manyItems is 0.
        // However, in the case that manyItems*2 + 1 is beyond
        // Integer.MAX_VALUE, there will be an arithmetic overflow and
        // the bag will fail.
        ensureCapacity(manyItems*2 + 1);
    }

    data[manyItems] = element;    ←—— See Self-Test Exercise 22
    manyItems++;                         for an alternative approach
}                                        to these steps.
```

Within a method we can activate other methods, such as the way that the add implementation activates ensureCapacity to increase the capacity of the array.

The addAll Method. The addAll method has this heading:

```
public void addAll(IntArrayBag addend)
```

implementing addAll

The bag that activates addAll is increased by adding all the elements from addend. Our implementation follows these steps:

1. Ensure that the capacity of the bag is large enough to contain its current elements plus the extra elements that will come from addend, as shown here:

    ```
    ensureCapacity(manyItems + addend.manyItems);
    ```

By the way, what happens in this statement if addend is null? Of course, a null value violates the precondition of addAll, but a programmer could mistakenly provide null. In that case, a NullPointerException will be thrown, and this possibility is documented in the specification of addAll on page 120.

2. Copy the elements from addend.data to the next available positions
in our own data array. In other words, we will copy addend.many-
Items elements from the front of addend.data. These elements go
into our own data array beginning at the next available spot,
data[manyItems]. We could write a loop to copy these elements, but
a quicker approach is to use Java's System.arraycopy method, which
has these five arguments:

```
System.arraycopy(source, si, destination, di, n);
```

The arguments source and destination are two arrays, and the other
arguments are integers. The method copies n elements from source
(starting at source[si]) to the destination array (with the elements
being placed at destination[di] through destination[di+n-1]). For
our purposes, we call the arraycopy method:

the arraycopy method

```
System.arraycopy
    (addend.data, 0, data, manyItems, addend.manyItems);
```

3. Increase our own manyItems by addend.manyItems:

```
manyItems += addend.manyItems;
```

These three steps are shown in the addAll implementation of Figure 3.3.

The addMany Method. This method has a variable number of parameters, as
indicated in its heading:

```
public void addMany(int... elements)
```

FIGURE 3.3   Implementation of the Bag's addAll Method

Implementation

```
public void addAll(IntArrayBag addend)
{
    // If addend is null, then a NullPointerException is thrown.
    // In the case that the total number of items is beyond
    // Integer.MAX_VALUE, there will be
    // arithmetic overflow and the bag will fail.
    ensureCapacity(manyItems + addend.manyItems);

    System.arraycopy(addend.data, 0, data, manyItems, addend.manyItems);
    manyItems += addend.manyItems;
}
```

FIGURE 3.4	Implementation of the Bag's addMany Method

Implementation

```
public void addMany(int... elements)
{
     if (manyItems + elements.length > data.length)
     {   // Ensure twice as much space as we need.
         ensureCapacity((manyItems + elements.length)*2);
     }

     System.arraycopy(elements, 0, data, manyItems, elements.length);
     manyItems += elements.length;
}
```

*implementing
addMany*

When the method is activated, the Java runtime system will take the actual arguments and put them in an array that the implementation can access with the parameter name (elements). For example, if we activate b.addMany(4,8,4), then elements will be an array containing the three integers 4, 8, and 4. One possible implementation is to activate the ordinary add method once for each integer in the elements array. This would work fine, but a more efficient approach uses System.arraycopy, as shown in Figure 3.4.

The remove Method. The remove method takes several steps to remove an element named target from a bag. In the first step, we find the index of target in the bag's array and store this index in a local variable named index. For example, suppose that target is the number 6 in this bag:

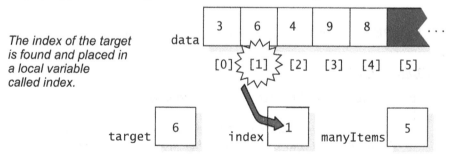

The index of the target is found and placed in a local variable called index.

In this example, target is a parameter to the remove method, index is a local variable in the remove method, and manyItems is the bag instance variable. As you can see in the drawing, the first step of remove is to locate the target (6) and place the index of the target in the local variable called index.

Once the index of the target is found, the second step is to take the *final* element in the bag and copy it to data[index]. The reason for this copying is so that all the bag's elements stay together at the front of the partially filled array, with no "holes." In our example, the number 8 is copied to data[index]:

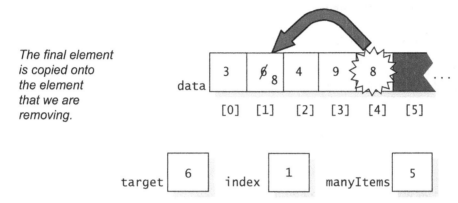

The final element is copied onto the element that we are removing.

The third step is to reduce manyItems by one—in effect reducing the used part of the array by one. In our example, manyItems is reduced from 5 to 4:

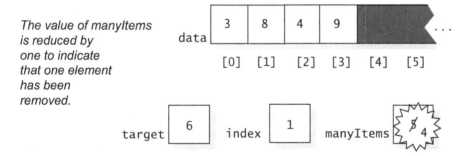

The value of manyItems is reduced by one to indicate that one element has been removed.

The code for the remove method, shown in Figure 3.5, follows these three steps. There is also a check that the target is actually in the bag. If we discover that the target is not in the bag, then we do not need to remove anything. Also note that our method works correctly for the boundary values of removing the first or last element in the array.

Before we continue, we want to point out a programming technique. Look at the following loop from Figure 3.5:

implementing remove

```
index = 0;
while ( (index < manyItems) && (target != data[index]) )
    index++;
```

FIGURE 3.5   Implementation of the Bag's Method to Remove an Element

Implementation

```
public boolean remove(int target)
{
    int index; // The location of target in the data array

    // First, set index to the location of target in the data array,
    // which could be as small as 0 or as large as manyItems-1.
    // If target is not in the array, then index will be set equal to manyItems.
    index = 0;
    while ((index < manyItems) && (target != data[index]))
        index++;

    if (index == manyItems)
        // The target was not found, so nothing is removed.
        return false;
    else
    {   // The target was found at data[index].
        manyItems--;
        data[index] = data[manyItems]; ◄─────── See Self-Test Exercise 22 for an
        return true;                            alternative approach to this step.
    }
}
```

The boolean expression indicates that the loop continues as long as `index` is still a location in the used part of the array (i.e., `index < manyItems`) and we have not yet found the target (i.e., `target != data[index]`). Each time through the loop, the `index` is incremented by one. No other work is needed in the loop. But take a careful look at the expression `data[index]` in the boolean test of the loop. The valid indexes for data range from 0 to `manyItems-1`. But if the target is not in the array, then `index` will eventually reach `manyItems`, which could be an invalid index. At that point, with `index` equal to `manyItems`, we must not evaluate the expression `data[index]`. Trying to evaluate `data[index]` with an invalid `index` will cause an `ArrayIndexOutOfBoundsException`.

```
┌─────────────────────────────────────────────────────┐
│     Using an Array Index in a Boolean Expression     │
│     Never use an invalid index, even in a simple test. │
└─────────────────────────────────────────────────────┘
```

Avoiding the invalid index is the reason for the first part of the boolean test (i.e., index < manyItems). Moreover, the test for (index < manyItems) must appear *before* the other part of the test. Placing (index < manyItems) first ensures that only valid indexes are used. The insurance comes from a technique called *short-circuit evaluation,* which Java uses to evaluate boolean expressions. In **short-circuit evaluation**, a boolean expression is evaluated from left to right, and the evaluation stops as soon as there is enough information to determine the value of the expression. In our example, if index equals manyItems, then the first part of the boolean expression (index < manyItems) is false, so the entire && expression *must* be false. It doesn't matter whether the second part of the && expression is true or false. Therefore, Java doesn't bother to evaluate the second part of the expression, and the potential error of an invalid index is avoided.

short-circuit evaluation of boolean expressions

The countOccurrences Method. To count the number of occurrences of a particular element in a bag, we step through the used portion of the partially filled array. Remember that we are using locations data[0] through data[manyItems-1], so the correct loop is shown in this implementation:

```java
public int countOccurrences(int target)
{
    int answer;
    int index;

    answer = 0;
    for (index = 0; index < manyItems; index++)
        if (target == data[index])
            answer++;
    return answer;
}
```

implementing the countOccurrences method

The union Method. The union method is different from our other methods. It is a *static* method, which means it is not activated by any one bag object. Instead, the method must take its two parameters (bags b1 and b2), combine these two bags together into a third bag, and return this third bag. The third bag is declared as a local variable called answer in the implementation of Figure 3.6. The capacity of the answer bag must be the sum of the capacities of b1 and b2, so the actual answer bag is allocated by the statement:

implementing the union method

```java
answer = new IntArrayBag(b1.getCapacity( ) + b2.getCapacity( ));
```

This calls the IntArrayBag constructor to create a new bag with an initial capacity of b1.getCapacity( ) + b2.getCapacity( ).

The union implementation also makes use of the System.arraycopy method to copy elements from b1.data and b2.data into answer.data.

FIGURE 3.6   Implementation of the Bag's union Method

Implementation

```
public static IntArrayBag union(IntArrayBag b1, IntArrayBag b2)
{
    // If either b1 or b2 is null, then a NullPointerException is thrown.
    // In the case that the total number of items is beyond Integer.MAX_VALUE,
    // there will be an arithmetic overflow and the bag will fail.

    IntArrayBag answer =
        new IntArrayBag(b1.getCapacity( ) + b2.getCapacity( ));

    System.arraycopy(b1.data, 0, answer.data, 0, b1.manyItems);
    System.arraycopy(b2.data, 0, answer.data, b1.manyItems, b2.manyItems);
    answer.manyItems = b1.manyItems + b2.manyItems;

    return answer;
}
```

The clone Method. The clone method of a class allows a programmer to make a copy of an object. For example, the IntArrayBag class has a clone method to allow a programmer to make a copy of an existing bag. The copy is separate from the original so that subsequent changes to the copy won't change the original, nor will subsequent changes to the original change the copy.

The IntArrayBag clone method will follow the pattern introduced in Chapter 2 on page 82. Therefore, the start of the clone method is:

```
public IntArrayBag clone( )
{ // Clone an IntArrayBag object.
    IntArrayBag answer;

    try
    {
        answer = (IntArrayBag) super.clone( );
    }
    catch (CloneNotSupportedException e)
    {
        throw new RuntimeException
        ("This class does not implement Cloneable.");
    }
    ...
```

As explained in Chapter 2, this code uses the super.clone method to make answer be an exact copy of the bag that activated the clone method. But for the bag class, an exact copy is not quite correct. The problem occurs because super.clone copies each instance variable of the class without concern for whether the instance variable is a primitive type (such as an int) or a more complicated type (such as an array or some other kind of reference to an object).

To see why this causes a problem, suppose we have a bag that contains three elements:

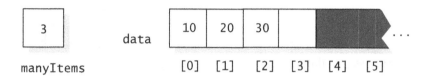

This drawing uses the "array shorthand" that we've been using—just putting the name of the array right next to it. But in fact, as with every array, the instance variable data is actually a reference to the array, so a more accurate picture looks like this drawing:

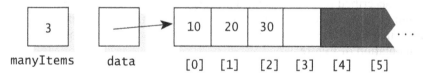

Now, suppose we activate clone( ) to create a copy of this bag. The clone method executes the statement answer = (IntArrayBag) super.clone( ). What does super.clone() do? It creates a new IntArrayBag object, and answer will refer to this new IntArrayBag. But the new IntArrayBag has instance variables (answer.manyItems and answer.data) that are merely copied from the original. So, after the statement answer = (IntArrayBag) super.clone( ), the situation looks like this (where manyItems and data are the instance variables from the original bag that activated the clone method):

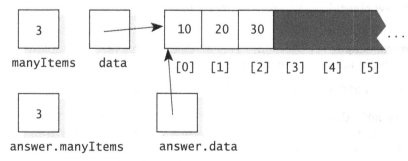

As you can see, answer.manyItems has a copy of the number 3, and that is fine. But answer.data merely refers to the original's array. Subsequent changes to answer.data will affect the original and vice versa. This is incorrect behavior for a clone. To fix the problem, we need an additional statement before the return of the clone method. The purpose of the statement is to create a new array for the clone's data instance variable to refer to. Here's the statement:

```
answer.data = data.clone( );
```

After this statement, answer.data refers to a separate array:

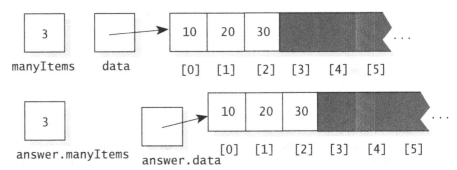

The new answer.data array was created by creating a clone of the original array (as described on page 107). Subsequent changes to answer will not affect the original, nor will changes to the original affect answer. The complete clone method, including the extra statement at the end, is shown as part of the full implementation of Figure 3.7.

ⓘ PROGRAMMING TIP

CLONING A CLASS THAT CONTAINS AN ARRAY

If a class has an instance variable that is an array, then the clone method needs extra work before it returns. The extra work creates a new array for the clone's instance variable to refer to.

The class may have other instance variables that are references to objects. In such a case, the clone method also carries out extra work. The extra work creates a new object for each such instance variable to refer to.

The ensureCapacity Method. This method ensures that a bag's array has at least a certain minimum length. Here is the method's heading:

```
public void ensureCapacity(int minimumCapacity)
```

The method determines whether the bag's array has a length below minimumCapacity. If so, the method allocates a new larger array with a length of minimumCapacity. The elements are copied into the larger array, and the data instance variable is then made to refer to the larger array. Part of Figure 3.7 shows our implementation, which follows the steps we have outlined.

The Bag ADT—Putting the Pieces Together

Three bag methods remain to be implemented: `size` (which returns the number of elements currently in the bag), `getCapacity` (which returns the current length of the bag's array, including the part that's not currently being used), and `trimToSize` (which reduces the capacity of the bag's array to equal exactly the current number of elements in the bag).

The `size` and `getCapacity` methods are implemented in one line each, and `trimToSize` is similar to `ensureCapacity`, so we won't discuss these methods. But you should examine these methods in the complete implementation file of Figure 3.7. Also notice that the `IntArrayBag` class is placed in a package called `edu.colorado.collections`. Throughout the rest of this book, we will add other collection classes to this package.

FIGURE 3.7   Implementation File for the `IntArrayBag` Class

Implementation

```
// File: IntArrayBag.java from the package edu.colorado.collections
// Complete documentation is in Figure 3.1 on page 119 or from the IntArrayBag link at
// http://www.cs.colorado.edu/~main/docs/.

package edu.colorado.collections;

public class IntArrayBag implements Cloneable
{
    // Invariant of the IntArrayBag class:
    //   1. The number of elements in the Bag is in the instance variable manyItems.
    //   2. For an empty Bag, we do not care what is stored in any of data;
    //      for a non-empty Bag, the elements in the Bag are stored in data[0]
    //      through data[manyItems-1], and we don't care what's in the rest of data.
    private int[ ] data;
    private int manyItems;

    public IntArrayBag( )
    {
        final int INITIAL_CAPACITY = 10;
        manyItems = 0;
        data = new int[INITIAL_CAPACITY];
    }
```

(continued)

(FIGURE 3.7 continued)

```java
public IntArrayBag(int initialCapacity)
{
    if (initialCapacity < 0)
        throw new IllegalArgumentException
        ("initialCapacity is negative: " + initialCapacity);
    manyItems = 0;
    data = new int[initialCapacity];
}

public void add(int element)
{
    if (manyItems == data.length)
    {
        // Double the capacity and add 1; this works even if manyItems is 0. However, in
        // the case that manyItems*2 + 1 is beyond Integer.MAX_VALUE, there will be an
        // arithmetic overflow and the bag will fail.
        ensureCapacity(manyItems*2 + 1);
    }
    data[manyItems] = element;
    manyItems++;
}

public void addAll(IntArrayBag addend)
{
    // If addend is null, then a NullPointerException is thrown.
    // In the case that the total number of items is beyond Integer.MAX_VALUE, there will
    // be an arithmetic overflow and the bag will fail.
    ensureCapacity(manyItems + addend.manyItems);

    System.arraycopy(addend.data, 0, data, manyItems, addend.manyItems);
    manyItems += addend.manyItems;
}

public void addMany(int... elements)
{
    if (manyItems + elements.length > data.length)
    {   // Ensure twice as much space as we need.
        ensureCapacity((manyItems + elements.length)*2);
    }

    System.arraycopy(elements, 0, data, manyItems, elements.length);
    manyItems += elements.length;
}
```

(continued)

(FIGURE 3.7 continued)

```java
public IntArrayBag clone( )
{  // Clone an IntArrayBag object.
   IntArrayBag answer;

   try
   {
      answer = (IntArrayBag) super.clone( );
   }
   catch (CloneNotSupportedException e)
   {
      // This exception should not occur. But if it does, it would probably indicate a
      // programming error that made super.clone unavailable. The most common
      // error would be forgetting the "Implements Cloneable" clause at the start of
      // this class.
      throw new RuntimeException
      ("This class does not implement Cloneable.");
   }

   answer.data = data.clone( );

   return answer;
}


public int countOccurrences(int target)
{
   int answer;
   int index;

   answer = 0;
   for (index = 0; index < manyItems; index++)
      if (target == data[index])
         answer++;
   return answer;
}

public void ensureCapacity(int minimumCapacity)
{
   int[ ] biggerArray;

   if (data.length < minimumCapacity)
   {
      biggerArray = new int[minimumCapacity];
      System.arraycopy(data, 0, biggerArray, 0, manyItems);
      data = biggerArray;
   }
}
```

(continued)

(FIGURE 3.7 continued)

```
public int getCapacity( )
{
    return data.length;
}

public boolean remove(int target)
{
    int index; // The location of target in the data array

    // First, set index to the location of target in the data array,
    // which could be as small as 0 or as large as manyItems-1.
    // If target is not in the array, then index will be set equal to manyItems.
    index = 0;
    while ((index < manyItems) && (target != data[index]))
        index++;

    if (index == manyItems)
        // The target was not found, so nothing is removed.
        return false;
    else
    {   // The target was found at data[index].
        manyItems--;
        data[index] = data[manyItems];  ←————— See Self-Test Exercise 22 for an
        return true;                            alternative approach to this step.
    }
}

public int size( )
{
    return manyItems;
}

public void trimToSize( )
{
    int[ ] trimmedArray;

    if (data.length != manyItems)
    {
        trimmedArray = new int[manyItems];
        System.arraycopy(data, 0, trimmedArray, 0, manyItems);
        data = trimmedArray;
    }
}
```

(continued)

(FIGURE 3.7 continued)

```java
public static IntArrayBag union(IntArrayBag b1, IntArrayBag b2)
{
    // If either b1 or b2 is null, then a NullPointerException is thrown.
    // In the case that the total number of items is beyond Integer.MAX_VALUE, there will
    // be an arithmetic overflow and the bag will fail.
    IntArrayBag answer = new IntArrayBag(b1.getCapacity( ) + b2.getCapacity( ));

    System.arraycopy(b1.data, 0, answer.data, 0, b1.manyItems);
    System.arraycopy(b2.data, 0, answer.data, b1.manyItems, b2.manyItems);
    answer.manyItems = b1.manyItems + b2.manyItems;
    return answer;
}

}
```

PROGRAMMING TIP

DOCUMENT THE ADT INVARIANT IN THE IMPLEMENTATION FILE

The invariant of an ADT describes the rules that dictate how the instance variables are used. This information is important to the programmer who implements the class. Therefore, you should write this information in the implementation file, just before the declarations of the private instance variables. For example, the invariant for the IntArrayBag class appears before the declarations of manyItems and data in the implementation file of Figure 3.7 on page 137.

This is the best place to document the ADT's invariant. In particular, do not write the invariant as part of the class's specification, because a programmer who uses the ADT does not need to know about private instance variables. But the programmer who implements the ADT does need to know about the invariant.

The Bag ADT—Testing

Thus far, we have focused on the design and implementation of new classes and their methods. But it's also important to continue practicing the other aspects of software development, particularly testing. Each of the bag's new methods must be tested. As shown in Chapter 1, it is important to concentrate the testing on boundary values. At this point, we will alert you to only one potential pitfall and will leave the complete testing to Programming Project 2 on page 169.

FIGURE 3.8	Wrong Implementation of the Bag's addAll Method

A Wrong Implementation

```
public void addAll(IntArrayBag addend)
{
    int i; // An array index

    ensureCapacity(manyItems + addend.manyItems);
    for (i = 0; i < addend.manyItems; i++)
        add(addend.data[i]);
}
```

> *WARNING!*
>
> *There is a bug in this implementation. See Self-Test Exercise 23.*

  PITFALL

AN OBJECT CAN BE AN ARGUMENT TO ITS OWN METHOD

A class can have a method with a parameter that is the same data type as the class itself. For example, one of the IntArrayBag methods, addAll, has a parameter that is an IntArrayBag itself, as shown in this heading:

```
public void addAll(IntArrayBag addend)
```

An IntArrayBag can be created and activate its addAll method using itself as the argument. For example:

```
IntArrayBag b = new IntArrayBag( );
b.add(5);                  ──── b now contains a 5 and a 2.
b.add(2);    ◄──
b.addAll(b); ◄──           ──── Now b contains two 5s and two 2s.
```

The highlighted statement takes all the elements in b (the 5 and the 2) and adds them to what's already in b, so b ends up with two copies of each number.

In the highlighted statement, the bag b is activating the addAll method, but this same bag b is the actual argument to the method. This is a situation that must be carefully tested. As an example of the danger, consider the incorrect implementation of addAll in Figure 3.8. Do you see what goes wrong with b.addAll(b)? (See the answer to Self-Test Exercise 23.)

The Bag ADT—Analysis

We'll finish this section with a time analysis of the bag's methods. Generally, we'll use the number of elements in a bag as the input size. For example, if b is a bag containing n integers, then the number of operations required by b.countOccurrences is a formula involving n. To determine the operations, we'll see how many statements are executed by the method, although we won't need an exact determination since our answer will use big-O notation. Except for two declarations and two statements, all of the work in countOccurrences happens in this loop:

```
for (index = 0; index < manyItems; index++)
    if (target == data[index])
        answer++;
```

We can see that the body of the loop will be executed exactly n times—once for each element in the bag. The body of the loop also has another important property: The body contains no other loops or calls to methods that contain loops. This is enough to conclude that the total number of statements executed by countOccurrences is no more than:

$n \times$ (number of statements in the loop) $+ 4$

The extra $+4$ at the end is for the two declarations and two statements outside the loop. Regardless of how many statements are actually in the loop, the time expression is *always* $O(n)$—so the countOccurrences method is linear.

A similar analysis shows that remove is also linear, although remove's loop sometimes executes fewer than n times. However, the fact that remove *sometimes* requires less than $n \times$ (number of statements in the loop) does not change the fact that the method is $O(n)$. In the worst case, the loop does execute a full n iterations; therefore, the correct time analysis is no better than $O(n)$.

FIGURE 3.9   Time Analysis for the Bag Operations

Operation	Time Analysis	
Constructor	$O(c)$	c is the initial capacity
add without capacity increase	$O(1)$	Constant time
add with capacity increase	$O(n)$	Linear time
b1.addAll(b2) without capacity increase	$O(n_2)$	Linear in the size of the added bag
b1.addAll(b2) with capacity increase	$O(n_1 + n_2)$	n_1 and n_2 are the sizes of the bags
clone	$O(c)$	c is the bag's capacity

Operation	Time Analysis	
countOccurrences	$O(n)$	Linear time
ensureCapacity	$O(c)$	c is the specified minimum capacity
getCapacity	$O(1)$	Constant time
remove	$O(n)$	Linear time
size	$O(1)$	Constant time
trimToSize	$O(n)$	Linear time
Union of b1 and b2	$O(c_1 + c_2)$	c_1 and c_2 are the bags' capacities

The analysis of the constructor is a special case. The constructor allocates an array of initialCapacity integers, and in Java all array components are initialized (integers are set to zero). The initialization time is proportional to the capacity of the array, so an accurate time analysis is $O(\text{initialCapacity})$.

constant time
$O(1)$

Several of the other bag methods do not contain any loops or array allocations. This is a pleasant situation because the time required for any of these methods does not depend on the number of elements in the bag. For example, when an element is added to a bag that does not need to grow, the new element is placed at the end of the array, and the add method never looks at the elements that were already in the bag. When the time required by a method does not depend on the size of the input, the procedure is called **constant time**, which is written $O(1)$.

The add method has two distinct cases. If the current capacity is adequate for a new element, then the time is $O(1)$. But if the capacity needs to be increased, then the time increases to $O(n)$ because of the array allocation and copying of elements from the old array to the new array.

The time analyses of all methods are summarized in Figure 3.9.

Self-Test Exercises for Section 3.2

14. Draw a picture of mybag.data after these statements:
    ```
    IntArrayBag mybag = new IntArrayBag(10);
    mybag.add(1);
    mybag.add(2);
    mybag.addMany(1,3,4);
    mybag.remove(1);
    ```

15. The bag in the preceding question has a capacity of 10. What happens if you try to add more than 10 elements to the bag?

16. Write the invariant of the bag ADT.

17. Which bag methods do not have the bag invariant as part of their implicit precondition?

18. Why don't we list the bag invariant as part of the explicit precondition and postcondition of the bag methods?

19. The add method uses ensureCapacity(manyItems*2 + 1). What would go wrong if we forgot the +1"?

20. Would the add method work correctly if we used ensureCapacity(manyItems + 1) without the *2?

21. What is the meaning of a *static* method? How is activation different from that of an ordinary method?

22. Use the expression --manyItems (with the -- *before* manyItems) to rewrite the last two statements of remove (Figure 3.5 on page 132) as a single statement. If you are unsure of the difference between manyItems-- and --manyItems, then go ahead and peek at our answer

at the back of this chapter. Use manyItems++ to make a similar alteration to the add method.

23. Suppose we implement addAll as shown in Figure 3.8 on page 142. What goes wrong with b.addAll(b)?

24. Describe the extra work that must be done at the end of the clone method. Draw pictures to show what goes wrong if this step is omitted.

25. Use the arraycopy method to copy 10 elements from the front of an array x to the front of an array y.

26. Suppose x and y are arrays with 100 elements each. Use the arraycopy method to copy x[10]...x[25] to y[33]...y[48].

27. Write a new bag method that removes all copies of a specified target from a bag (rather than removing just one copy of the target). The return value should be the number of copies of the target that were removed from the bag.

28. Write a variable-arity version of the remove method. The return value is the total number of elements removed from the bag. Your implementation should use the array version of a for-loop from page 111.

29. Write a static bag method called intersection that creates a new bag from two other bags b1 and b2. The number of copies of an integer x in the new bag will always be the minimum of b1.countOccurrences(x) and b2.countOccurrences(x).

3.3 PROGRAMMING PROJECT: THE SEQUENCE ADT

You are ready to tackle a collection class implementation on your own. The data type is called a **sequence**. A sequence is similar to a bag—both contain a bunch of elements. Unlike a bag, however, the elements in a sequence are arranged one after another.

How does this differ from a bag? After all, aren't the bag elements arranged one after another in the partially filled array that implements the bag? Yes, but that's a quirk of our particular bag implementation, and the order is just happenstance. Moreover, there is no way that a program using the bag can refer to the bag elements by their position in the array. *how a sequence differs from a bag*

In contrast, the elements of a sequence are kept one after another, and the sequence's methods allow a program to step through the sequence one element at a time, using the order in which the elements are stored. Methods also permit a program to control precisely where elements are inserted and removed within the sequence.

The Sequence ADT—Specification

Our bag happened to be a bag of *integers*. We could have had a different underlying element type, such as a bag of *double* numbers or a bag of *characters*. In fact, in Chapter 5, we'll see how to construct a collection that can simultaneously handle many different types of elements rather than being restricted to one type of element. But for now, our collection classes will have just one kind of element for each collection. In particular, for our sequence class, each element will be a *double* number, and the class itself is called `DoubleArraySeq`. We could have chosen some other type for the elements, but double numbers are as good as anything for your first implementation of a collection class.

As with the bag, each sequence will have a current capacity, which is the number of elements the sequence can hold without having to request more memory. The initial capacity will be set by the constructor. The capacity can be increased in several different manners, which we'll see as we specify the various methods of the new class.

Constructor. The `DoubleArraySeq` has two constructors—one that constructs an empty sequence with an initial capacity of 10 and another that constructs an empty sequence with some specified initial capacity.

The `size` Method. The `size` method returns the number of elements in the sequence. Here is the heading:

```
public int size( )
```

For example, if `scores` is a sequence containing the values 10.1, 40.2, and 1.1, then `scores.size( )` returns 3. Throughout our examples, we will draw sequences vertically with the first element on top, as shown in the picture in the margin (where the first element is 10.1).

10.1
40.2
1.1

Methods to Examine a Sequence. We will have methods to build a sequence, but it will be easier to explain first the methods to examine a sequence that has already been built. The elements of a sequence can be examined one after another, but the examination must be in order from the first to the last. Three methods work together to enforce the in-order retrieval rule. The methods' headings are:

```
public void start( )
public double getCurrent( )
public void advance( )
```

When we want to retrieve the elements of a sequence, we begin by activating `start`. After activating `start`, the `getCurrent` method returns the first element of the sequence. Each time we call `advance`, the `getCurrent` method changes so that it returns the next element of the sequence. For example, if a sequence called numbers contains the four numbers 37, 10, 83, and 42, then we can write the following code to print the first three numbers of the sequence:

```
numbers.start( );
System.out.println(numbers.getCurrent( ));          Prints 37
numbers.advance( );
System.out.println(numbers.getCurrent( ));          Prints 10
numbers.advance( );
System.out.println(numbers.getCurrent( ));          Prints 83
```

*start,
getCurrent,
advance*

One other method cooperates with getCurrent. The isCurrent method returns a boolean value to indicate whether there actually is a current element for getCurrent to provide or whether we have advanced right off the end of the sequence.

isCurrent

Using all four of the methods with a for-loop, we can print an entire sequence, as shown here for the numbers sequence:

```
for (numbers.start( ); numbers.isCurrent( ); numbers.advance( ))
    System.out.println(numbers.getCurrent( ));
```

The addBefore and addAfter Methods.   There are two methods to add a new element to a sequence, with these headers:

```
public void addBefore(double element)
public void addAfter(double element)
```

The first method, addBefore, places a new element before the current element. For example, suppose that we have created the sequence shown in the margin and that the current element is 8.8. In this example, we want to add 10.0 to our sequence, immediately before the current element. When 10.0 is added before the current element, other elements in the sequence—such as 8.8 and 99.0— will move down in the sequence to make room for the new element. After the addition, the sequence has the four elements shown in the lower box.

> 42.1
> 8.8
> 99.0

The sequence grows by adding 10.0 before the current element.

If there is no current element, then addBefore places the new element at the front of the sequence. In any case, after the addBefore method returns, the new element will be the current element. In the example shown in the margin, 10.0 becomes the new current element.

> 42.1
> 10.0
> 8.8
> 99.0

The second method, addAfter, also adds a new element to a sequence, but the new element is added *after* the current element. If there is no current element, then the addAfter method places the new element at the end of the sequence (rather than at the front). In all cases, when the method finishes, the new element will be the current element.

Either addBefore or addAfter can be used on an empty sequence to add the first element.

The removeCurrent Method. The current element can be removed from a sequence. The method for a removal has no parameters, but the precondition requires that there is a current element; it is this current element that is removed, as specified here:

♦ **removeCurrent**
> public boolean removeCurrent( )
> Removes the current element from this sequence.
>
> **Precondition:**
> > isCurrent( ) returns true.
>
> **Postcondition:**
> > The current element has been removed from this sequence. If this was the final element of the sequence (with nothing after it), then after the removal there is no longer a current element; otherwise, the new current element is the one that used to be after the removed element.

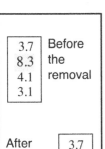

For example, suppose scores is the four-element sequence shown at the top of the box in the margin, and the highlighted 8.3 is the current element. After activating scores.removeCurrent( ), the 8.3 has been deleted, and the 4.1 is now the current element.

The addAll Method. The addAll method is similar to the bag's addAll method. It allows us to place the contents of one sequence at the end of what we already have. The method has this heading:

> public void addAll(DoubleArraySeq addend)

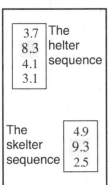

As an example, suppose we create two sequences called helter and skelter. The sequences contain the elements shown in the box in the margin (helter has four elements, and skelter has three). We can then activate the method:

> helter.addAll(skelter);

After the addAll activation, the helter sequence will have seven elements: 3.7, 8.3, 4.1, 3.1, 4.9, 9.3, and 2.5 (its original four elements followed by the three elements of skelter). The current element of the helter sequence remains where it was (at the number 8.3), and the skelter sequence still has its original three elements.

The concatenation Method. The **concatenation** of two sequences results in a new sequence obtained by placing one sequence after the other. We will implement concatenation with a static method that has the following two parameters:

> public static DoubleArraySeq concatenation
> (DoubleArraySeq s1, DoubleArraySeq s2)

A concatenation is somewhat similar to the union of two bags. For example:

```
DoubleArraySeq part1 = new DoubleArraySeq( );
DoubleArraySeq part2 = new DoubleArraySeq( );

part1.addAfter(3.7);
part1.addAfter(9.5);
part2.addAfter(4.0);
part2.addAfter(8.6);

DoubleArraySeq total = DoubleArraySeq.concatenation(part1, part2);
```

This computes the concatenation of the two sequences, putting the result in a third sequence.

After these statements, `total` is the sequence consisting of 3.7, 9.5, 4.0, and 8.6. The new sequence computed by `concatenation` has no current element. The original sequences, `part1` and `part2`, are unchanged.

Notice the effect of having a *static* method: `concatenation` is not activated by any one sequence. Instead, the activation of

```
DoubleArraySeq.concatenation(part1, part2)
```

creates and returns a new sequence that includes the contents of `part1` followed by the contents of `part2`.

The `clone` Method. As part of our specification, we require that a sequence can be copied with a `clone` method. The clone contains the same elements as the original. If the original had a current element, then the clone has a current element in the corresponding place. For example:

```
DoubleArraySeq s = new DoubleArraySeq( );
s.addAfter(4.2);
s.addAfter(1.5);
s.start( );
IntArrayBag t = (DoubleArraySeq) s.clone( );
```

At the point when the clone is made, the sequence s has two elements (4.2 and 1.5), and the current element is the 4.2. Therefore, t will end up with the same two elements (4.2 and 1.5), and its current element will be the number 4.2. Subsequent changes to s will not affect t, nor vice versa.

Three Methods That Deal with Capacity. The sequence class has three methods for dealing with capacity—the same three methods that the bag has:

```
public int getCapacity( )
public void ensureCapacity(int minimumCapacity)
public void trimToSize( )
```

As with the bag, the purpose of these methods is to allow a programmer to explicitly set the capacity of the collection. If a programmer does not explicitly set the capacity, then the class will still work correctly, but some operations will be less efficient because the capacity might be repeatedly increased.

The Sequence ADT—Documentation

The complete specification for this first version of our sequence class is shown in Figure 3.10. This specification is also available from the DoubleArraySeq link at the following web address:

```
http://www.cs.colorado.edu/~main/docs/
```

When you read the specification, you'll see that the package name is edu.colorado.collections. So you should create a subdirectory called edu/colorado/collections for your implementation.

The specification also indicates some limitations—the same limitations that we saw for the bag class. For example, an OutOfMemoryError can occur in any method that increases the capacity. Several of the methods throw an IllegalStateException to indicate that they have been illegally activated (with no current element). Also, an attempt to move the capacity beyond the maximum integer causes the class to fail by an arithmetic overflow.

After you've looked through the specifications, we'll suggest a design that uses three private instance variables.

The Sequence ADT—Design

Our suggested design for the sequence ADT has three private instance variables. The first variable, data, is an array that stores the elements of the sequence. Just like the bag, data is a partially filled array, and a second instance variable, called manyItems, keeps track of how much of the data array is currently being used. Therefore, the used part of the array extends from data[0] to data[manyItems-1]. The third instance variable, currentIndex, gives the index of the current element in the array (if there is one). Sometimes a sequence has no current element, in which case currentIndex will be set to the same number as manyItems (since this is larger than any valid index). The complete invariant of our ADT is stated as three rules:

1. The number of elements in the sequence is stored in the instance variable manyItems.

2. For an empty sequence (with no elements), we do not care what is stored in any of data; for a nonempty sequence, the elements of the sequence are stored from the front to the end in data[0] to data[manyItems-1], and we don't care what is stored in the rest of data.

3. If there is a current element, then it lies in data[currentIndex]; if there is no current element, then currentIndex equals manyItems.

| **FIGURE 3.10** | Specification for the DoubleArraySeq Class |

Class DoubleArraySeq

❖ **public class DoubleArraySeq from the package edu.colorado.collections**
A DoubleArraySeq keeps track of a sequence of double numbers. The sequence can have a special "current element," which is specified and accessed through four methods that are not available in the bag class (start, getCurrent, advance, and isCurrent).

Limitations:

(1) The capacity of a sequence can change after it's created, but the maximum capacity is limited by the amount of free memory on the machine. The constructor, addAfter, addBefore, clone, and concatenation will result in an OutOfMemoryError when free memory is exhausted.

(2) A sequence's capacity cannot exceed the largest integer, 2,147,483,647 (Integer.MAX_VALUE). Any attempt to create a larger capacity results in failure due to an arithmetic overflow.

Specification

◆ **Constructor for the DoubleArraySeq**
public DoubleArraySeq( )
Initialize an empty sequence with an initial capacity of 10. Note that the addAfter and addBefore methods work efficiently (without needing more memory) until this capacity is reached.

Postcondition:
This sequence is empty and has an initial capacity of 10.

Throws: OutOfMemoryError
Indicates insufficient memory for new double[10].

◆ **Second Constructor for the DoubleArraySeq**
public DoubleArraySeq(int initialCapacity)
Initialize an empty sequence with a specified initial capacity. Note that the addAfter and addBefore methods work efficiently (without needing more memory) until this capacity is reached.

Parameter:
initialCapacity – the initial capacity of this sequence

Precondition:
initialCapacity is non-negative.

Postcondition:
This sequence is empty and has the given initial capacity.

Throws: IllegalArgumentException
Indicates that initialCapacity is negative.

Throws: OutOfMemoryError
Indicates insufficient memory for new double[initialCapacity].

(continued)

(FIGURE 3.10 continued)

♦ addAfter and addBefore

```
public void addAfter(double element)
public void addBefore(double element)
```

Adds a new element to this sequence, either before or after the current element. If this new element would take this sequence beyond its current capacity, then the capacity is increased before adding the new element.

Parameter:

element – the new element that is being added

Postcondition:

A new copy of the element has been added to this sequence. If there was a current element, then addAfter places the new element after the current element, and addBefore places the new element before the current element. If there was no current element, then addAfter places the new element at the end of this sequence, and addBefore places the new element at the front of this sequence. In all cases, the new element becomes the new current element of this sequence.

Throws: OutOfMemoryError

Indicates insufficient memory to increase the size of this sequence.

Note:

An attempt to increase the capacity beyond Integer.MAX_VALUE will cause this sequence to fail with an arithmetic overflow.

♦ addAll

```
public void addAll(DoubleArraySeq addend)
```

Place the contents of another sequence at the end of this sequence.

Parameter:

addend – a sequence whose contents will be placed at the end of this sequence

Precondition:

The parameter, addend, is not null.

Postcondition:

The elements from addend have been placed at the end of this sequence. The current element of this sequence remains where it was, and the addend is also unchanged.

Throws: NullPointerException

Indicates that addend is null.

Throws: OutOfMemoryError

Indicates insufficient memory to increase the capacity of this sequence.

Note:

An attempt to increase the capacity beyond Integer.MAX_VALUE will cause this sequence to fail with an arithmetic overflow.

(continued)

(FIGURE 3.10 continued)

♦ **advance**
```
public void advance( )
```
Move forward so that the current element is now the next element in this sequence.

Precondition:
`isCurrent( )` returns `true`.

Postcondition:
If the current element was already the end element of this sequence (with nothing after it), then there is no longer any current element. Otherwise, the new element is the element immediately after the original current element.

Throws: `IllegalStateException`
Indicates that there is no current element, so advance may not be called.

♦ **clone**
```
public DoubleArraySeq clone( )
```
Generate a copy of this sequence.

Returns:
The return value is a copy of this sequence. Subsequent changes to the copy will not affect the original, nor vice versa. The return value must be typecast to a `DoubleArraySeq` before it is used.

Throws: `OutOfMemoryError`
Indicates insufficient memory for creating the clone.

♦ **concatenation**
```
public static DoubleArraySeq concatenation
    (DoubleArraySeq s1, DoubleArraySeq s2)
```
Create a new sequence that contains all the elements from one sequence followed by another.

Parameters:
`s1` – the first of two sequences
`s2` – the second of two sequences

Precondition:
Neither `s1` nor `s2` is null.

Returns:
a new sequence that has the elements of `s1` followed by the elements of `s2` (with no current element)

Throws: `NullPointerException`
Indicates that one of the arguments is null.

Throws: `OutOfMemoryError`
Indicates insufficient memory for the new sequence.

Note:
An attempt to increase the capacity beyond `Integer.MAX_VALUE` will cause this sequence to fail with an arithmetic overflow.

(continued)

(FIGURE 3.10 continued)

♦ **ensureCapacity**

```
public void ensureCapacity(int minimumCapacity)
```
Change the current capacity of this sequence.

Parameter:

minimumCapacity – the new capacity for this sequence

Postcondition:

This sequence's capacity has been changed to at least minimumCapacity.

Throws: OutOfMemoryError

Indicates insufficient memory for new double[minimumCapacity].

♦ **getCapacity**

```
public int getCapacity( )
```
Accessor method to determine the current capacity of this sequence. The addBefore and addAfter methods work efficiently (without needing more memory) until this capacity is reached.

Returns:

the current capacity of this sequence

♦ **getCurrent**

```
public double getCurrent( )
```
Accessor method to determine the current element of this sequence.

Precondition:

isCurrent( ) returns true.

Returns:

the current element of this sequence

Throws: IllegalStateException

Indicates that there is no current element.

♦ **isCurrent**

```
public boolean isCurrent( )
```
Accessor method to determine whether this sequence has a specified current element that can be retrieved with the getCurrent method.

Returns:

true (there is a current element) or false (there is no current element at the moment)

♦ **removeCurrent**

```
public void removeCurrent( )
```
Remove the current element from this sequence.

Precondition:

isCurrent( ) returns true.

Postcondition:

The current element has been removed from this sequence, and the following element (if there is one) is now the new current element. If there was no following element, then there is now no current element.

Throws: IllegalStateException

Indicates that there is no current element, so removeCurrent may not be called.   *(continued)*

(FIGURE 3.10 continued)

♦ **size**

    public int size( )

Accessor method to determine the number of elements in this sequence.

Returns:

the number of elements in this sequence

♦ **start**

    public void start( )

Set the current element at the front of this sequence.

Postcondition:

The front element of this sequence is now the current element (but if this sequence has no elements at all, then there is no current element).

♦ **trimToSize**

    public void trimToSize( )

Reduce the current capacity of this sequence to its actual size (i.e., the number of elements it contains).

Postcondition:

This sequence's capacity has been changed to its current size.

Throws: OutOfMemoryError

Indicates insufficient memory for altering the capacity.

As an example, suppose a sequence contains four numbers, with the current element at data[2]. The instance variables of the object might appear as shown here:

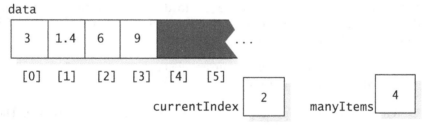

In this example, the current element is at data[2], so the getCurrent( ) method would return the number 6. At this point, if we called advance( ), then currentIndex would increase to 3, and getCurrent( ) would then return the 9.

Normally, a sequence has a current element, and the instance variable currentIndex contains the location of that current element. But if there is no current element, then currentIndex contains the same value as manyItems. In the preceding example, if currentIndex was 4, then that would indicate that there is no current element. Notice that this value (4) is beyond the used part of the array (which stretches from data[0] to data[3]).

The stated requirements for the instance variables form the invariant of the sequence ADT. You should place this invariant at the top of your implementation file (DoubleArraySeq.java). We will leave most of this implementation file up to you, but we will offer some hints and a bit of pseudocode.

The Sequence ADT—Pseudocode for the Implementation

The removeCurrent Method.   This method removes the current element from the sequence. First check that the precondition is valid (use isCurrent( )). Then remove the current element by shifting each of the subsequent elements leftward one position. For example, suppose we are removing the current element from this sequence:

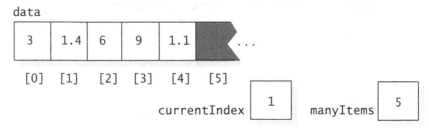

What is the current element in this picture? It is the 1.4 since currentIndex is 1 and data[1] contains 1.4.

In the case of the bag, we could remove an element such as 1.4 by copying the final element (1.1) onto the 1.4. But this approach won't work for the *sequence* because the elements would lose their sequence order. Instead, each element after the 1.4 must be moved leftward one position. The 6 moves from data[2] to data[1]; the 9 moves from data[3] to data[2]; and the 1.1 moves from data[4] to data[3]. This is a lot of movement, but a small for-loop suffices to carry out all the work. This is the pseudocode:

```
for (i = the index after the current element; i < manyItems; i++)
    Move an element from data[i] back to data[i-1];
```

When the loop completes, you should reduce manyItems by one. The final result for our example is:

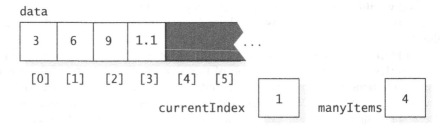

After the removal, the value in `currentIndex` is unchanged. In effect, this means that the element that was just after the removed element is now the current element. You must check that the method works correctly for boundary values— removing the first element and removing the end element. In fact, both these cases work fine. When the end element is removed, `currentIndex` will end up with the same value as `manyItems`, indicating that there is no longer a current element.

The addBefore Method.   If there is a current element, then `addBefore` must take care to put the new element just before the current position. Elements that are already at or after the current position must be shifted rightward to make room for the new element. We suggest that you start by shifting elements at the end of the array rightward one position each until you reach the position for the new element.

For example, suppose you are putting 1.4 at the location `data[1]` in this sequence:

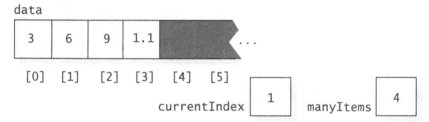

You would begin by shifting the 1.1 rightward from `data[3]` to `data[4]`; then you'd move the 9 from `data[2]` to `data[3]`; then the 6 moves from `data[1]` rightward to `data[2]`. At this point, the array looks like this:

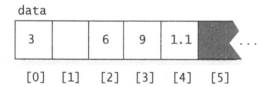

Of course, `data[1]` actually still contains a 6 because we just copied the 6 from `data[1]` to `data[2]`. But we have drawn `data[1]` as an empty box to indicate that `data[1]` is now available to hold the new element (the 1.4 that we are puting in the sequence). At this point, we can place the 1.4 in `data[1]` and add one to `manyItems`:

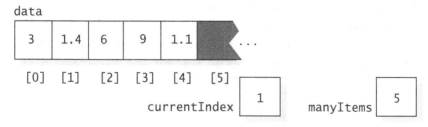

The pseudocode for shifting the elements rightward uses a for-loop. Each iteration of the loop shifts one element, as shown here:

```
for (i = manyItems;  data[i] is the wrong spot for element ;  i--)
    data[i] = data[i-1];
```

The key to the loop is the test `data[i]` is the wrong spot for `element`. How do we test whether a position is the wrong spot for the new element? A position is wrong when (`i > currentIndex`). Can you now write the entire method in Java? (See the solution to Self-Test Exercise 35 and don't forget to handle the special case when there is no current element.)

Other Methods. The other sequence methods are straightforward; for example, the `addAfter` method is similar to `addBefore`. Some additional useful methods are described in Programming Project 4 on page 169. You'll also need to be careful that you don't mindlessly copy the implementation of a bag method. For example, the `concatenation` method is similar to the bag's `union` method, but there is one extra step that concatenation must take. (It sets `currentIndex` to `manyItems`.)

Self-Test Exercises for Section 3.3

30. What elements will be in the sequence s after these statements?
    ```
    DoubleArraySeq s = new DoubleArraySeq( );
    s.addAfter(1);
    s.addAfter(2);
    s.start( );
    s.addAfter(3);
    ```

31. What are the instance variables for our sequence implementation?

32. Write some statements that declare a sequence and insert the numbers 1 through 100 into the sequence (in that order).

33. Suppose x is a double number (not an exact integer). Write some statements that insert x into the sequence from the previous exercise. The insertion should occur so that all the numbers of the sequence remain in order from smallest to largest.

34. Which of the sequence methods have implementations that could be identical to the bag methods?

35. Write the sequence's `addBefore` method.

36. Suppose a sequence has 24 elements, and there is no current element. According to the invariant of the ADT, what is `currentIndex`?

37. Suppose g is a sequence with 10 elements, and you activate g.start( ) and then activate g.advance( ) three times. What value is then in g.currentIndex?

38. What are good boundary values to test the `removeCurrent` method?

39. Write a demonstration program that asks the user for a list of family member ages and then prints the list in the same order it was given.

40. Write a new method to remove a specified element from a sequence. The method has one parameter (the element to remove).

41. For a sequence of numbers, suppose you insert 1, then 2, then 3, and so on, up to n. What is the big-O time analysis for the combined time of inserting all n numbers with `addAfter`? How does the analysis change if you insert n first, then $n-1$, and so on, down to 1—always using `add-Before` instead of `addAfter`?

42. Which of the ADTs—the bag or the sequence—*must* be implemented by storing the elements in an array? (Hint: We are not beyond asking a trick question.)

3.4   PROGRAMMING PROJECT: THE POLYNOMIAL

A one-variable **polynomial** is an arithmetic expression of the form:

$$a_k x^k + \ldots + a_2 x^2 + a_1 x^1 + a_0 x^0$$

The highest exponent, k, is called the **degree** of the polynomial, and the constants $a_0, a_1, \ldots$ are the **coefficients**. For example, here is a polynomial with degree three:

$$0.3x^3 + 0.5x^2 + (-0.9)x^1 + 1.0x^0$$

Each individual **term** of a polynomial consists of a real number as a coefficient (such as 0.3), the variable x, and a non-negative integer as an **exponent**. The x^1 term is usually written with just an x rather than x^1; the x^0 term is usually written with just the coefficient (since x^0 is always defined to be 1); and a negative coefficient may also be written with a subtraction sign, so another way to write the same polynomial is:

$$0.3x^3 + 0.5x^2 - 0.9x + 1.0$$

For any specific value of x, a polynomial can be evaluated by plugging the value of x into the expression. For example, the value of the sample polynomial at $x = 2$ is:

$$0.3(2)^3 + 0.5(2)^2 - 0.9(2) + 1.0$$

A typical algebra exercise is to plot the graph of a polynomial for each value of x in a given range. For example, Figure 3.11 plots the value of a polynomial for each x in the range of -2 to $+2$.

FIGURE 3.11   A Polynomial

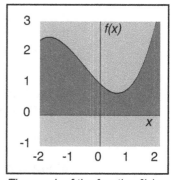

The graph of the function f(x) defined by the polynomial 0.3x³ + 0.5x² – 0.9x + 1.0

For this project, you should specify, design, and implement a class for polynomials. The coefficients are double numbers, and the exponents are non-negative integers. The coefficients should be stored in an array of double numbers, with the coefficient for the x^k term stored in location [k] of the array. The maximum index of the array needs to be at least as big as the degree of the polynomial so that the largest nonzero coefficient can be stored. For the example polynomial $0.3x^3 + 0.5x^2 - 0.9x + 1.0$, the start of the coefficient array contains these numbers:

$$[0] \quad [1] \quad [2] \quad [3] \quad [4] \quad [5]$$

In addition, the class should have an instance variable to keep track of the current degree of the polynomial. (You could manage without the degree variable, but having it around makes certain operations more efficient.)

The rest of this section lists some methods that you could provide to the class.

Constructors.
```
public Polynomial( )                    // No-arguments constructor
public Polynomial(double a0)            // Set the x⁰ coefficient only
public Polynomial(Polynomial source)    // Copy constructor
```

The no-arguments constructor creates a polynomial with all zero coefficients. The second constructor creates a polynomial with the specified parameter as the coefficient of the x^0 term, and all other coefficients are zero. For example:

```
Polynomial p = new Polynomial(4.2);
```

After this declaration, p has only one nonzero term, $4.2x^0$, which is the same as the number 4.2 (since x^0 is defined as equal to 1).

The third constructor will create a polynomial that is a copy of another polynomial (called the "source").

Clone Method.
```
public Polynomial clone( )
```

This is the usual clone method that returns a copy of the object that activates it.

Modification Methods.
```
public void add_to_coef(double amount, int k)
public void assign_coef(double new_coefficient, int k)
public void clear( )
public void reserve(int degree)
```

The `add_to_coef` method adds the specified amount to the coefficient of the x^k term. The `assign_coef` method sets the x^k coefficient to `new_coefficient`. The `clear` method sets all coefficients to zero. The `reserve` method is similar to `ensureCapacity` for the Bag class, making sure that the underlying array can hold a polynomial of the requested degree.

Accessor Methods.
```
public double coefficient(int k)
public int degree( )
public int next_term(int k)
```

The `coefficient` method returns the coefficient of the x^k term.

The `degree` method returns the degree of the polynomial. For a polynomial in which all coefficients are zero, our degree method returns -1.

The `next_term` method returns the exponent of the next term with a nonzero coefficient after x^k. For example, if the x^3 term of p is zero and the x^4 term of p is $6x^4$, then `p.next_term(2)` returns the exponent 4 (since 4 is the next exponent after 2 with a nonzero coefficient). If there are no nonzero terms after x^k, then `next_term(k)` should return the number -1.

Evaluation Method.
```
double eval(double x)
```

The `eval` method evaluates a polynomial at the given value of x. For example, if p is $0.3x^3 + 0.5x^2 - 0.9x + 1.0$, then `p.eval(2)` is $0.3(2)^3 + 0.5(2)^2 - 0.9(2) + 1.0$, which is 3.6.

Arithmetic Operators. You should include static methods with two polynomial parameters to perform the arithmetic operations of addition, subtraction, and multiplication of two polynomials in the usual manner. For example:

$$\text{Suppose } q = 2x^3 + 4x^2 + 3x + 1 \text{ and } r = 7x^2 + 6x + 5$$

$$\text{Then: } q + r = 2x^3 + 11x^2 + 9x + 6$$

$$q - r = 2x^3 - 3x^2 - 3x - 4$$

$$q \times r = 14x^5 + 40x^4 + 55x^3 + 45x^2 + 21x + 5$$

The product, $q \times r$, is obtained by multiplying each separate term of q times each separate term of r and adding the results together.

Other Operations. You might consider other methods, which are described online at `www.cs.colorado.edu/~main/javapoly.html`. Among other things, this online description includes operations that first-semester calculus students can connect to their calculus studies of derivatives, integration, and finding a root of a polynomial.

Self-Test Exercises for Section 3.4

43. Suppose you implement the polynomial class using an array called `coef`. What values will be stored in `coef` for the polynomial $0.3x^3 + 0.5x^2 - 0.9x^1 + 1.0$?

44. What is your guess for the running time required for the three arithmetic operators of addition, subtraction, and multiplication?

3.5   THE JAVA HASHSET AND ITERATORS

This section provides a first introduction to a one of Java's collection classes—the `HashSet`—including a feature called the *iterator*, which permits a programmer to easily step through all the elements of a collection.

The HashSet Class

java.util.HashSet   A `HashSet` (from `java.util.HashSet`) is one of several container classes that are part of the Java Class Libraries. Its primary purpose is to store a collection of Java objects, such as a collection of `String` objects. Unlike our bag, a `HashSet` stores references to objects rather than storing primitive values (such as `int` values). Also, a `HashSet` cannot contain two objects that are equal; a second addition of an object that is equal to one that's already in a `HashSet` will have no effect.

We'll start with a small example that creates a `HashSet` of strings:

```
HashSet<String> heroes = new HashSet<String>( );
heroes.add("Hiro");
heroes.add("Claire");        After these statements, heroes contains
heroes.add("Peter");         only three strings, since the same
heroes.add("Hiro");          string cannot be added twice.
```

The name of the data type is `HashSet`, but this name is augmented by `<String>` to indicate the type of elements that will reside in the set. This augmentation is called a *generic type instantiation*, and it differs from the way that we specified the underlying type for our own bag. We will learn how to write such *generic classes* of our own in Chapter 5, but for now we merely want to *use* a `HashSet` of strings, so we don't need to know how it is implemented.

Notice that in the example we tried to add four strings, but only the first three were added. That's because we cannot add the same string (`"Hiro"`) more than once to a single `HashSet`. The `HashSet`'s notion of "same string" is determined by using the `String`'s `equals` method (see page 77).

Some of the HashSet Members

Constructors. A default constructor creates an empty `HashSet`; a second constructor makes a copy of an existing `HashSet` (or, in fact, certain other kinds of collections). Remember that when you declare a HashSet, you must specify the type of elements that reside in the set, such as the String in HashSet<String>.

Members That Are Similar to the Bag. These members are similar to our bag:

```
boolean add(E element);
boolean remove(E element);
int size( );
```

E must be the data type of the elements in the HashSet

The HashSet's add method can be used exactly like the bag's add method to add an item to a HashSet. However, the HashSet's method has a boolean return value, which will be true in the case that the added element was not previously in the set and false otherwise. (In the false case, a second copy is not added.)

Iterators

An **iterator** is an object from java.util.Iterator that permits a programmer to easily step through all the items in a container, examining the items and (perhaps) changing them. Each of the collection classes in the Java Class Libraries has a standard method called iterator that returns an iterator providing access to the items in the container. The iterator itself is also a Java object with three methods that are illustrated in this small piece of code:

java.util.Iterator

```
// Declare a HashSet of Strings and an Iterator for that HashSet:
HashSet<String> heroes = new HashSet<String>( );
Iterator<String> it;

// Put three elements in the HashSet:
heroes.add("Hiro");
heroes.add("Claire");
heroes.add("Peter");

// Use the iterator to print all the Strings in the HashSet:
it = heroes.iterator( );
while (it.hasNext( ))
{
    System.out.println(it.next( ));
}
```

the iterator, hasNext, and next methods

The example shows a widely used pattern described here:

1. After the elements are all placed in the collection, call the iterator method of the collection to create an iterator object. The example does this with the statement it = heroes.iterator( );.

2. The iterator is now set up to step through the collection's elements one after another. The iterator's hasNext method controls the step-through process by returning true if there are more elements to step through. After the last element has been stepped through, hasNext returns false.

3. The iterator's next method returns a reference to one element in the collection; each time next is activated, it will return a different element from the collection, until eventually all the elements have been provided (at which point hasNext will return false). The precondition for next requires that hasNext returns true.

⟡ PITFALL

Do Not Access an Iterator's next Item When hasNext Is False

It is a programming error to activate it.next( ) when it.hasNext( ) returns false.

Here is the general pattern that you can use for an iterator it and a collection object c:

```
it = c.iterator( );
while (it.hasNext( ))
{
    ...statements to access the item it.next( )
}
```

Invalid Iterators

After an iterator has been set, it can easily move through its collection. However, changes to the collection—either additions or removals—can cause all of the collection's iterators to become invalid. When an iterator becomes invalid because of a change to its container, that iterator can no longer be used until it is assigned a new value.

⟡ PITFALL

Changing a Container Object Can Invalidate Its Iterators

When an iterator's underlying container changes (by an addition or a removal), the iterator generally becomes invalid. Unless the class documentation says otherwise, that iterator should no longer be used until it is reassigned a new value from the changed container.

For now, we've seen enough of Java's generic collection classes and their iterators. We'll return to them in detail in Chapter 5.

Self-Test Exercises for Section 3.5

45. What are the primary differences between a bag and a `HashSet`?

46. In general, how does an iterator become invalid?

47. Write a static method that has one parameter: a non-empty `HashSet` of strings. The return value is the average of the strings' lengths.

CHAPTER SUMMARY

- A *collection class* is an ADT in which each object contains a collection of elements. Bags and sequences are two examples of collection classes.

- The simplest implementations of collection classes use a *partially filled array*. Using a partially filled array requires each object to have at least two instance variables: the array itself and an `int` variable to keep track of how much of the array is being used.

- When a collection class is implemented with a partially filled array, the capacity of the array should grow as elements are added to the collection. The class should also provide explicit methods to allow a programmer to control the capacity of the array.

- In a collection class, some methods allocate additional memory (such as changing the capacity of an array). These methods have the possibility of throwing an `OutOfMemoryError` (when the machine runs out of memory).

- A class may have other instance variables that are references to objects or arrays. In such a case, the `clone` method must carry out extra work. The extra work creates a new object or array for each such instance variable to refer to.

- When you design an ADT, always make an explicit statement of the rules that dictate how the instance variables are used. These rules are called the *invariant of the ADT* and should be written at the top of the implementation file for easy reference.

- You don't have to write every collection class from scratch. The Java Class Libraries provide a variety of collection classes that are useful in many different settings (such as the `HashSet`). The `HashSet` requires the programmer to specify the specific generic type of the underlying elements, and it has iterators to step through the elements one after another.

? Solutions to Self-Test Exercises

1. Lowest is zero; highest is 41.

2. ```
   int i;
   int[ ] b;
   b = new int[1000];
   for (i = 1; i <= 1000; i++)
      b[i-1] = i;
   ```

3. ```
   int[ ] b = new int[ ] { 1,2,3,4,5 };
   ```

4. `b.length`

5. Either p[99] = 75 or s[99] = 75.

6. Only p[99] = 75.

7. 42 (since a and b refer to the same array)

8. 0 (since b is a clone of a)

9. `NullPointerException`

10. The array referred to by the parameter in the method is the same as the array referred to by the actual argument. So the actual argument will have its first component changed to 42.

11. ```
    public
    void copyFront(int[] a, int[] b, int n)
    // Precondition: a.length and b.length are
    // both greater than or equal to n.
    // Postcondition: n integers have been cop-
    // ied from the front of a to the front of b.
    {
       int i;
       for (i = 0; i < n; i++)
          b[i] = a[i];
    }
    ```

12. ```
    public void zero_some(int[] x)
    // Postcondition: Every even-index element
    // of x has been changed to zero.
    {
       int i;
       for (i = 0; i < x.length; i += 2)
          x[i] = 0;
    }
    ```
    After some_zero(a), these elements of a will be zero: a[0], a[2], and a[4].

13. ```
    public static int count
    (int[ ] a, int target)
    {
        int answer = 0;

        for (int item : a)
        {   // Check whether item is target.
            if (item == target)
                answer++;
        }

        return answer;
    }
    ```

14.

4	2	1	3
[0]	[1]	[2]	[3]

We don't care what appears beyond data[3].

15. When the 11th element is added, the add method will increase the capacity to 21.

16. See the two rules on page 126.

17. The constructors

18. Because the programmer who uses the bag class does not need to know this information.

19. If `manyItems` happens to be zero, then `manyItems*2` would also be zero, and the capacity would not increase.

20. The capacity would always be increased by one (which is enough for the one new element), but increasing one by one will be inefficient.

21. A static method is not activated by any one particular object. It is activated by writing the class name, a dot, the method name, and the argument list. For example:
    ```
    IntArrayBag.union(b1, b2)
    ```
    ```

22. The two statements can be replaced by one: `data[index] = data[--manyItems];`. When `--manyItems` appears as an expression, the variable `manyItems` is decremented by one, and the resulting value is the value of the expression. (On the other hand, if `manyItems--` appears as an expression, the value of the expression is the value of `manyItems` prior to subtracting one.) Similarly, the last two statements of `add` can be combined to `data[manyItems++] = element;`.

23. For the incorrect implementation of `addAll`, suppose we have a bag `b` and we activate `b.addAll(b)`. Then the private instance variable `manyItems` is the same variable as `addend.manyItems`. Each iteration of the loop adds 1 to `manyItems`; hence `addend.manyItems` is also increasing, and the loop never ends.

One warning: Some collection classes in the Java libraries have an `addAll` method that fails for the statement `b.addAll(b)`. So, before you use an `addAll` method, check the specification for restrictions.

24. At the end of the `clone` implementation, we need an additional statement to make a separate copy of the data array for the clone to use. If we don't make this copy, then our own data array and the clone's data array will be one and the same (see the pictures on page 135).

25. `System.arrayCopy(x, 0, y, 0, 10);`

26. `System.arrayCopy(x, 10, y, 33, 16);`

27.
```
public int removeAll(int target)
{
  int i;
  int count = 0;
  i = 0;
  while (i < manyItems)
  {
    if (data[i] == target)
    { // Delete data[i] by copying
      // the last element on top of it:
      manyItems--;
      data[i]=data[manyItems];
```
```
      count++;
    }
    else
      i++;
  }
  return count;
}
```

28.
```
public int removeMany(int... targets)
{
  int count = 0;

  for (int target : targets)
    count += remove(target);
  return count;
}
```

29.
```
public static
IntArrayBag intersection
(IntArrayBag b1, IntArrayBag b2)
{
  int i, j;
  int count;
  int it;
  IntArrayBag a;

  answer = new IntArrayBag;

  for (i = 0; i < b1.manyItems; i++)
  {
    it = b1.data[i];
    if (a.countOccurrences(it)==0)
    {
      count = Math.min(
        b1.countOccurrences(it),
        b2.countOccurrences(it)
      );
      for (j = 0; j < count; j++)
      {
        a.add(it);
      }
    }
  }
  return a;
}
```

30. 1, 3, 2 (in that order). The current element is the 3.

31. `data`, `manyItems`, `currentIndex`

32.
```
DoubleArraySeq s;
int i;
s = new DoubleArraySeq(100);
for (i = 1; i <= 100; i++)
    s.addAfter(i);
```

33.
```
s.start( );
while (
    s.isCurrent( )
    &&
    s.current( ) < x
    )
        s.advance( );
if (s.isCurrent( ))
    s.addBefore(x);
else
    s.addAfter(x);
```

34. addAll, getCapacity, size, trimToSize

35.
```
void addBefore(double element)
{
    int i;

    if (manyItems == data.length)
    {  // Try to double the capacity
        ensureCapacity(manyItems*2 + 1);
    }

    if (!isCurrent( ))
        currentIndex = 0;
    for
    (i=manyItems; i>currentIndex; i--)
        data[i] = data[i-1];
    data[currentIndex] = element;
    manyItems++;
}
```

36. 24

37. g.currentIndex will be 3 (since the 4th element occurs at data[3]).

38. The removeCurrent method should be tested when the sequence's size is just 1 and when the sequence is at its full capacity. At full capacity, you should try removing the first element and the last element of the sequence.

39. Your program can be similar to Figure 3.2 on page 123.

40. Here is our method's heading, with a postcondition:
```
void remove(int target);
// Postcondition: If target was in the
// sequence, then the first copy of target
// has been removed, and the element after
// the removed element (if there is one)
// becomes the new current element; other-
// wise the sequence remains unchanged.
```
The easiest implementation searches for the index of the target. If this index is found, then set currentIndex to this index and activate the ordinary removeCurrent method.

41. The total time to add $1, 2, ..., n$ with addAfter is $O(n)$. The total time to add $n, n-1, ..., 1$ with addBefore is $O(n^2)$. The larger time for the second approach is because an addition at the front of the sequence requires all of the existing elements to be shifted right to make room for the new element. Hence, on the second addition, one element is shifted. On the third addition, two elements are shifted. (And so on to the nth element, which needs $n-1$ shifts.) The total number of shifts is $1 + 2 + ... + (n-1)$, which is $O(n^2)$. To show that this sum is $O(n^2)$, use a technique similar to Figure 1.2 on page 20.

42. Neither of the classes *must* use an array. In later chapters, we will see both classes implemented without arrays.

43. coef[0] = 1.0; coef[1] = –0.9; coef[2] = 0.5; coef[3] = 0.3; the rest of coef is all zero.

44. Addition and subtraction are $O(n)$, where n is the larger degree of the two polynomials. Multiplication is $O(m \times n)$, where m and n are the degrees of the polynomials. (This assumes that m and n are nonzero.)

45. The bag class allows duplicate values in the container, whereas the HashSet class requires unique values; also, the data type of the elements in the HashSet is determined by its generic type parameter.

46. By changing its underlying collection

47. Here is one solution. We assume that java.util.HashSet and java.util.Iterator have been imported:

```
public static
double ave_len(HashSet<String> c)
{
   Iterator<String> it;
   double total = 0;
```

```
if (c.size( ) == 0)
   throw new
   IllegalArgumentException
   ("Empty HashSet!");

it = c.iterator( );
while (it.hasNext( ))
{
    total += it.next( ).length( );
}
return total/c.size( );
}
```

PROGRAMMING PROJECTS

1 For the IntArrayBag class, implement a new method called equals with a boolean return value and one parameter. The parameter, called b, is another IntArrayBag. The method returns true if b and the bag that activates the method have exactly the same number of every element. Otherwise, the method returns false. Notice that the locations of the elements in the data arrays are not necessarily the same. It is only the number of occurrences of each element that must be the same.

The worst-case time for the method should be $O(mn)$, where m is the size of the bag that activates the method and n is the size of b.

2 A **black box** test of a class is a program that tests the correctness of a class without directly examining the private instance variables of the class. You can imagine that the private instance variables are inside an opaque black box where they cannot be seen, so all testing must occur only through activating the public methods.

Write a noninteractive black box test program for the IntArrayBag class. Make sure you test the boundary values, such as an empty bag, a bag with just one element, and a full bag.

3 Study the BagApplet from Appendix I and write an expanded version that has three bags and buttons to activate any method of any bag. Also include a button that will carry out an action such as:

b1 = IntArrayBag.union(b2, b3).

4 Implement the sequence class from Section 3.3. You may wish to provide some additional useful methods, such as:
(1) a method to add a new element at the front of the sequence; (2) a method to remove the element at the front of the sequence; (3) a method to add a new element at the end of the sequence; (4) a method that makes the last element of the sequence become the current element; (5) a method that returns the ith element of the sequence (starting with the 0th at the front); and (6) a method that makes the ith element become the current element.

5 Using Appendix I as a guide, implement an applet for interactive testing of the sequence class from the previous project.

6 A bag can contain more than one copy of an element. For example, this chapter describes a bag that contains the number 4 and two copies of the number 8. This bag behavior is different from a **set**, which can contain only a single copy of any given element. Write a new collection class called `IntArraySet`, which is similar to a bag except that a set can contain only one copy of any given element. You'll need to change the specification a bit. For example, instead of the bag's `countOccurrences` method, you'll want a method such as this:

```
boolean contains(int target)
// Postcondition: The return value is true if
// target is in the set; otherwise, the return
// value is false.
```

Make an explicit statement of the invariant of the set ADT. Do a time analysis for each operation. At this point, an efficient implementation is not needed. For example, just adding a new element to a set will take linear time because you'll need to check that the new element isn't already present. Later we'll explore more efficient implementations.

You may also want to add additional methods to your set ADT, such as a method for subtracting one set from another.

7 Rewrite the sequence class using a new class name, `DoubleArraySortedSeq`. In the new class, the `add` method always puts the new element so that all the elements stay in order from smallest to largest. There is no `addBefore` or `addAfter` method. All the other methods are the same as in the original sequence ADT.

8 A one-variable **polynomial** is an arithmetic expression of the form:

$$a_0 + a_1 x + a_2 x^2 + \ldots + a_k x^k$$

Implement the polynomial class described in Section 3.4.

9 Specify, design, and implement a class that can be one player in a game of tic-tac-toe. The constructor should specify whether the object is to be the first player (Xs) or the second player (Os). There should be a method to ask the object to make its next move and a method that tells the object what the opponent's next move is. Also include other useful methods, such as a method to ask whether a given spot of the tic-tac-toe board is occupied and, if so, whether the occupation is with an X or an O. Also include a method to determine when the game is over and whether it was a draw, an X win, or an O win.

Use the class in two programs: a program that plays tic-tac-toe against the program's user and a program that has two tic-tac-toe objects that play against each other.

10 Specify, design, and implement a collection class that can hold up to five playing cards. Call the class `PokerHand`, and include a method with a boolean return value to allow you to compare two poker hands. For two hands x and y, the relation `x.beats(y)` means that x is a better hand than y. If you do not play in a weekly poker game yourself, you may need to consult a card rule book for the rules on the ranking of poker hands.

11 Specify, design, and implement a class that keeps track of rings stacked on a peg, rather like phonograph records on a spindle. An example with five rings is shown here:

Rings stacked on a peg

The peg may hold up to 64 rings, with each ring having its own diameter. Also, there is a rule that requires each ring to be smaller than any ring underneath it. The class's methods should include: (a) a constructor that places *n* rings on the peg (where *n* may be as large as 64), and these *n* rings have diameters from *n* inches on the bottom to one inch on the top; (b) an accessor method that returns the number of rings on the peg; (c) an accessor method that returns the diameter of the topmost ring; (d) a method that adds a new ring to the top (with the diameter of the ring as a parameter to the method); (e) a method that removes the topmost ring; and (f) a method that prints some clever representation of the peg and its rings. Make sure that all methods have appropriate preconditions to guarantee that the rule about ring sizes is enforced. Also spend time designing appropriate private instance variables.

12 In this project, you will design and implement a class called Towers, which is part of a program that lets a child play a game called Towers of Hanoi. The game consists of three pegs and a collection of rings that stack on the pegs. The rings are different sizes. The initial configuration for a five-ring game is shown here, with the first tower having rings from one inch (on the top) to five inches (on the bottom).

Initial configuration for a five-ring game of Towers of Hanoi

The rings are stacked in decreasing order of their size, and the second and third towers are initially empty. During the game, the child may transfer rings one at a time from the top of one peg to the top of another. The goal is to move all the rings from the first peg to the second peg. The difficulty is that the child may not place a ring on top of one with a smaller diameter. There is the one extra peg to hold rings temporarily, but the prohibition against a larger ring on a smaller ring applies to it as well as to the other two pegs. A solution for a three-ring game is shown at the top of the next page. The Towers class must keep track of the status of all three pegs. You might use an array of three pegs, where each peg is an object from the previous project. The Towers methods are specified here:

```
Towers(int n);
// Precondition: 1 <= n <= 64.
// Postcondition: The towers have been initialized
//   with n rings on the first peg and no rings on
//   the other two pegs. The diameters of the first
//   peg's rings are from one inch (on the top) to n
//   inches (on the bottom).

int countRings(int pegNumber)
// Precondition: pegNumber is 1, 2, or 3.
// Postcondition: The return value is the number
//   of rings on the specified peg.

int getTopDiameter(int pegNumber)
// Precondition: pegNumber is 1, 2, or 3.
// Postcondition: If countRings(pegNumber) > 0,
//   then the return value is the diameter of the top
//   ring on the specified peg; otherwise, the return
//   value is zero.

void move(int startPeg, int endPeg)
// Precondition: startPeg is a peg number
//   (1, 2, or 3), and countRings(startPeg) > 0;
//   endPeg is a different peg number (not equal
//   to startPeg), and if endPeg has at least one
//   ring, then getTopDiameter(startPeg) is
//   less than getTopDiameter(endPeg).
// Postcondition: The top ring has been moved
//   from startPeg to endPeg.
```

Also include a method so that a Towers object may be displayed easily.

Use the Towers object in a program that allows a child to play Towers of Hanoi. Make sure you don't allow the child to make any illegal moves.

13 This project is to implement a class that is similar to Java's Math.BigInteger class. Each object in your class keeps track of an integer with an unlimited number of digits in base 10. The digits can be stored in an array of int, and the sign of the number can be stored in a separate instance variable, which is +1 for a positive number and −1 for a negative number.

The class should include several convenient constructors, such as a constructor to initialize an object from an ordinary int. Also write methods to carry out the usual arithmetic operators and comparison operators (to carry out arithmetic and comparisons on these big numbers).

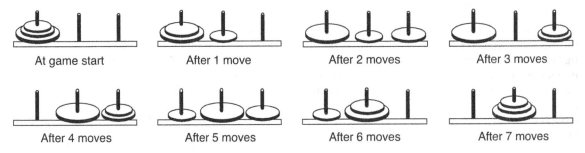

At game start	After 1 move	After 2 moves	After 3 moves
After 4 moves	After 5 moves	After 6 moves	After 7 moves

14 Revise the bag class so that it is a bag of strings rather than integers. For the methods that add strings to the bag, you should always use the string's `clone` method to make a copy of each string and put the copy into the clone rather than the original. Also, when you are comparing two strings for equality, make sure you use the string `equals` method rather than the `==` operator.

Modify the bag test applet from Appendix I to test your new string bag.

15 Implement the `Statistician` class from Project 2 on page 95, but include a new method that returns the median value of all the numbers. The median is a number that is greater than or equal to at least half of the numbers and is also less than or equal to at least half of the numbers.

Because of the new median calculation, the `Statistician` will need to keep track of all the numbers, perhaps using an array. The median calculation will be easiest if you keep these numbers in order from smallest to largest.

16 Implement the previous project with the following modification: All of the input numbers to the `Statistician` are required to be integers in the range from 0 to 100. This modification means that it's easier to keep track of all the input numbers using a single array (called `frequency`) with indexes from 0 to 100. At all times, the value of `frequency[i]` will be the number of times the number i has been given to the `Statistician`.

You will need to give it some thought to figure out how to use the frequency information to compute statistics such as the median and the mean.

17 Design, specify, and implement a collection class that is similar to an array of double numbers except that it automatically grows when needed and negative indexes are also permitted.

The class should include a method to put a double number into the "array" at a specified index. For example, suppose that v is an object of this class. Then `v.put(3.8, 7)` would put the number 3.8 at index 7 of the "array." Since negative indexes are also allowed, the statement `v.put(9.1, -3)` would put the number 9.1 at the index -3.

The class also includes a method to retrieve the number from a specified index. For example, `v.get(7)` would return the value of the number that is currently at index 7 of the "array." If a programmer tries to get a value that has not yet been put into the array, then the `get` method will return the Java constant `Double.NaN` (which is the way Java represents a double value that is not a real number).

The class should also have two methods that return the value of the largest and the smallest indexes that have ever been set with the `put` method. If no numbers have yet been put in the "array," then the "largest" index should be `Integer.MIN_VALUE` and the "smallest" index should be `Integer.MAX_VALUE`.

18 In this project, you will implement a new class called a **bag with receipts**. This new class is similar to an ordinary bag, but the data consists of strings, and the way that the strings are added and removed is different. Each time a string is added to a bag with receipts, the `insert` method returns a unique integer called the **receipt**. Later, when you want to remove a string, you must provide a copy of the receipt as a parameter to the remove method. The remove method removes the item whose receipt has been presented and also returns that item through its return value. You may also have a method that returns a copy of the string without removing it.

Here's an implementation idea: A bag with receipts can have a private array, like this:

```
private String[ ] data;
```

Some locations in this array may contain null, which means that that location is unused. When a new string is added, we will find the first spot that is currently unused and store the new string there. The receipt for the string is the index of the location where the string is stored.

19 Another way to store a collection of items is called a **keyed bag**. In this type of bag, whenever an item is added, the programmer using the bag also provides an integer called the **key**. Each item added to the keyed bag must have a unique key; two items cannot have the same key. For this project, implement a keyed bag in which the items to be stored are strings (perhaps people's names) and the keys are numbers (perhaps Social Security or other identification numbers). So, the insertion method has this specification:

```
public void insert
(String entry, int key);
// Precondition: size( ) < CAPACITY, and the
// bag does not yet contain any item
// with the given key.
// Postcondition: A new copy of entry has
// been added to the bag, with the given key.
```

When the programmer wants to remove or retrieve an item from a keyed bag, the key of the item must be specified rather than the item itself. The keyed bag should also have a boolean method that can be used to determine whether the bag has an item with a specified key.

A keyed bag differs from the bag with receipts (in the previous project). In a keyed bag, the programmer using the class specifies a particular key when an item is inserted. In contrast, for a bag with

receipts, the insert method returns a receipt, and the programmer using the class has no control over what that receipt might be.

Here's an implementation idea: A keyed bag can have two private arrays, one that holds the string data and one that holds the corresponding keys. The data at location data[i] has a key that is stored in key[i].

20 Specify, design, and implement a class where each object keeps track of a large integer with up to 100 digits in base 10. The digits are stored in an array of 100 elements, and the sign of the number is stored in a separate instance variable, which is +1 for a positive number and −1 for a negative number.

The class should include several convenient constructors, such as a constructor to initialize an object from an ordinary int. Also write methods to provide the usual arithmetic operations (such as addition), arithmetic comparisons (to carry out comparisons on these big numbers), an input method, and an output method.

21 Create a Person class that stores a name and birthday of a person. The name can be a String and the birthday can be a Date object from Project 19 of Chapter 2. The Person class should have both a clone method that creates a new string and a new Date object for the newly cloned Person. It should also have methods to set and get the name and date.

Use your Person class as part of a program that allows you to store and retrieve the birthdays of your friends.

22 Write a program that reads a list of nine-digit numbers from the keyboard. It stores the numbers in a bag, and then goes through the bag to determine whether there are any duplicate entries. For each duplicate entry, print a message that says how many times that entry occurred in the multiset.

23 Write a program that uses a HashSet of strings to keep track of a list of chores that you have to accomplish today. The user of the program can request several services: (1) add an item to the list of chores; (2) ask how many chores are in the list; (3) use the iterator to print the list of chores to the screen; (4) delete an item from the list; and (5) exit the program.

If you know how to read and write strings from a file, then have the program obtain its initial list of chores from a file. When the program ends, it should write all unfinished chores back to this file.

24 Write a program that contains two arrays called actors and roles, each of size *n*. For each i, actors[i] is the name of an actor and roles[i] is a HashSet of strings that contains the names of the movies that the actor has appeared in. The program reads the initial information for these arrays from files in a format that you design.

Once the program is running, the user can type in the name of an actor and receive a list of all the movies for that actor. Or the user may type the name of a movie and receive a list of all the actors in that movie.

25 An array can be used to store large integers one digit at a time. For example, the integer 1234 could be stored in the array a by setting a[0] to 1, a[1] to 2, a[2] to 3, and a[3] to 4. However, for this project, you might find it easier to store the digits backward, that is, place 4 in a[0], place 3 in a[1], place 2 in a[2], and place 1 in a[3].

Design, implement, and test a class in which each object is a large integer with each digit stored in a separate element of an array. You'll also need a private instance variable to keep track of the sign of the integer (perhaps a boolean variable). The number of digits may grow as the program runs, so the array may have to grow beyond its original size.

Discuss and implement other appropriate operators for this class (which is similar to Java's own BigInteger class).

26 Suppose that you want to implement a bag class to hold non-negative integers, and you know that the biggest number in the bag will never be more than a few thousand. One approach for implementing this bag is to have a private instance variable that is an array of integers called count with indexes from 0 to M (where M is the maximum number in the bag). If the bag contains six copies of a number n, then the object has count[n] equal to 6 to represent this fact.

For this project, reimplement the bag class from Figure 3.1 using this idea. You will have an entirely new set of private instance variables; for the public methods, you may delete the capacity methods, but please add a new method that the programmer can use to specify the maximum number that he or she anticipates putting into the bag. Also note that the add method must check to see whether the current maximum index of the array is at least as big as the new number. If not, then the array size must be increased.

CHAPTER **4**

Linked Lists

Linked Lists

*The simplest way to interrelate or link a set of elements is to
line them up in a single list... For, in this case, only a single
link is needed for each element to refer to its successor.*

NIKLAUS WIRTH
Algorithms + Data Structures = Programs

*linked lists are
used to
implement a list
of elements
arranged in
some kind of
order*

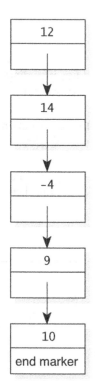

FIGURE 4.1
A Linked List
Made of Nodes
Connected with
Links

W̲e begin this chapter with a concrete discussion of a new
data structure, the *linked list*, which is used to implement a list of elements
arranged in some kind of order. The linked list structure uses memory that
shrinks and grows as needed but in a different manner than arrays. The discussion of linked lists includes the specification and implementation of a node
class, which incorporates the fundamental notion of a single element of a linked
list.

Once you understand the fundamentals, linked lists can be used as part of an
ADT, similar to the way that arrays have been used in previous ADTs. For
example, linked lists can be used to reimplement the bag and sequence ADTs.

By the end of the chapter, you will understand linked lists well enough to use
them in various programming projects (such as the revised bag and sequence
ADTs) and in the ADTs of future chapters. You will also know the advantages
and drawbacks of using linked lists versus arrays for these ADTs.

4.1 FUNDAMENTALS OF LINKED LISTS

A **linked list** is a sequence of elements arranged one after another, with each
element connected to the next element by a "link." A common programming
practice is to place each element together with the link to the next element,
resulting in a component called a **node**. A node is represented pictorially as a
box, with the element written inside the box and the link drawn as an arrow
pointing out of the box. Several typical nodes are shown in Figure 4.1. For
example, the topmost node has the number 12 as its element. Most of the nodes
in the figure also have an arrow pointing out of the node. These arrows, or **links**,
are used to connect one node to another.

The links are represented as arrows because they do more than simply connect
two nodes. The links also place the nodes in a particular order. In Figure 4.1, the
five nodes form a chain from top to bottom. The first node is linked to the second
node; the second node is linked to the third node; and so on, until we reach the
last node. We must do something special when we reach the last node since
the last node is not linked to another node. In this special case, we will replace
the link in this node with a note saying "end marker."

Declaring a Class for Nodes

Each node contains two pieces of information: an element (which is a number for these example nodes) and an arrow. But just *what* are those arrows? Each arrow points to another node, or you could say that each arrow *refers* to another node. With this in mind, we can implement a Java class for a node using two instance variables: an instance variable to hold the element and a second instance variable that is a reference to another node. In Java, the two instance variables can be declared at the start of the class:

```java
public class IntNode
{
    private int data;        // The element stored in this node
    private IntNode link;    // Refers to the next node in the list
    ...
```

We'll provide the methods later (in Sections 4.2 and 4.3). For now we want to focus on the two instance variables: data and link. The data is simply an integer element, though we could have had some other kinds of elements, perhaps double numbers, or characters, or whatever. The link is a reference to another node. For example, the link variable in the first node is a reference to the second node. Our drawings will represent each link reference as an arrow leading from one node to another. In fact, we have previously used arrows to represent references to objects in Chapters 2 and 3, so these links are nothing new.

Head Nodes, Tail Nodes

When a program builds and manipulates a linked list, the list is usually accessed through references to one or more important nodes. The most common access is through the list's first node, which is called the **head** of the list. Sometimes we maintain a reference to the last node in a linked list. The last node is the **tail** of the list. We could also maintain references to other nodes in a linked list.

Each reference to a node used in a program must be declared as a node variable. For example, if we are maintaining a linked list with references to the head and tail, then we would declare two node variables:

```java
IntNode head;
IntNode tail;
```

The program can now proceed to create a linked list, always ensuring that head refers to the first node and tail refers to the last node, as shown in Figure 4.2.

Building and Manipulating Linked Lists

Whenever a program builds and manipulates a linked list, the nodes are accessed through one or more references to nodes. Typically, a program includes a reference to the first node (the **head**) and a reference to the last node (the **tail**).

FIGURE 4.2 Node Declarations in a Program with a Linked List

Declaration from the `IntNode` Class

```
public class IntNode
{
    private int data;
    private IntNode link;
    ...
```

Declaring Two Nodes in a Program

```
IntNode head;
IntNode tail;
```

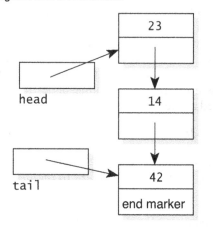

A computation might create a small linked list with three nodes, as shown here. The head and `tail` variables provide access to two nodes inside the list.

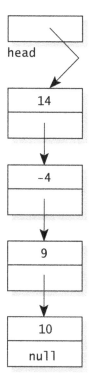

The Null Reference

Figure 4.3 illustrates a linked list with one new feature. Look at the link part of the final node. Instead of a reference, we have written the word null. The word null indicates the **null reference**, which is a special Java constant. You can use the null reference for any reference variable that has nothing to refer to. There are several common situations in which the null reference is used.

> ### The Null Reference and Linked Lists
>
> In Java, when a reference variable is first declared and there is not yet an object for it to refer to, it can be given an initial value of the null reference. Examples of this initial value are shown in Chapter 2 on page 54.
>
> The null reference is used for the link part of the final node of a linked list.
>
> When a linked list does not yet have any nodes, the null reference is used for the head and tail reference variables. Such a list is called the **empty list**.

In a program, the null reference is written as the keyword null.

FIGURE 4.3
Linked List with the
Null Reference at
the Final Link

PITFALL

NULLPOINTEREXCEPTIONS WITH LINKED LISTS

When a reference variable is null, it is a programming error to activate one of its methods or to try to access one of its instance variables. For example, a program may maintain a reference to the head node of a linked list, as shown here:

```
IntNode head;
```

Initially, the list is empty and head is the null reference. At this point, it is a programming error to activate one of head's methods. The error would occur as a NullPointerException.

The general rules: Never activate a method of the null reference. Never try to access an instance variable of the null reference. In both cases, the result would be a NullPointerException.

Self-Test Exercises for Section 4.1

1. Write the start of the class declaration for a node in a linked list. The data in each node is a double number.
2. Write another node declaration, but this time the data in each node should include both a double number and an integer. (Yes, a node can have many instance variables for data, but each instance variable needs to have a distinct name.)
3. Suppose a program builds and manipulates a linked list. What two special nodes would the program typically keep track of?
4. Describe two uses for the null reference in the realm of linked lists.
5. How many nodes are in an empty list? What are the values of the head and tail references for an empty list?
6. What happens if you try to activate a method of the null reference?

4.2 METHODS FOR MANIPULATING NODES

We're ready to write methods for the IntNode class, which begins like this:

```
public class IntNode
{
    private int data;       // The element stored in this node
    private IntNode link;   // Refers to the next node in the list
    ...
```

There will be methods for creating, accessing, and modifying nodes, plus methods and other techniques for adding or removing nodes from a linked list. We begin with a constructor that's responsible for initializing the two instance variables of a new node.

Constructor for the Node Class

The node's constructor has two arguments, which are the initial values for the node's data and link variables, as specified here:

◆ **Constructor for the IntNode**

```
public IntNode(int initialData, IntNode initialLink)
```
Initialize a node with specified initial data and a link to the next node. Note that the initialLink may be the null reference, which indicates that the new node has nothing after it.

Parameters:
  initialData – the initial data of this new node
  initialLink – a reference to the node after this new node (the reference may be null to indicate that there is no node after this new node)

Postcondition:
  This new node contains the specified data and a link to the next node.

The constructor's implementation copies its two parameters to the instance variables data and link:

```
public IntNode(int initialData, IntNode initialLink)
{
    data = initialData;
    link = initialLink;
}
```

As an example, the constructor can be used by a program to create the first node of the linked list shown in the margin.

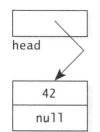

head

42

null

```
IntNode head;
head = new IntNode(42, null);
```

After these two statements, head refers to the head node of a small linked list that contains just one node with the number 42. We'll look at the formation of longer linked lists after we see four other basic node methods.

Getting and Setting the Data and Link of a Node

The node has an accessor method and a modification method for each of its two instance variables, as specified here:

getData,
getLink,
setData,
setLink

◆ **getData**

```
public int getData( )
```
Accessor method to get the data from this node.

Returns:
  the data from this node

♦ **getLink**

> `public IntNode getLink( )`
>
> Accessor method to get a reference to the next node after this node.
>
> **Returns:**
>
> > a reference to the node after this node (or the null reference if there is nothing after this node)

♦ **setData**

> `public void setData(int newdata)`
>
> Modification method to set the data in this node.
>
> **Parameter:**
>
> > `newData` – the new data to place in this node
>
> **Postcondition:**
>
> > The data of this node has been set to `newData`.

♦ **setLink**

> `public void setLink(IntNode newLink)`
>
> Modification method to set the reference to the next node after this node.
>
> **Parameter:**
>
> > `newLink` – a reference to the node that should appear after this node in the linked list (or the null reference if there should be no node after this node)
>
> **Postcondition:**
>
> > The link to the node after this node has been set to `newLink`. Any other node (that used to be in this link) is no longer connected to this node.

The implementations of the four methods are short. For example:

```
public void setLink(IntNode newLink)
{
    link = newLink;
}
```

Public Versus Private Instance Variables

In addition to `setLink`, there are the three other short methods (documented previously) that we'll leave for you to implement. You may wonder why you should bother having these short methods at all. Wouldn't it be simpler and more efficient to just make `data` and `link` public and do away with the short methods altogether? Yes, public instance variables probably are simpler, and the direct access of an instance variable is more efficient than calling a method. On the other hand, debugging can be easier with access and modification methods in place because we can set breakpoints to see whenever an instance variable is accessed or modified. Also, private instance variables provide good information hiding so that later changes to the class won't affect programs that use the class.

The public-versus-private question should be addressed for many of your classes, with the answer based on the intended use and required efficiency together with software engineering principles such as information hiding. For the classes in this text, we'll lean toward information hiding and avoid public instance variables.

Adding a New Node at the Head of a Linked List

New nodes can be added at the head of a linked list. To accomplish this, the program needs a reference to the head node of a list, as shown here:

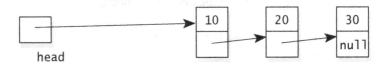

In this example, suppose we want to add a new node to the front of this list, with 5 as the data. Using the node constructor, we can write:

```
head = new IntNode(5, head);
```

how to add a new node at the head of a linked list

Let's step through the execution of this statement to see how the new node is added at the front of the list. When the constructor is executed, a new node is created with 5 as the data and with the link referring to the same node that head refers to. Here's what the picture looks like, with the link of the new node shaded:

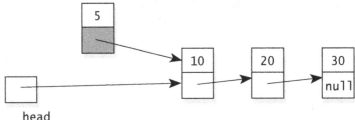

The constructor returns a reference to the newly created node, and in the statement, we wrote `head = new IntNode(5, head)`. You can read this statement as saying "make head refer to the newly created node." Therefore, we end up with this situation:

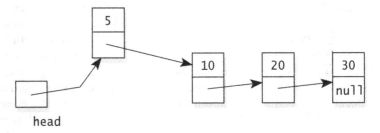

By the way, the technique works correctly even when we start with an empty   list (in which the head reference is null). In this case, the statement `head = new IntNode(5, head)` creates the first node of the list. To see this, suppose we start with a null head and execute the statement. The constructor creates a new node with 5 as the data and with head as the link. Since the head reference is null, the new node looks like this (with the link of the new node shaded):

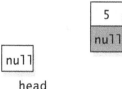

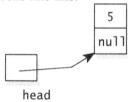
head

After the constructor returns, head is assigned to refer to the new node, so the final situation looks like this:

5
null

head

As you can see, the statement `head = new IntNode(5, head)` has correctly added the first node to a list. If we are maintaining a reference to the tail node, then we would also set the tail to refer to this one node.

Adding a New Node at the Head of a Linked List

Suppose head is the head reference of a linked list. Then this statement adds a new node at the front of the list with the specified new data:

    head = new IntNode(newData, head);

This statement works correctly even when we start with an empty list (in which case the head reference is null).

Removing a Node from the Head of a Linked List

Nodes can be removed from the head of the linked list. To accomplish this, we need a reference to the head node of a list:

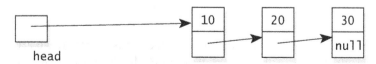
head

To remove the first node, we move the head so that it refers to the next node. This is accomplished with one statement:

```
head = head.getLink( );
```

how to remove a node from the head of a linked list

The right side of the assignment, `head.getLink( )`, is a reference to the second node of the list. So, after the assignment, head refers to the second node:

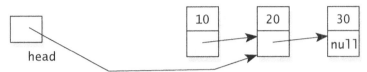

This picture is peculiar. It looks like we still have a linked list with three nodes containing 10, 20, and 30. But if we start at the head, there are only the two nodes with 20 and 30. The node with 10 can no longer be accessed starting at the head, so it is not really part of the linked list anymore. In fact, if a situation arises in which a node can no longer be accessed from anywhere in a program, then the Java runtime system recognizes that the node has strayed, and the memory used by that node will be reused for other things. This technique of rounding up stray memory is called **garbage collection**, and it happens automatically for Java programs. In other programming languages, the programmer is responsible for identifying memory that is no longer used and explicitly returning that memory to the runtime system.

automatic garbage collection has some inefficiency, but it's less prone to programming errors

What are the trade-offs between automatic garbage collection and programmer-controlled memory handling? Automatic garbage collection is slower when a program is executing, but the automatic approach is less prone to errors, and it frees the programmer to concentrate on more important issues.

Anyway, we'll remove a node from the front of a list with the statement `head = head.getLink( )`. This statement also works when the list has only one node, and we want to remove this one node. For example, consider this list:

In this situation, we can execute `head = head.getLink( )`. The `getLink( )` method returns the link of the head node—in other words, it returns `null`. So, the null reference is assigned to the head, ending up with this situation:

Now the head is null, which indicates that the list is empty. If we are maintaining a reference to the tail, then we would also have to set the tail reference to null. The automatic garbage collection will then take care of reusing the memory occupied by the one node.

Removing a Node from the Head of a Linked List

Suppose head is the head reference of a non-empty linked list (so that head is not null). Then this statement removes a node from the front of the list:

```
head = head.getLink( );
```

This statement works correctly even when the list has just one node (in which case the head reference becomes null).

Adding a New Node That Is Not at the Head

New nodes are not always placed at the head of a linked list. They may be added in the middle or at the tail of a list. For example, suppose you want to add the number 42 after the 20 in this list:

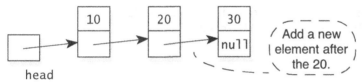

After the addition, the new, longer list has these four nodes:

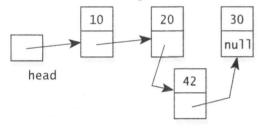

Whenever a new node is not at the head, the process requires a reference to the node that is just *before* the intended location of the new node. In our example, we would require a reference to the node that contains 20 since we want to place the new node after this node. This special node is called the "selected node," and the new node will go just after the selected node. We'll use the name selection for a reference to the selected node. So, to add an element after the 20, we would first have to set up selection this way:

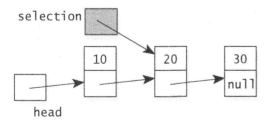

Once a program has calculated `selection`, the new node with data of 42 can be added with a method of the `IntNode` class, specified here:

addNodeAfter

♦ **addNodeAfter**
```
public void addNodeAfter(int element)
```
Modification method to add a new node after this node.

Parameter:
`element` – the data to be placed in the new node

Postcondition:
A new node has been created and placed after this node. The data for the new node is `element`. Any other nodes that used to be after this node are now after the new node.

Throws: `OutOfMemoryError`
Indicates that there is insufficient memory for a new `IntNode`.

For example, to add a new node with data of 42 after the selected node, we can activate `selection.addNodeAfter(42)`.

The implementation of addNodeAfter requires just one line:

```
public void addNodeAfter(int element)
{
    link = new IntNode(element, link);
}
```

Let's see exactly what happens when we set up `selection` as shown earlier and then execute `selection.addNodeAfter(42)`. The value of `element` is 42, so we have this situation:

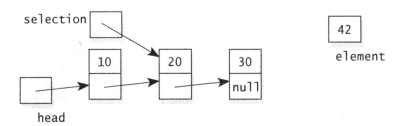

The method executes `link = new IntNode(element, link)`, where `element` is 42 and `link` is from the selected node—in other words, `link` is `selection.link`. On the right side of the statement, the `IntNode` constructor is executed, and a new node is created with 42 as the data and with the `link` of the new node being the same as `selection.link`. The resulting situation is shown next, with the new node shaded.

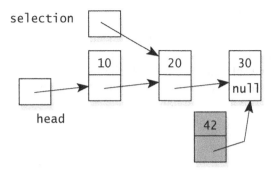

The constructor returns a reference to the newly created node, and in the assignment statement we wrote `link = new IntNode(element, link)`. You can read this statement as saying "change the link part of the selected node so that it refers to the newly created node." This change is made in the following drawing, which highlights the link part of the selected node:

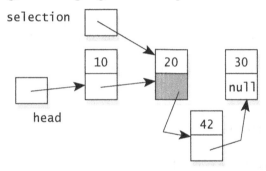

After adding the new node with 42, you can step through the complete linked list, starting at the head node 10, then 20, then 42, and finally 30.

The approach we have used works correctly even when the selected node is the tail of a list. In this case, the new node is added after the tail. If we were maintaining a reference to the tail node, then we would have to update this reference to refer to the newly added tail.

Adding a New Node That Is Not at the Head

Suppose `selection` is a reference to a node of a linked list. Activating the following method adds a new node after the selected node (using `element` as the new data):

```
selection.addNodeAfter(element);
```

The implementation of addNodeAfter needs only one statement to accomplish its work:

```
link = new IntNode(element, link);
```

Removing a Node That Is Not at the Head

It is also possible to remove a node that is not at the head of a linked list. The approach is similar to adding a node in the middle of a linked list. To remove a midlist node, we must set up a reference to the node that is just *before* the node we are removing. For example, to remove the 42 from the following list, we would need to set up `selection` as shown here:

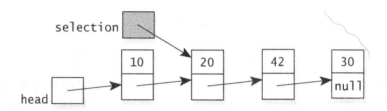

As you can see, `selection` does not actually refer to the node we are deleting (the 42); instead, it refers to the node that is just before the condemned node. This is because the link of the *previous* node must be reassigned; hence, we need a reference to this previous node. The removal method's specification is shown here:

removeNodeAfter   ♦ **removeNodeAfter**

  `public void removeNodeAfter( )`
  Modification method to remove the node after this node.

  Precondition:
    This node must not be the tail node of the list.

  Postcondition:
    The node after this node has been removed from the linked list. If there were further nodes after that one, they are still present in the list.

For example, to remove the 42 from the list drawn above, we would activate `selection.removeNodeAfter( )`. After the removal, the new list will look like this (with the changed link highlighted):

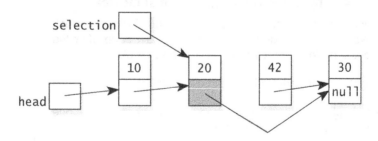

At this point, the node containing 42 is no longer part of the linked list. The list's first node contains 10; the next node has 20; and following the links we arrive at the third and last node, containing 30. Java's automatic garbage collection will reuse the removed node's memory.

The implementation of removeNodeAfter must alter the link of the node that activated the method. How is the alteration carried out? Let's go back to our starting position, but we'll put a bit more information in the picture:

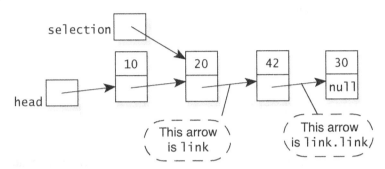

To work through this example, you need some patterns that can be used within the method to refer to the various data and link parts of the nodes. Remember that we activated selection.removeNodeAfter( ), so the node that activated the method has 20 for its data, and its link is indicated by the caption "This arrow is link." So we can certainly use these two names within the method:

data	This is the data of the node that activated the method (20).
link	This is the link of the node that activated the method. This link refers to the node that we are removing.

Because the name link refers to a node, we can also use the names link.data and link.link:

link.data	This notation means "go to the node that link refers to and use the data instance variable." In our example, link.data is 42.
link.link	This notation means "go to the node that link refers to and use the link instance variable." In our example, link.link is the reference to the node that contains 30.

In the implementation of removeNodeAfter, we need to make link refer to the node that contains 30. So, using the notation just shown, we need to assign link = link.link. The complete implementation is at the top of the next page.

```
public void removeNodeAfter( )
{
    link = link.link;
}
```

The notation `link.link` does look strange, but just read it from left to right so that it means "go to the node that `link` refers to and use the `link` instance variable that you find there." In our example, the final situation after assigning `link = link.link` is just what we want:

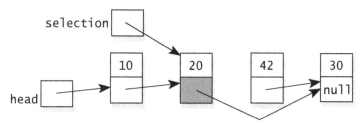

The `removeNodeAfter` implementation works fine, even when we want to remove the tail node. Here's an example in which we have set `selection` to refer to the node that's just before the tail of a small list:

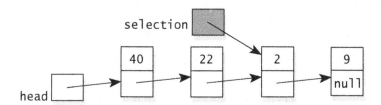

When we activate `selection.removeNodeAfter( )`, the link of the selected node will be assigned the value `null` (which is obtained from the link of the next node). The result is shown in this picture:

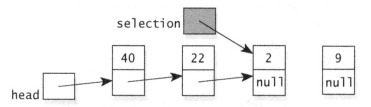

The tail node has been removed from the list. If the program maintains a reference to the tail node, then that reference must be updated to refer to the new tail.

In all cases, Java's automatic garbage collection takes care of reusing the removed node's memory.

Removing a Node That Is Not at the Head

Suppose `selection` is a reference to a node of a linked list. Activating the following method removes the node after the selected node:

```
selection.removeNodeAfter( );
```

The implementation of `removeNodeAfter` needs only one statement to accomplish its work:

```
link = link.link;
```

PITFALL

NULLPOINTEREXCEPTIONS WITH REMOVENODEAFTER

The `removeNodeAfter` method has a potential problem. What happens if the tail node activates `removeNodeAfter`? This is a programming error because `removeNodeAfter` would try to remove the node after the tail node, and there is no such node. The precondition of `removeNodeAfter` explicitly states that it must not be activated by the tail node. Still, what will happen in this case? For the tail node, `link` is the null reference, so trying to access the instance variable `link.link` will result in a `NullPointerException`.

When we write the complete specification of the node methods, we will include a note indicating the possibility of a `NullPointerException` in this method.

Self-Test Exercises for Section 4.2

7. Suppose head is a head reference for a linked list of integers. Write a few lines of code that will add a new node with the number 42 as the second element of the list. (If the list was originally empty, then 42 should be added as the first node instead of the second.)

8. Suppose head is a head reference for a linked list of integers. Write a few lines of code that will remove the second node of the list. (If the list originally had only one node, then remove that node instead; if it had no nodes, then leave the list empty.)

9. Examine the techniques for adding and removing a node at the head. Why are these techniques implemented as static methods rather than ordinary `IntNode` methods?

10. Write some code that could appear in a main program. The code should declare head and tail references for a linked list of integers and then create a list of nodes with the data being integers 1 through 100 (in that order). After each of the nodes is added, head and `tail` should still be valid references to the head and tail nodes of the current list.

4.3   MANIPULATING AN ENTIRE LINKED LIST

We can now write programs that use linked lists. Such a program declares some references to nodes, such as head and tail references. The nodes are manipulated with the methods and other techniques we have already seen. But all these methods and techniques deal with just one or two nodes at an isolated part of the linked list. Many programs also need techniques for carrying out computations on an entire list, such as computing the number of nodes in a list. This suggests that we should write a few more methods for the IntNode class—methods that carry out some computation on an entire linked list. For example, we can provide a method with this heading:

```
public static int listLength(IntNode head)
```

The listLength method computes the number of nodes in a linked list. The one parameter, head, is a reference to the head node of the list. For example, the last line of this code prints the length of a short list:

```
IntNode small; // Head reference for a small list
small = new IntNode(42, null);
small.addNodeAfter(17);
System.out.println(IntNode.listLength(small)); // Prints 2
```

By the way, the listLength return value is int so that the method can be used only if a list has fewer than Integer.MAX_VALUE nodes. Beyond this length, the listLength method will return a wrong answer because of arithmetic overflow. We'll make a note of the potential problem in the listLength specification.

Notice that listLength is a static method. It is not activated by any one node; instead, we activate IntNode.listLength. But why is it a *static* method? Wouldn't it be easier to write an ordinary method that is activated by the head node of the list? Yes, an ordinary method might be easier, but a static method is better because a static method can be used even for an empty list. For example, these two statements create an empty list and print the length of that list:

```
IntNode empty = null; // empty is null, representing an empty list
System.out.println(IntNode.listLength(empty)); // Prints 0
```

An ordinary method could not be used to compute the length of the empty list, because the head reference is null.

Manipulating an Entire Linked List

To carry out computations on an entire linked list, we will write static methods in the IntNode class. Each such method has one or more parameters that are references to nodes in the list. Most of the methods will work correctly even when the references are null (indicating an empty list).

Computing the Length of a Linked List

Here is the complete specification of the `listLength` method we've been discussing:

♦ **listLength**   *listLength*

```
public static int listLength(IntNode head)
```
Compute the number of nodes in a linked list.

Parameter:
head – the head reference for a linked list (which may be an empty list with a null head)

Returns:
the number of nodes in the list with the given head

Note:
A wrong answer occurs for lists longer than `Int.MAX_VALUE` because of arithmetic overflow.

The precondition indicates that the parameter, head, is the head reference for a linked list. If the list is not empty, then head refers to the first node of the list. If the list is empty, then head is the null reference (and the method returns zero since there are no nodes).

Our implementation uses a reference variable to step through the list, counting the nodes one at a time. Here are the three steps of the pseudocode, using a reference variable named `cursor` to step through the nodes of the list one at a time. (We often use the name `cursor` for such a variable since "cursor" means "something that runs through a structure.")

1. Initialize a variable named `answer` to zero. (This variable will keep track of how many nodes we have seen so far.)

2. Make `cursor` refer to each node of the list, starting at the head node. Each time `cursor` moves, add 1 to `answer`.

3. `return answer`.

Both `cursor` and `answer` are local variables in the method.

The first step initializes `answer` to zero because we have not yet seen any nodes. The implementation of Step 2 is a for-loop, following a pattern that you should use whenever *all of the nodes of a linked list must be traversed*. The general pattern looks like this:

```
for (cursor = head; cursor != null; cursor = cursor.link)
{

          . . .    Inside the body of the loop, you can
                   carry out whatever computation is
                   needed for a node in the list.

}
```
how to traverse all the nodes of a linked list

For the `listLength` method, the "computation" inside the loop is simple because we are just counting the nodes. Therefore, in our body, we will just add 1 to `answer`:

```
for (cursor = head; cursor != null; cursor = cursor.link)
    answer++;
```

Let's examine the loop in an example. Suppose the linked list has three nodes containing the numbers 10, 20, and 30. After the loop initializes (with `cursor = head`), we have this situation:

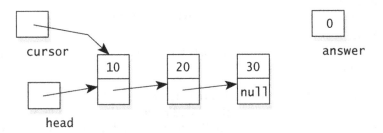

Notice that `cursor` refers to the same node that head refers to.

Since `cursor` is not `null`, we enter the body of the loop. Each iteration increments answer and then executes `cursor = cursor.link`. The effect of `cursor = cursor.link` is to copy the link part of the first node into `cursor` itself so that `cursor` ends up referring to the second node. In general, the statement `cursor = cursor.link` moves `cursor` to the next node. So, at the completion of the loop's first iteration, the situation is this:

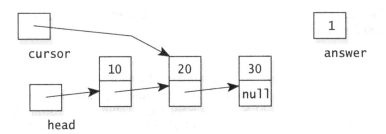

The loop continues. After the second iteration, answer is 2 and `cursor` refers to the third node of the list, as shown next.

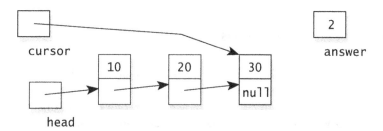

Each time we complete an iteration of the loop, `cursor` refers to some location in the list, and `answer` is the number of nodes *before* this location. In our example, we are about to enter the loop's body for the third and last time. During the last iteration, `answer` is incremented to 3, and `cursor` becomes `null`:

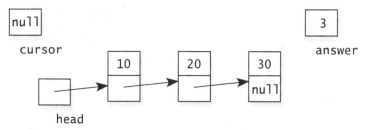

The variable `cursor` has become `null` because the loop control statement `cursor = cursor.link` copied the `link` part of the third node into `cursor`. Since this `link` part is `null`, the value in `cursor` is now `null`.

At this point, the loop's control test `cursor != null` is false. The loop ends, and the method returns the answer 3. The complete implementation of the `listLength` method is shown in Figure 4.4.

FIGURE 4.4   A Static Method to Compute the Length of a Linked List

Implementation

```
public static int listLength(IntNode head)
{
    IntNode cursor;
    int answer;

    answer = 0;
    for (cursor = head; cursor != null; cursor = cursor.link)
        answer++;                          Step 2 of the
                                           pseudocode
    return answer;
}
```

⬤ PROGRAMMING TIP

HOW TO TRAVERSE A LINKED LIST

You should learn the important pattern for traversing a linked list, as used in the listLength method (see Figure 4.4). The same pattern can be used whenever you need to step through the nodes of a linked list one at a time.

The first part of the pattern concerns moving from one node to another. Whenever we have a variable that refers to some node and we want the variable to refer to the next node, we must use the link part of the node. Here is the reasoning that we follow:

1. Suppose cursor refers to some node.
2. Then cursor.link refers to the next node (if there is one), as shown here:

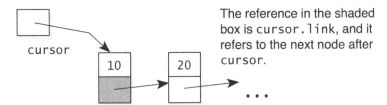

The reference in the shaded box is cursor.link, and it refers to the next node after cursor.

3. To move cursor to the next node, we use one of these assignment statements:

<pre>
          cursor = cursor.link;
            or
          cursor = cursor.getLink( );
</pre>

Use the first version, cursor = cursor.link, if you have access to the link instance variable (inside one of the IntNode methods). Otherwise, use the second version, cursor = cursor.getLink( ). In both cases, if there is no next node, then cursor.link will be null, and therefore our assignment statement will set cursor to null.

The key is to know that the assignment statement cursor = cursor.link moves cursor so that it refers to the next node. If there is no next node, then the assignment statement sets cursor to null.

The second part of the pattern shows how to traverse all of the nodes of a linked list, starting at the head node. The pattern of the loop looks like this:

<pre>
for (cursor = head; cursor != null; cursor = cursor.link)
{
          Inside the body of the loop, you can
   ...   *carry out whatever computation is*
          needed for a node in the list.
}
</pre>

You'll find yourself using this pattern continually in methods that manipulate linked lists.

FORGETTING TO TEST THE EMPTY LIST

Methods that manipulate linked lists should always be tested to ensure that they have the right behavior for the empty list. When head is null (indicating the empty list), our listLength method should return 0. Testing this case shows that listLength does correctly return 0 for the empty list.

Searching for an Element in a Linked List

In Java, a method can return a reference to a node. Hence, when the job of a subtask is to find a single node, it makes sense to implement the subtask as a method that returns a reference to that node. Our next method follows this pattern, returning a reference to a node that contains a specified element. The specification is given here:

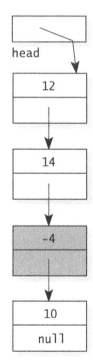

listSearch

♦ **listSearch**

> `public static IntNode listSearch(IntNode head, int target)`
> Search for a particular piece of data in a linked list.
> **Parameters:**
>> head – the head reference for a linked list (which may be an empty list with a null head)
>> target – a piece of data to search for
> **Returns:**
>> The return value is a reference to the first node that contains the specified target. If there is no such node, the null reference is returned.

As indicated by the return type of IntNode, the method returns a reference to a node in a linked list. The node is specified by a parameter named target, which is the integer that appears in the sought-after node. For example, the activation IntNode.listSearch(head, -4) in Figure 4.5 will return a reference to the shaded node.

Sometimes, the specified target does not appear in the list. In this case, the method returns the null reference.

The implementation of listSearch is shown in Figure 4.6. Most of the work is carried out with the usual traversal pattern, using a local variable called cursor to step through the nodes one at a time:

```
for (cursor = head; cursor != null; cursor = cursor.link)
{
    if (target == the data in the node that cursor refers to)
        return cursor;
}
```

FIGURE 4.5
Example for
listSearch

As the loop executes, cursor refers to the nodes of the list, one after another. The test inside the loop determines whether we have found the sought-after node, and if so, a reference to the node is immediately returned with the return

---

FIGURE 4.6   A Static Method to Search for a Target in a Linked List

Implementation

```
public static IntNode listSearch(IntNode head, int target)
{
    IntNode cursor;

    for (cursor = head; cursor != null; cursor = cursor.link)
        if (target == cursor.data)
            return cursor;

    return null;
}
```

---

statement `return cursor`. When a return statement occurs like this inside a loop, the method returns without ado, and the loop is not run to completion.

On the other hand, should the loop actually complete by eventually setting `cursor` to `null`, then the sought-after node is not in the list. According to the method's postcondition, the method returns `null` when the node is not in the list. This is accomplished with one more return statement— `return null`—at the end of the method's implementation.

Finding a Node by Its Position in a Linked List

Here's another method that returns a reference to a node in a linked list:

listPosition

♦ **listPosition**

    `public static IntNode listPosition(IntNode head, int position)`

    Find a node at a specified position in a linked list.

Parameters:

    head – the head reference for a linked list (which may be an empty list with a null head)

    position – a node number

Precondition:

    `position > 0`

Returns:

    The return value is a reference to the node at the specified position in the list. (The head node is position 1, the next node is position 2, and so on.) If there is no such position (because the list is too short), then the null reference is returned.

Throws: `IllegalArgumentException`

    Indicates that `position` is not positive.

In this method, a node is specified by giving its position in the list, with the head node at position 1, the next node at position 2, and so on. For example, with the linked list from Figure 4.7, `IntNode.listPosition(head, 3)` will return a reference to the shaded node. Notice that the first node is number 1, not number 0 as in an array. The specified position might also be larger than the length of the list, in which case the method returns the null reference.

The implementation of `listPosition` is shown in Figure 4.8. It uses a variation of the list traversal technique we have already seen. This variation is useful when we want to move to a particular node in a linked list and we know the ordinal position of the node (such as position number 1, position number 2, and so on). We start by setting a reference variable, `cursor`, to the head node of the list. A loop then moves the `cursor` forward the correct number of spots, as shown here:

```
cursor = head;
for (i = 1; (i < position) && (cursor != null); i++)
    cursor = cursor.link;
```

Each iteration of the loop executes `cursor = cursor.link` to move the cursor forward one node. Normally, the loop stops when i reaches `position` and `cursor` refers to the correct node. The loop can also stop if `cursor` becomes `null`, indicating that `position` was larger than the number of nodes in the list.

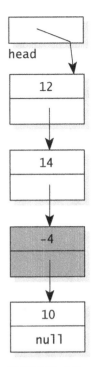

FIGURE 4.7
Example for
`listPosition`

FIGURE 4.8   A Static Method to Find a Particular Position in a Linked List

Implementation

```
public static IntNode listPosition(IntNode head, int position)
{
    IntNode cursor;
    int i;

    if (position <= 0)
        throw new IllegalArgumentException("position is not positive.");

    cursor = head;
    for (i = 1; (i < position) && (cursor != null); i++)
        cursor = cursor.link;

    return cursor;
}
```

Copying a Linked List

Our next static method makes a copy of a linked list, returning a head reference for the newly created copy. Here is the specification:

listCopy

♦ **listCopy**

```
public static IntNode listCopy(IntNode source)
```
Copy a list.

Parameter:
source – the head reference for a linked list that will be copied (which may be an empty list where source is null)

Returns:
The method has made a copy of the linked list starting at source. The return value is the head reference for the copy.

Throws: OutOfMemoryError
Indicates that there is insufficient memory for the new list.

For example, suppose that source refers to the following list:

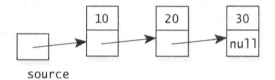

source

The listCopy method creates a completely separate copy of the three-node list. The copy of the list has its own three nodes, which also contain the numbers 10, 20, and 30. The return value is a head reference for the new list, and the original list remains intact.

The pseudocode begins by handling one special case—the case in which the original list is empty (so that source is null). In this case the method simply returns null, indicating that its answer is the empty list. So, the first step of the pseudocode is:

1. if (source == null), then return null.

After dealing with the special case, the method uses two local variables called copyHead and copyTail, which will be maintained as the head and tail references for the new list. The pseudocode for creating this new list is given in Step 2 through Step 4 on the top of the next page.

2. Create a new node for the head node of the new list we are creating. Make both `copyHead` and `copyTail` refer to this new node, which contains the same data as the head node of the source list.

3. Make `source` refer to the second node of the original list, then the third node, then the fourth node, and so on, until we have traversed all of the original list. At each node that `source` refers to, add one new node to the tail of the new list and move `copyTail` forward to the newly added node, as follows:

```
copyTail.addNodeAfter(source.data);
copyTail = copyTail.link;
```

4. After Step 3 completes, return `copyHead` (a reference to the head node of the list we created).

Step 3 of the pseudocode is completely implemented by this loop:

```
while (source.link != null)
{   // There are more nodes, so copy the next one.
    source = source.link;
    copyTail.addNodeAfter(source.data);
    copyTail = copyTail.link;
}
```

The while-loop starts by checking `source.link != null` to determine whether there is another node to copy. If there is another node, then we enter the body of the loop and move `source` forward with the assignment statement `source = source.link`. The second and third statements in the loop add a node at the tail end of the newly created list and move `copyTail` forward.

As an example, consider again the three-node list with data 10, 20, and 30. The first two steps of the pseudocode are carried out, and then we enter the body of the while-loop. We execute the first statement of the loop: `source = source.link`. At this point, the variables look like this:

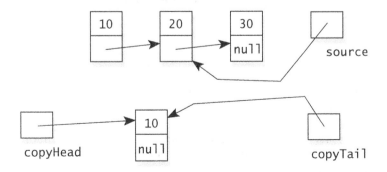

Notice that we have already copied the first node of the linked list. During the first iteration of the while-loop, we will copy the second node of the linked list—the node that is now referred to by source. The first part of copying the node works by activating one of our other methods, addNodeAfter:

```
copyTail.addNodeAfter(source.data);
```

This activation adds a new node to the end of the list we are creating (i.e., *after* the node referred to by copyTail), and the data in the new node is the number 20 (i.e., the data from source.data). Immediately after adding the new node, the variables look like this:

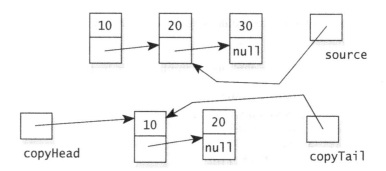

The last statement in the while-loop body moves copyTail forward to the new tail of the new list:

```
copyTail = copyTail.link;
```

This is the usual way in which we make a node reference "move to the next node," as we have seen in other methods, such as listSearch. After moving copyTail, the variables look like this:

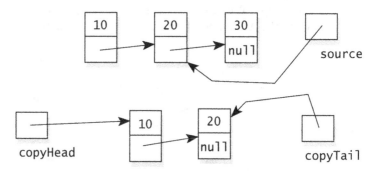

In this example, the body of the while-loop will execute one more time to copy the third node to the new list. Then the loop will end, and the method will return the new head reference, copyHead.

| **FIGURE 4.9** | A Static Method to Copy a Linked List |

Implementation

```
public static IntNode listCopy(IntNode source)
{
    IntNode copyHead;
    IntNode copyTail;

    // Handle the special case of an empty list.
    if (source == null)
        return null;

    // Make the first node for the newly created list.
    copyHead = new IntNode(source.data, null);
    copyTail = copyHead;

    // Make the rest of the nodes for the newly created list.
    while (source.link != null)
    {
        source = source.link;
        copyTail.addNodeAfter(source.data);
        copyTail = copyTail.link;
    }

    // Return the head reference for the new list.
    return copyHead;
}
```

The complete implementation of listCopy is shown in Figure 4.9.
Here's an example of how the listCopy method might be used in a program:

```
IntNode shortList;
IntNode copy;

shortList = new IntNode(10, null);
shortList.addNodeAfter(20);
shortList.addNodeAfter(20);
```

At this point, `shortList` is the head of a small list shown here:

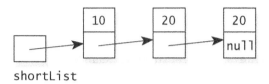

shortList

We could now use `listCopy` to make a second copy of this list:

```
copy = IntNode.listCopy(shortList);
```

Now we have two separate lists:

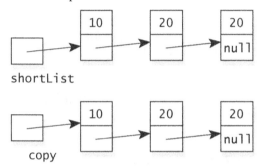

shortList

copy

why is listCopy a static method?

Keep in mind that `listCopy` is a static method, so we must write the expression `IntNode.listCopy(shortList)` rather than `shortList.listCopy( )`. This may seem strange—why not make `listCopy` an ordinary method? The answer is that an ordinary method could not copy the empty list (because the empty list is represented by the null reference).

A Second Copy Method, Returning Both Head and Tail References

Here's a second way to copy a list, with a slightly different specification:

listCopyWithTail

♦ **listCopyWithTail**
    `public static IntNode[ ] listCopyWithTail(IntNode source)`
    Copy a list, returning both a head and tail reference for the copy.
    Parameter:
        source – the head reference for a linked list that will be copied (which
            may be an empty list where source is null)
    Returns:
        The method has made a copy of the linked list starting at source. The
        return value is an array where the [0] element is a head reference for the
        copy and the [1] element is a tail reference for the copy.
    Throws: `OutOfMemoryError`
        Indicates that there is insufficient memory for the new list.

The `listCopyWithTail` method makes a copy of a list, but the return value is more than a head reference for the copy. Instead, the return value is an array with two components. The `[0]` component of the array contains the head reference for the new list, and the `[1]` component contains the tail reference for the new list. The `listCopyWithTail` method is important because many algorithms must copy a list and obtain access to both the head and tail nodes of the copy.

As an example, a program can create a small list and then create a copy with both a head and tail reference for the copy:

```
IntNode shortList;
IntNode copyInfo[ ];

shortList = new IntNode(10, null);
shortList.addNodeAfter(20);
shortList.addNodeAfter(20);
copyInfo = IntNode.listCopyWithTail(source);
```

At this point, `copyInfo[0]` is the head reference for a copy of the short list, and `copyInfo[1]` is the tail reference for the same list:

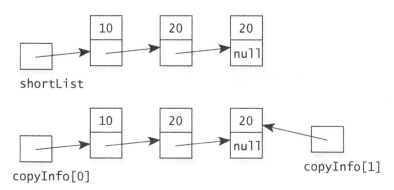

The implementation of `listCopyWithTail` is shown in the first part of Figure 4.10. It's nearly the same as `listCopy`, except there is an extra local variable called `answer`, which is an array of two `IntNode` components. These two components are set to the head and tail of the new list, and the method finishes with the return statement: `return answer`.

🎧 Programming Tip

A Method Can Return an Array

The return value from a method can be an array. This is useful when the method returns more than one piece of information. For example, `listCopyWithTail` returns an array with two components, containing the head and tail references for a new list.

FIGURE 4.10   A Second Static Method to Copy a Linked List

Implementation

```
public static IntNode[ ] listCopyWithTail(IntNode source)
{
    // Notice that the return value is an array of two IntNode components.
    // The [0] component is the head reference for the new list and
    // the [1] component is the tail reference for the new list.
    // Also notice that the answer array is automatically initialized to contain
    // two null values. Arrays with components that are references are always
    // initialized this way.
    IntNode copyHead;
    IntNode copyTail;
    IntNode[ ] answer = new IntNode[2];

    // Handle the special case of an empty list.
    if (source == null)
        return answer; // The answer has two null references.

    // Make the first node for the newly created list.
    copyHead = new IntNode(source.data, null);
    copyTail = copyHead;

    // Make the rest of the nodes for the newly created list.
    while (source.link != null)
    {
        source = source.link;
        copyTail.addNodeAfter(source.data);
        copyTail = copyTail.link;
    }

    // Return the head and tail references for the new list.
    answer[0] = copyHead;
    answer[1] = copyTail;
    return answer;
}
```

Copying Part of a Linked List

Sometimes a program needs to copy only part of a linked list rather than the entire list. The task can be done by a static method, listPart, which copies part of a list, as specified next.

◆ **listPart**

```
public static IntNode[ ] listPart
  (IntNode start, IntNode end)
```
Copy part of a list, providing a head and tail reference for the new copy.

Parameters:
start and end – references to two nodes of a linked list

Precondition:
start and end are non-null references to nodes on the same linked list, with the start node at or before the end node.

Returns:
The method has made a copy of part of a linked list, from the specified start node to the specified end node. The return value is an array in which the [0] component is a head reference for the copy and the [1] component is a tail reference for the copy.

Throws: IllegalArgumentException
Indicates that start and end do not satisfy the precondition.

Throws: OutOfMemoryError
Indicates that there is insufficient memory for the new list.

The listPart implementation is given as part of the complete IntNode class in Figure 4.11. In all, there is one constructor, five ordinary methods, and six static methods. The class is placed in a package called edu.colorado.nodes.

Using Linked Lists

Any program can use linked lists created from our nodes. Such a program must have this import statement:

```
import edu.colorado.nodes.IntNode;
```

The program can then use the various methods to build and manipulate linked lists. In fact, the edu.colorado.nodes package includes many different kinds of nodes: IntNode, DoubleNode, CharNode, etc. You can get these classes from http://www.cs.colorado.edu/~main/edu/colorado/nodes. (There is also a special kind of node that can handle many different kinds of data, but you'll have to wait until Chapter 5 for that.)

nodes with different kinds of data

To use our nodes, a programmer must have some understanding of linked lists and of our specific nodes. This is because we intend to use the node classes ourselves to build various collection classes. The different collection classes we build can be used by any programmer, with no knowledge of nodes and linked lists. This is what we will do in the rest of the chapter, providing two ADTs that use the linked lists.

| **FIGURE 4.11** | Specification and Implementation of the IntNode Class |

Class IntNode

❖ **public class IntNode from the package edu.colorado.nodes**

An IntNode provides a node for a linked list with integer data in each node. Lists can be of any length, limited only by the amount of free memory on the heap. But beyond Integer.MAX_VALUE, the answer from listLength is incorrect because of arithmetic overflow.

Specification

◆ **Constructor for the IntNode**

```
public IntNode(int initialData, IntNode initialLink)
```

Initialize a node with specified initial data and a link to the next node. Note that the initialLink may be the null reference, which indicates that the new node has nothing after it.

Parameters:

initialData – the initial data of this new node

initialLink – a reference to the node after this new node (this reference may be null to indicate that there is no node after this new node)

Postcondition:

This new node contains the specified data and a link to the next node.

◆ **addNodeAfter**

```
public void addNodeAfter(int element)
```

Modification method to add a new node after this node.

Parameters:

element – the data to be placed in the new node

Postcondition:

A new node has been created and placed after this node. The data for the new node is element. Any other nodes that used to be after this node are now after the new node.

Throws: OutOfMemoryError

Indicates that there is insufficient memory for a new IntNode.

◆ **getData**

```
public int getData( )
```

Accessor method to get the data from this node.

Returns:

the data from this node

◆ **getLink**

```
public IntNode getLink( )
```

Accessor method to get a reference to the next node after this node.

Returns:

a reference to the node after this node (or the null reference if there is nothing after this node)

(FIGURE 4.11 continued)

♦ listCopy

```
public static IntNode listCopy(IntNode source)
```

Copy a list.

Parameter:

source – the head reference for a linked list that will be copied (which may be an empty list where source is null)

Returns:

The method has made a copy of the linked list starting at source. The return value is the head reference for the copy.

Throws: OutOfMemoryError

Indicates that there is insufficient memory for the new list.

♦ listCopyWithTail

```
public static IntNode[ ] listCopyWithTail(IntNode source)
```

Copy a list, returning both a head and tail reference for the copy.

Parameters:

source – the head reference for a linked list that will be copied (which may be an empty list where source is null)

Returns:

The method has made a copy of the linked list starting at source. The return value is an array where the [0] element is a head reference for the copy and the [1] element is a tail reference for the copy.

Throws: OutOfMemoryError

Indicates that there is insufficient memory for the new list.

♦ listLength

```
public static int listLength(IntNode head)
```

Compute the number of nodes in a linked list.

Parameter:

head – the head reference for a linked list (which may be an empty list with a null head)

Returns:

the number of nodes in the list with the given head

Note:

A wrong answer occurs for lists longer than Int.MAX_VALUE because of arithmetic overflow.

(continued)

(FIGURE 4.11 continued)

◆ listPart

```
public static IntNode[ ] listPart(IntNode start, IntNode end)
```
Copy part of a list, providing a head and tail reference for the new copy.

Parameters:
   start and end – references to two nodes of a linked list

Precondition:
   start and end are non-null references to nodes on the same linked list, with the start node at or before the end node.

Returns:
   The method has made a copy of part of a linked list, from the specified start node to the specified end node. The return value is an array where the [0] component is a head reference for the copy and the [1] component is a tail reference for the copy.

Throws: IllegalArgumentException
   Indicates that start and end do not satisfy the precondition.

Throws: OutOfMemoryError
   Indicates that there is insufficient memory for the new list.

◆ listPosition

```
public static IntNode listPosition(IntNode head, int position)
```
Find a node at a specified position in a linked list.

Parameters:
   head – the head reference for a linked list (which may be an empty list with a null head)
   position – a node number

Precondition:
   position > 0

Returns:
   The return value is a reference to the node at the specified position in the list. (The head node is position 1, the next node is position 2, and so on.) If there is no such position (because the list is too short), then the null reference is returned.

Throws: IllegalArgumentException
   Indicates that position is 0.

◆ listSearch

```
public static IntNode listSearch(IntNode head, int target)
```
Search for a particular piece of data in a linked list.

Parameters:
   head – the head reference for a linked list (which may be an empty list with a null head)
   target – a piece of data to search for

Returns:
   The return value is a reference to the first node that contains the specified target. If there is no such node, the null reference is returned.

(continued)

(FIGURE 4.11 continued)

♦ **removeNodeAfter**

```
public void removeNodeAfter( )
```
Modification method to remove the node after this node.

Precondition:
This node must not be the tail node of the list.

Postcondition:
The node after this node has been removed from the linked list. If there were further nodes after that one, they are still present on the list.

Throws: `NullPointerException`
Indicates that this was the tail node of the list, so there is nothing after it to remove.

♦ **setData**

```
public void setData(int newdata)
```
Modification method to set the data in this node.

Parameters:
newData – the new data to place in this node

Postcondition:
The data of this node has been set to `newData`.

♦ **setLink**

```
public void setLink(IntNode newLink)
```
Modification method to set a reference to the next node after this node.

Parameters:
newLink – a reference to the node that should appear after this node in the linked list (or the null reference if there should be no node after this node)

Postcondition:
The link to the node after this node has been set to `newLink`. Any other node (that used to be in this link) is no longer connected to this node.

Implementation

```
// File: IntNode.java from the package edu.colorado.nodes
// Documentation is available from pages 208-211 or from the IntNode link at
// http://www.cs.colorado.edu/~main/docs/.

package edu.colorado.nodes;
```

(continued)

(FIGURE 4.11 continued)

```java
public class IntNode
{
    // Invariant of the IntNode class:
    //   1. The node's integer data is in the instance variable data.
    //   2. For the final node of a list, the link part is null.
    //      Otherwise, the link part is a reference to the next node of the list.
    private int data;
    private IntNode link;

    public IntNode(int initialData, IntNode initialLink)
    {
        data = initialData;
        link = initialLink;
    }

    public void addNodeAfter(int element)
    {
        link = new IntNode(element, link);
    }

    public int getData( )
    {
        return data;
    }

    public IntNode getLink( )
    {
        return link;
    }

    public static IntNode listCopy(IntNode source)
    || See the implementation in Figure 4.9 on page 203.

    public static IntNode[ ] listCopyWithTail(IntNode source)
    || See the implementation in Figure 4.10 on page 206.

    public static int listLength(IntNode head)
    || See the implementation in Figure 4.4 on page 195.
```

(continued)

(FIGURE 4.11 continued)

```java
public static IntNode[ ] listPart(IntNode start, IntNode end)
{
    // Notice that the return value is an array of two IntNode components.
    // The [0] component is the head reference for the new list,
    // and the [1] component is the tail reference for the new list.
    IntNode copyHead;
    IntNode copyTail;
    IntNode[ ] answer = new IntNode[2];

    // Check for illegal null at start or end.
    if (start == null)
        throw new IllegalArgumentException("start is null");
    if (end == null)
        throw new IllegalArgumentException("end is null");

    // Make the first node for the newly created list.
    copyHead = new IntNode(start.data, null);
    copyTail = copyHead;

    // Make the rest of the nodes for the newly created list.
    while (start != end)
    {
        start = start.link;
        if (start == null)
            throw new IllegalArgumentException
            ("end node was not found on the list");
        copyTail.addNodeAfter(start.data);
        copyTail = copyTail.link;
    }

    // Return the head and tail reference for the new list.
    answer[0] = copyHead;
    answer[1] = copyTail;
    return answer;
}
```

```java
public static IntNode listPosition(IntNode head, int position)
|| See the implementation in Figure 4.8 on page 199.
```

```java
public static IntNode listSearch(IntNode head, int target)
|| See the implementation in Figure 4.6 on page 198.
```

(continued)

(FIGURE 4.11 continued)

```
public void removeNodeAfter( )
{
    link = link.link;
}

public void setData(int newData)
{
    data = newData;
}

public void setLink(IntNode newLink)
{
    link = newLink;
}
}
```

Self-Test Exercises for Section 4.3

11. Look at http://www.cs.colorado.edu/~main/edu/colorado/nodes. How many different kinds of nodes are there? If you implemented one of these nodes, what extra work would be required to implement another?

12. Suppose locate is a reference to a node in a linked list (and it is not the null reference). Write an assignment statement that will make locate move to the next node in the list. You should write two versions of the assignment—one that can appear in the IntNode class itself and another that can appear outside of the class. What do your assignment statements do if locate was already referring to the last node in the list?

13. Which of the node methods use new to allocate at least one new node? Check your answer by looking at the documentation in Figure 4.11 on page 208 (to see which methods can throw an OutOfMemoryError).

14. Suppose head is a head reference for a linked list with just one node. What will head be after head = head.getLink( )?

15. What technique would you use if a method needs to return more than one IntNode, such as a method that returns both a head and tail reference for a list.

16. Suppose head is a head reference for a linked list. Also suppose douglass and adams are two other IntNode variables. Write one assignment statement that will make douglass refer to the first node in the list that contains the number 42. Write a second assignment statement that will make adams refer to the 42nd node of the list. If these nodes don't exist, then the assignments should set the variables to null.

17. Suppose a program sets up a linked list with an `IntNode` variable called head to refer to the first node of the list (or head is `null` if the list is empty). Write a few lines of Java code that will print all the numbers.

18. Implement a new static method for the `IntNode` class with one parameter that is a head reference for a linked list. The return value of the method is the number of times that the number 42 appears on the list.

19. Implement a new static method for the `IntNode` class with one parameter that is a head reference for a linked list. The return value of the method is a boolean value that is true if the list contains at least one copy of 42; otherwise, it is false.

20. Implement a new static method for the `IntNode` class with one parameter that is a head reference for a linked list. The return value of the method is the sum of all the numbers on the list.

21. Implement a new static method for the `IntNode` class with one parameter that is a head reference for a linked list. The function adds a new node to the tail of the list with the data equal to 42.

22. Implement a new static method for the `IntNode` class with one parameter that is a head reference for a linked list. The method removes the first node after the head that contains the number 42 (if there is such a node). Do not call any other methods to do any of the work.

23. Suppose p, q, and r are all references to nodes in a linked list with 15 nodes. The variable p refers to the first node, q refers to the 8th node, and r refers to the last node. Write a few lines of code that will make a new copy of the list. Your code should set *three* new variables called x, y, and z so that x refers to the first node of the copy, y refers to the 8th node of the copy, and z refers to the last node of the copy. Your code may not contain any loops, but it can use the other `IntNode` methods.

4.4   THE BAG ADT WITH A LINKED LIST

We're ready to write an ADT that is implemented with a linked list. We'll start with the familiar bag ADT, which we previously implemented with an array (in Section 3.2). At the end of this chapter, we'll compare the advantages and disadvantages of these different implementations. But first, let's see how a linked list is used in our second bag implementation.

Our Second Bag—Specification

The advantage of using a familiar ADT is that you already know most of the specification. The specification, given in Figure 4.12, is nearly identical to our previous bag. The major difference is that our new bag has no worries about capacity: There is no initial capacity and no need for an `ensureCapacity` method. This is because our planned implementation—storing the bag's elements on a linked list—can easily grow and shrink by adding and removing nodes from the linked list.

the new bag class is called IntLinkedBag

The new bag class will be called `IntLinkedBag`, meaning that the underlying elements are integers, the implementation will use a linked list, and the collection itself is a bag. The `IntLinkedBag` will be placed in the same package that we used in Chapter 3, `edu.colorado.collections`, as shown in the specification of Figure 4.12.

FIGURE 4.12   Specification and Implementation of the `IntLinkedBag` Class

Class IntLinkedBag

❖ **public class IntLinkedBag from the package edu.colorado.collections**
An `IntLinkedBag` is a collection of `int` numbers.
Limitations:
   (1) Beyond `Int.MAX_VALUE` elements, `countOccurrences`, `size`, and `grab` are wrong.
   (2) Because of the slow linear algorithms of this class, large bags have poor performance.

Specification

◆ **Constructor for the IntLinkedBag**
   `public IntLinkedBag( )`
   Initialize an empty bag.
   Postcondition:
   This bag is empty.

◆ **add**
   `public void add(int element)`
   Add a new element to this bag.
   Parameter:
   `element` – the new element that is being added
   Postcondition:
   A new copy of the element has been added to this bag.
   Throws: `OutOfMemoryError`
   Indicates insufficient memory for adding a new element.

(continued)

(FIGURE 4.12 continued)

♦ **addAll**

```
public void addAll(IntLinkedBag addend)
```
Add the contents of another bag to this bag.

Parameter:

addend – a bag whose contents will be added to this bag

Precondition:

The parameter, addend, is not null.

Postcondition:

The elements from addend have been added to this bag.

Throws: NullPointerException

Indicates that addend is null.

Throws: OutOfMemoryError

Indicates insufficient memory to increase the size of this bag.

♦ **addMany**

```
public void addMany(int... elements)
```
Add a variable number of new elements to this bag. If these new elements would take this bag beyond its current capacity, then the capacity is increased before adding the new elements.

Parameter:

elements – a variable number of new elements that are all being added

Postcondition:

New copies of all the elements have been added to this bag.

Throws: OutOfMemoryError

Indicates insufficient memory to increase the size of this bag.

♦ **clone**

```
public IntLinkedBag clone( )
```
Generate a copy of this bag.

Returns:

The return value is a copy of this bag. Subsequent changes to the copy will not affect the original, nor vice versa. The return value must be typecast to an IntLinkedBag before it is used.

Throws: OutOfMemoryError

Indicates insufficient memory for creating the clone.

♦ **countOccurrences**

```
public int countOccurrences(int target)
```
Accessor method to count the number of occurrences of a particular element in this bag.

Parameter:

target – the element that needs to be counted

Returns:

the number of times that target occurs in this bag

(continued)

(FIGURE 4.12 continued)

♦ **grab**

    `public int grab( )`

    Accessor method to retrieve a random element from this bag.

    Precondition:

      This bag is not empty.

    Returns:

      a randomly selected element from this bag

    Throws: `IllegalStateException`

      Indicates that the bag is empty.

♦ **remove**

    `public boolean remove(int target)`

    Remove one copy of a specified element from this bag.

    Parameter:

      `target` – the element to remove from the bag

    Postcondition:

      If `target` was found in this bag, then one copy of `target` has been removed, and the method
      returns `true`. Otherwise, this bag remains unchanged, and the method returns `false`.

♦ **size**

    `public int size( )`

    Accessor method to determine the number of elements in this bag.

    Returns:

      the number of elements in this bag

♦ **union**

    `public static IntLinkedBag union(IntLinkedBag b1, IntLinkedBag b2)`

    Create a new bag that contains all the elements from two other bags.

    Parameters:

      `b1` – the first of two bags
      `b2` – the second of two bags

    Precondition:

      Neither `b1` nor `b2` is null.

    Returns:

      a new bag that is the union of `b1` and `b2`

    Throws: `NullPointerException`

      Indicates that one of the arguments is null.

    Throws: `OutOfMemoryError`

      Indicates insufficient memory for the new bag.

The grab Method

The new bag has one other minor change, which is specified as part of Figure 4.12: Just for fun, we've included a new method called grab, which returns a randomly selected element from a bag. Later we'll use the grab method in some game-playing programs.

Our Second Bag—Class Declaration

Our plan has been laid. We will implement the new bag by storing the elements in a linked list. The class will have two private instance variables: (1) a reference to the head of a linked list that contains the elements of the bag, and (2) an int variable that keeps track of the length of the list. The second instance variable isn't really needed, because we could use listLength to determine the length of the list. But by keeping the length in an instance variable, the length can be quickly determined by accessing the variable (a constant time operation). This is in contrast to actually counting the length by traversing the list (a linear time operation).

In any case, we can now write an outline for our implementation. The class goes in the package edu.colorado.collections, and we import the node class from edu.colorado.nodes.IntNode. Then we declare our new bag class with two instance variables:

```
package edu.colorado.collections;
import edu.colorado.nodes.IntNode;

class IntLinkedBag
{
    private IntNode head;        // Head reference for the list
    private int manyNodes;       // Number of nodes in the list

    || Method implementations will be placed here later.
}
```

To avoid confusion over how we are using our linked list, we now make an explicit statement of the invariant for our second design of the bag ADT.

Invariant for the Second Bag ADT

1. The elements in the bag are stored in a linked list.
2. The head reference of the list is stored in the instance variable head.
3. The total number of elements in the list is stored in the instance variable manyNodes.

The Second Bag—Implementation

With our invariant in mind, we can implement each of the methods, starting with the constructor. The key to simple implementations is to use the node methods whenever possible.

Constructor. The constructor sets head to be the null reference (indicating the empty list) and sets manyNodes to 0. Actually, these two values (null and zero) are the default values for the instance variables, so one possibility is to not implement the constructor at all. When we implement no constructor, Java provides an automatic no-arguments constructor that initializes all instance variables to their default values. If we take this approach, then our implementation should include a comment to indicate that we are using Java's automatic no-arguments constructor.

However, we will actually implement the constructor:

constructor

```java
public IntLinkedBag( )
{
    head = null;
    manyNodes = 0;
}
```

Having an actual implementation makes it easier to make future changes. Also, without the implementation, we could not include a Javadoc comment to specify exactly what the constructor does.

The clone Method. The clone method needs to create a copy of a bag. The IntLinkedBag clone method will follow the pattern introduced in Chapter 2 on page 82. Therefore, the start of the clone method is the code shown here:

clone method

```java
public IntLinkedBag clone( )
{   // Clone an IntLinkedBag.
    IntLinkedBag answer;

    try
    {
        answer = (IntLinkedBag) super.clone( );
    }
    catch (CloneNotSupportedException e)
    {   // This exception should not occur. But if it does, it would
        // probably indicate a programming error that made
        // super.clone unavailable. The most common error would be
        // forgetting the "Implements Cloneable" clause.
        throw new RuntimeException
        ("This class does not implement Cloneable.");
    }
    ...
```

This is the same as the start of the `clone` method for our Chapter 3 bag. As with the Chapter 3 bag, this code uses the `super.clone` method to make `answer` be an exact copy of the bag that activated the `clone` method. With the Chapter 3 bag, we needed some extra statements at the end of the `clone` method; otherwise, the original bag and the clone would share the same array.

Our new bag, using a linked list, runs into a similar problem. To see this problem, consider a bag that contains three elements:

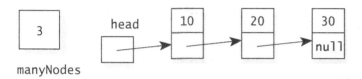

Now suppose we activate `clone( )` to create a copy of this bag. The clone method executes the statement `answer = (IntLinkedBag) super.clone( )`. What does `super.clone( )` do? It creates a new `IntLinkedBag` object, and `answer` will refer to this new `IntLinkedBag`. But the new `IntLinkedBag` has instance variables (`answer.manyNodes` and `answer.head`) that are merely copied from the original. So, after `answer = (IntLinkedBag) super.clone( )`, the situation looks like this (where `manyNodes` and `head` are the instance variables from the original bag that activated the `clone` method):

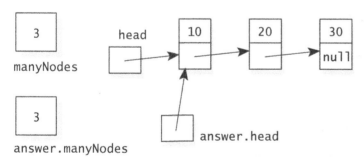

As you can see, `answer.head` refers to the original's head node. Subsequent changes to the linked list will affect both the original and the clone. This is incorrect behavior for a clone. To fix the problem, we need an additional statement before the return of the `clone` method. The purpose of the statement is to create a new linked list for the clone's head instance variable to refer to. Here's the statement:

```
answer.head = IntNode.listCopy(head);
```

This statement activates the `listCopy` method. The argument, `head`, is the head reference from the linked list of the bag we are copying. When the assignment

statement finishes, answer.head will refer to the head node of the new list.
Here's the situation after the copying:

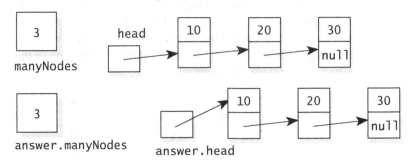

The new linked list for answer was created by copying the original linked list.
Subsequent changes to answer will not affect the original, nor will changes to
the original affect answer. The complete clone method, including the extra
statement at the end, is shown in Figure 4.13.

FIGURE 4.13 Implementation of the Second Bag's clone Method

Implementation

```
public IntLinkedBag clone( )
{
    // Clone an IntLinkedBag.
    IntLinkedBag answer;

    try
    {
        answer = (IntLinkedBag) super.clone( );
    }
    catch (CloneNotSupportedException e)
    {   // This exception should not occur. But if it does, it would probably indicate a
        // programming error that made super.clone unavailable. The most common
        // error would be forgetting the "Implements Cloneable"
        // clause at the start of this class.
        throw new RuntimeException
            ("This class does not implement Cloneable.");
    }

    answer.head = IntNode.listCopy(head);

    return answer;
}
```

*This step creates a new
linked list for answer. The
new linked list is
separate from the original
array so that subsequent
changes to one will not
affect the other.*

CLONING A CLASS THAT CONTAINS A LINKED LIST

If the instance variables of a class contain a linked list, then the clone method needs extra work before it returns. The extra work creates a new linked list for the clone's instance variable to refer to.

The remove Method. There are two approaches to implementing the remove method. The first approach uses the removal methods we have already seen—changing the head if the removed element is at the head of the list and using the ordinary removeNodeAfter to remove an element that is farther down the line. This first approach is fine, although it does require a bit of thought because removeNodeAfter requires a reference to the node that is just *before* the element you want to remove. We could certainly find this "before" node, but not by using the node's listSearch method.

The second approach actually uses listSearch to obtain a reference to the node that contains the element to be deleted. For example, suppose our target is the number 42 in this bag:

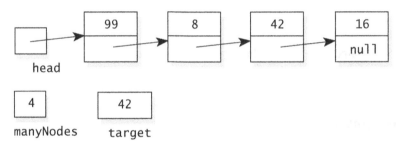

Our approach begins by setting a local variable named targetNode to refer to the node that contains our target. This is accomplished with the assignment targetNode = listSearch(head, target). After the assignment, the targetNode is set this way:

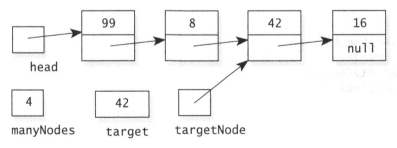

Now we can remove the target from the list with two more steps. First, copy the data from the head node to the target node, as shown at the top of the next page.

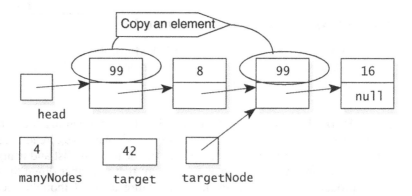

After this step, we have certainly removed the target, but we are left with two 99s. So, we proceed to a second step: Remove the head node (that is, one of the copies of 99). These steps are all implemented in the remove method shown in Figure 4.14. The only other steps in the implementation are a test to ensure that the target is actually in the bag and subtracting 1 from manyNodes.

FIGURE 4.14   A Method to Remove an Element from the Second Version of the Bag

---

Implementation

```
public boolean remove(int target)
{
    IntNode targetNode; // The node that contains the target

    targetNode = IntNode.listSearch(head, target);
    if (targetNode == null)
        // The target was not found, so nothing is removed.
        return false;
    else
    {   // The target was found at targetNode. So copy the head data to targetNode
        // and then remove the extra copy of the head data.
        targetNode.setData(head.getData( ));
        head = head.getLink( );
        manyNodes--;
        return true;
    }
}
```

PROGRAMMING TIP

HOW TO CHOOSE BETWEEN DIFFERENT APPROACHES

We have two possible approaches for the remove method. How do we select the better approach? Normally, when two different approaches have equal efficiency, we will choose the approach that makes better use of the node's methods. This saves us work and also reduces the chance of new errors from writing new code to do an old job. In the case of remove, we chose the second approach because it made better use of listSearch.

The countOccurrences Method.   Two possible approaches come to mind for the countOccurrences method. One of the approaches simply steps through the linked list one node at a time, checking each piece of data to see whether it is the sought-after target. We count the occurrences of the target and return the answer. The second approach uses listSearch to find the first occurrence of the target, then uses listSearch again to find the next occurrence, and so on, until we have found all occurrences of the target. The second approach makes better use of the node's methods, so that is the approach we will take.

As an example of the second approach to the countOccurrences method, suppose we want to count the number of occurrences of 42 in this bag:

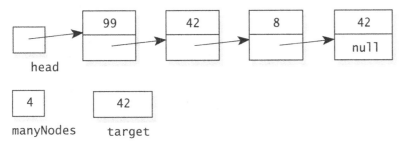

We'll use two local variables: answer, which keeps track of the number of occurrences we have seen so far, and cursor, which is a reference to a node in the list. We initialize answer to 0, and we use listSearch to make cursor refer to the first occurrence of the target (or to be null if there are no occurrences). After this initialization, we have this situation:

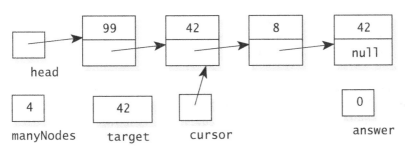

Next we enter a loop. The loop stops when `cursor` becomes `null`, indicating that there are no more occurrences of the target. Each time through the loop we do two steps: (1) Add 1 to `answer`, and (2) move `cursor` to refer to the next occurrence of the target (or to be `null` if there are no more occurrences). Can we use a node method to execute Step 2? At first, it might seem that the node methods are of no use since `listSearch` finds the *first* occurrence of a given target. But there is an approach that will use `listSearch` together with the `cursor` to find the *next* occurrence of the target. The approach begins by moving `cursor` to the next node in the list, using the statement `cursor = cursor.getLink( )`. In our example, this results in the following:

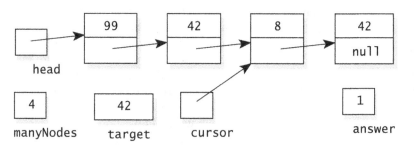

As you can see, `cursor` now refers to a node in the middle of a linked list. But any time that a variable refers to a node in the middle of a linked list, we can pretend that the node is the head of a smaller linked list. In our example, `cursor` refers to the head of a two-element list containing the numbers 8 and 42. Therefore, we can use `cursor` as an argument to `listSearch` in the assignment statement `cursor = IntNode.listSearch(cursor, target)`. This statement moves `cursor` to the next occurrence of the target. This occurrence could be at the `cursor`'s current spot, or it could be farther down the line. In our example, the next occurrence of 42 is farther down the line, so `cursor` is moved as shown here:

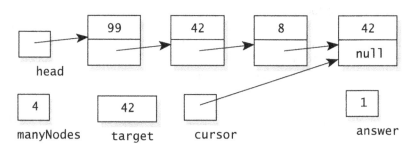

Eventually there will be no more occurrences of the target and `cursor` becomes `null`, ending the loop. At that point the method returns `answer`. The complete implementation of `countOccurrences` is shown in Figure 4.15.

FIGURE 4.15   Implementation of countOccurrences for the Second Version of the Bag

Implementation

```
public int countOccurrences(int target)
{
   int answer;
   IntNode cursor;

   answer = 0;
   cursor = IntNode.listSearch(head, target);
   while (cursor != null)
   {  // Each time that cursor is not null, we have another occurrence of target, so we
      // add 1 to answer and then move cursor to the next occurrence of the target.
      answer++;
      cursor = cursor.getLink( );
      cursor = IntNode.listSearch(cursor, target);
   }
   return answer;
}
```

Finding the Next Occurrence of an Element

The situation: A variable named cursor refers to a node in a linked list that contains a particular element called target.

The task: Make cursor refer to the next occurrence of target (or null if there are no more occurrences).

The solution:
```
    cursor = cursor.getLink( );
    cursor = IntNode.listSearch(cursor, target);
```

The grab Method. The bag has a new grab method, specified here:

◆ **grab**

```
public int grab( )
```
Accessor method to retrieve a random element from this bag.

Precondition:
This bag is not empty.

Returns:
a randomly selected element from this bag

Throws: IllegalStateException
Indicates that the bag is empty.

The implementation will start by generating a random int value between 1 and the size of the bag. The random value can then be used to select a node from the bag, and we'll return the data from the selected node. So the body of the method will look something like this:

```
i = some random int value between 1 and the size of the bag;
cursor = listPosition(head, i);
return cursor.getData( );
```

Of course, the trick is to generate "some random int value between 1 and the size of the bag." The Java Class Libraries can help. Within java.lang.math is a method that (sort of) generates random numbers, with this specification:

◆ **Math.random**

```
public static double random( )
```
Generates a pseudorandom number in the range 0.0 to 1.0.

Returns:
a pseudorandom number in the range 0.0 to 1.0 (this return value may be zero, but it's always less than 1.0)

The values returned by Math.random are not truly random. They are generated by a simple rule. But the numbers *appear* random, and so the method is referred to as a **pseudorandom number generator.** For most applications, a pseudorandom number generator is a close enough approximation to a true random number generator. In fact, a pseudorandom number generator has one advantage over a true random number generator: The sequence of numbers it produces is repeatable. If run twice with the same initial conditions, a pseudorandom number generator will produce exactly the same sequence of numbers. This is handy when you are debugging programs that use these sequences. When an error is discovered, the corrected program can be tested with the *same* sequence of pseudorandom numbers that produced the original error.

Math.random   But at this point we don't need a complete memoir on pseudorandom numbers. All we need is a way to use Math.random to generate a number between 1 and the size of the bag. The following assignment statement does the trick:

```
// Set i to a random number from 1 to the size of the bag:
i = (int) (Math.random( ) * manyNodes) + 1;
```

Let's look at how the expression works. The method `Math.random` gives us a number that's in the range 0.0 to 1.0. The value is actually in the "half-open range" of [0 .. 1), which means that the number could be from zero up to, but not including, 1. Therefore, the expression `Math.random( ) * manyNodes` is in the range zero to `manyNodes`—or to be more precise, from zero up to, but not including, `manyNodes`.

The operation `(int)` is an operation that truncates a double number, keeping only the integer part. Therefore, `(int) (Math.random( ) * manyNodes)` is an `int` value that could be from zero to `manyNodes-1`. The expression cannot actually be `manyNodes`. Since we want a number from 1 to `manyNodes`, we add 1, resulting in `i = (int) (Math.random( ) * manyNodes) + 1`. This assignment statement is used in the complete `grab` implementation shown in Figure 4.16.

The Second Bag—Putting the Pieces Together

The remaining methods are straightforward. For example, the `size` method just returns `manyNodes`. All these methods are given in the complete implementation in Figure 4.17. Take particular notice of how the bag's `addAll` method is implemented. The implementation makes a copy of the linked list for the bag that's being added. This copy is then attached at the front of the linked list for the bag that's being added to. The bag's `union` method is implemented by using the `addAll` method.

FIGURE 4.16 Implementation of a Method to Grab a Random Element

Implementation

```
public int grab( )
{
   int i; // A random value between 1 and the size of the bag
   IntNode cursor;

   if (manyNodes == 0)
      throw new IllegalStateException("Bag size is zero.");

   i =  (int) (Math.random( ) * manyNodes) + 1;
   cursor = IntNode.listPosition(head, i);
   return cursor.getData( );
}
```

FIGURE 4.17	Implementation of Our Second Bag Class

Implementation

```java
// FILE: IntLinkedBag.java from the package edu.colorado.collections
// Documentation is available in Figure 4.12 on page 216 or from the IntLinkedBag link at
// http://www.cs.colorado.edu/~main/docs/.

package edu.colorado.collections;
import edu.colorado.nodes.IntNode;

public class IntLinkedBag implements Cloneable
{
    // INVARIANT for the Bag ADT:
    //    1. The elements in the Bag are stored in a linked list.
    //    2. The head reference of the list is in the instance variable head.
    //    3. The total number of elements in the list is in the instance variable manyNodes.
    private IntNode head;
    private int manyNodes;

    public IntLinkedBag( )
    {
        head = null;
        manyNodes = 0;
    }

    public void add(int element)
    {
        head = new IntNode(element, head);
        manyNodes++;
    }

    public void addAll(IntLinkedBag addend)
    {
        IntNode[ ] copyInfo;

        if (addend == null)
            throw new IllegalArgumentException("addend is null.");
        if (addend.manyNodes > 0)
        {
            copyInfo = IntNode.listCopyWithTail(addend.head);
            copyInfo[1].setLink(head); // Link the tail of the copy to my own head...
            head = copyInfo[0];         // and set my own head to the head of the copy.
            manyNodes += addend.manyNodes;
        }
    }
```

(continued)

(FIGURE 4.17 continued)

```java
public void addMany(int... elements)
{
    // Activate the ordinary add method for each integer in the elements array.
    for (int i : elements)
        add(i);
}

public IntLinkedBag clone( )
|| See the implementation in Figure 4.13 on page 222.


public int countOccurrences(int target)
|| See the implementation in Figure 4.15 on page 227.


public int grab( )
|| See the implementation in Figure 4.16 on page 229.


public boolean remove(int target)
|| See the implementation in Figure 4.14 on page 224.


public int size( )
{
    return manyNodes;
}


public static IntLinkedBag union(IntLinkedBag b1, IntLinkedBag b2)
{
    if (b1 == null)
        throw new IllegalArgumentException("b1 is null.");
    if (b2 == null)
        throw new IllegalArgumentException("b2 is null.");

    IntLinkedBag answer = new IntLinkedBag( );

    answer.addAll(b1);
    answer.addAll(b2);
    return answer;
}
}
```

Self-Test Exercises for Section 4.4

24. Which methods would need to be altered if you wanted to keep the numbers in order from smallest to largest in the bag's list? Would this allow some other methods to operate more efficiently?

25. Suppose you want to use a bag in which the elements are double numbers instead of integers. How would you do this?

26. Write a few lines of code to declare a bag of integers and place the integers 42 and 8 in the bag. Then grab a random integer from the bag, printing it. Finally, print the size of the bag.

27. In general, which is preferable: an implementation that uses the node methods or an implementation that manipulates a linked list directly?

28. Suppose that p is a reference to a node in a linked list of integers and p.getData( ) has a copy of an integer called d. Write two lines of code that will move p to the next node that contains a copy of d (or set p to null if there is no such node). How can you combine your two statements into just one?

29. Describe the steps taken by countOccurrences if the target is not in the bag.

30. Describe one of the boundary values for testing remove.

31. Write an expression that will give a random integer between –10 and 10.

32. Do big-*O* time analyses of the bag's methods.

33. What would go wrong if you forgot to include the listCopy statement in the bag's clone method?

4.5 PROGRAMMING PROJECT: THE SEQUENCE ADT WITH A LINKED LIST

In Section 3.3 on page 145 we gave a specification for a sequence ADT that was implemented using an array. Now you can reimplement this ADT using a *linked list* as the data structure rather than an array. Start by rereading the ADT's specification on page 151 and then return here for some implementation suggestions.

The Revised Sequence ADT—Design Suggestions

Using a linked list to implement the sequence ADT seems natural. We'll keep the elements stored on a linked list in their sequence order. The "current" element on the list can be maintained by an instance variable that refers to the node that contains the current element. When the start method is activated, we set this cursor to refer to the first node of the linked list. When advance is activated, we move the cursor to the next node on the linked list.

With this in mind, we propose five private instance variables for the new sequence class:

- The first variable, manyNodes, keeps track of the number of nodes in the list.

- head and tail—These are references to the head and tail nodes of the linked list. If the list has no elements, then these references are both null. The reason for the tail reference is the addAfter method. Normally this method adds a new element immediately after the current element. But if there is no current element, then addAfter places its new element at the tail of the list, so it makes sense to maintain a connection with the list's tail.

- cursor—Refers to the node with the current element (or null if there is no current element).

- precursor—Refers to the node before the current element (or null if there is no current element or if the current element is the first node). Can you figure out why we propose a *pre*cursor? The answer is the addBefore method, which normally adds a new element immediately *before* the current element. But there is no node method to add a new node before a specified node. We can only add new nodes after a specified node. Therefore, the addBefore method will work by adding the new element *after* the precursor node—which is also just *before* the cursor node.

The sequence class you implement could have integer elements, double number elements, or several other possibilities. The choice of element type will determine which kind of node you use for the linked list. If you choose integer elements, then you will use edu.colorado.nodes.IntNode. All the node classes, including IntNode, are available for you to view at http://www.cs.colorado.edu/~main/edu/colorado/nodes.

For this programming project, you should use double numbers for the elements and follow these guidelines:

- The name of the class is DoubleLinkedSeq.

- You'll use DoubleNode for your node class.

- Put your class in the package edu.colorado.collections.

- Follow the specification from Figure 4.18 on page 235. This specification is also available at the DoubleLinkedSeq link at
    http://www.cs.colorado.edu/~main/docs/.

Notice that the specification states a limitation that, beyond Int.MAX_VALUE elements, the size method does not work (though all other methods should be okay).

Here's an example of the five instance variables for a sequence with four elements and the current element at the third location:

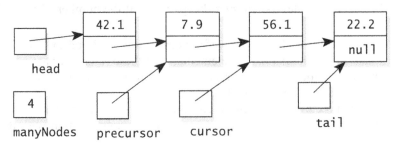

Notice that cursor and precursor are *references* to two nodes—one right after the other.

what is the invariant of the new list ADT?

Start your implementation by writing the invariant for the new sequence ADT. You might even write the invariant in large letters on a sheet of paper and pin it up in front of you as you work. Each of the methods counts on that invariant being true when the method begins, and each method is responsible for ensuring that the invariant is true when the method finishes.

As you implement each modification method, you might use the following matrix to increase your confidence that the method works correctly.

	manyNodes	head	tail	cursor	precursor
An empty list					
A non-empty list with no current element					
Current element at the head					
Current element at the tail					
Current element not at head or tail					

Here's how to use the matrix: Suppose you have just implemented one of the modification methods, such as addAfter. Go through the matrix one row at a time, executing your method with pencil and paper. For example, with the first row of the matrix, you would try addAfter to see its behavior for an empty list. As you execute each method by hand, keep track of the five instance variables and put five check marks in the row to indicate that the final values correctly satisfy the invariant.

The Revised Sequence ADT—Clone Method

The sequence class has a clone method to make a new copy of a sequence. The sequence you are copying activates the clone method, and we'll call it the "original sequence." As with all clone methods, you should start with the pattern from page 82. After activating super.clone, the extra work must make a separate copy of the linked list for the clone and correctly set the clone's head, tail, cursor, and precursor. We suggest that you handle the work with the following three cases:

- If the original sequence has no current element, then simply copy the original's linked list with listCopyWithTail. Then set both precursor and cursor to null.

- If the current element of the original sequence is its first element, then copy the original's linked list with listCopyWithTail. Then set the precursor to null and set cursor to refer to the head node of the newly created linked list.

- If the current element of the original sequence is after its first element, then copy the original's linked list in two pieces using listPart: The first piece goes from the head node to the precursor; the second piece goes from the cursor to the tail. Put these two pieces together by making the link part of the precursor node refer to the cursor node. The reason for copying in two separate pieces is to easily set the precursor and cursor of the newly created list.

FIGURE 4.18   Specification for the Second Version of the DoubleLinkedSeq Class

Class DoubleLinkedSeq

❖ **public class DoubleLinkedSeq from the package edu.colorado.collections**
A DoubleLinkedSeq is a sequence of double numbers. The sequence can have a special "current element," which is specified and accessed through four methods that are not available in the bag class (start, getCurrent, advance, and isCurrent).

Limitations:
Beyond Int.MAX_VALUE elements, the size method does not work.

Specification

◆ **Constructor for the DoubleLinkedSeq**
```
public DoubleLinkedSeq( )
```
Initialize an empty sequence.

Postcondition:
This sequence is empty.

(continued)

(FIGURE 4.18 continued)

♦ addAfter and addBefore

```
public void addAfter(double element)
public void addBefore(double element)
```

Adds a new element to this sequence either before or after the current element.

Parameter:

`element` – the new element that is being added

Postcondition:

A new copy of the element has been added to this sequence. If there was a current element, `addAfter` places the new element after the current element, and `addBefore` places the new element before the current element. If there was no current element, `addAfter` places the new element at the end of the sequence, and `addBefore` places the new element at the front of the sequence. The new element always becomes the new current element of the sequence.

Throws: `OutOfMemoryError`

Indicates insufficient memory for a new node.

♦ addAll

```
public void addAll(DoubleLinkedSeq addend)
```

Place the contents of another sequence at the end of this sequence.

Parameter:

`addend` – a sequence whose contents will be placed at the end of this sequence

Precondition:

The parameter, `addend`, is not null.

Postcondition:

The elements from `addend` have been placed at the end of this sequence. The current element of this sequence remains where it was, and the `addend` is also unchanged.

Throws: `NullPointerException`

Indicates that `addend` is null.

Throws: `OutOfMemoryError`

Indicates insufficient memory to increase the size of the sequence.

♦ advance

```
public void advance( )
```

Move forward so that the current element is now the next element in the sequence.

Precondition:

`isCurrent( )` returns `true`.

Postcondition:

If the current element was already the end element of the sequence (with nothing after it), then there is no longer any current element. Otherwise, the new element is the element immediately after the original current element.

Throws: `IllegalStateException`

Indicates that there is no current element, so advance may not be called.

(continued)

(FIGURE 4.18 continued)

♦ **clone**
> `public Object clone( )`
> Generate a copy of this sequence.
> **Returns:**
>> The return value is a copy of this sequence. Subsequent changes to the copy will not affect the original, nor vice versa. The return value must be typecast to a `DoubleLinkedSeq` before it is used.
> **Throws:** `OutOfMemoryError`
>> Indicates insufficient memory for creating the clone.

♦ **concatenation**
> `public static DoubleLinkedSeq concatenation`
> `(DoubleLinkedSeq s1, DoubleLinkedSeq s2)`
> Create a new sequence that contains all the elements from one sequence followed by another.
> **Parameters:**
>> `s1` – the first of two sequences
>> `s2` – the second of two sequences
> **Precondition:**
>> Neither `s1` nor `s2` is null.
> **Returns:**
>> a new sequence that has the elements of `s1` followed by `s2` (with no current element)
> **Throws:** `IllegalArgumentException`
>> Indicates that one of the arguments is null.
> **Throws:** `OutOfMemoryError`
>> Indicates insufficient memory for the new sequence.

♦ **getCurrent**
> `public double getCurrent( )`
> Accessor method to determine the current element of the sequence.
> **Precondition:**
>> `isCurrent( )` returns true.
> **Returns:**
>> the current element of the sequence
> **Throws:** `IllegalStateException`
>> Indicates that there is no current element.

♦ **isCurrent**
> `public boolean isCurrent( )`
> Accessor method to determine whether this sequence has a specified current element that can be retrieved with the `getCurrent` method.
> **Returns:**
>> `true` (there is a current element) or `false` (there is no current element at the moment)

(continued)

(FIGURE 4.18 continued)

◆ **removeCurrent**

```
public void removeCurrent( )
```
Remove the current element from this sequence.

Precondition:
isCurrent( ) returns true.

Postcondition:
The current element has been removed from the sequence, and the following element (if there is one) is now the new current element. If there was no following element, then there is now no current element.

Throws: IllegalStateException
Indicates that there is no current element, so removeCurrent may not be called.

◆ **size**

```
public int size( )
```
Accessor method to determine the number of elements in this sequence.

Returns:
the number of elements in this sequence

◆ **start**

```
public void start( )
```
Set the current element at the front of the sequence.

Postcondition:
The front element of this sequence is now the current element (but if the sequence has no elements at all, then there is no current element).

Self-Test Exercises for Section 4.5

34. Suppose a sequence contains your three favorite numbers, and the current element is the first element. Draw the instance variables of this sequence using our implementation.

35. Write a new method to remove a specified element from a sequence of double numbers. The method has one parameter (the element to remove). After the removal, the current element should be the element after the removed element (if there is one).

36. Which of the sequence methods use the new operator to allocate at least one new node?

37. Which of the sequence methods use DoubleNode.listPart?

4.6   BEYOND SIMPLE LINKED LISTS

Arrays Versus Linked Lists and Doubly Linked Lists

Many ADTs can be implemented with either arrays or linked lists. Certainly, the bag and the sequence ADT could each be implemented with either approach.

Which approach is better? There is no absolute answer, but there are certain operations that are better performed by arrays and others where linked lists are preferable. This section provides some guidelines.

Arrays Are Better at Random Access.   The term **random access** refers to examining or changing an arbitrary element that is specified by its position in a list. For example: *What is the 42nd element in the list?* Or another example: *Change the element at position 1066 to a 7.* These are constant time operations for an array. But in a linked list, a search for the ith element must begin at the head and will take $O(i)$ time. Sometimes there are ways to speed up the process, but even improvements remain linear time in the worst case.

If an ADT makes significant use of random-access operations, then an array is better than a linked list.

Linked Lists Are Better at Additions/Removals at a Cursor.   Our sequence ADT maintains a *cursor* that refers to a "current element." Typically, a cursor moves through a list one element at a time without jumping around to random locations. If all operations occur at the cursor, then a linked list is preferable to an array. In particular, additions and removals at a cursor generally are linear time for an array (since elements that are after the cursor must *all* be shifted up or back to a new index in the array). But these operations are constant time operations for a linked list. Also remember that effective additions and removals in a linked list generally require maintaining both a cursor and a *precursor* (which refers to the node before the cursor).

If an ADT's operations take place at a cursor, then a linked list is better than an array.

Resizing Can Be Inefficient for an Array.   A collection class that uses an array generally provides a method to allow a programmer to adjust the capacity as needed. But changing the capacity of an array can be inefficient. The new memory must be allocated and initialized, and the elements are then copied from the old memory to the new memory. If a program can predict the necessary capacity ahead of time, then capacity is not a big problem because the object can be given sufficient capacity from the outset. But sometimes the eventual capacity is unknown, and a program must continually adjust the capacity. In this situation, a linked list has advantages. When a linked list grows, it grows one node at a time, and there is no need to copy elements from old memory to new memory.

If an ADT is frequently adjusting its capacity, then a linked list might be better than an array.

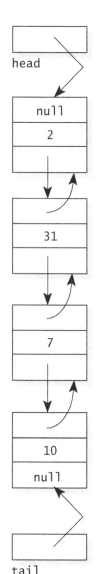

FIGURE 4.19
Doubly Linked
List

Doubly Linked Lists Are Better for a Two-Way Cursor. Sometimes list operations require a cursor that can move forward and backward through a list—a kind of **two-way cursor**. This situation calls for a **doubly linked list**, which is like an ordinary linked list except that each node contains two references: one linking to the next node and one linking to the previous node. An example of a doubly linked list of integers is shown in Figure 4.19 (in the margin) along with references to its head and tail. Here is the start of a declaration for a doubly linked list with integer data:

```
public class IntTwoWayNode
{
    private int data;
    private IntTwoWayNode backlink;
    private IntTwoWayNode forelink;
    ...
```

The backlink refers to the previous node, and the forelink refers to the next node in the list.

If an ADT's operations take place at a two-way cursor, then a doubly linked list is the best implementation.

Dummy Nodes

Many linked list operations require special treatment when the operation occurs on an empty list or the operation occurs at the head or tail node. The special treatment requires extra programming that results in more opportunity for programming errors. Because of this, programmers often create an extra node at the beginning of each list (called a **dummy head node**) and an extra node at the end of each list (called a **dummy tail node**). The data in these two dummy nodes is not part of the list. The nodes are present only to make it easier to program certain operations. Dummy nodes may be used with ordinary (singly linked) lists or with doubly linked lists.

A list with a dummy head node and a dummy tail node has another advantage: The references to the head and tail are set up just once (using the dummy nodes). After they are set up, the head and tail will never need to be changed and never need to refer to some other node. On the other hand, without dummy nodes, the head or tail will need to refer to new nodes whenever a node is inserted or removed at the front or back of the list.

For example, consider the problem of removing a node from a doubly linked list that is maintained with references to both the head and the tail, as in Figure 4.19. If there are no dummy nodes, then there are many cases to consider:

1. Suppose there is only one node in the list, and we are removing it. Then both the head and the tail must be set to null.

2. Suppose we are removing the head node from a list with more than one node. In this case, we must reset the head reference variable to

refer to the second node and also set the backward link of this new head node to null.

3. Suppose we are removing the tail node from a list with more than one node. In this case, we must reset the `tail` reference variable to refer to the next-to-last node and also set the forward link of this new tail to null.

4. Suppose we are removing a node from the middle of a list (neither the head nor the tail). In this case, we can set up two references: `before` (which refers to the node before the node we're removing) and `after` (which refers to the node after the node we're removing). Then, assuming we have methods to set the forward and backward links:

```
before.setForwardLink(after);
after.setBackwardLink(before);
```

There are lots of cases to consider and lots of cases that might go wrong. But if we have a dummy head node and a dummy tail node, then these dummy nodes are never removed, and from the four cases, only Case 4 is possible. Case 4 is also nice because it never needs to change head or `tail` reference variables.

If you are programming a linked list from scratch (with no preexisting methods to manipulate the list), then consider maintaining both a dummy head node and a dummy tail node. In this case, methods for searching the list may require extra care (to not search the dummy nodes), but both insertion and removal are significantly easier to program.

Java's List Classes

The Java Class Libraries have two basic list classes. One version (called `Array-List`) uses an array as its underlying data structure, and the other (called `LinkedList`) uses a linked list. The two different list classes have many (but not all) methods with the same names and specifications, although the implementations are different. In the next chapter, we'll see a mechanism (called an *interface*) that enforces these identical specifications, but for now we'll list only some of those common methods to allow you to use either of these classes in your own programs.

Constructors. As with the `HashSet` (Section 3.5), each list class's default constructor creates an empty list, and a second constructor makes a copy of an another existing collection (either an `ArrayList`, a `LinkedList`, a `HashSet`, or other collections that we'll see later). Also, as with the `HashSet`, when you declare a list, you must specify the type of elements that reside in the list, such as the `String` in `ArrayList<String>` or `LinkedList<String>`.

Basic methods. There are basic methods for adding elements, removing elements, and checking the size (in which E is the type of the elements in the list):

```
boolean add(E element);
void add(int index, E element);
boolean remove(E element);
E remove(int index);
int size( );
```

The first version of the add method adds the new element to the tail end of the list and then returns true. The true return value simply means that the add operation was successful, and this value is always true for the lists (although other kinds of collections, such as the HashSet, may fail and return false). The second version of add also adds an element, but it does so at a particular location. The number that specifies the location can range from 0 (meaning to insert at the head of the list) to the size of the list (meaning to insert at the tail). If the insertion is not at the tail, then one or more elements in the list will be shifted to higher locations. Can you imagine how the implementation of the add method differs between the ArrayList and the LinkedList?

There are also two remove methods. The first version searches for a specified element in the list. If the element is found, then its first occurrence is removed and the method returns true; otherwise, the method returns false. The second remove version has a precondition that the index parameter lies in the range from 0 up to, but not including, the size of the list. The function removes the element at that index. Notice that these indexes start at 0 rather than 1, so the indexing of these lists is similar to an ordinary array.

ListIterators

ListIterator

In Section 3.5, we first saw iterators in the context of a HashSet. Java's lists have a similar feature that's implemented via a data type called ListIterator. A ListIterator has a cursor that steps through its list, but unlike the cursor that we saw for our sequence class (Section 4.5), a ListIterator's cursor generally lies *in between* two of its list elements. For example, suppose we create a list with three strings: "Hiro", "Claire", and "Peter". Then, this code will create a ListIterator that lies between "Claire" and "Peter":

```
// Declare a list of Strings and an Iterator for that list:
LinkedList<String> heroes = new LinkedList<String>( );
ListIterator<String> it;

// Put elements in the list, and set iterator between "Claire" and "Peter":
heroes.add("Hiro");
heroes.add("Claire");
heroes.add("Peter");
it = heroes.listIterator(2);
```

The iterator returned by `heroes.listIterator(2)` will be on the `heroes` list; the argument, 2, indicates that the iterator will be positioned after the first two elements (`"Hiro"` and `"Claire"`) but before `"Peter"`.

Once a `ListIterator` is set, a program can use its add method to add a new element after the iterator's cursor. With our example list, we could write this code to add `"Sylar"` between `"Claire"` and `"Peter"`:

```
it = heroes.ListIterator(2);  // Cursor between "Claire" and "Peter"
it.add("Sylar");              // Put "Sylar" at this spot in the list
```

Here are a few other `ListIterator` methods (but not a complete list):

```
it.remove( )         // Remove the element that's just after the cursor
it.hasNext( )        // True if the cursor is not at the tail end of the list
it.next( )           // Move the cursor forward one element
it.hasPrevious( )    // True if the cursor is not at the start of the list
it.previous( )       // Move the cursor backward one element
```

remove, hasNext, next, hasPrevious, previous

Both the next and the previous functions return a reference to the element that the cursor jumps over.

Making the Decision

When you are implementing a new class or you are using one of the JCL classes, you're often faced with a decision about whether to use an array-based list or a linked list. The decision should be based on your knowledge of which operations occur in the ADT, which operations you expect to be performed most often, and whether you expect your arrays to require frequent capacity changes. Figure 4.20 summarizes these considerations.

FIGURE 4.20   Guidelines for Choosing Between an Array and a Linked List

Frequent random access operations	Use an array.
Operations occur at a cursor	Use a linked list.
Operations occur at a two-way cursor	Use a doubly linked list.
Frequent capacity changes	A linked list avoids resizing inefficiency.
Programming a linked list from scratch	Consider using a dummy head and tail.

Self-Test Exercises for Section 4.6

38. What underlying data structure is quickest for random access?

39. What underlying data structure is quickest for additions/removals at a cursor?

40. What underlying data structure is best when a cursor must move both forward and backward?

41. What is the typical worst-case time analysis for changing the capacity of a collection class that is implemented with an array?

42. For the `IntTwoWayNode` declaration on page 240, implement a method to remove a node from its list. The node that activates the method is the node to be removed. Assume that there are public methods to get or set the forward or backward link of a node.

CHAPTER SUMMARY

- A *linked list* consists of nodes; each *node* contains some data and a link to the next node in the list. The link part of the final node contains the null reference.

- Typically, a linked list is accessed through a *head reference* that refers to the *head node* (i.e., the first node). Sometimes a linked list is accessed elsewhere, such as through the *tail reference* that refers to the last node.

- You should be familiar with the methods of our node class, which provides fundamental operations to manipulate linked lists. These operations follow basic patterns that every programmer uses.

- Our linked lists can be used to implement ADTs. Such an ADT will have one or more private instance variables that are references to nodes in a linked list. The methods of the ADT will use the node methods to manipulate the linked list.

- You have seen two ADTs implemented with linked lists: a bag and a sequence. You will see more in the chapters that follow.

- ADTs often can be implemented in many different ways, such as with an array or with a linked list. In general, arrays are better at *random access*; linked lists are better at *additions/removals at a cursor*.

- A *doubly linked list* has nodes with two references: one to the next node and one to the previous node. Doubly linked lists are a good choice for supporting a cursor that moves forward and backward.

- Including dummy head and tail nodes on a linked list will simplify the programming for insertion and removal of nodes.

- The Java Class Libraries include sequence classes based on arrays (`ArrayList`) and based on linked lists (`LinkedList`).

1. ```
   public class DoubleNode
   {
      double data;
      DoubleNode link;
      ...
   ```

2. ```
   public class DINode
   {
      double d_data;
      int i_data;
      DINode link;
   ```

3. The head node and the tail node.

4. The null reference is used for the link part of the final node of a linked list; it is also used for the head and tail references of a list that doesn't yet have any nodes.

5. No nodes. The head and tail are `null`.

6. A `NullPointerException` is thrown.

7. Using techniques from Section 4.2:
   ```
   if (head == null)
       head = new IntNode(42, null);
   else
       head.addNodeAfter(42);
   ```

8. Using techniques from Section 4.2:
   ```
   if (head != null)
   {
       if (head.getLink( ) == null)
          head = null;
       else
          head.removeNodeAfter( );
   }
   ```

9. They cannot be implemented as ordinary methods of the `IntNode` class, because they must change the head reference (making it refer to a new node).

10. ```
    IntNode head;
    IntNode tail;
    ```

    ```
    int i;
    head = new IntNode(1, null);
    tail = head;
    for (i = 2; i <= 100; i++)
    {
        tail.addNodeAfter(i);
        tail = tail.getLink( );
    }
    ```

11. There are eight different nodes for the eight primitive data types (`boolean`, `int`, `long`, `byte`, `short`, `double`, `float`, and `char`). These are called `BooleanNode`, `IntNode`, and so on. There is one more class simply called `Node`, which will be discussed in Chapter 5. The data type in the `Node` class is Java's `Object` type. So there are nine different nodes in all.

    If you implement one of these nine node types, implementing another one takes little work: just change the type of the data and the type of any method parameters that refer to the data.

12. Within the `IntNode` class, you may write:
    ```
    locate = locate.link;
    ```
    Elsewhere, you must write:
    ```
    locate = locate.getLink( );
    ```
    If `locate` is already referring to the last node before the assignment statement, then the assignment will set `locate` to null.

13. The `new` operator is used in the methods add-NodeAfter, `listCopy`, `listCopyWithTail`, and `listPart`.

14. It will be the null reference.

15. The `listCopyWithTail` method does exactly this by returning an array with two `IntNode` components.

16. ```
    douglass =
        IntNode.listSearch(head, 42);
    adams =
        IntNode.listPosition(head, 42);
    ```

17.
```
IntNode cursor;
for (cursor = head;
        cursor != null;
        cursor = cursor.link;
    )
        System.out.print(cursor.data);
```

18.
```
public static int count42
(IntNode head)
{
    int count = 0;
    IntNode cursor;
    for (cursor = head;
            cursor != null;
            cursor = cursor.link;
        )
        {
            if (cursor.data == 42)
                count++;
        }
    return count;
}
```

19.
```
public static boolean has42
(IntNode head)
{
    IntNode cursor;
    for (cursor = head;
            cursor != null;
            cursor = cursor.link;
        )
        {
            if (cursor.data == 42)
                return true;
        }
    return false;
}
```

20.
```
public static int sum
(IntNode head)
{
    int count = 0;
    IntNode cursor;
    for (cursor = head;
            cursor != null;
            cursor = cursor.link;
        )
        {
            count += cursor.data;
        }
    return count;
}
```

21.
```
public static void tail42
(IntNode head)
{
    IntNode cursor;
```

```
    if (head = null)
        head = new IntNode(42, null);
    else
    {
        // Move cursor to tail...
        cursor = head;
        while(cursor.link != null)
            cursor = cursor.link;
        // ...and add the new node:
        cursor.addNodeAfter(42);
    }
}
```

22.
```
public static void remove42
(IntNode head)
{
    // Remove first node after the head that
    // contains a data of 42 (if there is one).
    IntNode cursor;
    if (head = null)
    {   // Empty list
        return;
    }

    // Step through each node of the list,
    // always looking to see whether the
    // next node has data of 42.
    cursor = head;
    while (cursor->link != null)
    {
        if (cursor->link->data == 42)
        {   // The next node's data is 42,
            // so remove the next node
            // and return.
            cursor->link =
                cursor->link->link;
            return;
        }
    }
}
```

23.
```
IntNode[ ] array;
array = IntNode.listPart(p. q);
x = array[0];
y = array[1];
array = IntNode.listPart(q.link, r);
y.link = array[0];
z = array[1];
```

24. These would change: add, addAll, remove, and union. You could then implement a more efficient countOccurrences that stopped when it found a number bigger than the target (but it would still have linear worst time).

25. Use DoubleNode instead of IntNode. There are a few other changes, such as changing some parameters from int to double.

26. We could write this code:
```
IntLinkedBag exercise =
    new IntLinkedBag( );
exercise.add(42);
exercise.add(8);
System.out.println
    (exercise.grab( ));
System.out.println
    (exercise.size( ));
```

27. Generally, we will choose the approach that makes the best use of the node methods. This saves us work and also reduces the chance of introducing new errors from writing new code to do an old job. The preference would change if the other approach offered better efficiency.

28. The two lines of code we have in mind:
```
p = p.getLink( );
p = listSearch(p, d);
```
These two lines are the same as this line:
```
p = listSearch(p.getLink( ), d);
```

29. When the target is not in the bag, the first assignment statement to cursor will set it to null. This means that the body of the loop will not execute at all, and the method returns the answer 0.

30. Test the case where you are removing the last element from the bag.

31. (int) (Math.random( ) * 21) - 10

32. All the methods are constant time except for remove, grab, countOccurrences, and clone (all of which are linear); the addAll method (which is *O(n)*, where *n* is the size of the addend); and the union method (which is *O(m+n)*, where *m* and *n* are the sizes of the two bags).

33. The new bag and the old bag would then share the same linked list.

34. manyNodes is 3; the other instance variables are shown at the top of the next column.

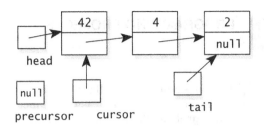

35. First check that the element occurs somewhere in the sequence. If it doesn't, then return with no work. If the element is in the sequence, then set the current element to be equal to this element and activate the ordinary remove method.

36. The two add methods both allocate dynamic memory, as do addAll, clone, and concatenation.

37. The clone method should use listPart, as described on page 235.

38. Arrays are quickest for random access.

39. Linked lists are quickest for additions/removals at a cursor.

40. A doubly linked list

41. At least $O(n)$, where n is the size of the array prior to changing the size. If the new array is initialized, then there is also $O(m)$ work, where m is the size of the new array.

42.
```
public void removeTwoWay
{
    IntTwoWayNode before;
    IntTwoWayNode after;

    before = backlink;
    after forelink;

    if (before != null)
        before.forelink = after;

    if (after != null)
        after.backlink = before;

    forelink = backlink = null;
}
```

PROGRAMMING PROJECTS

1 For this project, you will use the bag of integers from Section 4.4. The bag includes the `grab` method from Figure 4.16 on page 229. Use this class in an applet that has three components:

1. A button

2. A small text field

3. A large text area

Each time the button is clicked, the applet should read an integer from the text field and put this integer in a bag. Then a random integer is grabbed from the bag, and a message is printed in the text area—something like "My favorite number is now … ."

2 Write a new static method for the node class. The method has one parameter, which is a head node for a linked list of integers. The method computes a new linked list, which is the same as the original list but with all repetitions removed. The method's return value is a head reference for the new list.

3 Write a method with three parameters. The first parameter is a head reference for a linked list of integers, and the next two parameters are integers x and y. The method should write a line to `System.out` containing all integers in the list that are between the first occurrence of x and the first occurrence of y.

4 Write a method with one parameter that is a head reference for a linked list of integers. The method creates a new list that has the same elements as the original list but in the reverse order. The method returns a head reference for the new list.

5 Write a method that has two linked list head references as parameters. Assume that linked lists contain integer data, and on each list, every element is less than the next element on the same list. The method should create a new linked list that contains all the elements on both lists, and the new linked list should also be ordered (so that every element is less than the next element in the list). The new linked list should not eliminate duplicate elements (i.e., if the same element appears in both input lists, then two copies are placed in the newly constructed linked list). The method should return a head reference for the newly constructed linked list.

6 Write a method that starts with a single linked list of integers and a special value called the splitting value. The elements of the list are in no particular order. The method divides the nodes into two linked lists: one containing all the nodes that contain an element less than the splitting value and one that contains all the other nodes. If the original linked list had any repeated integers (i.e., any two or more nodes with the same element in them), then the new linked list that has this element should have the same number of nodes that repeat this element. It does not matter whether you preserve the original linked list or destroy it in the process of building the two new lists, but your comments should document what happens to the original linked list. The method returns two head references—one for each of the linked lists that were created.

7 Write a method that takes a linked list of integers and rearranges the nodes so that the integers stored are sorted into the order of smallest to largest, with the smallest integer in the node at the head of the list. Your method should preserve repetitions of integers. If the original list had any integers occurring more than once, then the changed list will have the same number of each integer. For concreteness you will use lists of integers, but your method should still work if you replace the integer type with any other type for which the less-than operation is defined. Use the following specification:

```
IntNode listSort(IntNode head)
// Postcondition: The return value is a head
// reference of a linked list with exactly the
// same entries as the original list (including
// repetitions, if any), but the entries
// in this list are sorted from smallest to
// largest. The original linked list is no longer
// available.
```

Your method will implement the following algorithm (which is often called **selection sort**): The algorithm removes nodes one at a time from the original list and adds the nodes to a second list until all the nodes have been moved to the second list. The second list will then be sorted.

```
// Pseudocode for selection sort:
while (the first list still has some nodes)
{
        1. Find the node with the largest element
           of all the nodes in the first list.
        2. Remove this node from the first list.
        3. Add this node at the head of the second
           list.
}
```

Note that your method will move entire nodes, not just elements, to the second list. Thus, the first list will get shorter and shorter until it is an empty list. Your method should not need to use the new operator since it is just moving nodes from one list to another (not creating new nodes).

8 Implement a new method for the bag class from Section 4.4. The new method allows you to subtract the contents of one bag from another. For example, suppose x has seven copies of the number 3 and y has two copies of the number 3. Then, after activating x.subtract(y), the bag x will have five remaining copies of the number 3.

9 Implement the sequence class from Section 4.5. You may wish to provide some additional useful methods, such as: (1) a method to add a new element at the front of the sequence; (2) a method to remove the element at the front of the sequence; (3) a method to add a new element at the end of the sequence; (4) a method that makes the last element of the sequence become the current element; (5) a method that returns the ith element of the sequence (starting with the 0th at the front); and (6) a method that makes the ith element become the current element.

10 You can represent an integer with any number of digits by storing the integer as a linked list of digits. A more efficient representation will store a larger integer in each node. Design and implement an ADT for unbounded whole numbers in which a number is implemented as a linked list of integers. Each node will hold an integer less than or equal to 999. The number represented is the concatenation of the numbers in the nodes. For example, if there are four nodes with the four integers 23, 7, 999, and 0, then this represents the number 23,007,999,000. Note that the number in a node is always considered to be three digits long. If it is not three digits long, then leading zeros are added to make it three digits long. Include methods for the usual integer operators to work with your new class.

11 Revise the set class (Programming Project 5 on page 169) so that it stores the items in a linked list instead of in an array.

12 Revise the sorted sequence (Project 7 on page 170) so that it stores the items on a linked list instead of in an array.

13 Implement a node class in which each node contains both an integer and a double number. Use this class to reimplement the polynomial class from Section 3.4 so that the coefficients and their exponents are stored in a linked list. This linked list should contain no more than one node for any particular exponent. Some of the operations will be easier to implement (or more efficient) if you keep the nodes in order from smallest to largest exponent. Also, some operations will be more efficient if you include an extra instance variable that is a reference to the most recently accessed node. (Otherwise, you would need to start over at the head of the list every time.)

14 Implement a node class in which each node contains a double number and each node is linked both forward and backward. Include methods that are similar to the node class from this chapter, but change the removal method so that the node that activates the method removes itself from the list.

15 Revise the `Statistician` with median (Programming Project 15 on page 172) so that it stores the input numbers on a doubly linked list using the doubly linked node class from the previous project. Rather than a head reference, you should have an instance variable that keeps track of the node that contains the current median and two instance variables that tell how many numbers are before and after this median. Keep the numbers in order from smallest to largest. Whenever a new item is inserted, you should check to see whether it goes before or after the median. After the new item is inserted, you might have to move the median pointer forward or backward.

16 Use a doubly linked list to implement the sequence class from Section 4.5. With a doubly linked list, there is no need to maintain a precursor. Your implementation should include a `retreat` member function that moves the cursor backward to the previous element. Also, use a dummy head and a dummy tail node. The data in these dummy nodes can be the Java constant `Double.NaN`, which is used for a double variable that is "not a number."

17 In this project, you will implement a variation of the linked list called a circular linked list. The link field of the final node of a circular linked list is not `NULL`; instead, the link member of the tail pointer points back to the first node. In this project, an extra reference variable is used to refer to the beginning of the list; this variable will be `NULL` if the list is empty. Revise the third bag class developed in this chapter to use a circular linked-list implementation.

18 Use a circular linked list to run a simple simulation of a card game called Crazy 8s. You can use any online rules that you find. The circular linked list is to hold the players (who sit in a circle while playing the game). Each player should be an object from a player class that you write yourself. You also design and use other relevant classes, such as a class for a single playing card and perhaps a class for a deck of cards.

19 Reimplement the bag class from Figure 4.17 so that the items of the bag are stored with a new technique. Here's the idea: Each node of the new linked list contains *two* integers. The first integer is called the *count*, and the second integer is called the *data*. As an example, if a node has a count of 6 and data of 10, then this means that the bag has six copies of the number 10.

The nodes of the linked list should be kept in order from the smallest data (at the head of the list) to the largest (at the tail of the list). You should never have two different nodes with the same data, and if the count in a node drops to zero (meaning there are no copies of that node's data), then the node should be removed from the linked list.

The public member functions of your new class should be identical to those in Figure 4.17.

Generic Programming

LEARNING OBJECTIVES

When you complete Chapter 5, you will be able to ...

- declare and use Java Object variables that can refer to any kind of object in a Java program.
- correctly use widening and narrowing to convert back and forth between Java Object variables and other object types.
- correctly use autoboxing and unboxing to convert back and forth between Java's primitive types and the Java wrapper classes.
- design, implement, and use generic methods that depend on a generic type parameter that varies from one activation to another.
- design, implement, and use generic collection classes where the data type of the underlying elements is specified by a generic type parameter.
- create classes that implement interfaces and generic interfaces from the Java API.
- design, implement, and use Java iterators for a collection class.
- use Java's enhanced for-loop for collections with iterators.
- find and read the API documentation for the Java classes that implement the Collection interface (such as Vector) and the Map interface (such as TreeMap) and use these classes in your programs.

CHAPTER CONTENTS

Generic Programming

I never knew just what it was, and I guess I never will.

TOM PAXTON
"The Marvelous Toy"

$\mathbf{P}$rofessional programmers often write classes that have general applicability in many settings. To some extent, our classes do this already. Certainly the bag and sequence classes can be used in many different settings. However, both our bag and our sequence suffer from the fact that they require the underlying element type to be fixed. We started with a bag of integers (IntArrayBag). If we later need a bag of double numbers, then a second implementation (DoubleArrayBag) is required. We can end up with eight different bags—one for each of Java's eight primitive types. But even then we're not done; we could use a bag of locations (with the Location class in Figure 2.5 on page 67) or a bag of strings (using Java's built-in String class, which is not one of the primitive types). It seems as if the onslaught of bags will never stop.

generic classes

A **generic class** is a new feature of Java that provides a solution to this problem. For example, a single generic bag can be used for a bag of integers, but it can also be used for a bag of double numbers, or strings, or whatever else is needed. By using Java's Object type, a generic bag can even hold a mixture of objects of different types.

This chapter shows how to build your own generic classes and how to use some of the generic collection classes that Java provides. In addition, you'll learn about related issues, such as the effective use of Java's Object type and wrapper classes, which are addressed in the first section of the chapter.

Eight Primitive Types
byte
short
int
long
float
double
char
boolean
...and everything else is a reference to an object

5.1   JAVA'S OBJECT TYPE AND WRAPPER CLASSES

A Java variable can be one of the eight primitive data types. Anything that's not one of the eight primitive types is a reference to an object. For example, if you declare a Location variable, that variable is capable of holding a reference to a Location object; if you declare a String variable, that variable is capable of holding a reference to a String object.

Java has an important built-in data type called Object. An Object variable is capable of holding a reference to any kind of object. To see how this is useful, let's look at how assignment statements can go back and forth between an Object variable and other data types.

Widening Conversions

Here's some code to show how an assignment can be made to an `Object` variable. The code declares a `String` with the value `"Objection overruled!"`. A second `Object` variable is then declared and made to refer to the same string.

```
String s = new String("Objection overruled!");
Object obj;

obj = s;
```

At this point, there is only one string—`"Objection overruled!"`—with both s and obj referring to this one string, as shown here:

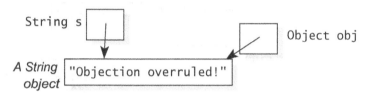

Assigning a specific kind of object to an `Object` variable is an example of a **widening conversion**. The term "widening" means that the `obj` variable has a "wide" ability to refer to different things; in fact, `obj` is very "wide" because it *could* refer to any kind of object. On the other hand, the variable s is relatively narrow with regard to the things that it can refer to—s can refer only to a `String`.

Widening Conversions with Reference Variables

Suppose x and y are reference variables. An assignment x = y is a **widening conversion** if the data type of x is capable of referring to a wider variety of things than the type of y.

Example:
```
String s = new String("Objection overruled!");
Object obj;
obj = s ;
```

Java permits all widening conversions.

Narrowing Conversions

After the widening conversion `obj = s`, our program can continue to do other things, perhaps even making s refer to a new string, as shown here:

```
String s = new String("Objection overruled!");
Object obj;

obj = s;
s = new String("Make it so.");
```

At this point, s refers to a new string, and obj still refers to the original string, as shown here:

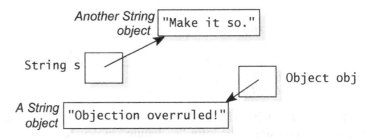

At a later point in the program, we can make s refer to the original string once again with an assignment statement, but the assignment needs more than merely `s = obj`. In fact, the Java compiler forbids the assignment `s = obj`. As far as the compiler knows, obj could refer to anything; it does not have to refer to a String, so the compiler forbids `s = obj`. The way around the restriction is to use the typecast expression shown here:

```
s = (String) obj;
```

The expression `(String) obj` tells the compiler that the reference variable obj is really referring to a String object. This is a typecast, as discussed in Chapter 2. With the typecast, the compiler allows the assignment statement, though you must still be certain that obj actually does refer to a String object. Otherwise, when the program runs, there will be a ClassCastException (see "Pitfall: ClassCastException" on page 82).

The complete assignment `s = (String) obj` is an example of a **narrowing conversion**. The term "narrowing" means that the left side of the assignment has a smaller ability to refer to different things than the right side.

Narrowing Conversion with Reference Variables

Suppose x and y are reference variables, and x has a smaller ability to refer to things than y. A narrowing conversion using a typecast can be made to assign x from y.

Example:
```
String s = new String("Objection overruled!");
Object obj;
obj = s;
...
s = (String) obj;
```

By using a typecast, Java permits all narrowing conversions, though a ClassCastException may be thrown at runtime if the object does not satisfy the typecast.

Narrowing conversions also occur when a method returns an Object and the program assigns that Object to a variable of a particular type. For example, the IntLinkedBag class from Chapter 4 has a clone method:

♦ **clone**
```
public IntLinkedBag clone( )
```
Generate a copy of this bag.

Returns:
The return value is a copy of this bag. Subsequent changes to the copy will not affect the original, nor vice versa. The return value must be typecast to an IntLinkedBag before it is used.

In the implementation of this method, we have the assignment:

```
IntLinkedBag answer;
answer = (IntLinkedBag) super.clone( );
```

The super.clone method from Java's Object class returns an Object. Of course, in this situation, *we* know that the Object is really an IntLinkedBag, but *the compiler* doesn't know that. Therefore, to use the answer from the super.clone method, we must insert the narrowing typecast, (IntLinkedBag). This tells the compiler that the programmer knows that the actual value is an IntLinkedBag, so it is safe to assign it to the answer variable.

Methods That Returns an Object

If a method returns an Object, then a narrowing conversion is usually needed to actually use the return value.

Wrapper Classes

For a programmer, it's annoying that *almost* everything is a Java object. It's those eight darn primitive types that cause the problem. Java's wrapper classes offer a partial solution to this annoyance. A **wrapper class** is a class in which each object holds a primitive value. For example, a wrapper class called `Integer` is designed so that each `Integer` object holds one `int` value. The two most important `Integer` methods are the constructor (which creates an `Integer` object from an `int` value) and the `intValue` method (which accesses the `int` value stored in an `Integer` object). Here are the specifications for these two `Integer` methods:

Primitive	Wrapper Class
byte	Byte
short	Short
int	Integer
long	Long
float	Float
double	Double
char	Character

◆ **Constructor for the Integer class**
```
public Integer(int value)
```
Construct an `Integer` object from an `int` value.

Parameter:
value – the int value for this `Integer` to hold

Postcondition:
This `Integer` has been initialized with the specified `int` value.

◆ **intValue**
```
public int intValue( )
```
Accessor method to retrieve the `int` value of this object.

Returns:
the `int` value of this object

Here's an example to show how an integer is placed into an `Integer` object (called a **boxing conversion**) and taken back out (an **unboxing conversion**):

```
int i = 42;
int j;
Integer example;
example = new Integer(i);  // The example has value 42 (boxing)
j = example.intValue( );   // j is now 42 too (unboxing)
```

Autoboxing and Auto-Unboxing Conversions

automatically convert from a primitive value to a wrapper object, or vice versa

Java has a convenience that simplifies the process of putting a primitive value into a wrapper object and taking it back out. In many situations, the Java compiler will recognize that a wrapper object is needed and automatically convert a primitive value to the wrapper object (an **autoboxing conversion**). Java will also convert from a wrapper object to the corresponding primitive type value in many situations (an **auto-unboxing conversion**). For example, the assignments shown above can be simplified:

```
example = i;   // Autoboxing occurs in an assignment statement
j = example;   // Auto-unboxing occurs in an assignment statement
```

In a similar way, if a method expects an `Integer` parameter, the actual argument may be a primitive `int` value, and an autoboxing conversion will occur. If a method expects an `int` parameter, the actual argument may be an `Integer` object, and an auto-unboxing conversion will occur.

Boxing and Unboxing Conversions

A **boxing conversion** occurs when a primitive value is converted to a wrapper object of the corresponding type. An **unboxing conversion** occurs when a wrapper object is converted to the corresponding primitive type. These may occur with an explicit conversion or automatically when the compiler detects the need for the conversion.

Examples:

```
int i = 42;
int j;
Integer example;
example = new Integer(i); // Boxing
example = i;              // Autoboxing
j = example.intValue( ); // Unboxing
j = example;             // Auto-unboxing
```

Advantages and Disadvantages of Wrapper Objects

The advantage of putting a value in a wrapper object is that the wrapper object is a full-blown Java object. For example, it can be put into the generic bag that we will create in Section 5.3. The disadvantage is that the ordinary primitive operations are no longer directly available. For example, suppose x, y, and z are Integer objects. Although the statement z = x + y; is legal, its evaluation is somewhat slow because the x and y Integer objects must first be auto-unboxed (converted to primitive int values) before the "+" operation can be applied. The answer must then undergo an autoboxing conversion before it can be stored back in the Integer z.

Self-Test Exercises for Section 5.1

1. Can an Object variable refer to a String? To a Location? To an IntArrayBag?

2. Write some code that includes both a widening conversion and a narrowing conversion. Draw a circle by the widening and a triangle by the narrowing.

3. Write an example of a narrowing conversion that will cause a `ClassCastException` at runtime.

4. Write some code that creates a `Character` wrapper object called `example`, initializing with the char `'w'`.

5. Describe an advantage and a disadvantage of wrapper objects.

6. Suppose that `x`, `y` and `z` are all `Double` objects. Describe all the boxing and unboxing that occurs in the assignment `z = x + y;`.

5.2   OBJECT METHODS AND GENERIC METHODS

Sometimes it seems that programmers intentionally make extra work for themselves. For example, suppose we write this method:

```
public static Integer middle(Integer[] data)
//  If the array is non-empty, then the function returns an element from
//  near the middle of the array; otherwise, the return value is null.
{
   if (data.length == 0)
   {  // The array has no elements, so return null.
      return null;
   }
   else
   {  // Return an element near the center of the array.
      return data[data.length/2];
   }
}
```

This is a fine method, reliably returning an element from near the middle of any non-empty array. Such a method is useful in certain kinds of searches. For example (with an `Integer` i and a non-empty `Integer` array `ia`):

```
i = middle(ia); // Set i to something from the middle of the array ia.
```

Now, suppose that tomorrow you have another program that needs to do the same thing with `Character` objects:

```
public static Integer middle(Integer[] data)...
```

we write lots of different middle methods

As you start writing the code, you realize that the only difference between this new method and the original version is that we must change every occurrence of the word `Integer` to `Character`. Later, if we want to carry out the same task with values of some other type, we might write another method, and another … . In fact, a single program might use many `middle` methods. When one of the functions is used, the compiler looks at the type of the argument and selects the appropriate version of the `middle` method. This works fine, but with this approach, you do need to write a different method for each different data type.

Object Methods

One way to avoid many different `middle` methods is to write just one method using the `Object` data type:

```
public static Object middle(Object[] data)
{
   if (data.length == 0)
   {  // The array has no elements, so return null.
      return null;
   }
   else
   {  // Return an element near the center of the array.
      return data[data.length/2];
   }
}
```

This approach also works fine. We can use this version of the `middle` method with an `Integer` array and a narrowing conversion to convert the return value from an `Object` to an `Integer`:

```
i = (Integer) middle(ia); // i is an Integer; ia is an Integer array.
```

We need only one version of the `Object` method, but there are some potential type errors that can't be caught until the program is running. For example, a programmer might accidentally use the `middle` method with a `Character` array, but assign the result to an `Integer` variable. Such a mistake would compile, but at run time there would be a `ClassCastException` from the illegal narrowing conversion. Another approach, called generic methods, offers a safer approach that cannot result in a type mismatch.

Generic Methods

A **generic method** is a method that is written with the types of the parameters not fully specified. Our `middle` method is written this way as a generic method:

```
public static <T> T middle(T[] data)
{
   if (data.length == 0)
   {  // The array has no elements, so return null.
      return null;
   }
   else
   {  // Return an element near the center of the array.
      return data[data.length/2];
   }
}
```

Notice that the name T appears in angle brackets (<T>) right before the return type in the method header. This name is called the **generic type parameter**. The generic type parameter indicates that the method depends on some particular class, but the programmer is not going to specify exactly what that class is. Perhaps T will eventually be an Integer, or a Character, or who knows what else. The name, T, that we used for the generic type parameter may be any legal Java identifier, but the designers of Java recommend single capital letters such as T (an abbreviation of "type") or E (an abbreviation of "element").

The generic type parameter always appears in angle brackets right before the return type of the method. This is how the compiler knows that the method is a generic method. In the rest of the method's implementation, the generic type may be used just like any other class name, and for most situations, it must be used at least once in the parameter list. In our example, T is used twice (once as the return type of the method and once as the data type of the array in the parameter list):

```
public static <T> T middle(T[] data)...
```

When a generic method is activated, the compiler infers the correct class for the generic type parameter. For example:

```
i = middle(ia); // i is an Integer; ia is an Integer array.
```

a generic method allows any class for the argument, and the compiler can detect certain type errors

In this case, the compiler sees the Integer array, ia, and determines that the data type of T must be Integer. This allows the compiler to detect potential type errors at compile time, before the program is running. For example:

```
c = middle(ia); // c is a Character; ia is an Integer array--type error!
```

For this assignment statement, the compiler will indicate that the Integer return value cannot be assigned to a Character variable.

Later, we will see generic methods with more than one generic type parameter. For example, here is a method with two generic type parameters, each of which occurs twice in the parameter list:

```
public static <S,T> bool most(S[] sa, S st, T[] ta, T tt)
// Returns true if st is in sa more often than tt is in ta.
```

🟊 PITFALL

GENERIC METHOD RESTRICTIONS

The data type inferred by the compiler for the generic type must always be a class type (not one of the primitive types). In addition, you may not call a constructor for the generic type, nor may you create a new array of elements of that type.

erasure

These restrictions are a consequence of a compilation technique called **erasure**, in which the exact data type of a generic type is unknown at run time when a generic method is running.

Generic Methods

A **generic method** is written by putting a generic type parameter in angle brackets before the return type in the heading of the method. For example:

```
static <T> T middle(T[] data)...
```

The generic data type is often named with a single capital letter, such as T for "type." The name T can then be used in the rest of the method implementation as if it were a real class name (with a few exceptions).

A programmer can activate a generic method just like any other method. The compiler will look at the data types of the arguments and infer a correct type for each generic type parameter. The inferred types help catch type errors at compile time. For example:

```
// i is an integer; ia is an Integer array; c is a Character

i = middle(ia); // This is fine
c = middle(ia); // Compile-time type error
```

Some additional features of generic methods, such as the ability to restrict the type of the argument to specific kinds of objects, will be covered in Chapter 13.

Self-Test Exercises for Section 5.2

7. Describe the main purpose of a generic method.

8. What is the principal disadvantage of using an object method as compared to a generic method?

9. What is the generic type parameter, and where does it first appear in the method implementation? Where else may it appear in the implementation? In what one other location does it nearly always appear?

10. Name two things that can usually be done with a class type but which are forbidden for a generic type.

11. Write a generic method for counting the number of occurrences of a target in an array. If the target is non-null, then use `target.equals` to determine equality.

12. Write the `most` method that was specified at the end of this section.

5.3 GENERIC CLASSES

Writing a Generic Class

A generic *method* is a method that depends on an unspecified underlying data type. In a similar way, when an entire *class* depends on an underlying data type, the class can be implemented as a **generic class**, resulting in the same typechecking advantages that you have seen for generic methods. For example, in this section, we'll convert our IntArrayBag (from Chapter 3) to a generic class, which means that the data type of the objects in the bag is left unspecified.

A generic class is written by putting a generic type parameter in angle brackets immediately after the class name in the class's implementation. For example, the implementation of a generic bag class might begin like this:

```
public class ArrayBag<E> implements Cloneable...
```

The name ArrayBag indicates that the bag will store its elements in an array. We can choose the name of the generic type parameter to be anything we like, but the designers of Java suggest using a single capital letter, such as E, to indicate that it is the unknown class of an "element" in the bag. Throughout the rest of the implementation of the bag, we can use the unknown class, E, as if it were any other class name. For example, our ArrayBag will have two private member variables, one of which is an array to hold the elements of type E, as shown here:

```
public class ArrayBag<E> implements Cloneable
{
    private            [ ] data;  // An array to hold the bag's elements
    private int manyItems;        // Number of items in the bag
```

programs cannot create arrays where the components are the generic type parameter

Notice that we've left out the data type of the array's components. That's because of a problem that we've already seen: A program cannot create an array where the components are a generic type parameter (see the pitfall on page 260). We'll solve this problem soon and see the entire implementation (which won't differ much from the original IntArrayBag), but first let's look at how a program uses a generic class.

Using a Generic Class

A program that wants to use a generic class must explicitly specify what class will be used for the generic type parameter. This process is called **instantiating** the generic type parameter. The syntax uses the name of the generic class followed by the name of the class that you want to use for the generic type parameter. For example, the following code will create a bag of strings and a bag of integers (using the default constructor in both cases):

```
ArrayBag<String> sbag = new ArrayBag<String>( );
ArrayBag<Integer> ibag = new ArrayBag<Integer>( );
```

We can then activate member functions such as sbag.add("Thunder") or ibag.add(42). This ibag activation will autobox the 42, so that the argument is an Integer object rather than a primitive int. However, the compiler will generate a typechecking error for a statement such as ibag.add("Thunder"). You cannot add a String object to a bag of Integer objects.

PITFALL ⓤ

GENERIC CLASS RESTRICTIONS

In a generic class, the type used to instantiate the generic type parameter must be a class (not a primitive type). In addition, within the implementation of the generic class, you may not call a constructor for the generic type, nor may you create a new array of elements of that type.

These restrictions are identical to the restrictions for a generic method (page 260), and are a consequence of the compilation method that Java uses for generic classes.

Details for Implementing a Generic Class

Figure 5.2 on page 271 gives the complete implementation of the generic ArrayBag class. The implementation is mostly unsurprising: We took the original IntArrayBag implementation, changed the class name to ArrayBag<E>, and throughout the implementation we use the unknown type E as the type of element in the bag (rather than int). Still, there are a few issues that you need to examine, and we'll discuss those next.

Creating an Array to Hold Elements of the Unknown Type

Within the generic class implementation, we are not allowed to create a new array of objects of the unknown type E. This causes a problem for our bag because we need an array that holds references to objects of type E. The solution is to declare data as an array of Java Objects (so the class has the private instance variable private Object[ ] data;), and we initialize it this way in the constructor:

```
public ArrayBag( )
{
    final int INITIAL_CAPACITY = 10;
    manyItems = 0;L
    data = new Object[INITIAL_CAPACITY];
}
```

In the rest of the ArrayBag code, we will ensure that we put only objects of type E into the array. (An alternative to this approach is briefly discussed in Figure 5.1 on the next page.)

FIGURE 5.1 An Older Approach to Implementing Generic Collection Classes

In our ArrayBag<E>, we use an array of objects, `private Object[ ] data;`, and our programming ensures that we put only E objects into the array. An alternative that has been used in older code uses an array of E objects instead: `private E[ ] data;`. In the constructor, the array is still created as an array of ordinary objects, and a typecast allows the data variable to refer to it, in this way:

```
public ArrayBag( )
{
    final int INITIAL_CAPACITY = 10;
    manyItems = 0;L
    data = (E[ ]) new Object[INITIAL_CAPACITY];
}
```

This alternative was used in earlier editions of this text and also in the original implementations of the Java generic collection classes. But the alternative is discouraged because it has a technical, uncaught type error at run time when the (E[ ]) variable is set to refer to an (Object[ ]) array. The latest version of the Java generic collection classes use `private Object[ ] data;` as we do in the text.

Retrieving E Objects from the Array

We know from our programming that the objects in the data array will always be E objects, but the Java compiler does not know this. Therefore, whenever we retrieve a component of the array, we must apply a typecast to the type E (as previously discussed on page 79). For example, the needed typecast is highlighted in this one statement of the ArrayBag's grab method:

```
return (E) data[i]; // From the end of the grab method
```

This typecast (E) is one of several places where Java compilers issue warnings about possible errors that can occur at run time. We discuss these situations next.

Warnings in Generic Code

Our ArrayBag implementation from Figure 5.2 on page 271 has several places where Java compilers will generate warnings. It's okay to have these warnings in your code, but you must be aware of the situations that cause the possible errors, so you can avoid these situations in your programming.

Typecasts. In our grab method, we take the Java object, data[i], and typecast it to an E object. This is safe because it was our own programming (such as the add method) that put the object into data[i], and at that point, we knew it was an E object.

But during run time, the information about the actual data type of a generic object is always unavailable. Therefore, there is no way for the program to check (while it is running) whether the typecast is correct. The warning that Java produces in this situation is an "unchecked cast" warning. This means that if the typecast is illegal at run time, then the error will not be caught as it usually is.

As a programmer, it is your responsibility to notice the warning and ensure that the value (`data[i]` in this case) actually is the correct data type (`E` in this case).

A second typecast that causes a similar problem is in the `ArrayBag`'s `clone` method at this statement:

```
answer = (ArrayBag<E>) super.clone( ); // From the clone method
```

In this case, the `super.clone( )` method returns a generic object that has had its type information erased at run time. Even though its type cannot be checked at run time, we know that this object is an `ArrayBag<E>` object, so the assignment is safe, despite the warning.

Variable Arity Methods. The `addMany` method of the `ArrayBag<E>` class is a variable arity method, meaning that it has a variable number of arguments that are put into an array for the `addMany` method to access (see page 115). This results in the compiler creating an array of generic objects, which usually is forbidden because it can result in unchecked typecast errors that are similar to those we have already seen.

Java compilers can issue warnings at two locations for this combination of variable arity and generic types. One location (starting with Java 1.7) is within the generic class at the declaration of the variable arity method. A second location (which occurs in only certain situations) is at the point where a program activates the variable arity method.

Provided that you access the array only as an array of `E` objects, then your programming is safe, and the warnings are not relevant.

PROGRAMMING TIP

SUPPRESSING UNCHECKED WARNINGS

If you write classes so that the possible runtime errors cannot occur, then you may document this and suppress the warnings with this annotation immediately before any method that contains a warning: `@SuppressWarnings("unchecked")`. Notice that there is no semicolon after this annotation; the line can be placed by itself just prior to any method declaration.

Starting with Java 1.7, there is a different annotation that can be used before a variable arity method: `@SafeVarargs`. This version of the annotation will suppress both the warning at the declaration of the variable arity method and the warnings that sometimes occur when the variable arity method is activated, but its use is restricted to only static or final methods.

Using ArrayBag as the Type of a Parameter or Return Value

The ArrayBag has several methods that have bags as parameters or as the return type. For example, our IntArrayBag has an addAll method:

```
public void addAll(IntArrayBag addend)...
```

When a program activates b1.addall(b2), all the integers from b2 are put in the bag b1.

For the generic bag, the way to implement such a parameter is to specify its data type as ArrayBag<E> (rather than just ArrayBag):

```
public void addAll(ArrayBag<E> addend)...
```

This will allow us to activate b1.addAll(b2) for two bags, b1 and b2, but only if the type of the elements in b1 is the same as the type of elements in b2.

For our array bag, all the uses of the ArrayBag data type within its own implementation will be written as ArrayBag<E>.

Counting the Occurrences of an Object

Counting the occurrences of an object in a bag requires some thought. Here's an example to get you thinking. Suppose you construct a bag of Location objects and create two identical Location objects with coordinates of $x = 2$, $y = 4$ (using the Location class from Section 2.4). The locations are then added to the bag:

```
ArrayBag<Location> spots = new ArrayBag<Location>( );
Location p1 = new Location(2, 4);   // x=2 and y=4
Location p2 = new Location(2, 4);   // Also at x=2 and y=4

spots.add(p1);
spots.add(p2);
```

The two locations are identical but separate objects, as shown in this drawing:

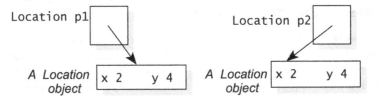

Keep in mind that the boolean expression (p1 == p2) is false because "==" returns true only if p1 and p2 refer to the exact same object (as opposed to two separate objects that happen to contain identical values). On the other hand, the Location class has an equals method with this specification:

♦ **equals (from the Location class)**

```
public boolean equals(Object obj)
```
Compare this Location to another object for equality.

Parameter:

> obj – an object with which this Location is compared

Returns:

> A return value of true indicates that obj refers to a Location object with the same value as this Location. Otherwise, the return value is false.

Both p1.equals(p2) and p2.equals(p1) are true.

So here's the question to get you thinking: With both locations in the bag, what is the value of spots.countOccurrences(p1)? In other words, how many times does the target p1 appear in the bag? The answer depends on exactly how we implement countOccurrences, with these two possibilities:

1. countOccurrences could step through the elements of the bag, using the "==" operator to look for the target. In this case, we find one occurrence of the target, p1, and spots.countOccurrences(p1) is 1.

2. countOccurrences could step through the elements of the bag, using equals to look for the target. In this case, both locations are equal to the target, and spots.countOccurrences(p1) is 2.

Every class has an equals method. For example, the equals method of the String class returns true when the two strings have the same sequence of characters. The equals method of the Integer wrapper class returns true when the two Integer objects hold the same int value. Because the equals method is always available, we'll use the second approach toward counting occurrences—and spots.countOccurrences(p1) is 2. Our bag documentation will make it clear that we count the occurrences of a non-null element by using its equals method.

> ### Generic Collections Should Use the equals Method
>
> When a generic collection tests for the presence of a non-null element, you should generally use the equals method rather than the "==" operator.

The Collection Is Really a Collection of References to Objects

There is another aspect of generic collections that you must understand. Although we use phrases such as "bag of objects," what we really have is a collection of *references* to objects. In other words, the bag does not contain separate copies of each object. Instead, the bag contains only references to each object that is added to the bag.

Let's draw some pictures to see what this means. Once again, we'll create two identical locations and put them in a bag:

```
ArrayBag<Location> spots = new ArrayBag<Location>( );
Location p1 = new Location(2, 4);   // x=2 and y=4
Location p2 = new Location(2, 4);   // Another at x=2 and y=4
spots.add(p1);
spots.add(p2);
```

Here's a picture of the two locations and the bag after the five statements:

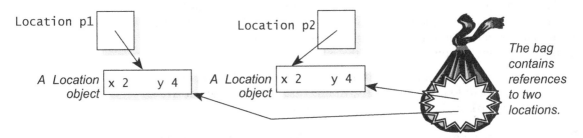

The references to the two locations are now in the bag. As we have already discussed, `spots.countOccurrences(p1)` is 2 because there are two locations with the coordinates $x = 2$, $y = 4$. What happens if we change p1 or p2? For example, after putting the two locations in the bag, we could execute this statement:

```
p1.shift(40, 0);
```

This shifts p1 by 40 units along the x-axis and leaves y alone, so p1 is now at $x = 42$, $y = 4$, as shown here:

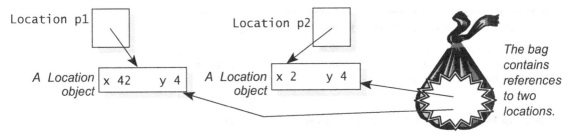

The bag still has two locations, but one of those locations has shifted to $x = 42$, $y = 2$. Therefore, `spots.countOccurrences(p1)` is now just 1 (there is one location in the bag with the coordinates of p1).

Set Unused References to Null

Our bag uses a partially filled array. For example, a bag might contain 14 elements, but the array could be much larger than 14. When the bag contained primitive data, such as integers, we didn't really care what values were stored in the unused part of the array. If a bag stored 14 integers, then we didn't care what was beyond the first 14 locations of the array.

However, our ArrayBag no longer uses primitive types. Instead, we have a partially filled array of references to objects. To help Java collect unused memory, we should write our methods so that the unused part of the array contains only null references. For our ArrayBag class, this means that whenever we remove an element, we will assign null to the array location we are no longer using.

Set Unused Reference Variables to Null

When a collection class is converted to a generic collection class, make sure any unused reference variables are set to null. This usually occurs in methods that remove elements from the collection. Setting these variables to null will allow Java to collect any unused memory.

Steps for Converting a Collection Class to a Generic Class

Here's a summary of exactly how we changed the IntArrayBag (from Section 3.2) into the generic ArrayBag class (in Figure 5.2 on page 271).

1. The Name of the Class. Each occurrence of the old class name, IntArray-Bag, is changed to the new name, ArrayBag<E>. The name ArrayBag indicates that we have an array implementation of a bag, but we do not have any single underlying data type (such as int) because the new bag is a generic bag that holds an unspecified kind of element.

Notice that the name of the constructors is just ArrayBag (without the <E>).

2. The Type of the Data Array. Change the type of the data array to the declaration `private Object[ ] data;`. Make sure that all the arrays that you create are Object arrays (such as in the constructor).

3. The Type of the Underlying Element. Find all the remaining spots where the old class used int to refer to an element in the bag. Change these spots to the generic type parameter E. For example, the old bag had a method with this heading to remove an element: `public boolean remove(int target)`. The new bag has `public boolean remove(E target)`. Be careful because some int values do not refer to elements in the bag, and those must stay int (such as the manyItems instance variable).

4. Change Static Methods to Generic Static Methods. The class may have some static methods. For example, the `IntArrayBag` had this static method:

```
public static IntArrayBag union
(IntArrayBag b1, IntArrayBag b2)...
```

Any static method that depends on the generic type E must be changed to a generic method, which means that <E> appears just before the return type in the method's heading, like this for our `ArrayBag`:

```
public static <E> ArrayBag<E> union
(ArrayBag<E> b1, ArrayBag<E> b2)...
```

5. Use Typecasts When an Element Is Retrieved from the Array. Our class has one location in the `grab` method where an item is retrieved from the array and returned from the method. We know that the retrieved item is actually an E object, so we may insert a typecast at this point in the code:

```
return (E) data[i];
```

6. Suppress Warnings. As discussed earlier, some code in generic collection classes generates "unchecked" warnings. Examine each of these spots, as discussed on page 264, and suppress the warnings (which is safe since our programming ensures that the data array contains only objects of type E).

7. Update Equality Tests. Find all the spots where the old class used "==" or "!=" to compare two elements. Change these spots so that they use the `equals` method instead. For example, instead of `target != data[index]`, we will write `!target.equals(data[index])`.

8. Decide How to Treat the Null Reference. The new bag stores references to objects. You must decide whether to allow the null reference to be placed in the bag. For our bag, we'll allow the null reference to be placed in the bag, and we'll indicate this in the documentation. Some of the bag's methods will need special cases to deal with null references. For example, `countOccurrences` will search for a null target using "==" to count the number of times that `null` is in the bag, but a non-null target is counted by using its `equals` method.

9. Set Unused Reference Variables to Null. For our bag, this occurs in the `remove` method. Each time we remove an element, there is one array location that is no longer being used, and we set that array location to null (rather than letting it continue to refer to an object).

10. Update All Documentation. All documentation must be updated to show that the bag is a collection of references to objects.

Any collection class can be converted to a collection of objects by following these steps. For example, Programming Project 1 on page 313 asks you to convert the Sequence class from Section 3.3.

As for the new ArrayBag class, its specification and implementation are given in Figure 5.2. The changes are marked in the figure, and you'll also find one other improvement: We have included a grab method to allow a program to grab a randomly selected object from the bag. The implementation of the new grab method is similar to the grab method in the linked list version of the bag (see Section 4.4).

Deep Clones for Collection Classes

The clone method creates a copy of an ArrayBag. As with other clone methods, adding or removing elements from the original will not affect the copy, nor vice versa. However, these elements are now references to objects; both the original and the copy contain references to the same underlying objects. Changing these underlying objects will affect both the original and the copy. An alternative cloning method, called **deep cloning**, can avoid the problem, as discussed in Programming Project 5 on page 313.

| **FIGURE 5.2** | Specification and Implementation for the ArrayBag |

Generic Class ArrayBag

❖ **public class ArrayBag<E> from the package edu.colorado.collections**
   An ArrayBag<E> is a collection of references to E objects.
   Limitations:
   (1) The capacity of one of these bags can change after it's created, but the maximum capacity is limited by the amount of free memory on the machine. The constructors, add, clone, and union will result in an OutOfMemoryError when free memory is exhausted.

   (2) A bag's capacity cannot exceed the largest integer, 2,147,483,647 (Integer.MAX_VALUE). Any attempt to create a larger capacity results in failure due to an arithmetic overflow.

   (3) Because of the slow linear algorithms of this class, large bags will have poor performance.

Specification

◆ **Constructor for the ArrayBag<E>**
   public ArrayBag( )
   Initialize an empty bag with an initial capacity of 10. Note that the add method works efficiently (without needing more memory) until this capacity is reached.
   Postcondition:
   This bag is empty and has an initial capacity of 10.
   Throws: OutOfMemoryError
   Indicates insufficient memory for new Object[10].   (continued)

(FIGURE 5.2 continued)

◆ Second Constructor for the ArrayBag<E>

```
public ArrayBag(int initialCapacity)
```

Initialize an empty bag with a specified initial capacity. Note that the add method works efficiently (without needing more memory) until this capacity is reached.

Parameter:

initialCapacity – the initial capacity of this bag

Precondition:

initialCapacity is non-negative.

Postcondition:

This bag is empty and has the given initial capacity.

Throws: IllegalArgumentException

Indicates that initialCapacity is negative.

Throws: OutOfMemoryError

Indicates insufficient memory for new Object[initialCapacity].

◆ add

```
public void add(E element)
```

Add a new element to this bag. If this new element would take this bag beyond its current capacity, then the capacity is increased before adding the new element.

Parameter:

element – the new element that is being added

Postcondition:

A new copy of the element has been added to this bag.

Throws: OutOfMemoryError

Indicates insufficient memory for increasing the capacity.

Note:

Creating a bag with capacity beyond Integer.MAX_VALUE causes arithmetic overflow.

◆ addAll

```
public void addAll(ArrayBag<E> addend)
```

Add the contents of another bag to this bag.

Parameter:

addend – a bag whose contents will be added to this bag

Precondition:

The parameter, addend, is not null.

Postcondition:

The elements from addend have been added to this bag.

Throws: NullPointerException

Indicates that addend is null.

Throws: OutOfMemoryError

Indicates insufficient memory to increase the size of this bag.

Note:

Creating a bag with capacity beyond Integer.MAX_VALUE causes arithmetic overflow.

(continued)

(FIGURE 5.2 continued)

♦ **addMany**
`public void addMany(E... elements)`
Add a variable number of new elements to this bag. If these new elements would take this bag beyond its current capacity, then the capacity is increased before adding the new elements.

Parameter:
`elements` – a variable number of new elements that are all being added

Postcondition:
New copies of all the elements have been added to this bag.

Throws: `OutOfMemoryError`
Indicates insufficient memory for increasing the capacity.

Note:
Creating a bag with capacity beyond `Integer.MAX_VALUE` causes arithmetic overflow.

♦ **clone**
`public ArrayBag<E> clone( )`
Generate a copy of this bag.

Returns:
The return value is a copy of this bag. Subsequent changes to the copy will not affect the original, nor vice versa.

Throws: `OutOfMemoryError`
Indicates insufficient memory for creating the clone.

♦ **countOccurrences**
`public int countOccurrences(E target)`
Accessor method to count the number of occurrences of a particular element in this bag.

Parameter:
`target` – the reference to an E object to be counted

Returns:
The return value is the number of times that `target` occurs in this bag. If `target` is non-null, then the occurrences are found using the `target.equals` method.

♦ **ensureCapacity**
`public void ensureCapacity(int minimumCapacity)`
Change the current capacity of this bag.

Parameter:
`minimumCapacity` – the new capacity for this bag

Postcondition:
This bag's capacity has been changed to at least `minimumCapacity`. If the capacity was already at or greater than `minimumCapacity`, then the capacity is left unchanged.

Throws: `OutOfMemoryError`
Indicates insufficient memory for `new Object[minimumCapacity]`.

(continued)

(FIGURE 5.2 continued)

◆ getCapacity

```
public int getCapacity( )
```

Accessor method to determine the current capacity of this bag. The add method works efficiently (without needing more memory) until this capacity is reached.

Returns:
the current capacity of this bag

◆ grab

```
public E grab( )
```

Accessor method to retrieve a random element from this bag.

Precondition:
This bag is not empty.

Returns:
a randomly selected element from this bag

Throws: IllegalStateException
Indicates that the bag is empty.

◆ remove

```
public boolean remove(E target)
```

Remove one copy of a specified element from this bag.

Parameter:
target – the element to remove from this bag

Postcondition:
If target was found in this bag, then one copy of target has been removed and the method returns true. Otherwise, this bag remains unchanged, and the method returns false.

◆ size

```
public int size( )
```

Accessor method to determine the number of elements in this bag.

Returns:
the number of elements in this bag

◆ trimToSize

```
public void trimToSize( )
```

Reduce the current capacity of this bag to its size (i.e., the number of elements it contains).

Postcondition:
This bag's capacity has been changed to its current size.

Throws: OutOfMemoryError
Indicates insufficient memory for altering the capacity.

(continued)

(FIGURE 5.2 continued)

♦ **union**

```
public static <E> ArrayBag<E> union(ArrayBag<E> b1, ArrayBag<E> b2)
```

Create a new bag that contains all the elements from two other bags.

Parameters:

b1 and b2 – two bags

Precondition:

Neither b1 nor b2 is null.

Returns:

a new bag that is the union of b1 and b2

Throws: NullPointerException

Indicates that one of the arguments is null.

Throws: OutOfMemoryError

Indicates insufficient memory for the new bag.

Note:

An attempt to create a bag with capacity beyond Integer.MAX_VALUE will cause the bag to fail with an arithmetic overflow.

Implementation

```
// File: ArrayBag.java from the package edu.colorado.collections
// Complete documentation is on pages 271–275 or from the ArrayBag link at:
// http://www.cs.colorado.edu/~main/docs/.

package edu.colorado.collections;

public class ArrayBag<E> implements Cloneable
{
    // Invariant of the ArrayBag<E> generic class:
    //   1. The number of elements in the bag is in the instance variable manyItems.
    //   2. For an empty bag, we do not care what is stored in any of data;
    //      for a non-empty bag, the elements in the bag are stored in data[0]
    //      through data[manyItems-1], and we don't care what's in the rest of data.
    private Object[ ] data;
    private int manyItems;

    public ArrayBag( )
    {
        final int INITIAL_CAPACITY = 10;
        manyItems = 0;
        data = new Object[INITIAL_CAPACITY];
    }
```

The new bag stores an array of Objects rather than an array of int values. At run time, each Object will actually have type E.

(continued)

(FIGURE 5.2 continued)

```
public ArrayBag(int initialCapacity)
{
   if (initialCapacity < 0)
      throw new IllegalArgumentException
      ("initialCapacity is negative: " + initialCapacity);
   manyItems = 0;
   data = new Object[initialCapacity];
}
```

```
public void add(E element)
```
‖ The implementation is unchanged from the original in Figure 3.7 on page 137.

```
public void addAll(ArrayBag<E> addend)
```
‖ The implementation is unchanged from the original in Figure 3.7 on page 137.

```
@SuppressWarnings("unchecked")
public void addMany(E... elements)
```
‖ The implementation is unchanged from the original in Figure 3.7 on page 137.

```
@SuppressWarnings("unchecked")
public ArrayBag<E> clone( )
{  // Clone an ArrayBag<E>.
   ArrayBag<E> answer;
```

See the discussion of warnings on page 265.

```
   try
   {
      answer = (ArrayBag<E>) super.clone( );
   }
   catch (CloneNotSupportedException e)
   {
      // This exception should not occur. But if it does, it would probably indicate a
      // programming error that made super.clone unavailable.
      // The most common error would be forgetting the "implements Cloneable"
      // clause at the start of this class.
      throw new RuntimeException
      ("This class does not implement Cloneable");
   }

   answer.data = data.clone( );
   return answer;
}
```

(continued)

(FIGURE 5.2 continued)

```
public int countOccurrences(E target)
{
   int answer;
   int index;

   answer = 0;

   if (target == null)
   {  // Count how many times null appears in the bag.
      for (index = 0; index < manyItems; index++)
         if (data[index] == null)
            answer++;
   }
   else
   {  // Use target.equals to determine how many times the target appears.
      for (index = 0; index < manyItems; index++)
         if (target.equals(data[index]))
            answer++;
   }

   return answer;
}

public void ensureCapacity(int minimumCapacity)
{
   Object[ ] biggerArray;

   if (data.length < minimumCapacity)
   {
      biggerArray = new Object[minimumCapacity];
      System.arraycopy(data, 0, biggerArray, 0, manyItems);
      data = biggerArray;
   }
}

public int getCapacity( )
```
The implementation is unchanged from the original in Figure 3.7 on page 140.

Special code is needed to handle the case where the target is null.

For a non-null target, we use target.equals instead of the "= =" operator.

(continued)

(FIGURE 5.2 continued)

```java
@SuppressWarnings("unchecked")    // See the warnings discussion on page 265.
public E grab( )
{
    int i;

    if (manyItems == 0)
        throw new IllegalStateException("Bag size is zero.");

    i =  (int) (Math.random( ) * manyItems); // From 0 to manyItems-1
    return (E) data[i];
}

public boolean remove(E target)
{
    int index; // The location of target in the data array

    // First, set index to the location of target in the data array.
    // If target is not in the array, then index will be set equal to manyItems.
    if (target == null)
    {   // Find the first occurrence of the null reference in the bag.
        index = 0;
        while ((index < manyItems) && (data[index] != null))
            index++;
    }
    else
    {   // Use target.equals to find the first occurrence of the target.
        index = 0;
        while ((index < manyItems) && (!target.equals(data[index])))
            index++;
    }

    if (index == manyItems)
        return false; // The target was not found, so nothing is removed.
    else
    {   // The target was found at data[index].
        manyItems--;
        data[index] = data[manyItems];
        data[manyItems] = null; ←
        return true;
    }

}

public int size( )
```
|| The implementation is unchanged from the original in Figure 3.7 on page 140.

The unused array location is set to null to allow Java to collect the unused memory.

(continued)

(FIGURE 5.2 continued)

```java
public void trimToSize( )
{
   Object[ ] trimmedArray;

   if (data.length != manyItems)
   {
      trimmedArray = new Object[manyItems];
      System.arraycopy(data, 0, trimmedArray, 0, manyItems);
      data = trimmedArray;
   }
}

public static <E> ArrayBag<E> union(ArrayBag<E> b1, ArrayBag<E> b2)
{
   // If either b1 or b2 is null, then a NullPointerException is thrown.
   ArrayBag<E> answer =
      new ArrayBag<E>(b1.getCapacity( ) + b2.getCapacity( ));

   System.arraycopy(b1.data, 0, answer.data, 0, b1.manyItems);
   System.arraycopy(b2.data, 0, answer.data, b1.manyItems, b2.manyItems);
   answer.manyItems = b1.manyItems + b2.manyItems;
   return answer;
}
}
```

Using the Bag of Objects

Using the bag of objects is easy. The program imports `edu.colorado.collec-tions.ArrayBag`, and then a bag of objects can be declared. The same program may have several different bags for different purposes, or it may even have some of the original bags, such as an `IntArrayBag`.

Figure 5.3 shows a demonstration program that uses three bags of strings. The program asks the user to type several adjectives and names. These words are placed in the bags, and then elements are grabbed out of the bags for the program to write a silly story called "Life."

FIGURE 5.3   Demonstration Program for the ArrayBag Generic Class

Java Application Program

```java
// FILE: Author.java
// This program reads some words into bags. Then a silly story is written using these words.
import edu.colorado.collections.ArrayBag;
import java.util.Scanner;

public class Author
{
    private static Scanner stdin = new Scanner(System.in);

    public static void main(String[ ] args)
    {
        final int WORDS_PER_BAG = 4;   // Number of items per bag
        final int MANY_SENTENCES = 3;  // Number of sentences in story

        ArrayBag<String> good  = new ArrayBag<String>(WORDS_PER_BAG);
        ArrayBag<String> bad   = new ArrayBag<String>(WORDS_PER_BAG);
        ArrayBag<String> names = new ArrayBag<String>(WORDS_PER_BAG);
        int line;

        // Fill the three bags with items typed by the program's user.
        System.out.println("Help me write a story.\n");
        getWords(good,  WORDS_PER_BAG, "adjectives that describe a good mood");
        getWords(bad,   WORDS_PER_BAG, "adjectives that describe a bad mood");
        getWords(names, WORDS_PER_BAG, "first names");
        System.out.println("Thank you for your kind assistance.\n");

        // Use the items to write a silly story.
        System.out.println("LIFE");
        System.out.println("by A. Computer\n");
        for (line = 1; line <= MANY_SENTENCES; line++)
        {
            System.out.print((String) names.grab( ));
            System.out.print(" was feeling ");
            System.out.print((String) bad.grab( ));
            System.out.print(", yet he/she was also ");
            System.out.print((String) good.grab( ));
            System.out.println(".");
        }
        System.out.println("Life is " + (String) bad.grab( ) + ".\n");
        System.out.println("The " + (String) good.grab( ) + " end.");
    }
```

The Scanner class is described in Appendix B.

(continued)

(FIGURE 5.3 continued)

```
public static void getWords(ArrayBag<String> b, int n, String prompt)
// Postcondition: The parameter, prompt, has been written as a prompt
// to System.out. Then n strings have been read using stdin.next,
// and these strings have been placed in the bag.
{
   String userInput;
   int i;

   System.out.print("Please type " + n + " " + prompt);
   System.out.println(", separated by spaces.");
   System.out.println("Press the <return> key after the final entry:");
   for (i = 1; i <= n; i++)
   {
      userInput = stdin.next( );
      b.add(userInput);
   }
   System.out.println( );
}
}
```

A Sample Dialogue

Help me write a story.

Please type 4 adjectives that describe a good mood, separated by spaces.
Press the <return> key after the final entry:
joyous   happy   lighthearted   glad

Please type 4 adjectives that describe a bad mood, separated by spaces.
Press the <return> key after the final entry:
sad   glum   melancholy   blue

Please type 4 first names, separated by spaces.
Press the <return> key after the final entry:
Michael   Janet   Tim   Hannah

Thank you for your kind assistance.

LIFE by A. Computer

Tim was feeling glum, yet he/she was also glad.
Michael was feeling melancholy, yet he/she was also joyous.
Hannah was feeling blue, yet he/she was also joyous.
Life is blue.

The lighthearted end.

Details of the Story-Writing Program

The bags are declared in the demonstration program as you would expect:

```
ArrayBag<String> good    = new ArrayBag<String>(WORDS_PER_BAG);
ArrayBag<String> bad;    = new ArrayBag<String>(WORDS_PER_BAG);
ArrayBag<String> names;  = new ArrayBag<String>(WORDS_PER_BAG);
```

The number, WORDS_PER_BAG, is 4 in the story program, so each of these bags has an initial capacity of 4. To get the actual words from the user, the program calls getWords, with this heading:

```
public static void getWords
(ArrayBag<String> b, int n, String prompt)
```

The method uses the third parameter, prompt, as part of a message that asks the user to type n words. For example, if prompt is the string constant "first names" and n is 4, then the getWords method writes this prompt:

```
Please type 4 first names, separated by spaces.
Press the <return> key after the final entry:
```

The method then reads n strings by using the Scanner class (described in Appendix B).

As the strings are read, the getWords method places them in the bag by activating b.add. In all, the main program activates getWords three times to get three different kinds of strings. The literary merit of the program's story is debatable, but the ability to use bags of objects is clearly important.

Self-Test Exercises for Section 5.3

13. We converted an IntArrayBag to a generic ArrayBag<E>. During the conversion, does every occurrence of int get changed to E?

14. Our bag is a bag of references to objects. Can the null reference be placed into our bag?

15. Write some code that declares a bag of integers and then puts the numbers 1 through 10 into the bag. The numbers are objects of the wrapper class, Integer, not the primitive class int.

16. The original countOccurrences method tested for the occurrence of a target by using the boolean expression **target == data[index]**. What different boolean expression is used in the countOccurrences method of the bag of objects?

17. What technique did the story-writing program use to read strings from the keyboard?

18. Consider the following code that puts a Location into a bag, changes the name, and then tests whether the original name is in the bag. The Location class is from Figure 2.5 on page 67. What does the code print?

```
ArrayBag<Location> points = new ArrayBag<Location>( );
Location origin = new Location(0,0);
Location moving = new Location(0,0);
points.add(moving);
moving.shift(5,10);
System.out.println(points.countOccurrences(origin));
System.out.println(points.countOccurrences(moving));
```

5.4   GENERIC NODES

Nodes That Contain Object Data

Our node class from Chapter 4 can also be converted to a generic class. In the conversion, the new class, called Node, allows us to build linked lists of nodes in which the type of data in each node is determined by the generic type parameter. Here is a comparison of the original IntNode declaration with our new generic class:

Original IntNode:

```
public class IntNode
{
    private int data;
    IntNode link;

    ║ The methods use
    ║ the int data.

}
```

Generic Node Class:

```
public class <E> Node
{
    private E data;
    Node<E> link;

    ║ The methods use
    ║ the E data.

}
```

With the new Node class, each node contains a piece of data that is a reference to an E object, but we don't specify exactly what E is. The implementation of the methods is based on the IntNode methods, following the same steps that we used before on page 269. The resulting Node class is online at http://www.cs.colorado.edu/~main/edu/colorado/nodes/node.java. You may find yourself using it beyond this book, too.

PITFALL ⊍

MISUSE OF THE EQUALS METHOD

When you convert a collection class to contain objects, it is tempting to blindly change every occurrence of the "==" operator to use the equals method instead. There are two pitfalls to beware of.

First, beware of null references. You cannot activate the equals method of a null reference. For example, here is the implementation of the new listSearch method from the generic Node class. The method searches the linked list for an occurrence of a particular target and returns a reference to the node that contains the target. If no such node is found, then the null reference is returned:

```java
public static <E> Node<E> listSearch(Node<E> head, E target)
{
    Node<E> cursor;

    if (target == null)
    { // Search for a node in which the data is the null reference.
        for (cursor = head; cursor != null; cursor = cursor.link)
            if (cursor.data == null)
                return cursor;
    }
    else
    { // Search for a node that contains the non-null target.
        for (cursor = head; cursor != null; cursor = cursor.link)
            if (target.equals(cursor.data))
                return cursor;
    }

    return null;
}
```

The target may be the null reference; in that case, we're searching for a node in which the data is null. This search is carried out in the first part of the large if-statement. We test whether a particular node contains null data with the boolean expression `cursor.data == null`. On the other hand, for a non-null target, the search is carried out in the else-part of the large if-statement. We test whether a particular node contains a non-null target with the boolean expression `target.equals(cursor.data)`.

In general, the `equals` method may be used only when you know that the target is non-null.

The second thing to beware of: You should change an equality test "==" to the `equals` method only where the program is comparing data. Don't change other comparisons. For example, here is the `listPart` method of the generic Node class:

```java
public static <E> Object[] listPart(Node<E> start, Node<E> end)
{
    Node<E> copyHead;
    Node<E> copyTail;
    Node<E> cursor;
    Object[ ] answer = new Object[2];

    // Check for illegal null at start or end.
    if (start == null)
        throw new IllegalArgumentException("start is null.");
```

Note that the return type must now be an array of Objects since generic arrays are forbidden.

```
    if (end == null)
        throw new IllegalArgumentException("end is null.");

    // Make the first node for the newly created list.
    copyHead = new Node<E>(start.data, null);
    copyTail = copyHead;
    cursor = start;

    // Make the rest of the nodes for the newly created list.
    while (cursor != end)
    {
        cursor = cursor.link;
        if (cursor == null)
            throw new IllegalArgumentException
            ("end node was not found on the list.");
        copyTail.addNodeAfter(cursor.data);
        copyTail = copyTail.link;
    }

    // Return the head and tail references.
    answer[0] = copyHead;
    answer[1] = copyTail;
    return answer;
}
```

The method copies part of a linked list, extending from the specified `start` node
to the specified end node. The large while-loop does most of the work, and this
loop continues while `cursor != end`. This boolean expression is checking
whether `cursor` refers to a different node than end. The expression becomes
`false` when `cursor` refers to the exact same node that end refers to, and at that
point the loop ends. Do not change this expression to use the `equals` method.

When the purpose of a boolean expression is to test whether two references
refer to the exact same object, then use the "`==`" or "`!=`" operator. Do not use the
`equals` method.

Other Collections That Use Linked Lists

Using the generic Node class, we can implement other collections that use
linked lists. For example, we can implement another bag of objects that stores
its objects in a linked list. In fact, we'll do exactly this in Section 5.6, but first
you need to see a Java feature called *interfaces* that supports generic programming.

Self-Test Exercises for Section 5.4

19. Why was extra code added to the new `listSearch` method?

20. Suppose the while-loop in `listPart` was changed to:

    ```
    while (!cursor.equals(end))
    ```

    Give an example in which this incorrect `listPart` method would not copy all of the nodes that it is supposed to copy.

21. Suppose x and y are non-null references to two nodes. The data in each node is a non-null `Object`. Write two boolean expressions: (1) an expression that is `true` if x and y refer to exactly the same node, and (2) an expression that is `true` if the data from the x node is equal to the data from the y node. Use the `equals` method where appropriate.

5.5   INTERFACES AND ITERATORS

Java provides another feature to support generic programming: *interfaces*, which allow methods to work with objects of a class when only a limited amount of information is known about that class. This section shows you how to use some basic interfaces that are provided as part of Java's Application Programming Interface (API). We concentrate on the `Iterator` interface, which is particularly important for data structures programming.

Programmers can also create new interfaces (that aren't part of the API), but we won't cover that topic here.

Interfaces

interface: a list of related methods for a class to implement

A Java **interface** is primarily a list of related methods that a programmer may want to implement in a single class. For example, Java's `AudioClip` interface indicates that a class that implements the `AudioClip` interface will have three methods with these headings:

```
public void loop( )
public void play( )
public void stop( )
```

advantages of implementing a known interface

The `AudioClip` interface is intended for classes in which each object can produce a sound on a computer with sound capabilities. For example, the `play` method is supposed to play the sound one time. A class that has these three methods (and perhaps other methods, too) is said to **implement the AudioClip interface**. If you're writing a class with these kinds of audio capabilities, then implementing the `AudioClip` interface will help other programmers understand your intentions and use your class in a way that is consistent with other classes that provide the same capabilities. In addition, using interfaces supports generic programming because programs can be written that use `AudioClip` variables, and these programs will work with any possible implementation of the interface.

How to Write a Class That Implements an Interface

Let's look at the steps to implement a Java interface. To illustrate each step, we'll outline a class called MP3Player, which implements the AudioClip interface. The MP3Player class is designed to allow a program to open and play a file that is stored in the popular MP3 music file format. The implementation follows these steps:

1. **Read the documentation that is provided for the interface.** This documentation is part of the Application Programming Interface (API) at:
   http://download.oracle.com/javase/7/docs/api/index.html.
   This web page lists all of the Java classes and interfaces in a menu on the left side of the page. Click on the AudioClip interface, and you'll see a list that describes the intended use of the three methods that are part of this interface (loop, play, and stop).

2. **Tell the compiler that you are implementing an interface.** When you write a class to implement an interface, the keyword implements is used in the class head to inform the compiler of your intent. For example, we are implementing the MP3Player class, which will implement the AudioClip interface. The required syntax for our example is:

   ```
   public class MP3Player implements AudioClip
   ```

   If a class implements several different interfaces, then the names of the interfaces appear one after another, separated by commas. For example, here is the beginning of a class that implements both the Cloneable and AudioClip interfaces:

   ```
   public class MP3Player implements Cloneable, AudioClip
   ```

3. **Implement the class in the usual way.** Make sure that you implement each of the specified methods. You may also include additional methods and other instance variables if needed. In the case of the MP3Player, you might have a constructor that creates an MP3Player object and connects it with an MP3 music file on your hard drive.

Generic Interfaces and the Iterable Interface

Just like an ordinary interface, a **generic interface** specifies a list of methods, but these methods *depend on one or more unspecified classes*. For example, Java defines a generic interface called Iterator<E> that depends on an unspecified class called E.

Any class that implements the Iterator<E> generic interface must be a generic class with its own generic type parameter, E. The class must provide methods with these headings:

generic interface: a list of related methods that depend on one or more unspecified classes

```
public boolean hasNext( )
public E next( )
public void remove( )
```

As with any generic class, we could have used some name other than E, but it's common practice to use the name E for "element."

Intuitively, an iterator is able to step through a sequence of elements, each of which is an E object. Usually, the sequence comes from a collection such as a generic bag. A program activates hasNext( ) to determine whether there are any more elements in the sequence. If there are more elements, then hasNext( ) returns true, and the program can then activate next( ) to obtain the next element.

An iterator also has a remove method. This method removes the element that was given by the most recent call to next( ). Sometimes an Iterator does not allow elements to be removed. In this case, activating the remove method results in an UnsupportedOperationException.

We could write many classes that implement the Iterator interface. We're going to write one particular generic class called Lister. When a Lister is constructed, it is given a reference to the head of a generic linked list of objects. The Lister stores a copy of this reference variable in its own instance variable, called current. Each subsequent activation of next returns one element from the linked list and moves current on to the next element. When the last element has been returned, hasNext will return false. The Lister does not allow removal of elements, so any attempt to activate remove results in an exception.

The specification and implementation of the Lister class are shown in Figure 5.4.

How to Write a Generic Class That Implements a Generic Interface

A generic class can implement a generic inferface by following the same three steps that we've seen for an ordinary interface:

1. **Read the interface's documentation.** For the Iterator generic interface, this documentation is at the Iterator link of http://download. oracle.com/javase/7/docs/api/index.html.

2. **Tell the compiler that you are implementing a generic interface.** For our gereric class, Lister, we write:

   ```
   public class <E> Lister implements Iterator<E>
   ```

3. **Implement the class in the usual way.** We'll discuss some of the Lister implementation details on page 291.

FIGURE 5.4   Specification and Implementation for the Lister Class

Generic Class Lister

❖ **public class Lister<E> from the package edu.colorado.nodes**

A Lister<E> implements Java's Iterator<E> generic interface for a linked list of objects of type E. Note that this implementation does not support the remove method. Any activation of remove results in an UnsupportedOperationException.

Specification

◆ **Constructor for the Lister<E>**

public Lister(Node<E> head)

Initialize a Lister with a particular linked list of objects.

Parameter:

head – a head reference for a linked list of objects

Postcondition:

Subsequent activations of next will return the elements from this linked list, one after another. If the linked list changes in any way before all the elements have been returned, then the subsequent behavior of this Lister is unspecified.

◆ **hasNext**

public boolean hasNext( )

Determine whether there are any more elements in this Lister.

Returns:

true if there are more elements in this Lister; false otherwise

◆ **next**

public E next( )

Retrieve the next element of this Lister.

Precondition:

hasNext( )

Returns:

The return value is the next element of this Lister. Note that each element is returned only once, and then the Lister automatically advances to the next element.

Throws: NoSuchElementException

Indicates that hasNext( ) is false.

◆ **remove**

public E remove( )

Although remove is part of the Iterator interface, it is not provided in this implementation.

Throws: UnsupportedOperationException

This exception is always thrown!

(continued)

(FIGURE 5.4 continued)

Implementation

```
// File: Lister.java from the package edu.colorado.nodes
// Documentation is available on the previous page or from the Lister link at
// http://www.cs.colorado.edu/~main/docs/.
package edu.colorado.nodes;

import java.util.Iterator;
import java.util.NoSuchElementException;
import edu.colorado.nodes.Node;

public class Lister<E> implements Iterator<E>
{
    // Invariant of the Lister class:
    //     The instance variable current is the head reference for the linked list that contains
    //     the elements that have not yet been provided by the next method. If there
    //     are no more elements to provide, then current is the null reference.
    private Node<E> current;

    public Lister(Node<E> head)
    {
        current = head;
    }

    public boolean hasNext( )
    {
        return (current != null);
    }

    public E next( )
    {
        E answer;

        if (!hasNext( ))
            throw new NoSuchElementException("The Lister is empty.");

        answer = current.getData( );
        current = current.getLink( );

        return answer;
    }

    public void remove( )
    {
        throw new UnsupportedOperationException("Lister has no remove method.");
    }
}
```

The Lister Class

We implement the Lister class as part of our package edu.colorado.nodes. It is a generic class that depends on an unspecified type, E, which is the type of element in a generic linked list. The Iterator interface is part of java.util, so the Lister implementation starts by importing java.util.Iterator. Also, the next method throws a NoSuchElementException to indicate that it has run out of elements, so we also import java.util.NoSuchElementException. The remove method also throws an exception, but no import statement is needed because UnsupportedOperationException is part of java.lang (which is automatically imported for any program).

Any program that creates linked lists can use the Lister class. For example, here's some code that creates a list of strings and then uses a Lister to step through those strings one at a time:

```
import edu.colorado.nodes.Node;
import edu.colorado.nodes.Lister;
...

Node<String> head;      // Head node of a small linked list
Node<String> middle;    // Second node of the same list
Node<String> tail;      // Tail node of the same list
Lister<String> print;   // Used to print the small linked list

// Create a small linked list.
tail   = new Node<String>("Larry", null);
middle = new Node<String>("Curly", tail);
head   = new Node<String>("Moe", middle);
// The list now has "Moe", "Curly", and "Larry". We'll print these strings.
print = new Lister<String>(head);
while (print.hasNext( ))
    System.out.println(print.next( ));
```

The while-loop steps through the elements of the list, printing the three strings:

```
Moe
Curly
Larry
```

 PITFALL

DON'T CHANGE A LIST WHILE AN ITERATOR IS BEING USED

The Lister contains one warning in the constructor documentation: If the linked list changes in any way before all the elements have been returned, then the subsequent behavior of the Lister is unspecified. In other words, while the Lister is being used, the underlying linked list must not be altered. The reason for this is that the Lister uses the original linked list rather than making a copy of that list. This is the way that many of Java's built-in iterators work. However, an alternative is to make a copy of the original linked list, which we will ask you to do in a self-test exercise.

The Comparable Generic Interface

Java has a generic interface called Comparable<T> that requires just one method:

```
public int compareTo(T obj)
```

This interface is intended for any class in which two objects x and y can always be compared to each other with one of three possible results:

- x is less than y
- x and y are equal to each other
- y is less than x

Many classes have this kind of natural ordering among objects. For example, two Integer objects can be compared. Therefore, Java's Integer class is implemented as:

```
public class Integer implements Comparable<Integer>...
```

Because the Integer class implements the Comparable<Integer> interface, it must have a compareTo method with this heading (where the generic type parameter has been instantiated as Integer):

```
public int compareTo(Integer obj)
```

FIGURE 5.5 Some Java Classes That Implement a Comparable Interface

In each case, a negative return value means that the value of x is less than the value of y; a zero return value means that the two values are equal; a positive return value means that the value of x is greater than the value of y.

Java class	Implements	What is compared by x.compareTo(y)
Character	Comparable<Character>	The ASCII values of x and y
Date	Comparable<Date>	A Date is a specific point in time on a specific date. When x.compareTo(y) is negative, the Date x occurred before the Date y.
Double	Comparable<Double>	The double values of x and y.
Integer	Comparable<Integer>	The int values of x and y.
String	Comparable<String>	The strings x and y are compared lexicographically, which means that strings of lowercase letters are compared alphabetically. When x.compareTo(y) is negative, it means that x is alphabetically before y (if they are strings of lowercase letters).

The documentation for the compareTo method is lengthy, but the gist is simple: Any two objects x and y of the class can be compared by activating x.compareTo(y). The method returns an integer that is negative (if x is less than y), zero (if x and y are equal), or positive (if x is greater than y).

The Comparable interface uses the name T for the generic type parameter (rather than E). We could have used any name instead of T, but T is common because it refers to any "type" rather than an "element" in a collection class.

Figure 5.5 shows some of the other Java classes that implement a Comparable interface.

Parameters That Use Interfaces

Interfaces support generic programming because it is often possible to implement a method based only on knowledge about an interface. For example, we can write a method that plays an AudioClip a specified number of times:

```
public static void playRepeatedly(AudioClip clip, int n)
{  // Play clip n times.
   int i;

   for (i = 0; i < n; i++)
      clip.play( );
}
```

The data type of the actual argument for the clip parameter may be any data type that implements the AudioClip interface.

Using an Interface as the Type of a Parameter

When an interface name is used as the type of a method's parameter, the actual argument must be a data type that implements the interface.

A generic method may use a generic interface as the data type of a parameter. For example, we can write a method that computes how many of the elements in an array of T objects are less than some non-null target, provided that the data type of the target is some type that implements Comparable<T>. The method's implementation looks like this, depending on the generic type parameter T (as indicated by <T> before the return type):

```
public static <T> int smaller(T[] data, Comparable<T> target)
{   // The return value is the number of objects in the data array that
    // are less than the non-null target b (using b.compareTo to compare
    // b to each object in the data array).
    int answer = 0;

    for (T next : data)
    {
        if (b.compareTo(next) > 0)
        {   // b is greater than the next element of data.
            answer++
        }
    }
    return answer;
}
```

In this example, the argument for data could be a `String` array, and target could be a `String` (since the `String` class implements `Comparable<String>`). Or data could be an `Integer` array, and target could be an `Integer`. Or data could be any array of T objects, so long as the type of target implements `Comparable<T>`.

In each of these examples, we used an interface as the type of a parameter. This results in restrictions on what type of argument can be used with the method. In Chapter 13, we'll see how to formulate other, more powerful restrictions.

Using instanceof to Test Whether a Class Implements an Interface

A programmer can test whether a given object actually does implement a specified interface. For example, suppose you are writing a method to test whether an object called `info` implements the `AudioClip` interface. If so, the `play` method is activated; otherwise, some other technique is used to display some information about the object. The method could begin like this:

```
if ((information instanceof AudioClip)
    information.play( );
else
    ...
```

The test is carried out with the `instanceof` operator, with the general form:

variable `instanceof` interface-or-class-name

The test is `true` if the variable on the left is a reference to an object of the specified type. Notice that the type name can be an ordinary class name (such as `(information instanceof String)`), or it may be the name of an interface (such as `(information instanceof AudioClip)`).

You can also test whether an object implements a generic interface. You can test for a specific instantiation of the generic interface, such as this:

```
if ((example instanceof Iterator<String>) ...
```

For example, the boolean expression just shown will be true if `example` is a `Lister<String>` object, since the `Lister<String>` class implements the `Iterator<String>` interface.

The Cloneable Interface

Throughout the book, all of our collection classes have implemented the `Cloneable` interface, which has a somewhat peculiar meaning. You might think that the `Cloneable` interface specifies that the class must implement a `clone` method, but this is wrong; there are no methods specified in the `Cloneable` interface. So what's the purpose of the `Cloneable` interface? The purpose comes from the behavior of the `clone( )` method of Java's `Object` class. That `clone` method carries out these two steps:

1. Check to see whether the class has implemented the `Cloneable` interface. If not, a `CloneNotSupportedException` is thrown.

2. Otherwise, the clone is made by copying each of the instance variables of the original.

As you can see, the `Object clone` method checks to see whether the object has implemented the `Cloneable` interface. It does this by using the boolean test `(obj instanceof Cloneable)`, and in fact, the only real purpose of implementing the `Cloneable` interface is so the `Object clone` method can test `(obj instanceof Cloneable)`. Therefore, if you write a `clone` method of your own and that `clone` method activates `super.clone` from Java's `Object` type, then your class must implement `Cloneable` to avoid a `CloneNot-SupportedException`.

Self-Test Exercises for Section 5.5

22. Find the documentation for Java's `CharacterSequence` interface in the API. What methods does this interface require?

23. Write a generic method with one parameter that is a head reference for a linked list of nodes. The method looks through all the nodes of the list and returns a count of the number of nodes that contain null data. Use a `Lister` object to search through the linked list.

24. Write a generic method with one parameter that is a head reference for a linked list of nodes and a second parameter x that is a `Comparable<T>` object. The precondition of the method requires that x is non-null. The method returns a reference to the data in the first node that it finds in

which the data is greater than or equal to x. If there is no such node, then the method returns null.

25. Reimplement the Lister constructor so that a copy of the original linked list is used, rather than using the original linked list directly.

26. Write a boolean expression that will be true if and only if the data type of a variable x implements the Comparable<String> interface.

27. How many methods are required for a class that implements Cloneable?

28. Write a class, ArrayIterator, which implements the Iterator<E> interface. The constructor has one argument, which is an array of E objects. The ArrayIterator returns the components of the array one at a time through its next method.

5.6   A GENERIC BAG CLASS THAT IMPLEMENTS THE ITERABLE INTERFACE (OPTIONAL SECTION)

Normally, when a program needs to keep track of some elements, it puts the elements into a bag or some other collection rather than building a linked list in a haphazard manner. Then, if the program needs to step through the elements, it will ask the bag to provide an iterator that contains all of the elements.

With this in mind, we'll implement one more bag class. The bag will be called LinkedBag in the package edu.colorado.collections, with these features:

- It is a generic bag of objects (with a generic type parameter E).

- The elements are stored in a linked list.

the generic Iterable interface requires one method that returns an iterator

- The bag implements a generic interface called Iterable, which requires one method:

```
public Iterator<E> iterator( )
```

This new method returns an iterator that can be used to step through all the elements currently in the bag. (In fact, the iterator that it returns will be a Lister<E> object, using the generic Lister class from the previous section.)

Here's part of a program that uses the new iterator method:

```
import edu.colorado.collections.LinkedBag;
import java.util.Iterator;
...

LinkedBag<String> stooges = new LinkedBag<String>( );
Iterator<String> print;    // Used to print the strings from the bag
```

```
// Put a few strings in the bag.
stooges.add("Larry");
stooges.add("Curly");
stooges.add("Moe");

// The bag now has "Moe", "Curly", and "Larry". We'll print these strings.
print = stooges.iterator( );
while (print.hasNext( ))
    System.out.println(print.next( ));
```

The while-loop will print the strings "Moe", "Curly", and "Larry"—although the order of printing depends on exactly how the bag stores the elements in the linked list.

PROGRAMMING TIP

ENHANCED FOR-LOOPS FOR THE ITERABLE INTERFACE

Java includes an enhanced version of the for-loop that can be used with any class that implements the `Iterable` interface. In the case of the `stooges` bag shown above, we could rewrite the loop to print the names as follows:

```
// The bag now has "Moe", "Curly", and "Larry". We'll print these strings.
for (String next : stooges)
    System.out.println(next);
```

The new version of the for-loop is similar to the enhanced for-loops for arrays (page 111). The general format is shown here:

This form of the for-loop is called **iterating over a collection**. The general format is given here, although you can use any variable name instead of `item`:

```
for (type of the collection elements  item :  name of the collection)
{
    // Do something with item.
    // The first time through the loop, item will be set equal to the
    // first element that the collection's iterator provides; the second time
    // through the loop, item will be set equal to the iterator's next
    // element; and so on.
    . . .
}
```

This form of the for-loop can be used with any collection that implements the `Iterable` interface.

Implementing a Bag of Objects Using a Linked List and an Iterator

For the most part, the implementation of the new bag is the same as the Chapter 4 class `IntLinkedBag`, which stored its elements in a linked list. To convert to a bag of Java Objects, we'll follow the steps listed on page 269. We'll also implement the new `iterator` method, which needs only one line to construct a `Lister` that contains all the elements. Here's the implementation:

```
public Iterator<E> iterator( )
// Method of the LinkedBag class to return an Iterator that
// contains all the elements that are currently in the bag.
{
    return (Iterator<E>) new Lister<E>(head);
}
```

In this implementation, `head` is the bag's instance variable that is a reference to the head node of the linked list where the bag keeps its elements. There's little new in the rest of the implementation of `edu.colorado.collections.LinkedBag`, so we've put it online at `http://www.cs.colorado.edu/~main/edu/colorado/collections/LinkedBag.java`.

ⓘ PROGRAMMING TIP

EXTERNAL ITERATORS VERSUS INTERNAL ITERATORS

The `iterator` method of the bag class provides an iterator for all the elements in the bag. This kind of iterator is called an **external iterator** because it is an object separate from the bag. This is different from our original bags (which had only a countOccurrences method to examine elements). The `iterator` method also differs from the sequence class of Section 3.3. With a sequence, a program can step through the elements, but only by accessing the sequence's current element. This kind of access, directly through a method of the class, is called an **internal iterator**.

Internal iterators are a simple solution to the problem of stepping through the elements of a collection class, but internal iterators also have a problem. Suppose your program needs to step through the elements of a bag in two different ways. With an internal iterator, the two traversals of the collection elements must occur sequentially—stepping through all the elements for the first time, then restarting the iterator, and finally stepping through all the elements for the second time. However, sometimes you would like to have the two different traversals occurring simultaneously. The first traversal could start, stepping through part of the elements, but before the first traversal is finished, the second traversal starts its work. Simultaneous traversals are not easily handled with internal iterators.

The problem is solved by having a method that provides an external iterator—an object that is separate from the bag. The bag's `iterator` method does just this. If we need to step through the elements of a bag two different times, then we can create two separate external iterators for the bag.

In general, a method that provides an external iterator (and thus implements the `Iterable` interface) is better than providing just an internal iterator.

Summary of the Four Bag Implementations

If nothing else, you should now know how to program your way out of a paper bag using one of the four bag classes listed in Figure 5.6. The bag class is a good example to show all these different approaches to implementing a collection class, but keep in mind that the same approaches can be used for other collection classes.

Self-Test Exercises for Section 5.6

29. What is the primary difference between the `LinkedBag` suggested in this section and the `IntLinkedBag` from Section 4.4?

30. What is the primary difference between the generic `LinkedBag` suggested in this section and the generic `ArrayBag` from Section 5.3?

31. Write some code that allows the user to type in 10 strings. Each string is put in a bag (using the `LinkedBag` from Section 5.6). When the user is finished, the 10 strings are printed.

32. Compare the benefits of an internal iterator to a method that provides an external iterator.

33. What kind of collection can be used in Java's enhanced for-loop?

FIGURE 5.6 Our Four Bag Classes

Approach	Class	Where to find it
Store integer elements in an array.	edu.colorado. collections.IntArrayBag	Figure 3.1 on page 119 and Figure 3.7 on page 137
Store integer elements in a linked list.	edu.colorado. collections.IntLinkedBag	Figure 4.12 on page 216 and Figure 4.17 on page 230
Generic class storing elements in an array.	edu.colorado. collections.ArrayBag	Figure 5.2 on page 271
Generic class with a linked list. This version also has a method to provide an iterator.	edu.colorado. collections.LinkedBag	http:// www.cs.colorado.edu/ ~main/edu/colorado/ collections/ LinkedBag.java

5.7   THE JAVA COLLECTION INTERFACE AND MAP INTERFACE (OPTIONAL SECTION)

Java provides several generic interfaces intended for collection classes that store Java objects. The two most basic of these interfaces are Collection and Map.

The Collection Interface

The methods of our own generic Bag are based on the generic Collection<E> interface, although we wanted to focus on basics, so we did not implement all of the Collection methods shown in Figure 5.7. Still, your experience with collection classes in Chapters 3 through 5 has prepared you for reading the documentation and using any of Java's classes that do implement the Collection interface. Some of the methods in that interface use a question mark as a data type, which is a feature that we'll discuss fully in Chapter 13.

Vector
Set
LinkedList
ArrayList
SortedSet
HashSet

The simplest Java Collection class is called Vector, which is similar to an array because you can place an object at a particular index. But unlike an array, a Vector automatically grows if you place an object at a location beyond its current capacity. Other classes that implement Collection include Set, LinkedList, ArrayList, SortedSet, and HashSet, some of which are discussed in Appendix D.

The Map Interface and the TreeMap Class

A *map class* is similar to a collection class in that a group of elements can be stored. However, the elements added to a map are called **keys**, and each key can have another object attached to it, called its **value**. The keys are usually small objects, such as a Social Security number or a name. The values might be small bits of information, or they could be huge objects containing lots of information. The important concept about a map is that after a key/value pair is added to a map, the entire pair can be retrieved or removed simply by specifying its key. For example, we might build a map in which a student's ID number is the key and the value is an object that contains the student's entire academic record. When we need to retrieve a student's record, we can do so by specifying just the student's ID number.

Maps

A **map** is a collection class in which key/value pairs may be added.
A pair can be retrieved or removed by specifying just its key.

Java has an interface called Map, and there are eight Java classes that implement this interface. One Java class that implements the Map interface is the HashMap (similar to the HashSet in Section 3.5). Another class that implements the Map is the TreeMap class, which we discuss next.

FIGURE 5.7	Part of the API Documentation for the `Collection` Interface

From the Collection link at `http://download.oracle.com/javase/7/docs/api/index.html`

Interface Collection<E>

Method	Summary
`boolean`	`add(E o)` Ensures that this collection contains the specified element.
`boolean`	`addAll(Collection<? extends E> c)` Adds all of the elements in the specified collection to this collection.
`void`	`clear( )` Removes all of the elements from this collection.
`boolean`	`contains(E o)` Returns `true` if this collection contains the specified element.
`boolean`	`containsAll(Collection<?> c)` Returns `true` if this collection contains all of the elements in the specified collection.
`boolean`	`equals(E o)` Compares the specified object with this collection for equality.
`int`	`hashCode( )` Returns the hash code value for this collection.
`boolean`	`isEmpty( )` Returns `true` if this collection contains no elements.
`Iterator<E>`	`iterator( )` Returns an iterator over the elements in this collection.
`boolean`	`remove(E o)` Removes a single instance of the specified element from this collection, if it is present.
`boolean`	`removeAll(Collection<?> c)` Removes all of this collection's elements that are also contained in the specified collection.
`boolean`	`retainAll(Collection<?> c)` Retains only the elements in this collection that are contained in the specified collection.
`int`	`size( )` Returns the number of elements in this collection.
`Object[ ]`	`toArray( )` Returns an array containing all of the elements in this collection.

The TreeMap Class

The generic TreeMap class has two generic type parameters: K for the keys and V for the type of the values. However, Java's java.util.TreeMap class (which implements the Map interface) has one extra requirement: The keys must come from a class that implements the Comparable<K> interface (from page 292). This allows a TreeMap to activate k1.compareTo(k2) to compare two keys k1 and k2.

TreeMap from java.util

Java's TreeMap<K,V> implements the Map interface in an efficient way in which the keys are required to come from a class (such as String) that implements the Comparable interface.

The most important TreeMap operations are specified in Figure 5.8.

To illustrate the TreeMap operations, we will write a program that uses a TreeMap to keep track of the number of times various words appear in a text file. We will use the words as the keys, and the value for each word will be an integer. For example, if the word "starship" appears in the text file 42 times, then the key/value pair of "starship"/42 will be stored in the map. With this in mind, we will write some examples of TreeMap operations using these three variables:

```
TreeMap<String, Integer> frequencyData;
String word;    // A word from our text file, to be used as a key
Integer count;  // The number of times that the word appeared
                // in our text file, to be used as a value in the TreeMap
```

Notice that keys will be strings, which allows us to use a TreeMap since the Java String class does implement the Comparable<String> interface. Also, the variable count is an Integer rather than a simple int. This is because the values in a map must be objects rather than primitive values.

FIGURE 5.8   Partial Specification for the TreeMap Class, Which Implements the Map Interface

---

Generic Class TreeMap<K,V>

❖ **public class TreeMap from the package java.util**

A TreeMap<K,V> implements Java's Map interface for a collection of key/value pairs. The keys (of type K) in a TreeMap are required to implement the Comparable<K> interface so that for any two keys x and y, the return value of x.compareTo(y) is an integer value that is:

— negative if x is less than y

— zero if x and y are equal

— positive if x is greater than y   (continued)

(FIGURE 5.8 continued)

Partial Specification (see the API documentation for complete specification)

♦ **Constructor for the TreeMap<K,V> (see the API documentation for more constructors)**
```
public TreeMap( )
```
Initialize a TreeMap with no keys and values.

♦ **clear**
```
public void clear( )
```
Remove all keys and values from this TreeMap.

Postcondition:
This TreeMap is now empty.

♦ **containsKey**
```
public boolean containsKey(K key)
```
Determine whether the TreeMap has a particular key.

Parameter:
key – the key to be searched for

Precondition:
The key can be compared to other keys in the TreeMap using the comparison operation.

Returns:
The return value is true if this TreeMap has a key of the specified value; otherwise, it's false.

Postcondition:
This TreeMap is now empty.

Throws: ClassCastException or NullPointerException
Indicates that the specified key cannot be compared to other keys currently in the TreeMap.
(The NullPointerException means that the specified key is null, and the comparison
operation does not permit null.)

♦ **get**
```
public V get(K key)
```
Gets the value that is currently associated with the specified key.

Parameter:
key – the key whose associated value is to be returned

Precondition:
The key can be compared to other keys in the TreeMap using the comparison operation.

Returns:
The value for the specified key within this TreeMap; if there is no such value, then the return
value is null.

Throws: ClassCastException or NullPointerException
Indicates that the specified key cannot be compared to other keys currently in the TreeMap.
(The NullPointerException means that the specified key is null, and the comparison
operation does not permit null.) (continued)

(FIGURE 5.8 continued)

♦ **keySet**
```
public Set<K> keySet( )
```
Obtain a Set that contains all the current keys of this TreeMap.

Returns:
The return value is a Java Set from the class java.util.Set. This Set is a container that contains all of the keys currently in this TreeMap.

Note:
Format for a loop that steps through every key in a TreeMap t (assuming the keys are strings):
```
String key;
while (K nextKey : t.keySet( ))
{
    ...process the next key, which is stored in nextKey...
}
```

♦ **put**
```
public V put(K key, V value)
```
Put a new key and its associated value into this TreeMap.

Parameters:
key and value – the key and its associated value to put into this TreeMap

Precondition:
The key can be compared to other keys in the TreeMap using the comparison operation.

Postcondition:
The specified key and its associated value have been inserted into this TreeMap. The return value is the value that was previously associated with the specified key (or null if there was no such key previously in the TreeMap).

Throws: ClassCastException or NullPointerException
Indicates that the specified key cannot be compared to other keys currently in the TreeMap. (The NullPointerException means that the specified key is null, and the comparison operation does not permit null.)

Note:
The return value does not need to be used. For example, t.put(k,v) can be a statement on its own.

♦ **size**
```
public int size( )
```
Obtain the number of key/value pairs currently in this TreeMap.

Returns:
The number of key/value pairs currently in this TreeMap.

Here are the common tasks we'll need to do with our `TreeMap`:

1. Putting a Key/Value Pair into a TreeMap. A key and its associated value are put into a `TreeMap` with the put method. For our example, we will read an English word into the variable word and compute the count of how many times the word occurs. Then we can put the word and its count into the `frequencyData` `TreeMap` with the statement:

```
frequencyData.put(word, count);
```

This adds a new key (word) with its value (count) to the `frequencyData`. If the word was already present in the `TreeMap`, then its old value is replaced by the new count.

2. Checking Whether a Specified Key Is Already in a TreeMap. The boolean method `containsKey` is used for this task. For example, the expression `frequencyData.containsKey(word)` will be true if the map already has a key that is equal to word.

3. Retrieving the Value That Is Associated with a Specified Key. The get method retrieves a value for a specified key. For example, the return value of `frequencyData.get(word)` is the `Integer` value associated with the key word. For our program, this return value is a Java `Integer` object.

4. Stepping Through All the Keys of a TreeMap. For any `TreeMap`, we can use the enhanced form of the for-loop to step through all the different keys currently in the map. The pattern for doing this uses the `keySet` method, as shown here for our word counting program:

```
for(String word : wordMap.keySet( ))
{
    ... do processing for this key, which is in the variable word ...
```

This programming pattern works because the return value of `keySet` is a collection class that implements the `Iterable` interface.

The Word Counting Program

Using a `TreeMap` and the four operations we have just described, we can write a small program that counts the number of occurrences of every word in a text file. The program we write will just read the words (which are expected to be separated by spaces) and then print a table of this sort:

```
------------------------------------------------------------
    Occurrences   Word
             2    aardvark
            10    dog
             1    not
             1    shower
------------------------------------------------------------
```

In this example, the file contained four different words ("aardvark," "dog," "not," and "shower"). The word "aardvark" appeared twice, "dog" appeared 10 times, and the other two words appeared once each.

One of the key tasks in our program is to open the input file (which will be called words.txt) and read all the words in the file, compute the correct counts as we go, and store these counts in a TreeMap called frequencyData. The pseudocode for this task follows these steps:

A. *Open the words.txt file for reading. We will use a Scanner object to do this (see Appendix B).*

B. *while there is still input in the file*
   {

       word = the next word (read from the file)

       Get the current count (from frequencyData) of how many times the word has appeared in the file.

       Add one to that current count and store the result back in the count variable.

       frequencyData.put(word, count);
   }

The implementation of this pseudocode is given in the readWordFile method of Figure 5.9, along with the implementations of three other methods for the application. The getCount method is needed to get the current count (from frequencyData) of a word. In addition to getting the count, it converts from an Integer to an ordinary int. The printAllCounts method is particularly interesting because it uses an enhanced for-loop, as discussed in Section 5.6.

Self-Test Exercises for Section 5.7

34. Write a Java statement that will put a key k into a TreeMap t with an associated value v. What will this statement do if t already has the key k?

35. Write an expression that will be true if a TreeMap t has a specific key k.

36. Suppose that a `TreeMap` t has a key k and that the value associated with k is an array of double numbers. Write a Java statement that will retrieve the value associated with k and assign it to an array variable called v.

37. Suppose t is a `TreeMap` with keys that are strings. Write a few Java statements that will print a list of all the keys in t, one per line.

FIGURE 5.9   Implementation of the `WordCounter` Program to Illustrate the Use of a `TreeMap`

Java Application Program

```java
// File: WordCounter.java
// Program from Section 5.7 to illustrate the use of TreeMaps and Iterators.
// The program opens and reads a file called words.txt.
// Each line in this file should consist of one or more English words separated by spaces.
// The end of each line must not have any extra spaces after the last word.
// The program reads the file, and then a table is printed of all words and their counts.

import java.util.*; // Provides TreeMap, Iterator, and Scanner
import java.io.*;   // Provides FileReader and FileNotFoundException

public class WordCounter
{
    private static void main(String[ ] args)
    {
        TreeMap<String, Integer> frequencyData =
            new TreeMap<String, Integer>( );

        readWordFile(frequencyData);
        printAllCounts(frequencyData);
    }

    private static int getCount
    (String word, TreeMap<String, Integer> frequencyData)
    {
        if (frequencyData.containsKey(word))
        {  // The word has occurred before, so get its count from the map.
            return frequencyData.get(word); // Auto-unboxed
        }
        else
        {  // No occurrences of this word
            return 0;
        }
    }
}
```

(continued)

(FIGURE 5.9 continued)

```java
    private static void printAllCounts
    (TreeMap<String, Integer> frequencyData)
    {
        System.out.println("-----------------------------------------------");
        System.out.println("    Occurrences    Word");

        for(String word : frequencyData.keySet( ))
        {
            System.out.printf("%15d    %s\n", frequencyData.get(word), word);
        }

        System.out.println("-----------------------------------------------");
    }


    private static void readWordFile
    (TreeMap<String, Integer> frequencyData)
    {
        Scanner wordFile;
        String word;       // A word read from the file
        Integer count;     // The number of occurrences of the word

        try
        {  // Try to open the words.txt file:
            wordFile = new Scanner(new FileReader("words.txt"));
        }
        catch (FileNotFoundException e)
        {  // If the file failed, then print an error message and return without counting words:
            System.err.println(e);
            return;
        }

        while (wordFile.hasNext( ))
        {
            // Read the next word and get rid of the end-of-line marker if needed:
            word = wordFile.next( );

            // Get the current count of this word, add 1, and then store the new count:
            count = getCount(word, frequencyData) + 1; // Autobox
            frequencyData.put(word, count);
        }
    }

}
```

CHAPTER SUMMARY

- A Java variable can be one of the eight primitive data types. Anything that's not one of the eight primitive types is a reference to a Java Object.

- An assignment x = y is a **widening conversion** if the data type of x is capable of referring to a wider variety of things than the type of y. It is a **narrowing conversion** if the data type of x is capable of referring to a smaller variety of things than the type of y. Java always permits widening conversions, but narrowing conversions require a typecast.

- A **wrapper class** is a class in which each object holds a primitive value. Java provides wrapper classes for each of the eight primitive types. In many situations, Java will carry out automatic conversions from a primitive value to a wrapper object (**autoboxing**) or vice versa (**auto-unboxing**).

- A **generic method** is similar to an ordinary method with one importnat difference: The definition of a generic method can depend on an underlying data type. The underlying data type is given a name, such as T, but T is not pinned down to a specific type anywhere in the method's implementation.

- When a class depends on an underlying data type, the class can be implemented as a **generic class**. Converting a collection class to a generic class that holds objects is usually a small task. For example, we converted the IntArrayBag to an ArrayBag by following the steps on page 269.

- An interface provides a list of methods for a class to implement. By writing a class that implements one of the standard Java interfaces, you make it easier for other programmers to use your class. There may also be existing programs already written that work with some of the standard interfaces.

- Java's Iterator<E> generic interface provides an easy way to step through all the elements of a collection class. A class that implements Java's Iterator interface must provide two methods:
    ```
    public boolean hasNext( )
    public E next( )
    ```
An Iterator must also have a remove method, although if removal is not supported, then the remove method can simply throw an exception.

- Two classes in this chapter have wide applicability, and you'll find them useful in the future: (1) the Node class from Section 5.4, which is a node from a linked list of objects; and (2) the LinkedBag class from Section 5.6, which includes a method to generate an Iterator for its elements.

- Java provides several different standard collection classes that implement the Collection interface (such as Vector) and the Map interface (such as TreeMap).

? Solutions to Self-Test Exercises

1. Yes, yes, yes.

2. This code has both a widening conversion (marked with the circle) and a narrowing conversion (marked with a triangle):
```
String s = new String("Liberty!");
Object obj;
obj = s; ●
s = (String) obj; △
```

3. Here is one example that causes a ClassCast-Exception at run time:
```
String s = new String("Liberty!");
Integer i;
Object obj;
obj = s;
i = (Integer) obj;
```

4.
```
Character example
    = new Character('w');
```

5. Advantage: When a primitive value is placed in a wrapper object, it can be treated just like any other Java object. Disadvantage: A wrapper object can no longer use the primitive operations, such as the arithmetic operations.

6. First, x and y are unboxed. Then the double numbers are added, resulting in a double answer. This answer is boxed and assigned to z.

7. A generic method is a type-safe way to write a single method that can be used with a variety of different types of parameters.

8. The compiler can discover more type errors with a generic method than with an object method.

9. The generic type parameter first appears in angle brackets before the return type of the generic method. It may later appear within the return type, the parameter list, or the implementation of the generic method. Almost all situations require it to appear at least once in the method's parameter list.

10. Create a new object of that type, or create an array with that type of element.

11.
```
public static <E> int
count(E[] data, E target)
{
    int answer = 0;
    if (target == null)
    {
        for (E next : data)
        {
            if (next == null)
                answer++;
        }
    }
    else
    {
        for (E next : data)
        {
            if (target.equals(next))
                answer++;
        }
    }
    return answer;
}
```

12. We use the count method from the previous exercise:
```
static <S,T> bool most(
    S[] sa, S starget,
    T[] ta, T ttarget
    )
{
    return count(sa, starget)
            > count(ta, ttarget);
}
```

13. No. The only conversions from int to E are the places where the data type refers to an element in the bag. For example, the return value from size remains an int.

14. Yes, we allow add(null), but we also need special code in countOccurrences and remove to handle the null reference.

15. Here is the code:
```
ArrayBag numbers;
int i;
numbers = new ArrayBag( );
for (i = 1; i <= 10; i++)
    numbers.add(new Integer(i));
```

16. In the new countOccurrences, we use this for non-null targets:
```
target.equals(data[index])
```

17. It used stdin.stringInput, where stdin is an EasyReader from Appendix B.

18. A reference to the moving object was put in the bag. When the moving object changes its position, the original location is no longer in the bag. So, the first countOccurrences prints 0, and the second prints 1.

19. To handle searching for a null target.

20. Suppose the data in the first node was equal to the data in the end node. Then the boolean expression will be false right at the start, and only one node will be copied.

21. The expression (x == y) is true if x and y refer to exactly the same node. The expression (x.data.equals(y.data)) is true if the data in the two nodes is the same.

22. The methods are charAt, length, subSequence, and toString.

23.
```
public static <T> int countNull
(Node<T> head)
{
    int answer = 0;
    Lister<T> it =
        new Lister<T>(head);
    while (it.hasNext( ))
    {
        if (it.next( ) == null)
            count++;
    }
    return count;
}
```

24.
```
public static <T> T find
(Node<T> head, Comparable x)
{
    Lister<T> it =
        new Lister<T>(head);
    T d;
    while (it.hasNext( ))
    {
        d = it.next( );
        if (x.compareTo(d) == 0)
            return d;
    }
    return null;
}
```

25.
```
public Lister(Node<T> head)
{
    current = Node<T>.listCopy(head);
}
```

26. (x instanceOf Comparable<Integer>)

27. None. The only purpose of the Cloneable interface is to allow a method to check whether an object is an instance of Cloneable.

28.
```
import java.util.Iterator;

public class ArrayIterator<E>
implements Iterator<E>
{
    private E[ ] array;
    private int index;

    public ArrayIterator
    (E[ ] things)
    {
        array = things;
        index = 0;
    }
    public boolean hasNext( )
    {
        return (index < array.length);
    }
    public E next( )
    {
        return array[index++];
    }
    ... See page 290 for remove ...
}
```

29. The elements in the new bag are Java objects rather than integers. Also, the new bag has an `iterator` method to return a `Lister`.

30. The bag from this section stores its elements in a linked list rather than in an array. Also, the new bag has an `iterator` method to return a `Lister`.

31. This uses three import statements:

```
import java.util.Scanner;
import
  edu.colorado.collections.LinkedBag;
import edu.colorado.nodes.Lister;
```

The code is:

```
Scanner stdin =
  new Scanner(System.in);
LinkedBag<String> b =
  new LinkedBag<String>( );
Lister<String> list;
String s;
int i;
for (i = 1; i <= 10; i++)
{
    System.out.print("Next: ");
    s = stdin.next( );
    b.add(s);
}
```

```
list = b.iterator( );
while (list.hasNext( ))
{
    s = list.next( );
    System.out.println(s);
}
```

32. An internal iterator is quick to implement and use, but an external iterator provides more flexibility, such as the ability to have two or more iterators active at once.

33. Any collection that implements the `Iterable` interface.

34. `t.put(k,v)`; If k is already a key in t, then the put method will replace the old value with the new value v, and the return value of `put` will be the old value.

35. `t.containsKey(k)`

36. `v = (double [ ]) t.get(k);`

37.
```
Iterator it = t.keySet( ).iterator;
while (it.hasNext( ))
{
    System.out.println(it.next( ));
}
```

PROGRAMMING PROJECTS

1 Implement a generic class for a sequence of Java objects. You can store the objects in an array (as in Section 3.3) or in a linked list (as in Section 4.5). The class should also implement the `Iterable` interface.

2 Write a program that uses a bag of strings to keep track of a list of chores you have to accomplish today. The user of the program can request several services: (1) Add an item to the list of chores; (2) ask how many chores are in the list; (3) print the list of chores to the screen; (4) delete an item from the list; (5) exit the program.

If you know how to read and write strings from a file, then have the program obtain its initial list of chores from a file. When the program ends, it should write all unfinished chores back to this file.

3 For this project, you will use the bag class from Section 5.6, including the grab method that returns a randomly selected element. Use this ADT in a program that does the following:

1. Asks the user for a list of 10 nouns.
2. Asks the user for a list of 10 verbs.
3. Prints some random sentences using the provided nouns and verbs.

For example, if two of the nouns were "monkey" and "piano" and two of the verbs were "eats" and "plays," we can expect any of these sentences:

```
The monkey eats the piano.
The monkey plays the piano.
The piano eats the monkey.
The piano plays the monkey.
```

Needless to say, the sentences are not entirely sensible. Your program will need to declare two bags: one to store the nouns and one to store the verbs. Use an appropriate top-down design.

4 Write a program for keeping a course list for each student in a college. The information about each student should be kept in an object that contains the student's name and a list of courses completed by the student. The courses taken by a student are stored as a linked list in which each node contains the name of a course, the number of units for the course, and the course grade. The program gives a menu with choices that include adding a student's record, deleting a student's record, adding a single course record to a student's record, deleting a single course record from a student's record, and printing a student's record to the screen. The program input should accept the student's name in any combination of upper and lowercase letters. A student's record should include the student's GPA (grade point average) when displayed on the screen. When the user is done with the program, the program should store the records in a file. The next time the program is run, the records should be read back out of the file, and the list should be reconstructed. (Ask your instructor if there are any rules about what type of file you should use.)

5 The bag's `clone` method creates a copy of an `ArrayBag`. As with other `clone` methods, adding or removing elements from the original bag will not affect the copy, nor vice versa. However, these elements are now references to objects; both the original and the copy contain references to the same underlying objects. Changing these underlying objects can affect both the original and the copy.

An alternative cloning method, called **deep cloning**, can avoid the problem. A deep cloning method has one extra step: Each reference to an object in the bag's array is examined to see whether that object itself can be cloned. If so, then the object is cloned, and the new bag is given a reference to the clone of the object rather than a reference to the same object that the original bag contains. Rewrite the bag's `clone` method to perform a deep cloning.

Note: Each element in the bag's array, such as `data[i]`, is a Java object, and unfortunately you

---

FIGURE 5.10 Setting `answer.data[i]` Equal to a Deep Clone of `data[i]`

```
java.lang.Class my_class;
java.lang.reflect.Method my_clone_method;
try
{  // Try to set answer.data[i] equal to a clone made by data[i].clone:
   my_class = data[i].getClass( );
   my_clone_method = my_class.getMethod("clone", new Class[0]);
   answer.data[i] = my_clone_method.invoke(data[i], new Object[0]);
}
catch (Exception e)
{
   // The clone method for data[i] wasn't available, so we have to accept the shallow clone.
}
```

cannot call `data[i].clone( )` directly to make a copy (since the `clone` method is not public for the `Object` class). The solution to this problem uses two classes, `java.lang.Class` and `java.lang.reflect.Method`, as shown in Figure 5.10.

6 Modify the bag from the previous exercise so that all of the add methods attempt to make a clone of any item that is added to the bag.

These clones are then put in the bag (rather than just putting a reference to the original item into the bag). Because you don't know whether the type of items in the bag have a public `clone` method, you'll need to attempt to clone in a manner that is similar to Figure 5.10.

7 Rewrite the word counting program from Section 5.7 so that the user can specify the name of the input file. Also, modify the pro-so that all non-letters are removed from each word as it is read, and all uppercase letters are converted to the corresponding lowercase letter.

8 Write an interactive program that uses a `TreeMap` to store the names and phone numbers of your friends.

9 Write a group of generic static methods for examining and manipulating a collection of items via the collection's iterator.

For example, one of the methods might have this heading:

```
public static <E> E find(
    Iterator<E> it,
    E target
    );
```

When the `find` method is activated, the iterator, `it`, is already in some collection. The method searches the collection via the iterator. If one of the collection's elements is equal to the target (using the `equals` method), then a reference to that element is returned; if the target is never found in the range, then the null reference is returned (and the iterator is left at a position that is just after the target).

Discuss and design other methods for your toolkit that manipulate a collection. As a starting point, please use the linked-list methods from the previous chapter.

CHAPTER **6**

Stacks

When you complete Chapter 6, you will be able to ...

- follow and explain stack-based algorithms using the usual computer science terminology of push, pop, and peek.
- use a Java Stack class to implement stack-based algorithms, such as the evaluation of arithmetic expressions.
- implement a Stack class of your own using either an array or a linked list data structure.

6

Stacks

The pushdown store is a "first in–last out" list. That is, symbols may be entered or removed only at the top of the list.

JOHN E. HOPCROFT AND JEFFREY D. ULLMAN
Formal Languages and Their Relation to Automata

This chapter introduces a data structure known as a *stack* or, as it is sometimes called, a *pushdown store*. It is a simple structure, even simpler than a linked list. Yet it turns out to be one of the most useful data structures known to computer science.

6.1 INTRODUCTION TO STACKS

The drawings in the margin depict some stacks. There is a stack of pancakes, some stacks of coins, and a stack of books. A *stack* is an ordered collection of items that can be accessed only at one end. That may not sound like what you see in these drawings, but think for a moment. Each of the stacks is ordered from top to bottom; you can identify any item in a stack by saying it is the top item, second from the top, third from the top, and so on. Unless you mess up one of the neat stacks, you can access only the top item. To remove the bottom book from the stack, you must first remove the two books on top of it. The abstract definition of a stack reflects this intuition.

Stack Definition

A **stack** is a data structure of ordered items such that items can be inserted and removed only at one end (called the **top**).

When we say that the items in a stack are *ordered,* all we mean is that there is one that can be accessed first (the one on top), one that can be accessed second (just below the top), a third one, and so forth. We do *not* require that the items can be compared using the < operator. The items can be of any type.

Stack items must be removed in the reverse order of that in which they are placed on the stack. For example, you can create a stack of books by first placing a dictionary, placing a thesaurus on top of the dictionary, and placing a novel on top of those so that the stack has the novel on top. When the books are removed, the novel must come off first (since it is on top), then the thesaurus, and finally the dictionary. Because of this property, a stack is called a "last-in/first-out" data structure (abbreviated LIFO).

Of course, a stack that is used in a program stores information rather than physical items such as books or pancakes. Therefore, it may help to visualize a stack as a pile of papers on which information is written. To place some information on the stack, you write the information on a new sheet of paper and place this sheet of paper on top of the stack. Getting information out of the stack is also accomplished by a simple operation since the top sheet of paper can be removed and read. There is just one restriction: Only the top sheet of paper is accessible. To read the third sheet from the top, for example, the top two sheets must be removed from the stack.

A stack is analogous to a mechanism that is used in a popular candy holder called a *Pez® dispenser*, shown in the margin. The dispenser stores candy in a slot underneath an animal head figurine. Candy is loaded into the dispenser by pushing each piece into the hole. There is a spring under the candy with the tension adjusted so that when the animal head is tipped backward, one piece of candy pops out. If this sort of mechanism were used as a stack data structure, the data would be written on the candy (which may violate some health laws, but it still makes a good analogy). Using this analogy, you can understand why adding an item to a stack is called a **push** operation and removing an item from a stack is called a **pop** operation.

> **LIFO**
>
> A stack is a last-in/first-out data structure. Items are taken out of the stack in the reverse order of their insertion.

Pushing

Popping

The Stack Class—Specification

The key methods of a stack class are specified in Figure 6.1. Our specification lists a stack constructor and five methods. The most important methods are push (to add an item at the top of the stack) and pop (to remove the top item). Another method, called peek, allows a programmer to examine the top item without actually removing it. There are no methods that allow a program to access items other than the top. To access any item other than the top one, the program must remove items one at a time from the top until the desired item is reached.

FIGURE 6.1   Specification of the Key Methods of a Generic Stack Class

Specification

These are the key methods of a stack class, which we will implement in several different ways. Although this is a specification for a generic stack, we could also implement a stack that contains primitive values (such as `int`) directly. The Java Class Libraries also provide a generic stack class called `java.util.Stack`, which has these same key methods.

♦ **Constructor for the Generic Stack<E>**
```
public Stack( )
```
Initialize an empty stack.
   Postcondition:
   This stack is empty.

(continued)

(FIGURE 6.1 continued)

♦ **isEmpty**

`public boolean isEmpty( )`

Determine whether this stack is empty.

Returns:

`true` if this stack is empty; otherwise, `false`

♦ **peek**

`public E peek( )`

Get the top item of this stack without removing the item.

Precondition:

This stack is not empty.

Returns:

the top item of the stack

Throws: `EmptyStackException`

Indicates that this stack is empty.

♦ **pop**

`public E pop( )`

Get the top item, removing it from this stack.

Precondition:

This stack is not empty.

Postcondition:

The return value is the top item of this stack, and the item has been removed.

Throws: `EmptyStackException`

Indicates that this stack is empty.

♦ **push**

`public void push(E item)`

Push a new item onto this stack. The new item may be the null reference.

Parameter:

`item` – the item to be pushed onto this stack

Postcondition:

The item has been pushed onto this stack.

Throws: `OutOfMemoryException`

Indicates insufficient memory for pushing a new item onto this stack.

♦ **size**

`public int size( )`

Accessor method to determine the number of items in this stack.

Returns:

the number of items in this stack

If a program attempts to pop an item off an empty stack, it is asking for the impossible; this error is called **stack underflow**. The pop method indicates a stack underflow by throwing an `EmptyStackException`. This exception is defined in `java.util.EmptyStackException`. To help you avoid a stack underflow, the class provides a method to determine whether a stack is empty. There is also a method to obtain the stack's current size.

We Will Implement a Generic Stack

Later we will implement the stack in several different ways. Some of our implementations will have extra methods beyond the five given in the figure. Also, each of our implementations will be a *generic* stack that depends on an unspecified data type for the stack's elements. We'll call the class `Stack`, but just like any generic class, it can be used only with Java objects. For example, we can't put primitive `int` values into our `Stack` without a boxing conversion. Because of this, it might sometimes be useful to have a stack that contains primitive values directly. Although we won't show those simpler stacks in this chapter, you can find source code for them in this book's online resources at `http://www.cs.colorado.edu/~main/dsoj.html`.

The stacks implemented in this chapter are generic stacks

The Java Class Libraries also provide a stack of objects called `java.util.Stack`, with the same five methods from Figure 6.1.

PROGRAMMING EXAMPLE: Reversing a Word

Stacks are very intuitive—even cute—but are they good for anything? Surprisingly, they have many applications. Most compilers use stacks to analyze the syntax of a program. Stacks are used to keep track of local variables when a program is run. Stacks can be used to search a maze or a family tree or other types of branching structures. In this book, we will discuss examples related to each of these applications. But before we present any complicated applications of the stack ADT, let us first practice with a simple problem so that we can see how a stack is used.

uses for stacks

Suppose you want a program to read in a word and then write it out backward. If the program reads in NAT, then it will output TAN. If it reads in TAPS, it will output SPAT. The author Roald Dahl wrote a book called ESIOTROT, which our program converts to TORTOISE. One way to accomplish this task is to read the input one letter at a time and place each letter in a stack of characters. After the word is read, the letters in the stack are written out, but because of the way a stack works, they are written out in reverse order. The outline is shown here:

```
// Reversing the spelling of a word
```
Declare a stack of characters.

`while` (there are more characters of the word to read)
    Read a character and push the character onto the stack.
`while` (the stack is not empty)
    Pop a character off the stack and write that character to the screen.

FIGURE 6.2 Using a Stack to Reverse Spelling

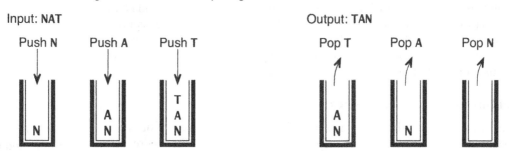

This computation is illustrated in Figure 6.2. At all times in the computation, the only available item is on "top." Figure 6.2 suggests another intuition for thinking about a stack. You can view a stack as a hole in the ground and view the items as being placed in the hole one on top of the other. To retrieve an item, you must first remove the items on top of it.

Self-Test Exercises for Section 6.1

1. Suppose a program uses a stack of characters to read in a word and then write the word out backward as described in this section. Now suppose the input word is DAHL. List all the activations of the push and pop methods. List them in the order in which they will be executed, and indicate the character that is pushed or popped. What is the output?

2. Consider the stack class given in Figure 6.1 on page 317. The peek method lets you look at the top item in the stack without changing the stack. Describe how you can define a new method that returns the second item from the top of the stack without permanently changing the stack. (If you temporarily change the stack, then change it back before the method ends.) Your description will be in terms of peek, pop, and push. Give your solution in pseudocode, not in Java.

6.2 STACK APPLICATIONS

As an exercise to learn about data structures, we will eventually implement the stack class ourselves. For now, though, we'll look at some example applications that use Java's generic stack from `java.util.Stack`. Our first example uses a stack that contains characters to analyze a string of parentheses.

PROGRAMMING EXAMPLE: **Balanced Parentheses**

Later in this chapter, we will describe how stacks can be used to evaluate arithmetic expressions. At the moment, we will describe a simpler method called isBalanced that does a closely related task. The algorithm checks an expres-

sion to see when the parentheses match correctly. It allows three kinds of parentheses: ( ), [ ], or { }. Any symbol other than one of these parentheses is
ignored.

For example, consider the string "{[X + Y*(Z + 7)]*(A + B)}". Each of the
left parentheses has a corresponding right parenthesis. Also, as the string is read
from left to right, there is never an occurrence of a right parenthesis that cannot
be matched with a corresponding left parenthesis. Therefore, the activation of
`isBalanced("{[X + Y*(Z + 7)]*(A + B)}")` returns `true`.

On the other hand, consider the string "((X + Y*{Z + 7}*[A + B])". The
parentheses around the subexpression Z + 7 match each other, as do the parentheses around A + B. And one of the left parentheses in the expression matches the
final right parenthesis. But the other left parenthesis has no matching right parenthesis. Hence, `isBalanced("((X + Y*{Z + 7}*[A + B])")` returns `false`.

The technique used is simple: The algorithm scans the characters of the string
from left to right. Every time a left parenthesis occurs, it is pushed onto the stack.
Every time a right parenthesis occurs, a matching left parenthesis is popped off
the stack. If the correct kind of left parenthesis is not on top of the stack, then the
string is unbalanced. For example, when a curly right parenthesis '}' occurs in
the string, the matching curly left parenthesis '{' should be on top of the stack.

All symbols other than parentheses are ignored. If all goes smoothly and the
stack is empty at the end of the expression, then the parentheses match. On the
other hand, three things might go wrong: (1) The stack is empty when the algorithm needs to pop a symbol; (2) the wrong kind of parenthesis appears at some
point; or (3) symbols are still in the stack after all the input has been read. In each
of these cases, the parentheses are not balanced.

Let's look at some examples. Since no symbols other than parentheses can
affect the results, we will use expressions of just parentheses symbols. All of the
following are balanced (shading and arrows help find matching parentheses):

If you think about these examples, you can begin to understand the algorithm. In
the first example, the parentheses match because they have the same number
of left and right parentheses, but the algorithm does more than just count parentheses. The algorithm actually matches parentheses. Every time it encounters a
')', the symbol it pops off the stack is the matching '('. When it encounters
a ']', the symbol it pops off the stack is the matching '['. When it encounters
a '}', the symbol it pops off the stack is the matching '{'.

The complete sequences of stack configurations from two executions of the
algorithm are shown in Figure 6.3. The stacks shown in the figure show the configuration after processing each character of the expression.

In general, the stack works by keeping a stack of the unmatched left parentheses. Every time the algorithm encounters a right parenthesis, the corresponding

left parenthesis is deleted (popped) from the stack. If the parentheses in the input match correctly, things work out perfectly, and the stack is empty at the end of the input line.

The balancing algorithm is implemented by the isBalanced method of Figure 6.4. Notice that the method uses a stack of Character objects. We can push ordinary char values onto the stack (through autoboxing), and we can use the popped values as if they were ordinary char values (through auto-unboxing). One technique in the implementation may be new to you: acting on the string's next character via a *switch* statement. We'll discuss this technique after you've looked through the program.

FIGURE 6.3 Stack Configurations for the Parentheses Balancing Algorithm

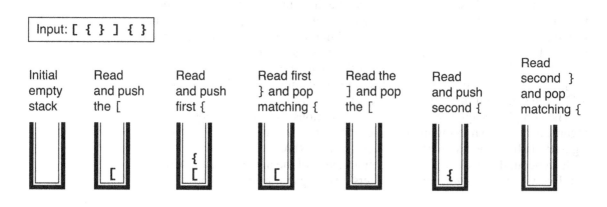

FIGURE 6.4   A Method to Check for Balanced Parentheses

A Method Implementation

```
public static boolean isBalanced(String expression)
// Postcondition: A true return value indicates that the parentheses in the
// given expression are balanced. Otherwise, the return value is false.
// Note that characters other than ( ), { }, and [ ] are ignored.
{
   // Meaningful names for characters
   final char LEFT_NORMAL  = '(';
   final char RIGHT_NORMAL = ')';
   final char LEFT_CURLY   = '{';
   final char RIGHT_CURLY  = '}';
   final char LEFT_SQUARE  = '[';
   final char RIGHT_SQUARE = ']';

   Stack<Character> store = new Stack<Character>; // From java.util.Stack
   int i;                          // An index into the string
   boolean failed = false;         // Change to true for a mismatch

   for (i = 0; !failed && (i < expression.length( )); i++)
   {
      switch (expression.charAt(i))
      {
         case LEFT_NORMAL:
         case LEFT_CURLY:
         case LEFT_SQUARE:
            store.push(expression.charAt(i));
            break;
         case RIGHT_NORMAL:
            if (store.isEmpty( ) || (store.pop( ) != LEFT_NORMAL))
               failed = true;
            break;
         case RIGHT_CURLY:
            if (store.isEmpty( ) || (store.pop( ) != LEFT_CURLY))
               failed = true;
            break;
         case RIGHT_SQUARE:
            if (store.isEmpty( ) || (store.pop( ) != LEFT_SQUARE))
               failed = true;
            break;
      }
   }

   return (store.isEmpty( ) && !failed);
}
```

ⓘ Programming Tip

The Switch Statement

The for-loop in Figure 6.4 processes character number i of the expression during each iteration. There are several possible actions, depending on what kind of character appears at `expression.charAt(i)`. An effective statement to select among many possible actions is the switch statement, with the general form:

```
switch (<Control value>)
{
    <Body of the switch statement>
}
```

When the switch statement is reached, the control value is evaluated. The program then looks through the body of the switch statement for a matching case label. For example, if the control value is the character 'A', then the program looks for a case label of the form `case 'A':`. If a matching case label is found, then the program goes to that label and begins executing statements. Statements are executed one after another, but if a **break** statement (of the form `break;`) occurs, then the program skips to the end of the body of the switch statement.

If the control value has no matching case label, then the program will look for a **default label** of the form `default:`. This label handles any control values that don't have their own case label.

If there is no matching case label and no default label, then the whole body of the switch statement is skipped.

The control value may be an integer, character, short integer, byte, enumerated value, or (starting with Java SE 7) a string value.

For the `isBalanced` method of Figure 6.4, the switch statement has one case label for each of the six possible kinds of parentheses. The three kinds of left parentheses are all handled together by putting their case statements one after another. Each of the right parentheses is handled with its own case statement. For example, one of the right parentheses is the character RIGHT_NORMAL, which is an ordinary right parenthesis ')'. The RIGHT_NORMAL character is handled as shown here:

```
switch (expression.charAt(i))
{
    ...
    case RIGHT_NORMAL:
        if (store.isEmpty( ) || (store.pop( ) != LEFT_NORMAL))
            failure = true;
        break;
    ...
}
```

Evaluating Arithmetic Expressions

In this next programming example, we will design and write a calculator program. This will be an example of a program that uses two stacks: a stack of characters and a stack of double numbers.

Evaluating Arithmetic Expressions—Specification

The program takes as input a fully parenthesized numeric expression such as the following:

input to the calculator program

```
((((12 + 9)/3) + 7.2)*((6 - 4)/8))
```

The expression consists of integers or double numbers, together with the operators +, -, *, and /. To focus on the use of the stack (rather than on input details), we require that each input number be non-negative. (Otherwise, it is hard to distinguish the subtraction operator from a minus sign that is part of a negative number.) We will assume that the expression is formed correctly so that each operation has two arguments. Finally, we will also assume that the expression is fully parenthesized with ordinary parentheses '(' and ')', meaning that each operation has a pair of matched parentheses surrounding its arguments. We can later enhance our program so that these assumptions are no longer needed.

The output will simply be the value of the arithmetic expression.

output of the calculator program

Evaluating Arithmetic Expressions—Design

Most of the program's work will be carried out by a method that reads one line of input and evaluates that line as an arithmetic expression. To get a feel for the problem, let's start by doing a simple example by hand. Consider the following expression:

```
(((6 + 9)/3)*(6 - 4))
```

do an example by hand

If we were to evaluate this expression by hand, we might first evaluate the innermost expressions, (6 + 9) and (6 - 4), to produce the smaller expression:

```
((15/3)*2)
```

Next, we would evaluate the expression (15/3) and replace this expression with its value of 5. That would leave us with the expression (5 * 2). Finally, we would evaluate this last operation to get the answer of 10.

To convert this intuitive approach into a fully specified algorithm that can be implemented, we need to do things in a more systematic way: We need a specific way to find the expression to be evaluated next and a way to remember the results of our intermediate calculations.

First let's find a systematic way of choosing the next expression to be evaluated. (After that, we can worry about how we will keep track of the intermediate results.) We know that the expression to be evaluated first must be one of the innermost expressions—which is a subexpression that has just one operation. Let's decide to evaluate the leftmost of these innermost expressions. For instance, consider our example of:

```
(((6 + 9)/3)*(6 - 4))
```

The innermost expressions are (6 + 9) and (6 – 4), and the leftmost one of these is (6 + 9). If we evaluate this *leftmost of the innermost expressions*, we obtain:

```
((15/3)*(6 - 4))
```

We could now go back and evaluate the other innermost expression (6 – 4), but why bother? There is a simpler approach that spares us the trouble of remembering any other expressions. After we evaluate the leftmost of the innermost expressions, we are left with another simpler arithmetic expression, namely ((15/3)*(6 – 4)), so we can simply repeat the process with this simpler expression: We again evaluate the leftmost of the innermost expressions of our new, simpler expression. The entire process will look like the following:

1. Evaluate the leftmost of the innermost expressions in

   ```
   (((6 + 9)/3)*(6 - 4))
   ```

   to produce the simpler expression ((15/3)*(6 - 4)).

2. Evaluate the leftmost of the innermost expressions in

   ```
   ((15/3)*(6 - 4))
   ```

   to produce the simpler expression (5*(6 - 4)).

3. Evaluate the leftmost of the innermost expressions in

   ```
   (5*(6 - 4))
   ```

   to produce the simpler expression (5 * 2).

4. Evaluate the leftmost of the innermost expressions in

   ```
   (5 * 2)
   ```

   to obtain the final answer of 10.

translating the hand method to an algorithm   This method works fine with pencil and paper, but the algorithm must read the input one character at a time from left to right. How does the algorithm find *the leftmost of the innermost expressions*? Look at the preceding example. The end of the expression to be evaluated is always a right parenthesis ')', and moreover, it is always the *first* right parenthesis. After evaluating one of these innermost expressions, there is no need to back up; to find the next right parenthesis, we can just keep reading left to right from where we left off. The next right parenthesis will indicate the end of the next expression to be evaluated.

Now we know how to find the expression to be evaluated next, but how do we keep track of our intermediate values? For this, we use two stacks. One stack will contain numbers; there will be numbers from the input as well as numbers that were computed when subexpressions were evaluated. The other stack will hold symbols for the operations that still need to be evaluated. Because a stack processes data in a last-in/first-out manner, it will turn out that the correct two numbers are on the top of the numbers stack at the same time that the appropriate operation is at the top of the stack of operations. To better understand how the process works, let's evaluate our sample expression one more time, this time using the two stacks.

We begin by reading up to the first right parenthesis; the numbers we encounter along the way are pushed onto the numbers stack, and the operations we encounter along the way are pushed onto the operations stack. When we reach the first right parenthesis, our two stacks look like this:

Characters read so far (shaded):
(((6 + 9) / 3) * (6 − 4))

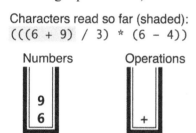

Whenever we reach a right parenthesis, we combine the top two numbers (on the numbers stack) using the topmost operation (on the character stack). In our example, we compute 6 + 9, yielding 15, and this number 15 is pushed back onto the numbers stack:

Characters read so far (shaded):
(((6 + 9) / 3) * (6 − 4))

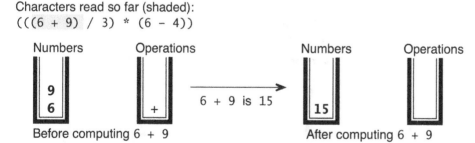

Notice that the leftmost operand (6 in this example) is the *second* number popped off the stack. For addition, this does not matter—who cares whether we have added 6 + 9 or 9 + 6? But the order of the operands does matter for subtraction and division.

Next, we simply continue the process by reading up to the next right parenthesis, pushing the numbers we encounter onto the numbers stack, and pushing the operations we encounter onto the operations stack. When we reach the next right parenthesis, we combine the top two numbers using the topmost operation. Here's what happens in our example when we reach the second right parenthesis:

Characters read so far (shaded):
(((6 + 9) / 3) * (6 − 4))

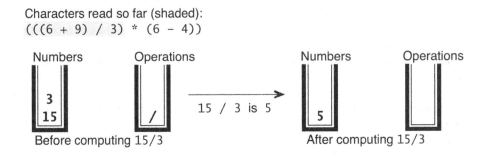

Again, the leftmost operand (15) is the second number popped off the stack, so the correct evaluation is 15/3, not 3/15. Continuing the process, we obtain:

Characters read so far (shaded):
(((6 + 9) / 3) * (6 − 4))

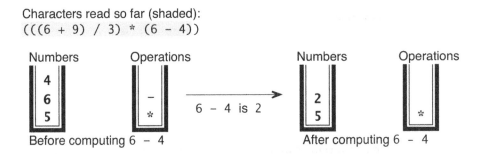

Finally, continuing the process one more time does not add anything to the stacks, but it does read the last right parenthesis and does combine two numbers from the numbers stack with an operation from the operations stack:

Characters read so far (shaded):
(((6 + 9) / 3) * (6 − 4))

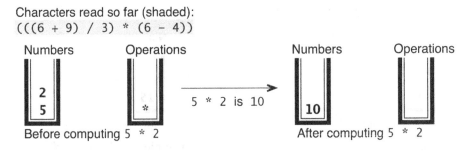

At this point, there is no more input, and there is exactly one number in the number stack, namely 10. That number is the answer. Notice that when we used the two stacks, we performed the exact same evaluations as we did when we first evaluated this expression in a simple pencil-and-paper fashion.

To evaluate our expression, we only need to repeatedly handle the input items according to the following cases:

cases for evaluating an arithmetic expression

Numbers. When a number is encountered in the input, the number is read and pushed onto the numbers stack. We allow the numbers to be any double number, but we do not allow a + or - sign at the front of the number. So, we can have numbers such as 42.8 and 0.34, but not -42.8 or -0.34. This restriction is because we haven't yet developed the algorithm for distinguishing between a + or - sign that is part of a number and a + or - sign that is an arithmetic addition or subtraction.

Operation Characters. When one of the four operation characters is encountered in the input, the character is read and pushed onto the operations stack.

Right Parenthesis. When a right parenthesis is read from the input, an "evaluation step" takes place. The step pops the top two numbers from the number stack and pops the top operation from the operation stack. The two numbers are combined using the operation (with the second number popped as the left operand). The result of the operation is pushed back onto the numbers stack.

Left Parenthesis or Blank. The only other characters that appear in the input are left parentheses and blanks. These are read and thrown away, not affecting the computation. A more complete algorithm would need to process the left parentheses in some way to ensure that each left parenthesis is balanced by a right parenthesis, but for now we are assuming that the input is completely parenthesized in a proper manner.

The processing of input items halts when the end of the input line occurs, indicated by '\n' in the input. At this point, the answer is the single number that remains in the number stack.

We now have our algorithm, which we plan to implement as a method called evaluate. The parameter to evaluate is a string that provides the arithmetic expression. The return value is the value of the arithmetic expression as a double number. For example, evaluate("(((60 + 40)/50) * (16 - 4))") returns 24.0.

Implementation of the evaluate Method

Our implementation of evaluate requires some understanding of the Scanner class from Appendix B. This class is often attached to keyboard input, but in our evaluate implementation, we create a Scanner called input that contains all the characters from the arithmetic expression. This allows us to more easily read the expression, detecting which parts are numbers and which parts are operations. In particular, we use these items:

- The method input.hasNext( ) returns true if there are still more parts of the expression to be processed.

- The expression input.hasNext(UNSIGNED_DOUBLE) is true if the next part of the input expression is a double number (with no + or - sign in front). This uses a constant UNSIGNED_DOUBLE that is defined and discussed in Appendix B.

- The statement next = input.findInLine(UNSIGNED_DOUBLE) sets the string next equal to the next part of the input expression, which must be a double number. Once the double number is in the string next, we can convert it to a Double value and push it onto the stack with:

```
numbers.push(new Double(next));
```

- Similarly, next = input.findInLine(CHARACTER) sets next equal to the next single character (skipping spaces) in the input expression.

Our implementation also uses one other method, evaluateStackTops, which appears along with the evaluate method in Figure 6.5. In order to compile these methods, you will need to include the definitions of UNSIGNED_DOUBLE and CHARACTER from Appendix B; the code also requires these import statements:

```
import java.util.Stack;    // Provides the generic Stack class
import java.util.Scanner;  // Provides the Scanner class
import java.util.Pattern;  // Provides the Pattern class
```

FIGURE 6.5   A Method to Evaluate a Fully Parenthesized Arithmetic Expression

Method Specification and Implementation

♦ **evaluate**

```
public static double evaluate(String expression)
```
The evaluate method evaluates the arithmetic expression.

Parameter:
expression– a fully parenthesized arithmetic expression

Precondition:
The expression must be a fully parenthesized arithmetic expression formed from double numbers (with no + or – sign in front), any of the four arithmetic operations (+, –, *, or /), and spaces.

Returns:
the value of the arithmetic expression

Throws: IllegalArgumentException
Indicates that the expression had the wrong format.

(continued)

(FIGURE 6.5 continued)

```java
public static double evaluate(String expression)
{
    // Two generic stacks to hold the expression's numbers and operations:
    Stack<Double> numbers = new Stack<Double>( );
    Stack<Character> operations = new Stack<Character>( );

    // Convert the expression to a Scanner for easier processing. The next String holds the
    // next piece of the expression: a number, operation, or parenthesis.
    Scanner input = new Scanner(expression);
    String next;

    while (input.hasNext( ))
    {
        if (input.hasNext(UNSIGNED_DOUBLE))
        {   // The next piece of the expression is a number
            next = input.findInLine(UNSIGNED_DOUBLE);
            numbers.push(new Double(next));
        }
        else
        {   // The next piece of the input is an operation (+, -, *, or /) or a parenthesis.
            next = input.findInLine(CHARACTER);
            switch (next.charAt(0))
            {
            case '+': // Addition
            case '-': // Subtraction
            case '*': // Multiplication
            case '/': // Division
                operations.push(next.charAt(0));
                break;
            case ')': // Right parenthesis (the evaluateStackTops function is on the next page)
                evaluateStackTops(numbers, operations);
                break;
            case '(': // Left parenthesis
                break;
            default : // Illegal character
                throw new IllegalArgumentException("Illegal character");
            }
        }
    }
    if (numbers.size( ) != 1)
        throw new IllegalArgumentException("Illegal input expression");
    return numbers.pop( );
}
```

> This code requires
> java.util.Stack,
> java.util.Scanner, and
> java.util.Pattern.
>
> See Appendix B for
> UNSIGNED_DOUBLE and
> CHARACTER, which we use
> here to simplify reading from
> a Scanner.

(continued)

(FIGURE 6.5 continued)

Method Specification and Implementation

♦ **evaluateStackTops**
```
    public static void evaluateStackTops
       (Stack<Double> numbers, Stack<Character> operations)
```
This method applies an operation to two numbers taken from the numbers stack.

Precondition:
There must be at least two numbers on the numbers stack, and the top character on the operations stack must be the character '+', '-', '*', or '/'.

Postcondition:
The top two numbers have been popped from the numbers stack, and the top operation has been popped from the operations stack. The two numbers have been combined using the operation (with the second number popped as the left operand).

Throws: IllegalArgumentException
Indicates that the stacks fail the precondition.

```
public static void evaluateStackTops
(Stack<Double> numbers, Stack<Character> operations)
{
    double operand1, operand2;

    // Check that the stacks have enough items, and get the two operands.
    if ((numbers.size( ) < 2) || (operations.isEmpty( )))
        throw new IllegalArgumentException("Illegal expression");
    operand2 = numbers.pop( );
    operand1 = numbers.pop( );

    // Carry out an action based on the operation on the top of the stack.
    switch (operations.pop( ))
    {
        case '+': numbers.push(operand1 + operand2);
                break;
        case '-': numbers.push(operand1 - operand2);
                break;
        case '*': numbers.push(operand1 * operand2);
                break;
        case '/': // Note: A division by zero is possible. The result would be one of the
                // constants Double.POSITIVE_INFINITY or Double.NEGATIVE_INFINITY.
                numbers.push(operand1 / operand2);
                break;
        default : throw new IllegalArgumentException("Illegal operation");
    }
}
```

Evaluating Arithmetic Expressions—Testing and Analysis

As usual, you should test your program on boundary values that are most likely *testing*
to cause problems. For this program, one kind of boundary value consists of
the simplest kind of expressions: those that combine only two numbers. To test
that operations are performed correctly, you should test simple expressions for
each of the operations +, -, *, and /. These simple expressions should have
only one operation. Be sure to test the division and subtraction operations carefully to ensure that the operations are performed in the correct order. After all,
3/15 is not the same as 15/3, and 3 – 15 is not the same as 15 – 3. These are
perhaps the only boundary values. But it is important also to test some cases
with nested parentheses, and you can test an illegal division such as 15/0.
What does the program do? It throws an `IllegalArgumentException` in the
`evaluateStackTops` method.

Let's estimate the number of operations that our program will use on an *time analysis*
expression of length *n*. We will count each of the following as one program operation: reading or peeking at a symbol, performing one of the arithmetic operations (+, -, *, or /), pushing an item onto one of the stacks, and popping an item
off of one of the stacks. We consider each kind of operation separately.

Time Spent Reading Characters. There are only *n* symbols in the input, so
the program can read at most *n* symbols. No character is "peeked" at more than
once either, so this aspect of the program has no more than 2*n* operations.

Time Spent Evaluating Arithmetic Operations. Each arithmetic operation
performed by the program is the evaluation of an operation symbol in the input.
Because there are no more than *n* arithmetic operations in the input, there are at
most *n* arithmetic operations performed. In actual fact, there are far fewer than *n*
operations since many of the input symbols are digits or parentheses. But there
are certainly no more than *n* arithmetic operation symbols, so it is safe to say that
there are no more than *n* arithmetic operations performed.

Number of Push Operations. Since there are no more than *n* arithmetic operation symbols, we know that there are at most *n* operation symbols pushed onto
the operations stack. The numbers stack may contain input numbers and numbers
obtained from evaluating arithmetic expressions. Again, an upper bound will suffice: There are at most *n* input numbers and at most *n* arithmetic operations evaluated. Thus, at most, 2*n* numbers are pushed onto the numbers stack. This gives
an upper bound of 3*n* total push operations onto the stacks.

Number of Pop Operations. Once we know the total number of items that are
pushed onto the two stacks, we have a bound on how many things can be popped
off of the two stacks. After all, you cannot pop off an item unless it was first
pushed onto the stack. Thus, there is an upper bound of 3*n* pop operations from
any of the stacks.

Total Number of Operations. Now let's total things up. The total number of operations is no more than $2n$ reads/peeks, plus n arithmetic operations performed, plus $3n$ items pushed onto a stack, plus $3n$ items popped off of a stack—for a grand total of $9n$. The actual number of operations will be less than this because we have used generous upper bounds in several estimates, but $9n$ is enough to conclude that the algorithm for this program is $O(n)$; this is a linear algorithm in the number of stack operations.

Evaluating Arithmetic Expressions—Enhancements

The program in Figure 6.5 on page 330 is a fine example of how to use stacks. As a computer scientist, you will find yourself using stacks in this manner in many different situations. However, the program is not a fine example of a finished program. Before we can consider it to be a finished product, we need to add a number of enhancements to make the program more robust and friendly.

Some enhancements are easy. It is useful (and easy) to write a main program that repeatedly gets and evaluates arithmetic expressions. Another nice enhancement would be to permit expressions that are not fully parenthesized and to use the Java precedence rules to decide the order of operations when parentheses are missing. We will discuss topics related to this enhancement in Section 6.4, where (surprise!) we'll see that a stack is useful for this purpose, too.

Self-Test Exercises for Section 6.2

3. How would you modify the calculator program in Figure 6.5 on page 330 to allow the symbol ∧ to be used for exponentiation? Describe the changes; do not write out the code.

4. How would you modify the calculator program in Figure 6.5 on page 330 to allow for comments in the calculator input? Comments appear at the end of the expression, starting with a double slash // and continuing to the end of the line. Describe the changes; do not write out the code.

5. Write some illegal expressions that are caught by the calculator program in Figure 6.5 on page 330, resulting in an `IllegalArgumentException`.

6. Write some illegal expressions that are not caught by the calculator program in Figure 6.5 on page 330.

7. Carry out the operations of `evaluate` by hand on the input expression `( ( (60 + 40)/50) * (16 - 4) )`. Draw the two stacks after each push or pop.

8. What kind of expressions cause the `evaluation` stacks to grow large?

9. What is the time analysis, in big-O notation, of the `evaluation` method? Explain your reasoning.

6.3 IMPLEMENTATIONS OF THE STACK ADT

We will give two implementations of our generic stack class: an implementation using an array and an implementation using a linked list. Each implementation will be for a generic class, but as we discussed earlier, we could just as easily implement the stack to hold one of Java's primitive types.

Array Implementation of a Stack

Figure 6.6 gives the specification and implementation of a generic `ArrayStack` class that includes all the earlier methods we mentioned (from Figure 6.1 on page 317). The class stores its items in an array, so the class also has extra methods for explicitly dealing with capacity. The class implementation uses two instance variables described here:

Invariant of the ArrayStack Class

1. The number of items in the stack is stored in the instance variable `manyItems`.

2. The items in the stack are stored in a partially filled array called `data`, with the bottom of the stack at `data[0]`, the next item at `data[1]`, and so on, to the top of the stack at `data[manyItems-1]`.

In other words, our stack implementation is simply a partially filled array implemented in the usual way: an array and a variable to indicate how much of the array is being used. The stack bottom is at `data[0]`, and the top position is the last array position used. Each method (except the constructor) can assume that the stack is represented in this way when the operation is activated. Each method has the responsibility of ensuring that the stack is still represented in this manner when the method finishes.

the stack items are stored in a partially filled array

The methods that operate on our stack are now straightforward. To initialize the stack, set the instance variable `manyItems` to zero, indicating an empty array and hence an empty stack. The constructor also makes the data array, which (as discussed in Section 5.3) is an array of Java objects.

implementing the stack operations

To add an item to the stack (in the `push` method), we store the new item in `data[manyItems]`, and then we increment `manyItems` by 1. To look at the top item in the stack (the peek method), we simply look at the item in array position `data[manyItems-1]`. To remove an item from the stack (in the pop method), we decrement `manyItems` and then return the value of `data[manyItems]` (which is the value that was on top prior to the pop operation). The methods to test for emptiness and to return the size of the stack work by examining the value of `manyItems`.

FIGURE 6.6	Specification and Implementation of the Array Version of the Generic Stack Class

Generic Class ArrayStack

❖ **public class ArrayStack<E> from the package edu.colorado.collections**

An ArrayStack<E> is a stack of references to E objects.

Limitations:

(1) The capacity of one of these stacks can change after it's created, but the maximum capacity is limited by the amount of free memory on the machine. The constructors, clone, ensureCapacity, push, and trimToSize will result in an OutOfMemoryError when free memory is exhausted.

(2) A stack's capacity cannot exceed the largest integer, 2,147,483,647 (Integer.MAX_VALUE). Any attempt to create a larger capacity results in failure due to an arithmetic overflow.

Specification

◆ **Constructor for the ArrayStack<E>**

public ArrayStack( )

Initialize an empty stack with an initial capacity of 10. Note that the push method works efficiently (without needing more memory) until this capacity is reached.

Postcondition:

This stack is empty and has an initial capacity of 10.

Throws: OutOfMemoryError

Indicates insufficient memory for new Object[10].

◆ **Second Constructor for the ArrayStack<E>**

public ArrayStack(int initialCapacity)

Initialize an empty stack with a specified initial capacity. Note that the push method works efficiently (without needing more memory) until this capacity is reached.

Parameter:

initialCapacity – the initial capacity of this stack

Precondition:

initialCapacity is non-negative.

Postcondition:

This stack is empty and has the given initial capacity.

Throws: IllegalArgumentException

Indicates that initialCapacity is negative.

Throws: OutOfMemoryError

Indicates insufficient memory for new Object[initialCapacity].

(continued)

(FIGURE 6.6 continued)

♦ **clone**
```
public ArrayStack<E> clone( )
```
Generate a copy of this stack.

Returns:
> The return value is a copy of this stack. Subsequent changes to the copy will not affect the original, nor vice versa.

Throws: OutOfMemoryError
> Indicates insufficient memory for creating the clone.

♦ **ensureCapacity**
```
public void ensureCapacity(int minimumCapacity)
```
Change the current capacity of this stack.

Parameter:
> minimumCapacity – the new capacity for this stack

Postcondition:
> This stack's capacity has been changed to at least minimumCapacity. If the capacity was already at or greater than minimumCapacity, then the capacity is left unchanged.

Throws: OutOfMemoryError
> Indicates insufficient memory for new Object[minimumCapacity].

♦ **getCapacity**
```
public int getCapacity( )
```
Accessor method to determine the current capacity of this stack. The push method works efficiently (without needing more memory) until this capacity is reached.

Returns:
> the current capacity of this stack

♦ **isEmpty—peek—pop—push—size**
```
public boolean isEmpty( )
public E peek( )
public E pop( )
public void push(E item)
public int size( )
```
These are the standard stack specifications from Figure 6.1 on page 318.

♦ **trimToSize**
```
public void trimToSize( )
```
Reduce the current capacity of this stack to its actual size (i.e., the number of items it contains).

Postcondition:
> This stack's capacity has been changed to its current size.

Throws: OutOfMemoryError
> Indicates insufficient memory for altering the capacity.

(continued)

(FIGURE 6.6 continued)

Implementation

```
// File: ArrayStack.java from the package edu.colorado.collections
// Complete documentation is available on pages 336–337 or from the Stack link at
// http://www.cs.colorado.edu/~main/docs/.

package edu.colorado.collections;
import java.util.EmptyStackException;

public class ArrayStack<E> implements Cloneable
{
   // Invariant of the ArrayStack class:
   //    1. The number of items in the stack is in the instance variable manyItems.
   //    2. For an empty stack, we do not care what is stored in any of data; for a
   //       non-empty stack, the items in the stack are stored in a partially filled array called
   //       data, with the bottom of the stack at data[0], the next item at data[1], and so on,
   //       to the top of the stack at data[manyItems-1].
   private Object[ ] data;
   private int manyItems;

   public ArrayStack( )
   {
      final int INITIAL_CAPACITY = 10;
      manyItems = 0;
      data = new Object[INITIAL_CAPACITY];
   }

   public ArrayStack(int initialCapacity)
   {
      if (initialCapacity < 0)
         throw new IllegalArgumentException
         ("initialCapacity too small " + initialCapacity);
      manyItems = 0;
      data = new Object[initialCapacity];
   }
```

(continued)

(FIGURE 6.6 continued)

```java
@SuppressWarnings("unchecked")      // See the warnings discussion on page 265.
public ArrayStack<E> clone( )
{   // Clone an ArrayStack.
    ArrayStack<E> answer;

    try
    {
        answer = (ArrayStack<E>) super.clone( );
    }
    catch (CloneNotSupportedException e)
    {
        // This exception should not occur. But if it does, it would probably indicate a
        // programming error that made super.clone unavailable.
        // The most common error would be forgetting the "implements Cloneable"
        // clause at the start of this class.
        throw new RuntimeException
        ("This class does not implement Cloneable.");
    }

    answer.data = data.clone( );

    return answer;
}

public void ensureCapacity(int minimumCapacity)
{
    Object[ ]biggerArray;

    if (data.length < minimumCapacity)
    {
        biggerArray = new Object[minimumCapacity];
        System.arraycopy(data, 0, biggerArray, 0, manyItems);
        data = biggerArray;
    }
}

public int getCapacity( )
{
    return data.length;
}

public boolean isEmpty( )
{
    return (manyItems == 0);
}
```

(continued)

(FIGURE 6.6 continued)

```java
@SuppressWarnings("unchecked")    // See the warnings discussion on page 265.
public E peek( )
{
    if (manyItems == 0)
        // EmptyStackException is from java.util, and its constructor has no argument.
        throw new EmptyStackException( );
    return (E) data[manyItems-1];
}

@SuppressWarnings("unchecked")    // See the warnings discussion on page 265.
public E pop( )
{
    E answer;
    if (manyItems == 0)
        // EmptyStackException is from java.util, and its constructor has no argument.
        throw new EmptyStackException( );
    answer = (E) data[--manyItems];
    data[manyItems] = null; // For the garbage collector
    return answer;
}

public void push(E item)
{
    if (manyItems == data.length)
    {
        // Double the capacity and add 1; this works even if manyItems is 0. However, in
        // case that manyItems*2 + 1 is beyond Integer.MAX_VALUE, there will be an
        // arithmetic overflow and the stack will fail.
        ensureCapacity(manyItems * 2 + 1);
    }
    data[manyItems] = item;
    manyItems++;
}

public int size( )
{
    return manyItems;
}

public void trimToSize( )
{
    Object[ ] trimmedArray;

    if (data.length != manyItems)
    {
        trimmedArray = new Object[manyItems];
        System.arraycopy(data, 0, trimmedArray, 0, manyItems);
        data = trimmedArray;
    }
}
}
```

Linked List Implementation of a Stack

A linked list is a natural way to implement a stack as a dynamic structure whose size can grow and shrink one item at a time. The head of the linked list serves as the top of the stack. Figure 6.7 contains the specification and implementation for a stack class that is implemented with a linked list. The class is called LinkedStack to distinguish it from our earlier ObjectStack. Here is a precise statement of the invariant of this version of the new stack ADT:

Invariant of the Generic LinkedStack Class

1. The items in the stack are stored in a linked list, with the top of the stack stored at the head node, down to the bottom of the stack at the final node.

2. The instance variable top is the head reference of the linked list of items.

As usual, all methods (except the constructors) assume that the stack is represented in this way when the method is activated, and all methods ensure that the stack continues to be represented in this way when the method finishes.

Because we are using a linked list, there are no capacity worries. Thus, there are no methods that deal with capacity. A program could build a stack with more than Integer.MAX_VALUE items, limited only by its amount of memory. However, beyond Integer.MAX_VALUE, the return value of the size method will be wrong because of arithmetic overflow.

As a further consequence of using a linked list, it makes sense to utilize the generic Node<E> class from http://www.cs.colorado.edu/~main/edu/colorado/nodes/Node.java. Thus, in Figure 6.7 you will find this import statement:

```
import edu.colorado.nodes.Node;
```

By using the Node<E> class, many of the stack methods can be implemented with just a line or two of code.

Discussion of the Linked List Implementation of the Stack

The constructor, size, and isEmpty each require just one line of code. The size method actually uses the node's listLength method to do its work since we are not maintaining an instance variable that keeps track of the number of nodes. Because the head node of the list is the top of the stack, the implementation of peek is easy: peek just returns the data from the head node. The operations push and pop work by adding and removing nodes, always working at the head of the linked list. Adding and removing nodes at the head of the linked list is straightforward using the techniques of Section 4.2. The clone method makes use of the node's listCopy method to copy the original stack to the clone.

FIGURE 6.7   Specification and Implementation for the Linked List Version of the Generic Stack Class

Generic Class LinkedStack

❖ **public class LinkedStack<E> from the package edu.colorado.collections**
   A LinkedStack is a stack of references to E objects.

   Limitations:
   Beyond Int.MAX_VALUE items, size is wrong.

Specification

◆ **Constructor for the LinkedStack<E>**
```
public LinkedStack( )
```
   Initialize an empty stack.

   Postcondition:
   This stack is empty.

◆ **clone**
```
public LinkedStack<E> clone( )
```
   Generate a copy of this stack.

   Returns:
   The return value is a copy of this stack. Subsequent changes to the copy will not affect the original, nor vice versa.

   Throws: OutOfMemoryError
   Indicates insufficient memory for creating the clone.

◆ **isEmpty—peek—pop—push—size**
```
public boolean isEmpty( )
public E peek( )
public E pop( )
public void push(E item)
public int size( )
```
   These are the standard stack specifications from Figure 6.1 on page 318.

Implementation

```
// File: LinkedStatck.java from the package edu.colorado.collections
// Complete documentation is available above or from the LinkedStack link at
// http://www.cs.colorado.edu/~main/docs/,

package edu.colorado.collections;
import java.util.EmptyStackException;
import edu.colorado.nodes.Node;
```

(continued)

(FIGURE 6.7 continued)

```java
public class LinkedStack<E> implements Cloneable
{
    // Invariant of the LinkedStack class:
    //    1. The items in the stack are stored in a linked list, with the top of the stack stored
    //       at the head node, down to the bottom of the stack at the final node.
    //    2. The instance variable top is the head reference of the linked list of items.
    private Node<E> top;

    public LinkedStack( )
    {
        top = null;
    }

    public LinkedStack<E> clone( )
    {   // Clone a LinkedStack.
        LinkedStack<E> answer;

        try
        {
            answer = (LinkedStack<E>) super.clone( );
        }
        catch (CloneNotSupportedException e)
        {
            // This exception should not occur. But if it does, it would probably indicate a
            // programming error that made super.clone unavailable. The most common error
            // is forgetting the "implements Cloneable" clause at the start of this class.
            throw new RuntimeException
            ("This class does not implement Cloneable.");
        }

        answer.top = Node.listCopy(top); // Generic listCopy method
        return answer;
    }

    public boolean isEmpty( )
    {
        return (top == null);
    }

    public E peek( )
    {
        if (top == null)
            // EmptyStackException is from java.util, and its constructor has no argument.
            throw new EmptyStackException( );
        return top.getData( );
    }
```

(continued)

(FIGURE 6.7 continued)

```java
public E pop( )
{
    E answer;

    if (top == null)
        // EmptyStackException is from java.util, and its constructor has no argument.
        throw new EmptyStackException( );

    answer = top.getData( );
    top = top.getLink( );
    return answer;
}

public void push(E item)
{
    top = new Node<E>(item, top);
}

public int size( )
{
    return Node.listLength(top); // Generic listLength method
}
}
```

Self-Test Exercises for Section 6.3

10. For the array version of the stack, which element of the array contains the top of the stack? In the linked list version, where is the stack's top?

11. For the array version of the stack, write a new member function that returns the maximum number of items that can be added to the stack without stack overflow.

12. Give the full implementation of an accessor method that returns the second item from the top of the stack without actually changing the stack. Write separate solutions for the two different stack versions.

13. For the linked list version of the stack, do we maintain references to both the head and the tail?

14. Is the constructor really needed for the linked list version of the stack? What would happen if we omitted the constructor?

15. Do a time analysis of the size method for the linked list version of the stack. If the method is not constant time, then can you think of a different approach that is constant time?

16. What kind of exception is thrown if you try to pop an empty stack? Which Java Class Library defines this exception?

6.4 MORE COMPLEX STACK APPLICATIONS

Evaluating Postfix Expressions

infix versus prefix notation

We normally write an arithmetic operation between its two arguments; for example, the + operation occurs between the 2 and the 3 in the arithmetic expression 2 + 3. This is called *infix notation*. There is another way of writing arithmetic operations that places the operation in front of the two arguments; for example, + 2 3 evaluates to 5. This is called **Polish prefix notation**, or simply **prefix notation**.

the origin of the notation

A **prefix** is something attached to the front of an expression. You may have heard about similar prefixes for words, such as the prefix *un* in *unbelievable*. Thus, it makes sense to call this notation *prefix notation*. But why *Polish*? It is called Polish because it was devised by the Polish mathematician Jan Łukasiewicz. It would be more proper to call it *Łukasiewicz notation*, but apparently non-Polish-speaking people have trouble pronouncing *Łukasiewicz* (lü-kä-**sha**-vēch).

Using prefix notation, parentheses are completely unneeded. For example, the expression (2 + 3) * 7 written in Polish prefix notation is:

The curved lines under the expression indicate groupings of subexpressions (but the lines are not actually part of the prefix notation).

postfix notation

If we prefer, we can write the operations after the two numbers being combined. This is called **Polish postfix notation**, or more simply **postfix notation** (or sometimes **reverse Polish notation**). For example, the expression (2 + 3) * 7 written in Polish postfix notation is:

Once again, the curves merely clarify the groupings of subexpressions, and these curves are not actually part of the postfix notation.

Here's a longer example. The postfix expression 7 3 5 * + 4 − is equivalent to the infix expression (7 + (3 * 5)) − 4. Notice that an operation is applied to the two numbers that are immediately before it, so the multiplication is 3 * 5. Sometimes one or both numbers for an operation are computed from a subexpression; for example, the + operation in the example is applied to the "number" 3 * 5 and the number before that (the 7), resulting in 7 + (3 * 5).

Do not intermix prefix and postfix notation. You should consistently use one or the other and not mix them together in a single expression.

Postfix notation is handy because it does not require parentheses and because it is particularly easy to evaluate (once you learn to use the notation). In fact, postfix notation often is used internally for computers because of the ease of

our goal: evaluation of postfix expressions

evaluation. We will describe an algorithm to evaluate a postfix expression. When converted to a Java program, the postfix evaluation is similar to the calculator program (Figure 6.5 on page 330)—although, from our comments, you might guess that the postfix evaluation is actually simpler than the infix evaluation required in the calculator program.

There are two input format issues that we must handle. When entering postfix notation, we will require a space between two consecutive numbers so that you can tell where one number ends and another begins. For example, the input

35 6

consists of two numbers, 35 and 6, with a space in between. This is different from the input

356

which is just a single number, 356. A second input issue: You probably want to restrict the input to non-negative numbers to avoid the complication of distinguishing the negative sign of a number from a binary subtraction operation.

postfix evaluation algorithm

Our algorithm for evaluating a postfix expression uses only one stack, which is a stack of numbers. There is no need for a second stack of operation symbols because *each operation is used as soon as it is read*. In fact, the reason why postfix evaluation is easy is precisely because each operation symbol is used as soon as it is read. In the algorithm, we assume that each input entry is either a number or an operation. For simplicity, we will assume that all the operations take two arguments. The complete evaluation algorithm is given in Figure 6.8, along with an example computation.

Let's study the example to see how the algorithm works. Each time an operation appears in the input, the operands for the operation are the two most recently seen numbers. For example, in Figure 6.8(c), we are about to read the * symbol. Since we have just pushed 3 and 2 onto the stack, the * causes a multiplication of 3 * 2, resulting in 6. The result of 6 is then pushed onto the stack, as shown in Figure 6.8(d).

Sometimes the "most recently seen number" is not actually an input number; instead, it is a number that we computed and pushed back onto the stack. For example, in Figure 6.8(d), we are about to read the first +. At this point, 6 is on top of the stack (as a result of multiplying 3 * 2). Below the 6 is the number 5. So the "two most recently seen numbers" are the 6 (that we computed) and the 5 (underneath the 6). We add these two numbers, resulting in 11 (which we push onto the stack, as shown in Figure 6.8(e)).

And so the process continues: Each time we encounter an operation, the operation is immediately applied to the two most recently seen numbers, which always reside in the top two positions of the stack. When the input is exhausted, the number remaining in the stack is the value of the entire expression.

| **FIGURE 6.8** | Evaluating a Postfix Expression |

Pseudocode

1. Initialize a stack of double numbers.
2. do
       `if` (the next input is a number)
           Read the next input and push it onto the stack.
       `else`
       {
           Read the next character, which is an operation symbol.
           Pop two numbers off the stack.
           Combine the two numbers with the operation (using the *second* number
           popped as the *left* operand) and push the result onto the stack.
       }
     `while` (there is more of the expression to read);

3. At this point, the stack contains one number, which is the value of the expression.

Example

> Evaluate the postfix expression
>   5 3 2 * + 4 − 5 +

(a) Input so far (shaded):
5 3 2 * + 4 − 5 +

```
| 5 |
```

(b) Input so far (shaded):
5 3 2 * + 4 − 5 +

```
| 3 |
| 5 |
```

(c) Input so far (shaded):
5 3 2 * + 4 − 5 +

```
| 2 |
| 3 |
| 5 |
```

(d) Input so far (shaded):
5 3 2 * + 4 − 5 +

```
| 6 |
| 5 |
```

(e) Input so far (shaded):
5 3 2 * + 4 − 5 +

```
| 11 |
```

(f) Input so far (shaded):
5 3 2 * + 4 − 5 +

```
| 4  |
| 11 |
```

(g) Input so far (shaded):
5 3 2 * + 4 − 5 +

```
| 7 |
```

(h) Input so far (shaded):
5 3 2 * + 4 − 5 +

```
| 5 |
| 7 |
```

(i) Input so far (shaded):
5 3 2 * + 4 − 5 +

```
| 12 |
```
The result of the computation is 12.

infix expression

postfix expression

Translating Infix to Postfix Notation

Because it is so easy to evaluate a postfix expression, one strategy for evaluating an ordinary infix expression is to first convert it to postfix notation and then evaluate the postfix expression. This is what compilers often do. In this section, we will present an algorithm to translate an infix expression to a postfix expression. The algorithm's input is an expression in infix notation, and the output is an equivalent expression in postfix notation. We will develop the algorithm as pseudocode and will not specify any precise form of input or output.

Until now, we have assumed that the operands in our arithmetic expressions were all numbers. That need not be true. For example, an arithmetic expression may also contain variables. In this example, we will assume that the arithmetic expression can also contain variables such as the variable x in $x + 7$. In fact, the operands may be anything at all, so long as we have a way of recognizing an operand when our algorithm encounters one. However, in our examples, we will assume that the operands are either numbers or variables. We will also assume that all the operations are **binary operations** (which have two operands) such as addition and subtraction. There will be no **unary operations** (which have only one operand) such as sqrt for the square root function. We will present two algorithms, one for fully parenthesized expressions and one for more realistic expressions that omit some parentheses. Our algorithms apply to any sort of operations working on any sort of operands; so, in particular, our algorithms will work on boolean expressions as well as arithmetic expressions. However, to keep matters uncluttered, we will consider only arithmetic expressions in our examples.

algorithm for fully parenthesized expressions

If the infix expression is fully parenthesized, the algorithm is simple. All that's needed to convert from infix to postfix notation is to move each operation symbol to the location of the right parenthesis corresponding to that operation and then remove all parentheses. For example, the following infix expression will have its operation symbols moved to the locations indicated by the arrows:

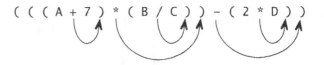

The result is the postfix expression:

```
A 7 + B C / * 2 D * -
```

This process of moving each operation to the location of its corresponding right parenthesis is more of an idea than a complete algorithm. A complete algorithm should read the expression from left to right and must somehow remember the operations and then determine when the corresponding right parenthesis has been found. We have some work to do before this idea becomes an algorithm.

First, observe that the operands (that is, the numbers and variables) in the equivalent postfix expression are in the same order as the operands in the corresponding infix expression we start out with. So our algorithm can simply copy the infix expression operands, omitting parentheses and inserting the operations, such as +, *, and so forth, at the correct locations. The problem is finding the location for inserting the operations in the postfix expression. How do we save the operations, and how do we know when to insert them? Look back at our example. If we push the operations onto a stack, then the operations we need will always be on top of the stack. When do we insert an operation? We insert an operation into the output whenever we encounter a right parenthesis in the input. Hence, the heart of the algorithm is to push the operations onto a stack and to pop an operation every time we encounter a right parenthesis. The algorithm is given in Figure 6.9. The algorithm does some checking to ensure that the input expression is fully parenthesized with balanced parentheses, although there is no checking to ensure that each operation appears between its operands (rather than before or after its operands).

FIGURE 6.9   Converting a Fully Parenthesized Infix Expression to a Postfix Expression

---

Pseudocode

1. Initialize a stack of characters to hold the operation symbols and parentheses.
2. do
   ```
   if (the next input is a left parenthesis)
       Read the left parenthesis and push it onto the stack.
   else if (the next input is a number or other operand)
       Read the operand and write it to the output.
   else if (the next input is one of the operation symbols)
       Read the operation symbol and push it onto the stack.
   else
   {
   ```
   Read and discard the next input symbol (which should be a right parenthesis). There should be an operation symbol on top of the stack, so pop this symbol and write it to the output. (If there is no such symbol, then print an error message indicating that there were too few operations in the infix expression and halt.) After popping the operation symbol, there should be a left parenthesis on the top of the stack, so pop and discard this left parenthesis. (If there was no left parenthesis, then the input did not have balanced parentheses, so print an error message and halt.)
   ```
   }
   while (there is more of the expression to read);
   ```

3. At this point, the stack should be empty. If it's not, print an error message indicating that the expression was not fully parenthesized.

Using Precedence Rules in the Infix Expression

So far, we have been assuming that our infix expression is fully parenthesized. However, in practice, infix expressions are usually not fully parenthesized, and the computer must rely on precedence rules to determine the order of operations for the missing parentheses. This adds a significant complication.

Let's start with an example. We will use the usual Java precedence rules in our example. Consider the following expression:

```
2 * (A - B) + 3 + C
```

In this case, the subtraction is performed first, then the multiplication, and finally the two additions are performed from left to right. The subtraction is first because the parentheses indicate that (A − B) must be evaluated before combining the result with any other operands. The multiplication is performed next—before the additions—because multiplication has *higher precedence* than addition. The two additions are of equal precedence, and there are no parentheses to tell us which addition to perform first. Operations of equal precedence are performed in left-to-right order (when parentheses do not indicate some other order). Thus, the left-hand addition occurs before the right-hand addition. This order of evaluation means the expression is the same as this fully parenthesized expression:

```
(((2 * (A - B)) + 3) + C)
```

To help determine the order of evaluation for arithmetic expressions, we have been referring to the *precedence* of operations such as +, −, and *. A **precedence** is just an ordering from high to low for the operations. Operations with a higher precedence are evaluated before operations with a lower precedence. Sometimes, two different operations (such as + and −) have equal precedence, in which case we must specify whether the operations are to be evaluated left to right or right to left. We need to know only when one operation has higher precedence than another and the direction of evaluation (left to right or right to left) for operations with equal precedence. For example, in Java, * and / have equal precedence; + and − also have equal precedence, but * and / have higher precedence than + and −. That is why we perform multiplication before addition (when there are no parentheses indicating otherwise).

rules for using precedence

Just to make sure they are fresh in our minds, let's review the Java rules for evaluating arithmetic expressions that are not fully parenthesized:

1. Parentheses, when they are present, determine the order of operations. Everything inside a pair of matching parentheses is evaluated, and that value is then combined with results outside the parentheses.

2. If the order is not indicated by parentheses, operations of higher precedence are performed before operations of lower precedence.

3. Arithmetic operations of equal precedence are performed in left-to-right order unless parentheses indicate otherwise.

In Figure 6.9, we gave an algorithm to convert a fully parenthesized infix expression to an equivalent postfix expression. Now we can make our algorithm more general. The new version (in Figure 6.10) does not require full parentheses for the input; the algorithm uses precedence to decide which operation to perform first. In other words, the expressions can be written as we normally write them, with parentheses omitted in some cases. Figure 6.11 contains an example computation of our algorithm as it translates an infix expression into the corresponding postfix expression. Study the example now, and then turn to page 353 to read the details of the algorithm.

FIGURE 6.10   Converting an Infix Expression to a Postfix Expression (General Case)

Pseudocode

1. Initialize a stack of characters to hold the operation symbols and parentheses.
2. do
       `if` (the next input is a left parenthesis)
           Read the left parenthesis and push it onto the stack.
       `else if` (the next input is a number or other operand)
           Read the operand and write it to the output.
       `else if` (the next input is one of the operation symbols)
       {
           Pop and print operations off the stack until one of three things occurs: (1) The
           stack becomes empty, (2) the next symbol on the stack is a left parenthesis,
           or (3) the next symbol on the stack is an operation with lower precedence than
           the next input symbol. When one of these situations occurs, stop popping, read
           the next input symbol, and push this symbol onto the stack.
       }
       `else`
       {
           Read and discard the next input symbol (which should be a right parenthesis).
           Pop and print operations off the stack until the next symbol on the stack is a
           left parenthesis. (If no left parenthesis is encountered, then print an error message
           indicating unbalanced parentheses and halt.) Finally, pop and discard the
           left parenthesis.
       }
     `while` (there is more of the expression to read);

3. Pop and print any remaining operations on the stack. (There should be no remaining left parentheses; if there are, the input expression did not have balanced parentheses.)

FIGURE 6.11   Example Computation for the Algorithm of Figure 6.10

Example

Convert the infix expression:
3   *   X   +   (Y   −   12)   −   Z

(a) Input so far (shaded):
3 * X + (Y − 12) − Z
The operand 3 is printed.

Output so far:
3

(b) Input so far (shaded):
3 * X + (Y − 12) − Z
The * is pushed.

Output so far:
3

(c) Input so far (shaded):
3 * X + (Y − 12) − Z
The operand X is printed.

Output so far:
3 X

(d) Input so far (shaded):
3 * X + (Y − 12) − Z
Pop and print the * since it
has higher precedence than
the +; then push the +.

Output so far:
3 X *

(e) Input so far (shaded):
3 * X + (Y − 12) − Z
Push the parenthesis.

Output so far:
3 X *

(f) Input so far (shaded):
3 * X + (Y − 12) − Z
The operand Y is printed.

Output so far:
3 X * Y

(g) Input so far (shaded):
3 * X + (Y − 12) − Z
The − is pushed.

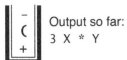

Output so far:
3 X * Y

(h) Input so far (shaded):
3 * X + (Y − 12) − Z
The operand 12 is printed.

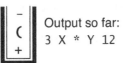

Output so far:
3 X * Y 12

(i) Input so far (shaded):
3 * X + (Y − 12) − Z
Pop until left parenthesis.

Output so far:
3 X * Y 12 −

(j) Input so far (shaded):
3 * X + (Y − 12) − Z
Pop and print the + since it
has precedence equal to
the −; then push the −.

Output so far:
3 X * Y 12 − +

(k) Input so far (shaded):
3 * X + (Y − 12) − Z
The operand Z is printed.

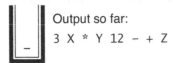

Output so far:
3 X * Y 12 − + Z

(l) Input so far (shaded):
3 * X + (Y − 12) − Z
Pop any remaining operations.

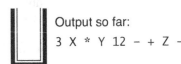

Output so far:
3 X * Y 12 − + Z −

Correctness of the Conversion from Infix to Postfix

For the conversion algorithm to be correct, we need to check these items:

1. The postfix expression contains the correct operands in the correct order.

2. The postfix expression evaluates subexpressions in the way indicated by the parentheses in the infix expression.

3. The postfix expression handles operations of differing precedence according to the precedence rules.

4. A sequence of operations of equal precedence in the infix expression is handled correctly when translated into the postfix expression.

Let's consider each of these four issues. First we need to know that the operands (the numbers and variables) in the postfix expression are in the same order as they were in the input infix expression, but this is easy to see. Because operands are written out as soon as they are read in, they are clearly in the same order as in the input infix expression.

1. the operands are in the right order

Parentheses are a way of grouping subexpressions. Everything inside a pair of matching parentheses is treated as a single unit by anything outside the parentheses. The parentheses give the following message to the operations outside of the parentheses: *Don't look inside these parentheses. We will work things out among ourselves and deliver a single value for you to combine with other operands.* This means that all operations between a set of matching parentheses in the infix expression should form a subexpression of the postfix expression, and with this algorithm they do just that. To see that they do form a subexpression, we will show the following:

2. the parentheses are done correctly

**How the Infix-to-Postfix Algorithm
Translates Subexpressions**

Claim: All of the operations between a pair of matching parentheses (and no other operations) are output in the time between reading the opening parenthesis and reading the closing parenthesis.

Once we show that this claim is true, we will know that all the operations between a pair of matching parentheses in the infix expression will be together in a group within the output postfix notation, and so they will form a subexpression of the postfix expression. So, let's see exactly why the claim is valid.

The algorithm keeps track of expressions within matching parentheses by using the stack. When the algorithm encounters an opening parenthesis—that is, a ' ('—it pushes this parenthesis onto the stack. Now consider what happens between pushing the opening parenthesis and encountering the matching closing parenthesis—that is, the matching ')'. The algorithm will never output an operation from the stack that is below the opening parenthesis, '('. Thus, it outputs only operations that are within the pair of matching parentheses in the input (infix) expression. Moreover, it outputs all of these operations. When it encounters the matching closing parenthesis, it outputs all the remaining operations on the stack all the way down to that matching opening parenthesis.

3. the precedence is handled correctly

When the infix expression contains an operation with low precedence followed by an operation with a higher precedence, then the algorithm should output these operations in reverse order. In other words, the higher precedence operation must be written first. A check of the algorithm will show that the operations are indeed output in reverse order.

4. operations of equal precedence are handled correctly

When the infix expression contains a sequence of operations of equal precedence, they represent an evaluation that goes from left to right. That means the operations should be output from left to right. If you check the algorithm, you will see that this is true. Operations are pushed onto the stack, but when the next operation of equal precedence is encountered, the operation in the stack is output, and the new operation is pushed onto the stack. To confirm this, first check the algorithm for the case in which the stack is empty at the time the operations are encountered. That is the easiest case to see. After that, the other cases will be clearer because they are similar.

Self-Test Exercises for Section 6.4

17. Evaluate the postfix expression 2 3 – 43 +.

18. Why does a postfix evaluation algorithm need only one stack?

19. Write the following expression in both prefix and postfix notation: ((7 + 3) * 2)

20. Trace the algorithm from Figure 6.8 on page 347 to evaluate the postfix expression 15 9 6 * + 12 – 15 +. Draw the stack after each push or pop.

21. Trace the algorithm from Figure 6.10 on page 351 to create a postfix expression from 3 / A + (B + 12) – C.

CHAPTER SUMMARY

- A stack is a last-in/first-out data structure.
- Adding an item to a stack is called a *push* operation. Removing an item from a stack is called a *pop* operation.
- Attempting to pop an item off an empty stack is an error known as a *stack underflow*. A method can throw java.util.EmptyStackException to indicate this error.
- A stack can be implemented as a partially filled array or as a linked list. The Java Class Libraries also provide a generic stack class: java.util.Stack.

- Each of our stack implementations was a generic stack of objects, but the implementations can be changed to any other type, such as a stack of `int`, without the trouble of obtaining a new implementation.
- Stacks have many uses in computer science. The evaluation and translation of arithmetic expressions are two common uses.

Solutions to Self-Test Exercises

1. Push a D; push an A; push an H; push an L; pop an L; pop an H; pop an A; pop a D; the output is LHAD.

2. Pop one item, storing it in a local variable called `top`. Then peek at the next item, storing it in another local variable called `result`. Push the `top` back on the stack and return the `result`.

3. Add a new case to the switch statements in both `evaluate` and `evaluateStackTops`. In `evaluateStackTops`, the new case calculates `operand1` raised to the power of `operand2` and pushes the result back onto the numbers stack.

4. The modification is most easily accomplished in the method `evaluate`. Within this method, you can add a bit of code in the section that reads an operator symbol. The new code should look ahead to see whether the very next character of the `Scanner` is a slash (as described in Appendix B). If so, read and discard the rest of the line (instead of pushing the operator onto the stack).

5. Here are some illegal expressions that are caught: too many right parentheses (3+4)), a missing operand (3 4), a missing right parenthesis (3+4.

6. Here are some illegal expressions that are not caught: too many left parentheses ((3+4), missing left parenthesis 3+4).

7. The solution is the same as the example that starts on page 327, but the numbers are changed. The final value is 24.

8. The numbers stack grows large if the input expression has parentheses that are nested deeply. For example, consider the input expression (1 + (2 + (3 + (4 + 5)))). By the time the 5 is read and pushed onto the stack, the 1, 2, 3, and 4 are already on the numbers stack. In this example, there are four nested subexpressions, and we need to push five numbers onto the numbers stack. So, the general stack size will be one more than the depth of the nesting.

9. The `evaluation` method is linear. If n is the length of the input expression, then the main loop cannot execute more than n times (since each iteration of the loop reads and processes at least one character). Moreover, each iteration performs no more than a constant number of operations, so n iterations will do no more than a constant times n operations.

10. The array version: `data[manyItems-1]`. The linked list version has the top at the head of the list.

11. The function should return `data.length` minus `manyItems`.

12. Here is one of the two solutions (for the linked list):

```
public E second( )
{
   if (top == null)
      throw
      new EmptyStackException( );
   if (top.link == null)
      throw
      new NoSuchElementException( );

   return top.link.data;
}
```

13. We maintain only a head reference.

14. The constructor isn't needed, because any instance variable that is a reference is automatically initialized to `null`.

15. Our `size` implementation uses `listSize`, which is linear time. For a constant-time implementation, you could maintain another private instance variable to continually keep track of the list length.

16. An `EmptyStackException`, which is defined in `java.util.EmptyStackException`.

17. 42

18. There is no need for a second stack of operation symbols because each operation is used as soon as it is read.

19. Prefix: `* + 7 3 2`   Postfix: `7 3 + 2 *`

20. The trace is the same as the computation at the bottom of Figure 6.8 on page 347, except that the numbers are three times as large.

21. The trace is much the same as the computation in Figure 6.11 on page 352, except that the operations are different.

 PROGRAMMING PROJECTS

1 | Write an applet that is a simple stack-based calculator. The calculator should have a text field where you can enter a double number and a text area that displays a stack of numbers. There should be an `enter` button that reads the number from the text field and pushes this number onto the stack. There are also several buttons for operations such as +, −, *, and /. When an operation button is pressed, the top two numbers are popped off the stack, and the operation is applied. The first number popped is always the second operand.

2 | Choose one of the stack implementations and implement a method with this specification:

```
Object itemAt(int n)
// Precondition: 0 <= n and n < size( ).
// Postcondition: The return value is the
// item that is n from the top (with the top at
// n = 0, the next at n = 1, and so on). The
// stack is not changed.
```

Throw a `NoSuchElementException` if the precondition is violated (from `java.util.NoSuchElementException`).

3 | In this exercise, you will need the `itemAt` method from the previous programming project. Write a program that prints all strings with at most *n* letters, where the letters are chosen from a range `first` ... `last` of characters. The following is an outline for an algorithm to do this using a stack. Your program should use a stack to implement this algorithm:

```
// Writing all strings of 1 to n letters:
Push first onto the stack.
while (the stack is not empty)
{
    Print all of the stack (using itemAt).
    if (the stack contains fewer than n letters)
        Push first onto the stack.
    else
    {
```

Pop characters off the stack until the stack is empty or there is a character other than last on the top. (Note: If the top character is not last, then nothing is popped off the stack.)

```
        if (the stack is not empty)
```

Pop a character c off the stack and push c+1 (i.e., the next letter) onto the stack.

```
    }
}
```

4 Enhance the calculator program given in Figure 6.5 on page 330 so that it has all of the following features: After one expression is evaluated, the user is asked if he or she wants to evaluate another expression and is allowed to choose between evaluating another expression and quitting the program. Expressions need not be fully parenthesized, and when parentheses are missing, the usual Java precedence rules are followed. If the arithmetic expression entered is not well formed, then the user is told that it is not well formed and is asked to re-enter the expression.

5 In Figure 6.5 on page 330, we presented a program to evaluate arithmetic expressions. In this exercise, you will write a similar program to evaluate boolean expressions. Rather than arithmetic operations, the input expressions for this program will use the operations && (the "and" operation), || (the "or" operation), and ! (the "not" operation). Rather than combining numbers, the input expression will combine simple boolean comparisons of numbers such as (1 < 2) and (6 < 3). Assume all the numbers in these simple comparisons are integers. Allow the following comparison operations: <, >, <=, >=, ==, and !=. At first assume that all boolean expressions are fully parenthesized and well formed. Be sure to note that "not" is a unary operation. You can assume that the argument to "not" (which follows the !) is enclosed in parentheses. Your program should allow the user to evaluate additional expressions until the user wishes to end the program.

For a more difficult assignment, enhance your program by adding any or all of the following features: (a) The numbers need not be integers. (b) The expression need not be fully parenthesized, and if parentheses are missing, then the Java precedence rules apply. (Note that innermost expressions such as (1 < 2) are still assumed to be in parentheses.) (c) The expression need not be well formed, and if it is not well formed, then the user is asked to re-enter the expression.

6 Write a program that evaluates an arithmetic expression in postfix notation. The basic algorithm is contained in "Evaluating Postfix Expressions" on page 345. Assume the input contains numbers (but no variables) as well as the arithmetic operations +, -, *, and /. Your program should allow the user to evaluate additional expressions until the user wants to end the program. You might also enhance your program so that the expression need not be well formed, and if it is not well formed, then the user must re-enter the expression.

7 Write a program that takes as input an infix expression and outputs the equivalent postfix expression. The basic algorithm is contained in "Translating Infix to Postfix Notation" on page 348. Assume that the input may contain numbers, variables, and arithmetic operations (+, -, *, and /), as well as parentheses. However, the expression need not be fully parenthesized, and when parentheses are missing, the usual Java precedence rules are used to determine the order of evaluation. Your program should allow the user to enter additional expressions until the user wishes to end the program. For a more difficult assignment, enhance your program so that the expression need not be well formed, and if it is not well formed, then the user is asked to re-enter the expression.

8 Redo the calculator program given in Figure 6.5 on page 330, but this time implement it in a different way. To evaluate the arithmetic expression, your program will first convert the expression to postfix notation. After that, it will evaluate the postfix expression. Pseudocode for both of these subtasks is given in this chapter. For this exercise, you should not assume that expressions are fully parenthesized. When parentheses are missing, the usual Java precedence rules are used to determine the order of evaluation. Your program should allow the user to evaluate additional expressions until the user wants to end the program.

9 Write a program that evaluates an arithmetic expression in infix notation, without full parentheses. Use the following algorithm: There are two stacks: a numbers stack and an operators stack. When a number appears, push it onto the numbers stack. Any parenthesis or operator should be treated as described in Step 2 of Figure 6.10 on page 351—with one change. Whenever you pop an operation off the stack, you should immediately use that operation by popping two numbers, applying the operation, and pushing the answer back on the numbers stack.

10 Suppose that you have n queens from a chess game, and that you also have an *n*-by-*n* chess board. Is it possible to place all *n* queens on the board so that no two queens are in the same row, no two queens are in the same column, and no two queens are on the same diagonal? For example, a solution with *n* = 5 is shown here:

Solution to the
5-queens problem

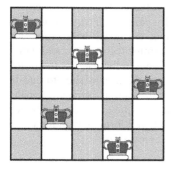

This problem is called the *n*-queens problem. For this project, you are to write a method that has one integer parameter, *n*, and determines whether there is a solution to the *n*-queens problem. If a solution is found, then the procedure prints the row and column of each queen (or displays the result graphically in an applet). Your program should solve the problem by making a sequence of choices such as "Try placing the row 1 queen in column 1" or "Try placing the row 7 queen in column 3." Each time a choice is made, the choice is pushed onto a stack that already contains all the previously made choices. The purpose of the stack is to make it easy to fix incorrect choices, as shown in this pseudocode:

Push information onto the stack indicating the first choice is a queen in row 1, column 1.

```
success = false;

while (!success && !s.isEmpty( ))
{
```

Check whether the most recent choice (on top of the stack) is in the same row, same column, or same diagonal as any other choices (below the top). If so, we say there is a conflict; otherwise, there is no conflict.

```
    if (there is a conflict)
```
Pop items off the stack until the stack becomes empty or the top of the stack is a choice that is not in column *n*. If the stack is now not empty, then increase the column number of the top choice by 1.

```
    else if (no conflict and the stack size is n)
```
Set `success` to `true` because we have found a solution to the *n*-queens problem.

```
    else
```
Push information onto the stack indicating that the next choice is to place a queen at row number `s.size( )`+1 and column number 1.

```
}
```

This technique is called **backtracking** since we keep our choices on a stack and *back up* to correct any mistakes that are made. Notice that when you check for a conflict, you will need access to the entire stack (not just the top), so you should use the `itemAt` method from Programming Project 2 on page 356.

11 In our first case study on evaluating arithmetic expressions, we used two stacks that held different types of data. In some other applications, we might need two stacks with the same type of data. If we implement the stacks as arrays, there is a chance that one array (and hence one stack) will become filled, causing our computation to end prematurely. This might be a shame since the other array (stack) might have plenty of room. One way around this problem is to implement two stacks as one large array rather than two smaller arrays. Write a class for a pair of stacks. A pair of stacks is simply an object with two stacks. Call these stacks *StackA* and *StackB*. There should be separate operations for each stack, for example, `pop_a` and `pop_b`. Implement the stack pair as a single array. The two stacks grow from the two ends of the array, so for example, one stack could fill up one quarter of the array while the other fills up three quarters.

Use `int` for the underlying type of the stack data.

12 Choose one of your stack implementations and write a static method to display the contents of a stack from top to bottom. Then, implement a static method to display the stack bottom to top.

13 Write a method that compares two stacks for equality. The method takes two stacks as parameters and returns `true` if they are identical. The stacks should remain unchanged after the function returns to the calling program. Hint: Either write a method that examines the elements directly, or pop the stacks and save the popped elements so that the stacks can be restored.

14 In this project, you will use stacks to recognize palindromes. Palindromes are strings that read the same backward as forward (for example, "madam"). Write a program to read a line and print whether or not it is a palindrome. Hint: You will need three stacks to implement the program. (In Chapter 7, you will utilize a stack and a queue to implement the palindrome program more efficiently.)

15 For any of your stack implementations, please write a new method called `flip` with no parameters. After a stack x activates the `flip` method, x should contain the same items, but the order of those items should be reversed.

16 Here's a new idea for implementing the sequence class from Section 4.5. Instead of the items being stored on a linked list, they will be stored using two stacks as private member variables with the following:
1. The bottom of the first stack is the beginning of the sequence.
2. The elements of the sequence continue up to the top of the first stack.
3. The next element of the sequence is then the top of the second stack.
4. And the elements of the sequence then continue down to the bottom of the second sequence (which is the end of the sequence).
5. If there is a current element, then that element is at the top of the first stack.

Don't change any of the specifications for any of the public methods.

All of the public methods should take constant time, with one exception. Which one takes linear time?

Queues

When you complete Chapter 7, you will be able to ...

- follow and explain queue-based algorithms using the usual computer science terminology of front, rear, entering the queue, and exiting the queue.
- use a Queue class to implement stack-based algorithms, such as scheduling first-come, first-served tasks.
- recognize situations that require a priority queue rather than an ordinary queue.
- implement Queue, PriorityQueue, and Deque classes of your own using either an array or a linked list data structure.

Queues

He who comes first, eats first.

EIKE VON REPGOW
Sachsenspiegel

A *queue* is a first-in/first-out data structure similar to a line of people at a ticket window. It can be used whenever you need a data structure that allows items to "wait their turn." Impressive algorithms that explore mazes of interconnected rooms use queues to keep track of which options have not yet been explored (though, of course, computer scientists have their own terminology—you'll see it as *breadth-first search* in Chapter 14—for such problems). In this chapter, we discuss applications of the queue data structure, give two implementations of a queue ADT, and discuss the differences between queues and stacks. We also discuss and implement two more flexible kinds of queue called a *priority queue* and a *double-ended queue* (also called a *deque*, pronounced "deck").

7.1 INTRODUCTION TO QUEUES

The word "queue" is pronounced as if you were saying the letter Q; it means the same thing as the word "line" when used in phrases like "waiting in a line." Every time you get in line at a supermarket or a bank or a ticket window, you are adding yourself to a queue. If everybody is polite, then people add themselves to the rear of the queue (the rear of the line), and the person at the front of the queue is always the person who is served first. The queue data structure works in the same way, and the abstract definition of a queue reflects this intuition.

> **Queue Definition**
>
> A **queue** is a data structure of ordered items such that items can be inserted only at one end (called the **rear**) and removed at the other end (called the **front**). The item at the front end of the queue is called the **first item**.

When we say that the items in a queue are *ordered,* we are referring to the items' position in the queue. There is a first one (the front one), a second one, a third one, and so forth. We do *not* require that the items can be compared using the < operator. The items can be of any type. In this regard, the situation is the same as it was for a stack.

Because items must be removed in exactly the same order as they were added to the queue, a queue is called a first-in/first-out data structure (abbreviated FIFO). This differs from a stack, which is a last-in/first-out data structure, but

stacks versus queues

apart from this difference, a stack and a queue are similar data structures. They differ only in the rule that determines which item is removed first. The contrast between stacks and queues is illustrated in Figure 7.1. In both structures, the items depicted are entered in the order A, B, C, and D. With a queue, they are removed in the same order: A, B, C, D. With a stack, they are removed in the reverse order: D, C, B, A.

FIFO

A queue is a first-in/ first-out data structure. Items leave the queue in the same order in which they were put into the queue.

The Queue Class

In Figure 7.2, we specify the key methods of a queue. The specification follows the same general pattern as the generic stack of Chapter 6. As with our stack, the queue is a generic queue of objects, but this underlying type can be changed to any primitive data type without problems. Later we will implement the queue as a Java class in two different ways: The first stores the items in an array, whereas the second uses a linked list.

The queue's methods include operations to remove the item from the front of the queue, to add an item to the rear of the queue, and so on. The method for adding an item to the queue is often called an **insert** or **enqueue** operation (pronounced *en-q*), which is a shortening of "*en*tering the *queue*." But for adding an item, we will use the alternative name add, which is the name that Java uses. The method for removing an item from the queue is often called a **getFront** or **dequeue** operation (pronounced *de-cue*), which means "*de*leting from the *queue*," but we will use the Java name remove.

If a program attempts to remove an item from an empty queue, that is a kind of error called **queue underflow**. This is similar to stack underflow (popping an empty stack), though there is one difference. Java provides a specific exception, EmptyStackException, to indicate a stack underflow. There is no specific exception for a queue underflow, so our remove method will throw NoSuchElementException to indicate an underflow. (NoSuchElementException is part of java.util, and many collection classes use it to indicate some kind of underflow.) Anyway, to help you avoid these errors, the queue class provides a boolean method to test for an empty queue and a second method to return the current number of items in the queue. (Java's queue also provides two alternative methods, offer and poll, that a queue can use instead of add and remove. The alternatives have a different kind of failure behavior that does not throw exceptions.)

FIGURE 7.1   Contrasting a Stack and a Queue

Input: **ABCD**

Stack

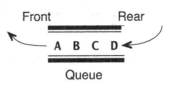

Queue

FIGURE 7.2 Specification of the Key Methods of a Generic Queue Class

Specification

These are the key methods of a typical queue class, which is based on Java's generic Queue<E> interface. Although this is a specification for a generic queue, we could also have a queue that contains primitive values (such as `int`) directly.

♦ **Constructor for the Generic Queue<E>**
    `public Queue( )`
    Initialize an empty queue.
    Postcondition:
       This queue is empty.

♦ **add**
    `public void add(E item)`
    Add a new item to the rear of this queue. The new item may be the null reference.
    Parameter:
       `item` – the item to be added to this queue
    Postcondition:
       The item has been added to the rear of this queue.
    Throws: `OutOfMemoryError`
       Indicates insufficient memory for adding a new item to this queue.
    Note:
       Java's version of this method returns a boolean value that is always true for a queue.

♦ **isEmpty**
    `public boolean isEmpty( )`
    Determine whether this queue is empty.
    Returns:
       `true` if this queue is empty; otherwise, `false`

♦ **remove**
    `public E remove( )`
    Get the front item, removing it from this queue.
    Precondition:
       This queue is not empty.
    Postcondition:
       The return value is the front item of this queue, and the item has been removed.
    Throws: `NoSuchElementException`
       Indicates that this queue is empty.

♦ **size**
    `public int size( )`
    Accessor method to determine the number of items in this queue.
    Returns:
       the number of items in this queue

We could add other operations, such as a method to look at the front item of the queue without removing it from the queue, but this minimal set of operations will be enough for our purposes.

Uses for Queues

Uses for queues are easy to find; we often use queues in our everyday affairs, such as when we wait in line at a bank. To get a feel for using a queue in an algorithm, we will first consider a simple example.

copying a word

Suppose you want a program to read a word and then write the word. This is so simple that you may wonder why we bother to consider this task, but it is best to start with a simple example. One way to accomplish this task is to read the input one letter at a time and place each letter in a queue. After the word is read, the letters in the queue are written out. Because a queue is a first-in/first-out data structure, the letters are written in the same order in which they were read. Here is the pseudocode for this approach:

```
// Echoing a word
1. Declare a queue of characters.
2. while (there are more characters of the word to read)
   {
       Read a character.
       Insert the character into the queue.
   }
3. while (the queue is not empty)
   {
       Get the front character from the queue.
       Write the character to the screen.
   }
```

simulation programs

Because queues occur in real-life situations, they are frequently used in simulation programs. For example, a program to simulate the traffic at an intersection might use a software queue to simulate the real-life situation of a growing line of automobiles waiting for a traffic light to change from red to green.

input/output buffering

Queues also appear in computer system software, such as the operating system that runs on your PC. For example, consider a program that reads input from the keyboard. We think of a program as directly reading its input from the keyboard. However, if you think of what actually happens when you give a line of input to a program, you will realize that the program does not necessarily read a character when the corresponding keyboard key is pressed. This allows you to type input to the program, and that input is saved in a queue by software that is part of the operating system. When the program asks for input, the operating system provides characters from the front of its queue. This is called **buffering** the input, and it is controlled by the PC's operating system software. In reality, a more sophisticated data structure is used rather than a queue, allowing you to back up and retype part of the line. Also, this form of buffering data in a queue is often used when one computer component is receiving data from another, faster computer component. For example, if your fast CPU (central processing unit) is sending data to your printer, which is slow by comparison, then the data is buffered in a queue. By using the queue in this way, the CPU need not wait for the printer to finish printing the first character before the CPU sends the next character.

Self-Test Exercises for Section 7.1

1. What are the meanings of LIFO and FIFO?
2. What are the traditional names for the queue operations that add an item and remove an item from a queue?
3. What queue method can a programmer use to avoid queue underflow?
4. Suppose a program uses a queue of characters to read a word and echo it to the screen. For the input word LINE, trace the algorithm, giving all the activations of the operations add and remove.
5. Name some common situations in which a PC's operating system uses some kind of a queue.
6. Write pseudocode for an algorithm that reads an even number of characters. The algorithm then prints the first character, third character, fifth character, and so on. On a second output line, the algorithm prints the other characters. Use two queues to store the characters.

7.2 QUEUE APPLICATIONS

Java Queues

Before we actually implement the queue class, we'll show two applications that use a generic queue. In particular, our first application will use a Java queue that is declared in this way:

```
import java.util.LinkedList;
import java.util.Queue;
...
Queue<Character> q = new LinkedList<Character>( );
```

how to declare a simple Queue in Java

This looks unusual because the data type of the variable is Queue<Character>, but we are calling Java's LinkedList constructor. The reason is that Java does not actually have a separate Queue class. Instead, it has a Queue interface (as described in Section 5.5). Since Queue is only an interface, we cannot create Queue objects in Java, but there are several other Java classes (such as LinkedList) that implement the Queue interface. This interface includes all of the methods from Figure 7.2 on page 363 (as well as many other methods).

In any case, if you want a simple Java queue, consider using the Queue interface and the LinkedList class as shown on the previous page.

PROGRAMMING EXAMPLE: Palindromes

A **palindrome** is a string that reads the same forward and backward; that is, the letters are the same whether you read them from right to left or from left to right. For example, the one-word string "radar" is a palindrome. A more complicated example of a palindrome is the following sentence:

```
Able was I ere I saw Elba
```

Palindromes are fun to make up, and they even have applications in at least one area—the analysis of genetic material.

Suppose we want a program to read a line of text and tell us whether the line is a palindrome. We can do this by using both a stack and a queue. We will read the line of text into both a stack and a queue and then write out the contents of the stack and the contents of the queue. The line that is written using the queue is written forward, and the line that is written using the stack is written backward. Now, if those two output lines are the same, then the input string must be a palindrome. Of course, the program need not actually write out the contents of the stack and the queue. The program can simply compare the contents of the stack and the queue character by character to see if they would produce the same string of characters.

A program that checks for palindromes in the way we just outlined is given in Figure 7.3. This program uses Java's stack class defined in Figure 6.1 on page 317 as well as a queue that is declared using the technique on page 365. In this program, we treat both the uppercase and lowercase versions of a letter as being the same character. This is because we want to consider a sentence as reading the same forward and backward even though it might start with an uppercase letter and end with a lowercase letter. For example, the string "Able was I ere I saw Elba" when written backward reads "ablE was I ere I saw elbA". The two strings match, provided we agree to consider upper- and lowercase versions of a letter as being equal. The treatment of the letters' cases is accomplished with a *the toUpperCase method converts lowercase letters to uppercase letters* useful Java method Character.toUpperCase. This method has one character as an argument. If this character is a lowercase letter, then the method converts it to the corresponding uppercase letter and returns this value. Otherwise, the method returns the character unchanged.

Our program also ignores many characters, requiring only that the *alphabetic letters* on the line read the same forward and backward. This way, we can find more palindromes. If we look only at alphabetic letters, discarding spaces and punctuation, then there are many more palindromes. However, they are not always easy to spot. For example, you might not immediately recognize the following as a palindrome:

```
Straw? No, too stupid a fad. I put soot on warts.
```

Depending on your current frame of mind, you may think that discovering such sentences is a stupid fad, but nevertheless, our program ignores blanks and punctuation. Therefore, according to our program, the preceding is a palindrome. The determination of whether a character is a letter is accomplished with another Java method. The method, called Character.isLetter, returns true if its single argument is one of the alphabetic characters.

the isLetter method determines which characters are letters

A sample dialogue from the palindrome program is shown at the end of Figure 7.3. As we often do, we have presented a minimal program to concentrate on the new material being presented. Before the program is released to users, it should be enhanced in a number of ways to make it more robust (such as better handling of a possible stack or queue overflow) and more friendly (such as allowing more than one sentence to be entered).

FIGURE 7.3   A Program to Recognize Palindromes

Java Application Program

```java
// FILE: Palindrome.java
// This program reads strings from the keyboard and determines whether each input
// line is a palindrome. The program ignores everything except alphabetic letters, and it
// ignores the difference between upper- and lowercase letters.

import java.util.LinkedList;  // See page 365 for why we use a Linked List.
import java.util.Queue;       // Provides the Queue interface
import java.util.Stack;       // Provides the Stack class
import java.util.Scanner;     // Provides the Scanner class (see Appendix B)

public class Palindrome
{
    public static void main(String[ ] args)
    {
        Scanner stdin = new Scanner(System.in); // Keyboard input
        String line;                            // One input line

        do
        {
            System.out.print("Your expression (or return to end): ");
            line = stdin.nextLine( );
            if (is_palindrome(line))
                System.out.println("That is a palindrome.");
            else
                System.out.println("That is not a palindrome.");
        }
        while (line.length( ) != 0);
    }
```

(continued)

(FIGURE 7.3 continued)

```
public static boolean is_palindrome(String input)
// The return value is true if and only if the input string is a palindrome.
// All non-letters are ignored, and the case of the letters is also ignored.
// See page 365 for an explanation of using Java's LinkedList class as a queue.
{
    Queue<Character> q = new LinkedList<Character>( );
    Stack<Character> s = new Stack<Character>( );
    Character letter;   // One character from the input string
    int mismatches = 0; // Number of spots that mismatched
    int i;              // Index for the input string

    for (i = 0; i < input.length( ); i++)
    {
        letter = input.charAt(i);
        if (Character.isLetter(letter))
        {
            q.add(letter);
            s.push(letter);
        }
    }

    while (!q.isEmpty( ))
    {
        if (q.remove( ) != s.pop( ))
            mismatches++;
    }

    // If there were no mismatches, then the string was a palindrome.
    return (mismatches == 0);
}

}
```

Part of a Sample Dialogue

```
Your expression (or return to end):
Straw? No, too stupid a fad. I put soot on warts.
That is a palindrome.
Your expression (or return to end):
Able were you ere you saw Elba.
That is not a palindrome.
```

You may have thought of other ways to solve the palindrome problem. (If not, give it a try now!) Your alternative solution may be simpler in some ways than the solution that uses a stack and a queue, but using the stack and queue has another advantage to keep in mind: Once the stack and queue classes are implemented, they can be used in many algorithms without worrying about their implementation details. This is a primary advantage of using existing implementations of abstract data types.

advantages of using existing implementations

PROGRAMMING EXAMPLE: **Car Wash Simulation**

The *Handy-Dandy Hand Car Wash Company* has decided to modernize and change its image. It has installed a fast, fully automated car-washing mechanism that can wash a car in one to 10 minutes. It will soon reopen under its new name, *The Automatic Auto Wash Emporium.* The company wants to know the most efficient way to use its new car-washing mechanism. If the mechanism is used on the fast setting, it can wash a car in one minute, but because of the high pressure required to operate at such speed, the mechanism uses a great deal of water and soap at this setting. At slower settings, it takes longer to wash a car but uses less soap and water. The company wants to know how many customers will be served and how long customers will have to wait in line when the washing mechanism is used at one of the slower speeds. The company also wants to know whether its new motto, "You Ought to Autowash your Auto," will be effective. We respectfully refuse comment on the motto, but we agree to write a program that will simulate automobiles waiting in line for a car wash. This way, the manager of the car wash can see how the speed of the car wash, the length of the line, and various other factors interact.

Car Wash Simulation—Specification

Our specification for the simulation consists of input and output descriptions.

Input. The program has three input items: (1) the amount of time needed to wash one car (in total seconds); (2) the probability that a new customer arrives during any given second (we assume that, at most, one customer arrives in a second); and (3) the total length of time to be simulated (in seconds).

Output. The program produces two pieces of output information: (1) the number of customers serviced in the simulated time; and (2) the average time that a customer spent in line during the simulation (in seconds).

Car Wash Simulation—Design

We will carry out a design of the program in a way that is common for many simulation tasks. The approach is to propose a collection of related object types that correspond to real-world objects in the situation we are simulating. There

the queue

propose a list of related object types

write pseudocode indicating how the objects are used

are many possibilities, but our particular approach focuses on the use of our queue class, which will be used to simulate a line of customers waiting to have their cars washed. We first discuss the queue and then go on to propose the other objects needed for the simulation.

We need to simulate a queue of customers, but we do not have real live customers, so we must decide how we will represent them. There are many ways to represent customers: We could use their names and place them in a queue of names; we could assign an arbitrary number to each customer and store that number in a queue of numbers; we could represent each customer by the make and year of the customer's automobile or even by how dirty the automobile is. However, none of these representations has any relevance to the specified simulation. For this simulation, all we need to know about a customer is how long the customer waits in the queue. Hence, a good way to represent a customer is to use a number that represents the time at which the customer entered the queue. Thus, our queue will be a queue of numbers. In a more complex simulation, it would be appropriate to implement the customers as objects, and one of the customer's methods would return the customer's arrival time.

The numbers that record the times at which customers enter the queue are called **time stamps**. Our simulation works in seconds, so a time stamp is just the number of simulated seconds that have passed since the start of the simulation. When the customer (represented by the time stamp) is removed from the queue, we can easily calculate the time the customer spent waiting: The time spent waiting is the total number of seconds simulated so far minus the time stamp.

Now let's discuss other objects that will be useful in the simulation program. In addition to the queue, we propose three other object types, listed here:

Washer.   A washer is an object that simulates the automatic car-washing mechanism.

BooleanSource.   An object of this class provides a sequence of boolean values. Some of the values in the sequence are `true`, and some are `false`. During the simulation, we will have one `BooleanSource` object that we query once per simulated second. If the query returns `true` as its response, this indicates that a new customer has arrived during the simulated second; a `false` return value indicates that no customer has arrived during the simulated second.

Averager.   An averager computes the average of a group of numbers. For example, we might send the following four numbers into an averager: 10, 20, 2, and 12. The averager could then tell us that the average of these numbers is 11.0. The averager can also tell us how many numbers it has processed—in our example, the averager processed four numbers. We'll use an averager to keep track of the average waiting time and the total number of cars washed.

A good way to design a simulation program is to first write pseudocode illustrating how the proposed objects will be used. From this pseudocode, we then extract the necessary methods for each object. The simulation program we have in mind will carry out the simulation using one-second intervals, and to make the

FIGURE 7.4	The Car Wash Simulation

Pseudocode

1. Declare a queue of integers, which will be used to keep track of arrival times of customers who are waiting to wash their cars. We also declare the following objects:

   (a) A Washer: The washer's constructor has an argument indicating the amount of time (in seconds) needed by the washer to wash one car.

   (b) A BooleanSource: The constructor has an argument that specifies how frequently the BooleanSource returns true (indicating how often customers arrive).

   (c) An Averager.

2. for (currentSecond = 0; currentSecond < the simulation length; currentSecond++)
   {
   > Each iteration of this loop simulates the passage of one second of time, as follows:
   > Ask the BooleanSource whether a new customer arrives during this second, and if so, enter the currentSecond into the queue.
   > if (the Washer is not busy and the queue is not empty)
   > {
   >> Remove the next integer from the queue and call this integer next.
   >> This integer is the arrival time of the customer whose car we will now wash.
   >> So, compute how long the customer had to wait (currentSecond - next) and send this value to the Averager. Also, tell the Washer that it should start washing another car.
   > }
   > Indicate to the Washer that another simulated second has passed. This allows the Washer to correctly determine whether it is still busy.
   }

3. At this point, the simulation is completed. We can get and print two items of information from the Averager: (1) how many numbers the Averager was given (i.e., the number of customers whose cars were washed); and (2) the average of all the numbers it was given (i.e., the average waiting time for the customers, expressed in seconds).

---

simulation simpler, we assume that at most one customer arrives during any particular second. The simulation contains a loop that is iterated once for each simulated second. In each loop iteration, all the activities that take place in one second, such as the possible arrival of a new customer or the removal of a customer from the queue, will be simulated. When the loop terminates, the simulation is over, and the needed output values are obtained from the averager. The basic pseudocode for the simulation is shown in Figure 7.4.

Next, we'll discuss the the three object types (BooleanSource, Averager, and Washer) in more detail.

BooleanSource. During each simulated second, the BooleanSource provides us with a single boolean value indicating whether a new customer has arrived during that second. A true value indicates that a customer has arrived; false indicates that no customer arrived. With this in mind, we propose two methods: a constructor and a method called query.

The constructor for the BooleanSource has one argument, which is the probability that the BooleanSource returns true to a query. The probability is expressed as a decimal value between 0 and 1. For example, suppose our program uses the name arrival for its BooleanSource, and we want to simulate the situation in which a new customer arrives during 1% of the simulated seconds. Then our program would have the following declaration:

```
BooleanSource arrival = new BooleanSource(0.01);
```

The second method of the BooleanSource can be called to obtain the next value in the BooleanSource's sequence of values. Here is the specification:

♦ **query (method of the BooleanSource)**
```
public boolean query( )
```
Get the next value from this BooleanSource.
Returns:
    The return value is either true or false; the probability of a true value is determined by the argument that was given to the constructor.

There are several ways of generating random boolean values, but at this specification stage, we don't need to worry about such implementation details.

Averager. The averager has a constructor that initializes the averager so that it is ready to accept numbers. The numbers will be given to the averager one at a time through a method called addNumber. For example, suppose our averager is named waitTimes, and the next number in the sequence is 10. Then we will activate waitTimes.addNumber(10); the averager also has two methods to retrieve its results: average and howManyNumbers, as specified here:

♦ **Constructor for the Averager**
```
public Averager( )
```
Initialize an Averager so that it is ready to accept numbers.

♦ **addNumber**
```
public void addNumber(double value)
```
Give another number to this Averager.

♦ **average**
```
public double average( )
```
The return value is the average of all numbers given to this Averager.

♦ **howManyNumbers**
```
public int howManyNumbers( )
```
Provide a count of how many numbers have been given to this Averager.

Notice that the argument to addNumber is actually a double number rather than an integer. This will allow us to use the averager in situations in which the sequence is more than just whole numbers. Also, the class will have some limitations (for example, the total count of numbers given to an averager cannot exceed Integer.MAX_VALUE). But we'll deal with those limitations during the implementation stage.

Washer. The simulation program requires one washer object. This washer is initialized with its constructor, and each time another second passes, the simulation program indicates the passage of a second to the washer. This suggests the following constructor and method:

◆ **Constructor for the Washer**
   public Washer(int s)
   Initialize a Washer.

   Postcondition:
      This Washer has been initialized so that it takes s seconds to complete one wash cycle.

◆ **reduceRemainingTime**
   public void reduceRemainingTime( )
   Reduce the remaining time in the current wash cycle by one second.

   Postcondition:
      If a car is being washed, then the remaining time in the current wash cycle has been reduced by one second.

The other two responsibilities of a washer are to tell the simulation program whether the washing mechanism is currently available and to begin the washing of a new car. These responsibilities are accomplished with two methods:

◆ **startWashing**
   public void startWashing( )
   Start a wash cycle for this Washer.

   Precondition:
      isBusy( ) is false.

   Postcondition:
      This Washer has started simulating one wash cycle.

   Throws: IllegalStateException
      Indicates that this Washer is busy.

◆ **isBusy**
   public boolean isBusy( )
   Determine whether this Washer is currently busy.

   Returns:
      true if this Washer is busy (in a wash cycle); otherwise, false

Car Wash Simulation—Implementing the Car Wash Classes

We have completed a specification for the three new classes that will be used in the car wash simulation. We'll implement these three classes in separate files: Averager.java (Figure 7.5 on page 376), BooleanSource.java (Figure 7.6 on page 378), and Washer.java (Figure 7.7 on page 379). All three are part of the package edu.colorado.simulations. The implementations are straightforward, but we'll provide a little discussion.

Implementation of the Averager. The implementation of the averager is a direct implementation of the definition of "average" and some straightforward details. The class has two instance variables: one to keep track of how many numbers the averager has been given and another to keep track of the sum of all those numbers. When the average method is activated, the method returns the average calculated as the sum of all the numbers divided by the count of how many numbers the averager was given.

Notice that the averager does *not* need to keep track of all the numbers individually. It is sufficient to keep track of the sum of the numbers and the count of how many numbers there were. However, the specification does indicate some limitations connected with possible arithmetic overflows.

Implementation of the BooleanSource. The BooleanSource class has one instance variable, probability, which stores the probability that an activation of query will return true. The implementation of the query method first uses the Math.random method to generate a random number between 0 and 1 (including 0 but not 1). Hence, if the instance variable probability is the desired probability of returning true, then query should return true provided the following relationship holds: Math.random( ) < probability.

For example, suppose we want a 10% chance that query returns true so that probability is 0.1. If random returns a value less than 0.1, then query will return true. The chance that rand returns a value less than 0.1 is 10% since 0.1 marks a point that is 10% of the way through random's output range. Therefore, there is about a 10% chance that Math.random( ) < probability will be true. It is this boolean expression that is used in the return statement of query.

Implementation of the Washer. The Washer class has two instance variables. The first instance variable, secondsForWash, is the number of seconds needed for one complete wash cycle. This variable is set by the constructor and remains constant thereafter. The second instance variable, washTimeLeft, keeps track of how many seconds until the current wash is completed. This value can be zero if the washer is not currently busy.

The washer's reduceRemainingTime method is activated to subtract one second from the remaining washing time. So the reduceRemainingTime method checks whether a car is currently being washed. If there is a car being washed, then the method subtracts 1 from washTimeLeft.

The washer's `isBusy` method simply checks whether `washTimeLeft` is greater than zero. If so, there is a car in the washing mechanism. Otherwise, the washing mechanism is ready for another car.

When the car-washing mechanism is not busy, the `startWashing` method can be activated to start another car through the washer. The method starts the wash by setting `washTimeLeft` equal to `secondsForWash`.

Car Wash Simulation—Implementing the Simulation Method

We can now implement the simulation pseudocode from Figure 7.4 on page 371. The implementation is shown as a method in Figure 7.8 on page 381. This method could be activated from a main program that interacts with a user. There are three parameters for the method: (1) an integer, `washTime`, which is the amount of time needed to wash one car; (2) a double number, `arrivalProb`, which is the probability that a customer arrives during any particular second; and (3) another integer, `totalTime`, which is the total number of seconds to be simulated. The method writes a copy of its parameters to the screen and then runs the simulation.

Most of the simulation work is carried out in the large for-loop, where the local variable `currentSecond` runs from 1 to `totalTime`. This loop parallels the large loop from the original pseudocode (Step 2 in Figure 7.4 on page 371).

After the loop finishes, the simulation method obtains two pieces of information from the averager and writes these items to `System.out`.

Self-Test Exercises for Section 7.2

7. How would you modify the palindromes program so that it indicates the first position in the input string that violates the palindrome property? For example, consider the input "Able were you ere you saw Elba." This looks like a palindrome until you see the first "e" in "were," so a suitable output would be:

```
That is not a palindrome.
Mismatch discovered at: Able we
```

8. How would you modify the palindromes program so that uppercase and lowercase versions of letters are considered different? In the modified program, the string "able was I ere I saw elba" would still be considered a palindrome, but the string "Able was I ere I saw Elba" would no longer be considered a palindrome since, among other things, the first and last letters, "A" and "a," are not the same under these changed rules.

9. Can a single program use both a stack and a queue?

10. Describe at least one assumption we made about the real-world car wash in order to make the simulation more manageable.

11. Use short sentences to describe the three main actions that occur during each second of simulated time in the car wash simulation.

12. When the car wash simulation finishes, there could still be some numbers in the queue. What do these numbers represent from the real world? (For a method of handling these leftover numbers, see Programming Project 8 on page 407.)

13. Our method in Figure 7.8 on page 381 uses an averager, and the method does not check that we don't give the averager more than Integer. MAX_VALUE numbers. Is this a potential problem for a long simulation?

FIGURE 7.5	Specification and Implementation for the Averager Class

Class Averager

❖ **public class Averager from the package edu.colorado.simulations**
An Averager computes an average of a sequence of numbers.

Specification

♦ **Constructor for the Averager**
```
public Averager( )
```
Initialize an Averager.

Postcondition:
This Averager has been initialized and is ready to accept a sequence of numbers.

♦ **addNumber**
```
public void addNumber(double value)
```
Give another number to this Averager.

Parameter:
value – the next number to give to this Averager

Precondition:
howManyNumbers( ) < Integer.MAX_VALUE

Postcondition:
This Averager has accepted value as the next number in the sequence of numbers.

Throws: IllegalStateException
Indicates that howManyNumbers( ) is Integer.MAX_VALUE.

♦ **average**
```
public double average( )
```
Provide an average of all numbers given to this Averager.

Returns:
the average of all the numbers that have been given to this Averager

Note:
If howManyNumbers( ) is zero, then the answer is Double.NaN ("not a number") because the average of an empty set of numbers is not defined. The answer may also be Double.POSITIVE_INFINITY or Double.NEGATIVE_INFINITY if there has been an arithmetic overflow during the summing of all the numbers. *(continued)*

(FIGURE 7.5 continued)

- ◆ **howManyNumbers**

   ```
   public int howManyNumbers( )
   ```
   Provide a count of how many numbers have been given to this Averager.

   Returns:

   the count of how many numbers have been given to this Averager

Implementation

```java
// File: Averager.java from the package edu.colorado.simulations
// Complete documentation is available on page 376 or from the Averager link at
// http://www.cs.colorado.edu/~main/docs/.

package edu.colorado.simulations;

public class Averager
{
   private int count;   // How many numbers have been given to this averager
   private double sum;  // Sum of all the numbers given to this averager

   public Averager( )
   {
      count = 0;
      sum = 0;
   }

   public void addNumber(double value)
   {
      if (count == Integer.MAX_VALUE)
         throw new IllegalStateException("Too many numbers.");
      count++;
      sum += value;
   }

   public double average( )
   {
      if (count == 0)
         return Double.NaN;
      else
         return sum/count;
   }

   public int howManyNumbers( )
   {
      return count;
   }
}
```

FIGURE 7.6	Specification and Implementation of the `BooleanSource` Class

Class BooleanSource

❖ **public class BooleanSource from the package edu.colorado.simulations**
A `BooleanSource` provides a random sequence of boolean values.

Specification

◆ **Constructor for the BooleanSource**
   `public BooleanSource(double p)`
   Initialize a `BooleanSource`.
   Precondition: 0 `<=` p and p `<=` 1.
   Postcondition:
   This `BooleanSource` has been initialized so that p is the approximate probability of returning true in any subsequent activation of the `query` method.
   Throws: `IllegalArgumentException`
   Indicates that p is outside of its legal range.

◆ **query (method of the BooleanSource)**
   `public boolean query( )`
   Get the next value from this `BooleanSource`.
   Returns:
   The return value is either `true` or `false`, with the probability of a `true` value being determined by the argument that was given to the constructor.

Implementation

```
// File: BooleanSource.java from the package edu.colorado.simulations
// Complete documentation is listed above, or available from the BooleanSource link at
// http://www.cs.colorado.edu/~main/docs/.

package edu.colorado.simulations;
public class BooleanSource
{
    private double probability; // The probability of query( ) returning true.

    public BooleanSource(double p)
    {
        if ((p < 0) || (1 < p))
            throw new IllegalArgumentException("Illegal p: " + p);
        probability = p;
    }

    public boolean query( )
    {
        return (Math.random( ) < probability);
    }
}
```

| **FIGURE 7.7** | Specification and Implementation for the Washer Class |

Class Washer

❖ **public class Washer from the package edu.colorado.simulations**
    A Washer simulates a simple washing machine.

Specification

◆ **Constructor for the Washer**
    public Washer(int s)
    Initialize a Washer.

   Parameter:
    s - the number of seconds required for one wash cycle of this Washer

   Postcondition:
    This Washer has been initialized so that it takes s seconds to complete one wash cycle.

◆ **isBusy**
    public boolean isBusy( )
    Determine whether this Washer is currently busy.

   Returns:
    true if this Washer is busy (in a wash cycle); otherwise, false

◆ **reduceRemainingTime**
    public void reduceRemainingTime( )
    Reduce the remaining time in the current wash cycle by one second.

   Postcondition:
    If a car is being washed, then the remaining time in the current wash cycle has been reduced
    by one second.

◆ **startWashing**
    public void startWashing( )
    Start a wash cycle for this Washer.

   Precondition:
    isBusy( ) is false.

   Postcondition:
    This Washer has started simulating one wash cycle. Therefore, isBusy( ) will return true
    until the required number of simulated seconds has passed.

   Throws: IllegalStateException
    Indicates that this Washer is busy.

(continued)

(FIGURE 7.7 continued)

Implementation

```
// File: Washer.java from the package edu.colorado.simulations
// Complete documentation is available on page 379 or from the Washer link at
// http://www.cs.colorado.edu/~main/docs/.

package edu.colorado.simulations;

public class Washer
{
    private int secondsForWash;   // Seconds for a single wash
    private int washTimeLeft;      // Seconds until this washer is no longer busy

    public Washer(int s)
    {
        secondsForWash = s;
        washTimeLeft = 0;
    }

    public boolean isBusy( )
    {
        return (washTimeLeft > 0);
    }

    public void reduceRemainingTime( )
    {
        if (washTimeLeft > 0)
            washTimeLeft--;
    }

    public void startWashing( )
    {
        if (washTimeLeft > 0)
            throw new IllegalStateException("Washer is already busy.");
        washTimeLeft = secondsForWash;
    }

}
```

FIGURE 7.8	Specification and Implementation of the Car Wash Method

Specification

◆ **carWashSimulate**
```
public static void carWashSimulate
(int washTime, double arrivalProb, int TotalTime)
```
Simulate the running of a car washer for a specified amount of time.

Parameters:
washTime - the number of seconds required to wash one car
arrivalProb - the probability of a customer arriving in any second; for example, 0.1 is 10%
totalTime - the total number of seconds for the simulation

Precondition:
washTime and totalTime are positive; arrivalProb lies in the range 0 to 1.

Postcondition:
The method has simulated a car wash in which washTime is the number of seconds needed to wash one car, arrivalProb is the probability of a customer arriving in any second, and totalTime is the total number of seconds for the simulation. Before the simulation, the method has written its three parameters to System.out. After the simulation, the method has written two pieces of information to System.out: (1) the number of cars washed, and (2) the average waiting time for customers that had their cars washed. (Customers that are still in the queue are not included in this average.)

Throws: IllegalArgumentException
Indicates that one of the arguments violates the precondition.

Sample Output

The carWashSimulate method could be part of an interactive or noninteractive Java program. For example, a noninteractive program might activate

```
carWashSimulate(240, 0.0025, 6000);
```

which can produce this output:

```
Seconds to wash one car: 240
Probability of customer arrival during a second: 0.0025
Total simulation seconds: 6000
Customers served: 13
Average wait: 111.07692307682308 sec
```

The actual output may be different because of variations in the random number generator that is used in the BooleanSource.

(continued)

(FIGURE 7.8 continued)

Implementation

```java
public static void carWashSimulate
(int washTime, double arrivalProb, int totalTime)
{
    Queue<Integer> arrivalTimes = new LinkedList<Integer>( );
    int next;
    BooleanSource arrival = new BooleanSource(arrivalProb);
    Washer machine = new Washer(washTime);
    Averager waitTimes = new Averager( );
    int currentSecond;

    // Write the parameters to System.out.
    System.out.println("Seconds to wash one car: " + washTime);
    System.out.print("Probability of customer arrival during a second: ");
    System.out.println(arrivalProb);
    System.out.println("Total simulation seconds: " + totalTime);

    // Check the precondition:
    if (washTime <= 0 || arrivalProb < 0 || arrivalProb > 1 || totalTime < 0)
        throw new IllegalArgumentException("Values out of range.");

    for (currentSecond = 0; currentSecond < totalTime; currentSecond++)
    {   // Simulate the passage of one second of time.

        // Check whether a new customer has arrived.
        if (arrival.query( ))
            arrivalTimes.add(currentSecond);

        // Check whether we can start washing another car.
        if ((!machine.isBusy( ))  &&  (!arrivalTimes.isEmpty( )))
        {
            next = arrivalTimes.remove( );
            waitTimes.addNumber(currentSecond - next);
            machine.startWashing( );
        }

        // Subtract one second from the remaining time in the current wash cycle.
        machine.reduceRemainingTime( );
    }

    // Write the summary information about the simulation.
    System.out.println("Customers served: " + waitTimes.howManyNumbers( ));
    if (waitTimes.howManyNumbers( ) > 0)
        System.out.println("Average wait: " + waitTimes.average( ) + " sec");
}
```

7.3   IMPLEMENTATIONS OF THE QUEUE CLASS

A queue seems conceptually simpler than a stack because we notice queues in our everyday lives. However, the implementation of a queue, although similar to that of a stack, is more complicated than the stack's implementation. As was the case with the stack class, we will give two implementations of our queue class: an implementation that stores the items in an array and an implementation using a linked list. Each implementation will be a generic `Queue` of Java objects, but as we discussed earlier, we could easily build a queue of any of the Java primitive types to obtain other queues.

Array Implementation of a Queue

As we did with the stack class, we will implement the queue class as a partially filled array. With a queue, we add items at one end of the array and remove them from the other end. Hence, we will be accessing the used portion of the array at both ends, increasing the size of the used portion at one end and decreasing the size of the used portion at the other end. This differs from our use of a partially filled array for a stack in that the stack accessed just one end of the array.

Because we now need to keep track of both ends of the used portion of the array, we will have *two* variables to keep track of how much of the array is used: One variable, called `front`, indicates the first index currently in use, and one variable, called `rear`, indicates the last index currently in use. If `data` is the array name, then the queue items will be in the array components:

keeping track of both ends of the partially filled array

    data[front], data[front + 1], ..., data[rear].

To add an item, we increment `rear` by 1 and then store the new item in the component `data[rear]`, where `rear` is now 1 larger than it was before. To get the next item from the queue, we retrieve `data[front]` and then increment `front` by 1 so that `data[front]` is then the item that used to be second.

There is one problem with this plan. The variable `rear` is incremented but never decremented. Hence, it will quickly reach the end of the array. At that point, it seems as if adding more items requires the array to increase capacity. Yet there is likely to be room in the array. In a normal application, the variable `front` would also be incremented from time to time (when items are removed from the queue). This will free up the array locations with index values less than `front`. There are several ways to reuse these freed locations.

One straightforward approach for using the freed array locations is to maintain all the queue items so that `front` is always equal to 0 (the first index of the array). When `data[0]` is removed, we move all the items in the array down one location, so the value of `data[1]` is moved to `data[0]`, and then all other items are also moved down one. This approach will work, but it is inefficient. Every time we remove an item from the queue, we must move every item in the queue. Fortunately, there is a better approach.

circular array

We do not need to move all the array elements. When the `rear` index reaches the end of the array, we can simply start using the available locations at the front of the array. One way to think of this arrangement is to think of the array as being bent into a circle so that the first component of the array is immediately after the last component of the array. In this way. the successor of the last array index is the first array index. In this circular arrangement, the free index positions are always "right after" `data[rear]`.

For example, suppose we have a queue of characters with a capacity of 5, and the queue currently contains three items, `'A'`, `'B'`, and `'C'`. Perhaps these values are stored with `front` equal to 0 and `rear` equal to 2, as shown here:

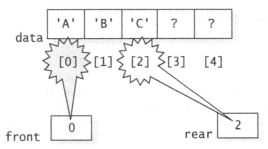

The question marks indicate unused spots in the array.

Let's remove two items (the `'A'` and `'B'`) and add two more items to the rear of this queue, perhaps the characters `'D'` and `'E'`. The result is shown here:

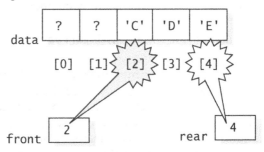

At this point, `front` is 2, `rear` is 4, and the queue items range from `data[2]` to `data[4]`. Suppose that now we add another character, `'F'`, to the queue. The new item cannot go after `rear` because we have hit the end of the array. Instead, we go to the front of the array, adding the new `'F'` at location `data[0]`, as shown here:

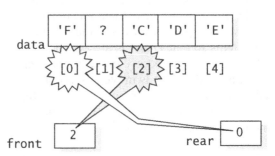

This may look peculiar with the `rear` index of 0 being *before* the `front` index of 2. But keep in mind the *circular* view of the array. With this view, the queue's items start at `data[front]` and continue forward. If you reach the end of the array, then come back to `data[0]` and keep going until you find the rear. It may help to actually view the array as bent into a circle, with the final array element attached back to the front, as shown here:

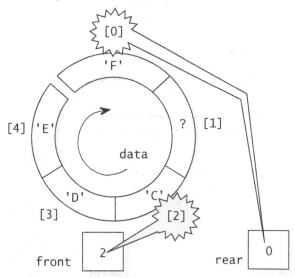

An array used in this way is called a **circular array**.

We now turn to a detailed presentation of our queue using the idea of a circular array. The specification and implementation for our queue are given in Figure 7.9 on page 387. The queue's items are held in an array, `data`, which is a private instance variable. The private instance variables `front` and `rear` hold the indexes for the front and the rear of the queue, as we have discussed. Whenever the queue is non-empty, the items begin at the location `data[front]`, usually continuing forward (to higher indexes) in the array. If the items reach the end of the array, then they continue at the first location, `data[0]`. In any case, `data[rear]` is the last item in the queue. One other private instance variable, `manyItems`, records the number of items that are in the queue. We will use many-Items to check whether the queue is empty and also to produce the value returned by the `size` method.

The `Queue` class implementation also has a new feature: a *private* method called `nextIndex`. This is a method that we think will be useful for the implementation, but it is not part of the public specification. We don't want other programmers to use this method; it is just for our own use in implementing a specific kind of queue. A private method such as this is called a **helper method**.

The `nextIndex` helper method allows us to step easily through the array, *the nextIndex* one index after another, with wraparound at the end. The activation of *helper method* `nextIndex(i)` usually returns `i+1`, with one exception: When `i` is equal to the last index of the array, `nextIndex(i)` returns 0 (the first index of the array).

ⓘ PROGRAMMING TIP

USE HELPER METHODS TO IMPROVE CLARITY

When a class requires some small computation that is likely to be used several times, consider implementing the computation with a helper method (that is, a private method). This will improve the clarity of your other code. Because a helper method is private, it does not need to be included in the documentation that's intended for other programmers, but you may write a precondition/postcondition contract for your own use.

The remaining implementation details are a straightforward implementation of a circular array, following this invariant:

Invariant of the ArrayQueue Class

1. The number of items in the queue is stored in the instance variable manyItems.

2. For a non-empty queue, the items are stored in a circular array beginning at data[front] and continuing through data[rear].

3. For an empty queue, manyItems is zero and data is a reference to an array, but we are not using any of the array, and we don't care about front and rear.

---

ensureCapacity implementation

The ensureCapacity method requires a bit of thought. The implementation starts by checking whether the current length of the data array is at least as big as the requested capacity. If so, the array is already big enough, and we return with no work. Otherwise, we must allocate a new, larger array and copy the elements from the original array to the new array. The allocation and copying are handled with three cases:

- If manyItems is zero, then we just allocate the new, larger array. There are no items to copy.

- If manyItems is nonzero and front ≤ rear, then we allocate the new array and copy data[front] ... data[rear] into the new array. This is not difficult because all the items are contiguous. We copy them into the new array with a single activation of System.arraycopy.

- If manyItems is nonzero and front > rear, then we allocate the new array, but it takes more care to copy the items into the new array. The items at the front of the queue are located at data[front] to the end of data. These items are followed by the items from data[0] to data[rear]. These two segments of items are copied into the new array by two separate activations of System.arraycopy, as shown at the top of the next page.

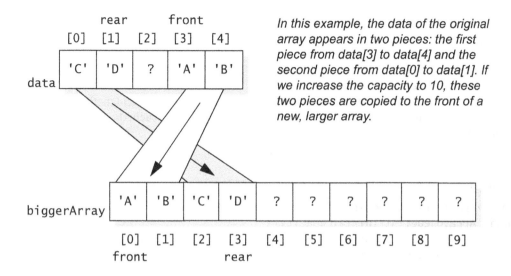

In this example, the data of the original array appears in two pieces: the first piece from data[3] to data[4] and the second piece from data[0] to data[1]. If we increase the capacity to 10, these two pieces are copied to the front of a new, larger array.

The `trimToSize` method has three cases that are similar to the `ensure-Capacity` method.

All the methods and their specifications are given in Figure 7.9.

FIGURE 7.9   Specification and Implementation of the Array Version of the Generic Queue Class

Generic Class ArrayQueue

❖ **public class ArrayQueue<E> from the package edu.colorado.collections**

An `ArrayQueue` is a queue of references to E objects.

Limitations:

(1) The capacity of one of these queues can change after it's created, but the maximum capacity is limited by the amount of free memory on the machine. The constructors, `clone`, `ensureCapacity`, `add`, and `trimToSize` will result in an `OutOfMemoryError` when free memory is exhausted.

(2) A queue's capacity cannot exceed the largest integer, 2,147,483,647 (`Integer.MAX_VALUE`). Any attempt to create a larger capacity results in failure due to an arithmetic overflow.

(continued)

(FIGURE 7.9 continued)

Specification

♦ **Constructor for the ArrayQueue<E>**

```
public ArrayQueue( )
```

Initialize an empty queue with an initial capacity of 10. Note that the add method works efficiently (without needing more memory) until this capacity is reached.

Postcondition:

This queue is empty and has an initial capacity of 10.

Throws: OutOfMemoryError

Indicates insufficient memory for new Object[10].

♦ **Second Constructor for the ArrayQueue<E>**

```
public ArrayQueue(int initialCapacity)
```

Initialize an empty queue with a specified initial capacity. Note that the add method works efficiently (without needing more memory) until this capacity is reached.

Parameter:

initialCapacity – the initial capacity of this queue

Precondition:

initialCapacity is non-negative.

Postcondition:

This queue is empty and has the given initial capacity.

Throws: IllegalArgumentException

Indicates that initialCapacity is negative.

Throws: OutOfMemoryError

Indicates insufficient memory for new Object[initialCapacity].

♦ **add—isEmpty—remove—size**

```
public void add(E)
public boolean isEmpty( )
public E remove( )
public int size( )
```

These are the standard queue specifications from Figure 7.2 on page 363.

♦ **clone**

```
public ArrayQueue<E> clone( )
```

Generate a copy of this queue.

Returns:

The return value is a copy of this queue. Subsequent changes to the copy will not affect the original, nor vice versa.

Throws: OutOfMemoryError

Indicates insufficient memory for creating the clone.

(continued)

(FIGURE 7.9 continued)

♦ **ensureCapacity**
   `public void ensureCapacity(int minimumCapacity)`
   Change the current capacity of this queue.
   Parameter:
   `minimumCapacity` – the new capacity for this queue
   Postcondition:
   This queue's capacity has been changed to at least `minimumCapacity`. If the capacity was already at or greater than `minimumCapacity`, then the capacity is left unchanged.
   Throws: `OutOfMemoryError`
   Indicates insufficient memory for `new Object[minimumCapacity]`.

♦ **getCapacity**
   `public int getCapacity( )`
   Accessor method to determine the current capacity of this queue. The add method works efficiently (without needing more memory) until this capacity is reached.
   Returns:
   the current capacity of this queue

♦ **trimToSize**
   `public void trimToSize( )`
   Reduce the current capacity of this queue to its actual size (i.e., the number of items it contains).
   Postcondition:
   This queue's capacity has been changed to its current size.
   Throws: `OutOfMemoryError`
   Indicates insufficient memory for altering the capacity.

Implementation

```
// File: ArrayQueue.java from the package edu.colorado.collections
// Complete documentation is available on pages 387–389 or from the ArrayQueue link at
// http://www.cs.colorado.edu/~main/docs/.

package edu.colorado.collections;
import java.util.NoSuchElementException;

public class ArrayQueue<E> implements Cloneable
{
    // Invariant of the ArrayQueue class:
    //    1. The number of items in the queue is in the instance variable manyItems.
    //    2. For a nonempty queue, the items are stored in a circular array beginning at
    //        data[front] and continuing through data[rear].
    //    3. For an empty queue, manyItems is zero and data is a reference to an array, but
    //        we don't care about front and rear.
    private Object[ ] data;
    private int manyItems;
    private int front;
    private int rear;
```

(continued)

(FIGURE 7.9 continued)

```java
public ArrayQueue( )
{
   final int INITIAL_CAPACITY = 10;
   manyItems = 0;
   data = new Object[INITIAL_CAPACITY];
   // We don't care about front and rear for an empty queue.
}

public ArrayQueue(int initialCapacity)
{
   if (initialCapacity < 0)
      throw new IllegalArgumentException
      ("initialCapacity is negative: " + initialCapacity);
   manyItems = 0;
   data = new Object[initialCapacity];
   // We don't care about front and rear for an empty queue.
}

public void add(E item)
{
   if (manyItems == data.length)
   {
      // Double the capacity and add 1; this works even if manyItems is 0. However, in
      // case that manyItems*2 + 1 is beyond Integer.MAX_VALUE, there will be an
      // arithmetic overflow and the bag will fail.
      ensureCapacity(manyItems*2 + 1);
   }

   if (manyItems == 0)
   {
      front = 0;
      rear = 0;
   }
   else
      rear = nextIndex(rear);

   data[rear] = item;
   manyItems++;
}
```

(continued)

(FIGURE 7.9 continued)

```java
@SuppressWarnings("unchecked")     // See the warnings discussion on page 265.
public ArrayQueue<E> clone( )
{   // Clone an ArrayQueue<E>.
    ArrayQueue<E> answer;

    try
    {
        answer = (ArrayQueue<E>) super.clone( );
    }
    catch (CloneNotSupportedException e)
    {
        // This exception should not occur. But if it does, it would probably indicate a
        // programming error that made super.clone unavailable.
        // The most common error would be forgetting the "Implements Cloneable"
        // clause at the start of this class.
        throw new RuntimeException
        ("This class does not implement Cloneable.");
    }

    answer.data = data.clone( );

    return answer;
}

public int getCapacity( )
{
    return data.length;
}

public boolean isEmpty( )
{
    return (manyItems == 0);
}

private int nextIndex(int i)
{
    || See the answer to Self-Test Exercise 17.
}
```

(continued)

(FIGURE 7.9 continued)

```java
public void ensureCapacity(int minimumCapacity)
{
   Object[ ] biggerArray;
   int n1, n2;

   if (data.length >= minimumCapacity)
      // No change needed.
      return;
   else if (manyItems == 0)
      // Just increase the size of the array because the queue is empty.
      data = new Object[minimumCapacity];
   else if (front <= rear)
   {  // Create larger array and copy data[front] ... data[rear] into it.
      biggerArray = new Object[minimumCapacity];
      System.arraycopy(data, front, biggerArray, front, manyItems);
      data = biggerArray;
   }
   else
   {  // Create a bigger array, but be careful about copying items into it. The queue items
      //  occur in two segments. The first segment goes from data[front] to the end of the
      //  array, and the second segment goes from data[0] to data[rear]. The variables n1
      //  and n2 will be set to the number of items in these two segments. We will copy
      //  these segments to biggerArray[0 ... manyItems-1].
      biggerArray = new Object[minimumCapacity];
      n1 = data.length - front;
      n2 = rear + 1;
      System.arraycopy(data, front, biggerArray, 0, n1);
      System.arraycopy(data, 0, biggerArray, n1, n2);
      front = 0;
      rear = manyItems-1;
      data = biggerArray;
   }
}


@SuppressWarnings("unchecked")      // See the warnings discussion on page 265.
public E remove( )
{
   E answer;

   if (manyItems == 0)
      throw new NoSuchElementException("Queue underflow.");
   answer = (E) data[front];
   front = nextIndex(front);
   manyItems--;
   return answer;
}
```

(continued)

(FIGURE 7.9 continued)

```java
    public int size( )
    {
        return manyItems;
    }

    public void trimToSize( )
    {
        // See the answer to Self-Test Exercise 18.
    }
}
```

Linked List Implementation of a Queue

A queue can also be implemented as a linked list. One end of the linked list is the front, and the other end is the rear of the queue. The approach uses two references to nodes. One refers to the first node (`front`), and the other refers to the last node (`rear`), as diagrammed here for a queue with three items:

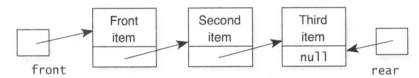

Figure 7.10 on page 395 shows the specification and implementation for a queue class that is implemented in this way. The class, called `LinkedQueue`, has no capacity problems, so it is considerably simpler than the array version. Here is the invariant we use in the linked list implementation:

Invariant of the LinkedQueue Class

1. The number of items in the queue is stored in the instance variable `manyNodes`.

2. The items in the queue are stored in a linked list, with the front of the queue stored at the head node and the rear of the queue stored at the final node.

3. For a non-empty queue, the instance variable `front` is the head reference of the linked list of items, and the instance variable `rear` is the tail reference of the linked list. For an empty queue, both `front` and `rear` are the null reference.

Each of the queue methods (except the constructors) can assume that the invariant is valid when the method is activated, and each method must ensure that the invariant is valid when the method finishes its work. Notice that the invariant includes an instance variable called `manyNodes` to keep track of the total number of items in the queue. We could get by without `manyNodes`, but its presence makes the `size` method quicker.

Most of the methods' work will be accomplished by the methods of our generic Node class that we developed in Chapters 4 and 5 (with a complete implementation in Appendix E). We'll look at the implementations of two queue methods—add and `remove`—in some detail.

The add Method. The add operation adds a node at the rear of the queue. For example, suppose we start with three items as shown here:

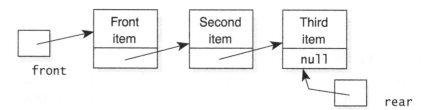

After adding a fourth item, the list would look like this:

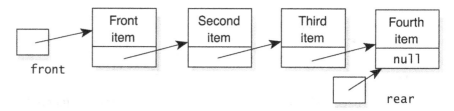

The new fourth item is placed in a newly created node at the end of the list. Normally, this is accomplished by two statements:

```
rear.addNodeAfter(item);
rear = rear.getLink( );
```

To add the first item, we need a slightly different approach because the empty list has only null references for the front and rear. In this case, we should add the new item at the front of the list and then assign `rear` to also refer to the new node, as shown in this code:

```
if (isEmpty( ))
{   // Insert first item.
    front = new Node<E>(item, null);
    rear = front;
}
else
{   // Insert an item that is not the first.
    rear.addNodeAfter(item);
    rear = rear.getLink( );
}
```

In fact, this code is most of the add method. The only other work is to add one to the manyNodes instance variable.

The remove Method. The remove method removes a node from the front of the queue. For example, suppose we start with this queue:

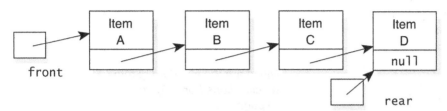

In this example, the remove method will return the item that is labeled "Item A." This item will also be removed from the queue so when remove returns, the list will have only the three items shown here:

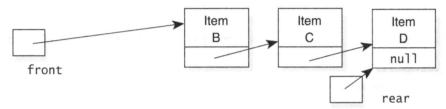

The implementation of remove uses the technique from page 183 to remove a node from the head. Most of the work is carried out by these statements:

```
E answer;
...
answer = front.getData( );
front = front.getLink( );
...
return answer;
```

The only other work in the complete implementation is to check the precondition (that the queue has some items), and if we remove the final item of the queue, then we must also set rear to null.

FIGURE 7.10 Specification and Implementation for the Linked List Version of the Queue Class

Generic Class LinkedQueue

❖ **public class LinkedQueue<E> from the package edu.colorado.collections**
A LinkedQueue<E> is a queue of references to E objects.
Limitations:
Beyond Int.MAX_VALUE items, size is wrong.

(continued)

(FIGURE 7.10 continued)

Specification

◆ **Constructor for the LinkedQueue<E>**
```
public LinkedQueue( )
```
Initialize an empty queue.
Postcondition:
This queue is empty.

◆ **add—isEmpty—remove—size**
```
public void add( )
public boolean isEmpty( )
public E remove( )
public long size( )
```
These are the standard queue specifications from Figure 7.2 on page 363.

◆ **clone**
```
public E clone( )
```
Generate a copy of this queue.
Returns:
The return value is a copy of this queue. Subsequent changes to the copy will not affect the original, nor vice versa.
Throws: OutOfMemoryError
Indicates insufficient memory for creating the clone.

Implementation

```
// File: LinkedQueue.java from the package edu.colorado.collections
// Complete documentation is written above or is available from the LinkedQueue link at
// http://www.cs.colorado.edu/~main/docs/

package edu.colorado.collections;
import java.util.NoSuchElementException;
import edu.colorado.nodes.Node;

public class LinkedQueue<E> implements Cloneable
{
    // Invariant of the LinkedQueue<E> class:
    //    1. The number of items in the queue is stored in the instance variable manyNodes.
    //    2. The items in the queue are stored in a linked list, with the front of the queue
    //       stored at the head node and the rear of the queue at the final node.
    //    3. For a non-empty queue, the instance variable front is the head reference of the
    //       linked list of items, and the instance variable rear is the tail reference of the
    //       linked list. For an empty queue, both front and rear are the null reference.
    private int manyNodes;
    private Node<E> front;
    private Node<E> rear;

    public LinkedQueue( )
    {
        front = null;
        rear = null;
    }
```

(continued)

(FIGURE 7.10 continued)

```java
public void add(E item)
{
   if (isEmpty( ))
   {  // Insert first item.
      front = new Node<E>(item, null);
      rear = front;
   }
   else
   {  // Insert an item that is not the first.
      rear.addNodeAfter(item);
      rear = rear.getLink( );
   }
   manyNodes++;
}

public LinkedQueue<E> clone( )
|| See the answer to Self-Test Exercise 19.

public boolean isEmpty( )
{
   return (manyNodes == 0);
}

public E remove( )
{
   E answer;

   if (manyNodes == 0)
      // NoSuchElementException is from java.util, and its constructor has no argument.
      throw new NoSuchElementException("Queue underflow.");
   answer = front.getData( );
   front = front.getLink( );
   manyNodes--;
   if (manyNodes == 0)
      rear = null;
   return answer;
}

public int size( )
{
   return manyNodes;
}

}
```

PITFALL

FORGETTING WHICH END IS WHICH

We implemented our queue with the front of the queue at the head of the list and the rear of the queue at the tail of the list. As it turns out, this was not an arbitrary choice. Can you see why? What would have happened if we had tried to do things the other way around, as shown in this wrong diagram?

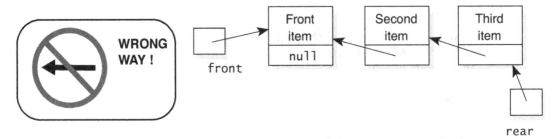

With this wrong arrangement of the queue's front and rear, we can still implement the add operation, adding a new node at the rear of the queue. We also have easy access to the front item. But it will be difficult to actually remove the front item. After the removal, the front must be positioned so that it refers to the next node in the queue, and there is no constant-time algorithm to accomplish that (though a linear-time algorithm could start at the rear and move through the whole list).

So, keep in mind that it's easy to insert and remove at the head of a linked list, but insertion is the only easy operation at the tail.

Self-Test Exercises for Section 7.3

14. Under what circumstances is a helper method useful?

15. Write a new accessor method that returns a copy of the item at the rear of the queue. Use the array version of the queue.

16. A programmer who sees our array implementation of a queue shown in Figure 7.9 on page 387 gives us the following suggestion: "Why not eliminate the manyItems instance variable since the number of items in the queue can be determined from the values of front and rear?" Is there a problem with this suggestion?

17. Implement the nextIndex method for the array version of the queue.

18. Implement the trimToSize method for the array version of the queue.

19. Implement the clone method for the linked list version of the queue. You should use Node.listCopyWithTail.

20. Write a new accessor method that returns a copy of the item at the rear of the queue. Use the linked list version of the queue.

21. Write another accessor method that returns a copy of the item at the *rear* of the queue. Use the linked list version of the queue.

22. What goes wrong if we try to put the front of the queue at the tail of the linked list?

7.4 DEQUES AND PRIORITY QUEUES (OPTIONAL SECTION)

Double-Ended Queues

One variation on the queue is a *double-ended queue*, also called a *deque* (pronounced like the word "deck"). The key property of a deque is that entries can be quickly inserted and removed at both ends. This differs from a stack (which uses only one end) and an ordinary queue (in which things enter at one end and leave at the other). The ends of the deque are called "front" and "back," but these designations are arbitrary since the same operations can occur at both ends.

In Java, deques are an interface (`java.util.Deque`) that includes all of the queue interface plus additional methods such as `addFirst` (to add an element to the front end) and `removeLast` (to remove an element from the back end). The key methods of the `Deque` interface are shown in Figure 7.11.

The most straightforward implementations of a deque are similar to the queue implementations that we have seen using a circular array or linked list—but a special technique must be used for a linked list. See if you can guess that special technique before looking at the answers to the Self-Test Exercises.

FIGURE 7.11   Key Methods of the Java Deque Interface

These are the key methods of the `java.util.Deque<E>` interface, which depends on the generic type parameter E.

Operation	At the front end use ...	At the back end use ...

add an element	`void push(E element)`
	or
	`void addFirst(E element)`
		`void add(E element)`
		or
		`void addLast(E element)`

remove an element and return a reference to the removed element	`E remove( )`
	or
	`E pop( )`
	or
	`E removeFirst( )`
		`E removeLast( )`

retrieve an element without removing it	`E peek( )`
	or
	`E peekFirst( )`
		`E peekLast( )`

Priority Queues

Using a queue ensures that customers are served in the exact order in which they arrive. However, we often want to assign priorities to customers and serve the higher-priority customers before those of lower priority. For example, a hospital emergency room will handle the most severely injured patients first, even if they are not "first in line." A computer operating system that keeps a queue of programs waiting to use some resource, such as a printer, may give interactive programs a higher priority than batch-processing programs that will not be picked up by the user until the next day, or it might give higher priority to short programs and lower priority to longer programs. A **priority queue** is a data structure that stores items along with a priority for each item. Items are removed in order of priority. The highest-priority item is removed first. If several items have equally high priorities, then the one that was placed in the priority queue first is the one removed first.

higher numbers indicate a higher priority

For example, suppose the following customer names and priorities are entered into a priority queue in the order given:

Ginger Snap, priority 0
Natalie Attired, priority 3
Emanual Transmission, priority 2
Gene Pool, priority 3
Kay Sera, priority 2

The higher numbers indicate a higher priority. The names would be removed in the following order: first Natalie Attired (with the highest priority), then Gene Pool, then Emanual Transmission, then Kay Sera, and finally Ginger Snap (with the lowest priority). Note that both Natalie Attired and Gene Pool have priority 3, which is the highest priority, but Natalie Attired entered the priority queue before Gene Pool, so Natalie Attired is removed before Gene Pool.

Priority Queue ADT—Specification

Figure 7.12 gives the specification for some methods of a priority queue class. When an item is added to a priority queue, it is entered with a specified priority, which is an integer in the range 0 ... highest, where highest is a parameter of the priority queue constructor. Items are removed from the queue in order of priority. For example, suppose highest is 2. In that case, items of priority 2 are removed first. When there are no items of priority 2 left, then items of priority 1 are removed. When there are no items of priority 1 left, then items of priority 0 are removed. Items with the same priority are removed in the order in which they were entered into the priority queue.

FIGURE 7.12   Specification of the Key Methods of a Generic `PriorityQueue` Class

Specification

These are the constructor, `remove`, and `add` methods of a generic priority queue class.

> ◆ **Constructor for the PriorityQueue<E>**
>> `public PriorityQueue(int highest)`
>> Initialize an empty priority queue.
>>
>> **Parameter:**
>>> `highest` – the highest priority allowed in this priority queue
>>
>> **Precondition:**
>>> `highest >= 0`.
>>
>> **Postcondition:**
>>> This priority queue is empty.
>>
>> **Throws:** `IllegalArgumentException`
>>> Indicates that `highest` is negative.
>
> ◆ **add**
>> `public void add(E item, int priority)`
>> Add a new item to this priority queue.
>>
>> **Parameters:**
>>> `item` – the item to be added to this queue
>>> `priority` – the priority of the new item
>>
>> **Precondition:**
>>> `0 <= priority` and `priority` is no more than the highest priority.
>>
>> **Postcondition:**
>>> The item has been added to this priority queue.
>>
>> **Throws:** `IllegalArgumentException`
>>> Indicates an illegal priority.
>>
>> **Throws:** `OutOfMemoryError`
>>> Indicates insufficient memory for adding a new item to this priority queue.
>
> ◆ **remove**
>> `public E remove( )`
>> Get the highest-priority item, removing it from this priority queue.
>>
>> **Precondition:**
>>> This queue is not empty.
>>
>> **Postcondition:**
>>> The return value is the highest-priority item of this queue, and the item has been removed. If several items have equal priority, then the one that entered first will be removed first.
>>
>> **Throws:** `NoSuchElementException`
>>> Indicates that this queue is empty.

Priority Queue Class—An Implementation That Uses an Ordinary Queue

You may have noticed that the priority queue has a lot in common with the ordinary queue. We used the same names for the methods, and only add has an extra parameter for the priority of the new item. This suggests that much of the priority queue work has already been accomplished in the queue implementation—but what is the best way to take advantage of this?

One possibility is to provide the priority queue with an array of ordinary queues. For example, suppose highest is 2. In this case, a priority queue can be implemented using three ordinary queues: one to hold the items with priority 0, another queue for the items of priority 1, and a third queue for the lofty items with priority 2. Using this idea, we could implement a priority queue by defining a private instance variable that is an array of ordinary queues, as shown in the highlighted line here:

```
// Import a class for an ordinary Queue:
import edu.colorado.collections.ArrayQueue;

public class PriorityQueue<E>
{
    private ArrayQueue<E>[ ] queues
    ...
```

an array of ordinary queues

In this implementation, the constructor allocates the memory for the array of queues with the statement:

```
queues = (ArrayQueue<E>[]) new Object[highest+1];
```

The array has highest+1 elements (from queues[0] through queues[highest]).

The items with priority 0 are stored in the ordinary queue called queues[0]; items with priority 1 are stored in queues[1]; and so on, up to the ordinary queue called queues[highest]. To enter an item into the priority queue with a given priority, all we need to do is enter the item into the correct ordinary queue. For example, suppose highest is 3 and items are put into the priority queue in the following order:

Ginger Snap, priority 0
Natalie Attired, priority 3
Emanual Transmission, priority 2
Gene Pool, priority 3
Kay Sera, priority 2

each item of the priority queue is placed in one of the ordinary queues

After these items, the array of ordinary queues looks like this:

queues[3]: Natalie Attired (at the front), followed by Gene Pool
queues[2]: Emanual Transmission (at the front), followed by Kay Sera
queues[1]: empty
queues[0]: Ginger Snap

When an item needs to be removed, we move down through the ordinary queues, starting with the highest priority, until we find a non-empty queue. We then remove the front item from this non-empty queue. This process could be made more efficient if we also keep a member variable to indicate which is the highest-numbered ordinary queue that is non-empty.

With this approach, we can implement a priority queue as an array of ordinary queues and do not need to duplicate a lot of the previous work. In fact, it is possible to implement the priority queue with no instance variables other than the queues array. However, some efficiency is gained by adding two other instance variables.

The first is a number, totalSize, which keeps track of the total number of items in all of the queues. With this instance variable, a size method for the priority queue can operate in constant time.

The second extra instance variable is an integer, which keeps track of the highest priority that is currently in the priority queue. This makes remove more efficient because, without the extra instance variable, we must always search from highest downward until we find a non-empty queue. With the extra private instance variable, remove can go straight to the correct queue and remove an item. (Of course, this extra instance variable also must be maintained correctly so that its value is always the priority of the highest item.) We leave the remainder of the details of writing this array-based implementation for Programming Project 4 on page 407.

Priority Queue ADT—A Direct Implementation

If the number of possible priorities is large, then an array of queues might be impractical. In this case, you might think of several alternatives. One possibility is to implement the priority queue as an ordinary linked list in which the data in each node contains two things: the item from the queue and the priority of that item. This implementation works, regardless of how large the priority range is. We will leave the details of the implementation as another exercise (Programming Project 5 on page 407).

Java's Priority Queue

Java has a different form of a priority queue in java.util.PriorityQueue. This generic class, PriorityQueue<E>, has a generic type parameter for the elements in the queue, and these elements are usually comparable to each other (rather than having a separate priority value for each insertion into the queue).

Self-Test Exercises for Section 7.4

23. Suppose you are storing the items of a deque in an array. Why do you need to use a circular array rather than putting all the items at the front?

24. Suppose you are using a linked list to implement a deque. What kind of linked list would be best?

25. Implement the add method of the priority queue. Use the implementation that has an array called queues of ordinary queues.

26. Suppose you know that the number of priorities that will be used in a priority queue application is small, but you do not know what the actual priorities will be. For example, suppose you know that the priorities can be any integer values in the range 0 to 1,000,000, but you also know that there will be at most 25 different numbers used. How might you implement the priority queue as an array of ordinary queues in such a way that the array size is much smaller than 1,000,000?

CHAPTER SUMMARY

- A queue is a first-in/first-out data structure.
- A queue can be used to buffer data that is being sent from a fast computer component to a slower component. Queues also have many other applications: in simulation programs, operating systems, and elsewhere.
- A queue can be implemented as a partially filled circular array.
- A queue can be implemented as a linked list.
- When implementing a stack, you need to keep track of only one end of the list of items, but when implementing a queue, you need to keep track of both ends of the list.
- A double-ended queue, or *deque,* can be implemented with a circular array or a doubly linked list.
- A priority queue can be implemented as an array of ordinary queues or in various ways as a linked list.

? Solutions to Self-Test Exercises

1. LIFO (last-in/first-out) and FIFO (first-in/first-out) refer to the order in which entries must be removed.

2. For adding: insert or enqueue ("enter queue"); for removing: getFront and dequeue ("delete from queue")

3. The isEmpty function tests for an empty queue.

4. The operations are add 'L', add 'I', add 'N', add 'E', followed by four remove operations that return 'L', then 'I', then 'N', then 'E'.

5. Reading input from a keyboard and sending output to a printer.

6. Read the characters two at a time. Each pair of characters has the first character placed in

queue number 1 and the second character placed in queue number 2. After all the reading is done, print all characters from queue number 1 on one line, and print all characters from queue number 2 on a second line.

7. A straightforward approach is to use a second queue, called `line`. As the input is being read, each character is placed in the `line` queue (as well as being placed in the original stack and queue). During the comparison phase, we also keep track of how many characters correctly match. If a mismatch occurs, we can then print an appropriate amount of the `line` queue as part of the error message.

8. Do not apply the `toUpperCase` method.

9. Yes.

10. We assumed that no more than one customer arrives during any particular second.

11. (1) Sometimes add a new customer to the arrivals queue; (2) sometimes start a new car through the washer; (3) tell the washer that another second has passed.

12. These are cars that arrived during the simulation, but they are still waiting in line at the end of the simulation.

13. The total number of cars can never exceed `Integer.MAX_VALUE` because there is at most one car per second and the total number of seconds in the simulation is an integer.

14. A helper method is a private method that is useful when a class requires an operation that does not need to be part of the public interface.

15. The body of the method should check that `size( ) > 0` and then return `data[rear]`.

16. The main problem is that you cannot tell when the queue is empty because `front` and `rear` have no meaning for an empty queue.

17. Here's the private method with its precondition/postcondition contract:
    ```
    private int NextIndex(int i)
    // Precondition: 0 <= i and i < data.length.
    // Postcondition: If i+1 is data.length,
    //   then the return value is zero;
    //   otherwise, the return value is i+1.
    {
        if (++i == data.length)
            return 0;
        else
            return i;
    }
    ```

18. The `trimToSize` method should handle these cases: (1) If the length of the array is already equal to the number of items, then do no work; (2) if the number of items is zero, then change `data` to an array of capacity zero and return with no other work; (3) if (`front<=rear`), then allocate a new array of the correct size and activate `System.array-copy` once to copy the items from the old array to the new array; (4) if (`front>rear`), then allocate a new array of the correct size and activate `System.arraycopy` twice to copy the two segments into the new array.

    The fourth case is similar to the final case of `ensureCapacity`. If you copy the items into the front of the new array, then make sure you also change `front` and `rear` to reflect the new positions of the items.

19. Here's the extra work after initially setting answer with super.clone:
    ```
    Node[ ] cloneInfo;
    cloneInfo =
        Node.listCopyWithTail(front);
    answer.front = cloneInfo[0];
    answer.rear = cloneInfo[1];
    return answer;
    ```

20. The body of the method should check that rear is not `null` and then return with:
    ```
    return rear.getData( );
    ```

21. The body of the method should check that `size( ) > 0` and then return with:
    ```
    return rear.getData( );
    ```

22. Removals will be hard to implement.

23. If all the items were kept at the front of the array, then it would be time-consuming to add or remove at the front.

24. For inserting at both ends, an ordinary singly linked list is fine. A singly linked list is also fine for removing at the front, but for removing at the back, a doubly linked list is needed.

25. The implementation should check that the priority is valid. Then activate the method `queues[priority].add[item]`. If you are keeping track of other items (such as the current highest priority and the total size), then those items should be updated, too.

26. Since you know that there are at most 25 different priorities, you could get by with an array of only 25 ordinary queues plus a second array of integers called `value`. The number in `value[i]` would be the priority of all the items in `queues[i]`. It might also make sense to keep the arrays sorted according to priority.

PROGRAMMING PROJECTS

1 In Figure 7.3 on page 367, we presented a program that checks a string to see if the letters in the string read the same forward and backward. These strings are called palindromes. Another kind of palindrome is one in which we look at words rather than letters. A **word-by-word palindrome** is a string of words such that the words read the same forward and backward. For example, the quote "You can cage a swallow, can't you, but you can't swallow a cage, can you?" is a word-by-word palindrome. Write a program to test an input string and tell whether or not it is a word-by-word palindrome. Consider upper- and lowercase letters to be the same letter. Define a word as any string consisting of only letters or an apostrophe and bounded at each end with one of the following: a space, a punctuation mark, the beginning of the line, or the end of the line. Your program should have a friendly interface and allow the user to check more lines until the user wishes to quit the program.

2 In Figure 7.3 on page 367, we presented a program that checks a string to see if the letters in the string read the same forward and backward. The previous exercise performed a similar check using words in place of letters. In this exercise, you are to write a program that runs a similar check using lines rather than words or letters.

Write a program that reads in several lines of text and decides if the passage reads the same, whether you read the lines top to bottom or bottom to top; this is yet another kind of palindrome. For example, the following poem reads the same from top to bottom and from bottom to top:

> *As I enter my time machine or*
> *maybe not,*
> *I wonder whether free will exists.*
> *Change?*
> *Change!*
> *I wonder whether free will exists—*
> *maybe not*
> *as I enter my time machine, or...*

Consider upper- and lowercase versions of a letter to be the same letter. Consider word boundaries to be significant, so for example, the words in the first line must read the same as the words in the last line in order to pass the test (as opposed to just the letters reading the same). However, consider all word delimiters as being equivalent; i.e., a punctuation mark, any number of spaces, or any combination of these are all considered to be equivalent. The end of the passage should be marked by a line containing only the word "end," spelled with any combination of upper- and lowercase letters and possibly with blanks before and/or after it. Your program should have a friendly interface and allow the user to check more passages until the user wishes to quit the program. Note that to test your program, you need not use such well-   constructed poems. Your program will check any passage, regardless of its literary merit.

3 Enhance the car wash simulation method in Figure 7.8 on page 381 so that it has the following additional property. There is an additional parameter, which is a maximum length for the queue. When the queue gets as long as this maximum, any customer who arrives will leave without entering the queue (because the customer does not want to wait that long). There should also be one additional simulation result that is printed. In addition to the output shown in Figure 7.8, the method should print the number of simulated customers who left because the queue was too long. Embed the method in a program that allows the user to repeat simulations with different arguments until the user wishes to quit the program.

4 Give a complete implementation of a priority queue using an array of ordinary queues. For your ordinary queue, use the version from `edu.colorado.collections.ArrayQueue` in Figure 7.9 on page 387.

5 Give a complete implementation of a priority queue using the idea from the direct implementation on page 403.

6 In this chapter, we gave a linked list implementation of a queue. This implementation used two references, called `front` and `rear`, to refer to the front and the rear nodes of the queue (linked list). A **circular linked list** is similar to a regular linked list, except that the link field in the "last node" refers back to the "first node." (Of course, after this change, it is no longer clear which node, if any, is intrinsically "first.") If we use a circular linked list, then we need only one reference to implement a queue since the front node and the rear node are adjacent nodes, as at the top of the next column.

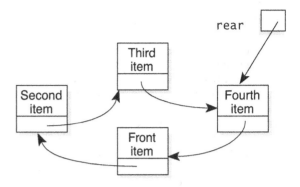

In the diagram, we have called the single reference `rear` because it refers to the last node in the queue. It turns out that this gives a more efficient implementation than having it refer to the first node in the queue. Redo the queue class using a circular linked list.

7 A **double-ended queue** is a list that allows the addition and removal of items from either end. One end is arbitrarily called the **front** and the other the **rear**, but the two ends behave identically. Specify, design, and implement a class for a double-ended queue. Include operations to check if it is empty and to return the number of items in the list. For each end, include operations for adding and deleting items. Implement the double-ended queue as a doubly linked list. Call your class Deque (pronounced "deck").

8 Make improvements to the car wash simulation program from Section 7.2. One particular improvement you should make is to handle the customers who are still in the queue at the end of the simulation. These customers should have their cars washed one after another, but no new customers should be allowed to join the queue during this time. The wait times of these leftover customers should be counted along with all the other customers.

9 Write a simulation program for a small airport that has only one runway. There will be a queue of planes waiting to land and a queue of planes waiting to take off. However, only one plane can use the runway at a time, so there can be only one takeoff or one landing in progress at any one time. Assume that all takeoffs take the same amount of time. Assume that all landings take the same amount of time, but this need not be the same as the takeoff time. Assume that planes arrive for landing at random times but with a specified probability of a plane arriving during any given minute. Similarly, assume that planes arrive at the takeoff queue at random times but with a (possibly different) specified probability of a departure. (Despite the fact that takeoffs and landings are scheduled, delays make this a reasonable assumption.) Since it is more expensive and more dangerous to keep a plane waiting to land than it is to keep a plane waiting to take off, landings will have priority over takeoffs. Thus, as long as some plane is waiting to land, no plane can take off. Use a clock that is an integer variable that counts the number of minutes simulated. Use a random number generator to simulate arrival and departure times of airplanes.

This simulation can be used, among other things, for deciding when the air traffic has become so heavy that a second runway must be built. Hence, the simulation will simulate disaster conditions in which planes crash because they run out of fuel while waiting too long in the landing queue. By examining the simulated situation, the airport authority hopes to avoid real tragedy. Assume all planes can remain in the queue for the same amount of time before they run out of fuel. If a plane runs out of fuel, your simulation will not discover this until the simulated plane is removed from the queue; at that point, the fact that the plane crashed is recorded, that plane is discarded, and the next plane is processed. A crashed plane is not considered in the calculation of waiting time. At the end of the simulated time, the landing queue is examined to see whether any of the planes in the simulated queue have crashed. You can disregard the planes left in the queue at the end of the simulation, other than those that crashed for lack of sufficient fuel. Use the following input and output specifications:

Input: (1) The amount of time needed for one plane to land; (2) the amount of time needed for one plane to take off; (3) the average amount of time between arrival of planes to the landing queue; (4) the average amount of time between arrival of planes to the takeoff queue; (5) the maximum amount of time that a plane can stay in the landing queue without

running out of fuel and crashing; and (6) the total length of time to be simulated.

Output: (1) The number of planes that took off in the simulated time; (2) the number of planes that landed in the simulated time; (3) the number of planes that crashed because they ran out of fuel before they could land; (4) the average time that a plane spent in the takeoff queue; and (5) the average time that a plane spent in the landing queue.

10 Do an airplane simulation that is more complex than the previous project. In this version, planes arrive for landing with a random amount of fuel, which determines how long they can remain in the air. A plane will crash unless it lands within the time assigned to it. Your simulation will keep planes in a priority queue, in which the priority of a plane is equal to the number of minutes before midnight that the plane will crash.

11 Write a simulation program of the lines at a grocery store. The program will be similar to the car wash simulation, except that there are multiple queues instead of one. You might use an array (or vector) of queues to simulate the lines. Assume that there are five cashier lines at the grocery store. Customers enter randomly to check out, and then enter the shortest line. If the lines are equal, then the first available line is chosen. Each transaction takes a random amount of time to complete.

For additional work, expand the grocery line program to allow shoppers to:

- avoid a line if all lines are a certain length
- leave a line if they have waited beyond a certain time
- check if another line is shorter at specified time intervals
- switch lines if another line is shorter

12 Write a program that uses a priority queue to store a list of prioritized chores.

13 Use a circular array or a doubly linked list to implement a deque.

Recursive Thinking

8

Recursive Thinking

"Well," said Frog, "I don't suppose anyone ever is completely self-winding. That's what friends are for." He reached for the father's key to wind him up again.

RUSSELL HOBAN
The Mouse and His Child

one of the subtasks is a simpler version of the same problem you are trying to solve in the first place

Often, during top-down design, you'll meet a remarkable situation: One of the subtasks to be solved is nothing more than a simpler version of the same problem you are trying to solve in the first place. In fact, this situation occurs so frequently that experienced programmers start *expecting* to find simpler versions of a large problem during the design process. This expectation is called **recursive thinking**. Programming languages such as Java support recursive thinking by permitting a method implementation to actually activate itself. In such cases, the method is said to use **recursion**.

In this chapter, we start encouraging you to recognize situations in which recursive thinking is appropriate. We also discuss recursion in Java, both how it is used to implement recursive designs and the mechanisms that occur during the execution of a recursive method.

8.1 RECURSIVE METHODS

We'll start with an example. Consider the task of writing a non-negative integer to the screen with its decimal digits stacked vertically. For example, the number 1234 should be written as:

1
2
3
4

a case with an easy solution ... and a case that needs more work

One version of this problem is quite easy: If the integer has only one digit, then we can just print that digit. But if the number has more than one digit, the solution is not immediately obvious, so we might break the problem into two subtasks: (1) print all digits except the last digit, stacked vertically; (2) print the last digit. For example, if the number is 1234, then the first step will write:

1
2
3

The second step will output the last digit, 4.

The main factor that influenced our selection of these two steps is the ease of providing the necessary data. For example, with our input number 1234, the first step needs the digits of 123, which is easily expressed as 1234/10 (since dividing an integer by 10 results in the quotient, with any remainder discarded). In general, if the integer is called number, and number has more than one digit, then the first step prints the digits of number/10, stacked vertically. The second step is equally easy: It requires us to print the last digit of number, which is easily expressed as number % 10. (This is the remainder upon dividing number by 10.) Simple expressions, such as number/10 and number % 10, are not so easy to find for other ways of breaking down the problem (such as printing only the first digit in the first step).

The pseudocode for our solution is as follows:

```
// Printing the digits of a non-negative number, stacked vertically
if (the number has only one digit)
    Write that digit.
else
{
    Write the digits of number/10 stacked vertically.
    Write the single digit of number % 10.
}
```

At this point, your recursive thinking cap should be glowing: One of the steps—*write the digits of* number/10 *stacked vertically*—is a simpler instance of the same task of writing a number's digits vertically. It is simpler because number/10 has one fewer digit than number. This step can be implemented by activating writeVertical itself. This is an example of a method activating itself to solve a smaller problem, which is a **recursive call**. The implementation, with a recursive call, is shown in Figure 8.1. This implementation is a static method that could be part of any class. Within this class itself, the static method can be activated by the simple name writeVertical(...). From outside the class, the method can be activated by giving the class name followed by ".writeVertical(...)".

one of the steps is a simpler instance of the same task

In a moment, we'll look at the exact mechanism that occurs during the activation of a recursive method, but first there are two notions to explain.

1. The Stopping Case. If the problem is simple enough, it is solved without recursive calls. In writeVertical, this occurs when number has only one digit. The case without any recursion is called the **stopping case** or **base case**. In Figure 8.1, the stopping case of writeVertical is implemented with the two lines:

```
if (number < 10)
    System.out.println(number); // Write the one digit.
```

2. The Recursive Call. In Figure 8.1, the method writeVertical makes a recursive call. The recursive call is the highlighted statement at the top of the next page.

```
        else
        {
            writeVertical(number/10);      // Write all but the last digit.
            System.out.println(number % 10); // Write the last digit.
        }
```

This is an instance of the writeVertical method activating itself to solve the simpler problem of writing all but the last digit.

| **FIGURE 8.1** | The writeVertical Method |

Specification

♦ **writeVertical**

    public static void writeVertical(int number)

    Print the digits of a non-negative integer vertically.

    Parameter:

    number - the number to be printed

    Precondition:

    number >= 0

    The method does not check the precondition, but the behavior is wrong for negative numbers.

    Postcondition:

    The digits of number have been written, stacked vertically.

Implementation

```
public static void writeVertical(int number)
{
    if (number < 10)
        System.out.println(number);              // Write the one digit.
    else
    {
        writeVertical(number/10);                // Write all but the last digit.
        System.out.println(number % 10);         // Write the last digit.
    }
}
```

Sample Results of writeVertical(1234)

```
1
2
3
4
```

Tracing Recursive Calls

During a computation such as writeVertical(3), what actually occurs? The first step is that the argument 3 is copied to the method's formal parameter, number. This is the way that all primitive types are handled as a parameter: The argument provides an initial value for the formal parameter.

Once the formal parameter has its initial value, the method's code is executed. Since 3 is less than 10, the boolean expression in the if-statement is true. So, in this case, it is easy to see that the method just prints 3 and does no more work.

Next, let's try an argument that causes us to enter the else-part, for example:

```
writeVertical(37);
```

When the method is activated, the value of number is set equal to 37, and the code is executed. Since 37 is not less than 10, the two statements of the else-part are executed. Here is the first statement:

```
writeVertical(number/10);   // Write all but the last digit.
```

In this statement, (number/10) is (37/10), which is 3. So this is an activation of writeVertical(3). We already know the action of writeVertical(3): Print 3 on a single line of output. After this activation of writeVertical is completely finished, the second line in the else-part executes:

example of a recursive call

```
System.out.println(number % 10);
```

This just writes number % 10. In our example, number is 37, so the statement prints the digit 7. The total output of the two lines in the else-part is:

```
3
7
```

The method writeVertical uses recursion. Yet we did nothing new or different in carrying out the computation of writeVertical(37). We treated it just like any other method. We simply substituted the actual argument for number and then executed the code. When the computation reached the recursive call of writeVertical(3), we simply activated writeVertical with the argument 3.

PROGRAMMING EXAMPLE: **An Extension of writeVertical**

Figure 8.2 shows an extension of writeVertical to a more powerful method called superWriteVertical, which handles all integers, including negative integers. With a negative input, the new method prints the negative sign on the first line of output, above any of the digits. For example:

```
superWriteVertical(-361)
```

FIGURE 8.2 The superWriteVertical Method

Specification

♦ **superWriteVertical**

    `public static void superWriteVertical(int number)`

    Print the digits of an integer vertically.

    Parameter:

    number - the number to be printed

    Postcondition:

    The digits of number have been written, stacked vertically. If number is negative, then a negative sign appears on top.

Implementation

```
public static void superWriteVertical(int number)
{
    if (number < 0)
    {
        System.out.println("-");              // Print a negative sign.
        superWriteVertical(-number);          // -1*number is positive.
        ‖ This is Spot #1 referred to in the text.
    }
    else if (number < 10)
        System.out.println(number);           // Write the one digit.
    else
    {
        superWriteVertical(number/10);        // Write all but the last digit.
        ‖ This is Spot #2 referred to in the text.
        System.out.println(number % 10);      // Write the last digit.
    }
}
```

This produces the following output with a minus sign on the first line:

```
-
3
6
1
```

How do we handle a negative number? The first step seems clear enough: Print the negative sign. After this, we must print the digits of number, which are the same as the digits of -1*number, which is *positive* (because number itself is negative). So the pseudocode for superWriteVertical is an extension of our original pseudocode:

```
if (the number is negative)
{
    Write a negative sign.
    Write the digits of -1*number stacked vertically.
}
else if (the number has only one digit)
    Write that digit.
else
{
    Write the digits of number/10 stacked vertically.
    Write the single digit of number % 10.
}
```

If you think recursively, you will recognize that the step *write the digits of -1*number stacked vertically* is a simpler version of our original problem (simpler because the negative sign does not need to be written). This suggests the implementation in Figure 8.2 with two recursive calls: one for the new case that writes the digits of -1*number and a second call for the original case that writes the digits of number/10. The implementation has one simplification using "-number" instead of "-1*number". We also have added comments in the code, identifying two particular locations, "Spot #1" and "Spot #2," to aid in taking a closer look at recursion.

A Closer Look at Recursion

The computer keeps track of method activations in the following way: When a method is activated, the computer temporarily stops the execution. Before actually executing the method, some information is saved that will allow the computation to return to the correct location after the method's work is completed. The computer also provides memory for the method's parameters and any local variables that the method uses. Next, the actual arguments are plugged in for the parameters, and the code of the activated method begins to execute.

If the execution should encounter an activation of *another* method—recursive or otherwise—then the first method's computation is temporarily stopped. This is because the second method must be executed before the first method can continue. Information is saved that indicates precisely where the first method should resume when the second method is completed. The second method is given memory for its own parameters and local variables. The execution then proceeds to the second method. When the method is completed, the execution returns to the correct location within the first method, and the first method resumes its computation. *how methods are executed*

This mechanism is used for both recursive and nonrecursive methods. As an example of the mechanism in a recursive method, let's completely trace the work of superWriteVertical(-36). Initially, we activate superWriteVertical with number set to -36. The actual argument, -36, is copied to the parameter, number, and we start executing the code. At the moment when the method's execution begins, all of the important information that the method needs to work is

Activation record for first call to
superWriteVertical

number: –36

When the method returns, the
computation should continue at
line 57 of the main program.

stored in a memory block called the method's **activation record**. The activation record contains information as to where the method should return when it is done with its computation, and it also contains the values of the method's local variables and parameters. For example, if our superWriteVertical method were called from a main program, then the activation record might contain the information shown to the left.

The return location specified in a real activation record does not actually refer to lines of code in the main program, but when you're imagining an activation record, you can think of a return location in this manner.

With the activation record in place, the method starts executing. Because the number is negative, the boolean test of the if-statement is true, and the negative sign is printed. At this point, the computation is about to make a recursive call, indicated here:

```
if (number < 0)
{
    System.out.println("-");
    superWriteVertical(-number);
    ‖ This is Spot #1 referred to in the text.
}
```

A recursive call is made in the superWriteVertical method.

This method generates its own activation record with its own value of number (which will be 36) and its own return location. The new activation record is placed on top of the other activation record, like this:

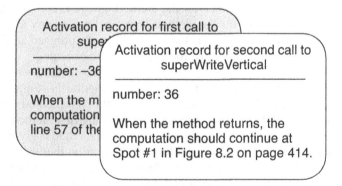

In fact, the collection of activation records is stored in a *stack* data structure called the **execution stack.** Each activation of a method pushes the next activation record on top of the execution stack.

In our example, the second call of superWriteVertical executes with its own value of number equal to 36. The method's code executes, taking the last branch of the if-else control structure, and arriving at another recursive call:

```
else                              Another recursive call is made in the
{                                 superWriteVertical method.
    superWriteVertical(number/10);
    ||  This is Spot #2 referred to in the text.
    System.out.println(number % 10);
}
```

To execute this recursive call, another activation record is created (with `number` now set to 3), and this activation record is pushed onto the execution stack, as shown here:

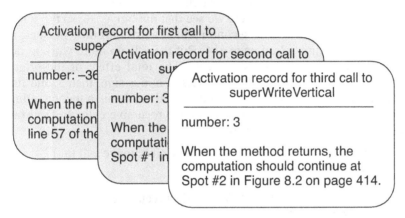

The `superWriteVertical` method begins executing once more. With `number` set to 3, the method enters the section to handle a one-digit number. At this point, the digit 3 is printed, and no other work is done during this activation.

When the third method activation ends, its activation record is popped off the stack. But just before it is popped, the activation record provides one last piece of information—telling where the computation should continue. In our example, the third activation record is popped off the stack, and the computation continues at Spot #2 in Figure 8.2 on page 414. At this point, we have the two remaining activation records shown here:

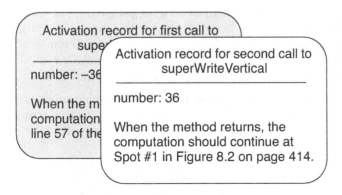

As we said, the computation is now at Spot #2 in Figure 8.2 on page 414. This is the highlighted location shown here:

```
else
{
    superWriteVertical(number/10);
    ‖ This is Spot #2 referred to in the text.
    System.out.println(number % 10);
}
```

The next statement is an output statement. What does it print? From the activation record on top of the stack, we see that number is 36, so the statement prints 6 (which is 36 % 10). The second method activation then finishes, returning to Spot #1 in Figure 8.2 on page 414. But there is no more work to do after Spot #1, so the first method also returns. The total effect of the original method activation was to print three characters: a minus sign, then 3, and finally 6. The tracing was all accomplished with the usual mechanism for activating a method; no special treatment was needed to trace recursive calls. In the example, there are two levels of recursive calls:

1. superWriteVertical(-36) made a recursive call to
   superWriteVertical(36).

2. superWriteVertical(36) made a recursive call to
   superWriteVertical(3).

In general, recursive calls may be much deeper than this, but even at the deepest levels, the activation mechanism remains the same as the example that we have traced.

General Form of a Successful Recursive Method

Key Design Concept

Find smaller versions of a problem within the larger problem itself.

Java places no restrictions on how recursive calls are used within a method. However, for recursive methods to be useful, any sequence of recursive calls must ultimately terminate with some piece of code that does not depend on recursion—in other words, there must be a *stopping case*. The method may call itself, and that recursive call may call the method again. The process may be repeated any number of times. However, the process will not terminate unless eventually one of the recursive calls does not itself make a recursive call. The general outline of a recursive method definition is as follows:

1. Suppose a problem has one or more cases in which some of the subtasks are simpler versions of the same problem you are trying to solve in the first place. These subtasks are solved by recursive calls.

2. A method that makes recursive calls must also have one or more cases in which the entire computation is accomplished without recursion. These cases without recursion are called **stopping cases** or **base cases**.

Often, a series of if-else statements determines which of the cases will be executed. A typical scenario is for the first method activation to execute a case that includes a recursive call. That recursive call may in turn execute a case that requires another recursive call. For some number of times, each recursive call produces another recursive call, but eventually one of the stopping cases applies. Every call of the method must eventually lead to a stopping case; otherwise, the execution will never end, because of an infinite sequence of recursive calls. In practice, infinite recursion will terminate with a Java exception called StackOverflowError, indicating that the execution stack has run out of memory for more activation records.

Self-Test Exercises for Section 8.1

1. What is the output produced by f(3) for each of the following?

```
public static void f(int n)      public static void f(int n)
{                                {
   System.out.println(n);           if (n > 1)
   if (n > 1)                          f(n-1);
      f(n-1);                       System.out.println(n);
}                                }
```

```
public static void f(int n)
{
    System.out.println(n);
    if (n > 1)
        f(n-1);
    System.out.println(n);
}
```

2. What is the output of the following method with an argument of 3?

```
public static void cheers(int n)
{
   if (n <= 1)
      System.out.println("Hurrah");
   else
   {
      System.out.println("Hip");
      cheers(n-1);
   }
}
```

3. Modify the cheers method from the preceding exercise so that it first prints "Hurrah" followed by n-1 "Hip"s. Make a further modification so that n-1 "Hip"s occur both before and after the "Hurrah". Make another modification so that approximately half of the "Hip"s occur before the "Hurrah" and half appear after.

4. Write a recursive method with a parameter that is a non-negative integer. The method writes that number of asterisks to the screen, followed by that number of exclamation points. Use no loops or local variables.

8.2 STUDIES OF RECURSION: FRACTALS AND MAZES

Recursive thinking makes its biggest impact on problems in which one of the *subtasks* is a simpler version of the *same* problem you are working on. For example, when we write the digits of a long number, our first step is to write the digits of the smaller number, number/10. This section provides additional examples of recursive thinking and the methods that recursion leads to.

FIGURE 8.3

The First Few Steps in Generating a Random Fractal

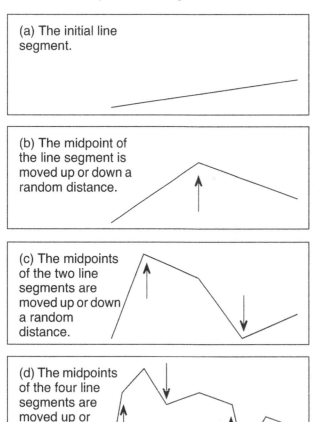

(a) The initial line segment.

(b) The midpoint of the line segment is moved up or down a random distance.

(c) The midpoints of the two line segments are moved up or down a random distance.

(d) The midpoints of the four line segments are moved up or down a random distance.

PROGRAMMING EXAMPLE:
Generating Random Fractals

Fractals are one of the techniques that graphics programmers use to artificially produce remarkably natural scenes of mountains, clouds, trees, and other objects. We'll explain fractals in a simple setting and develop a recursive method to produce a certain kind of fractal.

To understand fractals, think about a short line segment, as shown in Figure 8.3(a). Imagine grabbing the middle of the line and moving it vertically a random distance. The two endpoints of the line stay fixed, so the result might look like Figure 8.3(b). This movement has created two smaller line segments: the left half of the original segment and the right half. For each of these smaller line segments, we'll grab the midpoint and move it up or down a random distance. Once again, the endpoints of the line segments remain fixed, so the result of this second step might look like Figure 8.3(c). One more step might produce Figure 8.3(d). The process continues as long as you like, with each step creating a slightly more jagged line.

After several more steps, the line could appear as shown here:

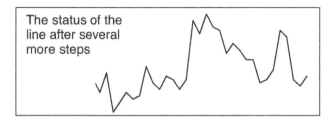

The status of the
line after several
more steps

Perhaps you can imagine that this jagged line is the silhouette of a mountain skyline.

The line that we're generating has an interesting property. Suppose that we carry out thousands of steps to create our line and then magnify a small portion of the result, as shown here:

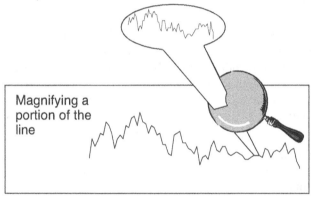

Magnifying a
portion of the
line

The magnified portion is not identical to the entire line, but there is a lot of similarity. **Fractal** is the term coined by the mathematician Benoît Mandelbrot to describe objects, such as our line, that exhibit some kind of similarity under magnification. In fact, the first fractals studied were mathematically defined sets that remained *completely unchanged* when magnified to certain powers. In nature, objects don't generally remain completely unchanged under magnification, but magnified views commonly exhibit similarities with the larger object (such as our line, or a cloud, or a fern). Also, in nature (and our line), the powers of magnification where the similarities occur are limited, so nature's fractals are really rough approximations of the more formal mathematical fractals. Even so, the term *fractal* is often applied to any object that exhibits similarities under some magnification. The jagged line we have described is called a **random fractal** because of the randomness in its generation.

fractals, nature's fractals, and random fractals

A Method for Generating Random Fractals—Specification

We wish to write a method that can draw a random fractal in the way we have described. The input to this method includes the locations of the two endpoints of the original line, measured from the top side and the left side of the drawing area. For example, consider the line segment shown here:

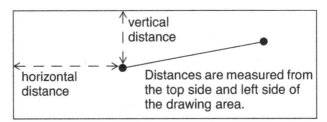

In computer graphics, these distances are measured in **pixels**, which are the individual dots on a computer screen. Today's typical screens have about 100 pixels per inch, so the endpoint just shown might have an *x* coordinate of 100 (the distance from the left side) and a *y* coordinate of 55 (the distance below the top side). These *y* coordinates are probably different from what you're used to because positive coordinates occur below the top side, whereas normal mathematics coordinates have positive numbers going upward—but that's the way computer graphics are usually measured, from the top down.

The *x* and *y* coordinates of both endpoints will be four of the parameters to the fractal-generating method. The method also has a fifth parameter called drawingArea. The drawingArea is a Java Graphics object, which is a class from the java.awt package. A Graphics object allows a program to draw images based on pixels. For example, one of the Graphics methods is specified here:

♦ **drawLine** (from the Graphics class)
   `public void drawLine(int x1, int y1, int x2, int y2)`
   Draw a line on this Graphics object.

   Parameters:
   x1 and y1 - the x and y pixel coordinates of one endpoint of the line
   x2 and y2 - the x and y pixel coordinates of the other endpoint of the line

   Postcondition:
   A line has been drawn on this Graphics object from (x1, y1) to (x2, y2).

Java programs have several ways to create Graphics objects, but we don't need to know about that yet. Instead, we'll provide the specification of the fractal method without worrying about exactly how the program generates a Graphics object. Here is a listing of the method with its five parameters:

```
public static void randomFractal(
    int leftX,
    int leftY,
    int rightX,
    int rightY,
    Graphics drawingArea
)
```

Now we must consider the method's behavior. Let's look at an example using an initial line segment shown here with its *x* and *y* coordinates:

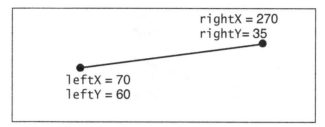

Notice that we're using pixel coordinates, so the higher point has the lower *y* coordinate.

Normally, the first step of randomFractal is to find the approximate *x* and *y*-coordinates of the segment's midpoint. We'll call these coordinates midX and midY, as shown here:

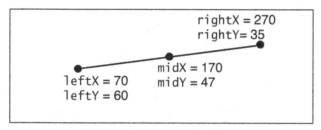

We are keeping track of the coordinates with integers, so the *y* midpoint is a bit inaccurate—the real midpoint is $47\frac{1}{2}$. The statements to compute the approximate midpoints use integer division (throwing away any remainder), as shown here:

```
midX = (leftX + rightX) / 2;
midY = (leftY + rightY) / 2;
```

Next, the *y* midpoint must be shifted up or down a random amount. To limit the rise and fall of the fractal, the complete shift will be no more than half of the distance from leftX to rightX. The amount of the shift is stored in a variable called delta, computed randomly with this statement:

```
delta = (int)((Math.random( ) - 0.5) * (rightX - leftX));
```

The random part of this expression, Math.random( ), provides a random double number from 0 up to, but not including, 1. So (Math.random( ) - 0.5) is from -0.5 to 0.5 (not including 0.5). The assignment to delta is this random number times the distance between the *x* coordinates and rounded to an integer.

Once we have delta, this value is added to midY with the statement:

```
midY += delta;
```

For example, suppose that delta is 25. Then the midY shifts down 25 pixels, as shown here:

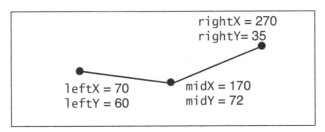

After computing the location of the displaced midpoint, we have two segments: from the left endpoint of the original segment to the displaced midpoint, and from the displaced midpoint to the right endpoint of the original segment. And what work do we have left to do? *We must generate a random fractal for each of these two smaller line segments.* This work can be accomplished with two recursive calls:

```
randomFractal(leftX, leftY,  midX,   midY,   drawingArea);
randomFractal(midX,  midY,   rightX, rightY, drawingArea);
```

two recursive calls solve two smaller versions of the original problem

The first of these recursive calls generates a random fractal for the leftmost smaller line segment. Let's examine the arguments of the first recursive call: The first two arguments are the left coordinates of the leftmost segment (leftX and leftY), the next two arguments are the right coordinates of the leftmost segment (midX and midY), and the final argument is the Graphics object that we are drawing on. The second recursive call handles the rightmost line segment in a similar way.

To summarize, the randomFractal method normally carries out these six statements:

```
midX = (leftX + rightX) / 2;
midY = (leftY + rightY) / 2;
delta = (int)((Math.random( ) - 0.5) * (rightX - leftX));
midY += delta;
randomFractal(leftX, leftY,  midX,   midY,   drawingArea);
randomFractal(midX,  midY,   rightX, rightY, drawingArea);
```

stopping case for the random fractal method

These six statements cannot be all of randomFractal. For one thing, no drawing takes place in these statements. For another, these statements on their own will lead to infinite recursion—there is no stopping case. The solution is a stopping case that's triggered when leftX and rightX get close to each other. In this case, the horizontal extent of the segment is small, and further subdividing the segment has little effect. So this will be our stopping case, and we will simply draw a line from the left endpoint to the right endpoint. This approach is taken in Figure 8.4 on the next page.

FIGURE 8.4   A Method to Generate a Random Fractal

Specification

♦ **randomFractal**
```
public static void randomFractal(
   int leftX,
   int leftY,
   int rightX,
   int rightY,
   Graphics drawingArea
)
```
Draws a random fractal on a Graphics object.

Parameters:
   leftX and leftY - the x and y pixel coordinates of one endpoint of a line segment
   rightX and rightY - the x and y pixel coordinates of the other endpoint of a line segment
   drawingArea - a Graphics object on which to draw a random fractal

Postcondition:
   A random fractal has been drawn on the Graphics object. The fractal extends from
   (leftX, leftY) to (rightX, rightY).

Implementation

```
public static void randomFractal
(
   int leftX,
   int leftY,
   int rightX,
   int rightY,
   Graphics drawingArea
)
{
   final int STOP = 4;
   int midX, midY;
   int delta;

   if ((rightX - leftX) <= STOP)
      drawingArea.drawLine(leftX, leftY, rightX, rightY);
   else
   {
      midX = (leftX + rightX) / 2;
      midY = (leftY + rightY) / 2;
      delta = (int)((Math.random( ) - 0.5) * (rightX - leftX));
      midY += delta;
      randomFractal(leftX,  leftY,  midX,   midY,   drawingArea);
      randomFractal(midX,   midY,   rightX, rightY, drawingArea);
   }
}
```

The Stopping Case for Generating a Random Fractal

The randomFractal method from Figure 8.4 reaches a stopping case when the distance from leftX to rightX gets small enough, as shown here:

```
if ((rightX - leftX) <= STOP)
    drawingArea.drawLine(leftX, leftY, rightX, rightY);
```

The constant, STOP, is defined as 4 at the top of the randomFractal method. In the stopping case, we use the Graphic drawLine method to draw a line segment from the left endpoint to the right endpoint.

Putting the Random Fractal Method in an Applet

There's one item you're probably still wondering about. How does a program get a Graphics object to draw on? One approach can be used by any applet that draws a single fixed image with no user interaction. This approach has five easy steps, though you must also be familiar with the general format of applets as described in Appendix I.

The fixed-image approach for an applet follows these steps:

1. Import java.awt.*, which provides the Graphics class and another class called Image.

2. The applet declares two private instance variables, like this:

   ```
   private Image display;
   private Graphics drawingArea;
   ```

   An Image is an area that can store a drawing. Sometimes these drawings are obtained from external files, but the drawings can also be created by the applet itself by attaching a Graphics object to the Image. This is what we plan to do; the drawingArea (a Graphics object) will be attached to the display (an Image).

3. The applet's init method initializes the Image and sets the Graphics object to draw on that image. This takes four statements:

   ```
   int height = getSize( ).height;
   int width = getSize( ).width;
   display = createImage(width, height);
   drawingArea = display.getGraphics( );
   ```

   The width and height variables are initialized with getSize( ).width and getSize( ).height, which provide the current size of a running applet. The createImage method is also part of any applet, and it creates an Image with a given width and height in pixels. The fourth statement sets drawingArea to a Graphics object that can be used to draw on the Image.

4. The rest of the applet's `init` method draws any items that you want to appear in the image. These are drawn using the `drawingArea` Graphics object. For example, we want an applet that draws a random fractal, so our `init` method will have this complete implementation:

```
public void init( )
{
   int height = getSize( ).height;
   int width = getSize( ).width;
   display = createImage(width, height);
   drawingArea = display.getGraphics( );

   randomFractal(0, height/2, width, height/2, drawingArea);
}
```

The last line of the `init` method does the actual drawing by calling the `randomFractal` method. The fractal will be drawn in `drawingArea`, which is the `Graphics` object that we set to draw in the `display` Image.

As with any applet, the `init` method is automatically called when the applet starts. This will put the `randomFractal` image in the `display` Image.

5. To actually show the image, we need to provide one more applet method, called `paint`. The `paint` method is called when the applet is started and whenever the applet's location or shape changes, such as moving from behind some other window. For the applet to draw a single fixed image, the `paint` method is simply this:

```
public void paint(Graphics g)
{
    g.drawImage(display, 0, 0, null);
}
```

The argument, g, is the underlying `Graphics` object where all applet drawing takes place. It is different from `drawingArea` (which is the `Graphics` object attached to the image that we drew). The one statement that we placed in the `paint` method will draw our `display` image in the applet's drawing area, aligned in the upper-left corner. (The first argument is the image we are drawing; the second and third arguments indicate the coordinates where the upper-left corner of the image will be placed in the applet; and the fourth argument is a Java object called an observer, but we can set it to `null` if we are not using this feature.)

As we said, any applet that draws a single fixed image can follow these five steps. A fractal-drawing applet following these steps is shown in Figure 8.5, along with a picture of how the applet looks when it runs.

FIGURE 8.5   Implementation of an Applet to Draw a Random Fractal

Java Applet Implementation

```
// File: Fractal.java
// This applet is a small example to illustrate the randomFractal method.

import java.applet.Applet;
import java.awt.*;              // Provides Graphics, Image

public class Fractal extends Applet
{
    private Image display;
    private Graphics drawingArea;

    public void init( )
    {
      int height = getSize( ).height;
      int width = getSize( ).width;
      display = createImage(width, height);
      drawingArea = display.getGraphics( );

      randomFractal(0, height/2, width, height/2, drawingArea);
    }

    public void paint(Graphics g)
    {
      g.drawImage(display, 0, 0, null);
    }

    public static void randomFractal
    (
      int leftX,
      int leftY,
      int rightX,
      int rightY,
      Graphics drawingArea
    )
    {
      || See Figure 8.4 on page 425.
    }
}
```

Sample of the Applet Running

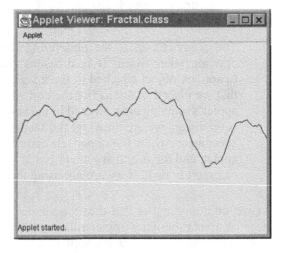

PROGRAMMING EXAMPLE: **Traversing a Maze**

Suppose your friend Jervis has a maze in his backyard. One day, Jervis mentions two facts about the maze:

1. Somewhere in the maze is a magic tapestry that contains the secret of the universe.

2. You can keep this tapestry (and its secret) if you can enter the maze, find the tapestry, and return to the maze's entrance. (So far, many have entered, but none have returned.)

The maze is built on a rectangular grid. At each point of the grid, there are four directions to move: north, east, south, or west. Some directions, however, may be blocked by an impenetrable wall. You decide to accept Jervis's challenge and enter the maze—but only with the help of your portable computer and a method that we'll write to guide you into the maze *and back out*.

Traversing a Maze—Specification

We plan to write a method, `traverseMaze`, which you can execute on a portable computer that you will carry through the maze. The method will give you directions and ask you questions to take you to the magic tapestry and back out. Here's the complete specification:

♦ **traverseMaze**
   `public static boolean traverseMaze( )`
   Provide interactive help to guide a user through a maze and back out.

   Precondition:
   The user of the program is facing an unblocked spot in the maze, and this spot has not previously been visited by the user.

   Postcondition:
   The method has asked a series of queries and provided various directions to the user. The queries and directions have led the user through the maze and back to the exact same position where the user started. If there was a magic tapestry that could be reached in the maze, then the user has picked up this tapestry, and the method returns `true`; otherwise, the method returns `false`.

Figure 8.6 shows a drawing of what the maze might look like, along with a sample dialogue. A sample dialogue written at this point—before we've written the program—is called a **script**, and it can help clarify a loose specification. As you might suspect, Jervis's actual maze is more complex than this sample dialogue might suggest, but simplicity often results in the best scripts.

FIGURE 8.6	Script for the Maze Traversal Method

A Sample Dialogue

Step forward & write your name on the ground.
Have you found the tapestry? [Y or N]
N
Please turn left 90 degrees.
Are you facing a wall? [Y or N]
N
Is your name written ahead of you? [Y or N]
N
Step forward & write your name on the ground.
Have you found the tapestry? [Y or N]
N
Please turn left 90 degrees.
Are you facing a wall? [Y or N]
Y
Please turn right 90 degrees.
Are you facing a wall? [Y or N]
N
Is your name written ahead of you? [Y or N]
N
Step forward & write your name on the ground.
Have you found the tapestry? [Y or N]
Y
Pick up the tapestry, and take a step backward.
Please turn right 90 degrees.
Please turn right 90 degrees.
Please step forward, then turn 180 degrees.
Please turn right 90 degrees.
Please turn right 90 degrees.
Please turn right 90 degrees.
Please step forward, then turn 180 degrees.

This dialogue supposes that the user starts at the entrance to the maze drawn below. The starting point of the user is represented by the arrow in a circle, with the arrow pointing in the direction that the user is facing. The large X is the magic tapestry.

Let's trace through this script to make sure it's correct. I'll pretend that I am the user and I'm standing, facing the entrance to the maze in Figure 8.6. The program asks me to step forward and write my name on the ground, which I do. I am now standing on the white square just inside the entrance, still facing in the same direction that I started, and my name is written in the dirt underneath me. Here's the bottom part of the maze at that point (the "MGM" is my name):

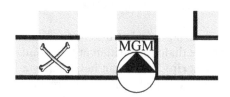

Next, the script asks me whether I have found the tapestry, and I answer N. I am then told to turn left 90 degress, which I do, placing me in this situation:

Am I facing a wall? (I answer N.) Is my name written ahead of me? (Again, I answer N because my name is not written in the square in front of me, which is the dark square just to the left of the entrance.) So, again, I am told to step forward and write my name on the ground, which I do:

My name is now written on the first two squares of the maze, and the program can use that information to determine which squares I have already visited. Once again, I am asked whether I have found the tapestry (I answer N) and then I'm told to turn left 90 degrees, like this:

Am I facing a wall? Yes, I am, so I am told to turn *right* 90 degrees. Kind of seems like I'm not getting anywhere because I've gone back to where I was a moment ago:

But even though I am back in a previous situation, the program has gained some information about one of the walls. If you continue following this particular script, you'll see that I pick up the tapestry and find my way back out of the maze. The exact instructions aren't that important. In fact, at this point, we might not even have a complete working script, just an idea that the script will ask me questions and give me orders that will take me to the tapestry and safely back out of the maze. So let's move on to apply recursive thinking to this problem of asking the questions and giving the orders to traverse the maze.

Traversing a Maze—Design

The traverseMaze method appears to perform a pretty complex task. When the method starts, all that's really known is that the user of the program is facing some spot in the maze, and that spot has not been previously visited. The method must take the user into the maze, eventually leading the user back to the exact starting spot. Hopefully, along the way, the user will find the magic tapestry. Recursive thinking can make the task easier.

We'll call the method's user Judy. We'll always start by asking Judy to take a step forward onto the spot she hasn't visited before. We'll also ask her to write her name on the ground so that later we can tell whether she's been to this spot before. After these two steps, we will ask her whether she has found the tapestry at this new spot and will place her true or false answer in a local variable named found.

the stopping case

Now there is one easy case: If the tapestry is at this spot, then we will have Judy pick up the tapestry and ask her to take a step backward to her starting spot. This is the stopping case, and the method returns true to indicate that the tapestry was found.

But what if Judy does not find the tapestry at this spot? In this case, there are three possible directions for Judy to explore: forward, left, or right. We won't worry about exploring backward, because that is the direction that Judy just came from. Also, sometimes we do not need to explore all three directions (forward, left, and right). A direction is a "dead end" if (a) there is a wall blocking that direction or (b) Judy's name is written on the ground in that direction (indicating she has already been there)—and there is no need to explore dead ends. We also don't need to explore a direction if Judy already found the tapestry in one of the other directions.

This description suggests the following steps if the user has not found the tapestry at this spot:

1. Have the user face left (the first direction to explore).

2. for each of the three directions
   {
       if (!found && the direction that is now being faced isn't a dead end)
       {
           Explore the direction that is now being faced, returning
           to this exact spot after the exploration and setting
           found to true if the tapestry was found.
       }
       Have the user turn 90 degrees to the right (the next direction).
   }

3. The user is now facing the direction she came from, so ask her to step forward and turn around (so that she is facing the same spot that she was facing before this method was activated).

Are you thinking recursively? The highlighted step—"Explore the direction that is now being faced ... "—is a simpler instance of the problem we are trying to solve. The instance is simpler because one spot in the maze has been eliminated from consideration; namely, the spot the user is at doesn't contain the tapestry. In our implementation, we'll solve this simpler problem with a recursive call.

Traversing a Maze—Implementation

Our implementation will benefit from two methods to carry out various sub-tasks. Figure 8.7 shows the methods we have in mind. The first method provides a simple way to ask a question and get a yes/no answer. The other method determines whether the user has reached a dead end.

A short discussion of these two methods appears after the figure.

FIGURE 8.7   Two Methods to Simplify the Maze Traversal

Specification

♦ **deadend**

    `public static boolean deadend( )`

    Determine whether the person traversing the maze has reached a dead end.

    Postcondition:

        The return value is `true` if the direction directly in front of the user is a dead end (that is, a direction that cannot contain the tapestry).

♦ **inquire**

    `public static boolean inquire(String query)`

    Ask a yes/no question and read the answer.

    Parameter:

        query - a question to ask

    Postcondition:

        The query has been printed to `System.out` and a one-character response read from `System.in` (skipping any whitespace characters). The method returns `true` if the user's response was `'Y'` or `'y'` and returns `false` if the user's response was `'N'` or `'n'`. (If the response is some other character, then the query is repeated and a new answer read.)

Implementation

```
public static boolean deadend( )
{
   return inquire("Are you facing a wall?")
        ||
        inquire("Is your name written in front of you?");
}
```

(continued)

(FIGURE 8.7 continued)

```java
public static boolean inquire(String query)
{
    char answer = 'N';

    do
    {
        System.out.println(query + " [Y or N]");
        try
        {
            do
                answer = (char) System.in.read( );
            while (Character.isWhitespace(answer));
        }
        catch (IOException e)
        {
            System.err.println("Standard input error: " + e);
            System.exit(0);
        }
        answer = Character.toUpperCase(answer);
    } while ((answer != 'Y') && (answer != 'N'));

    return (answer == 'Y');
}
```

The two methods in Figure 8.7 are:

- inquire: This method asks the user a yes/no question; it returns true if the user answers 'Y' or 'y' and returns false if the user answers 'N' or 'n'.
- deadend: This method determines whether the direction in front of the user is a dead end. Remember that dead ends are caused by a wall or by a direction that the user has already explored. The method returns true (for a dead end) or false (for no dead end).

The implementation of the deadend method is short, as shown here:

```java
return inquire("Are you facing a wall?")
       ||
       inquire("Is your name written in front of you?");
```

This implementation of deadend makes two activations of the inquire method and returns the "or" of the results (using the || operation). When the "or" expression is evaluated, the inquire method is called to ask the user, "Are you facing a wall?" If the user answers 'Y' or 'y', then the inquire method returns true, and the rest of the "or" expression will not be executed. This follows the general rule of **short-circuit evaluation** that we have seen before—meaning that the evaluation of a logical expression stops when there is enough information to determine whether the expression is true or false. On the other hand, if the user answers 'N' or 'n' to the first query, then the inquire method returns false, and the rest of the "or" expression will be executed (asking the second question, "Is your name written in front of you?").

In all, the method returns true if the user indicates that he or she is facing a wall or if the user says there is no wall and then answers 'Y' or 'y' to the second question (the user's name is written in front of him or her).

The actual traverseMaze method is given in Figure 8.8. You might enjoy knowing that the magic tapestry really does exist in a book called *Castle Roogna* by Piers Anthony. The hero of the book becomes part of the tapestry, whereupon his quest leads him to a *smaller* version of the *same* tapestry.

The Recursive Pattern of Exhaustive Search with Backtracking

The traverseMaze method of Figure 8.8 follows a recursive pattern that you may find useful elsewhere. The pattern is useful when a program is searching for a goal within a space of individual points that have connections between them. In the maze problem, the "points" are the individual squares of the maze, and the "connections" are the possible steps that the explorer can take in the four compass directions. Later you'll run into many data structures that have the form of "points and connections." In fact, our very next chapter introduces trees, which are such a structure.

The task of searching such a structure can often follow this pattern:

- Start by marking the current point in some way. In the maze, the mark was made by asking the explorer to write her name on the ground. The purpose of the mark is to ensure that we don't mistakenly return to this point and end up going around in circles, continually returning to this same spot.

   This "marking" step is not always necessary; sometimes there are other mechanisms to prevent unbounded repetitions of searching the same direction.

- Check whether the current point satisfies the goal. If so, return some value that indicates the success of the search.

- On the other hand, if the current point does not satisfy the goal, then one by one examine the other points that are connected to the current point. For each such point, check to see whether the point is marked; if so, we can ignore the point because we have already been there. On the other hand, if a connected point is not marked, then make a recursive call to continue the search from the connected point onward. If the recursive call finds the goal, then we won't bother checking any other points, but if the recursive call fails, then we will check each of the other unmarked connected points via further recursive calls.

This pattern is called **exhaustive search with backtracking**. The term *exhaustive search* means that all possibilities are tried. *Backtracking* is the process of a recursive call returning without finding the goal. When such a recursive call returns, we are "back where we started," and we can explore other directions with further recursive calls.

FIGURE 8.8 A Method to Traverse a Maze

Specification

♦ **traverseMaze**

```
public static boolean traverseMaze( )
```
Provide interactive help to guide a user through a maze and back out.

Precondition:

The program's user is facing an unblocked spot that has not been previously visited.

Postcondition:

The method has asked a series of questions and provided various directions to the user. The questions and directions have led the user through the maze and back to the exact same position where the user started. If there was a magic tapestry that could be reached in the maze, then the user has picked up this tapestry, and the method returns true; otherwise, the method returns false.

Implementation

```java
public static boolean traverseMaze( )
{
    int direction;   // Counts 1, 2, 3 for the three directions to explore.
    boolean found;   // Will be set to true if we find the tapestry.

    System.out.println("Step forward & write your name on the ground.");
    found = inquire("Have you found the tapestry?");

    if (found)
    { // Pick up the tapestry and step back from whence you came.
        System.out.println("Pick up the tapestry and take a step backward.");
    }
    else
    { // Explore the three directions (not counting the one that you just came from). Start
      // with the direction on your left, and then turn through each of the other directions.
        System.out.println("Please turn left 90 degrees.");
        for (direction = 1; direction <= 3; direction++)
        {
            if ( !found && !deadend( ) )
                found = traverseMaze( );
            System.out.println("Please turn right 90 degrees.");
        }
        // You're now facing the direction from whence you came, so step forward and turn
        // around. This will put you in the same spot when the method was activated.
        System.out.println("Please step forward, then turn 180 degrees.");
    }
    return found;
}
```

Exhaustive search with backtracking is most useful when the known search space doesn't get too large. But even with huge search spaces, programmers often use variants that try to cut down the search space in an intelligent manner. You'll find successful variants in programs that play games that have an enormous number of possibilities to search (such as chess). As one more recursive example, we'll write a method to play a game with a definite, small search space, so we won't need to cut down this space at all.

PROGRAMMING EXAMPLE: **The Teddy Bear Game**

Here are the rules of the Teddy Bear game: Your friend is going to give you a certain number of bears. The number of bears is called `initial`, and your goal is to end up with a particular number of bears, called the `goal` number.

There are two other integer parameters to the game: `increment` and n. At any point in the game, you have two choices: (a) You can ask for (and receive) `increment` more bears, or (b) if you have an even number of bears, then you can give half of them back to your friend. Each time you do (a) or (b), that is called a *step* in the game, and the goal must be reached in n steps or fewer. For example, if `initial` is 99, `increment` is 53, and n is at least 4, then the following sequence of steps will reach the goal of 91:

$$99 \xrightarrow[\text{step a}]{} 152 \xrightarrow[\text{step b}]{} 76 \xrightarrow[\text{step b}]{} 38 \xrightarrow[\text{step a}]{} 91$$

We want to write a recursive method, `bears`, that determines whether it is possible to reach a `goal` starting with some `initial` and `increment` numbers (allowing no more than n steps). The implementation follows the pattern from the previous page, although the first marking step of the pattern is not needed since we can prevent going around in circles by stopping when the parameter n reaches zero. So the pattern has only these two steps:

- Check whether the `initial` value is equal to the `goal`. If so, return `true` to indicate that the goal can be reached.

- On the other hand, if the `initial` value does not equal the `goal`, then we'll check that n is positive (otherwise, we have no more moves to make and must return `false` because the goal cannot be reached). When n is positive, we'll solve the problem by making one or two recursive calls. One call starts by taking an (a)-step and the other starts by taking a (b)-step—although this second call is made only if `initial` is an even number.

The implementation of the bear method appears in Figure 8.9. Notice the expression (`inital % 2 == 0`) to determine whether the initial number of bears is even.

Self-Test Exercises for Section 8.2

5. Suppose you activate `randomFractal` (Figure 8.4 on page 425) with the distance between the x coordinates equal to 24 and a stopping case when

this distance is less than or equal to 4. Then `randomFractal` will make two recursive calls, and each of those will make two more calls, and so on, until `width` is less than or equal to 4. How many total calls will be made of `randomFractal`, including the original activation?

6. Draw a copy of the maze from Figure 8.6 on page 430, moving the magic tapestry to a more difficult location. Run the `traverseMaze` method (Figure 8.8 on page 436), pretending that you are in this maze and following the method's directions. (Do not peek over the walls.)

7. Revise `randomFractal` (Figure 8.4 on page 425) so that the movements of the midpoints are not random. Instead, the first midpoint is moved upward by half the distance between the *x* coordinates; the midpoints at

---

FIGURE 8.9   A Method to Play the Teddy Bear Game

Specification

♦ **bears**

```
public static boolean bears(int initial, int goal, int increment, int n)
```
Determine whether the goal can be reached in the Teddy Bear game.

Precondition:
All parameters should be non-negative.

Postcondition:
The method has determined whether it is possible to reach the goal in the following Teddy Bear game. In the game, your friend gives you a certain number of bears. The number of bears is called `initial`, and your goal is to end up with a particular number of bears, called the `goal` number. At any point in the game, you have two choices: (a) You can ask for (and receive) `increment` more bears, or (b) if you have an even number of bears, then you can give half of them back to your friend. Each time you do (a) or (b), that is called a *step* in the game.
    The return value is `true` if and only if the goal can be reached in n steps or fewer.

Implementation

```
public static boolean bears(int initial, int goal, int increment, int n)
{
    if (initial == goal)
        return true;
    else if (n == 0)
        return false;
    else if (bears(initial+increment, goal, increment, n-1))
        return true;
    else if ((initial % 2 == 0) && bears(initial/2, goal, increment, n-1))
        return true;
    else
        return false;
}
```

the next level of recursion are moved down by half the distance between the *x* coordinates; the next level moves up again, then down, and so on.

8. Suppose you are exploring a rectangular maze containing 10 rows and 20 columns. What is the maximum number of recursive calls generated if you start at the entrance of the maze and activate `traverseMaze` (Figure 8.8 on page 436)? Include the initial activation as part of your count.

8.3   REASONING ABOUT RECURSION

After a lecture on cosmology and the structure of the solar system, William James was accosted by a little old lady.

"Your theory that the sun is the center of the solar system, and the earth is a ball which rotates around it has a very convincing ring to it, Mr. James, but it's wrong. I've got a better theory," said the little old lady.

"And what is that, madam?" inquired James politely.

"That we live on a crust of earth which is on the back of a giant turtle."

Not wishing to demolish this absurd little theory by bringing to bear the masses of scientific evidence he had at his command, James decided to gently dissuade his opponent by making her see some of the inadequacies of her position.

"If your theory is correct, madam," he asked, "what does this turtle stand on?"

"You're a very clever man, Mr. James, and that's a very good question," replied the little old lady, "but I have an answer to it. And it is this: the first turtle stands on the back of a second, far larger, turtle, who stands directly under him."

"But what does this second turtle stand on?" persisted James patiently.

To this the little old lady crowed triumphantly. "It's no use, Mr. James—it's turtles all the way down."

J.R. Ross
Constraints on Variables in Syntax

In all our examples of recursive thinking, the series of recursive calls eventually reaches a call that does not involve further recursion (that is, it reaches a *stopping case*). If, on the other hand, every recursive call produces another recursive call, then a recursive call will, in theory, run forever. This is called **infinite recursion**. In practice, such a method will run until the computer runs out of memory for the activation records and throws a `StackOverflowError`, indicating that the execution stack has run out of memory for activation records. Phrased another way, a recursive declaration should not be "recursive all the way down." Otherwise, like the lady's explanation of the solar system, a recursive call will never end, except perhaps in frustration.

In this section, we will show you how to reason about recursion, both to show that there is no infinite recursion and to show that a recursive method's results are correct. To illustrate how to do this reasoning, we will go through a series of methods, each of which incorporates a bit more recursion. The method is called `power`, and the activation of `power(x,n)` computes x^n so that `power(3.0, 2)` is

3.0^2 (which is 9.0), and power(4.2, 3) is 4.2^3 (which is 74.088). For any non-zero value of x, the value of x^0 is defined to be 1, so for example, power(9.1, 0) is 1. For a negative exponent, $-n$, the value returned is defined by:

$$x^{-n} = 1/x^n \quad \{ \ x \text{ is any real number, and } -n \text{ is a negative integer } \}$$

For example, power(3.0, -2) is $1/3.0^2$ (which is $\frac{1}{9}$). The only forbidden power is taking 0^n when n is not positive. The complete specification of the power method follows.

♦ **power**
```
public static double power(double x, int n)
```
Compute the value of x^n.

Precondition:
If x is zero, then n must be positive.

Returns:
x raised to the n power

Throws: IllegalArgumentException
Indicates that x is zero and n is not positive.

Our implementation begins by checking the precondition and then deals with several cases. The first case, when n is non-negative, is easy. This case is computed by setting a local variable, product, to 1 and then repeatedly multiplying product by x. The repeated multiplication occurs n times, in this loop:

```
if (n >= 0)
{
    product = 1;
    for (count = 1, count <= n; count++)
        product = product * x;
    return product;
}
```

To understand what's needed for a negative exponent, consider a concrete case. Suppose we are computing power(3.0, -2), which must return the value 3.0^{-2}. But this value is equal to $\frac{1}{3^2}$. Negative powers are the same as positive powers in the denominator. This means that if we know that the method returns the correct answer when n > 0, then we can calculate the correct value for power(3.0, -2) by the expression 1/power(3.0, 2). By thinking recursively, whenever n is negative, power can compute its answer with a recursive call, like this:

```
    return 1/power(x, -n); // When n is negative (and so -n is positive)
```

Remember, in this statement, n is negative (such as –2), so -n is positive, and therefore, the recursive call in the expression 1/power(x, -n) has a positive second argument. With a positive second argument, our power method makes no further recursive calls (i.e., a stopping case), and so the recursion ends.

This brings us to our first general technique for reasoning about recursion, which can be applied to the complete power method of Figure 8.10.

FIGURE 8.10 Implementation of the power Method with Only One Level of Recursion

Specification

♦ **power**
```
public static double power(double x, int n)
```
Compute the value of x^n.

Precondition:
If x is zero, then n must be positive.

Returns:
x raised to the n power

Throws: IllegalArgumentException
Indicates that x is zero and n is not positive.

Implementation

```
public static double power(double x, int n)
{
    double product; // The product of x with itself n times
    int count;

    if (x == 0 && n <= 0)
        throw new IllegalArgumentException("x is zero and n=" + n);

    if (n >= 0)
    {
        product = 1;
        for (count = 1; count <= n; count++)
            product = product * x;
        return product;
    }
    else
        return 1/power(x, -n);
}
```

Sample Results of the Method

Call with these arguments		Return value of the method
x	n	
3.0	2	9.0
2.0	-3	0.125
4.1	0	1.0
-2.0	3	-8.0

One-Level Recursion

Suppose every case is either a stopping case or makes a recursive call that is a stopping case. Then the deepest recursive call is only one level deep, and therefore no infinite recursion occurs.

How to Ensure That There Is No Infinite Recursion in the General Case

Recursive calls don't often stop just one level deep, but we needed to understand that case to form a base for deeper reasoning. Programmers have developed methods to reason about deeper recursive calls based on the principles of *mathematical induction.* The reasoning can increase your confidence that a recursive method avoids infinite recursion. As an example to show that there is no infinite recursion, let's rewrite the method power so that it uses more recursion.

The revision is based on the observation that for any number x and any positive integer n, the following relation holds: $x^n = x(x^{n-1})$. This formula means that an alternative way to define x^n is as follows:

- The value of x^n is undefined when $n \leq 0$ and $x = 0$.
- Otherwise, the value is 0 when $x = 0$.
- Otherwise, the value is 1 when $n = 0$.
- Otherwise, the value is x times x^{n-1} when $n > 0$.
- Otherwise, the value is $1/x^{-n}$ when $n < 0$.

an alternative algorithm for computing powers

The Java version of a recursive method that computes in this way is given in Figure 8.11. To avoid confusion, we have used a slightly different name, pow, for this version of the method.

FIGURE 8.11   Alternative Implementation of a Method to Compute Powers

Implementation

```java
public static double pow(double x, int n)
{
    if (x == 0 && n <= 0)
        throw new IllegalArgumentException("x is zero and n=" + n);
    else if (x == 0)
        return 0;
    else if (n == 0)
        return 1;
    else if (n > 0)
        return x * pow(x, n-1);
    else // x is nonzero, and n is negative.
        return 1/pow(x, -n);
}
```

Tracing a recursive method such as pow can quickly overwhelm you, but there are relatively simple ways of showing that there is no infinite recursion without actually tracing through the execution. The most common way to ensure that a stopping case is *eventually* reached is to define a numeric quantity called the *variant expression*. This quantity must associate each legal recursive call with a single number. In a moment, we'll discuss the properties that the variant expression should have, but first let's look at the kind of quantity we have in mind for the variant expression of the pow method. The variant expression for pow depends on whether n is negative or not. For a negative n, the variant expression is abs(n) + 1, which is one more than the absolute value of n. For a non-negative n, the variant expression is just the value of n itself.

With this definition, we can examine a sequence of recursive pow calls, beginning with pow(2.0, -3), as follows:

A Sequence of Recursive Calls

1. pow(2.0, -3) has a variant expression abs(n) + 1, which is 4; it makes a recursive call of pow(2.0, 3).

2. pow(2.0, 3) has a variant expression n, which is 3; it makes a recursive call of pow(2.0, 2).

3. pow(2.0, 2) has a variant expression n, which is 2; it makes a recursive call of pow(2.0, 1).

4. pow(2.0, 1) has a variant expression n, which is 1; it makes a recursive call of pow(2.0, 0).

5. pow(2.0, 0) has a variant expression n, which is 0; this is the stopping case.

There are two important points to this example: (a) Each time a recursive call is made, the variant expression is reduced by at least 1; and (b) when the variant expression reaches zero, there is a stopping case that terminates with no further recursive calls.

In general, a **variant expression** is a numeric quantity that is decreased by at least some fixed amount on each recursive call. Once the variant expression reaches a small enough value, a stopping case occurs. The "small enough value" that guarantees a stopping case is called the **threshold**.

variant expression and threshold

Variant Expression and Threshold

A **variant expression** is a numeric quantity that is decreased by at least some fixed amount on each recursive call. Once the variant expression reaches a small enough value (called the **threshold**), then the stopping case occurs.

In the pow example, the threshold is zero, and each recursive call reduces the variant expression by 1. A summary of the general technique for proving that a recursive call terminates is shown here:

Ensuring That There Is No Infinite Recursion

To prove that a recursive call does not lead to infinite recursion, it is enough to find a *variant expression* and a *threshold* with the following properties:

1. Between one call of the method and any succeeding recursive call of that method, the value of the variant expression decreases by at least some fixed amount.

2. If the method is activated and the value of the variant expression is less than or equal to the threshold, then the method terminates without making any recursive calls.

It is important that the reduction is at least a fixed amount. Otherwise, the variant expression might start at 1, then decrease to $\frac{1}{2}$, then to $\frac{1}{4}$, then to $\frac{1}{8}$, and so on, decreasing by ever-smaller amounts and never reaching the threshold. In the most common case, such as pow, the variant expression always decreases by at least 1, and the threshold is zero.

To see that these two conditions guarantee no infinite recursion, reason as follows. Suppose the two conditions hold. Since Condition 1 is true, every recursive call will decrease the variant expression. This means that either the method will terminate, which is fine, or the variant expression will decrease until it reaches the threshold. But if Condition 2 holds, then once the variant expression reaches the threshold, the method will terminate. That covers all the cases.

Inductive Reasoning about the Correctness of a Recursive Method

induction

In addition to checking that a recursive method terminates, you should also check that it always behaves correctly—in other words, that it meets its precondition/postcondition contract. The usual method for showing correctness of a recursive method is called **induction**. (And, in fact, the technique is the same as *mathematical induction,* which you may have used in math classes.) The induction approach requires a programmer to demonstrate the following facts about the method's behavior:

Induction Method to
Show That a Recursive Method Is Correct

To show that a recursive method meets its precondition/postcondition contract, first show that there is no infinite recursion (by showing Conditions 1 and 2), and then show that the following two conditions are also valid:

3. Whenever the method makes no recursive calls, then it meets its precondition/postcondition contract. (This is called the **base step**.)

4. Whenever the method is activated *and* all the recursive calls it makes meet their precondition/postcondition contract, then the original call will also meet its precondition/postcondition contract. (This is called the **induction step**.)

The conditions are numbered 3 and 4 to emphasize that they ensure correctness only if you know that there is no infinite recursion. You must also ensure that Conditions 1 and 2 hold for an appropriate variant expression and threshold.

Let's return to the method pow defined in Figure 8.11 on page 442. To complete our demonstration that it performs as desired, we must show that Conditions 3 and 4 hold.

It is easy to see that Condition 3 holds. The only way that the method can terminate without a recursive call is if the value of x is zero or n is zero. If x is zero, the method returns 0, which is the correct answer; if n is zero (and x is not zero), the method returns 1, which is also correct.

To see that Condition 4 holds, we need only recall the algebraic identities:

$$x^n = x(x^{n-1}) \quad \text{and} \quad x^n = 1/x^{-n}$$

To summarize how to reason about recursion: First, check that the method always terminates (no infinite recursion); next, make sure the stopping cases work correctly; and finally, for each recursive case, pretend that you know the recursive calls will work correctly and use this to show that each recursive case works correctly.

Self-Test Exercises for Section 8.3

9. Write a recursive method that computes the number of digits in an integer n. (You might recall from page 21 that this is $\lfloor \log_{10} n \rfloor + 1$ for positive numbers.) Do not use any local variables in your method declaration. Find a variant expression and threshold to show that your method has no infinite recursion.

10. Use inductive reasoning to show that your method from the preceding exercise is always correct.

11. Find variant expressions and thresholds to show that the methods randomFractal and traverseMaze (in Section 8.2) never result in infinite recursion.

12. Use induction to show that randomFractal meets its precondition/postcondition contract.

13. Rewrite the pow method using these two facts for x^n:
    • If n is positive and even, then $x^n = x^{n/2} \times x^{n/2}$.
    • If n is positive and odd, then $x^n = x \times x^{n-1}$.

14. Find a variant expression and threshold for the bears method from Figure 8.9 on page 438.

15. What kind of error is likely to occur if you write a method that results in infinite recursion?

16. Are there any methods that require recursion for their implementation?

CHAPTER SUMMARY

- If a problem can be reduced to smaller instances of the same problem, then a recursive solution is likely to be easy to find and implement.

- A recursive algorithm for a method implementation contains two kinds of cases: one or more cases that include a *recursive call* and one or more *stopping cases* in which the problem is solved without the use of any recursive calls.

- When writing recursive methods, always check to see that the method will not produce infinite recursion. This can be done by finding an appropriate *variant expression* and *threshold*.

- *Inductive reasoning* can be used to show that a recursive method meets its precondition/postcondition contract.

? Solutions to Self-Test Exercises

1. The top-left method prints 3, then 2, then 1. The top-right method prints 1, then 2, then 3. The bottom method prints 3, then 2, then 1, then 1 again, then 2 again, then 3 again.

2. The output is Hip, then Hip, then Hurrah, on three separate lines.

3. For the first modification, change the two lines in the else-block to:
```
cheers(n-1);
System.out.println("Hip");
```
For the second modification, change the lines to:
```
System.out.println("Hip");
cheers(n-1);
System.out.println("Hip");
```

For the third modification, change the lines to:
```
if (n % 2 == 0)
    System.out.println("Hip");
cheers(n-1);
if (n % 2 == 1)
    System.out.println("Hip");
```

4. The method's implementation is:
```
public static void exercise4(int n)
{
    if (n > 0)
    {
        System.out.print('*');
        exercise4(n-1);
        System.out.print('!');
    }
}
```

5. The original activation makes two calls with an *x* distance of 12. Each of those calls makes two calls with an *x* distance of 6, so there are four calls with an *x* distance of 6. Each of those four calls makes two more calls, again cutting the width in half, so there are eight calls with an *x* distance of 3. These eight calls do not make further calls, since width has reached the stopping point. The total number of calls, including the original call, is $1 + 2 + 4 + 8$, which is 15 calls.

6. Did you peek?

7. The easiest solution requires an extra parameter called `level`, which indicates how deep the recursion has proceeded. When the revised method is called from a program, the value of `level` should be given as 0. Each recursive call increases the level by 1. When the level is an even number, the midpoint is moved upward; when the level is odd, the midpoint is moved downward. The code to do the movement is as follows:
```
if (level % 2 == 0)
    midY += (rightX - leftX)/2;
else
    midY -= (rightX - leftX)/2;
```

8. Each recursive call steps forward into a location that has not previously been visited. Therefore, the number of calls can be no more than the number of locations in the maze, which is 200.

9. The method's implementation is:
```
int digits(int n)
{
    if (n < 10) && (n > -10))
        return 1;
    else
        return 1 + digits(n/10);
}
```
A good variant expression is "the number of digits in n," with the threshold of 1.

10. The stopping case includes numbers that are less than 10 and more than negative 10. All these numbers have one digit, and the method correctly returns the answer 1. For the induction case, we have a number *n* with more than one digit. The number of digits will always be one more than *n*/10 (using integer division), so if we assume that the recursive call of `digits(n/10)` returns the right answer, then `1 + digits(n/10)` is the correct number of digits in *n*.

11. For `randomFractal`, a good variant expression is `(rightX - leftX)`. If we make a recursive call, then this expression is greater than 4, and the recursive call cuts the expression in half. Therefore, each recursive call subtracts at least 2 from the expression. When the expression reaches 4 (or less), the recursion stops. Therefore, 4 is the threshold.

The method `traverseMaze` has a variant expression that is expressed in English as "the number of locations in the maze that do not yet have your name written on the ground." This value is reduced by at least 1 during each recursive call, and when this value reaches zero, there can be no further recursive calls. Therefore, 0 is the threshold.

12. We have already found a variant expression and threshold for Conditions 1 and 2, showing that `randomFractal` does not result in infinite recursion. For Condition 3, we must show that the method has correct behavior for the stopping case. In this case, `(rightX - leftX)` is no more than STOP, and therefore the line segment does not need further dividing. We only need to draw the current line segment, which is what the method does. In Condition 4 of the

inductive reasoning, we assume that the two recursive calls correctly generate a random fractal for the two smaller line segments we have created. Putting these two smaller random fractals together correctly gives us the larger random fractal.

13. In Figure 8.11 on page 442, we change the (n > 0) block to this:

```
if ((n > 0) && (n % 2 == 1))
    return x * pow(x, n-1);
else if ((n > 0) && (n % 2 == 0))
{
    double partial = pow(x, n/2);
    return partial * partial;
}
```

14. The variant expression is the number n, with a threshold of zero.

15. `StackOverflowError`

16. Explicit recursion can always be removed by using a stack to simulate the recursive calls.

PROGRAMMING PROJECTS

1 Write a method that produces the output shown below. This output was written by call number 1. In the example, the recursion stopped when it reached four levels deep, but your method should be capable of continuing to any specified level.

```
This was written by call number 2.
 This was written by call number 3.
  This was written by call number 4.
  This ALSO written by call number 4.
 This ALSO written by call number 3.
This ALSO written by call number 2.
This ALSO written by call number 1.
```

2 Write a method with two parameters, prefix (a string) and levels (a non-negative integer). The method prints the string prefix followed by "section numbers" of the form 1.1., 1.2., 1.3., and so on. The levels argument determines how many levels the section numbers have. For example, if levels is 2, then the section numbers have the form x.y. If levels is 3, then the section numbers have the form x.y.z. The digits permitted in each level are always '1'

through '9'. As an example, if prefix is the string "BOX:" and levels is 2, then the method would start by printing this:

```
BOX:1.1.
BOX:1.2.
BOX:1.3.
```

and finish by printing this:

```
BOX:9.7.
BOX:9.8.
BOX:9.9.
```

The stopping case occurs when levels reaches zero. The primary string manipulation technique that you will need is the ability to create a new string that consists of prefix followed by a digit and a period. If s is the string you want to create and i is the digit (an integer in the range 1 to 9), then the following statement will perform this task:

```
s = prefix + '.' + i;
```

The last part of the expression puts the character that corresponds to the integer i onto the end of the string. This new string, s, can be passed as a parameter to recursive calls.

3 Write a recursive method that has two parameters, `first` and `second`, that are both strings. The method should print all rearrangements of the letters in `first` followed by `second`. For example, if `first` is the string "CAT" and `second` is the string "MAN", then the method would print the strings CATMAN, CTAMAN, ACTMAN, ATCMAN, TACMAN, and TCAMAN. The stopping case of the method occurs when the length of `first` has zero characters. We'll leave the recursive thinking up to you, but we should mention three string techniques that will make things go more smoothly. These techniques are:

(1) The following expression is a string consisting of all of `first` followed by character number i from `second`:

```
first + second.charAt(i)
```

(2) The following expression is a string consisting of all of `second` with character i removed. The value of i must be less than the last index of the string. The first part of the expression is everything from location 0 to location i-1, and the second part of the expression is everything after location i.

```
second.substring(0, i)
+
second.substring(i+1);
```

(3) The following expression is a string consisting of all of `second` except the last character. For this to work, the string must be non-empty.

```
second.substring(0, s.length()-1)
```

The stopping case occurs when the length of the second string is zero (in which case you just print the first string). For the recursive case, make one recursive call for each character in the second string. During each recursive call, you take one character out of `second` and add it to the end of `first`.

4 Write an interactive program to help you count all of the boxes in a room. The program should begin by asking something like *How many unnumbered boxes can you see?* Then the program will have you number those boxes from 1 to *m*, where *m* is your answer. But remember that each box might have smaller boxes inside, so once the program knows you can see *m* boxes, it should ask you to open box number 1 and take out any box-

es you find, numbering those boxes 1.1, 1.2, and so on. It will also ask you to open box number 2 and take out any boxes you find there, numbering those boxes 2.1, 2.2, and so on. This continues for box 3, 4, and so on, up to *m*. And, of course, each time you number a box 1.1 or 3.8 or something similar, *that* box might have more boxes inside. Boxes that reside inside of 3.8 would be numbered 3.8.1, 3.8.2, and so on. At the end, the program should print a single number telling you the total number of boxes in the room.

5 Write a recursive method called `sumover` that has one argument *n*, which is a non-negative integer. The method returns a double value, which is the sum of the reciprocals of the first *n* positive integers. (The reciprocal of *x* is the fraction $1/x$.) For example, `sumover(1)` returns `1.0` (which is $1/1$); `sumover(2)` returns `1.5` (which is $1/1 + 1/2$); and `sumover(3)` returns approximately `1.833` (which is $1/1 + 1/2 + 1/3$). Define `sumover(0)` to be zero. Do not use any local variables in your method.

6 The formula for computing the number of ways of choosing *r* different things from a set of *n* things is the following:

$$C(n, r) = \frac{n!}{r!(n-r)!}$$

In this formula, the factorial function is represented by an exclamation point (!) and defined as the product:

$$n! = n \times (n-1) \times (n-2) \times \dots \times 1$$

Discover a recursive version of the $C(n, r)$ formula, and write a recursive method that computes the value of the formula. Embed the method in a program and test it.

7 Write a recursive method that has as arguments an array of characters and two bounds on array indexes. The method should reverse the order of those entries in the array whose indexes are between the two bounds (inclusive). For example, suppose the array is:

```
a[0] = 'A'   a[1] = 'B'   a[2] = 'C'
a[3] = 'D'   a[4] = 'E'
```

and the bounds are 1 and 4. Then, after the method is run, the array elements should be:

```
a[0] = 'A'   a[1] = 'E'   a[2] = 'D'
a[3] = 'C'   a[4] = 'B'
```

Embed the method in a program and test it.

8 Write a recursive method to produce a pattern of *n* lines of asterisks. The first line contains one asterisk, the next line contains two, and so on, up to the nth line, which contains *n* asterisks. Line number *n*+1 again contains *n* asterisks, the next line has *n*–1 asterisks, and so on, until line number 2*n*, which has just one asterisk.

9 Examine this pattern of asterisks and blanks, and write a recursive method that can generate exactly this pattern:

```
*
*  *
   *
*  *  *  *
      *
      *  *
         *
*  *  *  *  *  *  *  *  *
               *
               *  *
                  *
               *  *  *  *
                     *
                     *  *
                        *
```

With recursive thinking, the method needs only seven or eight lines of code (including two recursive calls). How is this pattern a fractal? Your method should also be capable of producing larger or smaller patterns of the same variety. Hint: Have two parameters. One parameter indicates the indentation of the leftmost line in the pattern; the other parameter indicates the number of stars in the longest line.

10 Write a program that asks the user to think of an integer between 1 and 1,000,000, and then guesses the number through a series of yes/no questions. To guess the number, the program calls a recursive method `guess` that has two parameters, `low` and `high`. The precondition for the method requires that the user's number lie in the range `low...high` so that the program's initial call is to `guess(1, 1000000)`. What is a good stopping case for `guess`, when it can guess the user's number with little or no work? Answer: If (`low == high`), then there is only one possible number, and the method can guess that number. On the other hand, if (`low < high`), then the method should calculate a point near the middle of the range:

```
midpoint = (low + high) / 2;
```

Then the method asks the user whether the midpoint is the correct number. If so, the method is finished. On the other hand, if the midpoint is not the user's number, then the method asks whether the correct number is larger than `midpoint`. If so, the method knows that the user's number lies in the range `midpoint + 1` to `high`, and a recursive call can be made to solve the smaller problem of finding a user's number in the range `midpoint + 1` to `high`. On the other hand, if the user's number is not larger than `midpoint`, then a recursive call can be made to solve the smaller problem of finding a user's number in the range `low` to `midpoint - 1`. This method of searching is called **binary search**, which we will explore further in Chapter 11.

11 This project uses the `Towers` class from Chapter 3's Programming Project 12 on page 171. For the project, write a recursive method that computes and prints a solution to the Towers of Hanoi game. The method should meet this specification:

```
public static void Hanoi(
    Towers t,
    int n,
    int start,
    int target,
    int spare
);
// Precondition: start, target, and spare are
// three different peg numbers of the game,
```

```
// and n is non-negative.
// Also, the n smallest rings currently are on
// the top of the start peg.
// Postcondition: The method has activated
// a sequence of moves for the tower t, so
// that the total effect of these moves is to
// shift the top n rings from the start peg to
// the target peg, using spare as the extra
// peg. None of the other rings has been
// disturbed. Each time a move is made,
// a message describing the move is
// printed.
```

Your solution should have a simple stopping case: When *n* is zero, there is no work to do. When *n* is more than zero, use a recursive call to move *n*–1 rings from the start peg to the spare peg. Then call the move method to move one ring from the start peg to the target peg. Finally, make another recursive call to move *n*–1 rings from the spare peg to the target peg.

12 For this project, you are to write a recursive method that prints all of the objects in a bag. Use the bag specification from Figure 4.12 on page 216, which is a bag of integers. The integers are to be printed in a random order—without using any of the bag private instance variables. For an empty bag, the method has no work to do (that is, it's the stopping case). For a non-empty bag, the method carries out four steps: (1) Grab a random integer from the bag, storing it in a local variable `oneItem`; (2) print `oneItem`; (3) print any items that remain in the bag; and (4) put `oneItem` back in the bag. You'll need to identify which of these steps is the "simpler version of the same problem."

13 Let's think about your computer science class for a moment. You might know several students, perhaps Judy, Jervis, Walter, and Michael. Each of those students knows several other students, and each of them knows more students, and so on. Now, there is one particular student named Dor that you would like to meet. One way to meet Dor would be if you had a mutual acquaintance. You know Judy, and Judy knows Dor, so Judy could introduce you to Dor. Or there might be a longer path of acquaintances. For example, you know Judy, and Judy knows Harry, and Harry knows Cathy, and Cathy knows Dor. In this case, Judy can introduce you to Harry, Harry can introduce you to Cathy, and Cathy can introduce you to Dor.

Write an interactive program to help you figure out whether there is a path of acquaintances from you to Dor. The program should include a recursive method that has one argument, `person`, which is the name of a person in your class. The method determines whether there is a path of acquaintances from `person` to Dor. Hint: This problem is similar to the maze problem in Section 8.2, but beware of potential infinite recursion! One way to avoid infinite recursion is to include a bag of student names that keeps track of the names of the students you have already visited on your search for a path to Dor.

14 A *pretty print* program takes a program that may not be indented in any particular way and produces a copy with the same program indented so that bracket pairs ({ and }) line up with inner pairs indented more than outer pairs (as we have been doing throughout the book). Write a program that reads a Java program from one text file and produces a pretty print version of the program in a second text file. To make it easier, simply do this for each method, ignoring the things outside of the methods.

15 Write a Java method that meets the following specification:

```
public static void digits(int c)
// Precondition: c is one of the ints 0 to 9.
// Postcondition: The method has printed a
// pattern of digits as follows:
// 1. If the parameter c is 0, then output is '0'.
// 2. For other values of c, the output consists of
// three parts:
// -- the output for the previous number (c-1);
// -- followed by the digit c itself;
// -- followed by a second copy of the output for
//    the previous number.
// There is no newline printed at the end of the
// output. Example output: digits(3) will print
// this to System.out: 010201030102010
```

16 Write a Java method with the following header:

```
public static void binaryPrint(int n)
```

The number n is non-negative. The method prints the value of n as a *binary* number. If n is zero, then a single zero is printed; otherwise, no leading zeros are printed in the output. The '\n' character is NOT printed at the end of the output. Your implementation must be recursive and not use any local variables.

EXAMPLES:
    n=0 Output: 0
    n=4 Output: 100
    n=27 Output: 11011

17 Write a Java method with the following header:

```
public static void numbers
(String prefix, int n)
```

The number k is non-negative. The argument called prefix is a String of 0s and 1s. The method prints a sequence of binary numbers. Each output number consists of the prefix followed by a suffix of exactly k more binary digits (0s or 1s). All possible combinations of the prefix and some k-digit suffix are printed. As an example, if the prefix is the string 00101 and the number of levels is 2, then the method would print the prefix followed by the four possible suffixes shown here:

```
0010100
0010101
0010110
0010111
```

The stopping case occurs when k reaches zero (in which case the prefix is printed once by itself followed by nothing else).

18 Rewrite the basic calculator program from Figure 6.5 on page 330 so that the method evaluate uses recursion instead of stacks.

19 Rewrite the recursive pow method from Figure 8.11 on page 442 so that the time to compute pow(x, n) is log(n). Hint: Use the formula $x^{2n} = x^n$ times x^n.

20 Write a recursive method to convert a character string of digits to an integer. Example: convert("1234") returns 1234. Hint: To convert a character to a number, subtract the ASCII value '0' from the character. For example, if the string s has but one character, then the function can return the value s[0] - '0'.

21 Ackermann's function, named after the German mathematician Wilhelm Ackermann, is used in the theory of recursive functions. There are several variants of this function. Their common properties are that the function takes two parameters (x and y) and grows very fast (much faster than polynomials or exponentials). Here is one variant:

  1. If $x = 0$, then Ackermann(x, y) = $2y$.
  2. If $x >= 1$ and $y = 0$, then Ackermann(x, y) = 0.
  3. If $x >= 1$ and $y = 1$, then Ackermann(x, y) = 2.
  4. If $x >= 1$ and $y >= 2$, then Ackermann(x, y) = Ackermann($x–1$, Ackermann($x, y–1$)).

Implement this variant of Ackermann's function with a recursive method.

Trees

When you complete Chapter 9, you will be able to ...

- follow and explain tree-based algorithms using the usual computer science terminology.
- design and implement classes for binary tree nodes and nodes for general trees.
- list the order in which nodes are visited for the three common binary tree traversals (in-order, pre-order, post-order) and implement these algorithms.
- list the rules for a binary search tree and determine whether a tree satisfies these rules.
- carry out searches, insertions, and removals by hand on a binary search tree and implement these algorithms using your binary tree node class.

CHAPTER

9

Trees

*Some people call it the Tree of Heaven. No matter where its
seed fell, it made a tree which struggles to reach the sky.*

BETTY SMITH
A Tree Grows in Brooklyn

*nonlinear
structures*

This chapter presents a new data structure, a tree, which is our
first example of a **nonlinear structure**. In a nonlinear structure, the components
do not form a simple sequence of first element, second element, third element,
and so on. Instead, there is a more complex linking between the components;
this is why they are called *non*linear. The nonlinear structure often allows dramatically improved efficiency for collection classes.

The chapter starts with definitions of various kinds of trees and their applications. We then show how to represent trees and implement a node class for building and manipulating trees. The node is useful for many ADTs, such as the binary
search tree used in the final section of this chapter.

a real tree...

9.1 INTRODUCTION TO TREES

Binary Trees

The first kind of tree we'll look at is a *binary tree*, which is the most commonly
used tree data structure. A binary tree is not too different from a real tree. The
real tree starts at its root, growing upward. At some point, the trunk splits into
two smaller branches. Each of the smaller branches continues, perhaps splitting
into two still smaller branches, and so forth, until each branch ends with some
leaves.

*...and a
computer
scientist's tree*

If you take that tree, pull it out of the ground, and stick its root in the air, you
will have a computer scientist's tree. You see, a computer scientist draws a tree
with the root at the top, branches below that, and leaves at the very bottom. And,
of course, a computer scientist's tree contains data of one kind or another. Let's
be more specific with a concrete example of a binary tree of integers, shown in
Figure 9.1.

Each of the boxes in Figure 9.1 is called a **node** of the tree, and each node
contains some data. In this case each piece of data is an integer, but we might
also have trees of double numbers, trees of strings, or even trees in which each
node's data is a complex type such as a stack or a queue. The node at the top of
the diagram, which has the number 14, is called the **root**. Each node in a binary
tree can have up to two nodes below it, one linked on its left and one linked on
its right. These are called the node's **left child** and **right child**. For example,
the root's left child is the node containing 17, and its right child contains 11.

Some nodes have only a left child, some have only a right child, and some have no children at all. A node with no children is called a **leaf**. In more general kinds of trees, a node can have more than two children, but for the **binary** trees we're discussing, each node is limited to at most two children. One other point: With the exception of the root, each node is the child of just one node; the root is not the child of any node.

Much of the terminology for trees comes from family relations, such as the word "child." Perhaps you can guess the meaning of some other terms: *parent, sibling, ancestor, descendant*. These definitions are given later, but first we'll provide a complete definition of a binary tree:

Binary Trees

A **binary tree** is a finite set of nodes. The set might be empty (no nodes, which is called the **empty tree**). But if the set is not empty, it follows these rules:

1. There is one special node, called the **root**.

2. Each node can be associated with up to two other different nodes, called its **left child** and its **right child**. If a node *c* is the child of another node *p*, then we say that "*p* is *c*'s **parent**."

3. Each node, except the root, has exactly one parent; the root has no parent.

4. If you start at a node and move to the node's parent (provided there is one), and then move again to that node's parent, and keep moving upward to each node's parent, you will eventually reach the root.

FIGURE 9.1   A Binary Tree of Integers

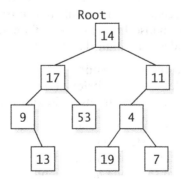

FIGURE 9.2 More Examples of Binary Trees

(a) A full binary tree. The depth of this tree is two because there are two links from the root to the farthest leaf.

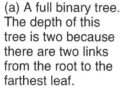

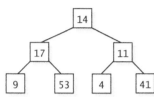

(b) A binary tree that is complete but not full.

(c) A binary tree that is neither complete nor full.

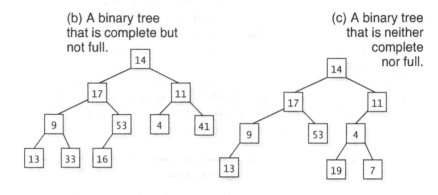

tree terminology

Here are some other terms used with trees, with examples selected from Figure 9.2.

Parent. The **parent** of a node is the node linked above it. More precisely, if a node c is the child of another node p, then we say that "p is c's **parent**." Except for the root, every node has just one parent, and the root has no parent. In Figure 9.2(a), the node containing 17 is the parent of the nodes containing 9 and 53.

Sibling. Two nodes are **siblings** if they have the same parent. In Figure 9.2(a), the nodes containing 9 and 53 are siblings.

Ancestor. A node's parent is its first ancestor. The parent of the parent is the next ancestor. The parent of the parent of the parent is the next ancestor ... and so forth, until you reach the root. The root is an ancestor of each other node.

Descendant. A node's children are its first descendants. The children's children are its next descendants. The children of the children of the children are ... well, you get the idea.

Subtree. Any node in a tree also can be viewed as the root of a new, smaller tree. This smaller tree contains the node we've picked as the new root and all of the new root's descendants. This is called a **subtree** of the original tree. In Figure 9.2(a), we may choose 17 as the root of a new subtree, and that subtree has three nodes: the nodes containing 17, 9, and 53.

Left and Right Subtrees of a Node. For a node in a binary tree, the nodes beginning with its left child and below are its **left subtree**. The nodes beginning with its right child and below are its **right subtree**.

Depth of a Node. Suppose you start at a node n and move upward to its parent. We'll call this "one step." Then move up to the parent of the parent—that's a second step. Eventually, you will reach the root, and the number of steps taken is called the **depth of the node** n. The depth of the root itself is zero; a child of the root has depth one. In Figure 9.2(b), the node containing 13 has depth three.

Depth of a Tree. The **depth of a tree** is the maximum depth of any of its leaves. In Figure 9.2(b), the leaf containing 13 has depth three, and there is no deeper leaf. So the depth of the example tree is three. If a tree has only one node, the root, then its depth is zero (since the depth of the root is zero). The empty tree doesn't have any leaves, so we use –1 for its depth. Just to confuse things, you'll often see the term *height* used instead of *depth*, but they both mean the same thing.

Full Binary Trees. In a **full binary tree**, every leaf has the same depth, and every non-leaf has two children. Figure 9.1 on page 455 is not a full tree, because it has leaves at different depths—some with depth two and some with depth three. Also, some of the non-leaves have only one child. In Figure 9.2, part (a) is full, but parts (b) and (c) are not full.

Complete Binary Trees. Suppose you take a full binary tree and start adding new leaves at a new depth from left to right. All the new leaves have the same depth—one more than where we started—and we always add leftmost nodes first. For example, if you add three nodes to Figure 9.2(a), then one possible result is Figure 9.2(b). The tree is no longer a full tree because some leaves are a bit deeper than others. Instead, we call this a **complete binary tree**. To be a complete tree, every level except the deepest must contain as many nodes as possible; and at the deepest level, all the nodes are as far left as possible. In run-time analysis, it's important to know that a complete binary tree of depth n has the maximum number of leaves for that depth (2^n) and the maximum number of total nodes ($2^{n+1} - 1$).

Binary Taxonomy Trees

Binary trees are useful in many situations. We'll look at one example, **binary taxonomy trees**, which can be used to store certain kinds of knowledge. The particular example we have in mind stores information about a collection of animals. Each leaf in a binary tree contains the name of an animal, and each non-leaf node contains a question about animals.

binary taxonomy trees store knowledge about a collection of animals

FIGURE 9.3 A Small Binary Taxonomy Tree

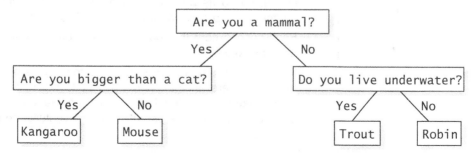

For example, suppose we want a taxonomy tree for four animals: a kangaroo, a mouse, a trout, and a robin. The tree might look like Figure 9.3. To use a binary taxonomy tree, you start at the root and ask the question that is written there. If the answer is "yes," you move to the left child, and if the answer is "no," you move to the right child. Eventually, you will reach a leaf, and the name at the leaf tells you which animal you have been examining—or at least it does if the animal is one of the animals that the tree knows about.

In general, computer scientists use the term **decision tree** for this kind of tree with a yes/no question at each non-leaf node.

More Than Two Children

Each node in a binary tree has at most two children. In fact, that's why the word "binary" is used. But in general, a node in a tree can have any number of children. Figure 9.4 shows an example in which some nodes have one child, some have two, and some have three. A node in a general tree might even have more than three children (although three is the most in Figure 9.4). In Figure 9.4, we have not written any data at the nodes, but we could have written integers or strings or whatever data type we were interested in storing.

There are other special kinds of trees. For example, Section 10.2 uses B-trees, which are trees in which the number of children of each node must lie between a certain minimum and a certain maximum.

FIGURE 9.4   A General Tree

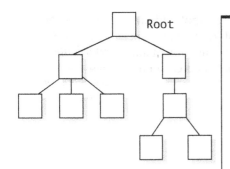

Root

> ### General Trees
>
> A **tree** is a finite set of nodes. The set might be empty (no nodes, which is called the **empty tree**). But if the set is not empty, then it must follow these rules:
>
> 1. There is one special node, called the **root**.
> 2. Each node can be associated with one or more different nodes, called its **children**. If a node *c* is the child of another node *p*, then we say that "*p* is *c*'s **parent**."
> 3. Each node except the root has exactly one parent; the root has no parent.
> 4. If you start at any node and move to the node's parent (provided there is one), and then move again to that node's parent (provided there is one), and keep moving upward to each node's parent, you will eventually reach the root.

Self-Test Exercises for Section 9.1

1. Draw a binary tree with 12 nodes. Circle the root, and put asterisks at each leaf. Find two nodes that are siblings and connect them with a wiggly line. Choose one of the leaves and shade all of its ancestors.

2. Draw a tree that contains members of your family. The root should contain your mother's mother. Her children nodes contain her actual children, and below those nodes are her children's children, and so on.

3. What is the depth of the tree from the preceding exercise? What is the depth of the node that contains *you*? Draw a circle around all nodes that are your ancestor nodes. Does each of these nodes contain one of your real-life ancestors? Draw a big square around all nodes that are descendants of your mother. Does each of these nodes contain one of her real-life descendants?

4. Create a binary taxonomy tree with 16 animals. Is your tree full? Is it complete?

5. How many nodes are in a complete binary tree of depth nine? How many leaves?

9.2   TREE REPRESENTATIONS

This section discusses two kinds of trees and how they typically are represented in a data structure. For the most part, if you understand these two representations, you can also manage other kinds of trees.

Array Representation of Complete Binary Trees

Complete binary trees have a simple representation using arrays. The representation may use a fixed-size array so that the number of nodes in the tree is limited to the size of the array. Or the representation can use an array that grows according to the number of nodes (as in the collection classes of Chapter 3).

Remember that in a complete binary tree, all of the depths are full, except perhaps for the deepest. At the deepest depth, the nodes are as far left as possible. For example, here is a complete binary tree with 10 nodes, in which the element contained in each node is a character. In this example, the first seven nodes completely fill the levels at depth zero (the root), depth one (the root's children), and depth two. There are three more nodes at depth three, and these nodes are as far left as possible.

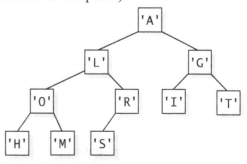

The 10 characters that the tree contains can be stored in an array of characters, starting with the root's character in the [0] location of the array, as shown here:

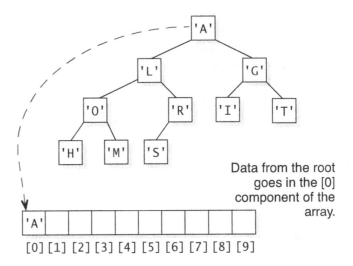

Data from the root goes in the [0] component of the array.

After the root, the two nodes with depth one are placed in the array, as shown here:

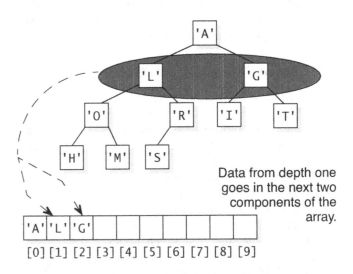

Data from depth one goes in the next two components of the array.

We continue in this way, placing the four nodes of depth two next and finishing off with the nodes of depth three. The entire representation of the tree by an array is shown at the top of the next page.

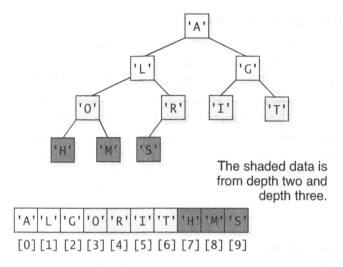

The shaded data is
from depth two and
depth three.

'A'	'L'	'G'	'O'	'R'	'I'	'T'	'H'	'M'	'S'
[0]	[1]	[2]	[3]	[4]	[5]	[6]	[7]	[8]	[9]

There are several reasons why the array representation is convenient:

formulas for storing data from a complete binary tree in the components of an array

1. The data from the root always appears in the [0] component of the array.

2. Suppose the data for a non-root node appears in component [i] of the array. Then the data for its parent is always at location [(i-1)/2] (using integer division).

3. Suppose the data for a node appears in component [i] of the array. Then its children (if they exist) always have their data at these locations:

> Left child at component [2i+1]
> Right child at component [2i+2]

These formulas make it easy to implement algorithms that traverse the tree, moving from node to node in various ways, processing data along the way.

Before long, you will implement some ADTs that store data in a tree. If the tree is a complete binary tree, then the ADT can store the complete binary tree in an array, using the formulas we have written. Such a class will have at least two private instance variables: (1) The array itself is one instance variable; and (2) a second instance variable keeps track of how much of the array is used. The actual links between the nodes are not stored. Instead, these links exist only via the formulas that determine where an element is stored in the array based on the element's position in the tree.

As a complete binary tree grows, the array size can be increased as necessary to handle more and more nodes.

Non-complete binary trees can also be implemented using an array, although a problem arises in determining which children of a node actually exist. We'll address this problem in Programming Project 3 on page 517. But for now, let's look at the other alternative: an implementation of a binary tree that allocates and releases nodes as needed.

Representing a Binary Tree with a Generic Class for Nodes

A binary tree can be represented by its individual nodes, where each node is an object of a generic binary tree node class that we will define, similar to the way in which we used a node class to build linked lists. Here is the basic idea:

Node Representation of Binary Trees

Each node of a binary tree can be stored as an object of a binary tree node class. The class contains private instance variables that are references to other nodes in the tree. An entire tree is represented as a reference to the root node.

For a binary tree, each node will contain references to its left child and right child. The node also has at least one instance variable to hold some data. The type of the data could be one of the eight primitive types, such as a char value, or the data type of a node could be defined by a generic type parameter. Here are two definitions we could use for binary tree nodes that contain data:

This implementation has char data in each node:

```
class CharBTNode
{
    private char data;
    private CharBTNode left;
    private CharBTNode right;
    ...
```

This implementation has data from a generic type parameter:

```
class BTNode<E>
{
    private E data;
    private BTNode<E> left;
    private BTNode<E> right;
    ...
```

When we get around to implementing the class, we'll use a generic type parameter for the data, but keep in mind that we could use one of the primitive types instead. In any implementation, the data instance variable of a node holds some information that occurs in the node. Each binary tree node also contains two instance variables, left and right, which refer to the left and right children of the node. When a reference to a child is null, it indicates that the particular child does not exist. We could include other references in a binary tree node: perhaps a reference to the node's parent, or to the root of the entire tree, or even to siblings. But many applications need only references to the children.

We can draw a boxes-and-arrows representation of a small tree, as in Figure 9.5. This is a tree of characters, so each node is stored in a CharBTNode, and the entire tree is accessed through a reference to the root node of the tree. Within the diagram, a null reference is drawn as a slash. The reference to the root node is similar to the head of a linked list, providing a starting point to access all the nodes in the tree. If the tree were empty (with no nodes), then the root reference would be null.

FIGURE 9.5 A Binary Tree Represented with the CharBTNode Class

(a) Example binary tree of characters.

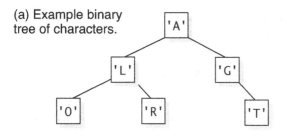

(b) Representation of the binary tree using the CharBTNode class. Each large box is a CharBTNode object, and each of the small shaded boxes is a reference to a CharBTNode.

A separate single variable is used to refer to the root node.

The slash represents the null reference.

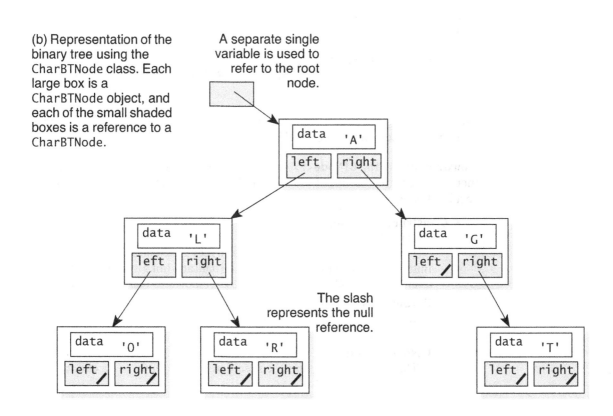

Self-Test Exercises for Section 9.2

6. Consider a complete binary tree with exactly 10,000 nodes, implemented with an array. Suppose a node has its value stored in location 4999. Where is the value stored for this node's parent? Where is the value stored for its left child? What can you say about its right child?

7. Draw a boxes-and-arrows representation of a small binary tree with three nodes containing integers. Put 10 in the root, 20 in the left child of the root, and 30 in the right child of the root.

8. Define the instance variables for a new generic node implementation that could be used for a tree in which each node has up to four children and each node also has a reference to its parent. Store the references to the children in an array of four references to nodes.

9.3 A CLASS FOR BINARY TREE NODES

We now have an understanding of the instance variables for a binary tree node. With this in hand, we're ready to write methods for the generic BTNode<E> class, which begins like this:

```
public class BTNode<E>
{
    private E data;         // The data stored in this node
    private BTNode<E> left;   // Reference to the left child
    private BTNode<E> right;  // Reference to the right child
    . . .
```

We begin with a constructor that's responsible for initializing the three instance variables of a new binary tree node.

Constructor for the BTNode<E> Class. The node's constructor has three arguments, which are the initial values for the node's data and link variables, as specified here:

♦ **Constructor for the BTNode<E>**
   public BTNode
     (E initialData, BTNode<E> initialLeft, BTNode<E> initialRight)
   Initialize a node with a specified initial data and links to children. Note that a reference to a child may be null, which indicates that there is no child.

   Parameters:
      initialData – the initial data of this new node
      initialLeft and initialRight – references to the children

   Postcondition:
      This new node contains the specified data and links to its children.

This constructor creates a new node with specified data. When the node is created, the programmer also specifies references to the left and right children. These references may be null to indicate that a child doesn't exist. The implementation merely fills in the three instance variables from the values of the three parameters, as shown here:

```
public BTNode(
    E initialData,
    BTNode<E> initialLeft,
    BTNode<E> initialRight
)
{
    data = initialData;
    left = initialLeft;
    right = initialRight;
}
```

Getting and Setting Data and Links.   There are three methods for setting the data and links of a node. Three other methods get the data and links. The headings of the get and set methods are given here:

```
public E getData( )               // Gets the data from this node
public BTNode<E> getLeft( )   // Gets reference to left child
public BTNode<E> getRight( ) // Gets reference to right child

public void setData(E newData)            // Set data of this node
public void setLeft(BTNode<E> newLeft)    // Set left child
public void setRight(BTNode<E> newRight) // Set right child
```

getData
getLeft
getRight
setData
setLeft
setRight

The six implementations are straightforward. Keep in mind that a node might not have children; for example, if there is no left child, then this implementation of getLeft will return the null reference:

```
public BTNode<E> getLeft( )
{
    return left;
}
```

Testing Whether a Node Is a Leaf.   Our next method tests whether a node is a leaf. You can write the specification yourself. Here is our implementation:

```
public boolean isLeaf( )
{
    return (left == null) && (right == null);
}
```

isLeaf

Getting Data from the Leftmost or Rightmost Node. Some applications need to retrieve the data from the leftmost or rightmost node of a tree. The leftmost node is obtained by starting at the root and following only left links. For example, consider this tree of strings:

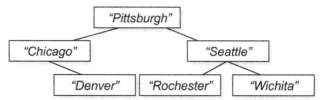

In this example, the leftmost node contains the string "Chicago" (not "Denver" since getting to "Denver" uses one right link). Here's the method to find the data from the leftmost node:

getLeftmostData
getRightmostData

♦ **getLeftmostData**

        public E getLeftmostData( )

Accessor method to get the data from the leftmost node of the tree starting with this node.

Returns:

> the data from the deepest node that can be reached from this node following left links

```
public E getLeftmostData( )
{
   if (left == null)
      return data;
   else
      return left.getLeftmostData( );
}
```

This is a recursive implementation. In the base case, there are no more left links to follow, so the method returns the data from the node that activated the method. On the other hand, if there is a left link, then we get the leftmost data by making the recursive call `left.getLeftmostData( )`, which gets the leftmost data from the left subtree.

You can write a similar method to get the data from the rightmost node.

Removing the Leftmost or Rightmost Node. Some programs remove the leftmost or rightmost node of a tree, resulting in a new, smaller tree. For example, if we remove the rightmost node from the tree of strings shown above, we end up with this smaller tree (without "Wichita"):

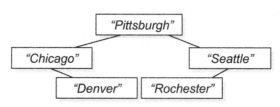

The specification of a method to remove the leftmost node is given here:

removeLeftmost
removeRightmost

♦ **removeLeftmost**

    `public BTNode<E> removeLeftmost( )`

    Remove the leftmost node of the tree with this node as its root.

    Postcondition:

        The tree starting at this node has had its leftmost node removed (i.e., the deepest node that can be reached by following left links). The return value is a reference to the root of the new (smaller) tree. This return value could be null if the original tree had only one node (since that one node has now been removed).

    Example:

        If n is a reference to a node in a tree and n has a right child, then we can remove the leftmost node of n's right subtree with this statement:

        `n.setRight(n.getRight( ).removeLeftmost( ));`

Let's look at the example from the specification. For this example, suppose n refers to the root node of this tree:

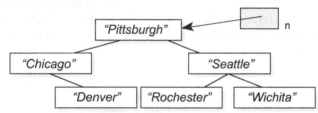

We would like to remove the leftmost node in n's right subtree, which is the node containing "Rochester." Now, `n.getRight( )` is a reference to the "Seattle" node, so `n.getRight( ).removeLeftmost( )` will remove "Rochester" and have a return value that is the reference to the root of the new, smaller subtree. We need to set n's right link to the new, smaller tree, so the complete statement to remove the leftmost node in n's right subtree is:

    `n.setRight(n.getRight( ).removeLeftmost( ));`

The resulting tree will look like this:

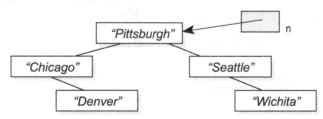

Notice that our statement for the removal actually sets n's right link to the root of the new, smaller subtree. This is important because, in some cases, the root of the subtree might now be null or could be a different node. For example, suppose we want to remove the leftmost node of n's right subtree a second time. We start from this situation:

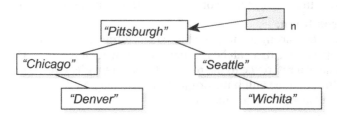

From this situation, we activate:

```
n.setRight(n.getRight( ).removeLeftmost( ));
```

The leftmost node of the right subtree now contains "Seattle" itself, so the activation of n.getRight( ).removeLeftmost( ) will remove the "Seattle" node and return a reference to the new, smaller subtree (which contains only "Wichita"). The right link of n is set to refer to the new, smaller tree, so we end up with this situation:

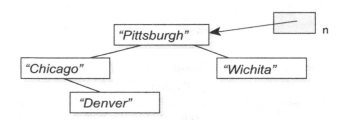

The implementation of removeLeftmost has a simple case when the node that activates removeLeftmost has no left child. This is the situation that we just saw, in which the "Seattle" node had no left child. In this case, the node that activates removeLeftmost is itself the leftmost node of the tree (or subtree). So we simply return a reference to the rest of the tree, which is on the right side. Thus, the implementation begins like this:

```
public BTNode<E> removeLeftmost( )
{
    if (left == null)
        return right;
    ...
```

For the preceding example, this code returns a reference to the node that contains "Wichita."

And what if there is a left child? In this case, we want to remove the leftmost node from the left subtree. For example, suppose the root of this tree activates `removeLeftmost`:

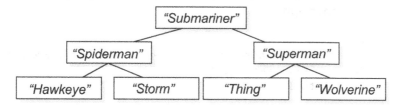

We must remove the leftmost node from the tree. Since the root has a left child, we can accomplish our task by removing the leftmost node from the left subtree (remove the leftmost node from the subtree has its root at "Spiderman"). This is a smaller version of the very problem we are trying to solve, and we can solve this smaller problem with a recursive call of `left.removeLeftmost( )`. The recursive call will remove the leftmost node from the left subtree (removing "Hawkeye") and return a reference to the new, smaller left subtree. This new, smaller left subtree may have a different root than the original left subtree, so we need to set our left link to refer to the new, smaller subtree. The complete statement to remove the leftmost node from the left subtree and set the left link to this new, smaller tree is:

```
left = left.removeLeftmost( );
```

This is a recursive call because we are using `removeLeftmost` to solve a smaller version of the `removeLeftmost` problem. After the recursive call, the tree looks like this:

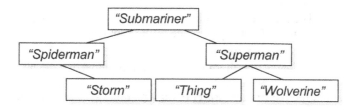

In this recursive solution, there is one last task. We must return a reference to the entire tree. This entire tree is now smaller than the tree we began with. ("Hawkeye" has been lost.) The root to this smaller tree is the very node that activated `removeLeftmost` in the first place—so how do we refer to that node so that we can use it in the method's return statement? The answer is Java's keyword `this`. Within any method, the keyword `this` is always a reference to the object that activated the method. So, `removeLeftmost` uses `this`, as shown in the following complete implementation.

```
public BTNode<E> removeLeftmost( )
{
    if (left == null)
    {  // The leftmost node is at the root because there is no left child.
        return right;
    }
    else
    {  // A recursive call removes the leftmost node from my left subtree.
        left = left.removeLeftmost( );
        return this;
    }
}
```

Notice the final line in the recursive case—return this—which returns a reference to the original node that activated the method. In the example at the bottom of the previous page, this would return a reference to the "Submariner" node.

You can implement removeRightmost yourself, using a similar recursive pattern.

Copying a Tree. Our last method is a static method that can be used at any time to copy an entire tree. The parameter of this method is a reference to the root node of a tree that we are copying, as shown here:

treeCopy

◆ **treeCopy**
    public static <E> BTNode<E> treeCopy(BTNode<E> source)
    Copy a binary tree.
    Parameter:
        source – a reference to the root node of a binary tree that will be copied
            (which may be an empty tree where source is null)
    Returns:
        The method has made a copy of the binary tree starting at source. The
        return value is a reference to the root of the copy.
    Throws: OutOfMemoryError
    Indicates that there is insufficient memory for the new tree.

Notice that the parameter, source, may be null. This would indicate that the tree we are copying is empty (has no nodes), and in this case, the treeCopy method returns the null reference. On the other hand, if the root reference is not null, then the tree has at least one node. The tree can be copied with these three steps (using local variables leftCopy and rightCopy, which are both references to nodes):

1. Make leftCopy refer to a copy of the left subtree (which might be empty).
2. Make rightCopy refer to a copy of the right subtree (which might be empty).
3. return new BTNode<E>(source.data, leftCopy, rightCopy);

The first two steps of the pseudocode are "smaller versions of the problem we are solving in the first place." Therefore, these two steps can be solved with recursive calls. The complete implementation of `treeCopy` is given here:

```
public static <E> BTNode<E> treeCopy(BTNode<E> source)
{
   BTNode<E> leftCopy, rightCopy;

   if (source == null)
      return null;
   else
   {
      leftCopy = treeCopy(source.left);
      rightCopy = treeCopy(source.right);
      return new BTNode<E>(source.data, leftCopy, rightCopy);
   }
}
```

By the way, do you see why `treeCopy` is a static method? The reason is that we may copy an empty tree. If it were an ordinary method, activated by the tree we are copying, then we could not activate `null.treeCopy( )`.

The specifications for the constructor, `isLeaf`, and `treeCopy` appear in Figure 9.6. We'll postpone the complete implementation for now because it will be include a few more methods we haven't mentioned yet. But even without these extra methods, we can look at a programming example beginning on page 473.

FIGURE 9.6   Specification of the Key Methods of a Generic Class for Binary Tree Nodes

Specification

These are the key methods of a generic class for binary tree nodes, which we will implement later. In this specification, each node contains data that is an E object. Our final implementation will contain additional methods that are discussed in Section 9.4.

♦ **Constructor for theGeneric BTNode<E>**
   `public BTNode(E initialData, BTNode<E> initialLeft, BTNode<E> initialRight)`
   Initialize a node with specified initial data and links to children. Note that a reference to a child may be null, which indicates that there is no child.
   Parameters:
      `initialData` – the initial data of this new node
      `initialLeft` and `initialRight` – references to the children of this new node
   Postcondition:
      This new node contains the specified data and links to its children.

(continued)

(FIGURE 9.6 continued)

♦ **getData—getLeft—getRight**

```
public E getData( )
public BTNode<E> getLeft( )
public BTNode<E> getRight( )
```

These are accessor methods to obtain this node's data or a reference to one of the children. Any of these objects may be null. A null reference to a child indicates that the child does not exist.

♦ **getLeftmostData**

```
public E getLeftmostData( )
```

Accessor method to get the data from the leftmost node of the tree below this node.

Returns:

The data from the deepest node that can be reached from this node following left links.

♦ **getRightmostData**

```
public E getRightmostData( )
```

Accessor method to get the data from the rightmost node of the tree below this node.

Returns:

The data from the deepest node that can be reached from this node following right links.

♦ **isLeaf**

```
public boolean isLeaf( )
```

Accessor method to determine whether a node is a leaf.

Returns:

`true` (if this node is a leaf); `false` otherwise.

♦ **setData—setLeft—setRight**

```
public void setData(E newData)
public void setLeft(BTNode<E> newLeft)
public void setRight(BTNode<E> newRight)
```

These are modification methods to set this node's data or a reference to one of the children. Any of these objects may be null. Setting a child to null indicates that the child does not exist.

♦ **removeLeftmost**

```
public BTNode<E> removeLeftmost( )
```

Remove the leftmost node of the tree with this node as its root.

Postcondition:

The tree starting at this node has had its leftmost node removed (i.e., the deepest node that can be reached by following left links). The return value is a reference to the root of the new (smaller) tree. This return value could be null if the original tree had only one node (since that one node has now been removed).

Example:

If n is a reference to a node in a tree and n has a right child, then we can remove the leftmost node of n's right subtree with this statement:

```
n.setRight(n.getRight( ).removeLeftmost( ));
```
(continued)

(FIGURE 9.6 continued)

♦ **removeRightmost**
   ```
   public BTNode<E> removeRightmost( )
   ```
   Remove the rightmost node of the tree with this node as its root.

   Postcondition:
   The tree starting at this node has had its rightmost node removed (i.e., the deepest node that can be reached by following right links). The return value is a reference to the root of the new (smaller) tree. This return value could be null if the original tree had only one node (since that one node has now been removed).

   Example:
   If n is a reference to a node in a tree and n has a left child, then we can remove the rightmost node of n's left subtree with this statement:
   ```
   n.setLeft(n.getLeft( ).removeRightmost( ));
   ```

♦ **treeCopy**
   ```
   public static <E> BTNode<E> treeCopy(BTNode<E> source)
   ```
   Copy a binary tree.

   Parameter:
   source – a reference to the root node of a binary tree that will be copied (which may be an empty tree where source is null)

   Returns:
   The method has made a copy of the binary tree starting at source. The return value is a reference to the root of the copy.

   Throws: OutOfMemoryError
   Indicates that there is insufficient memory for the new tree.

PROGRAMMING EXAMPLE: **Animal Guessing**

Now we'll write a small program that uses a binary tree. The program is a simple guessing game: You pretend that you are an animal, and the program asks questions to try to guess what animal you are. If the program guesses correctly, another round of the game is started. If the program can't figure out what you are, you provide some more knowledge to the program so that the next time the game is played, the program is a bit smarter.

As an example, suppose you are pretending to be a raccoon. The program might start by asking *"Are you a mammal?"* and you answer, "Yes." Next the program wants to know *"Are you bigger than a cat?"* and again you answer, "Yes." Finally, the program guesses: *"Are you a kangaroo?"* and with a smug smile you reply, "No, don't be ridiculous."

an animal-guessing program that gets smarter and smarter

At this point, the program says, *"I give up. What are you?"* You explain that you are a raccoon. You then provide the program with a question that the program can use in the future to distinguish a kangaroo from a raccoon—perhaps *"Are you a marsupial?"*—and you tell the program that the answer to this question is "Yes" for a kangaroo but "No" for a raccoon. The next time you are a raccoon, the program will have enough information to guess correctly. Here's a sample dialogue with the program:

```
Are you a mammal? [Y or N] Y
Are you bigger than a cat? [Y or N] Y
My guess is Kangaroo. Am I right? [Y or N] N
I give up. What are you? Raccoon
Please type a yes/no question that will distinguish a Raccoon
from a Kangaroo.
Your question: Are you a marsupial?
As a Raccoon, Are you a marsupial? Please answer [Y or N] N
Shall we play again? [Y or N] N
Thank you for teaching me a thing or two.
```

As you might guess, the data used by the program is stored in a binary taxonomy tree, as described on page 457, with each non-leaf node containing a question. When the program begins, it will know only four animals, and the taxonomy tree will look like this:

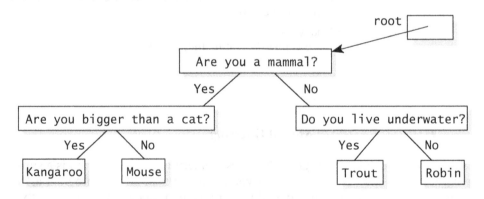

The program maintains a reference to a node called root, which is root of the binary taxonomy tree. As the game is being played, the program also maintains a second reference called current. The current reference starts at the root and travels down the tree according to the answers that the user provides.

For example, suppose the user answers "Yes" to the first question, *"Are you a mammal?"* Then the program will move its current to the left subtree, as shown at the top of the next page.

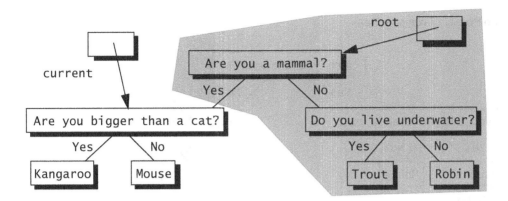

In the drawing, we have hidden part of the tree to indicate that only the left sub-tree is now relevant to the game. The rest of the tree and the reference to the root are still present, but they are not needed at this point in the game.

The program continues asking questions. Each time the user answers "Yes" to a question, the `current` reference is moved left. Each "No" answer moves `current` right. This continues until the program reaches a leaf. When a leaf is reached, the program guesses that you are the animal whose name is stored at the leaf. If the leaf contains the correct animal, then all is well. But if the guess is wrong, then the program elicits information from the user, and that information is used to improve the taxonomy tree.

In the sample dialogue where you were a raccoon, the program used the information to modify the taxonomy tree, resulting in the larger taxonomy tree of Figure 9.7(a). After playing several rounds of the game, the taxonomy tree might contain quite a few animals. Figure 9.7(b) shows what the tree could look like with seven animals. As an exercise, pretend you are a squid and follow the route that would be taken from the root to the squid leaf in this tree.

Animal-Guessing Program—Design and Implementation

Now that we have a general idea of how the program works, let's carry out a top-down design. The main method has three steps, shown in this pseudocode:

1. Print the instructions for the user.

2. Create a small initial taxonomy tree with four animals. The reference variable `root` refers to the root of this initial tree; each node contains a `String` as its data.

   the data at each node is a string

3. Repeat the following steps as often as the user wants:

   a. Activate a method called `play` that plays one round of the game, perhaps adding information to the bottom of the tree.

   b. Ask the user, "Shall we play again?" and read the answer.

FIGURE 9.7   Two Possible Taxonomy Trees

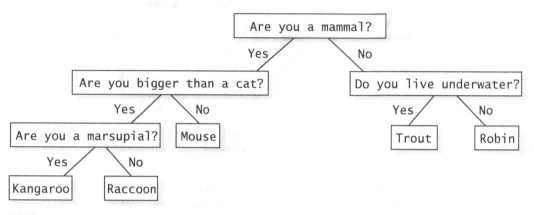

(a) Taxonomy tree after adding a raccoon

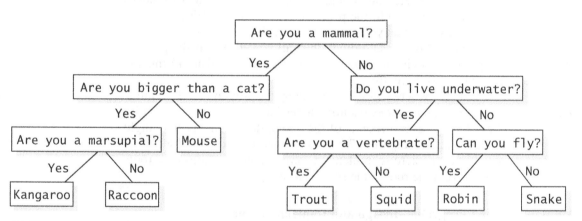

(b) Taxonomy tree with seven animals

The first two steps from our outline will be accomplished by methods we call instruct and beginningTree. For Step 3, the user's input will be read through a Scanner object (see Appendix B). The Scanner object will be a static instance variable, attached to System.in. It can be used by any method of the program that needs input from the user.

One of the methods that needs input is called play, which we'll design for Step 3a. Step 3b can be accomplished with another method that we'll write, called query. The query method asks a yes/no question, returning true if the user replies "Y" or "y" and returning false if the user replies "N" or "n." Putting the steps together, we can write the main method as shown next.

```
private static Scanner stdin = new Scanner(System.in);
public static void main(String[ ] args)
{
    BTNode<String> root;

    instruct( );
    root = beginningTree( );
    do
        play(root);
    while (query("Shall we play again?"));

    System.out.println
        ("Thanks for teaching me a thing or two.");
}
```

Notice that we are using a binary tree where the data in each node is a string. We discuss all the methods used in the main method next.

The instruct Method. This method prints instructions explaining the game. You can write it yourself with the heading public static void instruct( ).

The query Method. This method prints a prompt (using System.out.print) and reads the user's yes or no answer (using stdin.nextLine). If the user responds yes, then the method returns true; otherwise, the method returns false.

The beginningTree Method. This method creates the initial binary taxonomy tree and returns a reference to the root of this tree, as shown in this outline:

```
public static BTNode<String> beginningTree( )
{
    BTNode<String> root;
    BTNode<String> child;
```

1. Make root refer to a new node with the data "Are you a mammal?". Both children are initially null.

2. Make child refer to a new node with the data "Are you bigger than a cat?". Give it two leaves as children, with the data "Kangaroo" on the left and "Mouse" on the right. Then activate root.setLeft(child);.

3. Make child refer to a new node with the data "Do you live underwater?". Give it two leaves as children, with the data "Trout" on the left and "Robin" on the right. Then activate root.setRight(child);.

```
    4. return root;
}
```

The complete implementation will be shown as part of a program in a moment. For now, you should notice that the operations of beginningTree can be accomplished with the node's constructor, setLeft, and setRight. When beginningTree finishes, the root in the main program will refer to the root node of our initial taxonomy tree.

The play Method. The play method has one parameter, which initially is a reference to the root of the binary taxonomy tree, as shown in this specification:

♦ **play (for the Animal-Guessing Program)**
> `public static void play(BTNode<String> current)`
> Play one round of the animal-guessing game.
>
> **Parameter:**
>> current – a reference to the root node of a binary taxonomy tree that will be used to play the game
>
> **Postcondition:**
>> The method has played one round of the game and possibly added new information about a new animal.
>
> **Throws:** OutOfMemoryError
>> Indicates that there is insufficient memory to add information to the tree.

The method causes the current reference to move down the tree in response to the user's replies. (The root reference, back in the main program, will stay put at the root.) When the current reference reaches a leaf, an animal is guessed.

We'll use one other method to carry out some of play's work. The method, called learn, is used after the game reaches a leaf and the animal at the leaf is wrong. The method elicits information from the user and thereby improves the tree, as specified here:

♦ **learn (for the Animal-Guessing Program)**
> `public static void learn(BTNode<String> current)`
> Elicit information from the user to improve the binary taxonomy tree.
>
> **Parameter:**
>> current – a reference to a leaf node of a binary taxonomy tree
>
> **Precondition:**
>> current is a reference to a leaf in a binary taxonomy tree.
>
> **Postcondition:**
>> Information has been elicited from the user, and the tree has been improved.
>
> **Throws:** OutOfMemoryError
>> Indicates that there is insufficient memory to add information to the tree.

Using the methods we have described, the implementation of play is relatively short, as shown on the next page:

```
public static void play(BTNode<String> current)
{
   while (!current.isLeaf( ))
   {
      if (query(current.getData( )))
         current = current.getLeft( );
      else
         current = current.getRight( );
   }

   System.out.print("My guess is " + current.getData( ) + ". ");
   if (!query("Am I right?"))
      learn(current);
   else
      System.out.println("I knew it all along!");
}
```

Within this implementation, we used the `query` method to ask the questions, for example:

```
if (query(current.getData( ))) ...
```

Notice that the parameter to `query`, provided by `current.getData( )`, is a string. The `query` method prints this string as a prompt, and waits for the user to respond yes or no. We use `current.getData( )` in one other place, when the current node reaches a leaf of the taxonomy tree:

```
System.out.print("My guess is " + current.getData( ) + ". ");
```

So what's left to do? Implement the `learn` method, which we'll do now.

The `learn` Method. This method is activated when the game reaches a leaf and makes a wrong guess. The method takes several steps to improve the taxonomy tree. The method's argument is a reference to the node that contains the incorrect guess, as shown in this heading:

```
public static void learn(BTNode current)
```

For example, suppose we just made an incorrect guess of a kangaroo from this tree:

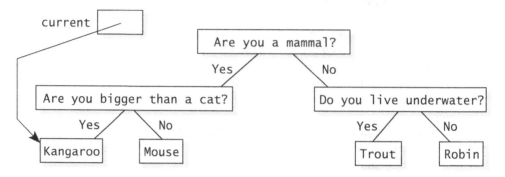

The learn method first sets three local String variables:

1. What animal was guessed? This is obtained from current.getData() and is stored in a local variable called guessAnimal. For this example, the guessAnimal is "Kangaroo."

2. What is the correct animal? The user's answer to this question is read into a local String variable called correctAnimal. To read the answer, we use the stdin.nextLine method. This method reads an entire line of input, including blanks, and returns this line as a String value. For this example, suppose the user's answer is "Raccoon," which is assigned to the local variable, correctAnimal.

3. What is a yes/no question that can distinguish the right animal from the animal that was guessed? In our example, we need a question that can distinguish a kangaroo from a raccoon. The user might provide the question "Are you a marsupial?" We'll read this question (with the nextLine method) and store it in another local String variable, newQuestion.

With the three strings set, we need one more piece of information. In particular, we need to know whether the correct animal answers "Yes" or "No" to the question that the user has just provided. In our example, we need to know whether a raccoon answers "Yes" or "No" to the question "Are you a marsupial?" Of course, a raccoon is not a marsupial, so based on this "No" answer, we can proceed with the these three steps:

- Copy the new question into current.data.
- Copy the *guessed* animal into a new leaf, which is created to be the left child of the current node.
- Copy the *correct* animal into a new leaf, which is created to be the right child of the current node.

In our example, these steps improve the taxonomy tree as shown here:

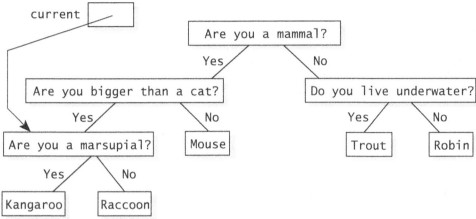

The other possibility is that the new animal has a "Yes" answer to the new question. For example, the question to distinguish a raccoon from a kangaroo could be "Do you have a ringed tail?" In this case, the new animal (raccoon) would be added as the left child of the new question, and the old animal (kangaroo) would be added on the right.

As an exercise, you should implement the learn method and add it to the complete program from Figure 9.8 on page 482. This program uses a BTNode class with the operations from Figure 9.6 on page 471. We'll actually implement the BTNode in the next section of this chapter.

Animal-Guessing Program—Improvements

Our animal program suffers from one problem: Each time the program is executed, it starts out knowing only four animals. An improvement will allow it to store the current taxonomy tree in a file and read that file whenever the program starts. This way, it remembers all the animals that you have taught it.

Self-Test Exercises for Section 9.3

9. Implement the learn method from the animal-guessing program.
10. Write a new BTNode method that computes the number of children that a node has.
11. Write a new BTNode method that computes the number of nodes in a binary tree. Add another method to compute the depth of a binary tree. Both methods should be static and work correctly for an empty tree.

FIGURE 9.8	The Animal-Guessing Program

Java Application Program

```java
// FILE: Animal.java
// This animal-guessing program illustrates the use of the binary tree node class.
import edu.colorado.nodes.BTNode; // For BTNode<String>
import java.util.Scanner;

public class Animal
{
   private static Scanner stdin = new Scanner(System.in);

   public static void main(String[ ] args)
   {
      BTNode<String> root;

      instruct( );
      root = beginningTree( );
      do
         play(root);
      while (query("Shall we play again?"));
      System.out.println("Thanks for teaching me a thing or two.");
   }


   public static void instruct( )
   | The implementation of this method is omitted—write it yourself!

   public static void learn(BTNode current)
   | The implementation of this method is Self-Test Exercise 9.

   public static void play(BTNode current)
   {
      while (!current.isLeaf( ))
      {
         if (query(current.getData( )))
            current = current.getLeft( );
         else
            current = current.getRight( );
      }

      System.out.print("My guess is " + current.getData( ) + ". ");
      if (!query("Am I right?"))
         learn(current);
      else
         System.out.println("I knew it all along!");
   }
```

(continued)

(FIGURE 9.8 continued)

```java
public static boolean query(String prompt)
{
    String answer;

    System.out.print(prompt + " [Y or N]: ");
    answer = stdin.nextLine( ).toUpperCase( );
    while (!answer.startsWith("Y") && !answer.startsWith("N"))
    {
        System.out.print("Invalid response. Please type Y or N: ");
        answer = stdin.nextLine( ).toUpperCase( );
    }

    return answer.startsWith("Y");
}

public static BTNode beginningTree( )
{
    BTNode root;
    BTNode child;

    final String ROOT_QUESTION = "Are you a mammal?";
    final String LEFT_QUESTION = "Are you bigger than a cat?";
    final String RIGHT_QUESTION = "Do you live underwater?";
    final String ANIMAL1 = "Kangaroo";
    final String ANIMAL2 = "Mouse";
    final String ANIMAL3 = "Trout";
    final String ANIMAL4 = "Robin";

    // Create the root node with the question "Are you a mammal?"
    root = new BTNode<String>(ROOT_QUESTION, null, null);
    // Create and attach the left subtree.
    child = new BTNode<String>(LEFT_QUESTION, null, null);
    child.setLeft(new BTNode<String>(ANIMAL1, null, null));
    child.setRight(new BTNode<String>(ANIMAL2, null, null));
    root.setLeft(child);
    // Create and attach the right subtree.
    child = new BTNode<String>(RIGHT_QUESTION, null, null);
    child.setLeft(new BTNode<String>(ANIMAL3, null, null));
    child.setRight(new BTNode<String>(ANIMAL4, null, null));
    root.setRight(child);

    return root;
}
}
```

9.4 TREE TRAVERSALS

And then he got up, and said: "And the only reason for making honey is so as I can eat it." So he began to climb the tree.

He climbed and he climbed and he climbed, and as he climbed he sang a little song to himself.

A. A. MILNE
Winnie-the-Pooh

We're almost ready to implement the BTNode, but first we'll look at one more action that can be taken on a binary tree—a tree traversal.

Traversals of Binary Trees

Programs that use tree structures often need to process all of the nodes in a tree, applying the same operation to each node. This processing is called a **tree traversal**. For example, suppose we have a tree in which each node contains an integer, and we need to print a list of all the integers in the tree. For a binary tree, there are three common ways of doing this kind of processing: **pre-order traversal, in-order traversal**, and **post-order traversal**. This section defines and implements the three traversal methods for binary trees. We also implement a modified pre-order traversal that uses indentation in a meaningful way for printing a tree. We start with a description of each method.

Pre-order Traversal. The word "pre-order" refers to when the root is processed; it is processed *pre*vious to its two subtrees. So a pre-order traversal has these three steps for a non-empty tree:

pre-order: the root is processed prior to its two subtrees

1. Process the root.

2. Process the nodes in the left subtree with a recursive call.

3. Process the nodes in the right subtree with a recursive call.

Let's look at the case in which we just want to be able to print the contents of each node. In this case, we could add this method to the BTNode of Section 9.3:

♦ **preorderPrint (for the generic BTNode<E> class)**

```
public void preorderPrint( )
```
Use a pre-order traversal to print the data from each node at or below this node of the binary tree.

Postcondition:
The data of this node and all its descendants have been written by System.out.println using a pre-order traversal.

Using recursion, the method's implementation is short, as shown next.

```
public void preorderPrint( )
{
    System.out.println(data);
    if (left != null)
        left.preorderPrint( );
    if (right != null)
        right.preorderPrint( );
}
```

Notice how the processing of the two subtrees is accomplished by activating left.preorderPrint( ) and right.preorderPrint( ). These are recursive calls of the preorderPrint method, with each recursive call responsible for solving a smaller version of the original problem.

Let's look at an execution of the pre-order traversal in more detail. We'll trace preorderPrint, applied to the binary tree shown below. This example tree consists of Integer objects, using Java's Integer wrapper class. Each Integer object contains a primitive int value, but it is also a full-blown Java Object, so it can be used as the data of a generic BTNode.

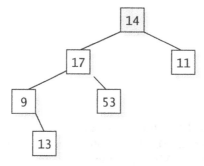

Suppose we activate preorderPrint for the shaded root in the diagram. The method's first step is to print the number at the root, so after this step, the only number printed is 14 (from the root).

The method's second step makes the recursive call left.preorderPrint( ). In effect, the recursive call says, "Do a pre-order traversal of the left subtree." To illustrate that we are now doing a traversal of a subtree, we will temporarily hide everything except the left subtree, as shown here:

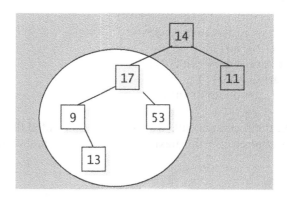

In this recursive call, the shaded node containing 17 has already activated preorderPrint. The first step of the recursive call is to print the number at the root of the subtree, so after that step, the total output contains two numbers:

14
17

The second step of the recursive call is to make yet another recursive call, for its own left subtree. In other words, this second recursive call will begin at the shaded node containing 9 in this drawing:

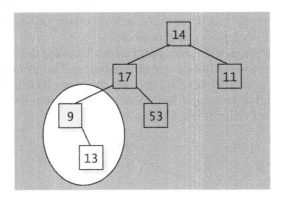

We now have three calls that are active: the original method activation by the root of the whole tree (containing 14), the first recursive call by the left child of the root (containing 17), and the second recursive call by the shaded node shown above (containing 9). This second recursive call carries out its appointed task by first printing a 9. After this, the total output consists of these three lines:

14
17
9

This time, the method does not make a recursive call to the left, because there is no left child. So the call continues executing the code at the spot marked here with an arrow:

```
System.out.println(data);
    if (left != null)
        left.preorderPrint( );
if (right != null)
        right.preorderPrint( );
```

At this point in the recursive call, we have already printed the 9 and dealt with the empty left subtree. So the next step will make another recursive call to process the right subtree. The node that activates this recursive call contains 13, as shown in this drawing:

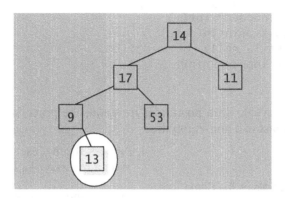

This recursive call prints the number 13 so that the entire output now has four numbers:

14
17
9
13

Both the left and right subtrees are empty for the node containing 13. So there are no further calls for those two empty subtrees. The recursive call, which printed 13, returns. Where does the method go from there? Can you finish tracing the pre-order traversal? By the time the last recursive call has returned, we've "visited" every node in the tree, and the numbers have been printed out, in this order:

14
17
9
13
53
11

In-order Traversal. The only change for an in-order traversal is that the root is processed *in* between the processing of its two subtrees. Here are the three steps for a non-empty tree:

in-order: the root is processed in between its two subtrees

1. Process the nodes in the left subtree with a recursive call.
2. Process the root.
3. Process the nodes in the right subtree with a recursive call.

The implementation of an in-order print method is a rearrangement of the pre-order print, as shown next.

```
public void inorderPrint( )
{
   if (left != null)
      left.inorderPrint( );
   System.out.println(data);
   if (right != null)
      right.inorderPrint( );
}
```

*post-order:
the root is
processed
after its two
subtrees*

Post-order Traversal. In a post-order traversal, the processing of the root is *post*poned until last in a non-empty tree:

1. Process the nodes in the left subtree with a recursive call.

2. Process the nodes in the right subtree with a recursive call.

3. Process the root.

We'll leave the implementation as an exercise in rearrangement.

Can you work out the order of the output numbers for the in-order and post-order traversals on an example such as Figure 9.5 on page 463? This is shown as one of the three traversals in Figure 9.9.

FIGURE 9.9 Three Different Traversals on the Same Tree

(a) Pre-order traversal

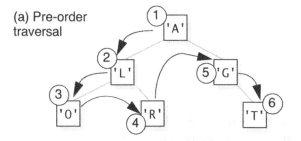

(b) In-order traversal

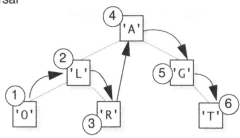

(c) Post-order traversal

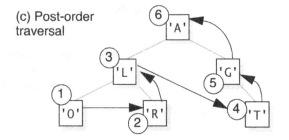

Printing a Tree with an Indentation to Show the Depth

There are times when you would like a quick display of a binary tree, in Java or some other programming language. In this case, you should consider implementing a pre-order traversal that prints each node with an indentation that indicates its depth. For example, consider the small tree shown at the top of the next page, along with output from a pre-order traversal with spaces at the start of each output line. The number of spaces on each line is four times the depth of the node, so that the indentation gives an indication of the depth.

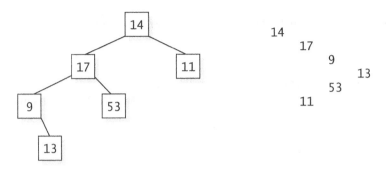

There's a small trick that will make the output more useful. The trick is to print a dash at any place where there is a child that has no sibling. For example, if a right child has no sibling to its left, then we print "--" to indicate the missing left child, as shown here:

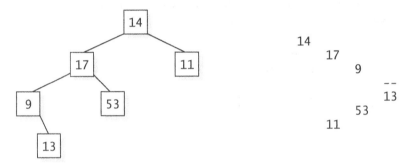

Why is this output useful? It's easy to interpret the tree structure: The root is the first number printed, with no indentation. Each node's children appear somewhere below it with an extra four spaces of indentation. A node with a single child has the dash "--" in place of the missing child. If necessary, you can easily draw lines by hand to connect a node to its children, as shown here:

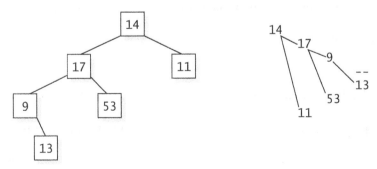

The specification and implementation of the print method are part of the complete generic BTNode given in Figure 9.10.

FIGURE 9.10	Specification and Implementation of the Generic Binary Tree Node Class

Generic Class BTNode

❖ **public class BTNode<E> from the package edu.colorado.nodes**

A BTNode<E> provides a node for a binary tree with a reference to an E object as the data in each node.

Limitations:

Beyond Int.MAX_VALUE elements, treeSize is wrong.

Specification

◆ **Constructor for the BTNode<E>**

    public BTNode(E initialData, BTNode<E> initialLeft, BTNode<E> initialRight)

Initialize a node with specified initial data and links to children. Note that a reference to a child may be null, which indicates that there is no child.

Parameters:

initialData – the initial data of this new node

initialLeft and initialRight – references to the children of this new node

Postcondition:

This new node contains the specified data and links to its children.

◆ **getData—getLeft—getRight**

    public E getData( )
    public BTNode<E> getLeft( )
    public BTNode<E> getRight( )

These are accessor methods to obtain this node's data or a reference to one of the children. Any of these objects may be null. A null reference to a child indicates that the child does not exist.

◆ **getLeftmostData**

    public E getLeftmostData( )

Accessor method to get the data from the leftmost node of the tree below this node.

Returns:

The data from the deepest node that can be reached from this node following left links.

◆ **getRightmostData**

    public E getRightmostData( )

Accessor method to get the data from the rightmost node of the tree below this node.

Returns:

The data from the deepest node that can be reached from this node following right links.

(continued)

(FIGURE 9.10 continued)

♦ **inorderPrint—postorderPrint—preorderPrint**
```
public void inorderPrint( )
public void postorderPrint( )
public void preorderPrint( )
```
Use a traversal to print the data from each node at or below this node of the binary tree.

Postcondition:
The data of this node and all its descendants have been written by System.out.println using one of three traversal techniques.

♦ **isLeaf**
```
public boolean isLeaf( )
```
Accessor method to determine whether a node is a leaf.

Returns:
true (if this node is a leaf); false otherwise.

♦ **print**
```
public void print(int depth)
```
Uses an in-order traversal to print the data from each node at or below this node of the binary tree, with indentation to indicate the depth of each node.

Parameter:
depth – the depth of this node (with 0 for the root, 1 for the root's children, and so on)

Precondition:
depth is the depth of this node.

Postcondition:
The data of this node and all its descendants have been written by System.out.println using an in-order traversal. The indentation of each line of data is four times its depth in the tree. A dash (--) is printed at any place where a child has no sibling.

♦ **removeLeftmost**
```
public BTNode<E> removeLeftmost( )
```
Remove the leftmost node of the tree with this node as its root.

Postcondition:
The tree starting at this node has had its leftmost node (i.e., the deepest node that can be reached by following left links) removed. The return value is a reference to the root of the new (smaller) tree. This return value could be null if the original tree had only one node (since that one node has now been removed).

Example:
If n is a reference to a node in a tree and n has a right child, then we can remove the leftmost node of n's right subtree with this assignment:
```
n.setRight(n.getRight( ).removeLeftmost( ));
```

(continued)

(FIGURE 9.10 continued)

♦ **removeRightmost**

```
public BTNode<E> removeRightmost( )
```
Remove the rightmost node of the tree with this node as its root.

Postcondition:

The tree starting at this node has had its rightmost node (i.e., the deepest node that can be reached by following right links) removed. The return value is a reference to the root of the new (smaller) tree. This return value could be null if the original tree had only one node (since that one node has now been removed).

Example:

If n is a reference to a node in a tree and n has a left child, then we can remove the rightmost node of n's left subtree with this assignment:

```
n.setLeft(n.getLeft( ).removeRightmost( ));
```

♦ **setData—setLeft—setRight**

```
public void setData(E newData)
public void setLeft(BTNode<E> newLeft)
public void setRight(BTNode<E> newRight)
```
These are modification methods to set this node's data or a reference to one of the children. Any of these objects may be null. Setting a child to null indicates that the child does not exist.

♦ **treeCopy**

```
public static <E> BTNode<E> treeCopy(BTNode<E> source)
```
Copy a binary tree.

Parameter:

source – a reference to the root node of a binary tree that will be copied (which may be an empty tree where source is null)

Returns:

The method has made a copy of the binary tree starting at source. The return value is a reference to the root of the copy.

Throws: OutOfMemoryError

Indicates that there is insufficient memory for the new tree.

♦ **treeSize**

```
public static <E> int treeSize(BTNode<E> root)
```
Compute the number of nodes in a binary tree.

Parameter:

root – the reference to the root of a binary tree (which may be an empty tree with a null root)

Returns:

the number of nodes in the tree with the given root

Note:

A wrong answer occurs for trees larger than Int.MAX_VALUE.

(continued)

(FIGURE 9.10 continued)

Implementation

```
// File: BTNode.java from the package edu.colorado.nodes
// Complete documentation is available from the BTNode link at
// http://www.cs.colorado.edu/~main/docs/.

package edu.colorado.nodes;

public class BTNode<E>
{
    // Invariant of the generic BTNode<E> class:
    //    1. Each node has one reference to an E Object, stored in data.
    //    2. The instance variables left and right are references to the node's children.
    private E data;
    private BTNode<E> left, right;

    public BTNode(E initialData, BTNode<E> initialLeft, BTNode<E> initialRight)
    {
        data = initialData;
        left = initialLeft;
        right = initialRight;
    }

    public E getData( )
    {
        return data;
    }

    public BTNode<E> getLeft( )
    {
        return left;
    }


    public E getLeftmostData( )
    {
        if (left == null)
            return data;
        else
            return left.getLeftmostData( );
    }

    public BTNode<E> getRight( )
    {
        return right;
    }
```

(continued)

(FIGURE 9.10 continued)

```
public E getRightmostData( )
{
   if (right == null)
      return data;
   else
      return right.getRightmostData( );
}

public void inorderPrint( )
{
   if (left != null)
      left.inorderPrint( );
   System.out.println(data);
   if (right != null)
      right.inorderPrint( );
}

public boolean isLeaf( )
{
   return (left == null) && (right == null);
}

public void postorderPrint( )
{
   if (left != null)
      left.postorderPrint( );
   if (right != null)
      right.postorderPrint( );
   System.out.println(data);
}

public void preorderPrint( )
{
   System.out.println(data);
   if (left != null)
      left.preorderPrint( );
   if (right != null)
      right.preorderPrint( );
}
```

(continued)

(FIGURE 9.10 continued)

```
public void print(int depth)
{
    int i;

    // Print the indentation and the data from the current node:
    for (i = 1; i <= depth; i++)
       System.out.print("    ");
    System.out.println(data);

    // Print the left subtree (or a dash if there is a right child and no left child).
    if (left != null)
       left.print(depth+1);
    else if (right != null)
    {
       for (i = 1; i <= depth+1; i++)
          System.out.print("    ");
       System.out.println("--");
    }

    // Print the right subtree (or a dash if there is a left child and no left child).
    if (right != null)
       right.print(depth+1);
    else if (left != null)
    {
       for (i = 1; i <= depth+1; i++)
          System.out.print("    ");
       System.out.println("--");
    }
}


public BTNode<E> removeLeftmost( )
{
    if (left == null)
    { // The leftmost node is at the root because there is no left child.
       return right;
    }
    else
    { // A recursive call removes the leftmost node from my own left child.
       left = left.removeLeftmost( );
       return this;
    }
}
```

(continued)

(FIGURE 9.10 continued)

```java
    public BTNode<E> removeRightmost( )
    {
       if (right == null)
       {  // The rightmost node is at the root because there is no right child.
          return left;
       }
       else
       {  // A recursive call removes the rightmost node from my own right child.
          right = right.removeRightmost( );
          return this;
       }
    }

    public void setData(E newData)
    {
       data = newData;
    }

    public void setLeft(BTNode<E> newLeft)
    {
       left = newLeft;
    }

    public void setRight(BTNode<E> newRight)
    {
       right = newRight;
    }

    public static <E> BTNode<E> treeCopy(BTNode<E> source)
    {
       BTNode<E> leftCopy, rightCopy;

       if (source == null)
          return null;
       else
       {
          leftCopy = treeCopy(source.left);
          rightCopy = treeCopy(source.right);
          return new BTNode<E>(source.data, leftCopy, rightCopy);
       }
    }

    public static <E> int treeSize(BTNode<E> root)
    {
       if (root == null)
          return 0;
       else
          return 1 + treeSize(root.left) + treeSize(root.right);
    }
}
```

BTNode, IntBTNode, and Other Classes

Figure 9.10 on page 490 shows the complete specification and implementation for the generic BTNode class. The class has one extra method, treeSize, which computes the number of nodes in a binary tree. We could add other methods; for example, Programming Project 6 on page 518 asks you to write traversals to create a Java Vector that contains all the elements from a binary tree.

The data in each BTNode is a Java Object, but we could have used other kinds of data. In all, there are nine implementations of binary tree nodes with the names shown in the box to the right. The generic verson, with a Java Object as the data, is called BTNode and is shown completely in Figure 9.10. You can modify the BTNode to obtain any of the other eight nodes, or you can find the complete implementations in the directory:

> *In the implementation of* BTNode, *we can change the* Object *to any of the primitive types, so we're really doing nine implementations at once:*
>
> BTNode
> BooleanBTNode
> ByteBTNode
> CharBTNode
> DoubleBTNode
> FloatBTNode
> IntBTNode
> LongBTNode
> ShortBTNode

        http://www.cs.colorado.edu/~main/edu/colorado/nodes/

Self-Test Exercises for Section 9.4

12. Look at the tree in Figure 9.5 on page 463. In what order are the letters printed for an in-order traversal? What about a post-order traversal?

13. Rewrite the pre-order traversal from page 484 so that it is a static method with one parameter (a reference to the root node of the tree). In what way is the static method more general than the nonstatic method?

14. Suppose we do a traversal of the tree in Figure 9.1 on page 455, printing out the numbers in the order 13, 9, 53, 17, 19, 7, 4, 11, 14. What kind of traversal did we do? In what order are the numbers printed for the other kinds of traversals?

15. Suppose you have a tree in which the left subtree contains 3000 nodes and the right subtree contains 100 nodes. For each of the different kinds of traversals, how many nodes are processed before the root node?

16. Here is an output from the tree-printing method for a tree of characters:

```
45
    9
        17
            20
            --
        3
    54
        53
        54
```

    For this exercise, draw pencil lines to show the links between the nodes in this tree.

17. Which of the traversal methods make sense for general trees in which there is no limit to the number of children that a node may have?

9.5 BINARY SEARCH TREES

Lucy looked very hard between the trees and could just see in the distance a patch of light that looked like daylight. "Yes," she said, "I can see the wardrobe door."

C.S. LEWIS
The Lion, the Witch and the Wardrobe

Perhaps you thought you would never see another bag after Chapter 3 (storing the bag's elements in an array), Chapter 4 (the linked list bag), and Chapter 5 (the generic bag). But binary trees offer yet another way to improve our bag, so we will have one last look at bags.

The Binary Search Tree Storage Rules

Binary trees offer an improved way of implementing the bag class. The improvement generally performs faster than our previous bags (or at least *sometimes* the improved approach may be taken). The improved implementation requires that the bag's elements can be compared to each other using operations such as the usual integer comparisons <, >, ==, <=, >=, and !=. These comparisons must form a *total order semantics*. Intuitively, a total order semantics requires that the different values of a class can all be placed on a single line, proceeding from smallest to largest along the line. This intuition is sufficient for most programming tasks, although you may sometimes need to know the more formal definition of a total order semantics, shown in Figure 9.11.

FIGURE 9.11 Total Order Semantics

A **total order semantics** for a class requires the six comparison operators (==, !=, >=, <=, >, <) to be defined, forming a total order that meets these requirements:

1. **Equality:** $(x == y)$ is true if and only if the two values, x and y, are identical.
2. **Totality:** For any two values x and y, exactly one of these three comparisons is true: $(x < y)$, $(x == y)$, or $(x > y)$.
3. **Consistency:** For any two values x and y:
   $(x > y)$ is the same as $(y < x)$
   $(x >= y)$ is the same as $((x > y) \;||\; (x == y))$
   $(x <= y)$ is the same as $((x < y) \;||\; (x == y))$
   $(x != y)$ is the same as $!(x == y)$
4. **Transitivity:** Whenever there are three values $(x, y, \text{and } z)$ with $(x < y)$ and $(y < z)$, then $(x < z)$ is also true.

We'll develop our bag as a bag of integers, but keep in mind that any data type could be used so long as there is some way to compare the elements using some total order semantics. The comparisons might be carried out with the usual operations (<, >, ==, and so on), or the comparisons might be incorporated by having the class implement the `Comparable` interface that we saw in Chapter 5. For example, Java's `String` class implements the `Comparable` interface, which means that it has the following method:

♦ **compareTo (method for the String class)**
> `public int compareTo(String str)`
> Compare this string to another string.

> **Returns:**
> > The return value is zero if this string is equal to `str`.
> > The return value is negative if this string is lexicographically before `str`.
> > The return value is positive if this string is lexicographically after `str`.

As you can see, `compareTo` returns zero if `str` is equal to the string that activates the method. If the strings are not equal, then they are compared in the **lexicographic order**, which is the normal alphabetical order for ordinary words of all lowercase letters. For example, if `s` is the string `"chaos"`, then `s.compareTo("order")` will return some negative number since `"chaos"` is alphabetically before `"order"`. On the other hand, `s.compareTo("action")` will return some positive integer. Therefore, our new bag could contain strings, which are compared to each other with the `compareTo` method.

Apart from requiring a total order semantics, the new bag class has a specification that is identical to our earlier bags. Therefore, a programmer who is using the bag class may switch to the new, improved bag without difficulty.

So, what good do we obtain from the total order semantics? We'll take advantage of the order to store the elements in the nodes of a binary tree, using a strategy that will make it easy to find elements. The strategy is to follow a collection of rules called the **Binary Search Tree Storage Rules**, defined here:

Binary Search Tree Storage Rules

In a **binary search tree**, the elements of the nodes can be compared with a total order semantics. These two rules are followed for every node *n*:

1. Every element in *n*'s left subtree is less than or equal to the element in node *n*.

2. Every element in *n*'s right subtree is greater than the element in node *n*.

FIGURE 9.12 Using a Binary Search Tree

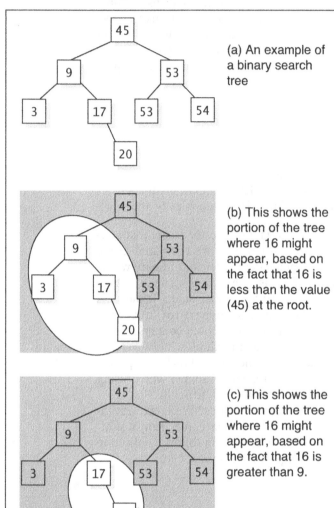

(a) An example of a binary search tree

(b) This shows the portion of the tree where 16 might appear, based on the fact that 16 is less than the value (45) at the root.

(c) This shows the portion of the tree where 16 might appear, based on the fact that 16 is greater than 9.

For example, suppose we want to store the numbers {3, 9, 17, 20, 45, 53, 53, 54} in a binary search tree. Figure 9.12(a) shows a binary search tree with these numbers. You can check that each node follows the Binary Search Tree Storage Rules. Binary search trees also can store a collection of strings, or real numbers, or *anything* that can be compared using some sort of total order semantics.

Can you see an advantage to storing a bag in a binary search tree rather than in an array or a linked list? The previous implementations of the bag ADT, using an array or a linked list, have a striking inefficiency: When we count the number of occurrences of an element in the bag, it is necessary to examine *every* element of the bag. Even if we are interested only in whether or not an element appears in the bag, we will often look at many elements before we stumble across the one we seek.

With a binary search tree, searching for an element is often much quicker. For example, suppose we're looking for the number 16 in the tree of Figure 9.12(a). We'll start at the root and compare 16 to the root's number. Since 16 is less than the root's number (45), we immediately know that 16 can appear only in the left subtree—if it appears at all. In Figure 9.12(b), we show the area where 16 might appear, based on knowing that 16 is less than the value at the root. Next we'll compare 16 with the root of the left subtree. Since 16 is greater than 9, this eliminates another portion of the tree, as shown in 9.12(c).

The number 16 is smaller than the next point on the tree (17), so we should continue to the left ... but we've run out of tree. At this point, we can stop and conclude that 16 is nowhere in the binary search tree, even though we only looked at the three numbers 45, 9, and 17. In fact, the most we'll ever have to look at is the depth of the tree plus one—four entries in this case.

This efficiency is the motivation for representing bags with a binary search tree. For the idea to work, the comparisons between entries must form a total order according to the rules of Figure 9.11 on page 498. In the remainder of this section, we'll use binary search trees to implement a bag of integers, as specified in Figure 9.13. This class is called an `IntTreeBag`, and it has the same methods as our earlier bags.

FIGURE 9.13   Specification of the `IntTreeBag` Class

Class IntTreeBag

❖ **public class IntTreeBag from the package edu.colorado.collections**
An `IntTreeBag` is a collection of `int` numbers.
Limitations:
Beyond `Integer.MAX_VALUE` elements, `countOccurrences` and `size` are wrong.

Specification

◆ **Constructor for the IntTreeBag**
`public IntTreeBag( )`
Initialize an empty bag.
Postcondition:
This bag is empty.

◆ **add**
`public void add(int element)`
Add a new element to this bag.
Parameter:
`element` – the new element that is being added
Postcondition:
A new copy of the element has been added to this bag.
Throws: `OutOfMemoryError`
Indicates insufficient memory for adding a new element.

(continued)

(FIGURE 9.13 continued)

◆ addMany

```
public void addMany(int... elements)
```

Add a variable number of new elements to this bag. If these new elements would take this bag beyond its current capacity, then the capacity is increased before adding the new elements.

Parameter:

elements – a variable number of new elements that are all being added

Postcondition:

New copies of all the elements have been added to this bag.

Throws: OutOfMemoryError

Indicates insufficient memory for increasing the capacity.

Note:

Creating a bag with capacity beyond Integer.MAX_VALUE causes arithmetic overflow.

◆ addAll

```
public void addAll(IntTreeBag addend)
```

Add the contents of another bag to this bag.

Parameter:

addend – a bag whose contents will be added to this bag

Precondition:

The parameter, addend, is not null.

Postcondition:

The elements from addend have been added to this bag.

Throws: IllegalArgumentException

Indicates that addend is null.

Throws: OutOfMemoryError

Indicates insufficient memory to increase the size of this bag.

◆ clone

```
public IntTreeBag clone( )
```

Generate a copy of this bag.

Returns:

The return value is a copy of this bag. Subsequent changes to the copy will not affect the original, nor vice versa. The return value must be typecast to an IntTreeBag before it is used.

Throws: OutOfMemoryError

Indicates insufficient memory for creating the clone.

◆ countOccurrences

```
public int countOccurrences(int target)
```

Accessor method to count the number of occurrences of a particular element in this bag.

Parameter:

target – the element that needs to be counted

Returns:

the number of times that target occurs in this bag

(continued)

(FIGURE 9.13 continued)

♦ remove

```
public boolean remove(int target)
```
Remove one copy of a specified element from this bag.

Parameter:

target – the element to remove from the bag

Postcondition:

If target was found in the bag, then one copy of target has been removed and the method returns true. Otherwise, the bag remains unchanged and the method returns false.

♦ size

```
public int size( )
```
Accessor method to determine the number of elements in this bag.

Returns:

the number of elements in this bag

♦ union

```
public static IntTreeBag union(IntTreeBag b1, IntTreeBag b2)
```
Create a new bag that contains all the elements from two other bags.

Parameters:

b1 – the first of two bags

b2 – the second of two bags

Precondition:

Neither b1 nor b2 is null.

Returns:

a new bag that is the union of b1 and b2

Throws: IllegalArgumentException

Indicates that one of the arguments is null.

Throws: OutOfMemoryError

Indicates insufficient memory for the new bag.

The Binary Search Tree Bag—Implementation of Some Simple Methods

Our new bag will have only one instance variable, which is a reference to the root of a binary search tree that contains the integers. If the bag is empty, then the root reference will be null. We could add other instance variables—such as a count of the number of nodes—but limiting ourselves to only the root will allow us to focus clearly on the necessary tree algorithms. Here's the start of the new class implementation:

```
public class IntTreeBag implements Cloneable
{
    // Invariant of the IntTreeBag class:
    //    1. The elements in the bag are stored in a binary search tree.
    //    2. The instance variable root is a reference to the root of the
    //       binary search tree (or null for an empty tree).
    private IntBTNode root;
    ...
```

Notice that we are using the IntBTNode class, which is the same as the BTNode class from Figure 9.10 on page 490 except that IntBTNode uses int elements instead of generic Java objects.

We're ready to dive into implementing the bag methods. For the most part, we will provide only pseudocode that you can implement yourself. Keep in mind that you should use the methods of the IntBTNode as much as possible.

Constructor. The constructor sets root to null. This isn't absolutely needed because a reference variable that is an instance variable is always initialized to null. So another alternative is not to bother implementing the constructor at all.

The clone Method. Since our bag uses dynamic memory, we must implement a clone method. The method can be implemented by following the three-step outline on page 82. The implementation will use the treeCopy method to carry out the actual copying of the tree.

The size Method. The size method simply returns the answer from Int-BTNode.treeSize(root), using the treeSize method from the IntBTNode class.

Counting the Occurrences of an Element in a Binary Search Tree

The countOccurrences method counts the number of occurrences of an element called target. We'll keep track of these occurrences in a local variable called count (which is initialized to zero). The important point is that we will not look at every element in the binary search tree. Instead, we'll have a local variable called cursor, which is initialized to the root. We'll use a loop to move the cursor down through the tree, always moving along the path where the target might occur. At each point in the tree, we have four possibilities:

1. The cursor can become null, indicating that we've moved off the bottom of the tree. In this case, we have counted all the occurrences of the target. So the loop can end, and we should return the current count.

2. The target might be smaller than the data at the cursor node. In this case, the target can appear only in the left subtree. For example, suppose we are counting occurrences of the integer 4 in the following binary search tree. The cursor's data might be 16, and the situation would look like this:

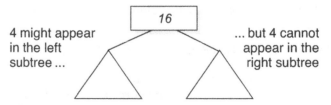

In this situation, we'll continue our search by assigning:

```
cursor = cursor.getLeft( );
```

3. The target might be larger than the data at the cursor node. This is similar to the previous case, except that we must continue our search to the right instead of the left, using this assignment:

```
cursor = cursor.getRight( );
```

4. The target might equal the data at the cursor node. In this case, we add 1 to the count and continue the search to the left (since elements to the left are less than *or equal to* the element at the cursor node).

The implementation of these steps is straightforward using a while-loop.

Adding a New Element to a Binary Search Tree

The add method puts a new element into a binary search tree, using this method header:

```
public void add(int element)
```

We suggest that you handle one special case first: When the first element is added, simply activate `root = new IntBTNode(element, null, null)`.

The other case is when there are already some other elements in the tree. In this case, we'll set a `cursor` to refer to the current root, and then we will pretend to search for the exact element we are trying to add. But the search runs a bit differently than a real search. The main difference is that we stop the search just before the cursor falls off the bottom of the tree, and we add the new element at the spot where the cursor was about to fall off. For example, consider the task of adding 16 to this binary search tree:

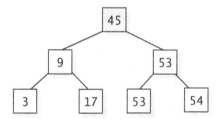

The cursor starts at the shaded node (with 45). If we were searching for the 16, we would continue the search to the left. So we move our cursor to the left, resulting in the cursor referring to the node that contains 9:

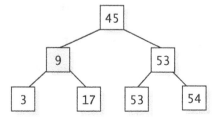

Again pretend that you are searching for the 16 instead of adding it, so that now the cursor moves right to the node containing 17:

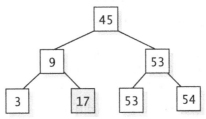

At this point, an ordinary search would continue to the left, stepping off the bottom of the tree. But instead, we add the new element at this position, resulting in this tree:

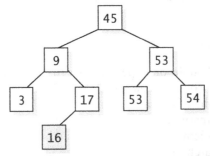

To implement the scheme, we suggest a boolean variable called done, which is initialized to `false`. We then have a loop that continues until done becomes `true`. Each iteration of the loop handles these two cases:

1. Suppose the new element is less than or equal to the data at the cursor node. In this case, check the left child. If `cursor.getLeft( )` is null, then create a new node containing the new element (setting the cursor's left child to this new node) and set done to `true`. On the other hand, if the left child is not null, then continue the search by moving the cursor to the left with this assignment statement:

   ```
   cursor = cursor.getLeft( );
   ```

2. Suppose the new element is greater than the data at the cursor node. In this case, follow the same procedure as Case 1, but use the right child instead of the left.

After the loop ends, the method has no more work.

Removing an Element from a Binary Search Tree

The `remove` method allows us to remove a specified element from a binary search tree, with this header:

```
public boolean remove(int target)
```

The method returns true if it finds and removes one copy of the target. Otherwise, it returns false without changing the tree.

The implementation has two parts. In the first part, we move a cursor down the tree to find the element that we are removing. To make the removal easier, we'll also maintain a variable called parentOfCursor, which usually refers to the parent of the cursor node. Once we find the target, there are several different cases for carrying out the actual removal. Here's the complete pseudocode:

public boolean remove(int target)

Start by setting up the cursor and parentOfCursor, which are both local IntBTNode variables. Initialize cursor to the root, and initialize parentOfCursor to null. Then move cursor down the tree until it either reaches the target or becomes null (meaning that the target is not in the tree). Also, whenever we are about to move the cursor downward, we will assign parentOfCursor = cursor . After moving the cursor, there are four possibilities:

1. The cursor could be null, indicating that the target was not in the tree. In this case, the method returns false with no further work.

2. The cursor could be at the root of the tree, but it has no left child. For example, we might be removing 45 from this tree:

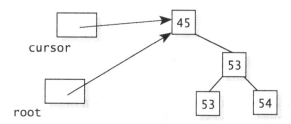

In this case, the 45 can be removed from the tree by moving the root rightward with the assignment root = root.getRight( ) . The result is:

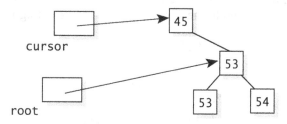

The node containing 45 still exists, but it is no longer part of the tree because it is not below the root. The method can return the value true to indicate that it found and removed the target. When the method does return, the local variable cursor will no longer be available, and Java's automatic garbage collection will eventually reuse the node that contains 45. The final tree without the 45 is shown here:

3. The cursor could be farther down the tree but still without a left child of its own. For example, we could be removing the 9 from this tree:

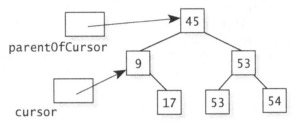

In this situation, we'll take one of the parent's links and shift it to the right child of the cursor. To be more specific, the link that connects the parent to the cursor node will be changed by this code:

```
if (cursor == parentOfCursor.getLeft( ))
{  // The cursor is on the left side of the parent,
   // so change parent's left link.
   parentOfCursor.setLeft( cursor.getRight( ) );
}
else
{  // The cursor is on the right side of the parent,
   // so change parent's right link.
   parentOfCursor.setRight( cursor.getRight( ) );
}
```

In our example, the cursor is on the left child of its parent, so we'll move the parent's left link down to the cursor's right child, resulting in this:

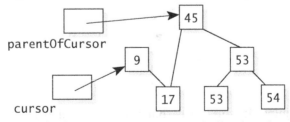

The method can now return `true`, indicating that it found and removed the target. When the method returns, the cursor is no longer available, and the node containing 9 will be garbage-collected, resulting in the final tree at the top of the next page.

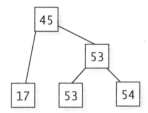

4. The cursor could be non-null and have a left child, so we can't simply ignore the left subtree of the cursor (as we did in cases 2 and 3). We could check whether there is a right child, and if not, we could have a plan that ignores the right subtree of the cursor—but we have a more general plan in mind. The plan is to find some element in the non-empty left subtree and move this element up to the cursor. But which element? Here's an example to help you figure out which element should be taken from the left subtree to replace the cursor's element. In this example, we are deleting 45 from this tree:

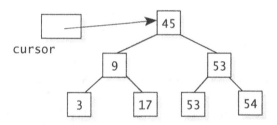

The plan is to replace the cursor's data with one of the three elements in the left subtree. Which of these elements can safely be moved to the cursor node? Not the 3 or 9, because a remaining element in the left subtree (the 17) would be larger than the new cursor (violating the Binary Search Tree Storage Rules). So we must select the 17 to move to the cursor node. The reason for this selection is that 17 is the largest element in the cursor's left subtree.

We'll actually carry out the movement in two steps. The first step is this statement:

```
cursor.setData(cursor.getLeft( ).getRightmostData( ));
```

This step sets the data in the cursor node to the rightmost element in the cursor's left subtree. The rightmost element in the cursor's left subtree is always the largest element in this subtree, so for our example, we now have the tree at the top of the next page.

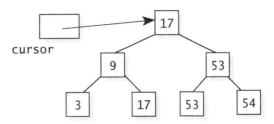

We have eliminated the 45, but we now have an extra copy of the 17. We must eliminate one of these extra 17s. We can do so with this statement:

```
cursor.setLeft(cursor.getLeft( ).removeRightmost( ));
```

This statement removes the rightmost node from the cursor's left subtree, and it sets the left link of the cursor to this new, smaller subtree. The end result is this tree:

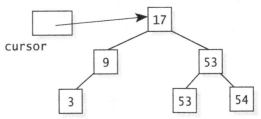

We're done with the pseudocode for the `remove` method. Case 4 was the most interesting step in the pseudocode. In this case, we had a node that was difficult to remove, so instead we found an easier node to remove (the rightmost node in the cursor's left subtree). We took the value from the "easy" node and copied this value on top of the element we wanted to remove. Then we removed the extra copy of the value that we copied (by removing the easy node).

By the way, you should check that Cases 2 and 3 also work correctly if the cursor happens to be a leaf. In Case 2, the pseudocode sets the root to null, indicating that we have just removed the final node from the tree. In Case 3, the pseudocode sets the parent's link to null, indicating that the parent no longer has a child on that side.

The addAll, addMany, and union Methods

The last three operations for the bag are the `addAll`, `addMany`, and `union` methods. The `addAll` method has this heading:

addAll

```
public void addAll(IntTreeBag addend)
```

When `b.addAll(c)` is activated, all the elements from the bag `c` are added to the bag `b`. This is an example of a method that will benefit from a private helper method. Private helper methods were described on page 386, and they may be used whenever there is a job to carry out, but you don't want other programmers to have access to the method that carries out the job. The helper method that we propose has this specification:

```
private void addTree(IntBTNode addroot)
// Precondition: addroot is a reference to the root of a binary search tree
// that is separate from the binary search tree of the bag that activated
// this method.
// Postcondition: All the elements from the addroot's binary search tree
// have been added to the binary search tree of the bag that activated this
// method.
```

Our intention is that this method is a new *private* method of the bag. Since the method is private, it won't be published for other programmers to use, and the specification can use private information, such as the fact that the bag is implemented with a binary search tree.

As a private method, the implementation of addTree must be placed with the other methods in the bag's implementation. The approach is to traverse the tree we are adding, putting a copy of each traversed element into the bag that activated the operator. For example, if we use a pre-order traversal, then the pseudocode for addTree is:

pseudocode for the private method addTree

```
if (addroot != null)
{
    add(addroot.getData( ));
    Make a recursive call to add all of addroot's left subtree.
    Make a recursive call to add all of addroot's right subtree.
}
```

Our pseudocode explicitly uses a pre-order traversal of the nodes. If you wish, you may use a post-order traversal instead. But avoid an in-order traversal. The problem with an in-order traversal is that the nodes of the added tree will be processed in order from smallest to largest. Therefore, these nodes will be added to the other bag from smallest to largest. This is a bad way to build a binary search tree. The resulting tree ends up with a single long, narrow path with only right children. Sometimes such long, narrow trees are hard to avoid. But do avoid such trees when you can because searching and other algorithms are inefficient when the trees lose their branching structure. In the next chapter, we will examine some specific ways to ensure that long, narrow trees are not created.

PITFALL

VIOLATING THE ADDTREE PRECONDITION

The specification of the addTree method indicates that the binary tree that is being added must be separate from the binary tree of the bag that activates the method. What goes wrong if we violate the precondition? An example can show the problem. For the example, suppose the binary search tree of a bag contains one element, the number 42, as shown next.

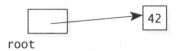

root

Now suppose we activate addTree with the parameter, addroot, being the same as root, as shown here:

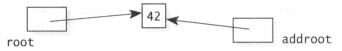

root   addroot

In this case, the first step of addTree will add a second copy of 42 to the tree, like this:

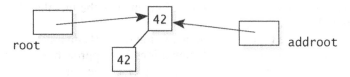

root   addroot

Now the second step of addTree makes a recursive call to add a copy of addroot's left subtree—but that left subtree has now changed from its original form (an empty tree) to a new, small subtree that contains 42. The consequence is that the recursive call adds another 42, makes another recursive call, and so on—an unbounded stream of 42s.

So, when we do use the private addTree method, we'll be careful to make sure that the parameter's tree is not the same as the bag's tree.

Implementing addAll

Here's the implementation of the public addAll method, using the private addTree:

```
public void addAll(IntTreeBag addend)
{
    IntBTNode addroot;

    if (root == addend.root)
    {   // addend is the same as the bag that activated this method.
        addroot = IntBTNode.treeCopy(addend.root);
        addTree(addroot);
    }
    else
        addTree(addend.root);
}
```

Notice that we do have a bit of complication when the addend is the same bag as the bag that activated the addAll method (as in the statement b.addAll(b)). In this case, we must make a second copy of the addend's tree and activate addTree, using the second copy rather than using the addend's tree directly. The reason for this complication is the restriction of addTree's precondition, which requires that the tree that's being added "is separate from the binary search tree of the bag that activated this method."

The union method is a static method with this heading:

the union method

```
public static IntTreeBag union(IntTreeBag b1, IntTreeBag b2)
```

This method's implementation can also use the addTree method. The answer bag should initially be empty. Then use answer.addTree to add the elements from b1, and use answer.addTree a second time to add the elements from b2.

Finally, the addMany method can be implemented by repeatedly calling the simpler add method.

Time Analysis and an Internal Iterator

With the descriptions we've given, you can put together the implementation file for the new bag. We'll carry out a time analysis of the operations after we've seen a few more trees (see Section 10.3).

You might also want to add methods that provide an internal or external iterator as described in Section 5.6. An iterator allows a programmer to step through the elements of the bag one at a time. One method for implementing an iterator utilizes a stack and is described in Programming Project 9 on page 519.

Self-Test Exercises for Section 9.5

18. Add a new method to the bag. The method should print all elements in the bag from smallest to largest. (Hint: Use a traversal.)

19. Write a static bag method called join with this heading:

```
public static void join(
    IntTreeBag top,
    IntTreeBag left,
    IntTreeBag right
)
```

The precondition of the method requires that top has just one element, that everything in left is less than or equal to the element in top, and that everything in right is greater than the element in top. The postcondition requires that top now contains its original element plus everything from left and right, and that left and right are now both empty. Your method should take constant time.

CHAPTER SUMMARY

- *Trees* are a nonlinear structure with many applications, including organizing information (such as taxonomy trees) and implementing an efficient version of the bag ADT (using binary search trees). The Programming Projects and the next chapter provide more examples of tree applications.

- Trees may be implemented with either arrays or dynamic data structures with nodes that contain references to other nodes. An array is particularly appropriate for *complete binary trees* because of the conditions that require the nodes of a complete tree to occur in specific locations.

- A *tree traversal* consists of processing a tree by applying some action to each node. Three common traversal methods—pre-order traversal, in-order traversal, and post-order traversal—differ only in the order in which the nodes are processed. A pre-order traversal with indentations is a quick and convenient way to print the data from a tree in a readable format.

- Binary search trees are one common application of trees that permit us to store a bag of ordered elements in a manner in which adding, removing, and searching for elements is potentially much faster than with a linear structure.

- Operations on trees are good candidates for recursive thinking. This is because many tree operations include a step to process one or more sub-trees, and this step is "a smaller version of the same problem."

? Solutions to Self-Test Exercises

1. Here is one possible solution:

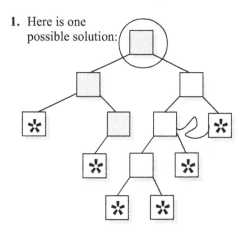

2. and 3. Here is a solution. The depth of this tree is three. The node containing "me!" has a depth of two. My ancestors are circled, and my mother's descendants have a big square around them.

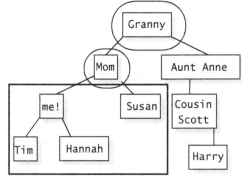

4. This solution is both full and complete. "Yes" answers move left and, "No" answers move right.

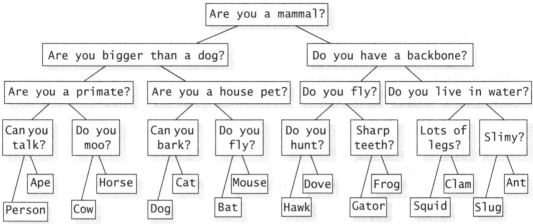

5. 512 leaves and 1023 nodes.

6. We use the formulas from page 461. The parent is stored at index 2499, which is (4999–1)/2. The left child is stored at index 9999, which is (2*4999)+1. If there were a right child, it would be stored at index 10,000 (which is (2*4999)+2). But since the last index is 9999, there is no right child.

7. A separate single reference variable is used to refer to the root node.

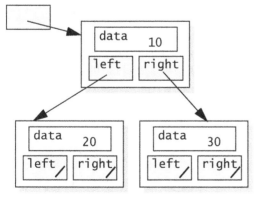

8.
```
public class TreeNode<E>
{ // The start of your definition:
    private E data;
    private TreeNode<E> parent;
    private TreeNode<E> links[ ];
```

9. See Figure 9.14 on page 516.

10. Here is one solution:
```
public int kids( )
// Postcondition: The return value is
// the number of children of this node.
{
    int answer = 0;
    if (left != null) answer++;
    if (right != null) answer++;
    return answer;
}
```

11. The node-counting method is `treeSize` from the bottom of Figure 9.10 on page 496. The depth method has a similar recursive implementation.

12. The in-order traversal prints O, L, R, A, G, T. The post-order traversal prints O, R, L, T, G, A.

13. This static method works correctly even when the parameter is the null reference:
```
public static <E> void pre
(BTNode<E> root)
{
    if (root != null)
    {
        System.out.println(root.data);
        pre(root.left);
        pre(root.right);
    }
}
```

FIGURE 9.14   The `learn` Method for the Solution to Self-Test Exercise 9

Implementation

```
public static void learn (BTNode<String> current)
// Precondition: current is a reference to a leaf in a taxonomy tree. This
// leaf contains a wrong guess that was just made.
// Postcondition: Information has been elicited from the user, and the tree
// has been improved.
{
    String guessAnimal;    // The animal that was just guessed
    String correctAnimal;  // The animal that the user was thinking of
    String newQuestion;    // A question to distinguish the two animals

    // Set Strings for the guessed animal, correct animal, and a new question.
    guessAnimal = current.getData( );
    System.out.println("I give up. What are you? ");
    correctAnimal = stdin.nextLine( );
    System.out.println("Please type a yes/no question that will distinguish a ");
    System.out.println(correctAnimal + " from a " + guessAnimal + ".");
    newQuestion = stdin.nextLine( );

    // Put the new question in the current node, and add two new children.
    current.setData(newQuestion);
    System.out.println("As a " + correctAnimal + ", " + newQuestion);
    if (query("Please answer"))
    {
        current.setLeft(new BTNode<String>(correctAnimal, null, null));
        current.setRight(new BTNode<String>(guessAnimal, null, null));
    }
    else
    {
        current.setLeft(new BTNode<String>(guessAnimal, null, null));
        current.setRight(new BTNode<String>(correctAnimal, null, null));
    }
}
```

14. This would be a post-order traversal. For in-order: 9, 13, 17, 53, 14, 19, 4, 7, 11. For pre-order: 14, 17, 9, 13, 53, 11, 4, 19, 7.

15. Pre-order: zero. Post-order: 3100. In-order: 3000.

16.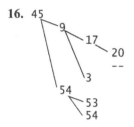

17. Pre-order would process a node before any of its children are processed. Post-order would process a node after all of its children are processed. In-order doesn't really make sense for a general tree.

18. For a non-empty bag, the body of your method should activate:
```
root.inorderPrint( );
```

19. The method needs four statements, as shown here:
```
top.root.setLeft(left.root);
left.root = null;
top.root.setRight(right.root);
right.root = null;
```

PROGRAMMING PROJECTS

1 This project deals with a simple kind of *expression tree*, in which there are two kinds of nodes:

(a) Leaf nodes, which contain a real number as their element;

(b) Non-leaf nodes, which contain either the character '+' or the character '*' as their element and have exactly two children.

For this project, implement a class for expression trees, including operations for building expression trees. Also include a recursive function to "evaluate" a non-empty expression tree using these rules:

(a) If the tree has only one node (which must be a leaf), then the evaluation of the tree returns the real number that is the node's element;

(b) If the tree has more than one node and the root contains '+', then first evaluate the left subtree, then evaluate the right subtree and add the results. If the root contains '*', then evaluate the two subtrees and multiply the results.

For example, consider the small expression tree shown to the right. The left subtree evaluates to 3+7, which is 10. The right subtree evaluates to 14. So the entire tree evaluates to 10*14, which is 140.

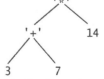

2 Specify, design, and implement a class for *complete* binary trees using the array representation from Section 9.2. You should have only one method that adds a new node (since there is only one place where a node may be added) and one method that removes the last node of the tree.

3 Specify, design, and implement a class for binary trees where the node's elements are stored in an array, similar to the way that a complete binary tree is usually stored. However, these binary trees do not need to be complete. Instead, you should have a second private instance variable that is an array of boolean values called isPresent. The isPresent array indicates which nodes actually exist in the tree. For example, if the tree has a root node, then isPresent[0] is true. If the root has a left child, then isPresent[1] is true. If the root has a right child, then isPresent[2] is true, and so on.

The class should have methods to create the first node and to move a cursor around the tree. After the first node, new nodes may be added only as children of the cursor.

4 Revise the animal-guessing program from Figure 9.8 on page 482 so that the initial knowledge tree is obtained by reading information from a file. Also, when the program ends, the knowledge tree at that point is written to the same file. You must carefully specify the format of the data in this file. The format should make it easy to do two things: (a) read the file and set the initial tree, and (b) write the knowledge tree to the file, using some kind of traversal.

5 This project requires that you know how to determine the actual time taken for a method to execute. Write a test program for the bag class from Section 9.5. The program should allow the user to specify an integer *n*. The program then adds *n* randomly selected integers to a bag and counts the number of occurrences of each integer between 1 and *n*, keeping track of the amount of time needed for the entirety of these operations. Also use the test program to test one of the earlier bag implementations. Graph the results of your tests on a plot that has elapsed time on the *y*-axis and *n* on the *x*-axis. (In the next chapter, we will do an analysis to explain these times.)

6 Implement a new method for the BTNode from Figure 9.10 on page 490. The new method creates a Java Vector that contains the data from all the nodes in a tree, as specified in Figure 9.15. Details about the Java Vector class are provided in Appendix D, although the only Vector method you'll use is addElement.

Also specify and implement similar methods that use in-order and post-order traversals instead of a pre-order traversal. Which of your three new methods creates a Vector with the entries sorted from smallest to largest?

7 Binary search trees have their best performance when they are *balanced*, which means that at each node *n*, the size of the left subtree of *n* is within one of the size of the right subtree of *n*. Write a static method that takes a sorted array of integers and produces a balanced binary search tree. (The array is sorted with smallest integers at the front and largest at the end.)

If useful, you can add extra parameters to the method, such as the total number of entries in the list. Hint: First build the left subtree of the root, then the right subtree of the root, then put the pieces to-

---

FIGURE 9.15   Method to Copy Data from the Nodes of a Binary Tree to a Java Vector

Specification

◆ **preorderVector (for the BTNode<E>)**
   `public void preorderVector(Vector<E> v)`
   The method does a pre-order traversal of all nodes at or below this node, appending the data from each node to a Vector.

   Parameter:
   v – the Vector that will have data appended to it

   Precondition:
   v is not null.

   Postcondition:
   The node and all its descendants have been traversed with a pre-order traversal, and all data has been appended to v using v.addElement.

   Throws: NullPointerException
   Indicates that v is null.

   Throws: OutOfMemoryError
   Indicates that there is insufficient memory for the Vector's append method to add a new element to the Vector.

gether with the `join` method from Self-Test Exercise 19 on page 513.

As an alternative, you can have the integer data come from a Java `Vector` rather than an array.

9 An *internal iterator* for a bag is a collection of methods that allows a programmer to step through the elements of a bag one at a time. For example, we might have an internal iterator consisting of four methods: `start`, `advance`, `isCurrent`, and `getCurrent`. The `start` method initializes the internal iterator; the `isCurrent` method is a boolean method that tells whether the iterator has a specified current element that can be retrieved with the `getCurrent` method; and the `advance` method moves the iterator to its next element.

For this project, add an internal iterator to the bag from Section 9.5. The implementation technique is to use a private instance variable called `s`. The instance variable `s` is a stack of references to nodes.

Each of the elements in the stack refers to a node whose element has not yet been processed by the internal iterator. The current element of the internal iterator is always in the node at the top of the stack. The pseudocode for the internal iterator methods is given here:

The `start` method: Clear the stack. For an empty tree, there is no more work. For a non-empty tree, do an in-order traversal of the tree's nodes, pushing a reference to each node onto the stack.

The `isCurrent` method: Return `true` if the stack is nonempty.

The `getCurrent` method: Check the precondition (the stack must be non-empty). Then peek at the top node on the stack (without removing it). Return the data element from this node.

The `advance` method: Check the precondition (the stack must be non-empty). Then pop the top node off the stack.

Changing the bag by adding or removing elements should invalidate the internal iterator (by clearing the stack).

When the internal iterator is started, use an in-order traversal to push node references onto the stack. As you pop the stack, these references come off in reverse order so that the iterator will advance through the elements from largest to smallest. If you

prefer a smallest-to-largest order, you could use a queue instead of a stack.

10 Write a class for a bag of strings, where the strings are stored in a binary search tree. In creating the binary search tree, you should use the string's `compareTo` method, which is described on page 499. The tree itself should use the BTNode class from Figure 9.10 on page 490.

11 Java has a generic interface called `Comparable<E>`. A class that implements the `Comparable` interface must have a method with this specification:

♦ **compareTo**

> `public boolean compareTo(E obj)`
> Compare this object to another object of the same type.

Returns:

> The return value is zero if this object is equal to `obj`; the return value is negative if this object is smaller than `obj`; the return value is positive if this object is larger than `obj`.

Throws: `ClassCastException`

> Indicates that `obj` is the wrong type of object to be compared with this object.

Write a generic class for a bag of `Comparable<E>` objects, where the objects are stored in a binary search tree. The tree itself should use the BTNode class from Figure 9.10 on page 490.

The first line of your new bag class should be:

```
public class ComparableTreeBag
<E extends Comparable<E>>
```

This tells the Java compiler that the `Comparable-TreeBag` is a generic class, but that any instantiation of the generic type parameter E must implement the `Comparable<E>` interface.

12 Expand the class from Project 10 or 11 so that there is an extra method that produces a Java `Iterator` for the bag. (The Java `Iterator` interface is discussed in Section 5.6.)

Tree Projects

LEARNING OBJECTIVES

When you complete Chapter 10, you will be able to ...

- list the rules for a heap or B-tree and determine whether a tree satisfies these rules.
- insert a new element into a heap or remove the largest element by following the insertion algorithm (with reheapification upward) and the removal algorithm (with reheapification downward)
- do a simulation by hand of the algorithms for searching, inserting, and removing an element from a B-tree.
- use the heap data structure to implement a priority queue.
- use the B-tree data structure to implement a set class.
- use Java's `DefaultMutableTreeNode` and `JTree` classes in simple programs that use trees.
- recognize which operations have logarithmic worst-case performance on balanced trees.

CHAPTER CONTENTS

Tree Projects

The great, dark trees of the Big Woods stood all around the house, and
beyond them were other trees and beyond them were more trees.

LAURA INGALLS WILDER
The Little House in the Big Woods

T his chapter outlines two programming projects involving trees. The projects are improvements of classes that we've seen before: the priority queue (Section 7.4) and the set (which is like a bag but does not allow more than one copy of an element). Both projects take advantage of *balanced* trees, in which the different subtrees below a node are guaranteed to have nearly the same height. We also discuss Java support for trees and analyze the time performance of tree algorithms, concentrating on a connection between trees and logarithms and explaining the advantages obtained from balanced trees.

10.1 HEAPS

Priority queues were introduced in Section 7.4 as a variation of an ordinary queue in which entries are given priority numbers that are used to determine which entries exit the queue first. This section describes a data structure called a heap that has many applications, including an efficient implementation of a priority queue.

The Heap Storage Rules

A **heap** is a binary tree in which the elements can be compared with each other using *total order semantics*. As we've seen before (Figure 9.11 on page 498), a total order semantics means that all the elements in the class can be placed in a single line, proceeding from smaller to larger along the line. In this way, a heap is similar to a *binary search tree*, but the arrangement of the elements in a heap follows some new rules that are different from a binary search tree:

Heap Storage Rules

If the elements of a set can be compared with a total order semantics, then these elements can be stored in a heap. A **heap** is a binary tree in which these two rules are followed:

1. The element contained by each node is greater than or equal to the elements of that node's children.

2. The tree is a complete binary tree, so that every level except the deepest must contain as many nodes as possible; at the deepest level, all the nodes are as far left as possible (see "Complete Binary Trees" on page 457).

As an example, suppose elements are integers. Of the three trees shown next, only one is a heap—which one?

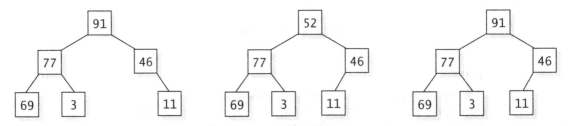

The tree on the left is not a heap, because it is not complete; a complete tree must have the nodes on the bottom level as far left as possible. The middle tree is not a heap, because one of the nodes (containing 52) has a value that is smaller than its child (which contains 77). The tree on the right *is* a heap.

implement heaps with a fixed array or with an array that grows and shrinks

A heap could be implemented with the binary tree nodes from the classes of Chapter 9. But wait! A heap is a *complete* binary tree, and a complete binary tree is more easily implemented with an array than with the node class (see the section "Array Representation of Complete Binary Trees" on page 459). If we know the maximum size of a heap in advance, then the array implementation can use an array with a single fixed size. If we are uncertain about the heap's maximum size, then the array can grow and shrink as needed.

In Self-Test Exercise 2 on page 527, you'll be asked to write definitions that would support the array implementation of a heap. The rest of this section will show how heaps can be used to implement an efficient priority queue; we won't worry much about the exact implementation.

The Priority Queue Class with Heaps

Priority queues were introduced in Section 7.4. A priority queue behaves much like an ordinary queue: Elements are placed in the queue and later taken out. But unlike in an ordinary queue, each element in a priority queue has an associated number called its priority. When elements leave a priority queue, the highest-priority elements always leave first. We have already seen one implementation of a priority queue using the specification from Figure 7.12 on page 401. Now we'll give an alternative implementation that uses the same specification of methods but uses a heap as the underlying data structure to store the queue's elements.

an alternative way to implement priority queues

In the heap implementation of a priority queue, each node of the heap contains one element along with the element's priority, and the tree is maintained so that it follows the heap storage rules using the elements' priorities to compare nodes. Therefore:

1. The element contained by each node has a priority that is greater than or equal to the priorities of the elements of that node's children.

2. The tree is a complete binary tree.

We'll focus on two priority queue operations: adding a new element (along with its priority) and removing the element with the highest priority. In both operations, we must ensure that the structure remains a heap when the operation concludes. Also, both operations can be described without worrying about precisely how we've implemented the underlying heap.

Adding an Element to a Heap

Let's start with the operation that adds a new element. As an example, suppose we already have nine elements that are arranged in a heap with the following priorities:

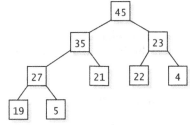

In this diagram, we have shown only the elements' priorities. In an actual priority queue, each element would also have some additional data in each node.

Suppose we are adding a new element with a priority of 42. The first step is to add this element in a way that keeps the binary tree complete. In this case, the new element will be the left child of the node with priority 21:

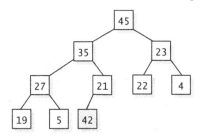

add the new element in a way that keeps the binary tree complete

But now the structure is no longer a heap since the node with priority 21 has a child with a higher priority. The algorithm fixes this problem by causing the new element (with priority 42) to rise upward until it reaches an acceptable location. This is accomplished by swapping the new element with its parent:

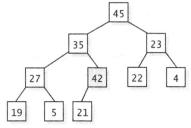

| **FIGURE 10.1** | Adding an Element to a Priority Queue |

Pseudocode for Adding an Element

The priority queue has been implemented as a heap.

1. Place the new element in the heap in the first available location. This keeps the structure as a complete binary tree, but it might no longer be a heap since the new element might have a higher priority than its parent.

2. `while` (the new element has a higher priority than its parent)
   Swap the new element with its parent.

Notice that the process in Step 2 will stop when the new element reaches the root or when the new element's parent has a priority that is at least as high as the new element's priority.

The new element is *still* bigger than its parent, so a second swap is done:

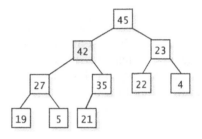

reheapification upward

Now the new element stops rising because its parent (with priority 45) has a higher priority than the new element. In general, the "new element rising" stops when the new element has a parent with a higher or equal priority or when the new element reaches the root. The rising process is called **reheapification upward**.

The steps for adding an element are outlined in Figure 10.1. Some of the details depend on how the underlying heap is implemented. For example, if the heap is implemented with a nongrowing array, then the first step must check that there is room for a new element. With an array that grows, the first step might need to increase the size of the array.

Removing an Element from a Heap

When an element is removed from a priority queue, we must always remove the element with the highest priority—the element that stands "on top of the heap." For example, consider this heap of 10 priorities:

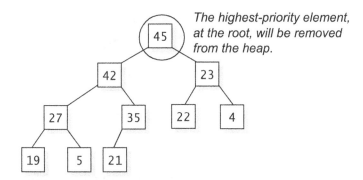

The element at the root, with priority 45, will be removed, and this is the element that is returned by the operation. But here we are ignoring a potential problem: There might be several elements with the highest priority. As described in Section 7.4, when several elements have equal priority, the elements should exit the priority queue in first-in/first-out (FIFO) order. Our adding and deleting mechanisms do not provide a way to determine which of several elements arrived first. So, in this discussion, we will suspend the requirement that elements with equal priority be treated in FIFO order. We will address this problem in Programming Project 1 on page 566.

The problem of removing the root from a heap remains. During the removal, we must ensure that the resulting structure remains a heap. If the root is the only element in the heap, then there is really no more work to do except to decrement the instance variable that is keeping track of the size of the heap. But if there are other elements in the tree, then the tree must be rearranged because a heap is not allowed to run around without a root. The rearrangement begins by moving the last element in the last level up to the root, like this:

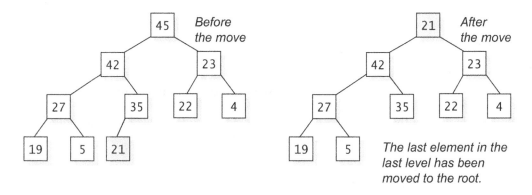

The structure is now a complete tree, but it is not a heap, because the root is smaller than its children. To fix this, we can swap the root with its larger child, as shown here:

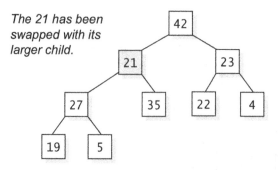

The 21 has been swapped with its larger child.

The structure is not yet a heap, so again we swap the out-of-place node with its larger child, giving us this tree:

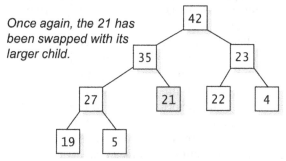

Once again, the 21 has been swapped with its larger child.

reheapification downward

At this point, the node that has been sinking has reached a leaf, so we can stop and the structure is a heap. The process would also stop when the sinking node no longer has a child with a higher priority. This process, called **reheapification downward**, is summarized in Figure 10.2.

FIGURE 10.2   Removing an Element from a Priority Queue

Pseudocode for Removing an Element

The priority queue has been implemented as a heap.

1. Copy the element at the root of the heap to the variable used to return a value.

2. Copy the last element in the deepest level to the root, and then take this last node out of the tree. This element is called the "out-of-place" element.

3. while (the out-of-place element has a priority that is lower than one of its children)
       Swap the out-of-place element with its highest-priority child.

4. Return the answer that was saved in Step 1.

Notice that the process in Step 3 will stop when the out-of-place element reaches a leaf or when the out-of-place element has a priority that is at least as high as its children.

Heaps have many other impressive applications, including collision detection in programs to simulate atomic particles, hidden surface removal in graphics programs, and a sorting algorithm that is discussed in Chapter 12.

Self-Test Exercises for Section 10.1

1. The most appropriate way to implement a heap is with an array rather than a linked structure. Why?
2. Define the instance variables for a Java class that would be appropriate for a priority queue implemented as a heap. Each node should have an integer priority and a piece of data that is a Java Object.
3. In the description of reheapification downward, we specified that the out-of-place element must be swapped with the larger of its two children. What goes wrong if we swap with the smaller child instead?
4. Start with an empty heap and enter 10 elements with priorities 1 through 10. Draw the resulting heap.
5. Remove three elements from the heap you created in the previous exercise. Draw the resulting heap.

10.2 B-TREES

Binary search trees were used in Section 9.5 to implement a bag ADT, but the efficiency of binary search trees can go awry. This section explains the potential problem and shows one way to fix it.

The Problem of Unbalanced Trees

Let's create a troublesome binary search tree of integers. The first number is 1, and then we add 2, 3, 4, and 5 in that order. The result appears in Figure 10.3(a). Perhaps you've spotted the problem. Suppose next we add 6, 7, 8, 9, and 10 in that order, ending up with Figure 10.3(b). The problem is that the levels of the tree are only sparsely filled, resulting in long, deep paths and defeating the purpose of binary trees in the first place. For example, if we are searching Figure 10.3(b) for the number 12, then we'll end up looking at every node in the tree. In effect, we are no better off

FIGURE 10.3 Two Troublesome Search Trees

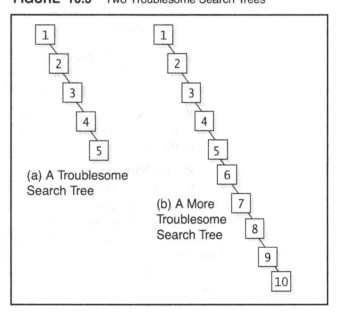

(a) A Troublesome Search Tree

(b) A More Troublesome Search Tree

than when we used the linked list implementation. Similar problems arise for adding and deleting elements.

The problem has several possible solutions, all of which involve trees in which the depth of the leaves remains small. For example, one solution is to balance the search trees periodically, as described in Programming Project 7 in Chapter 9 (page 518). Another solution uses a particular kind of tree called a B-tree, where leaves cannot become too deep (relative to the number of nodes). These trees were proposed by R. Bayer and E. M. McCreight in 1972 (see "Organization and Maintenance of Large Ordered Indexes" in *Acta Informatica,* Volume 1, Number 3 [1972], pages 173–189). The rest of this section discusses a B-tree implementation.

The B-Tree Rules

B-trees are <u>not</u> binary trees

A B-tree is a special kind of tree, similar to a binary search tree, where each node holds elements of some type. As with binary search trees, the implementation requires the ability to compare two elements via a total order semantics. But a B-tree is not a binary search tree; in fact, a B-tree is not even a *binary* tree, because *B-tree nodes have many more than two children.* Another important property of B-trees is that *each node contains more than just a single element.* The rules for a B-tree make it easy to search for a specified element, and the rules also ensure that leaves do not become too deep.

B-tree rules may be formulated for either a bag or a set

The precise B-tree rules may be formulated so that the B-tree stores a bag of elements similar to the bag implementations we have seen before. Alternatively, a B-tree may be formulated to store a *set* of elements. The difference between a set and a bag is that a given element can occur many times in a bag but only once in a set. We'll look at the set formulation of the B-tree rules, but keep in mind that a bag formulation is also possible.

The Elements in a B-Tree Node. Every B-tree depends on a positive constant integer called MINIMUM. The purpose of the constant is to determine how many elements are held in a single node, as shown in the first two B-tree rules:

> **B-Tree Rule 1:** The root can have as few as one element (or even no elements if it also has no children); every other node has at least MINIMUM elements.

> **B-Tree Rule 2:** The maximum number of elements in a node is twice the value of MINIMUM.

Although MINIMUM may be as small as 1, in practice much larger values are used—perhaps several hundred or even a couple thousand.

The many elements of a B-tree node are stored in an array so that we can talk about "the element at index 0" or "the element at index 1" and so on. Within the array, the elements must be sorted from smallest to largest. This provides our third B-tree rule:

B-Tree Rule 3: The elements of each B-tree node are stored in a partially filled array, sorted from the smallest element (at index 0) to the largest element (at the final used position of the array).

The Subtrees below a B-Tree Node. The number of subtrees below a node depends on how many elements are in the node. Here is the rule:

B-Tree Rule 4: The number of subtrees below a non-leaf node is always one more than the number of elements in the node.

For example, suppose a node has 42 elements. This node will have 43 children. We will refer to the many subtrees of a node from left to right as "subtree number 0, subtree number 1, ..." and so on, up to the last subtree.

The elements in each subtree are organized in a way that makes it easy to search the B-tree for any given element. Here is the rule for that organization:

B-Tree Rule 5: For any non-leaf node: (a) An element at index i is greater than all the elements in subtree number i of the node, and (b) an element at index i is less than all the elements in subtree number $i + 1$ of the node.

Let's look at an example to illustrate Rules 4 and 5. Suppose a non-leaf node contains two integer elements, the numbers 93 and 107. This node must have three subtrees, organized as follows:

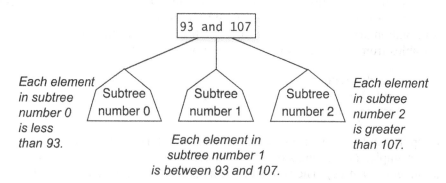

A B-Tree Is Balanced. The final B-tree rule ensures that a B-tree avoids the problem of an unbalanced tree:

B-tree Rule 6: Every leaf in a B-tree has the same depth.

An Example B-Tree

As another example, here is a complete B-tree of 10 integers (with MINIMUM set to 1). Can you verify that all six B-tree rules are satisfied?

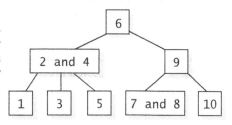

The Set Class with B-Trees

The rest of this section discusses the algorithms for implementing a set class using B-trees. For concreteness, the elements in our set are integers, but we could use any data type that can be ordered from smallest to largest. The class, called `IntBalancedSet`, has public methods for adding and removing elements and also for checking whether a given element is in the set. As you can see in our complete specification (Figure 10.4), the class also implements the `Cloneable` interface so that a programmer can make a clone of a set.

Figure 10.4 also provides an outline of the implementation. Let's examine the private instance variables that are used in this outline. The set class has two constants, shown here with a selection of 200 for `MINIMUM`:

```
private static final MINIMUM = 200;
private static final MAXIMUM = 2 * MINIMUM;
```

two private constants of the set

These constants are *private* because a programmer who *uses* the set class does not need to know about their existence. Access to these private values is needed only by the programmer who *implements* the set class. When you are actually implementing and testing the class, it's better to use smaller constants, perhaps `MINIMUM=1`. After debugging, you can increase `MINIMUM` and recompile.

After the declaration of the private constants, the set class has four private instance variables. The purpose of these four instance variables is to store all the information about the root node of the B-tree. Here are the first three instance variables from the set class in Figure 10.4 on page 531:

instance variables store information about the root of the B-tree

```
int dataCount;
int[ ] data = new int[MAXIMUM + 1];
int childCount;
```

Keep in mind that the instance variables store information about the *root* node. For example, dataCount stores the number of elements in the B-tree's root (not in the entire B-tree). The root's elements are stored in the partially filled array called data, ranging from data[0] through data[dataCount-1]. The complete size of the data array is MAXIMUM + 1, which allows space for one extra element beyond the usual maximum number. You'll see the benefit of this extra space when we discuss the implementations of the set's methods.

The number of children of the root node is stored in the instance variable childCount. The children of the root have an important property that will allow us to use *recursive thinking* in our implementations. Here is the property you should burn into your memory:

> Every child of the root node is also the root of a smaller B-tree.

(text continues on page 533)

FIGURE 10.4   The Set of Integers

Class IntBalancedSet

❖ **public class IntBalancedSet from the package edu.colorado.collections**
    An `IntBalancedSet` is a set of `int` numbers, stored in a B-tree.

Specification

◆ **Constructor for the IntBalancedSet**
    `public IntBalancedSet( )`
    Initialize an empty set.
    Postcondition:
        This set is empty.
    Throws: `OutOfMemoryError`
        Indicates insufficient memory for creating the set.

◆ **add**
    `public void add(int element)`
    Add a new element to this set.
    Parameter:
        `element` – the new element being added
    Postcondition:
        If the element was already in this set, then there is no change. Otherwise, the element has been added to this set.
    Throws: `OutOfMemoryError`
        Indicates insufficient memory for adding a new element.

◆ **clone**
    `public IntBalancedSet clone( )`
    Generate a copy of this set.
    Returns:
        The return value is a copy of this set. Subsequent changes to the copy will not affect the original, nor vice versa. The return value must be typecast to an `IntBalancedSet` before it is used.
    Throws: `OutOfMemoryError`
        Indicates insufficient memory for creating the clone.

(continued)

(FIGURE 10.4 continued)

♦ contains

```
public boolean contains(int target)
```

Accessor method to determine whether a particular element is in this set.

Parameter:

target – an element that may or may not be in this set

Postcondition:

true (if target is in this set) or false (if target is not in this set).

♦ remove

```
public boolean remove(int target)
```

Remove a specified element from this set.

Parameter:

target – the element to remove from this set

Postcondition:

If target was found in this set, then it has been removed and the method returns true. Otherwise, this set remains unchanged and the method returns false.

Implementation (outline)

```
//  FILE: IntBalancedSet.java from the package edu.colorado.collections
//  Documentation is available at the top of this figure or from the IntBalancedSet link at
//  http://www.cs.colorado.edu/~main/docs/.

package edu.colorado.collections;

public class IntBalancedSet implements Cloneable
{
    // INVARIANT for the IntBalancedSet ADT:
    //    1. The elements of the Set are stored in a B-tree, satisfying the six B-tree rules.
    //    2. The number of elements in the tree's root is in the instance variable dataCount, and
    //       the number of subtrees of the root is stored in the instance variable childCount.
    //    3. The root's elements are stored in data[0] through data[dataCount-1].
    //    4. If the root has subtrees, then subtree[0] through subtree[childCount-1] are
    //       references to these subtrees.
    private static final int MINIMUM = 200;
    private static final int MAXIMUM = 2*MINIMUM;
    int dataCount;
    int[ ] data = new int[MAXIMUM + 1];
    int childCount;
    IntBalancedSet[ ] subset = new IntBalancedSet[MAXIMUM + 2];
```

> You may implement the public methods here. The programmer who implements the class may wish to add further private methods, which are discussed in the text.

```
}
```

Let's look at an example to illustrate the rule "Every child of the root node is also the root of a smaller B-tree." For the example, consider the following B-tree (with MINIMUM equal to 1):

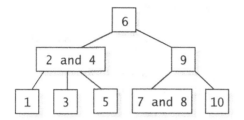

The root of this B-tree has two children, and each of these children is also the root of a smaller B-tree. These two smaller B-trees are clearly shown here:

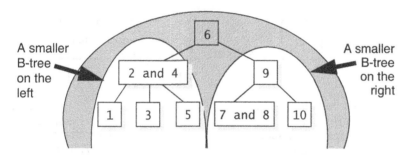

Each of the smaller B-trees also contains a set of elements. We will call these two smaller sets "subset number 0" and "subset number 1." If there were more children, we would continue with "subset number 2," and so on. The last subset is "subset number childCount-1."

Now consider how to store the subsets. The best solution is to store each subset as *an actual* IntBalancedSet *object*. In the root node itself, we will store *references* to these smaller IntBalancedSet objects. These references are stored in the fourth instance variable of the set class, declared here:

```
IntBalancedSet[ ] subset = new IntBalancedSet[MAXIMUM+2];
```

The instance variable subset is a partially filled array of references to smaller subsets. It is able to hold up to MAXIMUM + 2 such references—which is one more than the maximum number of children that a B-tree node may have. As with the elements, the benefit of this "space for one extra" will become evident shortly.

As an example, suppose a B-tree root has two children. Then subset[0] is a reference to "subset number 0," and subset[1] is a reference to "subset number 1." With this in mind, let's again consider the B-tree shown here:

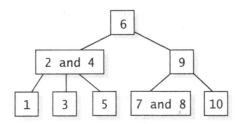

The root contains one element and two children, so the instance variables of the set object for this B-tree will look like this:

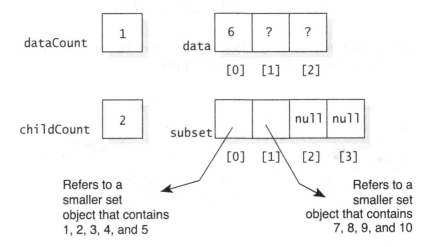

The important idea is that each `subset[i]` is a reference to another `IntBalancedSet` object. We will be able to use all of the `IntBalancedSet` methods with these objects in various recursive calls. Here is the complete invariant for our `IntBalancedSet` class:

Invariant for the Set ADT Implemented with a B-Tree

1. The elements of the set are stored in a B-tree, satisfying the six B-tree rules.

2. The number of elements in the tree's root is stored in the instance variable `dataCount`, and the number of subtrees of the root is stored in the instance variable `childCount`.

3. The root's elements are stored in `data[0]` through `data[dataCount-1]`.

4. If the root has subtrees, then `subset[0]` through `subset[childCount-1]` are references to these subtrees.

Searching for an Element in a B-Tree

The set class has a method, `contains`, that determines whether an element called `target` appears in the set. Searching for an element in a B-tree follows the same idea as searching for an element in a binary search tree, although there's more work needed to handle nodes that contain many elements instead of just one. The basic idea: Start with the entire B-tree, checking to see whether the target is in the root. If the target does appear in the root, the search is done— the method can return `true` to indicate that it found the target. A second possibility is that the target is not in the root and the root has no children. In this case, the search is also done—the method can return `false` to indicate that the target is not in the set. The final possibility is that the target is not in the root, but there are subtrees below. In this case, there is only one possible subtree where the target can appear, so the method makes a recursive call to search that one subtree for the target.

The entire method can benefit from one preliminary step, shown as the first step of this pseudocode:

// Searching for a target in a set

1. Make a local variable, `i`, equal to the first index such that `data[i] >= target`. If there is no such index, then set `i` equal to `dataCount`, indicating that none of the elements is greater than or equal to the target.

2. `if` (we found the target at `data[i]`)
        `return true;`
   `else if` (the root has no children)
        `return false;`
   `else`
        `return subset[i].contains(target);`

Be careful how you test the condition at the start of Step 2. To "find the target at `data[i]`," you must ensure that `i < dataCount` and that the target is actually equal to `data[i]`.

The recursive call in the pseudocode is highlighted. The recursive call works well in this situation because the subset is *smaller* than the entire set. Thus, the recursive call is solving a *smaller* version of the original problem.

As an example of executing the pseudocode, suppose we are searching for 10 in the following B-tree:

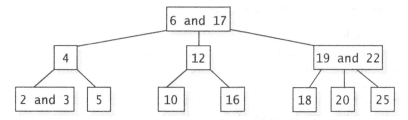

The search begins by finding the first element in the root that is greater than or equal to the target 10. This is the element 17, which occurs at data[1] in the root, so Step 1 sets i to the index 1. In Step 2, we notice that we have not found the target at data[1], but the root does have children. So we make a recursive call, searching subtree number 1 for the target 10. You can visualize the recursive call subtree[1].contains(10) as searching for a 10 in this part of this tree:

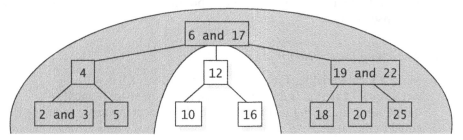

The recursive call of the contains method has its own copy of the local variable i. This variable i is set to 0 in Step 1 of the recursive call (since data[0] of the subtree is greater than or equal to the target 10). Again, we have not found the target, so the recursion continues, activating the contains method for the still smaller subtree shown here:

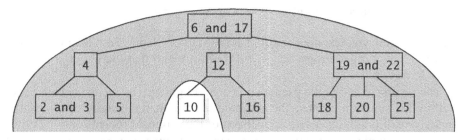

The recursive call finds the target, returning true to the previous recursive call. That previous recursive call then returns true to the original call, and the original call can also return true, indicating that the target was found somewhere in the set.

There are several parts of the pseudocode for you to clarify in your implementation. How do you determine whether the target was found at data[i]? How do you determine whether the root has children? The implementation of the first step of the pseudocode is smoother if you first implement a private method along these lines:

```
private int firstGE(int target)
// Postcondition: The return value x is the first location in the root such
//   that data[x] >= target. If there is no such location, then the return value
//   is dataCount.
```

PROGRAMMING TIP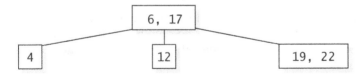

PRIVATE METHODS TO SIMPLIFY IMPLEMENTATIONS

Carefully selected private methods can simplify the implementations of other methods. You should write a specification for each private method, but these specifications do not need to be published for other programmers to see. Also, since the method is private, its specification can use information that only you know, such as the way that private instance variables are used.

Adding an Element to a B-Tree

The add method of the set class adds a new element to the B-tree. It is easier to add a new element to a B-tree if we relax one of the B-tree rules. In particular, we will allow a somewhat "loose addition" method to complete its work with the possibility that there is one element too many in the root node of the B-tree. In other words, a loose addition might result in MAXIMUM + 1 elements in the root. For example, consider this B-tree where MAXIMUM is 2:

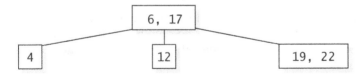

Suppose we want to add 18 to the tree. The end result of a loose addition could be the following illegal B-tree:

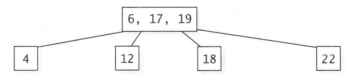

The B-tree is illegal because the root node has three elements, which is one more than the value of MAXIMUM. Notice that *only the root* may have an extra element after the "loose addition." Our plan is for the add method to begin by activating a private method that carries out a loose addition. After the loose addition, the usual add method will examine the root node. If the root node has too many elements, then the add method will fix that problem in a way that we'll describe later. For now, though, we'll turn our attention to the design of the loose addition method.

The Loose Addition Operation for a B-Tree

As discussed in the previous section, you can design a specification for a loose addition. The method will be a private method called looseAdd. The specification is given here:

```
private void looseAdd(int element)
// Precondition: The entire B-tree is valid.
// Postcondition: If the element was already in this set, then this set is
// unchanged. Otherwise, the element has been added to this set, and the
// entire B-tree is still valid EXCEPT that the number of elements in the root
// of this set might be one more than the allowed maximum.
```

Since this is a *private* method, it may violate the usual invariant for the set ADT. As you can see, the precondition does satisfy the usual invariant, but the postcondition allows for a violation of the invariant. This precondition/postcondition contract will not appear in the set's documentation. It is present only in the implementation file as an aid to the programmer who implements the class.

The first step of our approach for the loose addition is identical to the first step of the searching method. This step finds the first location in the root's data that is greater than or equal to the new element. Once we have this location, there are three possibilities listed in Step 2 of the pseudocode:

```
// Pseudocode for the looseAdd method
```

1. Make a local variable, i, equal to the first index such that data[i] >= element. If there is no such index, then set i equal to dataCount, indicating that none of the elements is greater than or equal to the target.

2. if (we found the new element at data[i])

pseudocode for the looseAdd method

2a. Return with no further work (since the new element is already in the set and we may not have two copies of the same element).

else if (the root has no children)

2b. Add the new element to the root at data[i]. (The original elements at data[i] and afterward must be shifted right to make room for the new element.)

else

{   2c.

subset[i].looseAdd(element);

If the root of subset[i] now has an excess element, then fix that problem before returning.

}

Looking through the pseudocode, Steps 2a and 2b are fairly easy. You already have a private method for Step 2a (firstGE on page 537), and you can write another private method for Step 2b. The more interesting work occurs in Step 2c, where we have not found the new element, nor are we ready to add the new element. In this case, we make a recursive call to do a loose addition of the new element in the appropriate subset. Since the recursive call is a *loose* addition, we may end up with one excess element in the root of our subset. This excess element must be dealt with before returning because the postcondition does not allow subsets to have nodes with extra elements.

As an example of executing the pseudocode, suppose we are making a loose addition of 18 into this B-tree (with MAXIMUM set to 2):

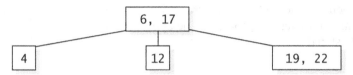

Step 1 of the pseudocode finds the first element in the root that is greater than or equal to the new element 18. As you see, none of the root elements is greater than or equal to 18, so what does Step 1 do instead? From the pseudocode, you see that the index i will be set to 2 (the number of elements in the root node).

In Step 2, we notice that we have not found the new element in the root, nor are we at a leaf. So we proceed to Step 2c, making a recursive call to add 18 to subtree number 2, as shown here:

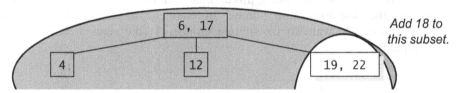

Add 18 to this subset.

The recursive call finds a small subtree with just a root. Following Step 2b, the recursive call adds the number 18 into the root of the subtree and then returns. After the recursive call returns, the entire tree looks like this:

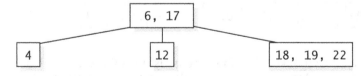

When the recursive call returns, we carry out the rest of Step 2c, checking whether the root of the subtree now has too many elements. Indeed, the root of subset[2] now has three elements, which is one more than the allowed maximum. We must fix this problem child, but how? It seems that fixing the child may take quite a bit of work, so we will propose another private method to carry out this work.

A Private Method to Fix an Excess in a Child

Here's the specification for the private method we have in mind:

```
private void fixExcess(int i)
// Precondition: (i < childCount) and the entire B-tree is valid EXCEPT that
// subset[i] has MAXIMUM + 1 elements.
// Postcondition: The tree has been rearranged so that the entire B-tree is
// valid EXCEPT that the number of elements in the root of this set might be
// one more than the allowed maximum.
```

Looking at the specification, you can see that the method starts with a problem child. When the method finishes, the child no longer has a problem, although the *root* may now have a problem. The approach of the fixExcess method can be simply stated:

Fixing a Child with an Excess Element

To fix a child with MAXIMUM + 1 elements, the child node is split into two nodes that each contain MINIMUM elements. This leaves one extra element, which is passed up to the parent.

Let's examine an example of this approach. In the example, suppose MINIMUM is 2 so that the maximum number of elements in a node is 4 (which is 2*MINIMUM). We want to fix subtree number 1 (the shaded subtree) in this example tree:

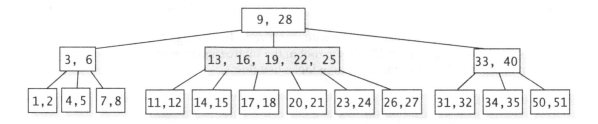

The approach taken by fixExcess is to split the problem node (with 2*MINIMUM + 1 elements) into two smaller nodes (with MINIMUM elements each). This leaves one element unaccounted for, and that one extra element will be passed upward to the parent of the split node. Therefore, the parent of the split node gains one additional child (from splitting the full node) and also gains one additional element (the extra element that is passed upward). For the example shown above, the result of the splitting is shown on the next page.

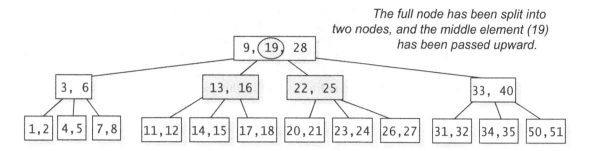

The full node has been split into two nodes, and the middle element (19) has been passed upward.

It is always the *middle* element of the split node that moves upward. Also, notice that the children of the split node have been equally distributed between the two smaller nodes.

As another example of fixExcess in action, suppose MAXIMUM is 2 and we have the problem child shown here:

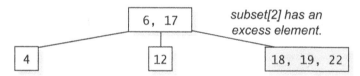

subset[2] has an excess element.

After fixExcess(2) returns, the problem child will be split into two nodes, with the middle element passed upward, as shown here:

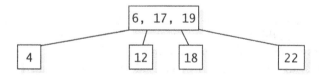

As you can see in this example, fixing the problem child can create a root with an excess element—but that is all right because the postcondition of fixExcess permits the root to have an extra element.

In your implementation of fixExcess, you will find it helpful to use the System.arraycopy method (see page 129), and you may also want to write more private methods to help with the work.

Back to the add Method

We need to finish the discussion of the original add method. By using the looseAdd method, the public add method has just two steps:

```
// Pseudocode for the public add method
looseAdd(element);
if (dataCount > MAXIMUM)
        Fix the root of the entire tree so that it no longer has too many elements.
```

pseudocode for add

In this pseudocode, how do we "fix the root of the entire tree so that it no longer has too many elements"? The step can be accomplished in two parts. The first part copies all instance variables from the root to a newly allocated node and clears out the root, giving it new arrays with only one child (which is the newly allocated node) and no elements. For example, suppose we do a loose addition, and then the B-tree looks like this (with MAXIMUM set to 2):

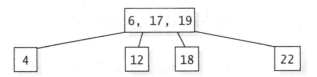

We will copy everything from the root to a new node and clear out the root. In the resulting tree, the root will have no elements, and everything else has moved down one level, as shown here:

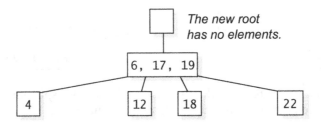

Once we have shifted things in this way, the problem is now with the child of the root. We can fix this problem by splitting the subset[0] of the root into two nodes and passing the middle element upward. In fact, if you are careful in writing fixExcess, this splitting can be carried out by activating fixExcess(0). Care must be taken because this root has no elements, so fixExcess must be prepared to deal with such a situation. (If you take this approach, you should document the extended ability of fixExcess in its precondition.)

In this example, after splitting subset[0], we have the completely valid B-tree shown here:

B-trees gain height only at the root

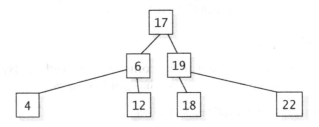

By the way, this growth at the root (within the add method) is the only point at which a B-tree gains height. This keeps all the leaves at the same depth.

Employing Top-Down Design

As you work on the project, keep in mind the top-down design that we have employed. As shown in Figure 10.5, the original add method activates the private method looseAdd. Both the ordinary add and the looseAdd methods activate fixExcess. The fixExcess method uses System.arraycopy, and you may have written other private methods to help with the fixExcess work.

FIGURE 10.5 Top-Down Design

The add method activates:
- looseAdd
- fixExcess

The looseAdd method is recursive and also activates:
- firstGE
- fixExcess

The fixExcess method activates:
- System.arraycopy
- Other private methods that you may write

Removing an Element from a B-Tree

The remove method of the set removes an element from the B-tree. Most of the removal work will be accomplished with a private method, looseRemove, which performs a *loose removal* that is analogous to the loose addition. The looseness in looseRemove occurs because it is allowed to leave a root that has one element too few. In other words, it might leave the root of the whole tree with zero elements (which is not permitted, unless there are also no children), or it might leave the root of an internal subtree with fewer than MINIMUM elements. The specification of looseRemove is given here:

```
private boolean looseRemove(int target)
// Precondition: The entire B-tree is valid.
// Postcondition: If target was in this set, then it has been removed from
// this set and the method returns true; otherwise, this set is unchanged
// and the method returns false. The entire B-tree is still valid
// EXCEPT that the number of elements in the root of this set might be one
// less than the allowed minimum.
```

Our complete remove method will first activate looseRemove. Afterward, if necessary, we can fix a root that may have been left with zero elements and one child. Thus, the remove pseudocode has just these steps:

```
// Pseudocode for the public remove method
answer = looseRemove(target);
if ((dataCount == 0) && (childCount == 1))
     Fix the root of the entire tree so that it no longer has zero elements.
return answer;
```

pseudocode for remove

In this pseudocode, how do we "fix the root of the entire tree so that it no longer has zero elements"? For example, we might have the tree shown here:

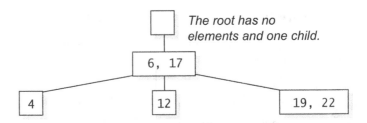

The root has no elements and one child.

Our solution for this problem is to reassign each of our four instance variables to equal the four instance variables from our only child. For example, the first assignment is `dataCount = subset[0].dataCount`. Make sure that the last of the four assignments is `subset = subset[0].subset`. (If you do this assignment too early, then you lose contact with `subset[0]`.) After this rearrangement, our tree will be one level shorter:

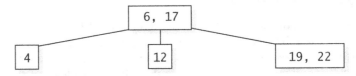

B-trees lose height only at the root

This shrinking at the root (within the `remove` method) is the only point at which a B-tree loses height.

The Loose Removal from a B-Tree

We are left with one more design task: the private `looseRemove` method. It starts in the same way as the `search` and `add` methods, by finding the first index `i` such that `data[i]` is greater than or equal to the target. Once we have found this index, there are four possibilities, shown here:

pseudocode for loose remove

```
// Removing a target from a set
```

1. Make a local variable, `i`, equal to the first index such that `data[i] >= target`. If there is no such index, then set `i` equal to `dataCount`, indicating that none of the elements is greater than or equal to the target.

2. Deal with one of these four possibilities:

   2a. The root has no children, and we did not find the target. In this case, there is no work to do, and the method returns `false`.

   2b. The root has no children, and we found the target. In this case, remove the target from the data array and return `true`.

   2c. The root has children, and we did not find the target (see page 545).

   2d. The root has children, and we found the target (see page 545).

Cases 2c and 2d require further development.

Case 2c. In this case, we did not find the target in the root, but the target still might appear in subset[i]. We will make a recursive call:

```
answer = subset[i].looseRemove(target);
```

The local variable answer is a boolean variable to keep track of whether the recursive call actually removed the target. If looseRemove did remove the target from subset[i], then we are left with the problem that the root of subset[i] might have only MINIMUM - 1 elements. If so, then we'll fix the problem by activating another private method with the specification shown here:

```
private void fixShortage(int i)
// Precondition: (i < childCount) and the entire B-tree is valid EXCEPT that
//  subset[i] has MINIMUM - 1 elements.
//  Postcondition: The tree has been rearranged so that the entire B-tree is
//  valid EXCEPT that the number of elements in the root of this set might be
//  one less than the allowed minimum.
```

After we fix any possible shortage, we should return answer to indicate whether target was removed from the set. We'll look at the design of fixShortage later.

Case 2d. In this case, we have found the target in the root, but we cannot simply remove it from the data array, because there are children below (and removing an element would thereby violate B-Tree Rule 4 on page 529). Instead, we will go into subset[i] and remove the *largest* element in this subset. We will take a copy of this largest element and place it into data[i] (which contains the target). The total effect is the same as removing the target.

For example, suppose we have found the target 28 at data[1] in the root of this B-tree:

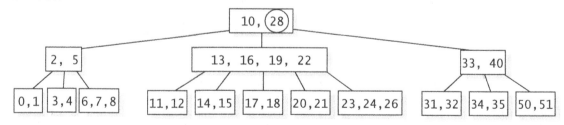

Our plan is to go into subset[1], remove the largest element (the 26), and place a copy of this 26 on top of the target. After these steps, the B-tree no longer has the 28:

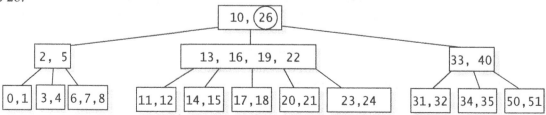

The combination of removing the largest element from subset[i] and placing a copy of the largest element into data[i] can be accomplished by activating another new private method, removeBiggest, with a specification shown here:

```
private int removeBiggest( )
// Precondition: (dataCount > 0) and this entire B-tree is valid.
// Postcondition: The largest element in this set has been removed, and the
// return value is this removed element. The entire B-tree is still valid,
// EXCEPT that the number of elements in the root of this
// set might be one less than the allowed minimum.
```

By using removeBiggest, most of Step 2d is done with one statement:

```
data[i] = subset[i].removeBiggest( );
```

After this statement finishes, we have deleted the largest element from subset[i] and placed a copy of this element into data[i] (replacing the target). The work that remains is to fix the possible shortage that may occur in the root of subset[i] (since the postcondition of subset[i].removeBiggest allows for the possibility that the root of subset[i] ends up with MINIMUM - 1 elements). How do we fix such a shortage? We can use the same fixShortage method that we used at the end of Step 2c. Thus, the entire code for Step 2d is the following:

```
data[i] = subset[i].removeBiggest( );
if (subset[i].dataCount < MINIMUM)
    fixShortage(i);
return true; // To indicate that we removed the target.
```

We have two more issues to deal with: the designs of fixShortage and removeBiggest.

A Private Method to Fix a Shortage in a Child

four situations for the fixShortage pseudocode

When fixShortage(i) is activated, we know that subset[i] has MINIMUM - 1 elements. How can we correct this problem? There are four situations that you can consider:

Case 1 of fixShortage: Transfer an Extra Element from subset[i-1].
Suppose subset[i-1] has more than the minimum number of elements. Then we can carry out these transfers:

a. Transfer data[i-1] down to the front of subset[i].data.
   Remember to shift over the existing elements to make room
   and add one to subset[i].dataCount.

b. Transfer the final element of subset[i-1].data up to replace
   data[i-1] and subtract one from subset[i-1].dataCount.

c. If subset[i-1] has children, transfer the final child of subset[i-1] over to the front of subset[i]. This involves shifting over the existing array subset[i].subset to make room for the new child at subset[i].subset[0]. Also add 1 to subset[i].childCount and subtract 1 from subset[i-1].childCount.

For example, let's activate fixShortage(2) for this tree (with MINIMUM set to 2):

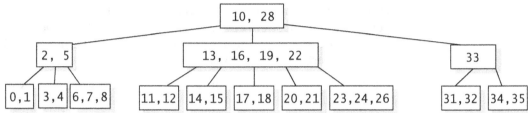

In this example, we need to fix subset[2], which has only one element. Following the steps outlined earlier, we can transfer an element from subset[1]. This transferred element is the 22, which gets passed up to data[1], and the 28 (from data[1]) comes down to be the new first element of the problem node. One child is also transferred from the end of subset[1] to the front of subset[2], as shown here:

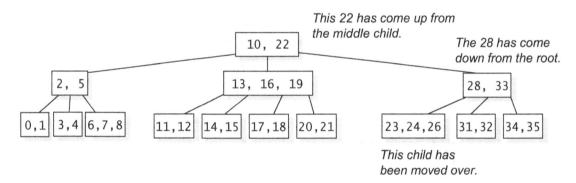

Case 2 for fixShortage: Transfer an Extra Element from subset[i+1].
Another possibility is to transfer an extra element from subset[i+1]. The work is similar to what you have just seen for transferring an element from subset[i-1].

Case 3 for fixShortage: Combine subset[i] with subset[i-1].
Suppose subset[i-1] is present (in other words, i > 0), but it has only MINIMUM elements. In this case, we cannot transfer an element from subset[i-1], but we can combine subset[i] with subset[i-1]. The combining occurs in these three steps:

a. Transfer data[i-1] down to the end of subset[i-1].data. This actually removes the element from the root, so shift data[i], data[i+1], and so on, leftward to fill in the gap. Also remember to subtract 1 from dataCount and add 1 to subset[i-1].dataCount.

b. Transfer all the elements and children from subset[i] to the end of subset[i-1]. Remember to update the values of subset[i-1].dataCount and subset[i-1].childCount.

c. Disconnect the node subset[i] from the B-tree by shifting subset[i+1], subset[i+2], and so on, leftward. Also reduce childCount by 1. (Once subset[i] is no longer part of the tree, Java's automatic garbage collector will reclaim its memory.)

For example, let's activate fixShortage(2) for the tree shown next (with MINIMUM set to 2).

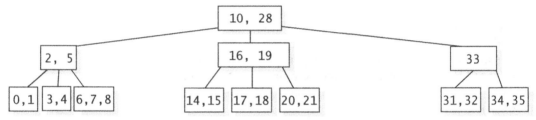

In this example, subset[2] is merged with its sibling to the left. During the merge, the 28 also is passed down from the root to become a new element of the merged nodes. The result is the following tree:

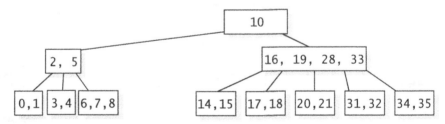

As you can see, this tree has too few elements in its own root, but that is okay because the postcondition of fixShortage allows the root of the resulting tree to have one less than the required number of elements.

Case 4 for fixShortage: Combine subset[i] with subset[i+1].
Our fourth case is to combine the problem subset with subset[i+1]. The work is similar to what you have just seen for combining with subset[i-1].

You now have enough information to write the fixShortage method. You should emphasize a clear, logical structure to determine which of the four approaches is appropriate. Your implementation will be cleaner if you provide four new private methods to do the actual work in each of the four cases.

Removing the Biggest Element from a B-Tree

Our last method has this specification:

```
private int removeBiggest( )
// Precondition: (dataCount > 0) and the entire B-tree is valid.
// Postcondition: The largest element in the set has been removed, and the
// value of this element is the return value. The entire B-tree is still valid,
// EXCEPT that the number of elements in the root of this
// set might be one less than the allowed minimum.
```

The work of `removeBiggest` is easy if the root has no children. In this case, we remove and return the last element of the partially filled data array with the single statement `return data[--dataCount]`. That's all! We might be left with a node that has one less than the allowed minimum number of elements, but according to the postcondition, that is okay.

What if the root has children? In this case, we make a recursive call to remove the largest element from the rightmost child. The recursive call is:

```
answer = subset[childCount-1].removeBiggest( );
```

The result of the recursive call is stored in a local variable, `answer`, so that the method can later return this value. But before returning, there is one remaining problem. The recursive call might leave the root of `subset[childCount-1]` with one element too few. How can we fix a child that has a shortage of elements? The `fixShortage` method can fix such a node. So, after the recursive call, you should check the number of elements in the root of `subset[childCount-1]`. If the number of elements is less than MINIMUM, then activate `fixShortage(childCount-1)`.

PROGRAMMING TIP

WRITE AND TEST SMALL PIECES

If you are implementing the entire set ADT, don't try to do the whole thing at once. Instead, write and test methods one at a time. In this project, you should also carry out a major testing after you have completed the add and `contains` methods and before you have started on any of the removal machinery.

When you start on the removal, draw a diagram of the top-down design you are implementing.

Test pieces as soon as you can. Early testing can be aided by initially implementing all of your planned methods with a single line that simply prints the name of the method, indicating that the method has been activated. A single line such as this is called a **stub**. With stubs in place, you can test any method as soon as you have written the complete version. For example, as soon as you implement the remove method, you can test it. You know that it should activate the `looseRemove` method, so you expect the `looseRemove` stub to print a message indicating that `looseRemove` has been activated.

Throughout your implementation work, it will be useful if you can print some representation of a B-tree. We suggest that you temporarily add a public `print` method, similar to the method shown in Figure 10.6.

For the output of the `print` method to be understandable, keep the value of MINIMUM small during testing—perhaps 1 or 2.

External B-Trees

Programmers may use B-trees to ensure quick behavior due to the fact that the trees are always balanced (all the leaves are at the same depth). If a balanced tree is your only objective, then the choice of the MINIMUM constant is not critical. Sometimes MINIMUM is simply 1, meaning that each node has one or two elements, and non-leaf nodes have *two or three* children. This situation is called a **2-3 tree**, which was proposed by John E. Hopcroft several years before B-trees were devised.

FIGURE 10.6   Implementing a Temporary Method That Prints a Set's B-Tree

Implementation

```
public void print(int indent)
// This is a temporary public method for use by the programmer who implements the
// class. The method prints a representation of the set's B-tree. The elements of the root node
// are printed with an indentation given by the parameter, and each subtree has an extra
// four spaces of indentation.
{
    final int EXTRA_INDENTATION = 4;
    int i;
    int space;

    // Print the indentation and the data from this node.
    for (space = 0; space < indent; space++)
       System.out.print(" ");
    for (i = 0; i < dataCount; i++)
       System.out.print(data[i] + " ");
    System.out.println( );

    // Print the subtrees.
    for (i = 0; i < childCount; i++)
       subset[i].print(indent + EXTRA_INDENTATION);
}
```

Sometimes B-trees become large—so large that the entire tree cannot reside in the computer's main memory at one time. For example, a residential phone book of the United States contains about 100 million entries. The set of elements can still be organized as a B-tree, but most of the nodes must be stored in slower, secondary memory, such as a hard drive or a CD-ROM. Typically, the root node is loaded into main memory, where it stays for the life of the program. But non-root nodes must be loaded from the secondary memory whenever they are needed. This situation is called an **external B-tree**.

most of the nodes reside in slower, secondary memory

A primary consideration with external B-trees is to reduce the total number of accesses to the secondary memory device. Therefore, the MINIMUM constant will be set quite large. With MINIMUM set to 1000, we can store more than one billion (10^9) elements with just the root and two levels below it. Because the root is always kept in memory, no search will ever require more than two nodes from the secondary memory device.

Another factor concerns the retrieval mechanism used by the secondary storage device. When a request is made to read from a hard disk or CD-ROM, there is a relatively long initial *access time* to position the disk's read head over the requested section of the disk. Once the head has been positioned, contiguous data can be read fairly quickly. This data is transferred in fixed-size blocks, using a relatively high *sustained transfer rate*. Today's 24X CD-ROM drives have an access time around $\frac{1}{10}$ of a second. Once the head is positioned, the drive transfers about 4 million bytes per second. With this in mind, you need to ensure that each node is stored in a contiguous area of the disk; if the node is spread out in several different areas, each area will require $\frac{1}{10}$ of a second of access time to reposition the head.

Self-Test Exercises for Section 10.2

6. What are the major differences between a B-tree and a binary search tree?

7. Suppose MINIMUM is 200 for a B-tree. What is the maximum number of elements that a node can contain? What is the minimum number of elements that a non-root node can have? What is the maximum number of children that a node can have? What is the minimum number of children that a non-leaf, non-root node can have?

8. Suppose MINIMUM is 1000 for a B-tree. The tree has a root and one level of 1000 nodes below that. What is the minimum number of elements that this tree might have? What is the maximum?

9. Start with an empty B-tree with MINIMUM set to 1. Enter the integers 1 through 10. Draw the resulting tree.

10. Remove the numbers 8, 3, and 6 from the tree you created in the previous exercise. Draw the resulting tree after each removal.

11. What is meant by loose insertion? How is a loose insertion eventually fixed?

10.3 JAVA SUPPORT FOR TREES

The Java Class Libraries provide several classes that allow programmers to incorporate tree data structures into programs. This section describes two of the classes: a class for tree nodes and a class for trees that includes support for graphical display.

The DefaultMutableTreeNode from javax.swing.tree

Support for general tree nodes is provided in Java by the class `Default-MutableTreeNode` from the package `javax.swing.tree`. A node created in this class may have a parent (which is another node), zero or more children (also other nodes), and a piece of data (called the **user object**). The most useful methods for this tree node class are listed in the first part of Figure 10.7 on page 554. These methods are similar to our earlier implementation of a node for binary trees (see Figure 9.6 on page 471).

Using the JTree Class to Display a Tree in an Applet

A program that needs a tree can be written using a `DefaultMutableTreeNode` that keeps track of the tree's root. However, Java provides several other classes for manipulating and displaying whole trees. One class, `JTree` from the `javax.swing` package, allows an applet to display an entire tree in an interactive format that lets the user expand or collapse the display of subtrees with the click of a mouse. We won't show the complete power of the `JTree` here, but we do have a small sample applet that creates and displays a `JTree` in the second part of Figure 10.7. We'll discuss a few aspects of this applet now.

The JApplet Class

The program in the second part of Figure 10.7 on page 556 uses an applet variation called `JApplet` from `javax.swing.JApplet`. This class is based on the applet class you may have used (see Appendix I), but it provides some extra support for displaying various data objects called the Java Swing components from the package `javax.swing`. Our sample `JApplet` has only one method (the applet's `init` method), which follows these steps:

1. Using the `DefaultMutableTreeNode`, we create a small sample tree with the variable `root` as its root. This tree is the taxonomy tree from Figure 9.3 on page 457.

2. Create a `JTree` using `root` as the root of the new `JTree`.

3. `sample.setShowsRootHandles(true);` The activation of this method ensures that each displayed node will have a small button that can be clicked with the mouse to expand or collapse the node. An expanded node will display all of its children; a collapsed node will not display its children.

4. Add the `JTree` to the components that the applets display.

There is one difference that you need to know about when you start using the `JApplet` class instead of `Applet`:

PROGRAMMING TIP 👆

ADDING A COMPONENT TO A JAPPLET

To add a component to an ordinary applet, you use the add method. For example:

```
add(sample);
```

But to add a component to a JApplet, you use the getContentPane( ).add method. For example:

```
getContentPane( ).add(sample);
```

What the TreeExample Applet Displays

When the `TreeExample` applet first starts, it will display the root and the root's children for the sample tree, as shown in the left picture below. The user of the applet can interact with the tree by expanding and collapsing the nodes. For example, if the user clicks on the node for "Are you bigger than a cat?", then that node will expand to show its children, as shown on the right.

 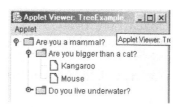

Self-Test Exercises for Section 10.3

12. Write a new method that computes the number of nodes in a tree with a specified root that is a `DefaultMutableTreeNode`. Add another method to compute the depth of a tree. Both methods should be static.

13. How is adding a component to a `JApplet` different than an `Applet`?

FIGURE 10.7 Specification of the Key Methods of the `DefaultMutableTreeNode` Class

Specification

These are the key methods of the `DefaultMutableTreeNode` class from `javax.swing.tree`. In each of these specifications, the `TreeNode` and `MutableTreeNode` data types can be an actual `DefaultMutableTreeNode` object or can be another kind of tree node implemented by the user.

♦ **Constructors for the DefaultMutableTreeNode**

```
public DefaultMutableTreeNode( )
public DefaultMutableTreeNode(Object userObject)
```

Initialize a node with no parent, no children. (These things can be added later.) The first version also has no user object, and the second version has the user object from its parameter. There is a third constructor that can be used to create a node that is forbidden from having children, but we won't use that constructor in our programs.

♦ **add**

```
public void add(MutableTreeNode newChild)
```

Add a new child to this node (at the rightmost end).

Parameter:
newChild – a reference to a node

Precondition:
The newChild is not null.

Postcondition:
The newChild has been disconnected from its current parent and added as the rightmost child of this node instead.

Throws: IllegalArgumentException
Indicates that newChild is null.

Throws: IllegalStateException
Indicates that this node is forbidden from having children.

♦ **getChildAt**

```
public TreeNode getChildAt(int index)
```

Get a reference to one of this node's children.

Parameter:
index – a number to specify a child of this node (index 0 is the leftmost child, then 1, 2, ...)

Precondition:
0 <= index and index < getChildCount( )

Returns:
areference to the specified child of this node

Throws: ArrayIndexOutOfBounds
Indicates that index violates the precondition.

(continued)

(FIGURE 10.7 continued)

♦ **getChildCount**
> `public int getChildCount( )`
> Get the number of children of this node.
> **Returns:**
>> the number of children of this node (which is zero for a leaf)

♦ **getFirstLeaf—getLastLeaf**
> `public DefaultMutableTreeNode getFirstLeaf( )`
> `public DefaultMutableTreeNode getLastLeaf( )`
> These are accessor methods to get a reference to a leaf that is at or below this node. The `getFirstLeaf` method returns the leftmost leaf that is at or below this node; the `getLastLeaf` returns the rightmost leaf that is at or below this node.

♦ **getParent**
> `public TreeNode getParent( )`
> Get a reference to this node's parent.
> **Returns:**
>> areference to this node's parent (or `null` if this node is the root)

♦ **getUserObject**
> `public Object getUserObject( )`
> Accessor method to get the user object from this node.
> **Returns:**
>> the user object from this node

♦ **insert**
> `public void insert(MutableTreeNode newChild, int childIndex)`
> Give this node a new child at a specified location.
> **Parameters:**
>> `newChild` – a reference to a node
>> `childIndex` – an integer index to indicate where the new child should be placed
> **Precondition:**
>> The `newChild` must not be `null` and must not already be an ancestor of this node. Also, `0 <= index` and `index <= getChildCount( )`.
> **Postcondition:**
>> The `newChild` has been disconnected from its current parent and added as the specified child of this node instead. Any previous children that were at or after this index have all been shifted rightward one spot to make room for the new child.
> **Throws:** `ArrayIndexOutOfBounds`
>> Indicates that `index` violates the precondition.
> **Throws:** `IllegalArgumentException`
>> Indicates that `newChild` is `null` or is already an ancestor of this node.
> **Throws:** `IllegalStateException`
>> Indicates that this node is forbidden from having children.

(continued)

(FIGURE 10.7 continued)

◆ isLeaf
```
public boolean isLeaf( )
```
Accessor method to determine whether a node is a leaf.

Returns:
true (if this node is a leaf); false otherwise

◆ remove
```
public void remove(int childIndex)
```
Remove a specified child from this node.

Parameter:
childIndex – a integer index to indicate which child should be removed (the leftmost child is number 0, and then 1, 2, ...)

Precondition:
Also, 0 <= index and index < getChildCount( ).

Postcondition:
The specified child has been removed as a child from this node.

Throws: ArrayIndexOutOfBounds
Indicates that index violates the precondition.

◆ removeFromParent
```
public void removeFromParent( )
```
Remove this node from its parent.

Postcondition:
This node has been removed from its parent, giving this node a null parent. Any children that this node has remain attached to it.

◆ setUserObject
```
public void setUserObject(Object userObject)
```
Set this node's user object.

Postcondition:
The user object of this node has been set to the specified value.

Java Applet Implementation

```
// File: TreeExample.java
// This applet is a small example to illustrate how to write an applet that uses trees from
// javax.swing.tree. This particular applet builds and displays a small tree.

import javax.swing.JApplet;
import javax.swing.JTree;
import javax.swing.tree.DefaultMutableTreeNode;
```

(continued)

(*FIGURE 10.7 continued*)

```java
public class TreeExample extends JApplet
{
    // The root of a small tree for this Applet to manipulate:
    private JTree sample;

    public void init( )
    {
        DefaultMutableTreeNode root;
        DefaultMutableTreeNode child;

        final String ROOT_QUESTION = "Are you a mammal?";
        final String LEFT_QUESTION = "Are you bigger than a cat?";
        final String RIGHT_QUESTION = "Do you live underwater?";
        final String ANIMAL1 = "Kangaroo";
        final String ANIMAL2 = "Mouse";
        final String ANIMAL3 = "Trout";
        final String ANIMAL4 = "Robin";

        // Create the root node:
        root = new DefaultMutableTreeNode(ROOT_QUESTION);

        // Create and attach the left subtree:
        child = new DefaultMutableTreeNode(LEFT_QUESTION);
        child.insert(new DefaultMutableTreeNode(ANIMAL1),0);
        child.insert(new DefaultMutableTreeNode(ANIMAL2),1);
        root.insert(child,0);

        // Create and attach the right subtree:
        child = new DefaultMutableTreeNode(RIGHT_QUESTION);
        child.insert(new DefaultMutableTreeNode(ANIMAL3),0);
        child.insert(new DefaultMutableTreeNode(ANIMAL4),1);
        root.insert(child,1);

        // Create the JTree and add it to the applet (with a handle on the root).
        // Note that a JApplet uses getContentPane( ).add rather than just add:
        sample = new JTree(root);
        sample.setShowsRootHandles(true);
        getContentPane( ).add(sample);
    }

}
```

10.4 TREES, LOGS, AND TIME ANALYSIS

The implementations in this chapter—heaps and B-trees—are efficient for a simple reason: The depth of the trees is kept small so that following a path from the root to a leaf does not examine too many nodes. In fact, we can make a strong statement relating the depth of a tree and the worst-case time required for the operations we have implemented:

Worst-Case Times for Tree Operations

The worst-case time performance for all the following operations is $O(d)$, where d is the depth of the tree:

1. Adding an element to a binary search tree, a heap, or a B-tree

2. Removing an element from a binary search tree, a heap, or a B-tree

3. Searching for a specified element in a binary search tree or a B-tree

These time results are valid provided that a node can be stored or retrieved through a pointer in constant time. An external B-tree may have worse time performance (because the time to retrieve a node depends on the external storage device), but the total number of nodes accessed is still $O(d)$ for all the operations.

For example, consider adding an element to a heap. The new element is placed at the next available location of the heap at the deepest level, d. The priority of the new element is then compared with its parent's priority, and the new element might be swapped with its parent. In the worst case, this process continues, comparing the new element with its parent and swapping, until the new element reaches the root. In this worst case, the new element had to be compared with its parent and swapped d times, where d is the depth at which the new element began its life. Since one comparison and swap requires a fixed number of operations, the total number of operations in the algorithm is a fixed number times d, which is $O(d)$. You can carry out a similar analysis for each of the other operations listed above.

This could be the end of our story, except that time analyses for these operations are more useful when they are given in terms of the number of elements in the tree rather than in terms of the tree's depth. To express the time analyses in these terms, we must first answer a secondary question: *What is the maximum depth for a tree with* n *elements?* We'll answer this question for binary search trees and heaps, leaving the case of B-trees for your exercises. Once this question is answered, we can provide worst-case time analyses in terms of the number of elements in a tree.

Time Analysis for Binary Search Trees

Suppose a binary search tree has n elements. What is the maximum depth the tree could have? A binary tree must have at least one node at each level. For example, a binary tree with depth two must have a root (at level 0), at least one child of the root (at level 1), and at least one child of the child (at level 2). If a tree has n nodes, then the first node may appear at the root level, the second node at level 1, the third node at level 2, and so on, until the nth node, which appears at depth $n-1$. So a binary tree with n elements could have a depth as big as $n-1$.

What does this say about the worst-case time analysis of the binary search tree operations in terms of the number of elements in a tree? Here's the analysis:

Worst-Case Times for Binary Search Trees

Adding an element, removing an element, or searching for an element in a binary search tree with n elements is $O(d)$, where d is the depth of the tree. Because d is no more than $n-1$, the operations are $O(n-1)$, which is $O(n)$ (since we can ignore constants in big-O notation).

Time Analysis for Heaps

In a heap, we can examine the relationship between depth and number of elements by first computing the smallest number of elements required for a heap to reach a given depth d. Remember that a heap is a complete binary tree, so each level must be full before proceeding to the next level. The first element goes at level 0 (the root level). The next two elements must go at level 1, the next four elements at level 2, the next eight elements at level 3, and so on. Let's present this information in a table.

Level	Number of Nodes to Fill the Level
0	1 node
1	2 nodes
2	4 nodes
3	8 nodes
4	16 nodes
. . .	
d	2^d nodes

The values in the table are the maximum number of nodes that can occur at each level. Using the table, we can obtain the total number of nodes needed to reach level d:

Number of nodes needed for a heap to reach depth d is
$$(1 + 2 + 4 + \ldots + 2^{d-1}) + 1$$

The first part of the formula, up to 2^{d-1}, is the number of elements required to completely fill the first d–1 levels, and the extra "+ 1" at the end is required because there must be at least one element in level d.

This formula can be simplified by shifting the +1 to the front:

Number of nodes needed for a heap to reach depth d is
$$1 + 1 + 2 + 4 + \ldots + 2^{d-1}$$

Why is this a simplification? Look at the start of the formula, which begins $1 + 1 \ldots$. Then combine the two 1s, like this:

$$1 + 1 + 2 + 4 + \ldots + 2^{d-1} \quad = \quad 2 + 2 + 4 + \ldots + 2^{d-1}$$

Now we have a formula that begins with two 2s, which can also be combined:

$$2 + 2 + 4 + \ldots + 2^{d-1} \quad = \quad 4 + 4 + \ldots + 2^{d-1}$$

Now we have a formula that begins with two 4s, and if we combine the 4s, we get two 8s, and so on, until we eventually end up with just $2^{d-1} + 2^{d-1}$. So:

Number of nodes needed for a heap to reach depth d is
$$= (1 + 2 + 4 + \ldots + 2^{d-1}) + 1$$
$$= 2^{d-1} + 2^{d-1}$$

This last formula, $2^{d-1} + 2^{d-1}$, is the same as 2^d, so we have the following result:

The number of nodes needed for a heap
to reach depth d is 2^d.

Expressed another way: The number of nodes in a heap is at least 2^d, where d is the depth of the heap.

This is certainly a simple formula, but to use it, we need to explain a bit about **base 2 logarithms**. For any positive number x, the base 2 logarithm of x is an exponent r such that:

$$2^r = x$$

The number r in this equation is usually written $\log_2 x$. For example:

$$2^0 = 1 \text{ so that } \log_2 1 = 0$$
$$2^1 = 2 \text{ so that } \log_2 2 = 1$$
$$2^2 = 4 \text{ so that } \log_2 4 = 2$$
$$2^3 = 8 \text{ so that } \log_2 8 = 3$$
$$2^4 = 16 \text{ so that } \log_2 16 = 4$$
$$2^d = 2^d \text{ so that } \log_2 2^d = d$$

The last line of this table is the key to our heap analysis. We know that in a heap, the number of elements, n, is at least 2^d, where d is the depth of the heap. Therefore:

$$\log_2 n \ \geq \ \log_2 2^d \ (\text{since } n \geq 2^d)$$

Since $\log_2 2^d = d,$ this implies that:

$$\log_2 n \ \geq \ d.$$

This is the relationship that we need between the number of elements, n, and the depth of a heap. Here's the analysis:

Worst-Case Times for Heap Operations

Adding or removing an element in a heap with n elements is $O(d)$, where d is the depth of the tree. Because d is no more than $\log_2 n$, the operations are $O(\log_2 n)$, which is $O(\log n)$ (since we can ignore log bases in big-O notation).

The time analysis for B-trees will also result in $O(\log n)$ time, as you'll be asked to show in Self-Test Exercise 15.

Omitting the subscript, 2, from $O(\log_2 n)$ may be a bit confusing, but to explain why the omission is valid, we need to look at logarithms in more depth. This look at logarithms will also give us a good understanding of the behavior that is expected from logarithmic algorithms, such as adding and deleting from a heap.

Logarithms

The definition of $\log_2 x$ is a number r such that $2^r = x$. The number 2 is called the **base of the logarithm,** and the definition extends to other bases. For example, $\log_{10} x$ is the number r such that $10^r = x$. Or consider base 16, where $\log_{16} x$ is the number r such that $16^r = x$.

Here are some specific examples for base 10:

$$10^0 = 1 \text{ so that } \log_{10} 1 = 0$$
$$10^1 = 10 \text{ so that } \log_{10} 10 = 1$$
$$10^{1.5} = \text{about } 32 \text{ so that } \log_{10} 32 = \text{about } 1.5$$
$$10^3 = 1000 \text{ so that } \log_{10} 1000 = 3$$

From these examples, you can see why we said in Chapter 1 that the number of digits in a positive integer n is approximately $\log_{10} n$. You can work out a little table:

For n in the range 1 to 9, $0 \leq \log_{10} n < 1$

For n in the range 10 to 99, $1 \leq \log_{10} n < 2$

For n in the range 100 to 999, $2 \leq \log_{10} n < 3$

For n in the range 1000 to 9999, $3 \leq \log_{10} n < 4$

Extrapolating from this table, you can find a precise relationship between the number of digits in a positive integer and base 10 logarithms (using $\lfloor \log_{10} n \rfloor$ to indicate rounding down the logarithm to an integer):

> The number of digits in a positive integer n is $\lfloor \log_{10} n \rfloor + 1$.

There is also a relationship between logarithms in one base and logarithms in another base:

> For any two bases a and b, and a positive number x:
> $$(\log_b a) \times (\log_a x) = \log_b x$$

This equation is the reason why bases generally are omitted from big-O notation. For example, if an algorithm requires $\log_2 n$ operations, then that is the same as $4 \times \log_{16} n$ operations since $\log_2 16$ is 4. In big-O notation, the multiplication by a constant (such as 4) is ignored, and this is why we write simply $O(\log n)$ rather than $O(\log_2 n)$.

Logarithmic Algorithms

Logarithmic algorithms are algorithms with worst-case time $O(\log n)$, such as adding and deleting from a heap. These algorithms have a characteristic time behavior:

Time Behavior of Logarithmic Algorithms

For a logarithmic algorithm, doubling the input size will make the time increase by a fixed number of new operations.

For example, consider adding a new element to a heap with n elements. The algorithm may look at as many as $\log_2 n$ nodes. If we double the number of nodes to $2n$, then the algorithm may look at as many as $\log_2 2n$ nodes—but $\log_2 2n$ is just one more than $\log_2 n$. (For example, $\log_2 1024 = 10$ and $\log_2 2048 = 11$.) So we can double the number of elements in a heap, and the process of adding a new element requires us to examine only one extra node.

Self-Test Exercises for Section 10.4

14. Evaluate the following logarithms:

   $\log_2 32$ $\qquad \log_5 125 \qquad \log_{16} 256$

   $\log_{10} 100 \qquad \log_{37} 1 \qquad \log_9 81$

15. Show that adding, removing, and searching in a B-tree have worst-case time $O(\log n)$.

16. Use the definition of logarithms to show that $\log_2 2n$ is always just one more than $\log_2 n$.

CHAPTER SUMMARY

- A *heap* is a complete binary tree that follows the rule that the element at any node is never less than any of its children's elements. Heaps provide an efficient implementation of priority queues.

- A *B-tree* is a tree for storing elements in a manner that follows six rules. The first two rules specify the minimum and maximum number of elements for each node. The third rule requires each node's elements to be sorted from smallest to largest. Rules 4 and 5 indicate how many subtrees a non-leaf node must have and provide an order for the elements of the subtrees. The last rule requires each leaf to be at the same depth.

- Java provides several classes to support trees, including a class for tree nodes (`DefaultMutableTreeNode`) and a class to display trees in JApplets (`JTree`).

- The tree algorithms we have seen for binary search trees, heaps, and B-trees all have worst-case time performance of $O(d)$, where d is the depth of the tree.

- The depth of a heap or B-tree is never more than $O(\log n)$, where n is the number of nodes. Hence, the operations on these structures are also $O(\log n)$.

? Solutions to Self-Test Exercises

1. Because a heap is a complete binary tree.

2. One approach is to store the complete binary tree of the heap in two separate arrays. One array, called `priority`, contains the priorities of the nodes. Another array, called `data`, contains the data of the nodes. For example, `priority[0]` and `data[0]` contain the priority and data of the root of the heap.

   With this idea, we can write a priority queue implementation, as shown here:

   ```
   public class PriorityQueue
   {
       private int[ ] priority;
       private Object[ ] data;
       int size;
       ...
   ```

   The `size` instance variable indicates how much of the arrays is currently being used. The constructor is responsible for allocating the initial arrays. The method that adds a new element to the priority queue may need to increase the size of these arrays.

3. If we swap with the smaller child, then the larger child will still have a priority that exceeds its parent's priority.

4. With our addition algorithm, you end up with this heap:

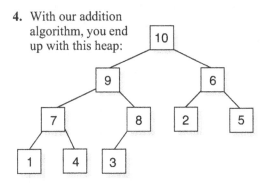

5. With our removal algorithm, you end up with this heap:

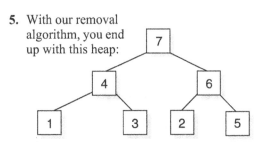

6. There are many differences that you might choose for this answer, but two fundamental differences are that each node in a B-tree may contain more than one entry (whereas a binary search tree has one entry per node), and the number of children for a non-leaf node in a B-tree is exactly one more than the number of entries (whereas in a binary search tree, each node has at most two children).

   When searching for an item in a binary search tree, the searcher must always choose between going left or right at each node. In a B-tree, the searcher must choose among more than just two possible children.

7. The maximum number of elements that a node can contain is 400, although during an addition we may temporarily have a node with 401 elements. The minimum number of elements that a non-root node can have is 200, although during a removal, we may temporarily have a node with 199 elements. The maximum number of children that a node can have is 401, although during an addition, we may temporarily have a node with 402 children. The minimum number of children that a non-leaf, non-root node can have is 201, although during a removal, we may temporarily have a node with 200 children.

8. The root has 999 elements, and each of the 1000 nodes at the next level has between 1000 and 2000 elements. Therefore, the total number of elements in the tree is between 1,000,999 and 2,000,999 elements.

9. With our addition algorithm, you end up with this B-tree:

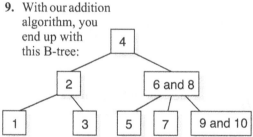

10. After removing the 8:

After removing the 3:

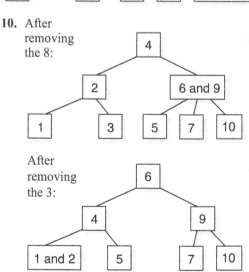

After removing the 6:

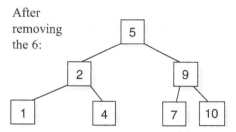

11. A loose insertion allows the top node of a subtree to temporarily hold one too many entries. The problem is fixed by splitting the node with too many entries. After the split, one new node contains the entries before the middle, another new node contains the entries after the middle, and the middle entry itself has been passed upward to a higher level.

12. Here is the `treeSize` method; the `depth` method has a similar recursive method:

```
public static int treeSize
(DefaultMutableTreeNode root)
{
    int count = root.getChildCount();
    int answer = 1;
    int i;
    for (i = 0; i < count; i++)
    {
        answer += treeSize
            (root.getChildAt(i));
    }
    return answer;
}
```

13. See the Programming Tip on page 553.

14. The logarithms are:

$$\log_2 32 = 5 \quad \log_5 125 = 3 \quad \log_{16} 256 = 2$$
$$\log_{10} 100 = 2 \quad \log_{37} 1 = 0 \quad \log_9 81 = 2$$

15. In all three algorithms, the number of total steps is a constant times the height of the B-tree. This height is no more than $\log_M n$, where M is the MINIMUM constant and n is the number of elements in the tree. Thus, the algorithms all require no more than $O(\log n)$ operations.

16. All logarithms in this solution are base 2:

$$2^{1 + \log n} = 2 \times 2^{\log n} = 2n = 2^{\log 2n}$$

Therefore, $1 + \log n = \log 2n$.

PROGRAMMING PROJECTS

1 Using a heap, implement the priority queue ADT from Section 7.4. You can store the heap in arrays, similar to the solution to Self-Test Exercise 1. To have FIFO behavior for elements with equal priority, you should have a third array called `entered`. The value of `entered[i]` tells when the data in node number `i` entered the priority queue. For example, the first element added has an entered value of 1, the second element has an entered value of 2, and so on. When you are comparing two elements with equal priority, use the entered value to "break the tie" (so that if two elements have the same priority number, then the one with the earlier entered value will come out of the priority queue first).

Make sure you keep track of how many elements are in the heap so that if the size of the heap reaches the size of the arrays, you can increase the size of the arrays.

2 Use a B-tree to implement the `Set` class from Figure 10.4 on page 531. Be sure to write and test small pieces.

3 The `java.lang.Math` class provides a static method `log(x)`, which returns the logarithm of `x` with a base that is approximately 2.71828. This base is written *e*, and the logarithms with this base are called **natural logarithms** or **Napierian logarithms**, after the Scottish mathematician John Napier (1550–1617) who invented these logarithms. The number *e* may seem like a strange choice for the base of a logarithm, but the choice is motivated by the fact that natural logarithms are easy to approximate as the sum of a series. Anyway, in this project, you are to write a method:

```
double log10(double x)
```

The method returns the base 10 logarithm of x. Make use of the `java.lang.Math.log` method and the formulas in Section 10.4. You can also use the fact that $\log_{10} e$ is about 0.4342944819032.

By the way, Napier also invented a calculator called "Napier's bones." The device performed multiplication and division through a series of connected rods with tables marked on them.

4 Use the material from Section 10.3 to reimplement the animal-guessing program from Figure 9.8 on page 482 as a `JApplet`. You'll need to research additional details of the Java classes.

5 Use the `DefaultMutableTreeNode` to reimplement one of these Chapter 9 projects:
   a. Expression trees (9.1)
   b. Bag of strings (9.10)

6 Use the `DefaultMutableTreeNode` to implement the B-tree set class from Section 10.2.

7 The heap in this chapter is referred to as a maxheap because the highest priority value is also the maximum value. Implement the heap as a minheap, in which the entry of the node with the highest priority has the minimum value in the heap, and an entry of a node is never more than the entries of the node's children.

8 Using the heap implementation of a priority queue from Project 1, implement a program that keeps track of the user's list of prioritized chores.

CHAPTER 11

Searching

Searching

"Compassion is what you're good at. I'm better at complex searches through organized data structures."

ORSON SCOTT CARD
Speaker for the Dead

Searching a list of values is a common computational task. An application program might retrieve a student record, bank account record, credit record, or any other type of record using a search algorithm. In this chapter, we present and analyze some of the most common (and most efficient) methods of searching for a particular element. The algorithms include serial search, binary search, and search by hashing.

We also use the search algorithms to develop additional techniques for analyzing the running times of algorithms, particularly average-time analyses and the analysis of recursive algorithms.

11.1 SERIAL SEARCH AND BINARY SEARCH

Serial Search

Our starting point is the searching algorithm, shown in Figure 11.1. This algorithm, called a **serial search** (also called a **linear** or **sequential** search), steps through part of an array one element at a time looking for a "desired element." The search stops when the element is found or when the search has examined each element without success. In the pseudocode, we did not specify the precise return value of the algorithm; it might return the actual index where the item is found (returning –1 if the element is not found), or it might return a boolean value to indicate whether the element was found, or perhaps there is some other action that the algorithm takes when it finds the element. In any case, the algorithm is easy to write and applicable to many situations.

Serial Search—Analysis

The running time of the serial search is easy to analyze, but some care is needed to specify the precise kind of analysis. As always, we will count the number of "operations" required by the algorithm rather than measuring actual elapsed time. For searching an array, a common approach is to count one operation each time the algorithm accesses an element of the array. With the serial search, the size of the array is one important factor in determining the number of array accesses, but even if we use a particular fixed array, the number of array accesses will still vary depending on precisely which target we are looking for. If the target is the first element in the array, then there will be only one array access. If the target is near the middle of the array, then the serial search accesses about half of the array elements.

Usually, when we discuss running times, we consider the "hardest" inputs, for example, a target that requires the algorithm to access the largest number of array elements. This is called the worst-case running time. For the serial search, the worst-case running time occurs when the target is not in the array. In this case, the algorithm accesses every element, and we have the following formula:

worst case

Worst-Case Time for Serial Search

For an array of *n* elements, the worst-case time for serial search requires *n* array accesses.

Most of the time, a serial search of an *n*-element array requires fewer than *n* array accesses. Thus, the worst-case expression "*n* array accesses" makes serial search sound worse than it often is. An alternative is the **average-case** running time, which is obtained by averaging the different running times for all different inputs of a particular kind. For example, we can develop an expression for the average-case running time of serial search based on all the targets that are actually in the array. To be concrete in this first example, suppose the array has 10

average case

FIGURE 11.1 Serial Search Algorithm

Pseudocode

// *Searches for a desired element in the n array elements starting at a[first]*

Set an `int` variable i to 0 (to use as an index), and set a `boolean` variable found to `false`.

while ((i < n) && !found)
{
    if (a[first+i] is the desired element)
        found = true;
    else
        i++;
}

if (found)
    The desired element is in a[first+i].
else
    The desired element does not appear in the n items starting at a[first].

elements so that there are 10 possible targets. If we are searching for the target that occurs at the first location, then there is just one array access. If we are searching for the target that occurs at the second location, then there are two array accesses, and so on, through the final target, which requires 10 array accesses. In all, there are 10 possible targets, which require 1, 2, 3, 4, 5, 6, 7, 8, 9, or 10 array accesses. The average of all these searches is:

$$\frac{1 + 2 + 3 + 4 + 5 + 6 + 7 + 8 + 9 + 10}{10} = 5.5$$

We can generalize this example so that the average-case running time of the serial search is written as an expression with part of the expression being the size of the array. Using n as the size of the array, this expression for the average-case running time is:

$$\frac{1 + 2 + \ldots + n}{n} = \frac{n(n+1)/2}{n} = (n+1)/2$$

The first equality in this formula is obtained from the formula we developed on page 20. We can summarize the average-case running time for serial search:

Average-Case Time for Serial Search

For an array of n elements, the average-case time for serial search to find an element that is in the array requires $(n + 1)/2$ array accesses.

You may have noticed that both the worst-case time and the average-case time are $O(n)$ expressions, but nevertheless, the average case is about half the time of the worst case.

best case   A third way to measure running times is called **best-case** running time, and as the name suggests, it takes the most optimistic view possible. The best-case running time is defined as the smallest of all the running times on inputs of a particular size. For serial search, the best case occurs when the target is found at the front of the array, requiring only one array access:

Best-Case Time for Serial Search

For an array of n elements, the best-case time for serial search is just one array access.

Unless the best-case behavior occurs with high probability, the best-case running time generally is not used during an analysis.

Binary Search

Serial search is easy to implement, easy to analyze, and fine to use when you are searching a small array only a few times. However, if a search algorithm will be used over and over, it is worthwhile to find a faster algorithm. A dramatically faster search algorithm is sometimes available. The algorithm, called *binary search,* may be used only if the array is sorted. Here are three examples for which binary search is applicable:

- Searching an array of integers in which the array is sorted from the smallest integer (at the front) to the largest integer (at the end of the array)

- Searching an array of strings in which the strings are sorted alphabetically

- Searching an array in which each component is an `Object` containing information about some item, such as an auto part, and the array is sorted by "part numbers" from the smallest to the largest

For concreteness, we'll develop the algorithm for the first of these three cases (searching a sorted array of integers), but keep in mind that the same algorithm applies to any other kind of sorted search space.

Our integer version of the binary search will be implemented with a static method called `search`. The parameter list for `search` has four parameters. The first three parameters provide the array itself, the starting index of the portion of the array that we are searching, and the number of elements to search. The fourth parameter is the target that we are searching for. For example, consider:

```
search(b, 17, 10, 42);
```

This example shows the four arguments needed to search for the number 42 occurring somewhere in the 10 elements from `b[17]` through `b[26]`.

The `search` method usually returns an index of the array—the index where the target was found. But if the target does not appear in the specified portion of the array, then the method returns –1 instead of an index. Here is the specification:

♦ **search**

  `public static int search(int[ ] a, int first, int size, int target)`
  Search part of a sorted array for a specified target.

  Parameters:
  a – the array to search
  `first` – the first index of the part of the array to search
  `size` – the number of elements to search, starting at a[`first`]
  `target` – the element to search for

  Precondition:
  If `size` > 0, then `first` through `first+size-1` must be valid indexes for the array a. Also, starting at a[`first`], the next `size` elements are sorted in increasing order from small to large.

Returns:
    If `target` appears in the array segment starting at `a[first]` and
    containing `size` elements, then the return value is the index of a location
    that contains `target`; otherwise, the return value is –1.

Throws: `ArrayIndexOutOfBoundsException`
    Indicates that some index in the range `first` through `first+size-1` is
    outside the range of valid indexes for the array a.

Binary Search—Design

Let's produce an algorithm to perform this search task. It will help to visualize
the problem in concrete terms. Suppose the array of numbers is a list of invalid
credit card numbers, and it is so long that it takes a book to list them. If you are
a clerk and are handed a credit card, you must check to see if it is on the list and
hence invalid. How would you proceed? Open the book to the middle and see
if it is there. If not and it is smaller than the middle number, then work toward
the beginning of the book. If it is larger than the middle number, then work
toward the back of the book. This idea produces our first draft of an algorithm,
shown in the following pseudocode.

```
if (size <= 0)
    return -1;
else
{
    middle = index of the approximate midpoint of the array segment;
    if (target == a[middle])
        the target has been found at a[middle], so return middle;
    else if (target < a[middle])
        search for the target in the area before the midpoint;
    else if (target > a[middle])
        search for the target in the area after the midpoint;
}
```

It is natural to use recursive calls for the two substeps that "search smaller
areas," and that is what our implementation will do. As with any recursive
method, we must ensure that the method terminates rather than producing infinite recursion. This insurance is provided by noting that each recursive call
searches a shorter area, and when the size reaches zero, there can be no further
recursive calls. This reasoning can be formalized as in Chapter 8 (see "How to
Ensure That There Is No Infinite Recursion in the General Case" on page 442).
Using the Chapter 8 technique, we see that the parameter `size` is a valid *variant
expression* with a *threshold* of zero. In other words, the `size` parameter is
always reduced by at least 1 on each recursive call, and when `size` reaches zero,
there is no further recursion.

Our complete implementation of the pseudocode is shown in Figure 11.2.

FIGURE 11.2   The Binary Search Method

Implementation

```
public static int search(int[ ] a, int first, int size, int target)
{
   int middle;

   if (size <= 0)
      return -1;
   else
   {
      middle = first + size/2;
      if (target == a[middle])
         return middle;
      else if (target < a[middle])
         // The target is less than a[middle], so search before the middle.
         return search(a, first, size/2, target);
      else
         // The target must be greater than a[middle], so search after the middle.
         return search(a, middle+1, (size-1)/2, target);
   }
}
```

Sample Results of `search(b, 2, 5, 42)` **when b contains this data:**

-7	3	8	39	42	63	70
[0]	[1]	[2]	[3]	[4]	[5]	[6]

The method returns the index 4 because `b[4]` is the target 42.

As an example of the binary search in action, suppose that we activate
`search(a, 0, 10, 42)` to search the following array for the number 42:

a

7	22	29	32	42	52	59	66	69	76
[0]	[1]	[2]	[3]	[4]	[5]	[6]	[7]	[8]	[9]

The binary search is searching the 10 elements of this array (`first` is 0 and
`size` is 10). The algorithm sets the variable `middle` to `first + size/2`, which is
5 in this example. Now `a[5]` is 52, which is greater than the target 42, so the
algorithm makes a recursive call, `search(a, 0, 5, 42)`, to search for the number
42 in the first five elements of the array. The part of the array that will be searched
by the recursive call is shown in the unshaded part of the following drawing:

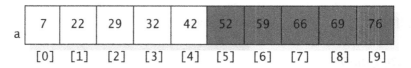

In the recursive call, the new local variable `middle` is assigned the value 2. Since a[2] is 29, which is smaller than 42, the next recursive call throws away everything at or before a[2]. This recursive call, search(a, 3, 2, 42), searches the two elements starting at a[3], as shown here:

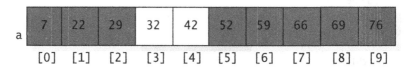

The important property of binary search is that each recursive call throws away at least half of the remaining elements.

In this example, the second recursive call sets its local variable `middle` to 4, and the search finds the target 42 at a[4]. Therefore, this recursive call returns the index 4 to the previous call, which returns 4 to the original call—and the final answer is 4.

   PITFALL

COMMON INDEXING ERRORS IN BINARY SEARCH IMPLEMENTATIONS

Binary search and similar array-based algorithms are notorious for having errors involving the array indexes. A common place for an error is the calculation of the size of the array for the recursive call. The implementation in Figure 11.2 has two recursive calls, and it's important to double-check the expression for the size of the array segment being searched in these recursive calls. For example, one of our recursive calls searches the segment that occurs before a[middle]. This segment begins at a[first] going up to (but not including) a[middle]. How many components are there in this segment? The answer is middle - first, which is the same as size/2, according to this calculation:

```
middle - first = (first + size/2) - first = size/2
```

In our recursive call, we use the expression size/2 for the argument that expresses the size of the array because this expression conveys the idea that the recursive call searches about half of the original array.

You should carry out a similar calculation to verify that the number of elements after a[middle] is (size - 1)/2. Hence, the size argument in our second recursive call is the expression (size - 1)/2.

Binary Search—Analysis

We want to estimate the running time for the binary search algorithm given in Figure 11.2. The algorithm tests to see if the middle element of the array has the target we are looking for. If it does, the algorithm stops, returning the index of this middle element. If our sought-after target is not in the middle of the array, the algorithm searches either the half above or the half below this midpoint. This narrows the search to about half of the array elements, and then another recursive call can take it to half of that, and then half of that, and so forth. The algorithm runs longest when the target is not in the array. If the target is not in the array, then eventually the algorithm will make a recursive call to search an array with zero elements. Of course, the target cannot occur in an empty array, so at that point, the algorithm returns and tells us that the target could not be found. We want to analyze this algorithm for worst-case running time.

The binary search algorithm is a recursive algorithm, so we need to compute the amount of time taken by all recursive calls, and recursive calls of recursive calls, etc. As in other cases, we will simply count the number of operations performed. The only operations mentioned in the algorithm are addition, subtraction, division, assignment, tests for equality or "less than," and the array access operation.

Let n be the number of elements in the array segment being searched (i.e., the value of `size`). We want to know how many operations the algorithm will perform in the worst case. As it turns out, the worst case is when the target is not in the array, so we will assume that `target` is not in the array.

When the algorithm starts out, it tests to see if the array segment is empty (`size <= 0`). This is a stopping case for the recursion. We'll charge one operation for this emptiness test.

one operation

After that, the algorithm computes the midpoint index, as follows:

three more operations

```
middle = first + size/2;
```

This adds an additional three operations, one each of division, addition, and assignment.

Next the algorithm tests to see whether the target equals `a[middle]`. This requires one array access and one application of `==`, so it counts as two more operations.

two more operations

We are assuming that the target is not in the array, so the algorithm then goes on to do this comparison:

```
(target < a[middle])
```

another two operations

This also requires two operations—one for the array access and one for the comparison.

The algorithm then makes a recursive call, which requires a few operations to provide the arguments. The exact number of operations depends on the way in which the methods are activated and the return value provided. Rather than selecting a particular number, let's just use the symbol c for the number of operations for passing the arguments and obtaining the return value. In addition, there will be the operations carried out by the recursive call, but we have not begun to worry about that yet.

If we total up all the operations used, we've estimated that the algorithm performs no more than $8 + c$ operations, not counting the work of the recursive call. The recursive call can produce another recursive call, which in turn produces another recursive call, until the procedure gets to a stopping case. Each of these recursive calls is preceded by $8 + c$ (or fewer) operations. The total number of operations is thus no more than $8 + c$ times the length of this chain of recursive calls, plus the number of operations performed in the stopping case. Using the symbol $T(n)$ for the worst-case running time to search an array of n elements, we therefore have:

$T(n) = (8 + c) \times$ (the length of the longest chain of recursive calls)
$+$
(the number of operations performed in the stopping case)

There are two possible stopping cases: when the size becomes zero or when the target is found. Since the worst case is when the target is not in the array, we assume that the target is not found. The stopping case when the target is not found requires two operations (a test of `size <= 0` and an operation to return the answer of negative 1).

Thus, the running time of the method is given by this formula:

$T(n) = (8 + c) \times$ (the length of the longest chain of recursive calls) $+ 2$

There is a standard term for the long phrase in parentheses, namely **the depth of recursive calls**.

Depth of Recursive Calls

The length of the longest chain of recursive calls in the execution of an algorithm is called the **depth of recursive calls** for that algorithm.

This definition allows us to replace the long phrase in our formula with this standard term and therefore obtain this slightly more compact formula:

$T(n) = (8 + c) \times$ (the depth of recursive calls) $+ 2$

Rather than compute the exact value for the depth of recursive calls, we will determine an upper-bound approximation to the number of recursive calls. The figure we obtain may be slightly larger than the actual number of calls, but it will be a close approximation. This is common practice when analyzing running times. It is often easier to calculate an upper bound than it is to calculate the exact running time. As long as we use an upper bound so that we are estimating higher than the true value, then we will always be safe. This way, our algorithm might turn out to be a bit faster than we thought, but never slower. Now let's calculate this upper bound on the length of the longest string of recursive calls.

The array contains n elements to be searched. Each recursive call is made on an array segment that contains, at most, half of the elements. Hence, to approximate the depth of recursive calls, all we need to do is determine how many times we can divide n in half, then divide that half in half again, then divide that result in half yet again, and so on, until the array is "all gone." The array is "all gone" when there are no elements to divide in half (that is, when `size` is zero).

Depth of Recursive Calls for Binary Search of an n-Element Array

The depth of recursive calls is, at most, the number of times that n can be divided by 2, stopping when the result is less than 1.

We can now estimate the number of operations performed by the binary search algorithm on an array with n elements. We know that the number of operations is at most $T(n) = (8 + c) \times$ (the depth of recursive calls) $+ 2$, which is:

$$= (8 + c) \times \text{(the number of times that } n \text{ can be divided by 2, stopping when the result is less than 1)} + 2$$

Let's denote the second expression in parentheses by $H(n)$ and call it the **halving function**.

The Halving Function

The **halving function** $H(n)$ is defined by $H(n) =$ (the number of times that n can be divided by 2, stopping when the result is less than 1).

With this new definition, we can express our estimate of the running time for the binary search algorithm compactly. The worst-case running time is closely approximated by:

$$T(n) = (8 + c) \times H(n) + 2$$

To get a feel for how fast this running time is, we must know a little about the function $H(n)$. As it turns out, $H(n)$ is nearly equal to the base 2 logarithm of n, which is written $\log_2 n$. To be even more precise, for any positive integer n:

Value of the Halving Function

$H(n) =$ (the number of times that n can be divided by 2, stopping when the result is less than 1) has the value:
$$H(n) = \lfloor \log_2 n \rfloor + 1$$

The symbols $\lfloor \; \rfloor$ mean that we round fractional numbers down to the next lowest whole number. For example, $\lfloor 3.7 \rfloor$ is 3. The notation $\lfloor \; \rfloor$ is called the **floor function**, and we used it before in Chapter 1 when we noted that the number of digits in a positive integer n is $\lfloor \log_{10} n \rfloor + 1$. Since $H(n)$ is a whole number and $\log_2 n$ might include a fractional part, they cannot always be exactly equal, but the preceding equality means that $H(n)$ and $\log_2 n$ will never differ by more than 1. Let's explore what this equality tells us about the running time of binary search.

For an array with n elements ($n > 0$), we have seen that the worst-case running time of the binary search algorithm is:

$$T(n) = (8 + c) \times H(n) + 2 = (8 + c) \times (\lfloor \log_2 n \rfloor + 1) + 2$$

binary search is an O(log n) algorithm

If we throw out the constants, the result says that the worst-case running time is *logarithmic* (that is, $O(\log n)$).

Worst-Case Time for Binary Search

For an array of *n* elements, the worst-case time for binary search is logarithmic.

An algorithm with logarithmic running time is fast because the logarithm of n is much smaller than n. Moreover, the larger n is, the more dramatic this difference becomes. For example, the base 2 logarithm of 2 is 1, the base 2 logarithm of 8 is 3, the base 2 logarithm of 64 is 6, the base 2 logarithm of a thousand is less than 10, and the base 2 logarithm of a million is less than 20.

This means that the binary search algorithm is very efficient. For example, suppose the constant c is 10. Then an array with a thousand elements has a running time of $18(\lfloor \log_2 n \rfloor + 1) + 2$, which is less than 182 operations. Even with a million elements, the worst-case time is fewer than 400 operations.

average time is also O(log n)

We won't give a rigorous analysis of the average running time for binary search, but we can tell you that the average running time for actually finding a number is $O(\log n)$. It is not hard to see why this is true. We have already seen that when a target is not found, the depth of recursion is $\lfloor \log_2 n \rfloor + 1$. In the worst case, even a found target requires a recursion depth of $\lfloor \log_2 n \rfloor$ (just one less than not finding a target). In some cases, the algorithm will not need that many recursive calls. If the sought-after target is found, the algorithm can terminate without additional recursive calls. Thus, on some inputs, the depth of recursive calls will be 0; on others it will be 1; on others 2; and so forth, up to $\lfloor \log_2 n \rfloor$. However, a more complete analysis would show that nearly half the keys in the array end up taking a recursion depth of $\lfloor \log_2 n \rfloor$. Even if the other half of the keys had no recursion at all, this would still result in an *average* recursion depth of one half of $\lfloor \log_2 n \rfloor$. Thus, the average number of recursive calls for finding a key is at least one half of $\lfloor \log_2 n \rfloor$. So the average case can save us only a factor of $\frac{1}{2}$ or less over the worst case. But constants like $\frac{1}{2}$ do not matter in big-O expressions; therefore, the average-case running time is $O(\log n)$, the same as the worst-case running time.

Java's Binary Search Methods

The Java Class Libraries include a class called `java.util.Arrays`, which contains many static methods for manipulating arrays. One group of these methods are designed to carry out a binary search on various kinds of arrays. For example, one of the methods searches a sorted array of integers:

```java
public static int binarySearch(int[] a, int target)
```

As with our own binary search method (in Figure 11.2 on page 573), the method searches the array for the specified target. Also, as with any binary search, the array must be in ascending order.

As you would expect, if the target is found, then `binarySearch` returns the index of the target; if the target occurs several times, then there is no guarantee of which occurrence will have its index returned—it might be the first occurrence, it might be the last, or it might be anywhere in between.

If the target is not in the array, the method returns a negative number, but unlike our method (which always returned −1 for an unfound number), the Java method returns a negative number that is calculated in a way that allows us to determine where the target *could be inserted* to keep the array sorted. In particular, when `binarySearch` returns a negative number −*i*, then that means that the target could be inserted at index *i*−1 and the list would remain sorted. (For example, a return value of −38 means that the target could be inserted at index 37.)

Figure 11.3 is a short demonstration program that shows the use of the binary search method with a small array.

Within `java.util.Arrays`, there are eight different `binarySearch` methods for searching arrays where the component is any of the seven basic types (such as `int` and `char`) or for an array of Java objects. In the case of objects, the array ordering comes from the implementation of a method called `compareTo`, which must be implemented for each object in the array and also for the target. We've seen `compareTo` before (page 292), and the requirement now is the same as the earlier occurrence: For any x and y, the result of x.`compareTo`(y) is:

- negative, if x is before y in the ordering on the set of objects,
- zero, if x is equal to y in the ordering on the set of objects, and
- positive, if x is after y in the ordering on the set of objects.

The precondition for `binarySearch` requires that the array parameter is sorted in ascending order with respect to the `compareTo` method that must be defined for all of the elements.

Java also provides static `binarySearch` methods in `java.util.Collections` to allow a programmer to search any collection class that implements Java's `List` interface (which is an extension of the `Collections` interface from Section 5.7).

| **FIGURE 11.3** | Testing the `binarySearch` Method from `java.util.Arrays` |

Implementation

```
import java.util.Arrays;
public class ArraySearcher
{
   // The main method prints a table of test results, searching for numbers
   // in an array that contains 2, 4, 6, 8, 10, 12, and 14.
   public static int search(String[ ] args)
   {
      final int[ ] DATA = { 2, 4, 6, 8, 10, 12, 14 };
      final int MINIMUM = -1;
      final int MAXIMUM = 16;
      int target;
      int answer;

      System.out.println("Searching for numbers in an array.");
      for (target = MINIMUM; target <= MAXIMUM; target++)
      {
         answer = Arrays.binarySearch(DATA, 0, DATA.length, target);
         System.out.print("Result searching for " + target + " is ");
         System.out.println("[" + answer + "].");
      }
      System.out.println("End of searching.");   }
}
```

Output

```
Searching for numbers in an array.
Result searching for -1 is [-1].
Result searching for 0 is [-1].
Result searching for 1 is [-1].
Result searching for 2 is [0].
Result searching for 3 is [-2].
Result searching for 4 is [1].
Result searching for 5 is [-3].
Result searching for 6 is [2].
Result searching for 7 is [-4].
Result searching for 8 is [3].
Result searching for 9 is [-5].
Result searching for 10 is [4].
Result searching for 11 is [-6].
Result searching for 12 is [5].
Result searching for 13 is [-7].
Result searching for 14 is [6].
Result searching for 15 is [-8].
End of searching.
```

Self-Test Exercises for Section 11.1

1. Reimplement the search method from Figure 11.2 on page 573 as a serial search. Use the pseudocode from Figure 11.1 on page 569 and make appropriate adjustments to the precondition/postcondition contract.

2. This exercise requires familiarity with Java's Comparable interface (Programming Project 11 on page 519). Rewrite the search method from Figure 11.2 on page 573 so that it searches an array of Comparable objects (similar to Java's own binarySearch method that we just saw).

3. Consider the search method from Figure 11.2 on page 573. Rewrite the method so that there is no size parameter. Instead, there is a parameter called last, which is the last index of the array segment being searched. Your precondition may require first <= last.

4. Compute the following values (H is the halving function): $H(1)$, $H(2)$, $H(4)$, $H(7)$, $H(8)$, $H(9)$.

11.2 OPEN-ADDRESS HASHING

In this section, we will present another approach to storing and searching for values. The technique, called *hashing,* has a worst-case behavior that is linear for finding a target, but with some care, hashing can be dramatically fast in the average case. Hashing also makes it easy to add and remove elements from the collection being searched, providing an advantage over binary search (since binary search must ensure that the entire list stays sorted when elements are added or removed).

As a bonus, Java has a standard hash table class, java.util.Hashtable, which can generally be used instead of implementing your own hash table. We'll look at the standard hash table after we've examined some of the issues involved in designing and implementing a hash table.

Introduction to Hashing

The Sixth Column Tractor Company sells all kinds of tractors with various stock numbers, prices, and other details. They want us to store information about each tractor in an inventory so that they can later retrieve information about any particular tractor simply by entering its stock number. To be specific, suppose the information about each tractor is an object in a class called Tractor. The Tractor class might have methods to return or change information about various tractor properties such as the tractor's cost, horsepower, stock number, and so on.

If the stock numbers have values ranging from 0 to 49, we could store the tractors in the following array, placing stock number i in location data[i]:

```
Tractor[ ] data = new Tractor[50]; // Array of 50 tractors
```

The tractor for stock number i can be retrieved immediately because we know it is in data[i].

But what if the stock numbers do not form a neat range like 0 ... 49. Suppose we know there will be 50 or fewer different stock numbers, but that they will be distributed in the range 0 through 4999. We could use an array with 5000 components, but that seems wasteful since only a small fraction of the array would be used. It appears that we have no alternative but to store the objects in an array with 50 elements and to use a serial search through the array whenever we wish to find a particular stock number. Things are not that bad. If we are clever, we can store the objects in a relatively small array and yet retrieve particular stock numbers much faster than we would by serial search.

To illustrate the trick involved, suppose an inside informer at the Sixth Column Tractor Company tells us that the stock numbers will be these:

```
0, 100, 200, 300, ..., 4800, 4900
```

In this case, we can store the objects in an array called data with only 50 components. The tractor with stock number i can be stored at data[i/100]. With this storage plan, we can make do with the indexes 0 through 49, even though the numbers become as large as 4900. If we want stock number 700, we compute 700/100 and obtain the index 7. The tractor for stock number 700 is stored in array component data[7].

hash function

This general technique is called **hashing**. Each element added to the table requires a unique identifying value called its **key**. In our example, the key was the tractor's stock number, but other, more complex keys are sometimes used. A computation, called the **hash function**, maps key values to array indexes. Suppose we implement our hash function as a method called hash. If an element has a key value of i, then we will try to store that element at location data[hash(i)]. Using the hash function to compute the correct array index is called **hashing the key to an array index**. The hash function must be chosen so that its return value is always a valid index for the array. The hash function may be either a Java method or a simple arithmetic expression. In our example, hash(i) was this expression:

```
i/100
```

collisions

In our example, every key produced a different index value when it was hashed. That is a perfect hash function, but unfortunately, a perfect hash function cannot always be found. Suppose we change the example so that we no longer have stock number 400, but we have 399 instead. Then the object with stock number 300 will be placed in data[3] as before, but where will stock number 399 be placed? Stock number 399 is supposed to be placed in data[399/100]. In other words, the object for stock number 399 is supposed to be placed in `data[3]`. There are now two different objects that belong in `data[3]`. This situation is known as a **collision**. In this case, we could redefine the hash function to avoid the collision. But in practice, you do not know the exact numbers that will occur as keys, and therefore you cannot design a hash function that is guaranteed to be free of collisions (unless, perhaps, your insider at the tractor company has a lot of pull). Something must be done to cope with the tractor collisions.

Typically, you do not know what numbers will be used as the key values, but you do know an upper bound on how many there will be. The usual approach is to use an array size that is larger than needed, and later we will see formulas that indicate how many extra positions are needed. The extra array positions make collisions less likely. A good hash function will distribute the key values uniformly through the index range of the array. If the array indexes range from 0 to 99, then you might use the following hash function to produce an array index for an object with a given key:

```
Math.abs(key) % 100
```

This hash function always produces a value in the range 0 to 99 (that is, the remainder when the absolute value of `key` is divided by 100).

Here's one way of dealing with collisions:

dealing with collisions

// *Basic storage by hashing algorithm*

1. For an object with key value given by `key`, compute the index `hash(key)`.

2. If `data[hash(key)]` does not already contain an object, then store the object in `data[hash(key)]` and end the storage algorithm.

3. If the location `data[hash(key)]` already contains an object, then try `data[hash(key)+1]`. If that location already contains an object, try `data[hash(key)+2]`, and so forth, until a vacant position is found. When the highest-numbered array position is reached, simply go to the start of the array. For example, if the array indexes are 0 ... 99 and the key is 98, then try 98, 99, 0, 1, and so on, in that order.

This storage algorithm is called **open-address hashing**, or more simply **open addressing**. In open addressing, collisions are resolved by placing the object in the next *open* spot of the array.

Noninteger Keys and Java's hashCode Method

Many applications require collections of objects with noninteger keys. For example, our tractors might have names such as "Big Bad Bruce" instead of stock numbers. In this case, we want to be able to retrieve a tractor by its name rather than a number. A clerk can ask for all the information about "Big Bad Bruce," and we're expected to use the string "Big Bad Bruce" as the key to retrieve information about a particular tractor.

String keys or other noninteger keys are usually handled by having an **encoding function** that converts the key into an integer value. This integer value is then hashed to an array index and is used in the same manner we've seen before. In fact, all Java classes include a method called hashCode, which is designed to convert an object to an integer value that can be used for hashing. For example, suppose we have:

- A String called key that we want to use as a key for an object
- A hash function called hash that converts integers to array indexes in our hash table

In this example, we would try to store the object at this location:

```
data[hash(key.hashCode( ))]
```

So the hashCode method allows us to use any Java Object as a key for adding something to a hash table. As you might guess, strings are the most common kind of object to use for such keys. In the case of strings, the hashCode method returns an integer that is an arithmetic computation based on the values of the string's characters. You don't need to know how the computation works to be able to use the hashCode method; all you need to know is that s.hashCode( ) is an integer value. (By the way, "Big Bad Bruce" is actually a bear from a Bill Peet story rather than a tractor. Java's hashCode for "Big Bad Bruce" is 2,136,477,814.)

◑ PITFALL

CLASSES OFTEN NEED A NEW HASHCODE METHOD

If you write a new class and write your own equals method (to determine when two objects are equal to each other), then you must often also write your own hashCode method for the class. The precondition/postcondition contract for hash-Code requires that two objects that are equal to each other must also have an identical value from the hashCode method. Two objects that are unequal may have equal or unequal hashCode values—but providing as many unequal hash codes as possible will reduce collisions.

The Table ADT—Specification

Storage by hashing forms the basis of the implementation of a new generic collection class called a table. A **table** is a collection of objects with operations for adding, removing, and locating objects. This sounds a lot like a bag, but the difference is that each table operation is controlled by a single key rather than being controlled by the entire object's value.

The Table class that we implement will actually be a reduced version of the standard java.util.Hashtable. The purpose of this implementation is to illustrate the ideas behind the implementation, but when you find yourself actually needing a hash table, you can use java.util.Hashtable instead.

The next few paragraphs specify the generic type parameters and six operations for our `Table` class.

The Generic Type Parameters.   The implementation of our `Table` class begins this way:

```
public class Table<K, E>
```

The class depends on *two* generic template parameters, K and E. The K parameter is the type of the key (which must have a `hashCode` method), whereas the E parameter is the type of the data for each item in the table.

The Constructor.   The `Table` class has a constructor that creates a hash table with a specified fixed capacity. Our table cannot grow beyond this capacity. There are several ways that we could allow for growing tables, but we will postpone that to focus on the table mechanism itself. So a typical `Table` declaration would be as follows:

```
// A table to hold up to 811 objects with Integer keys and Person data:
Table<Integer, Person> catalog = new Table<Integer, Person>(811);
```

In this declaration, the keys are `Integer` objects (which already have a `hashKey` method defined), and the data are objects of a type called `Person` (which could be any type, but presumably holds some information about a person).

The `size` and `capacity` Methods.   The `size` method returns the number of elements currently in the table. The `capacity` method returns the table's capacity, as determined by the argument to the constructor.

The put Method.   The `Table` class has a method to put a new object into the table. There are two possible outcomes from a `put` operation:

- There might already be an object with the same key as the new object. In this case, the old object is replaced by the new object with the same key.
- If the new object has a key that is not already in the table, then the new object is added to the table.

The complete specification of the `put` method is:

♦ **put**
    `public E put(K key, E element)`
    Add a new element to this table using the specified key.
    Parameters:
        key – the non-null key to use for the new element
        element – the new element that's being added to this table
    Precondition:
        If there is not already an element with the specified key, then this table's
        size must be less than its capacity (i.e., `size( ) < capacity( )`).
        Also, neither key nor element may be null.

Postcondition:
If this table already has an object with the specified key, then that object is replaced by element, and the return value is a reference to the replaced object. Otherwise, the new element is added with the specified key, and the return value is null.

Throws: IllegalStateException
Indicates that there is no room for a new object in this table.

Throws: NullPointerException
Indicates that key is null.

If the key is a new key (not already in the table), then the precondition of the put method requires that the table is not already full (otherwise, there won't be room for the new object). This is different from the standard java.util.Hashtable, which automatically grows as needed.

The containsKey and get Methods.   There are two accessor methods called containsKey and get. These methods search the table for an object with a particular key. Here are the specifications of the methods:

♦ **containsKey**
    public boolean containsKey(K key)
    Determine whether a specified key is in this table.

    Parameter:
        key – the non-null key to look for

    Precondition:
        key cannot be null.

    Returns:
        true (if this table contains an object with the specified key);
        false otherwise. Note that key.equals( ) is used to compare the key to the keys that are in the table.

    Throws: NullPointerException
        Indicates that key is null.

♦ **get**
    public E get(K key)
    Retrieve an object for a specified key.

    Parameter:
        key – the non-null key to look for

    Precondition:
        key cannot be null.

    Returns:
        A reference to the object with the specified key (if this table contains such an object); null otherwise. Note that key.equals( ) is used to compare the key to the keys that are in the table.

    Throws: NullPointerException
        Indicates that key is null.

The remove Method. This method removes an object with a specified key, as specified here:

♦ **remove**

```
public E remove(K key)
```
Remove an object for a specified key.

Parameter:
key – the non-null key to look for

Precondition:
key cannot be null.

Postcondition:
If an object was found with the specified key, then that object has been removed and a copy of the removed object is returned; otherwise, this table is unchanged and the null reference is returned. Note that key.equals( ) is used to compare the key to the keys that are in this table.

Throws: NullPointerException
Indicates that key is null.

The Table ADT—Design

Now we'll move on to the design and implementation of our Table class. The class will have four private instance variables, shown here:

```
public class Table<K, E>
{
    private int manyItems;
    private Object[ ] keys;
    private Object[ ] data;
    private boolean[ ] hasBeenUsed;
    ...
```

The variable manyItems indicates how many elements are currently in the table.

The elements themselves are stored in the data array, and the keys to the objects are stored in the keys array—but as we always do for generic classes, the actual arrays are arrays of type Object (see page 263). As an example, if an element is placed at data[i], then the key for that element will reside at keys[i].

The fourth instance variable, hasBeenUsed, is a boolean array. The value of hasBeenUsed[i] is true if data[i] and keys[i] have been used at some point, either now or in the past. Later, you will see that hasBeenUsed provides some efficiency to the containsKey, get, and remove methods. All three arrays are allocated by the table's constructor, with a length determined by the constructor's parameter.

Three Private Methods. During the process of adding a new element to the hash table, the first step will be to hash the key to an array index. This array index will be the preferred location for the new element, though if there is a collision, we will use open addressing to move forward to find an available position. The keys are objects, so we will hash the keys by first computing their hash code and then converting the hash code to a valid array index. In fact, the table will have a short private method to carry out this computation, as shown here:

```
private int hash(K key)
// The return value is a valid index of the table's arrays. The index is
// calculated as the remainder when the absolute value of the key's
// hash code is divided by the size of the table's arrays.
{
    return Math.abs(key.hashCode( )) % data.length;
}
```

nextIndex

A second private method will help us search the array for an open address. This method, called nextIndex, is used to step through the array one index after another, with wraparound at the end. The value of nextIndex(i) is usually i + 1, with one exception. When i is equal to the last index of the array, nextIndex(i) returns the first index of the array (zero).

findIndex

The third private method, called findIndex, is intended to find the array index of an object with a particular key. The value of findIndex(key) searches for the specified key. If the key is found, the method returns the index of the key in the keys array. Otherwise, the method returns –1 to indicate that the key is not in the keys array. This private method is similar to the public get method. The difference is that get returns a copy of the object with the specified key, whereas findIndex returns the array index of the specified key. The findIndex method will be useful for the implementor of the ADT because the implementor often needs to know where a particular key is located in the table. On the other hand, the programmer who uses the ADT doesn't need to know where a key is stored; in fact, that programmer doesn't even know that the elements happen to be stored in arrays.

Invariant for the Table ADT. With an understanding of the table's instance variables and the workings of the private methods, we can now state the complete invariant of the table ADT.

Invariant for the Table ADT

1. The number of elements in the table is in the instance variable manyItems.

2. The preferred location for an element with a given key is at index hash(key). If a collision occurs, then next-Index is used to search forward to find the next open address. When an open address is found at an index i, then the element itself is placed in data[i], and the element's key is placed at keys[i].

3. An index i that is not currently used has data[i] and keys[i] set to null.

4. If an index i has been used at some point (now or in the past), then hasBeenUsed[i] is true; otherwise, it is false.

The Table ADT—Implementation

The instance variables and three private methods have been defined for the Table class, and we know the ADT's invariant. The actual implementation is fairly straightforward. We'll discuss the methods one at a time.

The Constructor. Most of the table constructor's work involves allocating the three arrays, as shown here:

```
public Table(int capacity)
{
    // The manyItems variable is automatically set to zero, which is the
    // correct initial value. The three arrays are allocated to the specified
    // capacity. The boolean array is automatically initialized to all false,
    // and the other two arrays are automatically initialized to all null.
    if (capacity <= 0)
        throw new IllegalArgumentException("Capacity is negative.");
    keys = new Object[capacity];
    data = new Object[capacity];
    hasBeenUsed = new boolean[capacity];
}
```

Notice that the three arrays are allocated, but we don't need to put any initial values in the array components. The components of boolean arrays are automatically initialized to false, and the components of Object arrays are automatically initialized to null.

The put Method. This method's heading is public E put(K key, E element). The method puts the new element in the table with the specified key. If that key was already present in the table, then put returns a reference to the old element (which has been replaced); otherwise, the put method returns null. Our implementation starts by searching the table to determine whether the key is already in the table. The search is done with the statement index = findIndex(key). The private findIndex method was described on page 588, and it returns a –1 if it can't find the index of the specified key. After index is set, there are three cases shown in this pseudocode:

1. if (index != -1)
   The key is already in the table, so replace the data at the index.

2. else if (manyItems < data.length)
   // There is room for a new element to be added
   2a. Use a loop to set index so that data[index] is the first vacant location at or after data[hash(key)]. If the loop reaches the end of the array, then it should continue searching at data[0].
   2b. Set keys[index], data[index], and hasBeenUsed[index].
   2c. manyItems++;

3. else
   There's no room for another element, so throw an exception.

In Case 1, we will return a reference to the replaced data; in Case 2, we will return the null reference. This pseudocode is implemented at the top of Figure 11.4 on page 591. Notice that the loop in Step 2a uses the private method nextIndex in this assignment statement:

```
index = nextIndex(index);
```

This assignment moves index to the next available array index, wrapping back to the start of the array when index reaches the last valid array index. Also notice how the put method works if there is already an element with the same key as the new element. In this case, the new element replaces the old element (and the private instance variable manyItems remains unchanged).

The remove Method.   In our put method, we made use of the private method findIndex. The use of findIndex also simplifies the remove method, which has only three steps in its pseudocode (using local variables index and answer):

1. int index = findIndex(key);

2. E answer = null;

3. if (index != -1)

   An element has been found with the specified key. Set answer to data[index]; then set data[index] and keys[index] to null.

The remove implementation appears at the bottom of Figure 11.4.

The findIndex Method.   We have pushed a substantial amount of work into the findIndex method, which we will now implement. The method is responsible for finding the location in the array that contains a particular key value. Here is the specification of the private method:

```
private int findIndex(K key)
// Postcondition: If the specified key is found in the table, then the return
// value is the index of the specified key. Otherwise, the return value is - 1.
```

The method begins by hashing the key value to an array index and assigning this index to a local variable, i. The method then uses a loop to advance i through the possible indexes. Within the loop, we check whether we have found the index of the specified key. If so, we immediately return the value of i. On the other hand, if the loop determines that the key is not in the table, then the loop stops and the method returns −1.

   In our description of this work, just what does it mean to "determine that the key is not in the table"? One possibility is that we have examined every location in the table without finding the key. But sometimes it is possible to determine that the key is not in the table even though some locations have not been examined. Recall that if there is an element with its key equal to the parameter key, then this element should be at position hash(key) or in the first available position after that. Our method starts searching at array index hash(key). Should it ever encounter a position that has *never* held an element, then we have an interesting

FIGURE 11.4   Implementation of the put and remove Methods for the Open-Address Hash Table

Implementation

```java
@SuppressWarnings("unchecked")    // See the warnings discussion on page 265.
public E put(K key, E element)
{
    int index = findIndex(key);
    E answer;

    if (index != -1)
    {   // The key is already in the table.
        answer = (E) data[index];
        data[index] = element;
        return answer;
    }
    else if (manyItems < data.length)
    {   // The key is not yet in this table.
        index = hash(key);
        while (keys[index] != null)
            index = nextIndex(index);
        keys[index] = key;
        data[index] = element;
        hasBeenUsed[index] = true;
        manyItems++;
        return null;
    }
    else
    {   // The table is full.
        throw new IllegalStateException("Table is full.");
    }
}

@SuppressWarnings("unchecked")    // See the warnings discussion on page 265.
public void E remove(K key)
{
    int index = findIndex(key);
    E answer = null;

    if (index != -1)
    {
        answer = (E) data[index];
        keys[index] = null;
        data[index] = null;
        manyItems--;
    }

    return answer;
}
```

fact: If the key were ever put in the array, then it would have occurred at or before this vacant spot. Hence, the method knows that it has looked at every place that the key could possibly occur. Therefore, in the findIndex implementation, the loop terminates if it reaches a position that has never been used, as shown in this implementation of the loop (count is a local variable that keeps track of how many elements we have examined):

```
int count = 0;
int i = hash(key);
while ((count < data.length) && (hasBeenUsed[i]))
{
   if (key.equals(keys[i]))
      return i;
   count++;
   i = nextIndex(i);
}
return -1;
```

Notice that this technique for terminating the search cannot simply stop when it encounters a position that is *currently* vacant; the loop must continue until it encounters a position that has *never* held an element. We'll use an example to illustrate this after you've examined the findIndex and other implementations in Figure 11.5.

FIGURE 11.5   Implementation of the Table Class

Implementation

```
// FILE: Table.java from the package edu.colorado.collections
// Documentation is available starting on page 584 or from the Table link at
// http://www.cs.colorado.edu/~main/docs/.

package edu.colorado.collections;

public class Table<K, E>
{
   private int manyItems;
   private Object[ ] keys;
   private Object[ ] data;
   private boolean[ ] hasBeenUsed;

   public Table(int capacity)
   {
      if (capacity <= 0)
         throw new IllegalArgumentException("Capacity is negative.");
      keys = new Object[capacity];
      data = new Object[capacity];
      hasBeenUsed = new boolean[capacity];
   }
```

(continued)

(FIGURE 11.5 continued)

```
public boolean containsKey(K key)
|| See the answer to Self-Test Exercise 5.

private int findIndex(K key)
// Postcondition: If the specified key is found in the table, then the return
// value is the index of the specified key. Otherwise, the return value is -1.
{
   int count = 0;
   int i = hash(key);

   while ((count < data.length) && (hasBeenUsed[i]))
   {
      if (key.equals(keys[i]))
         return i;
      count++;
      i = nextIndex(i);
   }

   return -1;
}

@SuppressWarnings("unchecked")     // See the warnings discussion on page 265
public E get(K key)
{
   int index = findIndex(key);

   if (index == -1)
      return null;
   else
      return (E) data[index];
}

private int hash(Object key)
// The return value is a valid index of the table's arrays. The index is
// calculated as the remainder when the absolute value of the key's
// hash code is divided by the size of the table's arrays.
{
   return Math.abs(key.hashCode( )) % data.length;
}
```

(continued)

(FIGURE 11.5 continued)

```
private int nextIndex(int i)
// The return value is normally i+1. But if i+1 is data.length, then the return value is zero
// instead.
{
    if (i+1 == data.length)
        return 0;
    else
        return i+1;
}

private E put(K key, E element)
|| See the implementation in Figure 11.4 on page 591.

private E remove(K key)
|| See the implementation in Figure 11.4 on page 591.
}
```

A Practical Illustration of Open-Address Hashing

For an example of open addressing in action, I went to the undergraduate computing lab at the University of Colorado in Boulder. There were 1000 registered users of the lab. (I didn't make that up. Round numbers do occur sometimes!) Each person has a user record with information such as his or her full name and telephone number. I took the information from each user record and stored it in a Java `Object`. These objects were then placed in an open-address hash table, using the user's login name as the key. The table's capacity was 1231, a number that I chose using guidelines you'll see shortly.

Looking at parts of the resulting table can give you a good grasp of how open addressing works to solve collisions. For example, my own login name is `main`, and my entry happens to occur at entry 406 of the hash table, as shown in the margin on the next page. Let's go through the part of the hash table that is near my name. The records at indexes 402 and 403 were placed in their correct spots with no collisions. For example, the hash value for `landspar` is 402, and that spot was free when `landspar` entered the table.

What about `lcheng` with a hash value of 402? When `lcheng` entered the table, location 402 was already occupied by `landspar`, so the open-addressing algorithm moved to the next open location (403), which was also occupied. Finally, at 404, there was an open location where `lcheng` was placed.

When `lindr` entered the table, there was one collision (at 404), but 405 was open and `lindr` was placed there. When my own record, `main`, was placed in the table, the hash value was 405, but that location already contained `lindr`. However, 406 was open and `main` was placed there.

Finally, location 407 is a spot in the hash table that was not used.

If we search the table for the `main` record, the search will begin at `main`'s hash value of 405. Since that record does not contain `main`, the search continues forward and finds `main` in the next spot.

	· · ·
Index 402	Record for `landspar`, with a hash value of 402.
Index 403	Record for `harrisjm`, with a hash value of 403.
Index 404	Record for `lcheng`, with a hash value of 402.
Index 405	Record for `lindr`, with a hash value of 404.
Index 406	Record for `main`, with a hash value of 405.
Index 407	This spot has never been used to hold a record.
	· · ·

Let's also examine what happens when a record is removed from the table. Suppose the student `lindr` graduates. She will no doubt be happy, but she will have to leave the undergraduate lab, and her record will be removed from the hash table, as shown in the revised hash table shown here. The drawing shows that location 405 used to have a record, but it's now empty. In our hash table implementation, this would be indicated by setting `hasBeenUsed[405]` to `true`.

In this situation, what happens if we again search for `main`? The search starts at location 405, which is now unoccupied. But the search cannot stop; it must continue because `main` might be later in the table (caused by a collision with the element that used to be at location 405). In this case, the search continues and finds `main` at 406. (By the way, some search implementations will actually move `main` back to the earlier unoccupied spot when it has the chance, but our implementation does not do that.)

As a final example, suppose we are searching for the name `rickhall` with a hash value of 405. The search does not find `rickhall` at location 405 or 406. When the search examines location 407, it sees that

	·
Index 402	Record for `landspar`, with a hash value of 402.
Index 403	Record for `harrisjm`, with a hash value of 403.
Index 404	Record for `lcheng`, with a hash value of 402.
Index 405	This spot used to have a record, but it's now empty.
Index 406	Record for `main`, with a hash value of 405.
Index 407	This spot has never been used to hold a record.
	·

the spot has never been used (our implementation will have `hasBeenUsed[407]` set to `false`). Therefore, the search can conclude that `rickhall` is not in the table (since it would have been placed at or before location 407).

Out of interest, you might want to know that the undergraduate hash table has pretty good average behavior. There were 1000 used locations and 231 unused locations in the table. The average number of collisions during an insertion was 1.8, which means that a search examines only 2.8 elements on average. On the other hand, the worst entry, a user named `zhuj`, had a hash value of 863 and had 52 collisions, ending up at location 915. The problem was caused partly by the fact that the table was getting full (`zhuj` was one of the last entries placed in the table). It's interesting to look at the big group of 52 entries that `zhuj` collided with—most of them have fewer than two collisions—but the fact that there is a long sequence with no remaining openings is a real problem. Let's look at this problem, called *clustering*, along with techniques to reduce the overall number of collisions.

Choosing a Hash Function to Reduce Collisions

We have used a simple hash function that hashes a given key to the array index:

```
Math.abs(key.hashCode( )) % data.length
```

This kind of hash function depends on the remainder upon division and is therefore called a **division hash function**.

With a division hash function, certain table sizes are better than others at avoiding collisions that arise in data taken from real examples. C.E. Radke's 1970 study suggests that a good choice is a table size that is a prime number of the form $4k + 3$. For example, 1231 is a prime number equal to $(4 \times 307) + 3$.

Although division hash functions are the most common, you may sometimes encounter data that produces many collisions regardless of the table size. In this case, you can try two other common kinds of hash functions:

- **Mid-square hash function:** The key is converted to an integer and multiplied by itself. The hash function returns some middle digits of the result.
- **Multiplicative hash function:** The key is converted to an integer and multiplied by a constant less than 1. The hash function returns the first few digits of the fractional part of the result.

Double Hashing to Reduce Clustering

Consider what happens when you put a new element in a hash table and a collision occurs. The `put` moves forward from the original index until a vacant spot is found. For example, suppose a new key hashes to location 330, but this location is full. Then we will try location 331, then 332, then 333, and so on. Searching for a vacant spot in this manner is called **linear probing**.

There is a problem with linear probing. When several different keys are hashed to the same array location, the result is a small cluster of elements, one after another. As the table approaches its capacity, these clusters tend to merge into larger and larger clusters. This is the problem of **clustering**. If the key values happen to be consecutive numbers (such as a run of consecutive stock numbers in an inventory), then a "division hash function" makes clustering even worse. As clustering gets worse, adding a new element takes longer because the put method must step all the way through a cluster to find a vacant location. Elements are placed farther and farther from their correct hashed index, and searches require more time.

The most common technique to avoid clustering is called **double hashing**. The technique uses a second hash function to determine how we move through an array to resolve a collision. To see how this works, let's call the original hash function hash1 and call the second hash function hash2. When an element is added, double hashing begins by hashing the key to an array index using hash1. If there is a collision, then we calculate hash2(key) using the result to tell us how far forward to move through the array in looking for a vacant spot. For example, suppose a new key hashes to location 330 and hash2(key) is 7. If location 330 is occupied, then we move forward 7 spots and try location 337. If 337 is also occupied, then we move forward another 7 spots to location 344, and so on.

As we are stepping through the array, adding hash2(key) to the index at each step, there are two considerations:

- The array index must not leave the valid range of 0 to data.length - 1. We can keep the index in this range with the "%" operation. In particular, suppose that i is the index we have just examined (with a collision). Then the next index to examine is:

  (i + hash2(key)) % data.length

  For example, suppose data.length is 1231 and hash2(key) is 14. If a new key hashes to spot 1207 and there is a collision, then the next few spots we will try are 1221, then 4, then 18, then 32. Notice that the 4 is calculated as (1221 + 14) % data.length.

- As we step through the array, we must ensure that every array position is examined. With double hashing, this is a potential problem. We could come back to our starting position before we have examined every available location. There is an easy way to avoid this problem: Make sure the array's capacity is *relatively prime* with respect to the value returned by hash2. (In other words, these two numbers must not have any common factors apart from 1.) One way to accomplish this is to choose data.length as a prime number and have hash2 return values in the range 1 through data.length - 1. With this in mind, the preeminent computer scientist Donald Knuth suggests the following possibility (in which hash2 is never more than data.length - 2):

1. Both data.length and data.length - 2 should be prime numbers. For example, 1231 is prime and so is 1229. (Two such primes, separated by 2, are called **twin primes**.)

2. hash1(key) =

   Math.abs(key.hashCode( )) % data.length.

3. hash2(key) =

   1 + (Math.abs(key.hashCode( )) % (data.length-2)).

With our Table class from Figure 11.5 on page 592, double hashing can be incorporated in several ways. The easiest approach is to add another private method to compute hash2 and change nextIndex to return:

(i + hash2(key)) % data.length

This nextIndex method needs key as a second parameter.

At this point, you know enough to implement open-address hashing with linear probing or with double hashing. We'll delay the analysis of hashing until after the presentation of *chaining*, which is another way to resolve collisions. However, you might be interested in the results of double hashing for the undergraduate computer lab example. With double hashing, the average number of collisions drops from 1.8 to 1.0, and the maximum number of collisions drops from 52 to 21.

Self-Test Exercises for Section 11.2

5. Write the table's containsKey method.

6. Describe an idea for rewriting the Table class without the boolean array hasBeenUsed. Your idea should still be able to keep track of which locations have previously been used, but it should do so without having an explicit boolean array.

7. Suppose a hash table is full and you try to add a new element. What happens if the new element's key is already in the table? What happens if the new element's key is not already in the table?

8. In the implementation of the table's findIndex method, the method may sometimes find a key with a value of null. Why does the method need to continue to search?

9. An empty hash table has a capacity of 100, and you add six elements with hash codes 100, 0, 1199, 1299, 1399, and 2. Using linear probing and a division hash function, where will these elements be placed in the table? Where will they be placed with double hashing (with hash2(key) returning the value 1 + (Math.abs(key.hashCode( )) % 98))?

10. Write a quick program to determine whether there is a pair of twin primes between 800 and 850, with the upper prime having the form $4k + 3$ for some k. With this information, can you suggest a good size for a hash table that uses double hashing and has a capacity around 825?

11.3 USING JAVA'S HASHTABLE CLASS

Java has a standard hash table class called `java.util.Hashtable`. It has the same methods you have seen in the example `Table` class from the previous section, but the `Hashtable` class also grows automatically when it approaches full capacity. It also has a few additional methods that were not part of our `Table` class.

For example, the following statements create a hash table that stores phone numbers, using names as the keys. Both the phone numbers and the names are strings, and the sample statements put a few elements in the hash table:

```
import java.util.Hashtable;
...

// Both the keys and the data are strings, and the capacity is 811.
Hashtable<String, String> phonebook = new Hashtable<String, String>(811);
phonebook.put("Jean Luc", "622-1701");
phonebook.put("Katherine", "627-4656");
phonebook.put("Benjamin", "622-1764");
```

The statements have created a hash table with an initial capacity of 811. Java's hashtable is normally set to grow automatically when it becomes 75% full. After these statements, we could retrieve Katherine's phone number to store in a string variable with this statement:

```
String s = phonebook.get("Katherine");
```

Notice that the return value of the `get` method is a Java `String`, because the generic type of the table's data was set to `String`.

A summary of the `Hashtable` constructors and other methods is given in Appendix D. The summary includes information about how to change the point at which the table grows. For guidelines on setting the growth point, you can refer to "Time Analysis of Hashing" on page 605.

Hashtable versus HashMap

Java has a second collection class, `HashMap`, that uses a hash table to implement the `Map` interface you saw in Chapter 5. The `HashMap` has the advantage that both values and keys may be null, but it is not guaranteed to work correctly in programs that involve multiple threads (which are separate computations that occur concurrently, or at least appear to occur that way).

11.4 CHAINED HASHING

In open-address hashing, a collision is handled by probing the array for an unused position. Each array component can hold just one element. When the array is full, no more items can be added to the table. At that point, we could resize the array and rehash all the elements, placing each element in a new, larger array. But this would require a careful choice of the new size and would probably require each element to have a new hash value computed. An alternative approach uses a different collision-resolution method called chained hashing.

In **chained hashing**, also called **chaining**, the hash table contains an array in which each component can hold more than one element of the hash table. As with all hashing, we still hash the key of each element to obtain an array index. But if there is a collision, we don't worry too much. We simply place the new element in its proper array component along with other elements that happened to hash to the same array index.

How does chaining place more than one element in each component of the array? The answer is that each array component must have some underlying structure. The most common structure is to have each array component be a head reference for a linked list. Each node of the linked list is an object of the generic class shown here (similar to the generic node of Section 5.4):

```
class ChainedHashNode<K, E>
{
    K key;
    E element;
    ChainedHashNode<K, E> link;
}
```

Each object of this class has three instance variables, which are accessed directly rather than through methods. An implementation of a chained hash table can build an array of references to the heads of linked lists, where the nodes on the linked lists are objects of the ChainedHashNode<K, E> class. For example, if the size of the chained hash table is 811, then the class declaration for the chained hash table can begin like this:

```
public class ChainedTable<K, E>
{
    // For index i, the Object in table[i] is the head reference for a linked
    // list of all the elements for which hash(key) is equal to i.
    private Object[ ] table = Object[811];
```

This implementation has an array called table with 811 objects. Each of these objects is a head reference for a linked list. Ideally, this array would be declared as an array of type ChainedHashNode<K, E> objects, but remember that an array of generic objects is forbidden in Java (see page 263). Therefore, we use an array of Java objects in the declaration. Whenever we use the array in our code, we will ensure that the array contains references to the head of a linked list of ChainedHashNode<K, E> nodes.

In effect, the implementation has 811 separate linked lists, as shown here:

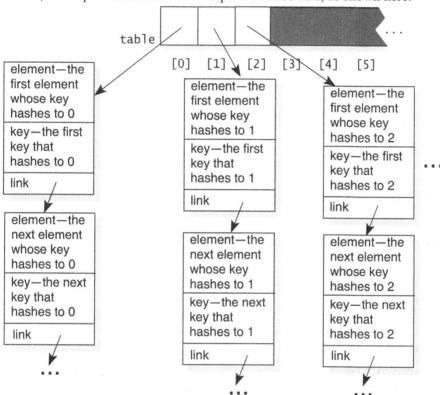

All the elements that hash to location i are placed on the linked list, which has its head reference stored in `table[i]`. Figure 11.6 shows an outline of the `Table` class declaration is using this scheme. In this outline, the table's size is determined by the constructor. The separate class, `ChainedHashNode<K,E>`, can be placed in the same file as the `ChainedTable<K, E>` class.

Self-Test Exercises for Section 11.4

11. Consider the chaining version of the table we have described. What value will be in each component of `table` after the constructor finishes?

12. Write a private method that can be used to carry out the first two shaded lines in the outline of Figure 11.6 on page 602.

13. Use your `put` method to place six items in a hash table with a table size of 811. Use the keys 811, 0, 1623, 2435, 3247, and 2.

14. In our new `ChainedTable` class, the array is still a fixed size. It never grows after the constructor allocates it. So, is there a limit to the number of elements in the chained hash table?

15. Suppose the keys can be compared using a `compareTo` method (such as in Programming Project 11 on page 519). Can you think of some advantage to keeping each linked list of the table sorted from smallest key to largest key?

FIGURE 11.6   Outline of the `ChainedTable` Class

Implementation

```
public class ChainedTable<K, E>
{
    private Object[ ] table;

    public ChainedTable(int tableSize)
    {
        if (tableSize <= 0)
            throw new IllegalArgumentException("Table size must be positive.");
        // Allocate the table, which is initially all null head references.
        table = new Object[tableSize];
    }

    @SuppressWarnings("unchecked")      // See the warnings discussion on page 265.
    public E put(K key, E element)
    {
        ChainedHashNode<K, E> cursor;
        E answer = null;

        if (key = null || element == null)
            throw new NullPointerException("key or element is null");
```

> You must write code here to set `cursor` to refer to the node that already contains the specified node. If there is no such node, then cursor is set to null.

```
        if (cursor == null)
        {   // Add a new node at the front of the list of table[hash(key)].
            int i = hash(key);
            cursor = new ChainedHashNode( );
            cursor.element = element;
            cursor.key = key;
            cursor.link = (ChainedHashNode<K, E>) table[i];
            table[i] = cursor;
        }
        else
        {   // The new element replaces an old node.
            answer = cursor.element;
            cursor.element = element;
        }
        return answer;
    }
```

> Other methods, such as `hash` and `get`, must be implemented here.

```
}
```

> The `ChainedHashNode` declaration from page 600 must appear here.

Each component of the array is a head reference for a linked list.

11.5 PROGRAMMING PROJECT: A TABLE CLASS IMPLEMENTED WITH JAVA'S VECTOR AND LINKEDLIST

A New Table Class

We have implemented hash tables with an array of records (for open-address hashing) and an array of linked lists (for chained hashing). The goal of this section is to implement a new version of a chained hash table by using existing collection classes from the Java Class Libraries. The new class, called NewTable, has the advantage of being able to easily access and modify data items using the methods and iterators of the underlying collection classes. A second advantage is that we no longer need to worry about the fact that Java forbids arrays of generic elements, because we'll never need such an array! Instead, we'll use the Java generic collection classes—and whoever implemented those classes can worry about the generic array problems.

Data Structures for the New Table Class

The public methods for the NewTable class will be identical to those we've already seen for the ChainedTable class, and the underlying data structures will be similar. The primary member variable of the NewTable will be a Java Vector, which is a data type that we saw briefly in Chapter 5 (see page 300 and the details in Appendix D). The functionality of a Vector v is similar to an array, but instead of using the v[i] notation to access the element at index i, there are two methods to retrieve and set individual elements. In particular, v.get(i) returns the element at index i, and v.set(i, value) sets the element at index i to a specified value.

The Vector member variable will be called table, like this:

```
public class NewTable<K, E>
{
    private Vector< ??? > table;
    ...
```

Notice that the NewTable is a generic class that depends on two underlying data types: K (the type of the table's keys) and E (the type of the table's elements). But we've omitted one piece of the table declaration! We must fill in the < *???* > part of the Vector declaration with the data type of the individual components of the table member variable. Since we are implementing a chained hash table, we require the component of the table at an index i to be a linked list containing all the hash table elements with hash(key) equal to i. However, we won't use our own homegrown linked list. Instead, we'll use Java's linked list class, along these lines:

```
public class NewTable<K, E>
{
    private Vector< LinkedList< ??? > > table;
    ...
```

So, we have a vector in which each component is a linked list. But once again, we've omitted a detail! What is the data type of the elements on the linked lists? Each element on each linked list is an entry in the hash table, so it must contain both a key (of type K) and a piece of data (of type E). We can put those two items into a tiny object of a class that we define ourselves, which leads us to this solution with two separate classes:

```
// Each object of this tiny public class holds the key and the data of one
//  entry in the hash table:
class HashPair<K, E>
{
    K key;
    E element;
}
```

```
// Our new hash table is implemented with a vector member variable.
// The component at index i of the vector is a linked list that contains all
//  the hash table entries with hash(key) equal to i.
public class NewTable<K, E>
{
    private Vector< LinkedList< HashPair<K,E> > > table;
    ...
```

In effect, this implementation has the same structure as the diagram at the top of page 601, but instead of using our own array and linked list, we are using Java's Vector and LinkedList classes.

Implementing the New Table Class

We're nearly ready to turn you loose on the entire implementation of the NewTable. But to get you started, we'll design and implement the put member function with the usual specification:

◆ **put**

    public E put(K key, E element)
    Add a new element to this table using the specified key.

   Parameters:
    key – the non-null key to use for the new element
    element – the new element that's being added to this table

   Precondition:
    If there is not already an element with the specified key, then this table's size must be less than its capacity (i.e., size( ) < capacity( )). Also, neither key nor element may be null.

Postcondition:
If this table already has an object with the specified key, then that object is replaced by `element`, and the return value is a reference to the replaced object. Otherwise, the new element is added with the specified key, and the return value is null.

Throws: `NullPointerException`
Indicates that `key` or `element` is null.

Our approach takes these three steps:

1. Check that neither the key nor the element is null. The key cannot be null because null has no hash value. The element cannot be null because null is used as a special return value from some of the member functions to indicate that there is no element with a given key.

2. Compute the hash value, `i`, of the given key and set up an iterator to go through the linked list at component number `i` of the `table`. The iterator looks at each element of that linked list. If it finds a `HashPair` with the given key, then it replaces the element of that `HashPair` with the new element (and returns a reference to the old element).

3. If the given key was not found in the linked list, then we add a new node to the list with the specified key and element.

These three steps are implemented in Figure 11.7.

Self-Test Exercises for Section 11.5

16. Suppose you are implementing the `NewTable` class. Which of these three classes must you write: `HashPair`, `LinkedList`, `Vector`?
17. What are the advantages of using Java's generic classes, such as `Vector` and `LinkedList`, rather than using an array?
18. Write the constructor for the `NewTable`. The constructor has one parameter, which is the size of the vector. The implementation must create that vector and also create all of the linked lists (which are initially empty).

11.6 TIME ANALYSIS OF HASHING

The worst case for hashing occurs when every key gets hashed to the same array index. We may end up searching through all the items to find the one we are after—a linear operation, just like serial search. However, with some reasonable assumptions, the average time for a search of a hash table is dramatically fast, requiring us to examine just a handful of elements. This section provides the information needed for an average-time analysis of our three hashing methods.

FIGURE 11.7   Partial Implementation of the `NewTable` Class

Implementation

```
package edu.colorado.collections;
import java.util.*;

class HashPair<K, E>
{
    K key;
    E element;
}

public class NewTable<K, E>
{
    private Vector< LinkedList< HashPair<K, E> > > table;

    public E put(K key, E element)
    {
        if (key == null || element == null)
            throw new NullPointerException("key or element is null");

        // Set up a ListIterator that can step through the one linked list that might
        // already have an element with the given key.
        int i = hash(key);
        LinkedList< HashPair<K, E> > oneList = table.get(i);
        ListIterator< HashPair<K, E> > cursor = oneList.listIterator(0);

        // Two other variables for the new HashPair (if needed) and the return value:
        HashPair<K, E> pair;
        E answer;

        // Step through the one linked list using the iterator (see page 287):
        while (cursor.hasNext( ))
        {
            pair = cursor.next( );
            if (pair.key.equals(key))
            {  // We found the given key already on the list.
                answer = pair.element;
                pair.element = element;
                return answer;
            }
        }

        // The specified key was not on oneList, so create a new node for the new entry:
        pair = new HashPair<K, E>;
        pair.key = key;
        pair.element = element;
        oneList.add(pair);
    }

    ‖ Other methods, such as hash and get, must be implemented here.

}
```

The Load Factor of a Hash Table

Analyzing the average-time performance of hashing is complex, particularly when removals are allowed. However, Knuth's *The Art of Programming, Volume 3*, provides formulas that can guide our choice of hash-table algorithms. Knuth's most useful formulas provide the average number of table elements that must be examined during a successful search for a key. There are three different formulas for the three versions of hashing: open addressing with linear probing, open addressing with double hashing, and chained hashing.

These three formulas depend on how many items are in the table. When the table has many items, there are many collisions, and the average time for a search is longer. With this in mind, we first define a fraction called the **load factor**, which is written α and is defined by the formula given here:

definition of the load factor, α

$$\alpha = \frac{\text{Number of elements in the table}}{\text{The size of the table's array}}$$

For open-address hashing, each array component holds at most one element, so the load factor can never exceed 1. But with chaining, each array component can hold many elements, and the load factor might be higher than 1.

Average Search Time for Open Addressing (Linear Probing). Open-address hash tables with linear probing have just one hash function. Collisions are resolved by stepping forward, probing consecutive array components. With linear probing and no removals, Knuth's formula for the time of a successful search is:

Searching with Linear Probing

In open-address hashing with linear probing, a nonfull hash table, and no removals, the average number of table elements examined in a successful search is approximately:

$$\frac{1}{2}\left(1 + \frac{1}{1 - \alpha}\right)$$

This formula is not exact, but it is a good approximation when the load factor (α) is below 1. You might notice that the formula completely fails when α is 1 since there is then a division by zero. But that situation would indicate a full hash table, and you should avoid getting close to full anyway. If you insist on a full hash table of n elements, Knuth shows that the average time for a successful search is approximately $\sqrt{n(\pi/8)}$—but better yet, steer clear of full tables, and you can use the formula in the box above. In addition to a nonfull table, the formula's derivation also assumes that we have not removed any elements and that the hash function does a good job of uniformly distributing all possible keys throughout the array (which is called **uniform hashing**).

As an example of how to use the formula, suppose we plan to put 649 elements into a table with a capacity of 811. This provides a load average of

649/811, or about 80%. On average, we expect successful searches to examine three table elements, as shown here:

$$\frac{1}{2}\left(1 + \frac{1}{1-\alpha}\right) = \frac{1}{2}\left(1 + \frac{1}{1-0.8}\right) = 3.0$$

Average Search Time for Open Addressing (Double Hashing). You have seen that open-address hash tables with double hashing provide some relief from clustering. The result is a smaller average time, given by the following formula (which uses "ln" to denote the natural logarithm of a number).

Searching with Double Hashing

In open-address hashing with double hashing, a nonfull hash table, and no removals, the average number of table elements examined in a successful search is approximately:

$$\frac{-\ln(1-\alpha)}{\alpha}$$

As with the previous formula, this estimate is approximate. It depends on a nonfull hash table, no removals, and using a hash function with uniform hashing.

You don't need to memorize the formula, but you should know how to use it along with the ln key on your calculator. For example, ln(0.2) is about –1.6, so with a load factor of 0.8, we expect to examine an average of two elements in a successful search, as shown here:

$$\frac{-\ln(1-\alpha)}{\alpha} = \frac{-\ln(0.2)}{0.8} = \frac{1.6}{0.8} = 2$$

This is an improvement over the linear probing with the same load factor.

Average Search Time for Chained Hashing. With chaining, each component of the table's array is a reference to the head of a linked list, and each of these linked lists may have several table elements. Therefore, the load factor may be higher than 1 in this formula:

Searching with Chained Hashing

In open-address hashing with chained hashing, the average number of table elements examined in a successful search is approximately:

$$1 + \frac{\alpha}{2}$$

FIGURE 11.8 Average Number of Table Elements Examined During a Successful Search

Load factor (α)	Open Addressing with Linear Probing $\frac{1}{2}\left(1 + \frac{1}{1-\alpha}\right)$	Open Addressing with Double Hashing $\frac{-\ln(1-\alpha)}{\alpha}$	Chained Hashing $1 + \frac{\alpha}{2}$
0.5	1.50	1.39	1.25
0.6	1.75	1.53	1.30
0.7	2.17	1.72	1.35
0.8	3.00	2.01	1.40
0.9	5.50	2.56	1.45
1.0			1.50
2.0	Not applicable		2.00
4.0			3.00

Once again, this estimate is approximate; it depends on using uniform hashing. Unlike the other two formulas, the chaining formula is valid even with removals.

With a load factor of 0.8, chained hashing expects to examine only 1.4 items during a successful search. Some other possible load factors are shown in Figure 11.8. You can compare the average numbers for the different hashing methods.

Self-Test Exercises for Section 11.6

19. Suppose you place 180 elements in a hash table with an array size of 200. What is the load factor? For each of the three hash methods, what is the average number of table elements you expect to have examined during a successful search?

20. You want to place 1000 elements in a hash table, and you'd like an average search to examine just two table elements. How big does the table's array need to be? Give separate answers for the three hash methods.

CHAPTER SUMMARY

- Serial search is quick to program but requires linear time to find an element in both the worst case and the average case.

- Binary search works well on a sorted array, requiring $O(\log n)$ time in both the worst case and the average case. As elements are added or removed, however, keeping the array in order may take considerable time (linear time for each addition or removal in the worst case).

- Hash tables are a good strategy for storing and retrieving elements with a key. In fact, it would be perfect if there were no collisions.

- One way to deal with collisions is **open addressing**. This scheme handles collisions by placing each new element in the first open location that is at or after the spot where the key hashes to. Two methods of searching for an open location are **linear probing** (which examines the array locations in consecutive order) and **double hashing** (which uses a second hash function to determine the size of the steps that are taken through the array). Double hashing is the better method because it avoids clustering.

- Another way to deal with collisions is **chaining**. In the chaining approach, each location of the hash table's array is able to hold multiple elements. A common way to implement chaining is for each array location to be a reference to the head of a linked list of elements.

- When you are implementing a new collection class (such as a chained hash table), there are advantages to using Java's generic classes (such as Vector and LinkedList) rather than directly using an array.

- The worst-case search time for a hash table is linear. But the average-case time is quite fast. Depending on the load factor and the precise method of hashing, the average case requires about two to five table elements to be examined during a successful search (see Figure 11.8 on page 609).

? Solutions to Self-Test Exercises

1. The precondition is modified so that the array no longer needs to be sorted. Here's the code:

```java
public static int search(
    int a[ ],
    int first, int size,
    int target
)
{
    int i = 0;
    boolean found = false;

    while ((i < size) && !found)
    {
        if (a[first+i] == target)
            found = true;
        else
            i++;
    }
    if (found)
        return first+i;
    else
        return -1;
}
```

2. See Figure 11.9.

3. The function is not difficult to write, but pay attention to the potential pitfalls from page 574.

4. $H(1) = 1, H(2) = 2, H(4) = 3, H(7) = 3, H(8) = 4, H(9) = 4$.

5. Here's one way to implement the method:

```java
public boolean
containsKey(Object key)
{
    return (findIndex(key) != -1);
}
```

6. One idea is to set keys[i] to null when the element at location i is removed, but keep data[i] so that it still refers to the removed data. Then we could tell when a spot has previously been used because data[i] would be non-null. The problem with this approach is

that it can interfere with Java's garbage collection. (The garbage collector would not collect the old data, because the program still has a reference to it.) So a better approach is to have some object declared as an instance variable in the `Table` class. The object can be called `previouslyUsed`, and when the element at location i is removed, we'll set `keys[i]` to null and set `data[i]` to refer to `previouslyUsed`.

7. If the key was already present, then the data with that key is overwritten. If the key was not already present, then the method tests whether there is room for a new element. When this test fails, the method throws an exception.

8. Suppose we start looking in the keys array at some index—say, 34—and we move forward until we find a null key. Perhaps this first null key is at index 36. If `hasBeenUsed[36]` is false, then that indicates that the location has never been used, and therefore no element with the given key appears in the table (since it would have been placed in this unused location or perhaps in location 34 or 35, which we have already examined).

On the other hand, if `hasBeenUsed[36]` is true, then this location has previously been used and since removed. In this case, it is possible that there is an element with the given key in the table at a location after 36. It might be after this location because, at the time it was added, location 36 might have been in use.

9. For linear probing, the key/index pairs are 100 at [0], 0 at [1], 1199 at [99], 1299 at [2], 1399 at [3], and 2 at [4]. For double hashing, the key/index pairs are 100 at [0], 0 at [1], 1199 at [99], 1299 at [25], 1399 at [27], and 2 at [2].

FIGURE 11.9   The Binary Search Method for Comparable Objects

```
// The method uses Java's Comparable interface from Programming Project 11 on page 519.
// Neither the target nor the array elements may be null references.
public static int search(Comparable[ ] a, int first, int size, Comparable target)
{
   int middle;
   int comparison;

   if (size <= 0)
      return -1;
   else
   {
      middle = first + size/2;
      comparison = target.compareTo(a[middle]);
      if (comparison == 0)
         return middle;
      else if (comparison < 0)
         // The target is less than a[middle], so search before the middle.
         return search(a, first, size/2, target);
      else
         // The target must be greater than a[middle], so search after the middle.
         return search(a, middle+1, (size-1)/2, target);
   }
}
```

10. There is a twin prime pair at 809 and 811, which suggests that 811 is a good table capacity.

11. An array of objects is automatically initialized with `null` at every component.

12. We call our new method `findNode`:
```
public ChainedHashNode
findNode(Object key)
{
   ChainedHashNode cursor;

   cursor = table[hash(key)];
   while (cursor != null)
   {
       if (key.equals(cursor.key)
          return cursor;
       cursor = cursor.link;
   }
   return null;
}
```

13. The `table[0]` list will have the keys 0 and 811. The `table[1]` list will have the key 1623. The `table[2]` list will have the keys 2 and 2435. The `table[3]` list will have the key 3247. All other lists are empty.

14. There is no limit because each component of the table is the head of a linked list that may contain many elements.

15. If the lists are kept in order, then a search can stop as soon as it reaches a key that is greater than the target.

16. `HashPair`

17. With a generic class rather than an array, various manipulations (such as searching) may be easier because of the class's methods. In addition, you avoid the problem that Java forbids an array component of a generic type.

18. Here is one solution:
```
public NewTable(int size)
{
   int i;

   if (size <= 0)
      throw new
      IllegalArgumentException
      ("Table size must be >= 0");

   // Create the vector and empty lists:
   table = new Vector
   <LinkedList<HashPair<K,E>>(size);
   for (i = 0; i < size; i++)
   {
      table.set(
      new LinkedList<HashPair<K,E>( );
   }
}
```

19. The load factor is 0.9 (i.e., 180/200). With linear probing, the expected average is 5.50; with double hashing, the expected average is 2.56; with chained hashing, the expected average is 1.45.

20. For linear probing, we need a load factor of 2/3, which requires a table capacity of 1500. For double hashing, we need a load factor of just less than 0.8, requiring a table capacity of about 1250. For chaining, we need a load factor of 2, requiring an array size of 500.

PROGRAMMING PROJECTS

1 Reimplement the binary search using a loop and no recursion. If you are familiar with Java's `Comparable` interface, then your implementation should search an array of `Comparable` objects rather than an array of `int`.

2 Use a binary search technique to write a game program that asks the user to think of an integer in a particular range and then tries to guess the number. The program may ask questions such as "Is your number bigger than 42?" Your result should have worst-case time of $O(\log n)$, where n is the size of the range of numbers.

3 For this project, you must first implement the `Polynomial` class from the Chapter 3 Programming Project 8 on page 170. Add a new method to the class with four parameters: a polynomial `f` and three double numbers `x`, `z`, and `epsilon`. The precondition requires that `epsilon` is positive and `f(x) <= 0 <= f(z)`.

The method searches for a number `y` between `x` and `z`, where `f(y)` is zero. Such a number is called a **root** of the polynomial. The method's return value might not be an exact root, but the difference between the return value and a real root should be no more than `epsilon`. The algorithm is a binary search of the numbers between `x` and `z`.

4 Use **double hashing** to reimplement the hash table from Figure 11.5 on page 592.

5 In our open-address hash tables, we have used linear probing or double hashing. Another probing method, which avoids some clustering, is called **quadratic probing**. The simplest version of quadratic probing works like this: Start by hashing the key to an array index. If there is a collision, then move to the next array index. If there is a *second* collision, then move forward *two* more spots through the array. After a *third* collision, move forward *three* more spots, and so on. For example, suppose a new key hashes to location 327 and this location is full. The next location we try is 328. If 328 is a second collision, then we move two spots forward to location 330. If 330 is a third collision, then we move three spots forward to location 333. If our calculation of the next spot takes us beyond the end of the array, then we "wrap around" to the front of the array (similar to double hashing). In general, if location `i` has just caused a collision and we have already examined `count` elements, then we increase `i` according to the assignment:

```
i = (i + count) % data.length;
```

In this formula, the "`% data.length`" causes the "wraparound" to the front of the array. For this approach to work correctly, the capacity must be a power of 2, such as $2^{10} = 1024$. Otherwise, the sequence of probes does not correctly examine all array items.

For this project, use quadratic hashing to reimplement the hash table from Figure 11.5 on page 592.

6 Rewrite one of your hash tables so that it has additional methods to provide statistics. You should include methods to calculate the load factor, the average number of items examined during a successful search, and the maximum number of items examined during a successful search.

Find a large collection of information to put in your hash table, perhaps the list of users at your computing site. Test how the statistics vary based on the capacity of the hash table.

7 Redesign the interface for a hash table to allow the data to be null and to allow multiple elements with the same key. You'll have to give some thought to the return value for the `get` function in the case where there is more than one entry with a given key.

8 Implement a dictionary program using a hash table. The user inputs a word, and then the word's definition is displayed. You'll need to use Java's hash table class with a string as both the key and the element types.

9 Implement the `NewTable` class from Section 11.5.

Sorting

When you complete Chapter 12, you will be able to ...

- do a simulation by hand of selectionsort, insertionsort, mergesort, quicksort, and heapsort.
- implement each of these sorting algorithms to sort an array of numbers or to sort any array of objects that satisfies Java's Comparable interface.
- explain the runtime advantage of insertionsort in the situation in which an array is nearly sorted to begin with.
- explain the advantage of mergesort for sorting a collection of data that is too large to fit in memory all at once.
- demonstrate situations where the poor choice of a pivot element can cause quadratic behavior for quicksort.

Sorting

A place for everything and everything in its place.

ISABELLA MARY BEETON
The Book of Household Management

One commonly encountered programming task is sorting a list of values. By way of examples, the list might consist of exam scores, and we may want to see them sorted from lowest to highest or from highest to lowest; the list might be a list of words that we have misspelled, and we may want to see them in alphabetical order; the list might be a list of student records, and we may want them sorted by student number or alphabetically by student name. In this chapter, we present and analyze a number of different sorting algorithms.

To maintain a sharp focus on the sorting algorithms, we will consider only arrays of integers and design algorithms to sort the integers into order from smallest to largest. However, if you are familiar with Java's Comparable interface (from Programming Project 11 on page 519), then you may easily adapt the algorithms to sort arrays of values of other types or to sort values according to other ordering relations. Other adaptations are also possible. For example, one common way of ordering objects is to choose one special instance variable, which is then called the **key field**, and to sort the objects according to that key field. Using a key field, we could sort a list of student records by student number (with the student number serving as the key field). We could sort the same records alphabetically by student name (with the student name serving as the key field).

sorting by key field

12.1 QUADRATIC SORTING ALGORITHMS

In this section, we develop and implement two algorithms to sort a list of numbers into increasing order.

Selectionsort—Specification

We have an array of integers that we wish to sort into order from smallest to largest. To be concrete, we'll use this heading and specification:

```
public static void selectionsort(int[ ] data, int first, int n)
// Precondition: data has at least n components starting at data[first].
// Postcondition: The elements of data have been rearranged so
//   that data[first] <= data[first + 1] <= ... <= data[first + n - 1].
```

The method is a static method that could be part of a class that needs to do some sorting, or it could be part of a class that provides static sorting methods for other classes to use.

Selectionsort—Design

One way to design an algorithm is to rely on the definition of the problem. Our problem is to sort part of an array from smallest to largest. In particular, we must rearrange the n values starting at data[first] so that data[first] is the smallest, data[first + 1] the next smallest, and so forth, up to data[first + n - 1], which is the largest. That definition yields an outline for a straightforward algorithm (i is a local variable):

```
for (i = 0; i < n; i++)
    Move the smallest element of the segment
    data[first + i]...data[first + n - 1] to location data[first + i].
```

This approach finds the smallest element, then the next smallest, and so on, placing the elements in data[first + 0], data[first + 1], ... as they are found. We can also work the approach the other way, finding the largest element, then the second largest, and so on:

```
for (i = n-1; i >= 0; i--)
    Move the largest element of the segment
    data[first]...data[first + i] to location data[first + i].
```

There are many ways to realize either of these general approaches. The details could be developed using two arrays and copying the elements from one array to the other in sorted order. However, one array is both adequate and economical, so we decided to develop the algorithm using only one array. To help in exploring the problem, we will use the concrete example shown here:

data

10	8	6	2	16	4	18	11	14	12
[0]	[1]	[2]	[3]	[4]	[5]	[6]	[7]	[8]	[9]

Consider sorting this entire array with a pencil and eraser according to the second version of the pseudocode we have outlined (finding and placing the largest element, then the next largest, and so on). Because we are sorting the entire array, the parameters for our selectionsort will have first equal to 0 and n equal to 10.

We begin by searching the array for the largest element, and we find this largest element at data[6], which is the 18. We next want to set the final element of the array equal to this value of 18. In doing so, we must be careful not to lose the original value of 12 that was stored in array location data[9]. A simple assignment statement like the following would destroy the 12:

```
data[9] = data[6]; // No good: destroys the original data[9].
```

The algorithm must not simply destroy the original value 12 that was in the final spot of the array. Fortunately, we have an array location in which to store it. We can place it in the location that used to have the largest element. In other words, we actually want to "swap" the largest element with the final element of the array. After the swap, the array looks like this:

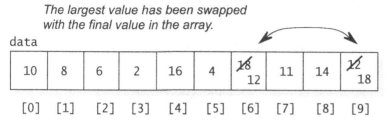

*The largest value has been swapped
with the final value in the array.*

data

10	8	6	2	16	4	~~18~~ 12	11	14	~~12~~ 18
[0]	[1]	[2]	[3]	[4]	[5]	[6]	[7]	[8]	[9]

The values of data[6] and data[9] have simply been swapped. A similar thing is done with the second-largest value of the array. We find this second-largest value (the 16 at data[4]) and swap it with the next-to-last element of the array (data[8]), resulting in this array:

*The second-largest value has been swapped
with the next-to-last value in the array.*

data

10	8	6	2	~~16~~ 14	4	12	11	~~14~~ 16	18
[0]	[1]	[2]	[3]	[4]	[5]	[6]	[7]	[8]	[9]

The entire array can be sorted by a series of swaps such as these. Any sorting algorithm that is based on swapping elements is called an **interchange sort**.

The simplest interchange sorting algorithm, which we have been describing, is called **selectionsort**. The algorithm is a refinement of our previous pseudo-code, as shown here:

```
for (i = n-1; i > 0; i--)
{
    Calculate big as the index of the largest value in
            data[first] through data[first + i];
    swap data[first + i] with data[big];
}
```

The control of the for-loop has one refinement from the original pseudocode: The loop executes only n-1 times, stopping as soon as i drops to zero. There is no need to execute the loop with i equal to zero, because when i reaches zero, all the larger elements are already in their correct spots. Therefore, data[0] must already have the smallest element.

How do we calculate the index of the largest value in data[first] through data[first + i]? We can start by assuming that the biggest value is at the front of the segment, data[first]. Then we can use a loop to search through the rest of the segment, up to data[first + i]. Each time we find a bigger element, we'll place the index of this bigger element in a variable called big, as shown in the following refinement. In this refinement, big and j are local int variables:

```
for (i = n-1; i > 0; i--)
{
    // Calculate big as the index of the largest value in
    // data[first]...data[first + i]:
    big = first;
    for (j = first + 1; j <= first + i; j++)
        if (data[big] < data[j])
            big = j;
    swap data[first + i] with data[big];
}
```

When the inner for-loop finishes, `big` is the index of the largest value in
`data[first]` through `data[first + i]`. At this point, we need to swap
`data[first + i]` with `data[big]`. Such a swap can be done with three assignment statements and one extra local variable (usually called `temp` because it is
needed for a short, *temp*orary time). The necessary assignment statements are
shown at the bottom of the complete implementation in Figure 12.1.

FIGURE 12.1   Selectionsort

Java Application Program

```
// FILE: Select.java
// A demonstration program for the selectionsort method
public class Select
{
    public static void selectionsort(int[ ] data, int first, int n)
    // Precondition: data has at least n components starting at data[first].
    // Postcondition: The elements of data have been rearranged so
    // that data[first] <= data[first + 1] <= ... <= data[first + n - 1].
    {
        int i, j; // Loop control variables
        int big;   // Index of largest value in data[first] ... data[first + i]
        int temp; // Used during the swapping of two array values

        for (i = n-1; i > 0; i--)
        {
            // Calculate big as the index of the largest value in data[first] ... data[first + i]:
            big = first;
            for (j = first + 1; j <= first + i; j++)
                if (data[big] < data[j])
                    big = j;

            // swap data[first + i] with data[big]:
            temp = data[first + i];
            data[first + i] = data[big];
            data[big] = temp;
        }
    }
}
```

(continued)

(FIGURE 12.1 continued)

```java
public static void main(String[ ] args)
{
    final String BLANKS = "  ";  // A String of two blanks
    int i;                       // Array index

    int[ ] data = { 80, 10, 50, 70, 60, 90, 20, 30, 40, 0 };

    // Print the array before sorting:
    System.out.println("Here is the original array:");
    for (i = 0; i < data.length; i++)
        System.out.print(data[i] + BLANKS);
    System.out.println( );

    // Sort the numbers, and print the result with two blanks after each number.
    selectionsort(data, 0, data.length);
    System.out.println("In sorted order, the numbers are:");
    for (i = 0; i < data.length; i++)
        System.out.print(data[i] + BLANKS);
    System.out.println( );
    }
}
```

Sample Output

```
Here is the original array:
80  10  50  70  60  90  20  30  40  0
In sorted order, the numbers are:
0 10   20   30   40   50   60   70   80   90
```

Figure 12.1 also contains a small `main` method to test `selectionsort`. The `main` method declares an array of 10 integers with the following declaration:

```java
int[ ] data = { 80, 10, 50, 70, 60, 90, 20, 30, 40, 0 };
```

A list like this, given after the declaration of an array variable, has two effects: *array* First, a new array of the correct size (10 elements in this case) is allocated, and *initialization* then the new array is initialized with the provided list of values.

Selectionsort—Testing

The `main` method in Figure 12.1 shows that `selectionsort` works correctly in one small situation. More testing should be carried out to improve confidence that we did not make a programming error. For sorting methods, it is important to test some random cases (such as the array in our `main` method), test the case in which the array starts out already sorted (to make sure the algorithm doesn't crash or mix up the order), test the case in which the array starts out completely backward, and test the boundary cases when the array size is one or zero. In the case of an array with zero elements, the method has no work to do (there are no elements to sort), and our selectionsort performs correctly. (The loop begins with i set to –1, and therefore the body of the loop never executes.)

Selectionsort—Analysis

We want to analyze the worst-case running time for the selectionsort algorithm that we implemented as the method selectionsort shown in Figure 12.1. Let's use n for the number of elements to be sorted. In outline form, the major work of the selectionsort algorithm is given here:

```
for (i = n-1; i > 0; i--)
    swap(data[first + i], data[suitable index]);
```

When i is equal to n-1, then data[suitable index] is the largest element in the portion of the array we are sorting; when i is equal to n-2, then data[suitable index] is the second-largest element; and so forth.

How many operations are performed by the above for-loop? The answer is not easy. Many of the operations are hidden. The loop control variable, i, is compared to zero at the start of each loop iteration. The actual swapping uses three assignment operations, and the calculation of the "suitable index" requires some work. The value of i is decremented at the end of each loop iteration. We could determine the precise number of operations for each of these subtasks in the loop. However, that is more detail than we need. We are looking only for a big-O approximation, which means that we do not need the exact values for constants. This will simplify our analysis significantly.

During each iteration of the loop, there is some constant number of operations in managing the loop control variable, and there is some constant number of operations involved in the swapping of two array elements. So *the number of operations in each loop iteration* is the sum:

some constant + the cost of finding the suitable index

Since there are n–1 loop iterations, the total count of the number of operations performed is given by the following product:

$(n - 1) \times$ (some constant + the cost of finding the suitable index)

To change this into a nice formula expressed in terms of n, we need to determine the cost of finding the "suitable index."

As it turns out, when the algorithm is looking for the value to place in location data[i], the "suitable index" is the index of the largest of the values:

data[0], data[1], …, data[i]

The selectionsort algorithm uses a loop that determines the location of this largest element and thereby the value of the "suitable index." The loop has the following form:

```
big = first;
for (j = first + 1; j <= first + i; j++)
    if (data[big] < data[j])
        big = j;
```

How much work is done each time these lines of code compute the "suitable index"? There are five operations to get things started: an assignment statement (big = first) before the loop, an addition/assignment (j = first + 1), and an addition/boolean test (j <= first + i) to initialize the loop. Each time through the body of the loop, we perform some limited number of operations to examine one of the array elements. The body of the loop executes i times, so the number of operations of this code is no more than 5 plus a constant times i. We could ignore the 5 at this point, but let's leave it in and simplify in a different way by noticing that i is always less than n. With this simplification, our estimate of the number of operations to find this "suitable index" is *at most 5 plus a constant times* n.

Putting this information together, we see that the total count of the number of operations performed in the selectionsort is this:

Total = $(n - 1) \times$ (some constant + the cost of finding the suitable index)

$\leq (n - 1) \times$ [some constant + 5 + (some other constant) $\times n$]

Now we need to estimate the quantity:

$(n - 1) \times$ [some constant + 5 + (some other constant) $\times n$]

If you multiply this out, there will be an n^2 term, an n term, and a constant term without any n. Thus, the number of operations performed is:

$n^2 \times$ (some new constant)

+

$n \times$ (some other new constant)

+

(yet another new constant)

This is our estimate of the worst-case run time for selectionsort. Because we are doing a big-O analysis, we can ignore the constants and consider only the highest exponent of n. Hence, we see that the worst-case running time for selectionsort is $O(n^2)$.

In arriving at the quadratic time analysis, we made one overestimate by replacing i with n. A more detailed time analysis would not make this simplification but would still end up with a quadratic time. Our analysis of the running time for selectionsort did not depend on the initial values in the array. The selectionsort algorithm performs the same number of operations no matter what values are in the array that it sorts. Thus, the average-case running time (and even the best-case running time) is the same as the worst-case running time.

Selectionsort Running Time

The worst-case running time, the average-case running time, and the best-case running time for selectionsort are all quadratic.

PROGRAMMING TIP 🌓

ROUGH ESTIMATES SUFFICE FOR BIG-O

We have just computed big-O expressions for the worst-case running time of the selectionsort algorithm. Notice that when we performed the big-O analysis, we did not compute exact formulas for some running times. For example, when we estimated the number of operations in one iteration of the primary loop used in the algorithm, we decided that the algorithm performed the following number of operations in each loop iteration:

some constant + the cost of finding the suitable index

We never computed the exact value of "some constant." Because big-O expressions are accurate only to "within a constant multiple," the exact value of the constant does not matter. If we want only a big-O expression, there is no reason to spend time computing an exact value for this constant.

Insertionsort

Another simple and natural sorting algorithm is based on the following illustration of sorting an array that contains this list of 10 integers:

(8, 2, 5, 3, 10, 7, 1, 4, 6, 9)

One way to proceed is to take the numbers one at a time and build up another sorted list of values. The first number is 8, so make a list that contains only the one number 8. That is certainly a sorted list. Next, take the 2 and combine it with the 8 to obtain a longer sorted list, namely (2, 8). Next, add the 5 to obtain the list (2, 5, 8).

If you keep adding numbers to the list, you will eventually obtain a sorted list containing all the numbers. The original list decreases by one on each iteration, and the list we are building increases by one on each iteration. The progress of this process is shown at the top of the next page for an example list.

```
(  )    ( 8,  2,  5,  3, 10,  7,  1,  4,  6,  9 )

( 8 )   ( 2,  5,  3, 10,  7,  1,  4,  6,  9 )

( 2,  8 )   ( 5,  3, 10,  7,  1,  4,  6,  9 )

( 2,  5,  8 )   ( 3, 10,  7,  1,  4,  6,  9 )

( 2,  3,  5,  8 )   ( 10,  7,  1,  4,  6,  9 )

( 2,  3,  5,  8, 10 )   ( 7,  1,  4,  6,  9 )

( 2,  3,  5,  7,  8, 10 )   ( 1,  4,  6,  9 )

( 1,  2,  3,  5,  7,  8, 10 )   ( 4,  6,  9 )

( 1,  2,  3,  4,  5,  7,  8, 10 )   ( 6,  9 )

( 1,  2,  3,  4,  5,  6,  7,  8, 10 )   ( 9 )

( 1,  2,  3,  4,  5,  6,  7,  8,  9, 10 )   (  )
```

   With the insertionsort, your first thought might be to use an additional array and copy values from one array to the other. The numbers in the left-hand lists in our drawings would be in one array, and the numbers in the right-hand lists would be in the other array. But, if you look carefully at the drawings, you will see that one list grows at exactly the same rate that the other list shrinks. So we need only one array. If we have 10 numbers, we need only 10 positions. One list can be kept at the front of the array and the other at the back of the array.

We can redraw the progress of the insertionsort in a way that makes it evident that one array is sufficient. At the start of the insertionsort, we have the same 10-element array that we have been working with:

data

8	2	5	3	10	7	1	4	6	9
[0]	[1]	[2]	[3]	[4]	[5]	[6]	[7]	[8]	[9]

We have called the array data. The first component, data[0], is shaded to indicate that even at the start, the front part of the array—with only the one shaded element—can be viewed as a tiny, sorted array on its own. The first actual work will be to insert the second element (data[1], which is a 2) into the tiny, sorted array, increasing the "sorted part" of the array to encompass two elements, as shown here:

data

2	8	5	3	10	7	1	4	6	9
[0]	[1]	[2]	[3]	[4]	[5]	[6]	[7]	[8]	[9]

So, at this point, the first two elements (2, 8) form a small sorted list, and we still need to insert the remaining elements (5, 3, 10, 7, 1, 4, 6, 9). After the insertion of the 5, we have the situation shown here:

data

2	5	8	3	10	7	1	4	6	9
[0]	[1]	[2]	[3]	[4]	[5]	[6]	[7]	[8]	[9]

The insertion process continues, taking the next element from the unsorted side of the array and inserting it into the sorted side of the array. Each insertion increases the size of the sorted side and decreases the unsorted side until the entire array is sorted.

All we need to do now is convert these ideas into a Java method with the heading and specification shown here:

```
public static void insertionsort(int[ ] data, int first, int n)
// Precondition: data has at least n components starting at data[first].
// Postcondition: The elements of data have been rearranged so
//   that data[first] <= data[first + 1] <= ... <= data[first + n-1].
```

This specification should seem familiar. It's the same specification we used for the selectionsort; only our algorithm will change.

The insertionsort can be accomplished with this pseudocode:

```
for (i = 1; i < n; i++)
    Insert the element from data[first + i] into the portion of the array
    from data[first] through data[first + i - 1] so that all of
    data[first] through data[first + i] is now sorted.
```

Let's look at an example to help refine the pseudocode in the body of the loop. In the example, suppose first is 10 so that we are sorting a portion of the array beginning at data[10]. Also suppose that i is 4 so that we are entering the loop for the fourth time. In this situation, data[10] through data[13] are already sorted, and we have the task of inserting data[14]. If the value of data[14] is 3, we might have this situation when the fourth iteration of the loop body begins:

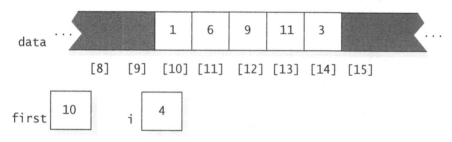

A useful initial step is to use a local variable to store a copy of the number we are inserting. If we call the local variable entry, then this first step is accomplished with the assignment entry = data[first + i] . After the assignment, we have this situation:

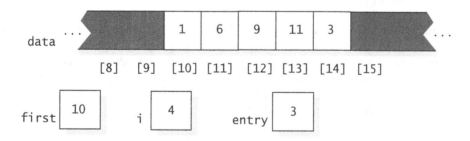

Once the extra copy of the new element has been made, we suggest you shift elements at the end of the array rightward one position each until you find the correct position for the new entry. In our example, you would begin by shifting the 11 rightward from data[13] to data[14]; then you'd move the 9 from data[12] to data[13]; then the 6 moves from data[11] to data[12]. At this point, the array contains the following values:

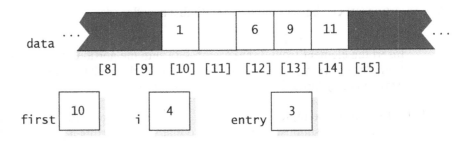

Of course, data[11] actually still contains a 6 because we just copied the 6 from data[11] to data[12]. But we have drawn data[11] as an empty box to indicate that data[11] is now available to hold the new entry (i.e., the 3 that we're inserting). At this point, we can place the 3 in data[11], as shown here:

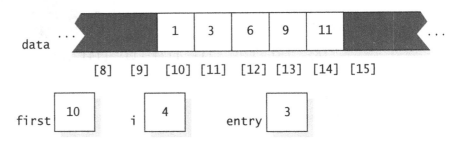

The pseudocode for shifting the elements rightward uses a for-loop. Each iteration of the loop shifts one element, as shown here:

```
for (j = first + i;  data[j] is the wrong spot for entry ; j--)
    data[j] = data[j-1];
```

The key to the loop is the test data[j] is the wrong spot for entry . A position is wrong if (j > first) and the element at data[j-1] is greater than the new entry. We know that such a position must be wrong because placing the new entry at this position would result in data[j-1] > data[j]. Can you now write the loop in Java and incorporate it into the actual insertionsort method? (See Self-Test Exercise 3 on page 629.)

Insertionsort—Analysis

We'll analyze the insertionsort in a slightly different manner, determining how many times the algorithm must access an element of the array—either for a comparison or for a swap of some sort. For many sorting algorithms, such as insertionsort, the count of array accesses is proportional to the total number of operations. Therefore, the final big-O analysis comes out the same.

We start by asking how many array accesses are required to insert just one new element, which occurs during each iteration of this pseudocode:

```
for (i = 1; i < n; i++)
    Insert the element from data[first + i] into the portion of the array
    from data[first] through data[first + i - 1] so that all of
    data[first] through data[first + i] is now sorted.
```

Our implementation of the loop starts by comparing the new element to the final element from data[first] through data[first + i - 1]. After this comparison, the algorithm works backward through the array until it finds the correct spot to insert a new element. In the worst case, the algorithm could compare and shift each element data[first] through data[first + i - 1], and therefore the total number of array accesses is limited to a constant times n. In fact, an iteration of the loop may need significantly fewer than $O(n)$ accesses because each iteration examines only i-1 elements of the array rather than all n. But $O(n)$ operations is a good overestimate because it is easy to express and easy to work with.

So the insertion of one new element takes $O(n)$ time, and there are n elements to insert. Thus, the total time for n separate insertions is no more than this:

$$\text{Total} = n \times (\text{the number of operations in an } O(n) \text{ algorithm})$$
$$= n \times (\text{some constant times } n)$$
$$= \text{some constant times } n^2$$
$$= O(n^2)$$

This analysis shows one important trick to remember:

Analysis for Quadratic Time

An $O(n)$ process that is performed n times results in a quadratic number of operations ($O(n^2)$).

In the case of insertionsort, we actually perform $n-1$ insertions rather than n, but the time for $n-1$ insertions is also quadratic.

Our analysis has used one major overestimation. We assumed that each insertion required the body of the loop to examine the full n elements of the array, but some insertions require the examination of far fewer elements. Will a more accurate estimate reduce the time analysis? The answer is no. A precise analysis of the worst-case running time still results in a quadratic formula. To see this, suppose that all the original elements are far from their correct places. In fact, these elements might be completely backward, as shown at the top of the next page.

data

10	9	8	7	6	5	4	3	2	1
[0]	[1]	[2]	[3]	[4]	[5]	[6]	[7]	[8]	[9]

In this case, the first insertion must insert the 9 in front of the 10, resulting in this array:

data

9	10	8	7	6	5	4	3	2	1
[0]	[1]	[2]	[3]	[4]	[5]	[6]	[7]	[8]	[9]

The next insertion must insert the 8 in front of everything else. And then the 7 is inserted, again at the front. With the elements starting out backward, each insertion must compare and shift all the elements in the currently sorted part of the array, placing the new element at the front. So, for an insertionsort to work on a completely backward array, it requires these comparisons and shifts:

1 compare and shift to insert the 1st element

+

2 compares and shifts to insert the 2nd element

+

3 compares and shifts to insert the 3rd element

+

...

+

$n-1$ compares and shifts to insert the $(n-1)^{st}$ element

The total number of compares and shifts is thus $1 + 2 + 3 + ... + (n-1)$. You can use a technique similar to Figure 1.2 on page 20 to evaluate this sum. The result is $n(n-1)/2$, which is $O(n^2)$. So the worst case for insertionsort is indeed quadratic time, the same as for selectionsort.

The analysis of the average-case running time for insertionsort is essentially the same as that for the worst case. The only difference is that a single insertion will, on the average, stop after accessing half of the elements from the sorted side rather than accessing them all. This means that the average-case running time is half that of the worst-case running time, but we know that a constant multiple, such as $\frac{1}{2}$, does not affect a big-O expression. Thus, the average-case running time for insertionsort is quadratic, the same as the worst-case running time.

On the other hand, the best-case running time for insertionsort is much better than quadratic. In particular, suppose that the array is *already sorted* before we begin our work. This is certainly an advantage, though the advantage does not help all sorting algorithms. For example, starting with a sorted array does not help selectionsort, which still requires quadratic time. But starting with a sorted array does help insertionsort. In this case, each insertion of a new element will examine only a single element from the array. This single-element examination is carried out once to insert each new element, and the result is an $O(n)$ time.

You probably think that starting with an already-sorted array does not happen too often, and perhaps you are right. But frequently an array is *nearly* sorted—perhaps a few new elements are out of place. Insertionsort is also quite quick for nearly sorted arrays.

Here is a summary of insertionsort times:

Insertionsort Running Time

Both the worst-case and the average-case running times are quadratic. But the best case (when the starting array is already sorted) is linear, and the algorithm is also quick when the starting array is nearly sorted.

Self-Test Exercises for Section 12.1

1. The `selectionsort` method in Figure 12.1 on page 618 sorts integers into increasing order. How would you change the method so that it sorts integers into decreasing order?

2. The `selectionsort` method in Figure 12.1 on page 618 sorts integers into increasing order. How would you change the function so that it sorts an array of strings into alphabetical order? All strings consist only of lowercase letters.

3. Give a complete implementation for insertionsort.

12.2 RECURSIVE SORTING ALGORITHMS

Divide-and-Conquer Using Recursion

Let's start with an explicit statement of a recursive design technique that we have used a few times in the past. The technique, called **divide-and-conquer**, is applicable to many problems. Here's the idea: When a problem is small, simply solve it. When the problem is large, divide the problem into two smaller subproblems, each of which is about half of the original problem. Solve each subproblem with a recursive call. After the recursive calls, extra work is sometimes needed to combine the solutions of the smaller problems, resulting in a solution to the larger problem.

Divide-and-conquer can work in slightly different ways, perhaps having more than two subproblems or having subproblems with unequal size, but the basic approach—two subproblems of roughly equal size—works best.

Key Design Concept

Divide-and-conquer works best with two equally sized subproblems, each of which is solved with a recursive call.

Applied to sorting, divide-and-conquer results in the following pattern:

The Divide-and-Conquer Sorting Paradigm

1. Divide the elements to be sorted into two groups of equal (or almost equal) size.
2. Sort each of these smaller groups of elements (by recursive calls).
3. Combine the two sorted groups into one large sorted list.

We will present two recursive sorting methods based on this divide-and-conquer paradigm.

Mergesort

The most straightforward implementation of the divide-and-conquer approach to sorting is the **mergesort** algorithm. Let's see how mergesort works with a small array. The first step divides the array into two equally sized groups, as shown in this cut:

After the cut, we have two smaller arrays with five elements each. These smaller arrays can be sorted separately with recursive calls, providing this result:

5	9	12	25	31

2	3	6	8	20

When the recursive calls return, the two half-arrays need somehow to be put together into one sorted array, as shown here:

2	3	5	6	8	9	12	20	25	31

As shown in this illustration, the mergesort algorithm divides the array near its midpoint, sorts the two half-arrays by recursive calls to the algorithm, and then merges the two halves to get a new sorted array of elements. The final "merging" step of the process will require some thought, so we'll postpone that part of the implementation by assuming that we have a separate method to carry out the merging. The specification for the separate merging method is shown here:

```
private static void merge
(int[ ] data, int first, int n1, int n2)
// Precondition: data has at least n1 + n2 components starting at
//  data[first]. The first n1 elements (from data[first] to
//  data[first + n1 - 1] are sorted from smallest to largest, and the
//  last n2 (from data[first + n1] to data[first + n1 + n2 - 1]) are also
//  sorted from smallest to largest.
// Postcondition: Starting at data[first], n1 + n2 elements of data
//  have been rearranged to be sorted from smallest to largest.
// Note: An OutOfMemoryError can be thrown if there is insufficient
//  memory for an array of n1+n2 ints.
```

This merge method will be used as the last step of our mergesort. Let's examine where the merge method is used within the mergesort method of Figure 12.2.

The stopping case for mergesort's recursion is when the array to be sorted consists of only one element. In this stopping case, there is no work to do because a single element does not need to be "rearranged." On the other hand, if there is more than one element, then mergesort carries out these steps:

1. Calculate the sizes of the two pieces of the array. The size of the first half, n1, is approximately half of the entire size (calculated by n/2, using integer division). The second size, n2, is whatever is left over (calculated by n - n1).

2. Use recursive calls to sort the two halves. Notice that the second recursive call, mergesort(data, first + n1, n2), indicates that its work should begin at data[first + n1], which is the starting point of the second half.

3. Finally, activate merge to combine the two sorted halves.

The operation of the merge method has some issues that we discuss next.

The merge Function

The algorithm for the merge method uses a second temporary array that we will call temp. Elements will be copied from the array data to the array temp in such a way that the elements are completely sorted. After that, the values are simply copied back to the array data. The merging algorithm uses the precondition that the two halves of the array (data[first] through data[first + n1 - 1] and data[first + n1] through data[first + n1 + n2 - 1]) are each sorted. Since they are both sorted, we know that data[first] contains the smallest element in the first half, and data[first + n1] contains the smallest element in the second half.

FIGURE 12.2   Mergesort

Specification

◆ **mergesort**

```
public static void mergesort(int data[ ], int first, int n)
```
Sort an array of integers from smallest to largest.

Parameters:

data – the array to be sorted

first – the start index for the portion of the array that will be sorted

n – the number of elements to sort

Precondition:

data[first] through data[first + n - 1] are valid parts of the array.

Postcondition:

If n is zero or negative, then no work is done. Otherwise, the elements of data have been rearranged so that data[first] <= data[first + 1] <= ... <= data[first + n - 1].

Throws: ArrayIndexOutOfBoundsException

Indicates that first + n - 1 is an index beyond the end of the array.

Throws: OutOfMemoryError

Indicates insufficient memory for creating a temporary array in the merge step.

Implementation

```
public static void mergesort(int data[ ], int first, int n)
{
    int n1; // Size of the first half of the array
    int n2; // Size of the second half of the array

    if (n > 1)
    {
        // Compute sizes of the two halves.
        n1 = n / 2;          The two subarrays are sorted
        n2 = n - n1;         with recursive calls.

        mergesort(data, first, n1);      // Sort data[first] through data[first + n1 - 1]
        mergesort(data, first + n1, n2); // Sort data[first + n1] to the end

        // Merge the two sorted halves.
        merge(data, first, n1, n2);
    }
}
```

Therefore, we know that the smallest element overall is either `data[first]` or `data[first + n1]`. The algorithm compares these two elements and copies the smallest one to the front of the temporary array (the location `temp[0]`). The algorithm then somehow marks the copied element as being "already copied." For example, suppose that `first` is 8 and both `n1` and `n2` are 5 so that the first half of the array goes from `data[8]` through `data[12]` and the second half goes from `data[13]` to `data[17]`. After the first element is copied to `temp`, we might have this situation:

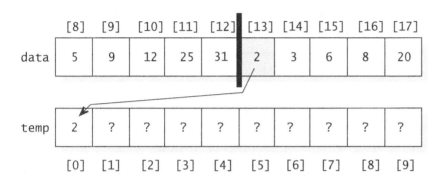

The drawing has a thick black line to separate the two halves of the `data` array. In this example, the 2 (at the front of the second half) is smaller than the 5 (at the front of the first half), so this 2 is copied to the first position of the temporary array. We marked the 2 as "already copied" by shading it in the diagram. In the actual algorithm, we'll keep track of which elements have been copied by maintaining three `int` variables:

```
int copied;   // Number of elements copied from data to temp
int copied1;  // Number copied from the first half of data
int copied2;  // Number copied from the second half of data
```

All three local variables are initialized to zero in the `merge` method. Each time we copy an element from the first half of `data` to the temporary array, we add 1 to both `copied` and `copied1`. Each time we copy an element from the second half of `data` to the temporary array, we add 1 to both `copied` and `copied2`. So, after copying the 2 in the preceding example, `copied` and `copied2` will both be 1, but `copied1` remains zero.

The merge algorithm proceeds by looking at the next uncopied elements from each half of the `data` array. The smaller of these two elements is copied to the next spot in the temporary array. In our example, we would next compare the 5 (from the first half) to the 3 (the next uncopied element from the second half).

Since the 3 is smaller, we copy the 3 to the next spot in the `temp` array, as shown here:

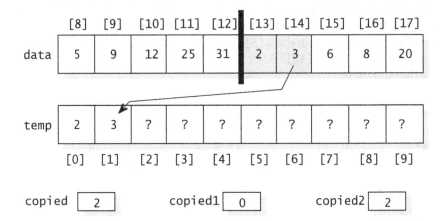

At this point, we have copied a total of two elements (because `copied` is 2). Both of the copied elements came from the second half (because `copied1` is 0 and `copied2` is 2).

The next step of the algorithm will compare the 5 (from the first half) to the 6 (from the second half). The 5 is lower, so it gets copied to the temporary array, as shown here:

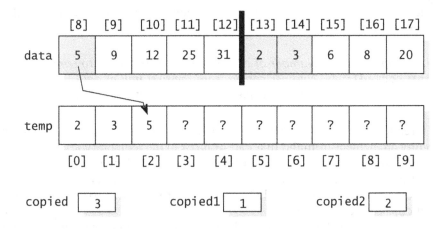

The loop proceeds in this way, moving through the two array halves. With this idea, we can write our first version of the pseudocode, shown next.

1. Allocate the `temp` array and set `copied`, `copied1`, and `copied2` to zero.

2. `while` (both halves of the array have more elements to copy)
   `if` (the next element of 1st half is <= the next element of the 2nd half)
   `{`
   > Copy the next element of 1st half to the next spot in `temp`.
   > Add 1 to both `copied` and `copied1`.

   `}`
   `else`
   `{`
   > Copy the next element of 2nd half to the next spot in `temp`.
   > Add 1 to both `copied` and `copied2`.

   `}`

Using the local variables `copied`, `copied1`, and `copied2`, we can refine the pseudocode a bit. The "next spot in temp" is `temp[copied]`, the "next element in the 1st half" is `data[first + copied1]`, and the "next element in the 2nd half" is at `data[first + n1 + copied2]`, as shown in this refinement:

1. Allocate the `temp` array and set `copied`, `copied1`, and `copied2` to zero.

2. `while` (both halves of the array have more elements to copy)
   `if` (`data[first + copied1]` <= `data[first + n1 + copied2]`)
   `{`
   > `temp[copied]` = `data[first + copied1]` ;
   > Add 1 to both `copied` and `copied1`.

   `}`
   `else`
   `{`
   > `temp[copied]` = `data[first + n1 + copied2]`;
   > Add 1 to both `copied` and `copied2`.

   `}`

In our actual implementation, the two assignment statements can be modified to also add 1 to `copied` and to the appropriate one of the other two local variables (`copied1` or `copied2`). The modified assignment statements make use of the ++ operator, as shown here:

1. Allocate the `temp` array and set `copied`, `copied1`, and `copied2` to zero.

2. `while` (both halves of the array have more elements to copy)
   `if` (data[first + copied1] <= data[first + n1 + copied2])
   `temp[copied++]` = `data[first + (copied1++)]`;
   `else`
   `temp[copied++]` = `data[first + n1 + (copied2++)]`;

Using an index such as `copied++` has the effect of using the *current* value of the variable `copied` as the index and *afterward* adding 1 to the variable. (If we wanted to add 1 before using the index, we would write `++copied` instead of `copied++`.)

This part of our algorithm works fine as long as neither half of the array runs out of elements. However, eventually one of the two halves will run out of elements. For our example, this will occur after we copy the last element (20) from the second half of the `data` array to the temporary array, as shown here:

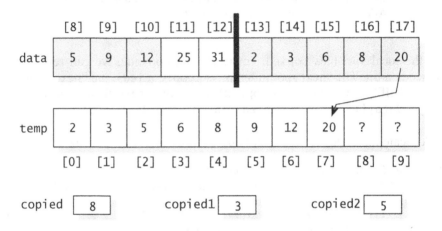

At a point like this, we want to copy the elements remaining in the uncompleted half into the temporary array. This yields the following, final version of our pseudocode for the `merge` function:

1. Allocate the `temp` array and set `copied`, `copied1`, and `copied2` to zero.

2. `while` (both halves of the array have more elements to copy)
   `if (data[first + copied1]` <= `data[first + n1 + copied2])`
     `temp[copied++]` = `data[first + (copied++)];`
   `else`
     `temp[copied++]` = `data[first + n1 + (copied2++)];`

3. Copy any remaining entries from the left or right subarray.

4. Copy the elements from `temp` back to `data`.

For the most part, this pseudocode translates to the Java method shown in Figure 12.3, although we did modify Steps 3 and 4 because extra elements at the end of the second section are already in the right spot (and hence, they do not need to be copied into `temp` and back again).

FIGURE 12.3   A Method to Merge Two Parts of an Array

Implementation

```
private static void merge
(int[ ] data, int first, int n1, int n2)
// Precondition: data has at least n1 + n2 components starting at data[first]. The first
// n1 elements (from data[first] to data[first + n1 - 1] are sorted from smallest
// to largest, and the last n2 (from data[first + n1] to data[first + n1 + n2 - 1]) are also
// sorted from smallest to largest.
// Postcondition: Starting at data[first], n1 + n2 elements of data
// have been rearranged to be sorted from smallest to largest.
// Note: An OutOfMemoryError can be thrown if there is insufficient
// memory for an array of n1+n2 ints.
{
    int[ ] temp = new int[n1+n2]; // Allocate the temporary array
    int copied  = 0; // Number of elements copied from data to temp
    int copied1 = 0; // Number copied from the first half of data
    int copied2 = 0; // Number copied from the second half of data
    int i;               // Array index to copy from temp back into data

    // Merge elements, copying from two halves of data to the temporary array.
    while ((copied1 < n1) && (copied2 < n2))
    {
        if (data[first + copied1] < data[first + n1 + copied2])
            temp[copied++] = data[first + (copied1++)];
        else
            temp[copied++] = data[first + n1 + (copied2++)];
    }

    // Copy any remaining entries in the left subarray (but not from the right subarray,
    // because those entries are already in the correct spot of the data array).
    while (copied1 < n1)
        temp[copied++] = data[first + (copied1++)];

    // Copy from temp back to the data array.
    for (i = 0; i < copied; i++)
        data[first + i] = temp[i];

}
```

Mergesort—Analysis

A complete analysis of mergesort's running time is beyond the scope of this book, but we can give the final result and hint at its derivation. First the result:

Mergesort Running Time

The worst-case running time, the average-case running time, and the best-case running time for mergesort are all $O(n \log n)$.

As usual, n is the number of elements to be sorted. Let's try to motivate this formula. In the case of mergesort, the algorithm performs similarly on all inputs, so our motivation will apply to the worst-case, average-case, and best-case running times. Let's diagram the first few levels of recursive calls made by a typical mergesort:

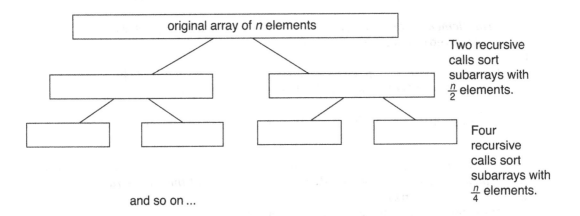

At the top level, we make two recursive calls to sort subarrays with $\frac{n}{2}$ elements each. At this level, we use merge once to merge those two $\frac{n}{2}$ pieces into a single n element array. At the second level, each $\frac{n}{2}$ piece is broken into two $\frac{n}{4}$ pieces. At this level, there will be two merge activations, each of which merges a pair of $\frac{n}{4}$ pieces to create the two $\frac{n}{2}$ pieces. Continuing this pattern, you can determine the total number of activations of merge, as shown at the top of the next page.

At the top level, one activation of merge creates an array with n elements

+

At the next level, two activations of merge to create two $\frac{n}{2}$ pieces

+

At the next level, four activations of merge to create four $\frac{n}{4}$ pieces

+

At the next level, eight activations of merge to create eight $\frac{n}{8}$ pieces

+

...

The pattern continues until we cannot further subdivide the pieces (because we have only a single element).

At each level of the pattern, the *total* work done by merging is $O(n)$. For example, at the top level, we have one merge activation to create an array with n elements, and the number of operations in this one activation is proportional to n. At the next level, there are two merge activations, but each of the activations does work that is proportional to $\frac{n}{2}$, so again the *total* work done at that level is $O(n)$. At the next level, we have four merge activations; each does work that is proportional to $\frac{n}{4}$. And so on.

Each level does *total* work proportional to n. So the total cost of mergesort is given by this formula:

(some constant) $\times n \times$ (the number of levels in the pattern)

The size of the array pieces is halved on each step down the pattern. So the number of levels in the pattern is approximately equal to the number of times that n can be divided by 2, stopping when the result is less than or equal to 1. That number of "halvings" is closely approximated by $\log_2 n$ (the base 2 logarithm of n). Therefore, mergesort appears to perform the following number of operations:

(some constant) $\times n \times \log_2 n$

As a big-O formula, we can throw out the multiplicative constant and also the constant 2 in the base of the logarithm. So the time is $O(n \times \log n)$. This time of n multiplied by a logarithm of n is usually written more simply as $O(n \log n)$, pronounced "big-O of n log n."

Our analysis has not been formal, but it is the correct answer, and a rigorous demonstration would follow the same outline as our intuitive explanation.

Mergesort has a worst-case running time of $O(n \log n)$ operations, which is faster than the quadratic running times for the selectionsort and insertionsort algorithms. But how much faster is it? We can get a feel for the difference by comparing the function $n \log_2 n$ with n^2. The table in Figure 12.4 gives some representative values for comparison. As you can see by studying the table, an $n \log_2 n$ running time is substantially faster than an n^2 running time, particularly if the array to be sorted is large.

FIGURE 12.4

Value of $n \log_2 n$ versus n^2

n	$n \log_2 n$	n^2
2	2	4
8	24	64
32	160	1024
128	896	16,384
512	4608	262,144
2048	22,528	4,194,304

Mergesort for Files

The mergesort algorithm is actually a poor choice for sorting arrays. Quicksort and heapsort, which we will describe in a moment, are better because they don't require a temporary array for the merge step. However, mergesort can be modified to sort a file, even when the file is too large to fit in the largest possible array. In the mergesort of a file, the file is divided into several pieces, and each piece is sorted (perhaps with a recursive call of the `mergesort` method). The sorted pieces are then merged into a single sorted file, and the separate pieces can be removed.

With this use of mergesort, the separate file pieces get smaller and smaller with each recursive call. Eventually, a piece gets small enough to fit into an array. At this point, the piece should be read into an array and sorted using quicksort or heapsort.

Quicksort

We developed the mergesort algorithm as a special case of a general sorting technique that is called divide-and-conquer sorting. In this section, we will develop another sorting algorithm based on this same basic divide-and-conquer approach. This sorting algorithm is called **quicksort**, and it was first devised by the computer scientist C. A. R. Hoare. It is similar to mergesort in many ways. It divides the elements to be sorted into two roughly equal groups, sorts the two groups by recursive calls, and combines the two sorted groups into a single array of sorted values. However, the method for dividing the array in half is much more sophisticated than the simple method we used for mergesort. On the other hand, the method for combining these two groups of sorted elements is trivial compared to the method used in mergesort. In mergesort, the division is trivial and the combining complicated. With quicksort, the division is complicated and the combining is trivial.

pivot element

The basic idea of quicksort is simple: Suppose you know some particular value that belongs in the middle of the array, or at least the approximate middle of the array. We will call this value the **pivot element**, or simply the **pivot**. Suppose we somehow put this pivot element into its correct location in the array, somehow put all the values less than or equal to the pivot in array positions before the pivot, and somehow put all the values greater than the pivot in array positions after the pivot element. At this point, we have not sorted the values less than the pivot element; we simply placed them in any order in array positions before the pivot element. Similarly, we have not yet sorted the values greater than the pivot; we simply placed them in any order in array positions after the pivot element.

After this initial moving of array elements, we have moved the array closer to being sorted. We know that the pivot element of the array is in the correct position. We also know that all other values are in the correct segment of the array, either the segment before the pivot element or the segment after the pivot element. However, although we know they are in the correct segment, those segments are still not sorted. One way to proceed is to sort the two segments separately. This works because we know that all values in the first segment are less than all values in the second segment, so no value ever needs to move from one segment to the other. How do we sort the two segments? These are smaller versions of the original sorting task, so we can sort the two smaller array segments by recursive calls. If we continue to divide the array into smaller portions in the way we outlined, we will eventually get down to array segments of size 1, and we can use that as a stopping case (requiring no work).

This idea is sound except for one problem: How do we find a pivot element and its correct final position in the sorted array? There is no obvious way to quickly find the midpoint value until after the array is sorted. Our solution will be to take an arbitrary array value and use it as the pivot element. As a result, we may not be dividing the array exactly in half, but as long as we divide it into smaller pieces, our algorithm will eventually sort the array. We perform the subtask of dividing the array elements with a private method called `partition`. The `partition` method chooses some arbitrary pivot element, places it at the correct index position, and divides the remaining array elements as we have described. The method will not necessarily do those three things in that order, but it will do them all. The method's specification is as follows:

```
private static int partition(int[ ] data, int first, int n)
// Precondition: n > 1, and data has at least n elements starting at
// data[first].
// Postcondition: The method has selected some "pivot value" that occurs
// in data[first] ... data[first + n – 1]. The elements of data have then been
// rearranged and the method returns a pivot index so that
//     -- data[pivot index] is equal to the pivot;
//     -- each element before data[pivot index] is <= the pivot;
//     -- each element after data[pivot index] is > the pivot.
```

We will formulate our sorting algorithm as a recursive method called quicksort, which uses the partition method. After the partitioning, the array and the pivot index look like this:

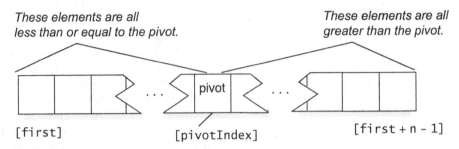

These elements are all
less than or equal to the pivot.

These elements are all
greater than the pivot.

[first]   [pivotIndex]   [first + n - 1]

After the partition, our quicksort method makes two recursive calls. The first recursive call sorts the elements before the pivot element, from data[first] to data[pivotIndex - 1]. The second recursive call sorts the elements after the pivot element, from data[pivotIndex + 1] to data[first + n - 1]. The recursive calls are part of the quicksort implementation in Figure 12.5. We still need to derive the code for the partition.

FIGURE 12.5   Quicksort

Implementation

```
public static void quicksort(int[ ] data, int first, int n)
// Precondition: data has at least n components starting at data[first].
// Postcondition: The elements of data have been rearranged so
// that data[first] <= data[first + 1] <= ... <= data[first + n - 1].
{
    int pivotIndex; // Array index for the pivot element
    int n1;         // Number of elements before the pivot element
    int n2;         // Number of elements after the pivot element

    if (n > 1)
    {
        // Partition the array, and set the pivot index.
        pivotIndex = partition(data, first, n);

        // Compute the sizes of the two pieces.
        n1 = pivotIndex - first;
        n2 = n - n1 - 1;

        // Recursive calls will now sort the two pieces.
        quicksort(data, first, n1);
        quicksort(data, pivotIndex + 1, n2);
    }
}
```

The Partition Method

Since we have no information about the values in the array, all values have an equal probability of being the value that belongs in the middle of the array. Moreover, we know that the algorithm will work no matter what value we use for the pivot element. So we arbitrarily choose the first array element to use as the pivot element. (On page 648, we discuss why this is not always the best choice and propose a method to fix the problem.)

The `partition` method will move all the values that are less than or equal to this pivot element toward the beginning of the array (that is, toward positions with lower-numbered indexes). All values that are greater than this pivot element are moved the other way, toward the tail end of the array with higher-numbered indexes. Because the pivot element is not necessarily the value that belongs at the exact midpoint position of the array, we do not know where the dividing line between the two array portions belongs. Hence, we do not know how far forward we need to move elements less than or equal to the pivot element, nor do we know how far toward the end of the array we must move elements that are greater than the pivot element. We solve this dilemma by working inward from the two ends of the array. We move smaller elements to the beginning of the array, and we move larger elements to the tail end of the array. In this way, we obtain two segments; one segment of smaller elements growing to the right from the beginning of the array, and one segment of larger elements growing to the left from the tail end of the array. When these two segments meet, we have correctly partitioned the array. The correct location for the pivot element is at the boundary of these two segments.

Starting at `data[first]`, the algorithm passes over smaller elements at the beginning of the array until it encounters an element that is larger than the pivot element. This larger element is not in the correct segment and must somehow move to the tail end segment. Starting at the other end of the array, the algorithm passes over larger elements at that end of the array until it encounters an element that is smaller than (or equal to) the pivot element. This smaller element is not in the correct segment and must somehow move to the beginning segment. At that point, we know that the elements in the two segments, up to but not including these out-of-place elements, are in the correct segment of the array. If we switch these two out-of-place elements, we will know that they also are in the correct portion of the array. Using this technique of locating and switching incorrectly placed elements at the ends of the array, our algorithm proceeds to continually expand the segment at the beginning of the array and the segment at the tail end of the array until these two segments meet.

For example, suppose the following represents our array (with `first` equal to zero and n equal to 11):

40	20	10	80	60	50	7	30	100	90	70

[0] [1] [2] [3] [4] [5] [6] [7] [8] [9] [10]

We choose the first value, 40, as our pivot element. Starting at the beginning of the array, we look for the first element that is greater than the pivot. That is the 80. Starting from the other end we look for the first value that is less than or equal to the pivot. That is the 30. We use two variables, called `tooBigIndex` and `tooSmallIndex`, to hold the indexes of these two array elements. After finding the two out-of-place elements, the array can be represented as follows:

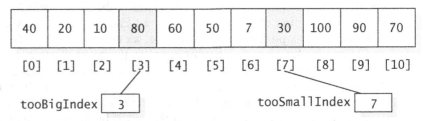

The two shaded elements are in incorrect segments of the array. If we interchange them, the array will be closer to being divided correctly. After the exchange, the array will contain these elements:

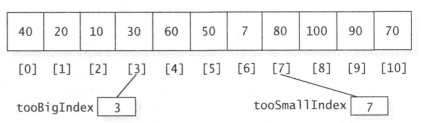

We now repeat the process. Continuing from the places we left off, we increment `tooBigIndex` until we find another element larger than the pivot; we decrement `tooSmallIndex` until we find another element less than or equal to the pivot element. This changes the values of the two index variables as shown here:

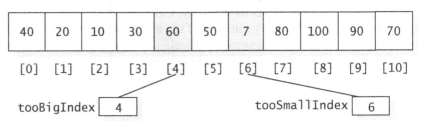

Exchanging these two elements places them in the correct array portions and yields the following array value:

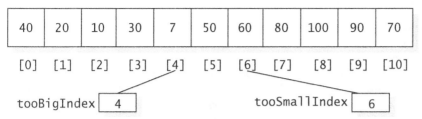

If we continue to look for elements to exchange, we will increment the tooBigIndex until it reaches the element that contains 50, and we will decrement the tooSmallIndex past the element 50 to the index of the element 7. At this point, the two indexes have crossed each other, as shown here:

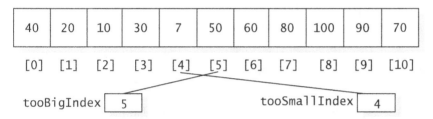

Once the indexes cross each other, we have partitioned the array. All elements less than or equal to the pivot element of 40 are in the first five positions.

All elements greater than the pivot element of 40 are in the last six positions. However, the pivot is not yet at the dividing point between the two parts of the array. At this point, the correct spot for the pivot will always be at the location given by the variable tooSmallIndex. The reason is because the tooSmallIndex has just hit the tail end of the first of the two array segments.

So, we exchange the values of data[first] and data[tooSmallIndex]. After moving the pivot element, the array configuration is as follows:

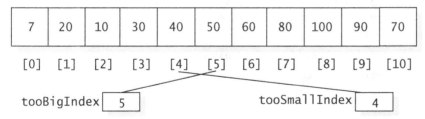

In addition to the local variables tooSmallIndex and tooBigIndex, our pseudocode for the complete partition method will also have a local variable called pivot to hold a copy of the pivot element. The array itself is called data, and the first element of the segment we are partitioning is data[first]. The total number of elements is n, and the precondition guarantees that n is at least 2. Here is the pseudocode:

```
private static int partition(int[ ] data, int first, int n)
// Precondition: n > 1, and data has at least n elements starting at
// data[first].
// Postcondition: The method has selected some "pivot value" that occurs
// in data[first]...data[first + n - 1]. The elements of data have then been
// rearranged and the method returns a pivot index so that
//      -- data[pivot index] is equal to the pivot;
//      -- each element before data[pivot index] is <= the pivot;
//      -- each element after data[pivot index] is > the pivot.
```

1. Initialize values:
   ```
   pivot = data[first];
   tooBigIndex = first + 1;        // Index of element after pivot
   tooSmallIndex = first + n - 1;  // Index of last element
   ```

2. Repeat the following until the two indexes cross each other (in other words, keep going while `tooBigIndex <= tooSmallIndex`):

   2a. `while tooBigIndex` is not yet beyond the final index of the part of the array that we are partitioning, and `data[tooBigIndex]` is less than or equal to the pivot, move `tooBigIndex` to the next index.

   2b. `while data[tooSmallIndex]` is greater than the pivot, move `tooSmallIndex` down to the previous index.

   2c. `if (tooBigIndex < tooSmallIndex)`, then there is still room for both end portions to grow toward each other, so swap the values of `data[tooBigIndex]` and `data[tooSmallIndex]`.

3. Move the pivot element to its correct position at `data[tooSmallIndex]`:

   3a. Move `data[tooSmallIndex]` (which still contains a value that is less than or equal to the pivot) to `data[first]` (which still contains the pivot).

   3b. `data[tooSmallIndex] = pivot;`

   3c. `return tooSmallIndex;` (i.e., the index where the pivot is).

Quicksort—Analysis

We want to estimate the running time of quicksort from Figure 12.5 on page 642. As always, *n* will be the number of elements to be sorted, and we will express our running times in terms of *n*. In the best situation, the analysis of quicksort is much like our mergesort analysis from page 638. In this situation, each partition places the pivot element in the precise middle so that each recursive call sorts about half of the current elements, as shown here:

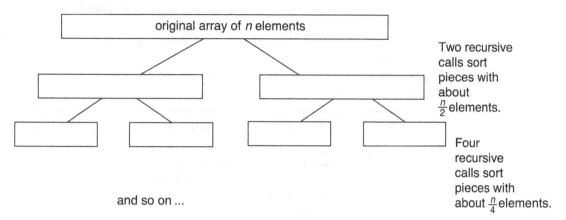

Two recursive calls sort pieces with about $\frac{n}{2}$ elements.

Four recursive calls sort pieces with about $\frac{n}{4}$ elements.

and so on ...

The total work carried out by the partitions on each level is $O(n)$ so that the total time for quicksort is:

(some constant) × n × (the number of levels in the pattern)

In the ideal case, with the pivot element near the middle of each piece, the number of levels is about $\log_2 n$ (just like in the mergesort analysis). This results in a running time of $O(n \log n)$, which is the *best* that quicksort can manage.

But sometimes quicksort is significantly worse than $O(n \log n)$. In fact, the worst time behavior occurs when the array is already sorted before activating quicksort. In this case, the first element is smaller than everything else. Because we have been using the first element for the pivot, the pivot element is smaller than everything else. This causes a miserable partition with everything to the right of the pivot, as shown here:

No elements are less than or equal to the pivot.

n–1 elements are greater than the pivot.

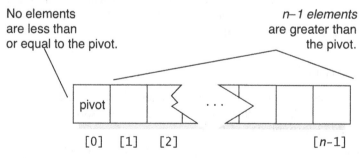

pivot

[0]   [1]   [2]   [n–1]

In this situation, the recursive call to sort the right-hand piece has a lot of work to do. It must sort $n-1$ elements. Even worse, when the recursive call does its own partitioning, its pivot element will be the smallest of its $n-1$ elements, and again a bad partitioning occurs. The recursive call at the next level will have to sort $n-2$ elements. This pattern of bad partitions continues with recursive calls to sort n–3, n–4, and so on, right down to 1. The total work done by all these recursive calls is proportional to the familiar sum: $n + (n–1) + (n–2) + (n–3) + ... + 1$. What's the big-$O$ analysis for this sum? It is $O(n^2)$ (see Figure 1.2 on page 20). So the *worst*-case running time for quicksort is quadratic.

Despite a poor worst-case time, quicksort generally is quite good. In fact, the average time (which we won't develop) turns out to be $O(n \log n)$. This is the same as mergesort, and we have the bonus of not needing to allocate an extra array for the merging process.

Quicksort Running Time

The worst-case running time of quicksort is $O(n^2)$ but the average-case running time and the best-case running time for quicksort are both $O(n \log n)$. Obtaining a good running time requires the choice of a good pivot element.

Quicksort—Choosing a Good Pivot Element

Our analysis of running times points out that the choice of a good pivot element is critical to the efficiency of the quicksort algorithm. If we can ensure that the pivot element is near the median of the array values, then quicksort is very efficient. One technique that is often used to increase the likelihood of choosing a good pivot element is to choose three values from the array and then use the middle of these three values as the pivot element. For example, if the three values chosen from the array are 10, 107, and 53—then 53 would be used as the pivot element. One possibility for the three values is to use the first array value, the last array value, and the value in the array position nearest to the midpoint of the array. However, with our particular partitioning pseudocode, using these three values actually has poor performance when the array starts in reverse order. A better choice is to use three randomly selected values from the array.

Several other common techniques to speed up quicksort are discussed in the Self-Test Exercises and Programming Projects.

Self-Test Exercises for Section 12.2

4. Suppose data is an array of 1000 integers. Write a line of code to activate the quicksort or mergesort method to sort the 100 elements data[222] through data[321].

5. Which recursive sorting technique always makes recursive calls to sort pieces that are about half the size of the original array?

6. In quicksort, what time performance is obtained when good "splitting" of arrays continues for all recursive calls? What time performance occurs if there is bad splitting, so that many recursive calls reduce the array size by only 1?

7. The `quicksort` method in Figure 12.5 on page 642 produces its worst-case running time when the array is already sorted. Suppose you know that the array might already be sorted or almost sorted. How should you modify the algorithm for quicksort?

8. One problem with both of our recursive sorting algorithms is that the recursion continues all the way down until we are sorting a piece with only one element. The one-element piece is our stopping case. This works fine, but once the size of a piece becomes fairly small, a lot of time is wasted making more and more recursive calls. To fix this problem, actual implementations usually stop making recursive calls when the size of an array segment becomes small. The definition of "small" can vary, but experiments have shown that somewhere around 15 elements is a good choice for small arrays. For this exercise, modify the recursive quicksort algorithm so that any small segment is sorted using insertionsort, and the process of partitioning and making recursive calls is done only for larger array segments.

stopping recursion before the pieces get too small

12.3 AN *O(N* LOG *N)* ALGORITHM USING A HEAP

Heapsort

Both mergesort and quicksort have an average-case running time that is $O(n \log n)$. Mergesort also has a worst-case running time that is $O(n \log n)$, whereas the worst-case running time for quicksort is $O(n^2)$. That makes mergesort sound preferable to quicksort. However, mergesort requires more storage because it requires an extra array. In this section, we present a sorting algorithm, called *heapsort*, that combines the time efficiency of mergesort and the storage efficiency of quicksort. Like mergesort, heapsort has a worst-case running time that is $O(n \log n)$, and like quicksort, it does not require an additional array.

Like selectionsort, heapsort is an interchange sorting algorithm that works by repeatedly interchanging pairs of array elements. Thus, heapsort needs only some small, constant amount of storage in addition to the array that holds the elements to be sorted. Heapsort is similar to selectionsort in another way as well. Selectionsort locates the largest value and places it in the final array position. Then it locates the next-largest value and places it in the next-to-last array position, and so forth. Heapsort uses a similar strategy, locating the largest value, then the next largest, and so on. However, heapsort uses a much more efficient algorithm to locate the array values to be moved.

heapsort is an interchange sorting algorithm

Heapsort works by first transforming the array to be sorted into a *heap*. This notion of a heap is the same data structure that was used in Section 10.1 to implement a priority queue. As a quick review, here is the definition of a heap:

the array is made into a heap

Heap Review
(from Section 10.1)

A **heap** is a binary tree in which the elements of the nodes can be compared with a total order semantics. In addition, these two rules are followed:

1. The element contained by a node is greater than or equal to the elements of the node's children.
2. The tree is a complete binary tree so that every depth except the deepest must contain as many nodes as possible; at the deepest level, all the nodes are as far left as possible (see "Complete Binary Trees" on page 457).

A heap is a *complete* binary tree, and we have an efficient method for representing a complete binary tree in an array. This representation was first shown in Section 9.2, following these rules:

- Data from the root of the complete binary tree goes in the [0] component of the array.
- The data from the children of the root is placed in the next two components of the array.
- We continue in this way, placing the four nodes of depth two in the next four components of the array, and so forth. For example, a heap with 10 nodes can be stored in a 10-element array, as shown here:

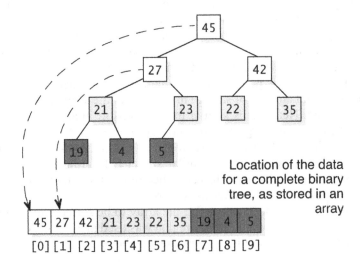

Location of the data for a complete binary tree, as stored in an array

To be more precise about the location of data in the array, we have these rules:

1. The data from the root always appears in the [0] component of the array.

2. Suppose the data for a non-root node appears in component [i] of the array. Then the data for its parent is always at location [(i-1)/2] (using integer division).

3. Suppose the data for a node appears in component [i] of the array. Then its children (if they exist) always have their data at these locations:

> Left child at component [2i+1]
> Right child at component [2i+2]

With these facts in mind, we can easily state the general idea that underlies a heapsort algorithm with this specification:

◆ **heapsort**

```
public static void heapsort(int data[ ], int n)
```
   Sort an array of integers from smallest to largest.

   Parameters:
   data – the array to be sorted
   n – the number of elements to sort (from data[0] through data[n-1])

   Precondition:
   data has at least n elements.

   Postcondition:
   If n is zero or negative, then no work is done. Otherwise, the elements of data have been rearranged so that data[0] <= data[1] <= ... <= data[n-1].

   Throws: ArrayIndexOutOfBoundsException
   Indicates that data has fewer than n elements.

Notice that heapsort sorts an array beginning at index [0]. This differs from our earlier sorting algorithms (which have a specified first index for the portion of the array that was being sorted). We could write heapsort so that it dealt with a specified first index, but the algorithm will be clearer with the requirement of starting at index [0]. So heapsort starts with an array of values to be sorted. The algorithm treats the array values as if they were values in a complete binary tree using the three rules just listed. That much is easy since any array of *n* values represents some complete binary tree with *n* nodes.

The first step of the heapsort algorithm is to rearrange the values in the array so that the corresponding complete binary tree is a heap. In other words, we rearrange the array so that the corresponding complete binary tree follows the heap storage rule: *The value contained in a node is never less than a value from one of the node's children.* For example, suppose the array begins with the 10 values at the top of the next page.

first the array is made into a heap

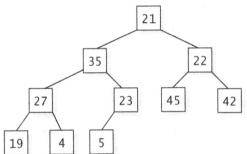

[0] [1] [2] [3] [4] [5] [6] [7] [8] [9]

This array can be interpreted as representing the complete binary tree shown here:

Of course, this complete binary tree is *not* a heap—for example, the data in the root's left child (35) is larger than the data in the root (21). So the first step of the heapsort is to rearrange the array elements so that the corresponding complete binary tree is a heap.

For the 10-element example that we have just seen, the first step of the heapsort might rearrange the array so that the elements are in the following order:

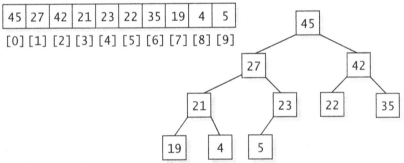

[0] [1] [2] [3] [4] [5] [6] [7] [8] [9]

After the rearrangement of the array elements, the corresponding complete binary tree is a heap, and to aid your visualization, we have drawn the tree beside the array. But keep in mind that the only place that the numbers are stored is in the array. The tree is just our visualization of how those elements are structured. In a moment, we'll provide the details of how the rearrangement into a heap occurs, but first let's look at the rest of the heapsort algorithm.

find the largest element and move it to the end of the array

Recall that the largest value in a heap is stored in the root, and that in our array representation of a complete binary tree, the root node is stored in the first array position. Thus, since the array represents a heap, we know that the largest array element is in the first array position. To get the largest value into the correct array position, we simply interchange the first and the final array elements. After interchanging these two array elements, we know that the largest array element is in the final array position, as shown on the next page.

5	27	42	21	23	22	35	19	4	45
[0]	[1]	[2]	[3]	[4]	[5]	[6]	[7]	[8]	[9]

The dark vertical line in the array separates the sorted side of the array (on the right) from the unsorted side. Moreover, the unsorted side (on the left) still represents a complete binary tree, which is *almost* a heap, as shown here:

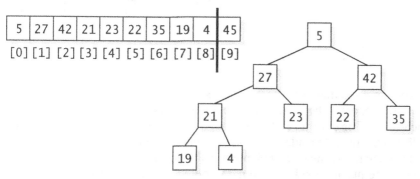

When we consider the *unsorted* side as a complete binary tree, it is only the root   *fix the heap* that violates the heap storage rule. This root is smaller than its children. So the next step of the heapsort is to reposition this one out-of-place value to restore the heap. In Section 10.1, we discussed this process of restoring the heap by repositioning the out-of-place root. The process, called *reheapification down-ward*, begins by comparing the value in the root with the value of each of its children. If one or both children are larger than the root, then the root's value is exchanged with the larger of the two children. This moves the troublesome value down one level in the tree. For our example, the out-of-place value (5) is exchanged with its larger child (42), as shown here:

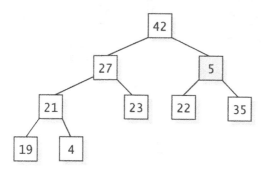

Of course, this exchange of values actually occurs within the array that represents the heap so that the array now looks like this:

42	27	5	21	23	22	35	19	4	45
[0]	[1]	[2]	[3]	[4]	[5]	[6]	[7]	[8]	[9]

In this example, the 5 is still out of place, so we will once again exchange it with its largest child, resulting in the array (and heap) shown here:

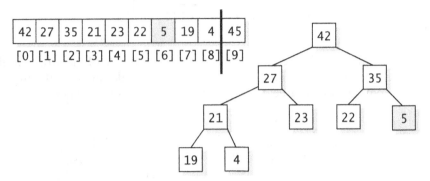

Keep in mind that only the unsorted side of the array must be maintained as a heap. In general, the reheapification continues until the troublesome value reaches a leaf or until it reaches a spot where it is no larger than its children.

When the unsorted side of the array is once again a heap, the heapsort continues by exchanging the largest element in the unsorted side with the rightmost element of the unsorted side. For our example, the 42 is exchanged with the 4, as shown here:

$$\boxed{4 \mid 27 \mid 35 \mid 21 \mid 23 \mid 22 \mid 5 \mid 19 \mid 42 \mid 45}$$
[0] [1] [2] [3] [4] [5] [6] [7] [8] [9]

As you can see, the sorted side has grown by one element. It now has the two largest elements, and the unsorted side is once again *almost* a heap, as shown here:

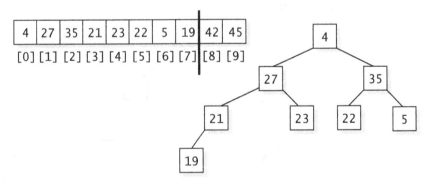

Only the root (4) is out of place, and that can be fixed by another reheapification downward. After the reheapification downward, the largest value of the unsorted side will once again reside at location [0], and we can continue to pull out the *next* largest value.

Here is the pseudocode for the heapsort algorithm we have been describing:

// Heapsort for the array called data with n elements

1. Convert the array of *n* elements into a heap.
2. `unsorted = n;` *// The number of elements in the unsorted side*
3. `while (unsorted > 1)`
   ```
   {
       // Reduce the unsorted side by 1.
       unsorted--;
       Swap data[0] with data[unsorted].
       The unsorted side of the array is now a heap with the root out of place.
       Do a reheapification downward to turn the unsorted side back into
       a heap.
   }
   ```

The implementation of this pseudocode is shown in Figure 12.6. In the implementation we use two methods, `makeHeap` and `reheapifyDown`, which we discuss next.

FIGURE 12.6 Heapsort

Implementation

```java
public static void heapsort(int[ ] data, int n)
{
    int unsorted; // Size of the unsorted part of the array
    int temp;     // Used during the swapping of two array locations

    makeHeap(data, n);

    unsorted = n;

    while (unsorted > 1)
    {
        unsorted--;

        // Swap the largest element (data[0]) with the final element of unsorted part
        temp = data[0];
        data[0] = data[unsorted];
        data[unsorted] = temp;

        reheapifyDown(data, unsorted);
    }
}
```

Making the Heap

At the start of the heapsort algorithm, we must rearrange the array elements so that they form a heap. This rearrangement is accomplished by using a private method with the following specification:

```
private static void makeHeap(int[ ] data, int n);
// Precondition: data is an array with at least n elements.
// Postcondition: The elements of data have been rearranged so that the
// complete binary tree represented by this array is a heap.
```

There are two common ways to build an initial heap from the array. One method is relatively easy to program, and we will show that method here. A second, more efficient method requires more difficult programming, which we will outline in Programming Project 5 on page 672..

The simple approach to makeHeap builds the heap one element at a time, starting at the front of the array. Initially, we start with just one element, and this one element forms a small heap of one node. For example, we might start with the array shown here:

21	35	22	27	23	45	42	19	4	5
[0]	[1]	[2]	[3]	[4]	[5]	[6]	[7]	[8]	[9]

the first array element forms a heap with one node

In this array, the area to the left of the vertical bar can be viewed as a heap with just one node, and the area to the right is still a jumble of random values.

The makeHeap method adds the array elements to the heap one at a time. In our example, we will next add the 35 to the heap, resulting in the following configuration. In this illustration, we have drawn both the array and the state of the heap that is formed from the elements to the left of the vertical bar.

21	35	22	27	23	45	42	19	4	5
[0]	[1]	[2]	[3]	[4]	[5]	[6]	[7]	[8]	[9]

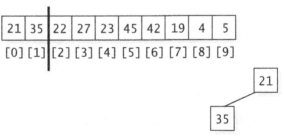

As you can see, just adding the node in this way does not actually create a heap because the newly added node (35) has a value that is larger than its parent. However, we can fix this problem by pushing the out-of-place node upward until it reaches the root or until it reaches a place with a larger parent. This process of pushing a new node upward is called *reheapification upward*. We have seen reheapification upward before in Section 10.1. In that section, reheapification upward was used whenever a new element was added to the priority queue (which was represented as a heap).

The pseudocode for makeHeap uses reheapification upward, as shown here (with two local int variables called i and k):

```
// Making a heap from an array called data with n elements
for (i = 1; i < n; i++)
{
   k = i; // The index of the new element
   while (data[k] is not yet the root, and data[k] is bigger than its parent)
       Swap data[k] with its parent, and reset k to be the index of its parent.
}
```

The complete implementation of this pseudocode for the makeHeap method is left up to you. The readability of your implementation can be improved if you also implement another method called parent, as shown here:

```
private static int parent(int k)
// Precondition: k > 0.
// Postcondition: The method assumes that k is the index of an array
// element, where the array represents a complete binary tree. The return
// value is the index of the parent of node k, using the formula from
// Rule 3 on page 651.
{
    return (k-1)/2;
}
```

Whenever k is an index of an element in the array and k is not zero, the value of parent(k) is the array index of the parent of data[k]. You can use this method whenever you need to calculate the index of the parent of a node.

Reheapification Downward

We have one more method to implement, the reheapification downward, with this specification:

```
private static void reheapifyDown(int[ ] data, int n)
// Precondition: n > 0, and data is an array with at least n elements. These
// elements form a heap, except that data[0] may be in an incorrect
// location.
// Postcondition: The data values have been rearranged so that the first
// n elements of data now form a heap.
```

The method works by continually swapping the out-of-place element with its largest child, as shown in the pseudocode at the top of the next page.

```
// Reheapification downward (for a heap where the root is out of place)
int current;          // Index of the node that's moving down
int bigChildIndex;    // Index of current's larger child
boolean heapOkay;     // Will become true when heap is correct

current = 0;
heapOkay = false;

while ((!heapOkay) && (the current node is not a leaf))
{
    Set bigChildIndex to be the index of the larger child of the current
    node. (If there is only one child, then bigChildIndex will be set to
    the index of this one child.)

    if (data[current] < data[bigChildIndex])
    {
        Swap data[current] with data[bigChildIndex].
        current = bigChildIndex;
    }
    else
        heapOkay = true;
}
```

The swapping stops when the out-of-place element reaches a leaf or when the out-of-place element is larger than both of its children.

Heapsort—Analysis

Let's count operations for the worst-case running time for the heapsort algorithm. As usual, we take the problem size n to be the number of elements to be sorted. If you look back at the implementation from Figure 12.6 on page 655, you will see that the total number of operations can be given as this sum:

(The operations to build the initial heap)
+
(The operations to pull the elements out of the heap one at a time)
+
(Some fixed number of operations for a few other assignments)

To refine this formula, we must calculate the number of operations to build the initial heap and the number of operations required when an element is pulled out of the heap.

Building the Initial Heap. To build the heap, we add the elements one at a time, using reheapification upward to push the new element upward until it reaches the root or until it reaches an acceptable spot (where the parent has a larger value). Since we actually add $n-1$ elements (rather than n), the total time is this:

$(n - 1) \times$ (number of operations for one reheapification upward)

The maximum number of operations for one reheapification upward is a constant times the depth of the heap. In Section 10.4, we showed that the depth of a heap is no more than $\log_2 n$. Therefore, the worst-case time for building the heap is the following:

$(n - 1) \times$ a constant $\times (\log_2 n)$

Removing the constants from this formula results in an $O(n \log n)$ running time to build the initial heap.

Pulling the Elements out of the Heap. Once the initial heap is built, we pull the elements out of the heap one at a time. After each element is removed, we perform a reheapification downward. We pull out a total of $n-1$ elements, and the number of operations in each reheapification downward is never more than a constant times the depth of the tree. Therefore, pulling all the elements out of the tree also requires $(n - 1) \times$ a constant $\times (\log_2 n)$ operations, which is an $O(n \log n)$ running time.

Total Time for Heapsort. We can now give a final estimate for the worst-case running time for the entire heapsort algorithm. Building the initial heap requires $O(n \log n)$ operations, and then pulling the elements out of the heap requires another $O(n \log n)$ operations. You might be tempted to write that the sum of all this work is $O(2n \log n)$, and you would be right. But remember that multiplication by a constant (such as 2) can be ignored in big-O notation, so in fact the entire algorithm from start to finish requires $O(n \log n)$ operations. *worst case for heapsort*

Although we won't give a derivation, it turns out that the average-case running time for heapsort is also $O(n \log n)$, the same as the worst-case running time. *average case for heapsort*

Heapsort Running Time

The worst-case running time and the average-case running time for heapsort are both $O(n \log n)$.

Self-Test Exercise for Section 12.3

9. How would you modify the heapsort algorithm so that it sorts integers into decreasing order rather than increasing order?

12.4 JAVA'S SORT METHODS

In the previous chapter, we saw the `java.util.Arrays.binarySearch` methods (page 579) that can carry out a binary search on any sorted array. Within `java.util.Arrays`, there are related static methods that can sort any array. The methods' headings are what you might expect. For example, with an `int` array, the heading is:

```
public static void sort(int[] a)
```

This version of the method sorts the entire array into ascending order. A second version allows you to search part of the array by specifying the indexes of the elements to be sorted:

```
public static void sort(int[] a, int fromIndex, int toIndex)
```

This second version sorts the array from `a[fromIndex]` up to, but not including, `a[toIndex]`. As with the `binarySearch` methods, there are seven versions of each `sort` method to sort any of the seven basic types of arrays (such as `int` or `char`).

There are additional methods to sort an array of Java objects or to sort any Java collection that implements the `List` interface. These additional methods define what it means to be in ascending order by using the same `compareTo` approach that was described for binary searches on page 579.

Self-Test Exercises for Section 12.4

10. Suppose that `data` is an array of 100 double numbers. Write a line of Java code that activates the `sort` method to sort the array into nondecreasing order.

11. Using the same array, write another line of code that sorts only the 10 elements that start at `data[42]`.

12.5 CONCURRENT RECURSIVE SORTING

Modern computers have a capability called *concurrency*, whereas allows a computer to carry out more than one computation. In practice, concurrency can be implemented in several different ways, some of which involve multiple computations that actually run at the same time (called *parallel processing*) while other techniques have the appearance of simultaneity that is achieved through other means (called *multitasking*).

Thread, RecursiveAction, and ForkJoinPool

One Java feature that supports concurrency is the `Thread` class. Each thread is a separate computation with the potential of being run simultaneously with other threads. However, in this section we'll use two higher-level classes—the `RecursiveAction` and `ForkJoinPool` classes—rather than using threads directly.

Mergesort with a Threshold

The concurrency example we'll develop in this section begins with this modification of the mergesort from Figure 12.2 on page 632:

```
// Sort the elements from data[first] up to (but not including) data[first + n].
public static void mergesort(int[ ] data, int first, int n)
{
    final int THRESHOLD = 20000;
    int n1; // Size of the first half of the array
    int n2; // Size of the second half of the array

    if (n > THRESHOLD)
    {
        // Compute sizes of the two halves:
        n1 = n / 2;
        n2 = n - n1;

        // Sort the two halves with recursive calls:
        mergesort(data, first, n1);
        mergesort(data, first + n1, n2);

        // Merge the two sorted halves with the function from page 637:
        merge(data, first, n1, n2);
    }
    else
    {   // Sort the whole array with some other method:
        java.util.Arrays.sort(data, first, first + n);
    }
}
```

For the most part, this is just the mergesort that we've already seen. The modification is that relatively small arrays (with fewer than 20,000 elements) are sorted by some other technique (the sort method from java.util.Arrays). The breakpoint between using recursion and sorting directly is called the *recursion threshold*.

The mergesort method is a great candidate for concurrency because the two recursive calls can be done independently of each other. For example, if we have two processors available, then we might ask each processor to carry out one of the recursive calls. The two processors can work concurrently, and the entire job will finish faster than a single processor that does the two recursive calls one after another.

Our conversion to use concurrency will employ a new class that first appeared in Java 7. The class, called RecursiveAction, was introduced precisely to make it easier to convert recursion to concurrency—but remember that it's not available prior to Java 7.

Ⓛ Pitfall

THE RECURSIVEACTION CLASS DID NOT APPEAR UNTIL JAVA 7

Java is not a static language. There is an ongoing process of proposing, testing, and revising new features. The new features are released in packages that can be installed on a variety of different kinds computers. For example, one of the new features of Java Standard Edition 7 (released at the end of July 2011) is the RecursiveAction class that we're using. If you have an earlier version of Java, then you won't be able to compile or run the programs from this section.

Java's RecursiveAction Class

In order to use concurrency on our recursive sorting problem, we must write a class with the structure shown here:

Sorter extends RecursiveAction

```
public class Sorter extends java.util.concurrent.RecursiveAction
{
    private Sorter(...)
    {  // The constructor...
```

> The parameters to the constructor contain all the information that's needed to solve one part of the overall problem. Those parameters are copied to local variables of the Sorter class.

```
    }

    private void compute( )
    {
```

> When the compute method is activated, it carries out the work to solve the part of the problem that was set up when the constructor was called.

```
    }
```

> And there will be public methods that we'll see soon.

```
}
```

We chose the name "Sorter" because the class is going to implement a concurrent mergesort. But what does the words "extends" mean in this context? This means that our Sorter class will add some things to the already existing RecursiveAction class. The underlying details of how these things are added are discussed in a later chapter (Chapter 13). For now, it's sufficient to know the syntax of "extends java.util.concurrent.RecursiveAction".

What about the compute method? Its purpose is to be called after the constructor has copied its parameters to the instance variables. When that compute method is activated, it must solve one piece of the overall problem. The piece that it solves is determined by the parameters that were given to the constructor. The compute will then carry out the work of actually sorting the array using the familiar mergesort algorithm. But when it comes to the two recursive calls, we'll arrange for the two calls to execute concurrently. (By the way, we have no choice about the name of this method. Because of requirements from the existing `RecursiveAction` class, we must use the name `compute`.)

You may have noticed that both the constructor and the `compute` method are private. That's not a requirement, but it is a frequent approach when you use the `RecursiveAction` class. The reason for this is that we don't want other programmers creating `Sorter` objects and activating the `compute` method directly. Instead, we'll provide some additional public static methods that can be used by other programmers.

So, now that you know the rough structure of the class that we're aiming for, let's look at the details, starting with its simple constructor.

The Sorter's Constructor

Here's the constructor we have in mind, along with the class's instance variables:

```
// Instance variables for the Sorter class will keep track of information
// about the portion of the array being sorted. Note that arrays smaller
// than the THRESHOLD will be sorted directly (no concurrency):
public final int THRESHOLD = 20000;
private int[ ] data;
private int first, n;

private Sorter(int[ ] data, int first, int n)
{
    // Check that the indexes are valid:
    if (first < 0 || n < 0 || first+n > data.length)
        throw new ArrayIndexOutOfBoundsException("Bad indexes");

    // Copy the parameters to the instance variables:
    this.data = data;
    this.first = first;
    this.n = n;
}
```

Note that we've used the same names for the instance variables and the parameters of the constructor. In this case, the longer name (such as this.data) is the instance variable, and the shorter name (such as data) is the parameter.

When we want to sort a portion of an array, we'll always begin by creating a new `Sorter` object with appropriate parameters. Then we'll arrange for the `compute` method to do its work on the array.

The Sorter's compute Method

The work of the compute method is based on the modifed mergesort from page 661. The only aspect that changes is the recursive calls, which we want to execute concurrently. To get concurrent execution, we use a method called invokeAll, as shown here:

```
// Sort the elements from data[first] up to (but not including)
// data[first + n]. The values of data, first, n, and THRESHOLD are all
// Sorter instance variables.
private void compute( )
{
    int n1; // Size of the first half of the array
    int n2; // Size of the second half of the array

    if (n > THRESHOLD)
    {
        // Compute sizes of the two halves:
        n1 = n / 2;
        n2 = n - n1;

        // Sort the two halves with concurrent recursive calls:
        invokeAll(                                          the invokeAll
            new Sorter(data, first, n1),                    method
            new Sorter(data, first + n1, n2)
        );

        // Merge the two sorted halves with the function from page 637:
        merge(data, first, n1, n2);
    }
    else
    {   // Sort the whole array with some other method:
        java.util.Arrays.sort(data, first, first + n);
    }
}
```

Here is a point-by-point description of the work and requirements of the invokeAll method:

ⓘ PROGRAMMING TIP

USING INVOKEALL

- invokeAll is a method from Java's RecursiveAction class. Its parameters are usually two or more newly created RecursiveAction objects (such as the two Sorter objects in our example).

- When `invokeAll` is activated, it starts all the compute methods of its arguments running concurrently.

- Remember that this concurrency might involve real simultaneity (parallel processing) or it could be an illusion achieved through multitasking. But as a programmer, you don't have to worry too much about that. It is wise, however, to ensure that the individual compute methods are not too small (since that would cause poor performance due to the overhead of starting many concurrent processes).

- When all of the separate compute methods finish their work, then the `invokeAll` method will also finish.

- There is one unusual requirement about the use of `invokeAll` within the compute method: The compute method itself must be activated using an object called a `ForkJoinPool`, as described in the next section.

Using a ForkJoinPool to Get Concurrent Recursion Started

As a Java programmer, you cannot just create a `Sorter` object and activate its compute method. Instead, `compute` must always be activated within a special kind of managed thread called a `ForkJoinPool`. Here are the required steps for getting things going:

1. Create a `Sorter` object to sort part of an array. For example, if you want to sort all of an array called `numbers`, then you can create this object:

   ```
   Sorter s = new Sorter(numbers, 0, numbers.length);
   ```

2. Create an object of the class `java.util.concurrent.ForkJoinPool`, like this:

   ```
   ForkJoinPool pool = new ForkJoinPool( );
   ```

   The purpose of a `ForkJoinPool` is to manage a bunch of concurrent computations. The name comes from two operations that it manages: the *fork* operation (in which computation splits into two or more computations), and the *join* operation (in which a computation waits for other computations to finish their work).

3. Start the compute method of your `Sorter` object running under the management of the `ForkJoinPool`. This is done by the `invoke` method of the `ForkJoinPool`, as shown here:

   ```
   pool.invoke(s);
   ```

We put these three steps into a new public static method, `concurrentSort`, of the complete `Sorter` class, shown in Figure 12.7. Notice that `concurrentSort` is the only method that we document fully, since it is the only public method of the class.

FIGURE 12.7   The Sorter Class

Class Sorter

❖ **public class Sorter from the package edu.colorado.concurrency**
   A Sorter provides a concurrent technique to sort an array.

Specification

The only public members of this class are a constant (Sorter.THRESHOLD) and this static method:

◆ **concurrentSort**
   public static concurrentSort(int[ ] data, int first, int n)
   Sort a portion of the array. Small arrays (less than the constant Sorter.THRESHOLD) are sorted directly by java.util.Arrays.sort. Bigger arrays are broken into two pieces, and these two pieces are sorted with concurrent recursion.

   Parameters:
   data – the array to be manipulated
   first – the index of the first entry in the portion of data to be sorted
   n – the size of the portion of data to be sorted.

   Precondition:
   0 <= first <= first + n <= data.length

   Postcondition:
   A portion of the array from data[first] up to, but not including, data[first + n]) has been sorted into nondecreasing order.

Implementation

*Requires
Java 7 or later!*

```
package edu.colorado.concurrent;
import java.util.Arrays;                         // Provides Arrays.sort
import java.util.concurrent.ForkJoinPool;        // Provides the ForkJoinPool class
import java.util.concurrent.RecursiveAction;     // Provides the RecursiveAction class

public class Sorter extends RecursiveAction
{
    // Instance variables for the Sorter class will keep track of information
    // about the portion of the array being sorted. Note that arrays smaller
    // than the THRESHOLD will be sorted directly (no concurrency):
    final int THRESHOLD = 200000000;
    int[] data;
    int first, n;
```

(continued)

(FIGURE 12.7 continued)

```java
private Sorter(int[ ] data, int first, int n)
{
    // Check that the indexes are valid:
    if (first < 0 || n < 0 || first + n > data.length)
        throw new ArrayIndexOutOfBoundsException("Bad indexes");

    // Copy the parameters to the instance variables.
    this.data = data;
    this.first = first;
    this.n = n;
}

private void compute( )
{
    int n1; // Size of the first half of the array
    int n2; // Size of the second half of the array

    if (n > THRESHOLD)
    {
        // Compute sizes of the two halves:
        n1 = n / 2;
        n2 = n - n1;

        // Sort the two halves with recursive calls:
        invokeAll(
            new Sorter(data, first, n1),
            new Sorter(data, first + n1, n2)
        );

        // Merge the two sorted halves with the function from page 637:
        merge(data, first, n1, n2);
    }
    else
    {   // Sort the whole array with some other method:
        Arrays.sort(data, first, first + n);
    }
}

private static void merge(int[] data, int first, int n1, int n2)
|| See the implementation in Figure 12.3 on page 637.
```

(continued)

(FIGURE 12.7 continued)

```
public static void concurrentSort(int[] data, int first, int n)
{
    Sorter s = new Sorter(data, first, n);
    ForkJoinPool pool = new ForkJoinPool( );
    pool.invoke(s);
}
}
```

Beyond the Simple Sorter Class

Our Sorter class is simple, but it provides a good basis for understanding concurrency. You can consider several expansions of the class's functionality. For example, you might add the recursion threshold as an extra parameter to the constructor. There is also an alternative approach: Instead of using a recursion threshold, the constructor can have a parameter that specifies an exact number of threads to be used. If this number of threads is equal to 1, then the compute method uses java.util.Arrays.sort to sort the array in a single thread. And if the number of threads is greater than 1, then the compute method allows one of the recursive calls to use half of the threads, and the other to use the rest (see the answer to Self-Test Exercise 14).

Java also has support for concurrency beyond the RecursiveAction class. For example, RecursiveTask<T> is a generic class similar to RecursiveAction in which the compute method returns a value of type T. In this case, the invokeAll method returns a collection of T objects that contains the results of all the separately invoked compute methods.

Self-Test Exercises for Section 12.5

12. How does parallel processing differ from multitasking?
13. In the example of this section, what are the parameters to invokeAll, and what is done with those parameters?
14. Assume that the Sorter constructor has an extra parameter, many-Threads, which it copies to an instance variable. Rewrite the compute method so that it behaves according to the description at the end of this section.

CHAPTER SUMMARY

- All the sorting algorithms presented in this chapter apply to any type of values sorted according to any reasonable ordering relation. The array values do not need to be integers.

- In the divide-and-conquer sorting method, the values to be sorted are divided into two approximately equal groups, the groups are sorted by a recursive call, and then the two sorted groups are combined into the final sorted list. Mergesort and quicksort are two examples of divide-and-conquer sorting algorithms.

- Selectionsort and insertionsort have quadratic running times in both the worst case and the average case. This is comparatively slow. However, if the arrays to be sorted are short or if the sorting program will be used only a few times, then they are reasonable algorithms to use. Insertionsort is particularly good if the array is nearly sorted beforehand.

- Mergesort and quicksort are much more efficient than selectionsort and insertionsort. They each have an average-case running time that is $O(n \log n)$. If you need to sort a large number of long lists, it would be worth the extra effort of coding and debugging one of these more complicated algorithms.

- Mergesort has the advantage that its worst-case running time is $O(n \log n)$, but it has the disadvantage of needing to allocate a second array to use in the merging process.

- Quicksort has the disadvantage of a quadratic worst-case time. However, with some care in the pivot selection process, we usually can avoid this bad time. Quicksort can be further improved by stopping the recursive calls when the subarrays become small (around 15 elements). These small subarrays can be sorted with an insertionsort.

- Heapsort works by creating a heap from all the array elements and then pulling the largest element out of the heap, then the next largest, and so on. The worst-case and average-case running times for heapsort are both $O(n \log n)$.

- One Java feature that supports concurrency is the `RecursiveAction` class, which can be used to allow separate recursive calls to execute in separate threads.

? **Solutions to Self-Test Exercises**

1. Instead of finding the index of the biggest element, find the index of the smallest element.

2. To sort strings, change each declaration of the array to an array of strings rather than an array of integers. The `temp` variable must also be changed to a string. Also, the comparison (`data[big] < data[j]`) is changed to compare strings:

   (`data[big].compareTo(data[j]) < 0`).

3. Here is one solution:
```
public static void insertionsort
(int[ ] data, int first, int n)
{
    int i, j;
    int entry;

    for (i = 1; i < n; i++)
    {
        entry = data[first+i];
        for (j = first+i; test ; j--)
            data[j] = data[j-1];
        data[j] = entry;
    }
}
```
The critical test in the implementation is (j>first) && (data[j-1] > entry).

4. quicksort(data, 222, 100);

5. Mergesort always makes recursive calls to sort subarrays that are about half the size of the original array, resulting in $O(n \log n)$ time.

6. When there is good splitting in quicksort, the resulting time is $O(n \log n)$. When there is bad splitting in quicksort, the result can be quadratic time.

7. See "Quicksort—Choosing a Good Pivot Element" on page 648.

8. Your new quicksort method should have an if-statement that tests whether (n <= 15). If so, activate insertionsort; otherwise, proceed as in the original quicksort.

9. Change the heap rule so that the value in every node is less than or equal to its children. Modify makeHeap to build this new kind of heap by changing the test in the while-loop to this:

    (k>0 && data[k] < data[parent(k)])

   In reheapifyDown, change the series of if-statements so that they find the index of the smaller child. If this smaller child is less than the current node, swap the current node with the smaller child and continue. Otherwise, the heap is okay.

10. Arrays.sort(data, 0, 100);

11. Arrays.sort(data, 42, 52);

12. In parallel processing, more than one computation is carried out simultaneously; in multitasking, there is only an illusion of simultaneity from rapid back-and-forth between the execution of several computations.

13. The parameters are Sorter objects. The invokeAll method causes all of the Sorter's compute methods to execute concurrently, finishing only when all of those compute methods have themselves finished.

14. The body of the if-statement is modified this way, using two new int variables t1 and t2:
```
if (manyThreads > 1)
{
    // Compute sizes of the two halves
    n1 = n / 2;
    n2 = n - n1;

    // Number of threads for each half
    t1 = manyThreads/ 2;
    t2 = manyThreads - t1;

    // Sort the halves with recursive calls
    invokeAll(
        new Sorter(data,first,n1,t1),
        new Sorter(data,first+n1,n2,t2)
    );

    // Merge the two sorted halves:
    merge(data, first, n1, n2);
}
```

1 If you are familiar with Java's `Comparable` interface (Programming Project 11 on page 519), then rewrite one of the sorting methods so that it sorts an array of `Comparable` objects. You may choose selectionsort, insertionsort, mergesort, quicksort, or heapsort. For example, with selectionsort, you would have the specification shown here:

```
public static void selectionsort
(Comparable[ ] data, int first, int n)
// Precondition: data has at least n non-null
// components starting at data[first], and
// they may all be compared with one another
// using their compareTo methods.
// Postcondition: The elements of data
// have been rearranged so that
// data[first] <= data[first + 1] <= ... <=
// data[first + n - 1].
```

2 Redo the insertionsort algorithm so that the values are inserted into a linked list rather than an array. This eliminates the need to move other values when a new value is inserted because your algorithm can simply insert a new node where the new value should go. Analyze your algorithm to obtain a big-*O* expression of the worst-case running time. Code your algorithm to produce a complete Java program that reads in a list of 10 integers, sorts the integers, and then writes out the sorted list. Your program should allow the user to repeat the process and sort another list until the user wants to exit the program.

3 One of the advantages of mergesort is that it can easily be adapted to sort a linked list of values. This is because the algorithm retrieves the values from the two lists being merged in the order that they occur in the lists. If the lists are linked lists, then that algorithm can simply move down the list node after node. With heapsort or quicksort, the algorithm needs to move values from random loca-

tions in the array, so they do not adapt as well to sorting a linked list. Write a program that sorts a linked list of integers using mergesort. The program will read the integers into a linked list and then sort the linked list using mergesort. This will require additional linked lists, but you should use linked lists, not arrays, for all your list storage.

4 Rewrite quicksort so that there are no recursive calls. The technique is to use a stack to keep track of which portions of the array still need to be sorted. Whenever we identify a portion of the array that still needs to be sorted, we will push two items onto the stack: (1) the starting index of the array segment and (2) the length of the array segment. The entire quicksort can now work as follows (with no recursion):

1. Push `first` and n onto the stack (indicating that we must sort the n-element array segment starting at `data[first]`).

2. `while` (the stack is not empty)

   2a. Pop a size n and a starting index i off the stack. We must now sort the n-element array segment starting at `data[i]`. To do this sort, first use the assignment:
   `pivotIndex = partition(data,i,n);`

   2b. If the area before the pivot index has more than one element, then we must sort this area. This area begins at `data[i]` and has `pivotIndex-i` elements, so push i and `pivotIndex-i` onto the stack.

   2c. If the area after the pivot index has more than one element, then we must sort this area. Compute the starting point and length of this area in two local variables and push their values onto the stack.

With this approach, in the worst case the stack must be as big as the array that's being sorted. This worst case occurs when we keep pushing two-element array segments onto the stack. However, there is a modification that reduces the maximum stack size. When you do steps 2b and 2c, make sure the *larger* array segment gets pushed onto the stack first. With this modification, the maximum necessary stack size is just $2 \log_2 n$. With this in mind, you can use a stack with a fixed size—for example, a 100-element stack is enough to sort an array with 2^{50} elements.

---

5 The discussion on page 656 shows our algorithm for building the initial heap in the heapsort algorithm. The algorithm is reasonably efficient, but we can make it even more efficient. The more efficient algorithm uses a method that creates a heap from a subtree of the complete binary tree. This method has the following specification:

```
private static void heapifySubtree(
   int[ ] data,
   int rootOfSubtree,
   int n
)
// Precondition: data is an array with at least
// n elements, and rootOfSubtree < n. We will
// consider data to represent a complete
// binary tree, and in this representation the
// node at data[rootOfSubtree] is the root of
// a subtree called s. This subtree s is already
// a heap, except that its root might be out of
// place.
// Postcondition: The subtree s has been
// rearranged so that it is now a valid heap.
```

You can write the heapifySubtree method yourself. Using this method, you can make an entire *n*-element array into a heap with the algorithm:

```
for (i = (n/2); i > 0; i--)
   heapifySubtree(data, i-1, n);
```

For example, with $n = 10$, we will end up making the following sequence of activations:

```
heapifySubtree(data, 4, 10);
heapifySubtree(data, 3, 10);
heapifySubtree(data, 2, 10);
heapifySubtree(data, 1, 10);
heapifySubtree(data, 0, 10);
```

It turns out that this method is actually $O(n)$ rather than $O(n \log n)$.

For this project, reimplement makeHeap, as outlined above.

---

6 On problem with mergesort is that it constantly needs a new temporary array. One solution to the problem is to rewrite the mergesort according to the following specification:

```
void mergesort(
   int data[ ],
   int first,
   int n,
   int temp[ ]
);
// Precondition: data[first] through
// data[first+n-1] are array elements in no
// particular order. The temp array has
// locations temp[first] through
// temp[first+n-1].
// Postcondition: The elements
// data[first] through data[first+n-1]
// have been rearranged so that they are
// ordered from smallest to largest. The array
// elements temp[first] through
// temp[first+n-1] have been used as
// temporary storage.
```

---

7 Rewrite the quicksort partition function so that the pivot is chosen by selecting the median of three random values from the array. Next, write a version using five random values. This may reduce the running time. Test both of these versions with sorted arrays, random arrays, and reverse order arrays, and display your results.

---

8 Choose one of the recursive sorting algorithms and vary the point where you cut off the recursion. Below this size, the array is sorted by a quadratic algorithm.

For each different recursion threshold, get a rough estimate of the time required to sort a random array of 10,000,000 integers. You can get an estimate of this kind by calling System.current-TimeMillis both before and after the sort. The difference between the two return values is the approximate number of milliseconds required by the sort method. (It is only approximate because the sort method does not have exclusive use of the computer during the time that it's executing.)

9 A radix sort is a technique for sorting non-negative integers (or other data that has individual characters or digits).

One version of radix sort works with a linked list of integers. In addition to the list that is being sorted, there are two extra lists called list0 and list1.

The algorithm begins by going through the list of elements to be sorted; every even number is transferred from the original list to the tail of list0, and every odd number is transferred to the tail of list1. After all numbers have been processed, put the two lists together (with list0 in front and list1 at the back), and then put the whole thing back in the original list.

This process of separating and splicing is repeated a second time, but now we separate based on the boolean expression $((n/2) \% 2 == 0)$. And then we separate and splice using $((n/4) \% 2 == 0)$. And so on, with larger and larger divisors 8, 16, 32, ..., . The process stops when the divisor is bigger than the largest number in the list.

Here is one way to implement the algorithm for ordinary integers (with a maximum value of $2^{31}-1$):

```
final int MAX_ITERATIONS = 31;
divisor = 1;
for (i = 0; i < MAX_ITERATIONS; ++i)
{
    Perform the separation and splice using
    ((n/divisor) % 2 == 0)
    to control the split.

    divisor = 2*divisor;
}
```

To improve performance, you can break out of the loop if the divisor ever exceeds the largest number in the list. But if you don't do so, the loop will still end when the divisor overflows the largest possible integer.

The algorithm is quick: Each iteration of the loop takes $O(n)$ time (where n is the size of the list), and the total number of iterations is about $\log_2 m$ (where m is the maximum number in the list). Thus, the entire time is $O(n \log m)$.

10 The performance of the radix sort from the previous project can be improved by using more supplementary lists (rather than just list0 and list1).

For example, you can have an array of 16 lists, which we'll call list[0] through list[15]. Each item of the original list is put into list[index], where the index is computed by the equation:

```
index = (n >> i) % 16;
```

During each iteration, you should add 4 to i and multiply the divisor by 16.

Reimplement this base 16 version of the radix sort, or use some larger base of your own choosing. Don't make the base too big, though, since the number of supplementary lists is equal to the base.

11 Work out an algorithm that uses a radix sort to sort strings of characters.

12 In 1959, the American computer scientist Donald Shell invented a technique that can be used to speed up many different sorting algorithms. For this project, you will apply Shell's method to insertionsort.

The basis of the technique is to get the items to move in big steps (rather than shifting elements to the next-higher index). These big-step shifts are done early in the algorithm, and they tend to put the array in nearly sorted order. Later in the algorithm, we use smaller steps (all the way down to steps of size 1, just like an ordinary insertionsort). But by the time that the small steps are being taken, the array is nearly sorted, and that's a situation where insertionsort is efficient.

The choice of the step sizes affects the performance of the algorithm, but one sequence that is empirically good starts at $n/2$, and each subsequent step size is about the previous size divided by 2.2.

The overall pseudocode is given here:

```
ss = n/2;
while (ss > 0)
{
```

Do an insertionsort on the elements
`data[0]`, `data[ss]`, `data[2*ss]`...

Also do an insertionsort on
`data[1]`, `data[ss+1]`, `data[2*ss+1]`...

And on
`data[2]`, `data[ss+2]`, `data[2*ss+2]`...

And so on. The last little insertionsort that you do starts at `data[ss-1]`.

```
    ss = round ss/2.2  to nearest integer;
}
```

13 Reimplement the concurrent `Sorter` class from Section 12.5 using a quicksort to control the recursion (rather than a mergesort).

CHAPTER **13**

Software Reuse with Extended Classes

LEARNING OBJECTIVES

When you complete Chapter 13, you will be able to ...

- recognize situations in which inheritance can simplify the implementation of a group of related classes.
- implement extended classes.
- recognize situations in which creating an abstract base class will allow the later implementation of many extended classes that share underlying features.
- use our abstract game class to implement many extended classes for playing two-player strategy games such as chess, checkers, Othello, and Connect Four.

CHAPTER CONTENTS

Software Reuse with Extended Classes

*It is indeed a desirable thing to be well descended, but the
glory belongs to our ancestors.*

PLUTARCH
Morals

Often you will find yourself with a class that is *nearly* what
you require, but not quite. Perhaps the class you require needs alterations to one
or two of the methods of an existing class, or maybe an existing class just needs
a few extra methods. Object-oriented languages provide support for this situation by allowing programmers to easily create new classes that acquire most of
their properties from an existing class. The original class is called the **superclass** (or *parent* class or *base* class—the lingo isn't entirely stabilized), and the
new, slightly different class is the **extended class** (or *derived* class, or *child*
class or *subclass*).

The first section of this chapter provides an introduction to extended classes.
The next two sections show two detailed programming examples, including an
illustration of how many of our previous ADTs might have benefited from using
an extended class.

13.1 EXTENDED CLASSES

One of the exercises in Chapter 2 was a Clock class to keep track of one
instance of a time value such as 9:48 P.M. (see Self-Test Exercise 7 on page 51).
One possible specification for this class is shown in Figure 13.1; we're not con-
cerned about the Clock implementation right now. Suppose you're writing a
program with various kinds of clocks: 12-hour clocks, 24-hour clocks, alarm
clocks, grandfather clocks, cuckoo clocks, maybe even a computer clock. Each
of these things is a Clock, but each of these also has additional properties that
don't apply to clocks in general. For example, a CuckooClock might have an
extra method, isCuckooing, that returns true if its cuckoo bird is currently
making noise. How would you implement a CuckooClock, which is a Clock
with one extra isCuckooing method?

One solution uses no new ideas: Make a copy of the original Clock.java file,
change the name of the class to CuckooClock, and add an extra method,
isCuckooing. Can you think of some potential problems with this solution?
We'll end up writing a separate class declaration for each different type of clock.
Even though all of these clocks have similar or identical constructors and methods, we'll still end up repeating the method implementations for each different
kind of clock.

The solution to the clock problem is a new concept called **extended classes**, described here:

Extended Classes

Extended classes use a concept called **inheritance**. In particular, once we have a class, we can then declare new classes that contain all of the methods and instance variables of the original class—plus any extras you want to throw in. This new class is called an **extended class** of the original class. The original class is called the **superclass**. The methods that the extended class receives from its superclass are called **inherited methods**.

FIGURE 13.1   Specification for the Clock Class

Class Clock

❖ **public class Clock from the package edu.colorado.simulations**
   A Clock object holds one instance of a time value such as 9:48 P.M.

Specification

◆ **Constructor for the Clock**
   public Clock( )
   Construct a Clock that is initially set to midnight.
   Postcondition:
   This Clock has been initialized with an initial time of midnight.

◆ **advance**
   public void advance(int minutes)
   Move this Clock's time by a given number of minutes.
   Parameter:
   minutes - the number of minutes to move this Clock's time
   Postcondition:
   This Clock's time has been moved forward by the indicated number of minutes. Note: A negative argument moves this Clock backward.

◆ **getHour**
   public int getHour( )
   Get the current hour of this Clock.
   Returns:
   the current hour (always in the range 1 ... 12)

(continued)

(FIGURE 13.1 continued)

◆ **getMinute**

```
public int getMinute( )
```

Get the current minute of this Clock.

Returns:

the current minute (always in the range 0 ... 59)

◆ **isMorning**

```
public boolean isMorning( )
```

Check whether this Clock's time is before noon.

Returns:

If this Clock's time lies from 12:00 midnight to 11:59 A.M. (inclusive), then the return value is true; otherwise, the return value is false.

◆ **setTime**

```
public void setTime(int hour, int minute, boolean morning)
```

Set the current time of this Clock.

Parameters:

hour – the hour at which to set this Clock

minute – the minute at which to set this Clock

morning – indication of whether the new time is before noon

Precondition:

$1 <=$ hour $<= 12$, and $0 <=$ minute $<= 59$.

Postcondition:

This Clock's time has been set to the given hour and minute (using the usual 12-hour time notation). If the third parameter, morning, is true, then this time is from 12:00 midnight to 11:59 A.M. Otherwise, this time is from 12:00 noon to 11:59 P.M.

Throws: IllegalArgumentException

Indicates that the hour or minute is illegal.

How to Declare an Extended Class

In the declaration of an extended class, the name of the extended class is followed by the keyword extends and then the name of the superclass. For example, suppose we want to declare an extended class CuckooClock using the existing Clock class as the superclass. The beginning of the CuckooClock class declaration would then look like this:

```
public class CuckooClock extends Clock
{
    ...
```

This declaration indicates that every CuckooClock is also an ordinary Clock. The primary consequence is that all of the public methods and instance variables of an ordinary Clock are immediately available as public members of a CuckooClock. These members are said to be **inherited** from the Clock.

Notice that it is the *public* members of the Clock that are accessible to the CuckooClock. In some sense, the private members of the Clock are also present in a CuckooClock—they must be present because some of the public methods access other private members. But these private members cannot be accessed directly in a CuckooClock.

There is another kind of access that can be provided to a method or instance variable. The access is called **protected**. In most respects, a protected member is just like a private member, but the programmer of an extended class has direct access to protected members. None of our examples will use protected members.

Now let's finish our CuckooClock declaration. Our complete CuckooClock is shown in Figure 13.2. This CuckooClock has one extra public method: a boolean method called isCuckooing, which returns true when the clock's cuckoo is making noise. In the implementation of isCuckooing, our cuckoos make noise whenever the current minute of the time is zero. In this implementation, we use the ordinary clock method, getMinute, to determine whether the current minute is zero.

Once the CuckooClock declaration is available, a program can declare CuckooClock objects using all the public Clock methods and also using the new isCuckooing method. In this usage, there are some special considerations for the constructors. We'll discuss these considerations next.

The Constructors of an Extended Class

An extended class may declare its own constructors, or it may use a no-arguments constructor that is inherited from the superclass. Other superclass constructors, with arguments, are not inherited by the extended class (which is why a constructor is not technically a "member"—members must be inheritable). For the cuckoo clock, the inherited no-arguments constructor from the ordinary clock is sufficient. For example, a program can allocate a new CuckooClock object with the statement:

```
CuckooClock noisy = new CuckooClock( );
```

This activates the inherited no-arguments constructor from the Clock to create a new CuckooClock.

Several important aspects of constructors for an extended class are:

1. If an extended class has new instance variables that are not part of the superclass, then an inherited no-arguments constructor will set these new values to their default values (such as zero for an int) and then do the work of the superclass's constructor.

2. Other superclass constructors, with arguments, are not inherited by the extended class.

3. If an extended class declares any constructors of its own, then none of the superclass constructors are inherited, not even the no-arguments constructor. Later we will examine the special format that should be used to write an extended class with its own declared constructors.

FIGURE 13.2   The CuckooClock Is an Extension of the Ordinary Clock

Class CuckooClock

- ❖ **public class CuckooClock from the package edu.colorado.simulations**
- ◆ **extends Clock**

    A CuckooClock is a Clock that cuckoos when the minute is zero. The primary purpose of this class is to demonstrate how an extended class is implemented.

Specification

In addition to the Clock methods, a CuckooClock has:

- ◆ **isCuckooing**

    ```
    public boolean isCuckooing( )
    ```
    Check whether this CuckooClock is currently cuckooing.

    Returns:
    If this CuckooClock's current minute is zero, then the return value is true; otherwise, the return value is false.

Implementation

```
//  File: CuckooClock.java from the package edu.colorado.simulations
//  Documentation is available at the top of this diagram or from the CuckooClock link at
//  http://www.cs.colorado.edu/~main/docs/.

package edu.colorado.simulations;

public class CuckooClock extends Clock
{
    public boolean isCuckooing( )
    {
        return (getMinute( ) == 0);
    }
}
```

Using an Extended Class

We now know enough to write a bit of code that uses an extended class. For example, here is a bit of code that declares a cuckoo clock, advances the cuckoo clock some number of minutes, and then prints a message about whether the cuckoo clock is currently cuckooing:

```
CuckooClock noisy = new CuckooClock( );
noisy.advance(42);
System.out.print("The noisy clock's time is now ");
System.out.println
    (noisy.getHour( ) + ":" + noisy.getMinute( ));
```

```
if (noisy.isCuckooing( ))
    System.out.println("Cuckoo cuckoo cuckoo.");
else
    System.out.println("All's quiet on the cuckoo front.");
```

The key feature is that a cuckoo clock may use ordinary clock methods (such as advance), and it may also use the new isCuckooing method. The inheritance is accomplished with little work on our part. We only need to write the body of isCuckooing; none of the ordinary clock methods need to be rewritten for the cuckoo clock.

There's another advantage to extended classes: An object of the extended class may be used at any location where the superclass is expected. For example, suppose you write a method to compare the times on two clocks, as shown in Figure 13.3. This method could be part of the Clock class, or it could be implemented elsewhere. We can use this method to compare two ordinary clocks, but we can also compare objects of the clock's extended classes. For example, consider the code shown here:

```
CuckooClock sunrise = new CuckooClock( );
CuckooClock yourTime = new CuckooClock( );
```

... code that sets the clocks to some time ...

```
if (earlier(yourTime, sunrise))
    System.out.println("That's before sunrise!");
else
    System.out.println("That's not before sunrise.");
```

In fact, we can even use the earlier method to compare an ordinary Clock with a CuckooClock or to compare two objects from different extended classes.

Any methods you write to manipulate a clock will also be able to manipulate all of the clock's extended classes. Without extended classes, we would need to write a separate method for each kind of clock that we want to manipulate.

Descendants and Ancestors

Two other terms for classes are borrowed from tree terminology: The **descendants** of a class are all of its extended classes, and their extended classes, and so on. For example, we will soon build a hierarchy of classes, shown in Figure 13.5 on page 688. Each class in the diagram is drawn below its superclass. The descendants of Animal are Herbivore, Elephant, Carnivore, Bird of Prey, and Tiger.

The **ancestors** of a class are the class's superclass, and the superclass of the superclass, and so on. For example, the ancestors of Tiger are Carnivore, Animal, Organism, and Java's Object class. In fact, Java's Object class is automatically an ancestor of every other class.

FIGURE 13.3   A Method to Compare the Time of Two Clocks

Implementation

```
public static boolean earlier (Clock c1, Clock c2)
// Postcondition: Returns true if the time on c1 is earlier than the time on c2 over a usual
// day (starting at midnight and continuing to 11:59 P.M.); otherwise, returns false.
{
    // Check whether one is morning and the other is not.
    if (c1.isMorning( ) && !c2.isMorning( ))
        return true;
    else if (c2.isMorning( ) && !c1.isMorning( ))
        return false;

    // Check whether one is 12 o'clock and the other is not.
    else if ((c1.getHour( ) == 12) && (c2.getHour( ) != 12))
        return true;
    else if ((c2.getHour( ) == 12) && (c1.getHour( ) != 12))
        return false;

    // Check whether the hours are different from each other.
    else if (c1.getHour( ) < c2.getHour( ))
        return true;
    else if (c2.getHour( ) < c1.getHour( ))
        return false;

    // The hours are the same, so check the minutes.
    else if (c1.getMinute( ) < c2.getMinute( ))
        return true;
    else
        return false;
}
```

Overriding Inherited Methods

Frequently, an extended class needs to perform some method differently from the way the superclass does. For example, the original clock provides the current hour via getHour, using a 12-hour clock. Suppose we want to implement an extended class that provides its hour on a 24-hour basis, ranging from 0 to 23. The new clock can be defined as an extended class called Clock24. The Clock24 class inherits everything from the ordinary clock, but it provides a new getHour method. This is called **overriding** an inherited method.

To override an inherited method, the extended class redefines the method within its own class declaration. For example, the Clock24 class in Figure 13.4 overrides the original getHour method of the original Clock. Within this implementation, we can use the name super.getHour to refer to the original getHour method of the superclass.

FIGURE 13.4   The Clock24 Class Overrides the Clock's getHour Method

Class Clock24

❖ **public class Clock24 from the package edu.colorado.simulations**
◆ **extends Clock**
> A Clock24 object is a Clock with its hour in 24-hour format (0 to 23) instead of 12-hour format. The purpose is to show how an extended class can override a method of the superclass.

Specification

In addition to the Clock methods, a Clock24 object has:

◆ **getHour (overriden from the superclass Clock)**
> public int getHour( )
> Get the current hour of this Clock24, in 24-hour format.
> **Returns:**
>> the current hour (always in the range 0 ... 23)

Implementation

```
// File: Clock24.java from the package edu.colorado.simulations
// Documentation is available at the top of this diagram or from the Clock24 link at
// http://www.cs.colorado.edu/~main/docs/.

package edu.colorado.simulations;

public class Clock24 extends Clock
{
    public int getHour( )
    {
        int ordinaryHour = super.getHour( );

        if (isMorning( ))
        {
            if (ordinaryHour == 12)
                return 0;
            else
                return ordinaryHour;
        }
        else
        {
            if (ordinaryHour == 12)
                return 12;
            else
                return ordinaryHour + 12;
        }
    }

}
```

Covariant Return Values

Beginning with Java 5.0, the data type of the return value of an overriding method may be any descendant of the data type of the return value of the original method. Using a descendant in this way is called a **covariant** return value. We have already seen one such example: When a class overrides the clone method of its superclass, the data type of the return value is changed to match the extending class. For example, in Chapter 3 we had a clone method for a generic bag with this heading:

```
public IntArrayBag clone( )
```

This method is overriding the Object clone method, which returns an object. Since we have changed the data type of the return value to an extended class, we are using a covariant return type.

Widening Conversions for Extended Classes

In Java, assignments are allowed from an extended class to the superclass. For example:

```
Clock ordinary;
Clock24 scientific = new Clock24( );
```

```
scientific.advance(780);
ordinary = scientific;
```
Advance the scientific clock to 1 P.M. and assign the ordinary clock to equal the scientific clock.

The assignment `ordinary = scientific` is an example of a *widening conversion*, which we first saw in Chapter 5 on page 253. It is a widening conversion because the variable `ordinary` is capable of referring to many different kinds of clocks (an ordinary Clock, or a CuckooClock, or a Clock24); thus, the `ordinary` variable has a wider variety of possibilities than the `scientific` variable (which may refer to a Clock24 object only). Assigning an object of the extended class to a variable of the superclass is always permitted, and the assignment acts like any other Java assignment. After the preceding statements, both `ordinary` and `scientific` refer to the same clock, and this clock is the Clock24 object that was allocated and advanced 780 minutes.

During the execution of a Java program, the Java runtime system keeps track of the class of each object. In the preceding code, the Java runtime system knows that the one clock object is really a Clock24 object, so we might diagram the situation like this (after the assignment statement):

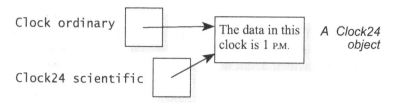

```
Clock ordinary   ┌────┐      ┌──────────────┐
                 │  ─────────▶│ The data in this │   A Clock24
                 └────┘      │ clock is 1 P.M.  │     object
                 ┌────┐    ▲  └──────────────┘
Clock24 scientific │   ────┘
                 └────┘
```

What happens when we activate scientific.getHour( )? The Clock24 getHour method is activated (from Figure 13.4 on page 683), and the answer 13 is returned (which is the hour corresponding to 1 P.M.). That's not surprising since scientific was declared as a Clock24 variable.

But what happens when we activate ordinary.getHour( )? In this situation, the answer is still 13, even though ordinary is declared as a Clock variable rather than a Clock24 variable. Here's the reason:

How Java Methods Are Activated

When a program is running and a method is activated, the Java runtime system checks the data type of the actual object and uses the method from that type (rather than the method from the type of the reference variable).

This technique of method activation is called **dynamic method activation** because the actual method to activate is not determined until the program is running. A method that behaves like this is called a **virtual method**. Some programming languages, such as C++, allow both virtual methods (in which the method to activate is determined by the actual object when the program is running) and nonvirtual methods (in which the method to activate is determined by the type of the variable during the compilation). But Java's nonstatic methods are always virtual.

Narrowing Conversions for Extended Classes

Assignments are also permitted from a superclass to one of its extended types, but the compiler needs a bit of extra reassurance to permit the assignment. For example, suppose that c is a Clock variable and fancy is a CuckooClock variable. To make an assignment from c to fancy, we must write:

```
fancy = (CuckooClock) c;
```

The typecast (CuckooClock) c tells the compiler that the reference variable c is really referring to a CuckooClock object, even though it was declared as a Clock. With the typecast in place, the assignment always compiles correctly, though during the execution there is an extra check. When the assignment is executed, the Java runtime system checks that c really does refer to a CuckooClock, and if it doesn't, then a ClassCastException is thrown.

The assignment `fancy = (CuckooClock) c` is an example of a *narrowing conversion*, which we first saw in Chapter 5 on page 254. In Java, a narrowing conversion always requires a typecast to reassure the compiler that you really did mean to make that assignment. Even with the typecast, a programming error can cause a `ClassCastException` at run time if the object is the wrong type.

Several features of extended classes remain to be seen, such as extended classes that require new private instance variables. These considerations will arise in the examples in the rest of this chapter.

Self-Test Exercises for Section 13.1

1. Design and implement an extended class called `DaylightClock`. A daylight clock is like a clock, except that it has one extra boolean method to determine whether it is currently daylight. Assume that daylight stretches from 7 A.M. through 6:59 P.M.

2. Using your `DayLightClock` from the preceding exercise, write an example of a widening conversion and a narrowing conversion.

3. Suppose an extended class does not declare any constructors of its own. What constructors is it given automatically?

4. Design and implement an extended class called `NoonAlarm`. A noon alarm object is just like a clock, except that whenever the advance method is called to advance the clock forward through 12 o'clock noon, an alarm message is printed (by the advance method).

5. Write a static method with one argument that is a Java `Vector` that contains `Clock` objects. The method returns `true` if at least one clock is in the morning; otherwise, the method returns `false`.

13.2 GENERIC TYPE PARAMETERS AND INHERITANCE

Perhaps your solution to Self-Test Exercise 5 above looked like this:

```java
public static boolean someMorning(Vector<Clock> clocks)
{
    for (Clock next : clocks)
    {
        if (next.isMorning( ))
            return true;
    }
    return false;
}
```

This is a reasonable solution, but it suffers from one surprising problem: The actual argument must always be a vector of `Clock` objects, not a vector of some extended class. For example, Java will not allow this:

```
Vector<Clock24> vc = new Vector<Clock24>( );
System.out.println( someMorning(vc) );
```

The problem with someMorning(vc) is that vc is a Vector<Clock24> object, but the parameter to someMorning is a Vector<Clock> object. Moreover, even though Clock is a superclass of Clock24, Java does not consider Vector<Clock> to be a superclass of Vector<Clock24>. Therefore, someMorning(vc) is illegal (since Java cannot apply a widening conversion to convert vc to a Vector<Clock>).

One solution to this problem is to write a generic method (see Section 5.2), but the generic method must employ a restriction on its type parameter, as described in the first option shown here.

Upper bounds for generic type parameters.   A generic type parameter of the form <T extends B> must be instantiated as the class B or one of its descendants. For example, we can write a generic method in which the generic type parameter T must be derived from our Clock class:

```
public static <T extends Clock> boolean someMorning(Vector<T> vc)
{
    for (T next : clocks)
    {
        if (next.isMorning( ))
            return true;
    }
    return false;
}
```

In a similar way, we might create a generic collection class that can be instantiated only with Clock or one of its descendants:

```
class ClockCollection<E extends Clock>...
```

Within the implementation of ClockCollection, the generic type parameter, E, is guaranteed to be a type that extends the Clock class. This allows us to activate Clock methods for any available E objects. Because of this, any use of the ClockCollection class must instantiate the generic type parameter as a Clock or a type that extends Clock. For example:

```
ClockCollection<Clock24> ccc;
```

Lower bounds for generic type parameters.   A generic type parameter of the form <T super X> must be instantiated as the type X or one of its ancestors.

Combining bounds.   Several bounds for a generic type parameter can be combined. For example, a generic type parameter <T extends B super X> must be instantiated as a type that is both a descendant of B and an ancestor of X.

An alternative approach to generics and inheritance is called *wildcard parameters*. We won't discuss this approach in detail, but we can mention that it allows for generic type parameters to be instantiated with a question mark, such as Vector<?> (which is a superclass of all other Vector instantiations) and Vector<? extends Clock> (which is a superclass of any Vector that is instantiated with a Clock or a Clock descendant).

Self-Test Exercise for Section 13.2

6. Write a static method with one argument that is a Java Vector that contains Clock objects. The method returns the clock that contains the earliest time. If the vector is empty, then the method returns null instead. Your method should work correctly with a Vector<Clock> argument, or with a vector of objects that are a class that extends Clock.

13.3 SIMULATION OF AN ECOSYSTEM

A is-a B means that A is a particular kind of B

There are many potential uses for extended classes, but one of the most frequent uses comes from the is-a relationship. "A is-a B" means that each A object is a particular kind of B object. For example, a cuckoo clock is a particular kind of clock. Some other examples of is-a relationships for living organisms are shown in Figure 13.5. The relationships are drawn in a tree called an **object hierarchy** tree. In this tree, each superclass is placed as the parent of its extended classes.

FIGURE 13.5 An Object Hierarchy

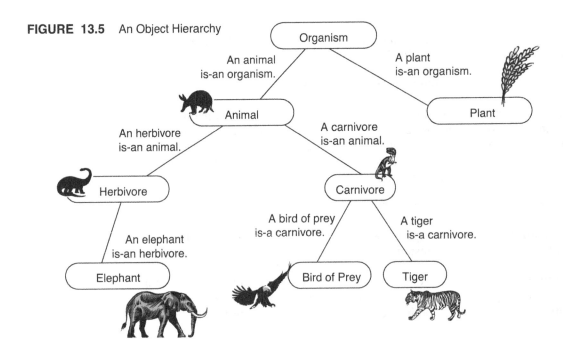

WHEN TO USE AN EXTENDED CLASS

Look at each line in the object hierarchy tree (see Figure 13.5). For each child and its parent, does it make sense to say "A is-a B"? Whenever it makes sense to say "A is-a B," consider implementing the class for A as an extended class of B. This lets the new A class benefit from inheriting all of B's public members.

Implementing Part of the Organism Object Hierarchy

We will implement four classes from the object hierarchy tree of living organisms and use these four classes in a program that simulates a small ecosystem. The four classes that we will implement are:

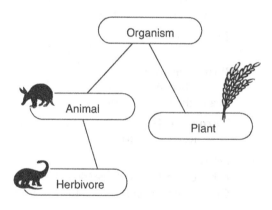

- A general class, called `Organism`, that can be used by a program to simulate the simplest properties of organisms, such as being born, growing, and eventually dying.

- Two classes that are extended from an `Organism`. The classes, called `Animal` and `Plant`, can do everything that an ordinary organism can do—but they also have extra abilities associated with animals and plants.

- The final class, called `Herbivore`, is extended from the `Animal` class. It is a special kind of animal that eats plants.

Keep in mind that the extended classes might have new instance variables as well as new methods.

The Organism Class

At the top of our object hierarchy tree is a class called `Organism`. Within a program, every organism is given an initial size, measured in ounces. Each organism is also given a growth rate, measured in ounces per week. A program that wants to simulate the growth of an organism will start by specifying an initial size and a growth rate as arguments to the organism's constructor. Throughout the computation, the program may activate a method called `simulateWeek`, which causes the organism to simulate the passage of one week in its life—in other words, activating `simulateWeek` makes the organism grow by its current growth rate. The `Organism` class has a few other methods specified in Figure 13.6 on page 690, and a usage of the `Organism` class is shown in Figure 13.7 on page 692.

FIGURE 13.6   Specification for the Organism Class

Class Organism

❖ **public class Organism from the package edu.colorado.simulations**
An Organism object simulates a growing organism, such as a plant or an animal.

Specification

♦ **Constructor for the Organism**
```
public Organism(double initSize, double initRate)
```
Construct an Organism with a specified size and growth rate.

Parameters:
initSize – the initial size of this Organism, in ounces
initRate – the initial growth rate of this Organism, in ounces per week

Precondition:
initSize >= 0. Also, if initSize is zero, then initRate must also be zero.

Postcondition:
This Organism has been initialized. The value returned from getSize( ) is now initSize, and the value returned from getRate( ) is now initRate.

Throws: IllegalArgumentException
Indicates that initSize or initRate violates the precondition.

♦ **alterSize**
```
public void alterSize(double amount)
```
Change the current size of this Organism by a given amount.

Parameter:
amount – the amount to increase or decrease the size of this Organism (in ounces)

Postcondition:
The given amount (in ounces) has been added to the size of this Organism. If this new size is less than or equal to zero, then expire is also activated.

♦ **expire**
```
public void expire( )
```
Set this Organism's size and growth rate to zero.

Postcondition:
The size and growth rate of this Organism have been set to zero.

(continued)

(FIGURE 13.6 continued)

◆ getRate
```
public double getRate( )
```
Get the growth rate of this Organism.

Returns:
the growth rate of this Organism (in ounces per week)

◆ getSize
```
public double getSize( )
```
Get the current size of this Organism.

Returns:
the current size of this Organism (in ounces)

◆ isAlive
```
public boolean isAlive( )
```
Determine whether this Organism is currently alive.

Returns:
If this Organism's current current size is greater than zero, then the return value is true; otherwise, the return value is false.

◆ setRate
```
public void setRate(double newRate)
```
Set the current growth rate of this Organism.

Parameter:
newRate – the new growth rate for this Organism (in ounces per week)

Precondition:
If the size is currently zero, then newRate must also be zero.

Postcondition:
The growth rate for this Organism has been set to newRate.

Throws: IllegalArgumentException
Indicates that the size is currently zero but the newRate is nonzero.

◆ simulateWeek
```
public void simulateWeek( )
```
Simulate the passage of one week in the life of this Organism.

Postcondition:
The size of this Organism has been changed by its current growth rate. If the new size is less than or equal to zero, then expire is activated to set both size and growth rate to zero.

FIGURE 13.7	Sample Program from the Movie *The Blob*

Java Application Program

```
// FILE: Blob.java
// This small demonstration shows how the Organism class is used.
import edu.colorado.simulations.Organism

public class Blob
{
    public static void main(String[ ] args)
    {
        Organism blob = new Organism(20.0, 100000.0);
        int week;

        // Untroubled by conscience or intellect, the Blob grows for three weeks.
        for (week = 1; week <= 3; week++)
        {
            blob.simulateWeek( );
            System.out.print("Week " + week + ":" + " the Blob is ");
            System.out.println(blob.getSize( ) + " ounces.");
        }

        // Steve McQueen reverses the growth rate to -80000 ounces per week.
        blob.setRate(-80000.0);
        while (blob.isAlive( ))
        {
            blob.simulateWeek( );
            System.out.print("Week " + week + ":" + " The Blob is ");
            System.out.println(blob.getSize( ) + " ounces.");
            week++;
        }
        System.out.println("The Blob (or its son) shall return.");
    }

}
```

Sample Dialogue

```
Week 1: The Blob is 100020.0 ounces.
Week 2: The Blob is 200020.0 ounces.
Week 3: The Blob is 300020.0 ounces.
Week 4: The Blob is 220020.0 ounces.
Week 5: The Blob is 140020.0 ounces.
Week 6: The Blob is 60020.0 ounces.
Week 7: The Blob is 0.0 ounces.
The Blob (or its son) shall return.
```

Can anyone stop the Blob?!

Steve McQueen comes to the rescue at the end of week 3!

The Organism class has methods to set a new growth rate, a method to alter the organism's current size, and methods to return information about the organism's current size and growth rate.

The Organism class is not hard to implement, and we'll leave its implementation up to you. But we will give one example of using the Organism class. Movie buffs may recall the 1958 film *The Blob*. The Blob came to Earth from outer space at a mere 20 ounces, but "untroubled by conscience or intellect," it absorbs anything and anyone in its path. Without giving away the whole plot, let's suppose the Blob grows at the astonishing rate of 100,000 ounces per week for three weeks. Then our hero (Steve McQueen) manages to reverse its growth to a rate of negative 80,000 ounces per week. A program to simulate the movie plot is shown in Figure 13.7.

The Animal Class: An Extended Class with New Private Instance Variables

Now we want to implement a class that can be used to simulate an animal. Because an animal *is-an* organism, it makes sense to declare the Animal class as an extended class of the Organism. In our design, an animal is an organism that must consume a given amount of food each week to survive. If a week has passed and the animal has consumed less than its required amount of food, then death occurs. With this in mind, the Animal class will have two new private instance variables that are not part of the Organism class, as shown at the front of this partial declaration:

```
public class Animal extends Organism
{
    private double needEachWeek;
    private double eatenThisWeek;

    || We discuss the animal's public methods in a moment.
    ...
```

the extended class has two new private instance variables

The first new instance variable, needEachWeek, keeps track of how many ounces of food the animal must eat each week to survive. The second new instance variable, eatenThisWeek, keeps track of how many ounces of food the animal has eaten so far this week.

When an extended class has some new instance variables, it will usually need a new constructor to initialize those instance variables. This is the first example we have seen in which an extended class has a new constructor rather than using the inherited constructors described on page 679.

How to Provide a New Constructor for an Extended Class

When an extended class has a new constructor, the implementation of the new constructor appears in the class declaration, just like any other constructor. The inherited no-arguments constructor can no longer be used to create an object of the extended class.

In the case of the animal, the new constructor will have three arguments. The first two arguments are the same as the arguments for any organism, providing the initial size and the initial growth rate. The third argument will indicate how much food the animal needs, in ounces per week. Thus, the start of the animal's declaration is given here:

```
public class Animal extends Organism
{
    public double needEachWeek;
    public double eatenThisWeek;

    public Animal
    (double initSize, double initRate, double initNeed)
    ...
```

The constructor has no argument for eatenThisWeek because we plan to have that instance variable initialized to zero, indicating that a newly constructed animal has not yet eaten.

The work of the animal's constructor is easy enough to describe: The first two arguments must somehow initialize the size and growth rate of the animal; the last argument initializes needEachWeek; and the value of eatenThisWeek is initialized to zero. But how do we manage to use initSize and initRate to initialize the size and growth rate of the animal? Most likely, the size and growth rate are stored as private instance variables of the Organism class, but the animal has no direct access to the organism's private instance variables.

Java provides a solution to this problem, called a **super constructor**. A super constructor is any constructor of the superclass. Usually, a constructor for an extended class will activate the super constructor in its first line of code. This is done with the keyword super, followed by the argument list for the super constructor.

Here is the implementation of our animal constructor, with the activation of the super constructor highlighted:

```
public Animal
(double initSize, double initRate, double initNeed)
{
    super(initSize, initRate);
    if (initNeed < 0)
        throw new IllegalArgumentException("negative need");
    needEachWeek = initNeed;
    // eatenThisWeek will be given its default value of zero.
}
```

If a constructor for an extended class does not activate the super constructor, then Java arranges for the superclass's no-arguments constructor to be automatically activated at the start of the extended class's constructor.

The Other Animal Methods

The animal has four new methods that deal with eating, and the `simulateWeek` method must also be overridden. The four new methods are called `eat`, `assignNeed`, `stillNeed`, and `getNeed`. We'll discuss each of these methods.

The `assignNeed` Method.   This method has this heading:

```
void assignNeed(double newNeed)
```

The method is activated when a simulation needs to specify how much food an animal must eat to survive a week. For example, if `spot` is an animal that needs 30 ounces of food to survive a week, then `spot.assignNeed(30)` is activated. During a simulation, the food requirements may change, so `assignNeed` can be activated several times with different arguments.

The `eat` Method.   Whenever the animal, `spot`, eats `m` ounces of food, the method `spot.eat(m)` records this event. Here's the heading of the method:

```
void eat(double amount)
```

The amount of food that has been eaten during the current week is stored in a private instance variable, `eatenThisWeek`. So activating `eat(m)` will simply add `m` to `eatenThisWeek`.

Two Accessor Methods.   There are two animal methods that are accessor methods called `getNeed` and `stillNeed`. The `getNeed` method returns the total amount of food that the animal needs in a week, and the `stillNeed` method returns the amount of food that the animal still needs in the current week (which is the total need minus the amount already eaten).

Overriding the `simulateWeek` Method.   The animal must do some extra work in its `simulateWeek` method. Therefore, it will override the organism's `simulateWeek` method. The animal's `simulateWeek` will first activate `super.simulateWeek` to carry out whatever work an ordinary organism does to simulate one week. Next, the animal's `simulateWeek` determines whether the animal has had enough food to eat this week. If `eatenThisWeek` is less than `needEachWeek`, then `expire` is activated. Also, `eatenThisWeek` is reset to zero to restart the recording of food eaten for the animal's next week.

   At the top of the next page, we show some example code to illustrate the coordination of the new methods. It begins by declaring a 160-ounce animal, `spot` (perhaps a cat). Spot is not currently growing (since `initRate` is zero in the constructor), but she does require 30 ounces of food per week.

```
Animal spot = new Animal(160, 0, 30);

spot.eat(10);        ◄──────────── Spot catches a 10-ounce fish
spot.eat(25);        ◄              and steals 25 ounces of
spot.simulateWeek( );               chicken from the kitchen.
if (spot.isAlive( ))
   System.out.println("Spot lives!"); ◄── Spot still lives at the
else                                        end of her first week.
   System.out.println("Spot has died.");


spot.eat(10);
spot.eat(15);                   Spot catches another 10-ounce
spot.simulateWeek( );           fish, but gets only 15 ounces
if (spot.isAlive( ))            of chicken this week.
   System.out.println("Spot lives!");
else                                 ◄── Sadly, Spot dies at the
   System.out.println("Spot has died."); end of her second week.
```

The specification and implementation for the animal appear in Figure 13.8. Because the animal is in the same package as the organism (edu.colorado.simulations), there is no need to import the Organism class.

The next class we'll build is a class to simulate a plant. The Plant class is extended from an organism, and it has one extra method—but the work is left up to you in the next few exercises.

Self-Test Exercises for the Middle of Section 13.3

7. Draw an object hierarchy diagram for various kinds of people.

8. Declare a new class called Plant, extended from Organism with one extra method:

   void NibbledOn(double amount)
   // Precondition: 0 <= amount <= getSize( ).
   // Postcondition: The size of this Plant has been decreased by
   // amount. If this reduces the size to zero, then expire is activated.

Suppose fern is a plant. Activating fern.NibbledOn(m) corresponds to some beast eating m ounces of fern. Notice that NibbledOn differs from the existing alterSize method, since in the NibbledOn method the amount is removed from the size (rather than adding to the size), and there is also a strict precondition on the amount eaten. The nibbledOn implementation should activate alterSize to do some of its work.

Your Plant class should have one constructor with the same parameters as the Organism constructor. The plant's constructor merely activates the super constructor with these same parameters.

9. Write a static method with one argument that is a Java Vector, as shown in this header:

```
public static <T extends Organism>double totalMass(Vector<T> organisms)
```

The return value is the total mass of all these organisms.

FIGURE 13.8   The Animal Class

Class Animal

* ❖ **public class Animal from the package edu.colorado.simulations**
* ◆ **extends Organism**
    An Animal is an Organism with extra methods that deal with eating.

Specification

In addition to the Organism methods, an Animal has a new constructor and these new methods:

◆ **Constructor for the Animal**
    public Animal(double initSize, double initRate, double initNeed)
    Construct an Animal with a specified size, growth rate, and weekly eating need.

Parameters:
    initSize – the initial size for this Animal, in ounces
    initRate – the initial growth rate for this Organism, in ounces per week
    initNeed – the initial weekly eating requirement for this Animal, in ounces per week

Precondition:
    initSize >= 0 and initNeed >= 0. Also, if initSize is zero, then initRate must also be zero.

Postcondition:
    This Animal has been initialized. The value returned from getSize( ) is now initSize; the value returned from getRate( ) is now initRate; and this Animal must eat at least initNeed ounces of food each week to survive.

Throws: IllegalArgumentException
    Indicates that initSize, initRate, or initNeed violates the precondition.

(continued)

(FIGURE 13.8 continued)

◆ **eat**

```
public void eat(double amount)
```
Have this Animal eat a given amount of food.

Parameter:
  amount – the amount of food for this Animal to eat (in ounces)

Precondition:
  amount >= 0.

Postcondition:
  The amount (in ounces) has been added to the food that this Animal has eaten this week.

Throws: IllegalArgumentException
  Indicates that amount is negative.

◆ **getNeed**

```
public double getNeed( )
```
Determine the amount of food that this Animal needs each week.

Returns:
  the total amount of food that this Animal needs to survive one week (measured in ounces)

◆ **setNeed**

```
public void setNeed(double newNeed)
```
Set the current weekly food requirement of this Animal.

Parameter:
  newNeed – the new weekly food requirement for this Animal (in ounces)

Precondition:
  newNeed >= 0.

Postcondition:
  The weekly food requirement for this Animal has been set to newNeed.

Throws: IllegalArgumentException
  Indicates that newNeed is negative.

◆ **simulateWeek (overriden from the superclass Organism)**

```
public void simulateWeek( )
```
Simulate the passage of one week in the life of this Animal.

Postcondition:
  The size of this Animal has been changed by its current growth rate. If the new size is less than or equal to zero, then expire is activated to set both size and growth rate to zero. Also, if this Animal has eaten less than its need over the past week, then expire has been activated.

◆ **stillNeed**

```
public double stillNeed( )
```
Determine the amount of food that this Animal still needs to survive this week.

Returns:
  the ounces of food that this Animal still needs to survive this week
  (which is the total need minus the amount eaten so far)   *(continued)*

(FIGURE 13.8 continued)   *Simulation of an Ecosystem*   **699**

Implementation

```
// File: Animal.java from the package edu.colorado.simulations
// Documentation is available on pages 697-698 or from the Animal link at
// http://www.cs.colorado.edu/~main/docs/.

package edu.colorado.simulations;

public class Animal extends Organism
{
   private double needEachWeek;      // Amount of food needed (in ounces per week)
   private double eatenThisWeek;     // Ounces of food eaten so far this week

   public Animal(double initSize, double initRate, double initNeed)
   {
      super(initSize, initRate);
      if (initNeed < 0)
         throw new IllegalArgumentException("negative need");
      needEachWeek = initNeed;
      // eatenThisWeek will be given its default value of zero.
   }

   public void eat(double amount)
   {
      if (amount < 0)
         throw new IllegalArgumentException("amount is negative");
      eatenThisWeek += amount;
   }

   public double getNeed( )
   {
      return needEachWeek;
   }

   public void setNeed(double newNeed)
   {
      if (newNeed < 0)
         throw new IllegalArgumentException("newNeed is negative");
      needEachWeek = newNeed;
   }
```

(continued)

(FIGURE 13.8 continued)

```
public void simulateWeek( )
{
    super.simulateWeek( );
    if (eatenThisWeek < needEachWeek)
        expire( );
    eatenThisWeek = 0;
}

public double stillNeed( )
{
    if (eatenThisWeek >= needEachWeek)
        return 0;
    else
        return needEachWeek - eatenThisWeek;
}
}
```

The Herbivore Class

We're almost ready to start designing a simulation program for a small ecosystem. The ecosystem will be a small pond containing weeds and weed-eating fish. The weeds will be modeled by the Plant class from Self-Test Exercise 8 on page 696, and the fish will be a new class that is extended from the animal class we have just completed.

The new class for the fish, called Herbivore, is an animal that eats plants. This suggests that an herbivore should have one new method, which we call nibble. The method will interact with a plant that the herbivore is nibbling, and this plant is a parameter to the new method. Here is the specification:

♦ **nibble (from the Herbivore class)**

    public void nibble(Plant meal)

Have this Herbivore eat part of a Plant.

Parameter:

    meal - the Plant that will be partly eaten

Postcondition:

Part of the Plant has been eaten by this Herbivore by activating both eat(amount) and meal.nibbledOn(amount). The amount is usually half of the Plant, but it will not be more than 10% of this Herbivore's weekly need nor more than the amount that this Herbivore still needs to eat to survive this week.

For example, suppose carp is an Herbivore and bushroot is a Plant. If we activate carp.nibble(bushroot), then carp will eat some of bushroot by activating two other methods: (1) its own eat method, and (2) the bushroot.nibbledOn( ) method.

The nibble method follows a few rules about how much of the plant is eaten. The rules state that carp.nibble(bushroot) will usually cause carp to eat half of bushroot, but a single nibble will not eat more than 10% of the herbivore's weekly need nor more than the amount that the herbivore still needs to eat to survive the rest of the week. In an actual model, these rules would be determined from behavior studies of real herbivores.

The complete herbivore documentation is shown in Figure 13.9, along with the implementation of the herbivore's methods.

FIGURE 13.9   The Herbivore Class

Class Herbivore

❖ **public class Herbivore from the package edu.colorado.simulations**
◆ **extends Animal**
   An Herbivore is an Animal with an extra method for eating a Plant.

Specification

In addition to the Animal methods, an Organism has a new constructor and the following new methods:

◆ **Constructor for the Herbivore**
   public Herbivore(double initSize, double initRate, double initNeed)
   This is the same as the Animal constructor.

◆ **nibble (from the Herbivore class)**
   public void nibble(Plant meal)
   Have this Herbivore eat part of a Plant.
   Parameter:
   meal - the Plant that will be partly eaten
   Postcondition:
   Part of the Plant has been eaten by this Herbivore by activating both eat(amount) and meal.nibbledOn(amount). The amount is usually half of the Plant, but it will not be more than 10% of this Herbivore's weekly need nor more than the amount that this Herbivore still needs to eat to survive this week.

(continued)

(FIGURE 13.9 continued)

Implementation

```java
// File: Herbivore.java from the package edu.colorado.simulations
// Documentation is available on the preceding page or from the Herbivore link at
// http://www.cs.colorado.edu/~main/docs/.

package edu.colorado.simulations;

public class Herbivore extends Animal
{
    public Herbivore(double initSize, double initRate, double initNeed)
    {
        super(initSize, initRate, initNeed);
    }

    public void nibble(Plant meal)
    {
        final double PORTION = 0.5;        // Eat no more than this portion of
                                           // the plant
        final double MAX_FRACTION = 0.1;   // Eat no more than this fraction of
                                           // the weekly need

        double amount;                     // How many ounces of the plant will
                                           // be eaten

        // Set amount to some portion of the Plant, but no more than a given maximum
        // fraction of the total weekly need, and no more than what this Herbivore still needs to
        // eat this week.
        amount = PORTION * meal.getSize( );
        if (amount > MAX_FRACTION * getNeed( ))
            amount = MAX_FRACTION * getNeed( );
        if (amount > stillNeed( ))
            amount = stillNeed( );

        // Eat the Plant.
        eat(amount);
        meal.nibbledOn(amount);
    }
}
```

The Pond Life Simulation Program

A simulation program can use objects such as our herbivores to predict the effects of changes to an ecosystem. We'll write a program along these lines to model the weeds and fish in a small pond. The program stores the pond weeds in a collection of plants. To be more precise, we have a Java Vector that will contain all the Plant objects of the simulation program. Check Appendix D if you need information on the Vector collection class.

For example, suppose the pond has 2000 weeds with an initial size of 15 ounces each and a growth rate of 2.5 ounces per week. Then we will create a Vector of 2000 plants, as shown here:

```
public static final int    MANY_WEEDS = 2000;
public static final double WEED_SIZE  =   15;
public static final double WEED_RATE  =  2.5;
...
Vector<Plant> weeds = new Vector<Plant>(MANY_WEEDS);

int i; // Loop control variable

for (i = 0; i < MANY_WEEDS; i++)
    weeds.addElement(new Plant(WEED_SIZE, WEED_RATE));
```

Let's start our explanation of this code with the highlighted expression new Plant(WEED_SIZE, WEED_RATE). This expression uses the new operator to allocate a new Plant object. After the type name, Plant, we have an argument list (WEED_SIZE, WEED_RATE). This is the form of new that allocates a new plant using a constructor with two arguments, WEED_SIZE and WEED_RATE. The statement weeds.addElement(new Plant(WEED_SIZE, WEED_RATE)) is executed 2000 times in the code. Each of the 2000 allocations results in a new plant, and references to these 2000 plants are placed in the weeds vector.

Our simulation has a second vector called fish, which is a vector of Herbivore objects. Initially, we'll stock the fish vector with 300 full-grown fish.

With the weeds and fish in place, our simulation may proceed. Throughout the simulation, various fish nibble on various weeds. Each week, every weed increases by its growth rate (stated as 2.5 ounces/week in the code). Some weeds will also be nibbled by fish, but during our simulation no weed will ever be completely eaten, so the weeds never die, nor do we ever create new weeds beyond the initial 2000. On the other hand, the number of fish in the pond may vary throughout the simulation. When a fish dies (because of insufficient nibbling), the reference to that fish is removed from the fish vector. New fish are also born each week at a rate that we'll explain in a moment. For now, though, you should be getting a good idea of the overall simulation. Let's lay out these ideas precisely with some pseudocode.

// Pseudocode for the pond life simulation

1. Create a bunch of new plants and put the references to these new plants in a vector called weeds. The exact number of weeds, their initial size, and their growth rate are determined by the static constants called MANY_WEEDS, WEED_SIZE, and WEED_RATE.

2. Create a bunch of new herbivores and put the references to these new herbivores in a vector called fish. The number of fish and their initial size are determined by static constants INIT_FISH and FISH_SIZE. In this simple simulation, the fish will not grow (their growth rate is zero), and their weekly need will be their initial size times a static constant called FRACTION.

3. For each week of the simulation, we will first cause some randomly selected fish to nibble on randomly selected weeds. On average, each fish will nibble on AVERAGE_NIBBLES weeds (where AVERAGE_NIBBLES is yet another constant in our program). After all these nibbles, we will activate simulateWeek for each fish and each weed. Dead fish will be removed from the fish vector. At the end of the week, we will give birth to some new fish. The total number of newly spawned fish is the current number of fish times a constant called BIRTH_RATE. To simplify the simulation, we will have the new fish born fully grown with a growth rate of zero.

At the end of each week (simulated in Step 3), our program prints a few statistics. These statistics show the number of fish that are currently alive and the total mass of the weeds.

Our program implementing the pseudocode is given in Figure 13.10. The top of the program lists the various constants we have mentioned, from MANY_WEEDS to BIRTH_RATE. Within the program, we use two static methods to carry out some subtasks. One of the methods, called pondWeek, carries out the simulation of one week in the pond, as described in Step 3 of the pseudocode. The other method, totalMass, computes the total mass of all the plants in the pond.

We discuss some implementation details starting on page 708.

FIGURE 13.10   The Pond Life Simulation

Java Application Program

```
//  FILE: PondLife.java
//  A simple simulation program to model the fish and weeds in a pond

import edu.colorado.simulations.*; // Provides Organism, Plant, Herbivore classes
import java.util.Vector;

public class PondLife
{
    // Number of weeds in the pond
    public static final int MANY_WEEDS = 2000;

    // Initial size of each weed, in ounces
    public static final double WEED_SIZE = 15;

    // Growth rate of weeds, in ounces/week
    public static final double WEED_RATE = 2.5;

    // Initial number of fish in the pond
    public static final int INIT_FISH = 300;

    // Fish size, in ounces
    public static final double FISH_SIZE = 50;

    // A fish must eat FRACTION times its size during one week, or it will die.
    public static final double FRACTION = 0.5;

    // Average number of weeds nibbled by a fish over a week
    public static final int AVERAGE_NIBBLES = 30;

    // At the end of each week, some fish have babies. The total number of new fish born is the
    // current number of fish times the BIRTH_RATE (rounded down to an integer).
    public static final double BIRTH_RATE = 0.05;

    // Number of weeks to simulate
    public static final int MANY_WEEKS  = 38;
```

(continued)

(FIGURE 13.10 continued)

```java
public static void main(String[ ] args)
{
    Vector<Herbivore> fish = new Vector<Herbivore>(INIT_FISH);
    Vector<Plant> weeds = new Vector<Plant>(MANY_WEEDS);
    int i;

    // Initialize the Vectors of fish and weeds:
    for (i = 0; i < INIT_FISH; i++)
        fish.addElement(new Herbivore(FISH_SIZE, 0, FISH_SIZE * FRACTION));
    for (i = 0; i < MANY_WEEDS; i++)
        weeds.addElement(new Plant(WEED_SIZE, WEED_RATE));

    // Print headings for the output, using tabs (\t) to separate columns of data:
    System.out.println("Week \tNumber \tPlant Mass");
    System.out.println("      \tof       \t(in ounces)");
    System.out.println("      \tFish");

    // Simulate the weeks:
    for (i = 1; i <= MANY_WEEKS; i++)
    {
        pondWeek(fish, weeds);
        System.out.print(i + "\t");
        System.out.print(fish.size( ) + "\t");
        System.out.print((int) totalMass(weeds) + "\n");
    }
}

public static double totalMass(Vector<? extends Organism>organisms)
{
    double answer = 0;

    for (Organism next : organisms)
    {
        if (next != null)
            answer += next.getSize( );
    }
    return answer;
}
```

(continued)

(FIGURE 13.10 continued)

```java
public static void pondWeek(Vector<Herbivore> fish, Vector<Plant> weeds)
{
    int i;
    int manyIterations;
    int index;
    Herbivore nextFish;
    Plant nextWeed;

    // Have randomly selected fish nibble on randomly selected plants:
    manyIterations = AVERAGE_NIBBLES * fish.size( );
    for (i = 0; i < manyIterations; i++)
    {
        index = (int) (Math.random( ) * fish.size( ));
        nextFish = fish.elementAt(index);
        index = (int) (Math.random( ) * weeds.size( ));
        nextWeed = weeds.elementAt(index);
        nextFish.nibble(nextWeed);
    }

    // Simulate the weeks for the fish:
    i = 0;
    while (i < fish.size( ))
    {
        nextFish = fish.elementAt(i);
        nextFish.simulateWeek( );
        if (nextFish.isAlive( ))
            i++;
        else
            fish.removeElementAt(i);
    }

    // Simulate the weeks for the weeds:
    for (i = 0; i < weeds.size( ); i++)
    {
        nextWeed = weeds.elementAt(i);
        nextWeed.simulateWeek( );
    }

    // Create some new fish, according to the BIRTH_RATE constant:
    manyIterations = (int) (BIRTH_RATE * fish.size( ));
    for (i = 0; i < manyIterations; i++)
        fish.addElement(new Herbivore(FISH_SIZE, 0, FISH_SIZE * FRACTION));
}
```

Pond Life—Implementation Details

The implementations of totalMass and pondWeek are part of Figure 13.10. The pondWeek implementation requires the ability to grab a random element out of a vector, and this is accomplished by generating a random integer via the Math.random method.

Both totalMass and pondWeek require the ability to step through the items of a vector one at a time. This could be accomplished by using an Iterator (as discussed in Section 5.5), but we just stepped through the elements one at a time in a for-loop, using the elementAt method. For example, within the pondWeek method, we activate simulateWeek for each plant by using the for-loop, as shown here:

```
// Simulate the weeks for the weeds:
for (i = 0; i < weeds.size( ); i++)
{
    nextWeed = weeds.elementAt(i);
    nextWeed.simulateWeek( );
}
```

A similar loop steps through the fish, simulating one week for each fish and removing dead fish.

Using the Pond Model

No doubt you have noticed that our pond model is not entirely rooted in reality. For example, each fish is born full-grown and does not continue to grow. Some extensions to make the model more realistic are given in the Programming Projects of this chapter. Nevertheless, even our simple program illustrates the principles of simulation programs. Let's look at one way that a simulation program such as ours could be used.

Suppose your friend Judy owns a pond with 2000 weeds, about 15 ounces each. Perhaps the pond is too choked with weeds for Judy's taste. One way to control the weeds is to introduce a weed-eating species of fish, and the pond life program can help us predict what will happen when a certain number of fish are put in the pond. For example, suppose we have a species of fish in which the program's constants (see Figure 13.10 on page 705) are accurate. When we run the program with these constants, we get the output in Figure 13.11 on page 709.

Actually, if you run the program, you may get slightly different output because of the use of the random factor in the selection of which fish nibble which weeds. What does the program predict will happen in the pond if we introduce 300 of this kind of fish? Each output line gives the fish population and the plant mass at the end of one more week. The model predicts that the mass of the weeds will decrease fairly rapidly. This is followed by a period of some oscillation in both the fish and plant populations, including a rather catastrophic week for the fish when their population drops from 359 to 144. Sudden declines such as this are observed in real ecosystems when a species is allowed to expand, limited only by its food supply.

This kind of model can provide predictions and test theories of interactions in an ecosystem. It's also important to remember that any predictions are only as accurate as the underlying model.

Self-Test Exercises for the End of Section 13.3

10. Write code to declare a Vector. Put 10 new organisms in the Vector with an initial size of 16 ounces and a growth rate of 1 ounce per week. Grab five random organisms and alter their growth rates to 2 ounces per week. Finally, calculate the total of all the organisms' growth rates and print the result.

11. In the preceding exercise, you started with 10 organisms growing at 1 ounce per week. Five random organisms had their growth rates changed to 2 ounces per week, so you might think that the total of all the organisms' rates would be 5*1 + 5*2, which is 15. But when I ran the program, the total was only 14. Why?

12. What advantages did we get by storing the fish and weeds in vectors rather than in a partially filled array?

FIGURE 13.11   Pond Life Results

Sample Output

Week	Number of Fish	Plant Mass (in ounces)
1	315	27500
2	330	24625
3	346	21375
4	363	17725
5	379	13654
6	359	9286
7	144	6462
8	109	7960
9	112	10245
10	117	12445
11	122	14520
12	128	16470
13	134	18270
14	140	19920
15	147	21420
16	154	22745
17	161	23895
18	169	24870
19	177	25645
20	185	26220
21	194	26595
22	203	26745
23	213	26670
24	223	26345
25	234	25770
26	245	24920
27	257	23795
28	268	22374
29	281	20674
30	292	18656
31	306	16356
32	313	13720
33	301	10984
34	244	8689
35	189	7812
36	163	8225
37	161	9176
38	164	10159

13. Design and implement a new class extended from the Animal class. The new class, called Carnivore, has one new method with the heading shown here:

```
public void chase(Animal prey, double chance)
```

When chase(prey, chance) is activated for some carnivore, the carnivore chases the prey. The probability of actually catching the prey is given by the parameter chance (which should lie between 0 and 1—for example, 0.75 for a 75% chance). If the prey is actually caught, then this will also activate the carnivore's eat method and (sadly) will activate the prey's expire method.

Note: You can use the Math.random method to determine whether the animal is caught, as shown here:

```
if (Math.random( ) < chance)
{
    || Code for catching and eating the prey
}
```

13.4 ABSTRACT CLASSES AND A GAME CLASS

This section demonstrates *abstract classes*, which are a new kind of class that allows the implementation of certain methods to be delayed until an extended class is implemented.

Introduction to the AbstractGame Class

To explain abstract classes, we'll present a class called AbstractGame, which will make it easier for us to write programs that play various two-player games such as chess, checkers, or Othello. The games we have in mind will pit a human player against the computer, with the computer making moves that are hopefully intelligent.

The key to the AbstractGame class is the realization that many aspects of these different games can be handled in a uniform way. For example, each game needs a general procedure for going back and forth between the human player and the computer, and each game needs a sensible procedure for selecting the computer's move from among the alternatives. So our proposal is to have an AbstractGame class that provides all these common operations and will serve as a superclass for many extended classes that play various two-player games.

The class provides a framework in which other games can be implemented. For example, a programmer who is writing a chess-playing program can implement an extended chess class that uses AbstractGame as the superclass.

Another programmer, writing a program to play Othello, can implement a derived `othello` class that also uses `AbstractGame` as its superclass.

The specification of our proposed game class is given in Figure 13.12. There's a lot of information in the `AbstractGame` class specification, and it uses several new techniques. We'll briefly explain each part of the specification, and then we'll come back to concentrate on how to write an extended class to play a game such as chess, or Othello, or—as our actual example—Connect Four.

FIGURE 13.12   Specification for the `AbstractGame` Class

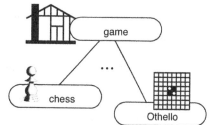

Class AbstractGame

❖ **public class AbstractGame from the package edu.colorado.games**

An `AbstractGame` provides basic methods for playing a two-player game such as chess, checkers, or Othello.

Specification of Public Members

◆ **Constructor for the AbstractGame**
```
public AbstractGame( )
```
Initialize a game so that it's ready to play. The human always moves first; the computer moves second.

◆ **play**
```
public final Player play(int depth)
```
Play one round of this game.

Parameters:
depth - Indicates how many moves the computer should look ahead (beyond its own move) when it is making its move. If this value is less than or equal to zero, then no lookahead is done.

Postcondition:
The first time this method is activated for a game, one round of this game is played; the return value is the outcome of the game which is one of three values (human, computer or nobody) from an enum type called `Player`. Each later activation of play will display the final state of the original game and return the winner of that game. (Use `repeatPlay` if you want to play a series of one game after another.)

(continued)

(FIGURE 13.12 continued)

◆ **repeatPlay**

```
public static final double repeatPlay(String name, int depth)
```
Create and play a series of games.

Parameters:

name – the name of the extended class that is to be played (for example, edu.colorado.games.Connect4 is the extended class given in Figure 13.3 on page 719).

depth – same as the parameter for play( )

Precondition:

The name must be the name of a class that extends AbstractGame.

Postcondition:

A series of the indicated game has been played. After each game, the user is given the choice of playing another. The return value is the fraction of games won by the user (counting a tie as if it were half a win).

Throws: IllegalArgumentException

Indicates that name was not a class that extends AbstractGame.

Specification of Protected Final Methods

These methods are protected and final. The protected keyword means that these methods may be used by any class that extends AbstractGame (and by any class in the edu.colorado.games package). The final keyword means that these methods may not be overridden.

◆ **movesCompleted**

```
protected final int movesCompleted( )
```
Get the number of moves that have been made in this game.

Returns:

The number of moves that have been played in this game (which is just the number of times that makeMove( ) has been activated). Note: Arithmetic overflow occurs if this goes larger than the largest integer.

◆ **nextMover**

```
protected final Player nextMover( )
```
Get the next player to move.

Returns:

The next player to move (human or computer) from the enum type, Player.

(continued)

(FIGURE 13.12 continued)

Specification of Protected Nonfinal Methods

These methods are `protected` but not `final`. The `protected` keyword means that they may be used by any class that extends `AbstractGame` (and by any class in the `edu.colorado.games` package). Because they are not `final`, they may be overridden by an extending class.

♦ **clone**

> `protected AbstractGame clone( )`
>
> Generate a copy of this `AbstractGame`. If an extended class uses any arrays or other objects, then this `clone` method must be overrridden so that cloned games do not share memory with the original.
>
> **Returns:**
>> The return value is a copy of this `AbstractGame`.
>
> **Throws:** `OutOfMemoryError`
>> Indicates insufficient memory for creating the clone.

♦ **displayMessage**

> `protected void displayMessage(String message)`
>
> Provide a message to the game's user. This method may be overridden to present the message to the user in a different way (such as in a message window of an applet).
>
> **Parameter:**
>> `message` – the message to be printed
>
> **Postcondition:**
>> The specified message has been printed to `System.out` followed by a new line.

♦ **getUserMove**

> `protected String getUserMove( )`
>
> All moves in the game must have a representation as a `String`. This method prompts the user for a move, then reads and returns the answer (which is not verified for legality). An extended class may override this method to provide a fancier interactive way of obtaining a user move.
>
> **Returns:**
>> the string typed by the user in response to a prompt

♦ **makeMove**

> `protected void makeMove(String move)`
>
> All moves in the game must have a representation as a `String`. This method makes the specified move for the player whose turn it is to move. Almost every extended class will override this method so that it can update its own state of the game. The first statement of any overriding `makeMove` must call `super.makeMove` (which is this method).
>
> **Parameter:**
>> `move` – the move to be made.
>
> **Precondition:**
>> `isLegal(move)`
>
> **Postcondition:**
>> This version of `makeMove` just updates data about how many moves have been made.
>
> **Throws: IllegalArgumentException**
>> Indicates that the move was not a legal move.

(continued)

(FIGURE 13.12 continued)

◆ winning

```
protected Player winning( )
```

Get who is winning the game. This activates `evaluate` to determine who is winning at the moment, but an extended class may override to provide a more sophisticated analysis.

Returns:

who is currently winning the game (`human`, `nobody`, or `computer`), which is a value from the enum class, `Player`.

Specification of Protected Abstract Methods

The keyword `abstract` means that all of these methods must be overridden by any extending class.

◆ computeMoves

```
protected abstract Vector<String> computeMoves( )
```

All moves in the game must have a representation as a `String`. This method computes all strings that are legal moves at the moment and puts them into a vector.

Postcondition:

The return value is a vector of all currently legal moves (which are strings); if the game is not over, then this includes at least one move.

◆ displayStatus

```
protected abstract void displayStatus( )
```

Display the current status of the game to the user, such as by printing the current game board.

◆ evaluate

```
protected abstract double evaluate( )
```

Evaluate the current status of the game.

Returns:

A positive number (not infinity) if the game status seems to favor the computer; a negative number (not infinity) for a human advantage. Zero indicates no advantage to either player. Values that are closer to zero indicate less advantage than values that are far away.

◆ isGameOver and isLegal

```
protected abstract boolean isGameOver( )
protected abstract boolean isLegal(String move)
```

Determine whether the game is over or whether a given move is currently legal.

The Player Class. Within the AbstractGame class, we make use of an enumeration type defined this way:

```
enum Player { human, nobody, computer }
```

how to define an enum class

The general form of an enum class is the keyword enum followed by the class name and a list of names for the constant values for objects of the enum type.

The Player class defines a simple class whose variables may be assigned any one of three values: Player.human, Player.nobody, or Player.computer. Some methods, such as AbstractGame.winning, have parameters or return values that are from the Player class. Assignments and other operations to objects of type Player use only the three defined values. For example, our game class will have an instance variable that keeps track of whose move it is, and the value of this object will always be Player.human or Player.computer.

Public Methods to Play a Game. The AbstractGame class has a no-arguments constructor (which may be used by the no-arguments constructor of any extended class) and two public methods to play a game:

```
public final int play(int depth)
public static final double repeatPlay(String name, int depth);
```

These methods are both inherited by any extended class. Any Java program can use these methods to play a single game (the play method) or a series of games (the repeatPlay method). For example, later we will write a class called edu.colorado.games.Connect4, which extends the AbstractGame class to a game called Connect Four. A simple main function that plays a Connect Four game looks like this:

```
import edu.colorado.games.Connect4;
public static void main(String args)
{
    final int DEPTH = 4;
    Connect4 instance = new Connect4( );
    Player winner;

    winner = instance.play(DEPTH);    ◀—  This plays one game of
    switch (winner)                        Connect Four.
    {
    case human:
        System.out.println("You win"); break;
    case computer:
        System.out.println("I win"); break;
    case nobody:
        System.out.println("A draw"); break;
    }
}
```

The DEPTH argument indicates how far ahead the computer will look when it's making its moves. A higher DEPTH will result in better moves for the computer but a longer running time. The game is interactive, letting the user type game moves at the keyboard (or, as we will see, the input can come in other ways). A method of the AbstractGame class directs the computer's moves, searching through all possible moves, looking at responses that the human might make to those moves, looking at possible responses to the human's responses, and so on.

You are probably wondering about the details of directing the computer's moves. We will discuss that at the end of this section, but for now, let's assume that some wise and generous programmer has given us the AbstractGame class, which we are going to use to implement games such as Connect Four. The wonderful feature of the AbstractGame class is that we don't need to know the details of how play works in order to write our extended class. We can just trust that our wise and generous programmer wrote the play method correctly. This is a benefit of any well-written superclass, whether it is abstract or not:

The Benefit of a Well-Written Superclass

With a well-written superclass in hand, a programmer can write extended classes without worrying about how the superclass accomplishes its work.

We're planning to write a class that extends AbstractGame. Among other things, our extended class will inherit the powerful play function. We have no immediate need to understand the details of the play function, but we do need to know more about the next part of the AbstractGame class specification, which provides a series of methods using the keywords final, protected, and abstract.

Protected Methods

The specification of the AbstractGame includes a series of methods that are declared with the protected keyword, such as:

```
protected void displayMessage(String message)
```

The keyword protected indicates that the member is somewhere between public and private. In particular, a **protected member** can be used (and overridden) by a extended class and also used anywhere within the current package (edu.colorado.games); apart from that, it cannot be used elsewhere.

Final Methods

Five of the methods use the keyword final. This keyword forbids any extended class from overriding the method. For example, the play method cannot be changed by any extended method. However, other methods do not use the keyword final (such as displayMessage and makeMove). These other methods can be overridden if an extended class wants to change how things are done. (In fact, makeMove is almost always overridden by an extended class.)

Abstract Methods

The last five methods in the AbstractGame specification use the keyword abstract. This keyword indicates that the method will not be implemented by the current class (AbstractGame), and therefore any extended class must implement these methods itself. These five methods all involve aspects of the game that AbstractGame cannot know about because it doesn't even know what the game is. For example, one of the abstract methods displays the current status of the game:

♦ **displayStatus**

> protected abstract void displayStatus( )
>
> Display the current status of the game to the user, such as by printing the current game board.

AbstractGame cannot implement this method because it doesn't even know what the game is (such as Connect Four), and it doesn't know where the data that describes the game is kept (in member variables of the extended class).

Because the AbstractGame class includes some abstract methods, there are extra aspects of its implementation:

Abstract Classes

1. Any class that includes some abstract members must also include the keyword abstract on the first line of the class definition. For example:

   ```
   public abstract class AbstractGame
   . . .
   ```

2. Usually, the name of an abstract class begins with the word Abstract (such as AbstractGame), though this is not a Java requirement.

3. Any class that extends an abstract class must either implement all of the abstract methods or be declared as an abstract class itself (using the keyword abstract on its first line).

4. A constructor for an abstract class is responsible for initializing all of its member variables. But a constructor for an abstract class cannot generally be called to create instances (because some of the methods are missing). Such a constructor can be called within the constructor of an extended class (using the super keyword as shown on page 694).

An Extended Class to Play Connect Four

We're ready to implement a Connect4 class that extends the AbstractGame class. The extended class will have member variables to keep track of the status of a Connect Four game as it is being played. The extended class will also override seven methods (including all five abstract methods) to provide the tasks that are needed for examining and manipulating the status of the game.

the rules of Connect Four

The rules of Connect Four are easy to describe. The game board consists of a transparent vertical tray with seven slots at the top. The players alternate dropping checkers into the slots: white (for player one), then black (player two), then white (player one), black (player two), and so on. The game ends when someone gets four of his or her checkers in a row (horizontally, vertically, or diagonally). For example, after the first player's third move, the board might look like the one in the margin.

In this situation, the black player needs to make the next move in the rightmost column; otherwise, the white player can win by getting four-in-a-row horizontally on the next move.

Each slot can hold up to six checkers, so it is possible that the game ends with no player having four-in-a-row (that would be a tie).

The Private Member Variables of the Connect Four Class

what the game class requires from its derived classes

Our Connect4 class definition will extend AbstractGame. Any such extended class must have member variables to keep track of the status of a single game. In the case of Connect Four, the Connect4 class must have member variables to keep track of the status of a single game of Connect Four as the game is played.

In addition, the extended class must implement at least the five abstract methods that allow the AbstractGame class to access the game status, and usually it will also override the clone and makeMove methods. Our overall plan for the Connect4 class is shown in Figure 13.13, including a two-dimensional array called data with six rows and seven columns:

```
public static final int ROWS = 6;
public static final int COLUMNS = 7;
private Player[ ][ ] data = new Player[ROWS][COLUMNS];
```

In Java, a **two-dimensional array** is an array (such as data) in which every component has two indexes rather than the usual one index. Programmers usually view a two-dimensional array as a grid of elements, where the first index provides the row number of a component and the second index provides the column number. The preceding data declaration declares a reference variable called data that is capable of refering to a two-dimensional array of Player values, and the new operation makes such an array with six rows and seven columns.

the purpose of the data member variables

Each spot in the data array corresponds to one spot on the game board. For example, if the game board has the computer's checker at row 1 and column 3, then data[1][3] will be set to computer (using the computer constant from AbstractGame). Any location without a checker will be recorded as nobody.

For example, after five moves, the data array might look like this (with row zero on the bottom, although programmers more often draw it on the top):

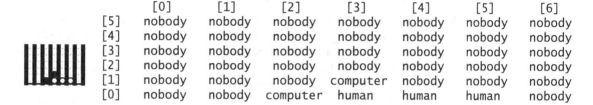

	[0]	[1]	[2]	[3]	[4]	[5]	[6]
[5]	nobody	nobody	nobody	nobody	nobody	nobody	nobody
[4]	nobody	nobody	nobody	nobody	nobody	nobody	nobody
[3]	nobody	nobody	nobody	nobody	nobody	nobody	nobody
[2]	nobody	nobody	nobody	nobody	nobody	nobody	nobody
[1]	nobody	nobody	nobody	computer	nobody	nobody	nobody
[0]	nobody	nobody	computer	human	human	human	nobody

FIGURE 13.13   Class Implementation for the Connect Four Game

---

Implementation

```
// File: Connect4.java from the package edu.colorado.games
// Documentation is available from the Connect4 link at
// http://www.cs.colorado.edu/~main/docs/.

package edu.colorado.games;
import java.util.Vector;

public class Connect4 extends AbstractGame implements Cloneable
{
    public static final int ROWS = 6;
    public static final int COLUMNS = 7;
    private Player[ ][ ] data = new Player[ROWS][COLUMNS];
    private int[ ] manyUsed = new int[COLUMNS];
    private int mostRecentColumn;
```

Although we won't show them here, the actual implementation includes these seven methods that override the AbstractGame methods:
```
protected Connect4 clone( )
protected Vector<String> computeMoves( )
protected void displayStatus( )
protected double evaluate( )
protected boolean isGameOver( )
protected boolean isLegal(String move)
protected void makeMove(String move)
```

```
}
```

In addition to the data array, we have two other private member variables:

```
private int[ ] manyUsed = new int[COLUMNS];
private int mostRecentColumn;
```

The value of manyUsed[i] is the number of checkers in column number i (which is useful when you're calculating where the next checker in that column should go). After the game is started, the value of mostRecentColumn will be the column where the last checker was placed. This is useful for reducing the calculations about whether the game has ended.

The only remaining work is to understand and implement the seven methods that Connect4 implements. We'll do this over the next few pages, sometimes providing an implementation and other times providing only a discussion.

Three Connect Four Methods That Deal with the Game's Status

Each class that extends AbstractGame must implement three abstract methods that allow the AbstractGame class to access the current state of the game:

The displayStatus Method. This void method has no parameters. It merely displays the current status of the game. Our implementation of displayStatus prints a grid representing the game, like this:

```
Current game status
(human = #   and   computer = @):
Most recent move in column 5
    .   .   .   .   .   .   .
    .   .   .   .   .   .   .
    .   .   .   .   .   .   .
    .   .   .   .   .   .   .
    .   .   .   @   .   .   .
    .   .   @   #   #   #   .
    0   1   2   3   4   5   6
Computer's turn to move...
```

In this grid, we used the character @ to represent a computer checker and the character # to represent the human's checker.

The isGameOver Method. This boolean method also has no parameters. Its return value is true if the current game is over. The game is over if the most recently placed checker is part of a four-in-a-row or if all the columns are full.

The evaluate Method. This method is the heart of the game. It examines the current status and provides a numerical estimate of how favorable the current status seems, providing a positive answer when the status is good for the computer and a negative answer when the status is good for the human. Larger magnitudes indicate a more certain answer, and an evaluation of zero indicates that the game is more or less even for both players.

The evaluation should be done in a fixed way that doesn't try to look ahead at possible future moves (because looking ahead is already built into the play method). There's no one right way to evaluate the game status, but we can tell you the idea we used, which was suggested by our colleague John Gillett: We examine every possible sequence of four consecutive locations, giving each such sequence a value as follows:

If the four locations have ...	Then the value is ...
...four computer checkers	+500
...1 to 3 computer checkers and none of the human's	+1 to +3
...no checkers or a mixture of both players	zero
...1 to 3 human checkers and none of the computer's	−1 to −3
...four of the human's checkers	−500

The result of our evaluation method returns the sum of all these values after examining every one of the possible sequences of four locations in the current game. The large numbers (+500 and −500) were selected so that the total evaluation would always favor the player who obtained four-in-a-row, even if the other locations completely favor the other player.

Three Connect Four Methods That Deal with Moves

Our classes need some way to represent a move in the game. Since the programmer of the AbstractGame class doesn't know much about the exact game being played, we decided to use strings to represent moves. The exact format of these "move strings" can be decided by the programmer who implements an extended class. In the case of Connect Four, our move strings will just be simple strings that contain one digit specifying the slot in which the player wants to place the next checker. For example, the string "3" represents the move of putting a checker into slot number 3.

Each extended class must provide three methods that deal with its move strings:

The isLegal Method. This boolean method has a string as its parameter. It returns true if the string is currently a legal move for the next player. Among other things, the AbstractGame class uses this method to determine whether a move typed by the user is currently legal. For Connect Four, a move is legal provided that it is a number from 0 to COLUMNS-1 and that the column is not already full.

The makeMove Method. This void method has a string move as its parameter. The string has already been checked to ensure that it is a legal move. The method is responsible for making this move (by updating the member variables that represent the status of the game). The method must also activate super.makeMove so that the superclass can update any of its member variables that deal with the status of the game.

The computeMoves Method.   The heading for this method is:

```
protected Vector<String> computeMoves( )
```

The method examines the current status of the game and determines what moves are currently legal. All these legal moves are then placed into the vector that is then returned. The method does not actually make any of these moves. (It just puts these moves into the vector.)

If the game is not yet over, there should always be at least one legal move put into the queue (although in some games, such as Othello, this one legal move could be a "pass" move).

The clone Method

Our Connect4 class must also provide a clone method to make a new copy of a Connect4 object.

As with any clone method, the implementation follows the usual format for making sure that the copy has its own arrays (for manyUsed and data) rather than sharing the arrays of the original object. But the process of making a new copy of a two-dimensional array requires a little loop that you might not have seen before, as shown in the highlighted code shown here:

```
protected Connect4 clone( )
{
    Connect4 answer;
    int i;

    answer = (Connect4) super.clone( );

    // Make new copies of the data and manyUsed arrays:
    answer.manyUsed = (int [ ]) manyUsed.clone( );
    answer.data = (int [ ][ ]) data.clone( );
    for (i = 0; i < ROWS; i++)
        answer.data[i] = (int [ ]) data[i].clone( );

    return answer;
}
```

No try/catch block is needed because we know that the Game superclass has implemented the clone method.

These lines make a copy of the two-dimensional data array.

The complicated copying procedure is needed because of the way that two-dimensional arrays are represented in Java, which looks like the picture on the top of the next page (where we've now put row number zero on top because it seems more natural, but remember that row zero is the bottom of the Connect Four board).

In this drawing, the variable data is a reference to an array of size six because data was declared to have six rows. Each of data[0] through data[5] is also a reference variable that refers to one of the rows of the two-dimensional array. For example, data[0] is a reference to row number zero. To copy this two-dimensional array, we must first create a new array that will hold the references to each of the six rows, like this:

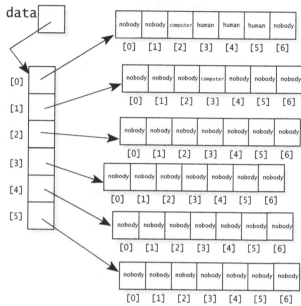

```
answer.data =
    data.clone( );
```

The second step of the copying process is to copy each of the six rows, with this loop:

```
for (i = 0; i < ROWS; i++)
    answer.data[i] = data[i].clone( );
```

Finally, notice that the clone method is simple, but it cannot be implemented by the AbstractGame itself because this superclass does not know what member variables the extended class will use.

Writing Your Own Derived Games from the AbstractGame Class

You could now write the Connect4 class yourself (for comparison to ours, visit http://www.cs.colorado.edu/~main/edu/colorado/games), or you could write other games derived from the AbstractGame class. Some useful resources are online:

http://www.cs.colorado.edu/~main/edu/colorado/games/

AbstractGame.java	Our AbstractGame class
Connect4.java	Our Connect4 class
gameideas.html	Ideas for other games to implement

It's interesting that you can write such clever games without knowing the details of the play method. In fact, we encourage you to write your extended classes without much concern for the workings of the superclass. On the other hand, it might be interesting to know a bit more about the play algorithm. You can download and read the entire AbstractGame class and see the algorithm that it uses (called minimax), which you might also study in a later course in artificial intelligence.

Self-Test Exercises for Section 13.4

14. What was the situation in this chapter where an abstract method was used?

15. What is the difference between a private and a protected member?

16. What is the purpose of the depth parameter for the play method?

17. Write a loop that makes a copy of a two-dimensional integer array called x. The copy should be put in a new variable called y.

18. Implement the makeMove method for the Connect4 class.

CHAPTER SUMMARY

- Object-oriented programming supports the use of *reusable components* by permitting new *extended classes* to be declared that automatically *inherit* all members of an existing superclass.

- When you implement a new class, ask yourself whether the new class is an example of an existing class with slightly different capabilities or extra capabilities. In these cases, the new class can be implemented as an extended class of the existing class.

- All members of a superclass are inherited by the extended class, but only the non-private members of the superclass can be accessed by the programmer who implements the extended class. This is why most of our examples of superclasses do not specify the precise form of the private members of the superclass.

- The connection between an extended class and its superclass can often be characterized by the *is-a* relationship. For example, an herbivore *is-a* particular kind of animal, so it makes sense to implement Herbivore as an extended class of the Animal superclass.

- An *abstract class* is a class that is intended to be used as a superclass for several different extensions. The abstract class implements the methods that are general enough to be shared by all extended classes. Other methods, called the *abstract methods*, need not be implemented by the superclass (but must be implemented by each different extended class).

FURTHER READING

This chapter has introduced the concepts of extended classes and inheritance, which are a central concepts for OOP programming. In your future programming, further inheritance is likely to be important. You can consult a comprehensive Java language guide such as *Just Java and Beyond* by Peter van der Linden or *Thinking in Java* by Bruce Eckel.

1. The declaration for the extended class is shown here, along with the implementation of the new method:

```
public class DaylightClock
extends Clock
{
    public boolean isDay( )
    {
        if (isMorning( ))
            return (getHour( ) >= 7);
        else
            return (getHour( ) < 7);
    }
}
```

2. Suppose d is a DayLightClock and c is a Clock. The assignment c = d is a widening conversion. An example of a narrowing conversion is d = (DayLightClock) c.

3. It inherits the no-arguments constructor of the superclass.

4. The NoonAlarm overrides the advance method of the ordinary clock. Here is one solution:

```
public class NoonAlarm extends Clock
{
    public void advance(int minutes)
    {
        int untilNoon;

        // Calculate number of minutes until
        // noon.
        if (isMorning( ))
            untilNoon =
                60 * (12-getHour( ))
                - getMinute( );
        else if (getHour( ) != 12)
            untilNoon =
                60 * (24 - getHour( ))
                - getMinute( );
        else
            untilNoon =
                60 * 24
                - getMinute( );
```

```
        // Maybe print an alarm message.
        if (minutes >= untilNoon)
            System.out.print("!!");

        // Activate the superclass method.
        super.advance(minutes);
    }
}
```

5. See the solutions at the start of Section 13.2.

6.
```
public static <T extends Clock>
<T> earliest(Vector<T> vc)
{
    T answer;
    int i;

    if (vc.isEmpty( ))
        return null;

    answer = vc.get(0);
    for (i = 1; i < vc.size( ); i++)
    {
        if (earlier(vc.get(i), answer))
            answer = vc.get(i);
    }
    return answer;
}
```

7.

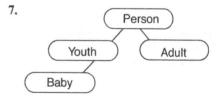

8. The Plant declaration is:
```
public class Plant extends Organism
{
    public Plant
    (double initSize, double initRate)
    {
        super(initSize, initRate);
    }
```

```
public void
NibbledOn(double amount)
{
    if (amount < 0)
        throw new
        IllegalArgumentException
        ("amount is negative");
    if (amount > getSize( ))
        throw new
        IllegalArgumentException
        ("amount is too big");
    alterSize(-amount);
}
}
```

9. See the solution in Figure 13.10 on page 706. Another approach would be to use the vector's iterator.

10. Here is one solution:
```
Vector<Organism> blob
    = new Vector<Organism>(10);
int i;
double answer;
Organism thing;

for (i = 1; i <= 10; i++)
    blobs.addElement
    (new Organism(16, 1));

for (i = 1; i <= 5; i++)
{
    thing = blobs.elementAt
      ((int) Math.random( ) * 10);
    thing.setRate(2);
}

answer = 0;
for (i = 0; i <= 10; i++)
{
    thing = blobs.elementAt(i);
    answer += things.getRate( );
}

System.out.println
(answer + " total of rates");
```

11. The random method must have selected one organism twice (and three other organisms were selected once each).

12. We didn't have to worry about the number of elements going beyond the size of the array. We also get to use various methods such as removeElementAt.

13. We'll leave some of this to you, but here is most of the new method:
```
public void chase
(Animal prey, double chance)
{
    ... check that chance is in 0 ... 1
    if (Math.random() < chance)
    {
        eat(prey.getRate( ));
        prey.expire( );
    }
}
}
```

14. An abstract method is needed when an abstract superclass does not have enough information to implement a method.

15. A private member may be used only within its own class; a protected member may also be used by other classes in the same package and by any class that extends the original class.

16. The depth parameter controls how far ahead the play method looks when it is evaluating potential moves for the computer to make.

17. Here is one implementation:
```
int i;
y = x.clone( );
for (i = 0; i < x.length; x++)
    y[i] = x[i].clone( );
```

18. Here is one implementation:
```
protected void makeMove(String move)
{
    int row, column;

    super.makeMove(move);
    column =
     Integer.valueOf(move).intValue( );
    row = manyUsed[column]++;
    data[row][column] = nextMover( );
    mostRecentColumn = column;
}
```

PROGRAMMING PROJECTS

1 A *set* is like a *bag*, except that a set does not allow multiple copies of any element. If you try to insert a new copy of an item that is already present in a set, then the set simply remains unchanged. For this project, implement a set as a new class that is extended from one of your bags.

2 Rewrite the pond life program from Figure 13.10 on page 705 so that the values declared at the start of the program are no longer constant. The program's user should be able to enter values for all of these constants. Also, improve the program so that the fish are more realistic. In particular, the fish should be born at a small size and grow to some maximum size. Each fish should also have a weekly food requirement that is proportional to its current size.

3 Rewrite the pond life program from Figure 13.10 on page 705 so that the output is presented as a graph in an applet window. The applet can use most of the same graphing techniques as the fractal applet from page 426 in Chapter 8. You should use different colors for graphing the populations of the weeds and the fish.

4 Extend the `Organism` object hierarchy from Section 13.3 so that there is a new class `Carnivore` as described in Self-Test Exercise 13 on page 710. Use the hierarchy in a model of life on a small island that contains shrubs, geese that eat the shrubs, and foxes that eat the geese. The program should allow the user to vary the initial conditions on the island (such as the number of foxes, the amount of food needed to sustain a fox, and so on).

5 Write an extended class that has all the operations of the `Bag<E>` class from Figure 5.2. Use Java's `Vector<E>` as the superclass.

6 Tic-Tac-Twice is a game invented by Pat Baggett and Andrzej Ehrenfeucht. It is distributed by the Aristoplay company. The rules are simple, starting with two 4x4 boards that each have a pattern of 16 letters (or other objects). If you use the letters A through P, then the two boards have these patterns:

Board 1

A	B	C	D
E	F	G	H
I	J	K	L
M	N	O	P

Board 2

B	K	M	H
P	E	C	J
G	N	L	A
I	D	F	O

The two players (human and computer) take alternate turns. During your turn, you can place a checker of your color on an empty spot on Board 1. At the same time, you put a checker of your color on the square in Block 2 with the same letter. For example, if you put your checker in the bottom-left corner of Board 1 (letter M), then you would simultaneously put one of your checkers on the third spot of the top row of Board 2 (also letter M).

You win the game by having four of your circles in a row (horizontally, diagonally, or vertically) on either of the boards. Note that you don't need four in a row on both boards, just on one of them.

Implement a class that lets a user play Tic-Tac-Twice against the computer. Use the `AbstractGame` class from Section 13.4 as your superclass.

Graphs

When you complete Chapter 14, you will be able to ...

- follow and explain graph-based algorithms using the usual computer science terminology.
- design and implement classes for labeled or unlabeled graphs.
- list the order in which nodes are visited for the two common graph traversals (breadth-first and depth-first) and implement these algorithms.
- simulate the steps of simple path algorithms (such as determining whether a path exists) and be able to design and implement such algorithms.
- simulate the steps of Dijkstra's shortest-path algorithm and be able to implement it.

Graphs

So many gods, so many creeds,
So many paths that wind and wind,
When just the art of being kind
Is all this sad world needs.

ELLA WHEELER WILCOX
"The World's Need"

Graphs are the most general data structure in this text. In fact, it's fair to say that graphs are the ultimate commonly used data structure. Many of the data structures you will study in the future can be expressed in terms of graphs. This chapter provides an introduction to graphs and their algorithms, including the implementation of a graph class in Java.

14.1 GRAPH DEFINITIONS

A graph, like a tree, is a nonlinear data structure consisting of nodes and links between the nodes. In the trees we have already seen, the nodes are somewhat orderly: The root is linked to its children, which are linked to their children, and so on, to the leaves. But in a graph, even this modicum of order is gone. Graph nodes can be linked in any pattern—or lack of pattern—depending only on the needs of an application.

Graphs occur in several varieties. We'll start with the simplest form: *undirected graphs*.

graphs occur in several varieties, the simplest of which is an undirected graph

Undirected Graphs

An undirected graph is a set of nodes and a set of links between the nodes. Each node is called a **vertex**, each link is called an **edge**, and each edge connects two vertices. Undirected graphs are drawn by putting a circle for each vertex and a line for each edge. For example, here is a drawing of an undirected graph with five vertices and six edges:

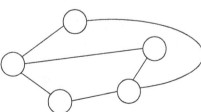

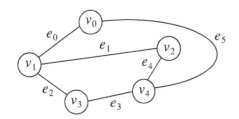

Often we'll need to refer to the vertices and edges of a graph, and we can do this by writing names next to each vertex and edge. For example, the graphs in the margin both have vertices named v_0, v_1, v_2, v_3, and v_4, whereas its edges are named e_0, e_1, e_2, e_3, e_4, and e_5. In drawings such as these, the actual placement of the vertices and edges is unimportant. The only important points are which vertices are connected and which edges are used to connect them.

in a drawing, the placement of the vertices and edges is unimportant

Here's a formal definition of these graphs:

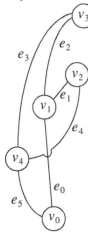

Undirected Graphs

An **undirected graph** is a finite set of vertices together with a finite set of edges. Both sets might be empty (no vertices and no edges), which is called the **empty graph**.

Each edge is associated with two vertices. We sometimes say that the edge **connects** its two vertices. The order of the two connected vertices is unimportant, so it does not matter whether we say "This edge connects vertices *u* and *v*," or "This edge connects vertices *v* and *u*."

An edge is even allowed to connect a single vertex to itself. We'll see examples of this later, and we'll also see several different variants of graphs. Many applications require additional data to be attached to each vertex or to each edge, but even without these extras, we can give the flavor of a graph application with an example.

PROGRAMMING EXAMPLE: Undirected State Graphs

As an example of a problem where graphs are useful, we'll look at a little game. To start the game, you place three coins on the table in a line, as shown here:

      The start of the game

At the start of the game, the middle coin is "tails" and the other two are "heads." The goal is to change the configuration of coins so that the middle coin is heads and the other two are tails, like this:

      The goal of the game

Now, this wouldn't be much of a game without a few good rules. Here are the rules:

1. You may flip the middle coin (from heads to tails or vice versa) whenever you want to.

2. You may flip one of the end coins (from heads to tails or vice versa) only when the other two coins are the same as each other (both heads or both tails).

You are not allowed to change the coins in any other way, such as shuffling them around. But within these rules you may flip coins. For example, if you start with the position *head-tail-head*, then the first rule allows you to flip the middle coin, resulting in three heads:

     From the start position, flip the middle coin.

If you play the game for a while, you'll soon figure out how to get from the starting position (*head-tail-head*) to the goal position (*tail-head-tail*) within the limits of the rules. But our *real* goal is to figure out how a graph can aid in solving this kind of problem—even if the rules were beyond human manageability. The graph we'll use is called an undirected state graph, which is a graph in which each of the vertices represents one of the possible configurations of the game. These configurations are called "states," and the coin game has eight states, ranging from *head-head-head* to *tail-tail-tail*. Therefore, these eight states are the vertices of the state graph for the coin game. Figure 14.1 shows each vertex as a large oval so that we have room inside the oval to draw the state

a graph may represent the legal moves in a game

FIGURE 14.1 Undirected State Graph for the Coin Game

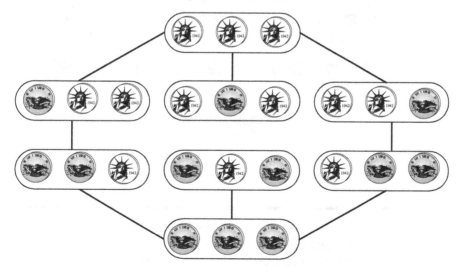

of the coins. Two vertices of the undirected state graph are connected by an edge whenever it is possible to move back and forth between the two states using one of the rules. For example, Rule 1 allows us to move between *head-head-head* and *head-tail-head*, so one of the edges in the graph goes from the topmost state in Figure 14.1 (*head-head-head*) to the state directly below it (*head-tail-head*). Figure 14.1 shows a total of eight edges: The four vertical edges come from Rule 1, and the four diagonal edges come from Rule 2. You may have noticed a curious fact about our rules: Whenever it is possible to move from one state to another (such as moving *head-head-head* to *head-tail-head*), it is also possible to move in the other direction (such as *head-tail-head* to *head-head-head*). If you study the rules, you will see that this is true. The way we have drawn the edges reflects this symmetry. The edges are drawn as line segments connecting two vertices, with no indication as to the direction in which a movement must proceed. In this game, if an edge connects two vertices v_0 and v_1, then a movement is permitted in both directions, from v_0 to v_1 or from v_1 to v_0. This property of the coin game is the reason why we can use an undirected state graph. Later we will see more complex games in which movements might be permitted in only one direction, and hence we will need more complex graphs.

Once we know the undirected state graph, the game becomes a problem of finding a path from one vertex to another, where the path is allowed only to follow edges. According to our rules, we need to find a path from the vertex *head-tail-head* to the vertex *tail-head-tail*, and one such path consists of edges 1 through 5, highlighted here:

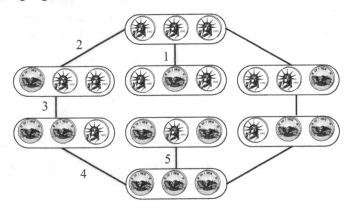

The coin game is a small problem, and the state graph isn't vital to the solution. But the important idea of the example goes beyond this small game.

Graphs in Problem Solving

Often a problem can be represented as a graph, and the solution to the problem is obtained by solving a problem on the corresponding graph.

Because of this wide applicability of graphs, we will study many different kinds of graphs, exploring how to implement the graphs and how to solve problems such as "Is there a path from here to there?" The rest of this section shows the kinds of graphs we'll study and some of the problems we'll solve.

Directed Graphs

The graphs we have seen so far are all *undirected*, which means that each edge connects two vertices with no particular orientation or direction. An edge just connects two vertices; there is no "first vertex" or "second vertex." But there is another kind of graph called a *directed graph* in which each edge has an orientation connecting its first vertex (called the edge's **source**) to its second vertex (the edge's **target**). Here is the formal definition of a directed graph:

Directed Graphs

A **directed graph** is a finite set of vertices together with a finite set of edges. Both sets might be empty (no vertices and no edges), which is called the **empty graph**.

Each edge is associated with two vertices, called its **source** and **target** vertices. We sometimes say that the edge **connects** its source to its target. The order of the two connected vertices *is* important, so it *does* matter whether we say "This edge connects vertex *u* to vertex *v*," or "This edge connects vertex *v* to vertex *u*."

Directed graphs are drawn as diagrams with circles representing the vertices and *arrows* representing the edges. Each arrow starts at an edge's source and has the arrowhead at the edge's target. For example:

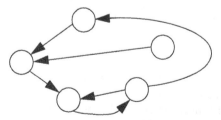

One application of directed graphs is a state graph for a game where reversing a move is sometimes forbidden. For such a game, the state graph might have an edge from a source v_1 to a target v_2 but *not* include the reverse edge from v_2 to v_1. This would indicate that the game's rules permit a move from state v_1 to state

v_2 but not the other way around. For example, we could use a large state graph to represent the different states in a game of tic-tac-toe. Two of the many possible states are shown next, with a directed edge between them.

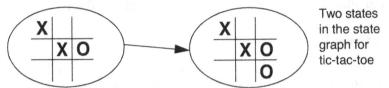

Two states in the state graph for tic-tac-toe

There is a directed arrow between these two states since it is possible to move from the first state to the second state (by placing an O), but it is not possible to move in the other direction (since once an O is placed, it may not be removed).

More Graph Terminology

Loop. A **loop** is an edge that connects a vertex to itself. In the diagrams that we've been using, this is drawn as a line (or arrow) with both ends at the same location. The highlighted edges at the left of these two graphs are both loops:

Path. A **path** in a graph is a sequence of vertices, $p_0, p_1, \ldots p_m$, such that each adjacent pair of vertices p_i and p_{i+1} are connected by an edge. In a directed graph, the connection must go from the source p_i to the target p_{i+1}.

Multiple Edges. In principle, a graph can have two or more edges connecting the same two vertices in the same direction. These are called **multiple edges**. In a diagram, each edge is drawn separately. For example:

Multiple edges in an undirected graph

Multiple edges in a directed graph

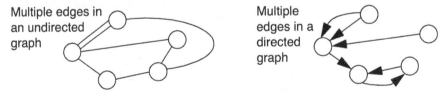

Note that the two edges at the bottom of the directed graph are not multiple edges, because they connect the two vertices in different directions. Many applications do not require multiple edges. In fact, many implementations of graphs do not permit multiple edges. Throughout the graph implementations of this chapter, we will specify which implementations permit multiple edges and which implementations forbid them.

Simple Graphs. The simplest of graphs have no loops and no multiple edges. Appropriately enough, these graphs are called **simple** graphs. Many applications require only simple directed graphs or even simple undirected graphs.

Airline Routes Example

Let's examine a directed graph that represents the flights of a small airline called Crocodile Airlines. Each vertex in the graph is a city, and each edge represents a regularly scheduled flight from one city to another. Crocodile's complete collection of flights is shown in Figure 14.2. Notice that the graph is directed; for example, it's possible to fly from Darwin to Canberra on a nonstop flight, but not the other way around.

    The point of expressing the flights as a graph is that questions about the airline can be answered by carrying out common algorithms on the graph. For example, a sheep farmer might wonder what is the fewest number of flights required to fly from Black Stump to Melbourne. This is an example of a *shortest path* problem, which we will solve in Section 14.4. With a small graph such as Figure 14.2, you can probably see that the shortest path from Black Stump to Melbourne consists of four edges, but a manual examination might not suffice for a larger graph.

airline routes form a directed graph

FIGURE 14.2 Crocodile Airlines Routes

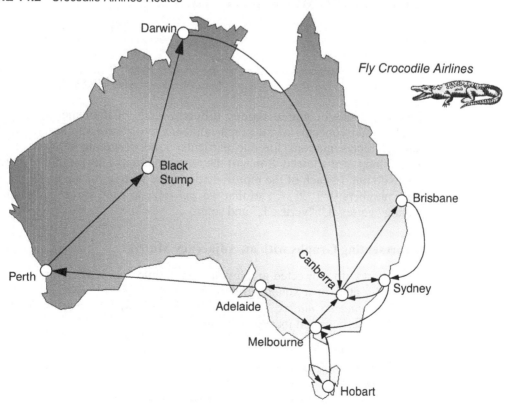

Self-Test Exercises for Section 14.1

1. How many vertices and edges does the graph in Figure 14.2 have? How many loops? How would you interpret a loop in this graph?

2. Is Figure 14.2 a simple graph? Why or why not?

3. Suppose we have four coins in the coin game instead of just three. At the start of the game, the coins are in a line, with the two end coins heads and the other two coins tails. The goal is to change the configuration so that the two end coins are tails and the other two coins are heads. There are three rules for this game: (1) Either of the end coins may be flipped whenever you want to; (2) a middle coin may be flipped from heads to tails only when the coin to its immediate right is already heads; and (3) a middle coin may be flipped from tails to heads only when the coin to its immediate left is already tails. Your mission: Draw the directed state graph for this game and determine whether it is possible to go from the start configuration to the goal. Why does the graph need to be directed?

14.2 GRAPH IMPLEMENTATIONS

"I could spin a web if I tried," said Wilbur, boasting. "I've just never tried."

E. B. WHITE
Charlotte's Web

Different kinds of graphs require different kinds of implementations, but the fundamental concepts of all graph implementations are similar. We'll look at several representations for one particular kind of graph: directed graphs in which loops are allowed. Some of the representations allow multiple edges, and some do not. In each of the representations, the vertices of the graph are named with numbers 0, 1, 2, ... , so that we can refer to each vertex individually by saying "vertex 0," "vertex 1," and so on.

Representing Graphs with an Adjacency Matrix

Let's start with a directed graph with no multiple edges. The graph's edges can be represented in a square grid of boolean (true/false) values, called the graph's *adjacency matrix*. The top of the next page shows an example of a graph with four vertices and its adjacency matrix.

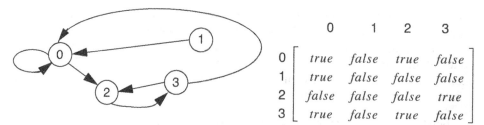

	0	1	2	3
0	*true*	*false*	*true*	*false*
1	*true*	*false*	*false*	*false*
2	*false*	*false*	*false*	*true*
3	*true*	*false*	*true*	*false*

Each component of the adjacency matrix indicates whether a certain edge is present. For example, is there an edge from vertex 0 to vertex 2? Yes, because `true` appears at row 0 of column 2. But is there also an edge from vertex 2 to vertex 0? No, because `false` appears at row 2 of column 0. The general rule for using an adjacency matrix is given here:

a true component at row i and column j indicates an edge from vertex i to vertex j

---

Adjacency Matrix

An **adjacency matrix** is a square grid of `true`/`false` values that represent the edges of a graph. If the graph contains *n* vertices, then the grid contains *n* rows and *n* columns. For two vertex numbers *i* and *j*, the component at row *i* and column *j* is `true` if there is an edge from vertex *i* to vertex *j*; otherwise, the component is `false`.

Using a Two-Dimensional Array to Store an Adjacency Matrix

In Java, an adjacency matrix can be stored in a **two-dimensional array** in which every component has two indexes rather than the usual one index. Programmers usually view a two-dimensional array as a grid of elements, where the first index provides the row number of a component and the second index provides the column number of a component. In a declaration of a two-dimensional array, the data type of the components is followed by two pairs of brackets, as shown here:

in a two-dimensional array, every component has two indexes

```
double[ ][ ] budget;
```

As with any array, the declaration just provides a reference variable that is capable of refering to a two-dimensional array. The actual array must be allocated with the new operator. For example, this allocates a two-dimensional array of double numbers with 12 rows and 8 columns, as declared here:

```
budget = new double [12][8];
```

allocating a two-dimensional array with 12 rows and 8 columns

Within the program, the individual components of a two-dimensional array can be accessed by providing both indexes. For example, we can assign the value 3.14 to row number 2 and column number 6 with this assignment statement:

```
budget[2][6] = 3.14;
```

As with an ordinary array, the index numbers begin with zero, so our budget has rows numbered from 0 to 11 and columns numbered from 0 to 7.

For an adjacency matrix, we use a two-dimensional array with one row and one column for each vertex of the graph. The components of the array are boolean `true`/`false` values. For example, the adjacency matrix for a graph with four vertices can be stored using this declaration of a two-dimensional array:

```
boolean[ ][ ] adjacent = new boolean[4][4];
```

The location `adjacent[i][j]` contains `true` if there is an edge from vertex *i* to vertex *j*. A `false` value indicates no edge. Edges of a graph can be added (by placing `true` in a location of the matrix) or removed (by placing `false`). Once the adjacency matrix has been set, an application can examine locations of the matrix to determine which edges are present and which are missing.

Representing Graphs with Edge Lists

Again, suppose we have a directed graph with no multiple edges. Such a graph can be represented by creating a linked list for each vertex. Here's an example:

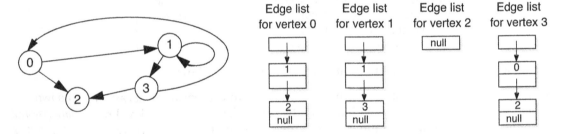

To understand the example, look at the linked list for vertex number 0. This list contains 1 and 2, which means that there is an edge from vertex 0 to vertex 1 and a second edge from vertex 0 to vertex 2. In general, the linked list for vertex number *i* is a list of vertex numbers following this rule:

Linked List Representation of Graphs

A directed graph with *n* vertices can be represented by *n* different linked lists. List number *i* provides the connections for vertex *i*. To be specific: For each entry *j* in list number *i*, there is an edge from *i* to *j*.

Loops are allowed in this representation; for example, look at the list for vertex 1 in the preceding edge lists. Number 1 appears on this list itself, so there is an edge from vertex 1 to vertex 1 in the graph. We may also have vertices that are not the source of any edge—for example, vertex 2 in the preceding graph. Since vertex 2 is not the source of any edge, the edge list for vertex 2 is empty. If we allow the same element to appear more than once on the list, then multiple edges could also be allowed. But often multiple edges are not allowed.

In a graph with *n* vertices, there are *n* edge lists. References to the heads of the *n* edge lists can be stored in an array of *n* node variables. When we need to determine whether an edge exists from vertex *i* to vertex *j*, we check to see whether *j* appears on list number *i*.

Representing Graphs with Edge Sets

Another implementation of graphs requires a previously programmed implementation of a set ADT. For example, suppose we have declared `IntSet` as a class capable of holding a set of integers. Presumably, the set class has operations to add an integer, check whether an integer is in the set, remove an integer, and so forth. To represent a graph with 10 vertices, we can declare an array of 10 sets of integers, as shown here:

```
IntSet[ ] connections = new IntSet[10];
```

Using this representation, a set such as `connections[i]` contains the vertex numbers of all of the vertices to which vertex *i* is connected. For example, suppose `connections[3]` contains the numbers 1 and 2. In this case, there is an edge from vertex 3 to vertex 1 and another edge from vertex 3 to vertex 2.

Which Representation Is Best?

If the space is available, then an adjacency matrix is easier to implement and is generally easier to use than edge lists or edge sets. But sometimes there are other considerations. For example, how often will you be doing each of the following operations?

1. Adding or removing edges

2. Checking whether a particular edge is present

3. Iterating a loop that executes one time for each edge with a particular source vertex

The first two operations require only a small constant amount of time with the adjacency matrixes. But in the worst case, both (1) and (2) require $O(n)$ operations with the edge list representation (where *n* is the number of vertices). This worst case occurs when the operation must traverse an entire edge list, and that edge list might contain as many as *n* edges. With edge sets, both (1) and (2) might also require $O(n)$ operations, but this time could be cut to $O(\log n)$ by using a fast set representation such as B-trees, covered in Section 10.2.

On the other hand, the edge lists are efficient for the third operation. With an edge list, the third operation can be carried out by simply stepping through the list one element at a time. The time required is $O(e)$, where e is the number of edges that have vertex i as their source. A good set ADT should also provide the operations to step through the elements of the set one at a time. In this way, both edge lists and edge sets are likely to require just $O(e)$ operations to step through the edges with a particular source vertex. But with an adjacency matrix, the act of stepping through the edges with source vertex i requires that each component of row i be examined. This traversal of the entire row is necessary just to see whether each entry is true or false. This always requires $O(n)$ time, where n is the number of vertices.

In general, your choice of representations should be based on your expectations as to which operations are most frequent. The availability of a previously programmed set ADT may also affect your choice. One last consideration is the average number of edges originating at a vertex. If each vertex has only a few edges (a so-called **sparse** graph), then an adjacency matrix is mostly wasted space filled with the value false.

PROGRAMMING EXAMPLE: Labeled Graph ADT

Now we'll implement a class called Graph for directed graphs with no multiple edges. This first ADT has only a few methods; for example, the number of vertices is set by the constructor, and there is no way to add or remove vertices later. An n-vertex graph always has its vertices numbered from zero to $n-1$. This simple form of the first Graph class provides a sharp focus on graphs and their algorithms.

With our Graph class, there are methods to add or remove edges between the vertices. The edges are stored in an adjacency matrix, which is implemented as the two-dimensional boolean array called edges. The edges array is allocated within the constructor, based on the number of vertices required for the graph.

Even though we're implementing our graph using an adjacency matrix, the class will also have a method, called neighbors, that computes an edge list for a specified vertex. This edge list will be provided as an array of integers that contains all of the vertex numbers for the targets of edges that start at a specified source. Here's an example to show the integer array that's computed and returned by g.neighbors(3) for a particular graph:

If g is the graph shown here,
then g.neighbors(3) returns the array:

0	2
[0]	[1]

This means that vertex 3 is the source of
two edges, going to vertices 0 and 2.

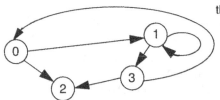

The neighbors method may take $O(n)$ time to compute one of its arrays, but once an array is available, it can be used to quickly traverse all the neighbors of a vertex. Notice that the length of the array computed by g.neighbors(i) is equal to the number of edges that have vertex i as the source, and this could even be zero (resulting in the unusual occurrence of an array with zero components).

Our Graph class will have one extra feature: The vertices will have information attached to them in the same way that we attached information to tree nodes. For example, in the airline route graph of Figure 14.2 on page 735, each vertex is associated with a city name. The addition of information at each vertex makes the graph a **labeled graph**, and the information itself is called a vertex's **label**. Of course, the information might be any data type—integers, doubles, strings, you name it—which suggests that the labeled graph should be a generic class with the type of the label determined by the generic type parameter. This does not allow us to use the eight primitive types for labels, though if we do want something like an integer label, we could use the Integer wrapper class described on page 256.

The labels of the vertices will be stored in a private instance variable named labels, which is an ordinary one-dimensional array. The label for vertex number i will be stored in labels[i]. Thus, our graph implementation has a total of two instance variables, as shown here:

```
public class Graph<E>
{
    private boolean[ ][ ] edges;
    private Object[ ] labels; // The vertex labels will be E objects

    || We'll discuss the methods in a moment.
}
```

The Graph Constructor and size Method

When a graph is initialized with the constructor, it has a given number of vertices and no edges, as shown in this specification of the constructor:

◆ **Constructor for the Graph<E>**
   public Graph(int n)
   Initialize a Graph with n vertices, no edges, and null labels.

   Parameter:
      n – the number of vertices for this Graph

   Precondition:
      n >= 0.

   Postcondition:
      This Graph has n vertices, numbered from 0 to n-1. It has no edges, and all vertex labels are null.

   Throws: OutOfMemoryError
      Indicates insufficient memory to create this Graph.

   Throws: NegativeArraySizeException
      Indicates that n is negative.

The only work in the implementation is the allocation of the two instance variables, which are both arrays, as shown here:

```
public Graph(int n)
{
    edges = new boolean[n][n];   // All values initially false
    labels = new Object[n];      // All values initially null
}
```

After construction, the current number of vertices can be obtained from an accessor method named `size`.

Methods for Manipulating Edges

Two methods, `addEdge` and `removeEdge`, allow us to add and remove edges. One other method, called `isEdge`, determines whether a specified edge is present. The methods have these specifications:

> ♦ **addEdge, isEdge, and removeEdge**
> ```
> public void addEdge(int source, int target)
> public boolean isEdge(int source, int target)
> public void removeEdge(int source, int target)
> ```
> Add an edge, test whether an edge exists, or remove an edge of this `Graph`.
>
> **Parameters:**
> source – the vertex number of the source of the edge
> target – the vertex number of the target of the edge
>
> **Precondition:**
> Both `source` and `target` are non-negative and less than `size( )`.
>
> **Postcondition:**
> For `addEdge`, the specified edge is added to this `Graph` (unless it was already present); for `isEdge`, the return value is `true` if the specified edge exists and is `false` otherwise; and for `removeEdge`, the specified edge is removed from this `Graph` (unless it was already not present).
>
> **Throws:** ArrayIndexOutOfBoundsException
> Indicates that the `source` or `target` was not a valid vertex number.

The implementations of these methods will be short. The `addEdge` method sets `edges[source][target]` to `true`, and the `removeEdge` method sets it to `false`. The `isEdge` method just returns the current value of `edges[source][target]`. In all cases, an illegal parameter will try accessing `edges[source][target]` and will result in an `ArrayIndexOutOfBoundsException`.

As we have already discussed, there is also a method called `neighbors` to generate an array that contains an edge list for a specified vertex.

Methods for Manipulating Vertex Labels

There are two methods for setting and retrieving the label of a vertex:

◆ **getLabel**
  `public E getLabel(int vertex)`
  Accessor method to get the label of a vertex of this Graph.
  Parameter:
  `vertex` – a vertex number
  Precondition:
  `vertex` is non-negative and less than `size( )`.
  Returns:
  the label of the specified vertex in this Graph
  Throws: `ArrayIndexOutOfBoundsException`
  Indicates that the `vertex` was not a valid vertex number.

◆ **setLabel**
  `public void setLabel(int vertex, E newLabel)`
  Change the label of a vertex of this Graph.
  Parameters:
  `vertex` – a vertex number
  `newLabel` – a vertex number
  Precondition:
  `vertex` is non-negative and less than `size( )`.
  Postcondition:
  The label of the specified `vertex` in this Graph has been changed to
  `newLabel`.
  Throws: `ArrayIndexOutOfBoundsException`
  Indicates that the `vertex` was not a valid vertex number.

For example, the following statements create the two-vertex graph shown in the
picture. In this graph, vertex number zero (v_0) has the string "bar" as its label,
and vertex number one (v_1) has the string "goo" as its label:

```
Graph<String> t = new Graph<String>(2);
```

```
t.setLabel(0, "bar");  // Provides vertex number 0 with label of "bar"
t.setLabel(1, "goo");  // Provides vertex number 1 with label of "goo"
t.addEdge(1, 0);       // Adds an edge from vertex 1 to vertex 0
```

Labeled Graph ADT—Implementation

The complete specification and implementation for the graph ADT are given in
Figure 14.3. In addition to the methods we have already mentioned, the Graph
class also implements the Cloneable interface.

FIGURE 14.3	Specification and Implementation of the Graph Class

Generic Class Graph

❖ **public class Graph<E> from the package edu.colorado.graphs**
  A Graph<E> is a labeled graph with a fixed number of vertices and labels of type E.

Specification

◆ **Constructor for the Graph<E>**
  `public Graph(int n)`
  Initialize a Graph with n vertices, no edges, and null labels.

  Parameter:
    n – the number of vertices for this Graph

  Precondition:
    n >= 0.

  Postcondition:
    This Graph has n vertices, numbered from 0 to n-1. It has no edges and all vertex labels are null.

  Throws: `OutOfMemoryError`
    Indicates insufficient memory to create this Graph.

  Throws: `NegativeArraySizeException`
    Indicates that n is negative.

◆ **addEdge, isEdge, and removeEdge**
  `public void addEdge(int source, int target)`
  `public boolean isEdge(int source, int target)`
  `public void removeEdge(int source, int target)`
  Add an edge, test whether an edge exists, or remove an edge of this Graph.

  Parameters:
    source – the vertex number of the source of the edge
    target – the vertex number of the target of the edge

  Precondition:
    Both source and target are non-negative and less than size( ).

  Postcondition:
    For addEdge, the specified edge is added to this Graph (unless it was already present); for isEdge, the return value is true if the specified edge exists and is false otherwise; and for removeEdge, the specified edge is removed from this Graph (unless it was already not present).

  Throws: `ArrayIndexOutOfBoundsException`
    Indicates that the source or target was not a valid vertex number.

(continued)

(FIGURE 14.3 continued)

◆ clone
```
public Graph<E> clone( )
```
Generate a copy of this Graph.

Returns:
The return value is a copy of this Graph. Subsequent changes to the copy will not affect the original, nor vice versa. The return value must be typecast to a Graph before it is used.

Throws: OutOfMemoryError
Indicates insufficient memory for creating the clone.

◆ getLabel
```
public E getLabel(int vertex)
```
Accessor method to get the label of a vertex of this Graph.

Parameter:
vertex – a vertex number

Precondition:
vertex is non-negative and less than size( ).

Returns:
the label of the specified vertex in this Graph

Throws: ArrayIndexOutOfBoundsException
Indicates that the vertex was not a valid vertex number.

◆ neighbors
```
public int[ ] neighbors(int vertex)
```
Accessor method to obtain a list of neighbors of a specified vertex of this Graph.

Parameter:
vertex – a vertex number

Precondition:
vertex is non-negative and less than size( ).

Returns:
The return value is an array that contains all the vertex numbers of vertices that are targets of edges with a source at the specified vertex.

Throws: ArrayIndexOutOfBoundsException
Indicates that the vertex was not a valid vertex number.

(continued)

(FIGURE 14.3 continued)

◆ **setLabel**
   ```
   public void setLabel(int vertex, E newLabel)
   ```
   Change the label of a vertex of this Graph.

   Parameters:
   vertex – a vertex number
   newLabel – a vertex number

   Precondition:
   vertex is non-negative and less than size( ).

   Postcondition:
   The label of the specified vertex in this Graph has been changed to newLabel.

   Throws: ArrayIndexOutOfBoundsException
   Indicates that the vertex was not a valid vertex number.

◆ **size**
   ```
   public int size( )
   ```
   Accessor method to determine the number of vertices in this Graph.

   Returns:
   the number of vertices in this Graph

Implementation

```
// File: Graph.java from the package edu.colorado.graphs
// Complete documentation is on pages 744–745 or from the Graph link at
// http://www.cs.colorado.edu/~main/docs/.

package edu.colorado.graphs;

public class Graph<E> implements Cloneable
{
    // Invariant of the Graph<E> class:
    //    1. The vertex numbers range from 0 to labels.length-1.
    //    2. For each vertex number i, labels[i] contains the label for vertex i.
    //    3. For any two vertices i and j, edges[i][j] is true if there is a vertex from i to j;
    //       otherwise, edges[i][j] is false.
    private boolean[ ][ ] edges;
    private Object[ ] labels;

    public Graph(int n)
    {
        edges = new boolean[n][n];     // All values initially false
        labels = (E[]) new Object[n];  // All values initially null
    }
```

(continued)

(FIGURE 14.3 continued)

```java
public void addEdge(int source, int target)
{
   edges[source][target] = true;
}

public Graph<E> clone( )
{  // Clone a Graph<E> object.
   Graph<E> answer;

   try
   {
      answer = (Graph<E>) super.clone( );
   }
   catch (CloneNotSupportedException e)
   {
      // This exception should not occur. But if it does, it would probably indicate a
      // programming error that made super.clone unavailable. The most common
      // error would be forgetting the "implements Cloneable"
      // clause at the start of this class.
      throw new RuntimeException
      ("This class does not implement Cloneable");
   }

   answer.edges = edges.clone( );
   answer.labels = labels.clone( );

   return answer;
}


@SuppressWarnings("unchecked")    // See the warnings discussion on page 265.
public E getLabel(int vertex)
{
   return (E) labels[vertex];
}

public boolean isEdge(int source, int target)
{
   return edges[source][target];
}
```

(continued)

(FIGURE 14.3 continued)

```java
public int[ ] neighbors(int vartex)
{
    int i;
    int count;
    int[ ] answer;

    // First count how many edges have the vertex as their source:
    count = 0;
    for (i = 0; i < labels.length; i++)
    {
        if (edges[vertex][i])
            count++;
    }

    // Allocate the array for the answer:
    answer = new int[count];

    // Fill the array for the answer:
    count = 0;
    for (i = 0; i < labels.length; i++)
    {
        if (edges[vertex][i])
            answer[count++] = i;
    }

    return answer;
}

public void removeEdge(int source, int target)
{
    edges[source][target] = false;
}

public void setLabel(int vertex, E newLabel)
{
    labels[vertex] = newLabel;
}

public int size( )
{
    return labels.length;
}
}
```

Self-Test Exercises for Section 14.2

4. Write a new Graph method to remove a specified number of vertices from a graph. The removed vertices should be the k vertices with the highest numbers. Write another method to add a specified number of new vertices.

5. Write a new Graph method that interchanges two specified vertices. For example, after interchanging vertices i and j, the original neighbors of vertex i will now be neighbors of vertex j, and vice versa.

6. We have assumed that there are no multiple edges in a graph, and therefore we could store simple true/false values in the adjacency matrix. Describe how adjacency matrixes might be used even if the graphs do have multiple edges.

7. Compare and contrast adjacency lists and edge lists.

8. Write a generic static method with one Graph<E> parameter g. The precondition requires g to have at least one vertex. The method's return value is the number of the vertex that is the source of the most edges. If there are several vertices with an equally high number of edges, then you may return whichever vertex number you prefer.

14.3 GRAPH TRAVERSALS

In the chapter on trees, we saw three different binary tree traversals. Each traversal visits all of a binary tree's nodes and does some processing at each node. The three traversals had similar recursive implementations, with the distinguishing factor being whether a node was visited before, after, or in between its two children. A graph vertex doesn't have children like a tree node, so the tree traversal algorithms are not immediately applicable to graphs. But there are two common ways of traversing a graph. One of the methods (breadth-first search) uses a queue to keep track of vertices that still need to be visited, and the other method (depth-first search) uses a stack. The depth-first search can also be implemented recursively in a way that does not explicitly use a stack of vertices.

This section discusses the two traversal algorithms in a general way and then provides implementations of the algorithms to traverse a Graph object (using the Graph class; see Figure 14.3 on page 744). Both of the traversal algorithms have the same underlying purpose: to start at one vertex of a graph (the "start" vertex), process the information contained at that vertex, and then move along an edge to process a neighbor. When the traversal finishes, all of the vertices that can be reached from the start vertex (via some directed path) have been processed.

when the traversal finishes, all of the vertices that can be reached from the start vertex have been processed

A traversal algorithm must be careful that it doesn't enter a repetitive cycle—for example, moving from the start vertex to a neighbor, from there to the neighbor's neighbor, from there back to the starting point and then back to the same neighbor, and so on. To prevent this potential "spinning your wheels," we will

include an ability to *mark* each vertex as it is processed. If a traversal ever returns
to a vertex that is already marked, then reprocessing is not done. If we are drawing the graphs, then we might indicate a marked vertex by shading it. For example, suppose a traversal starts at vertex 0 of this graph:

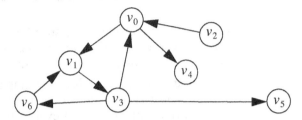

The traversal begins by processing vertex number 0. We don't really care what
kind of processing occurs; maybe the labels are printed out, or perhaps there is
more complicated processing. In any case, there will be some processing of vertex number 0, and then we will mark it as processed, looking like this:

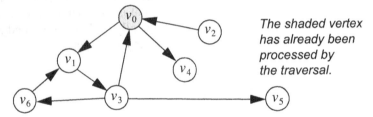

*The shaded vertex
has already been
processed by
the traversal.*

    The progress of a traversal after the start vertex depends on the traversal
method being used. We'll start by looking at how a depth-first search proceeds.

Depth-First Search

After processing vertex 0, a depth-first search moves along a directed edge to
one of vertex 0's neighbors. In our example, there are two possibilities: moving
to vertex 1 (along the edge from 0 to 1) or to vertex 4 (along the edge from 0 to
4). In our example, it is not possible to move from vertex 0 to 3 or from vertex 0
to 2, because the edges go in the wrong direction. So the traversal has a choice:
Move to vertex 1 or move to vertex 4. Right now, we won't worry about exactly
how the choice is made, so let's just assume that the next vertex processed is
vertex 1. After processing vertex 1, the picture looks like this:

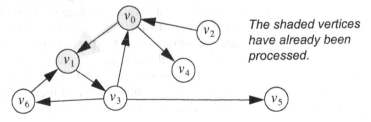

*The shaded vertices
have already been
processed.*

In the drawing, we have highlighted the edge from vertex 0 to vertex 1 to indicate the intuitive notion of "moving from one vertex to another."

From here, the traversal moves to one of vertex 1's neighbors. You may think of vertex 1 as being at the "leading edge" of the depth-first traversal. It is the vertex that has most recently been processed, so we will continue pushing forward from vertex 1, moving to one of vertex 1's unprocessed neighbors. In this example, there is only one unprocessed neighbor to consider, vertex 3. So we will move to vertex 3 and process it. At this point, we have processed three of the vertices, as shown here:

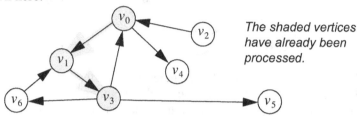

The shaded vertices have already been processed.

One of vertex 3's neighbors is vertex 0—but vertex 0 has already been marked as previously processed. So, to prevent the traversal from going around in circles, we will not move from 3 back to 0. In general, *we will never move forward to a marked vertex (because it has already been processed)*. But we will move to vertex 3's other neighbors (vertices 5 and 6). Suppose we move to vertex 5 first. After processing vertex 5, the picture looks like this:

to prevent going around in circles, never move forward to a marked vertex

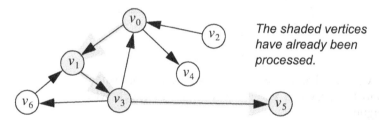

The shaded vertices have already been processed.

Since vertex 5 has no neighbors, the depth-first traversal cannot proceed forward any farther. Instead, the traversal comes back to see whether the previous vertex—vertex 3—has any more unmarked neighbors:

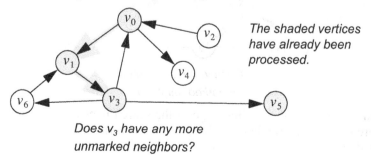

The shaded vertices have already been processed.

Does v_3 have any more unmarked neighbors?

In this drawing, you can see that four vertices have been processed, and the "leading edge" of the search has pulled back to vertex v_3. Does v_3 have any more unmarked neighbors where the search can proceed? Yes, v_6 is an unmarked neighbor of v_3, so again the search plunges forward, along the edge from v_3 to v_6. Vertex 6 is processed, giving the following picture:

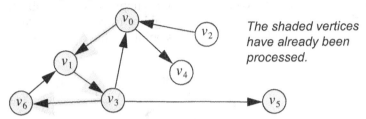

The shaded vertices have already been processed.

What now? Vertex 6 does have a neighbor—vertex 1—but v_1 has already been marked. So, since vertex 6 has no *unmarked* neighbors, the traversal again backs up to see whether v_3 has any more unmarked neighbors. After the backup, we have this situation:

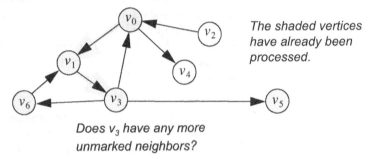

The shaded vertices have already been processed.

Does v_3 have any more unmarked neighbors?

Vertex 3 has no more unmarked neighbors (thank goodness!). So back we go to the previous vertex—vertex 1—to check whether it has any unmarked neighbors:

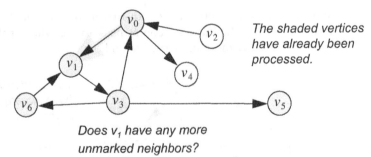

The shaded vertices have already been processed.

Does v_1 have any more unmarked neighbors?

You can see that the leading edge of the search is now at v_1, and that v_1 has no more unmarked neighbors, so back we go to vertex 0 to see if it has any unfinished business. This situation is drawn at the top of the next page.

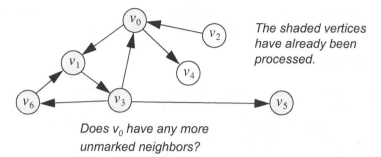

The shaded vertices have already been processed.

Does v₀ have any more unmarked neighbors?

From vertex 0, we can still travel to the unmarked vertex 4 and process it, as shown here:

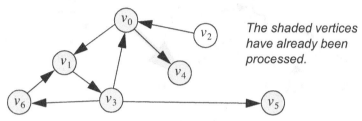

The shaded vertices have already been processed.

Vertex 4 has no neighbors, so we back up once more to vertex 0:

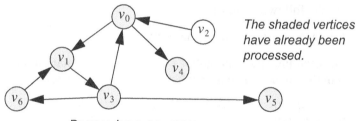

The shaded vertices have already been processed.

Does v₀ have any more unmarked neighbors?

Vertex 0 has no more unmarked neighbors—and since this was the starting point, there is no place left to back up to. That's the end of the traversal.

In this example, vertex 2 was never processed, because there was no path from the start vertex (vertex 0) to vertex 2. A traversal processes only those vertices that can be reached from the start vertex.

There's one other important point about a depth-first search: From the start vertex, the traversal proceeds to a neighbor and from there to another neighbor, and so on—always going as far as possible before it ever backs up. In describing this behavior, it seems as if there's a lot to keep track of: where we start, where we go from there, and where we go from there. But the actual implementation can use recursion to keep track of most of these details in a simple way. We'll tackle that recursive implementation after looking at an alternative method: breadth-first search.

some vertices are not processed, because they can't be reached from the start vertex

By the way, did you notice that the maze problem from Section 8.2 was solved by a recursive implementation of a depth-first search?

Breadth-First Search

A breadth-first search uses a queue to keep track of which vertices might still have unprocessed neighbors. The search begins with a starting vertex, which is processed, marked, and placed in the queue. For example, suppose we are processing this graph with vertex 0 as our starting point so that vertex 0 is the first vertex to be processed, marked, and placed into the queue:

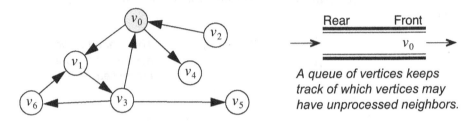

A queue of vertices keeps track of which vertices may have unprocessed neighbors.

Once the starting vertex has been processed, marked, and placed in the queue, the main part of the breadth-first search begins. This consists of repeatedly carrying out the following steps:

1. Remove a vertex, v, from the front of the queue.

2. For each unmarked neighbor u of v: Process u, mark u, and then place u in the queue (since u may have further unprocessed neighbors).

These two steps are repeated until the queue becomes empty. Let's look at our example to see how these two steps are carried out when vertex 0 is at the head of the queue. The vertex 0 is removed from the queue, and we note that it has two unprocessed neighbors: vertices 1 and 4. Vertices 1 and 4 will each be processed, marked, and placed in the queue. Let's assume that vertex 1 is placed in the queue first and then vertex 4. (The queuing could also occur the other way, with vertex 4 placed first; the algorithm is correct either way.) After 1 and 4 are in the queue, the situation looks like this:

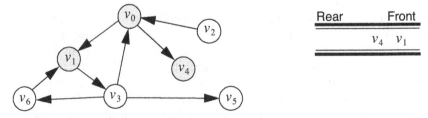

Since the queue still has entries, we repeat the two steps again: Remove the front entry (vertex 1), process and mark any unmarked neighbors of vertex 1, and enter these neighbors into the queue. The only unmarked neighbor of vertex 1 is vertex 3, so after processing, marking, and entering vertex 3, the situation looks like this:

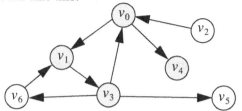

Next we remove vertex 4 from the front of the queue. Since vertex 4 has no neighbors, no new entries are processed or placed in the queue. The situation is now:

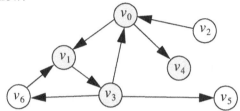

Vertex 3 comes out of the queue next. It has two unmarked neighbors (vertices 5 and 6) that are processed, marked, and placed in the queue, like this:

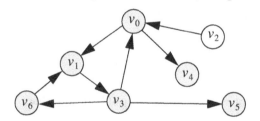

Notice that vertex 0 (which is also a neighbor of vertex 3) does not get reprocessed, because it is already marked.

At this point, we remove vertex 5 from the front of the queue, but it has no unmarked neighbors to worry about. We then remove vertex 6 from the queue. It also has no unmarked neighbors. The queue is finally empty, which ends the breadth-first search.

The effect of the breadth-first search is similar to the depth-first search: Vertices 0, 1, 3, 4, 5, and 6 have all been processed because they could all be reached from the starting point (vertex 0). Vertex 2 was not processed because there is no directed path from vertex 0 to vertex 2. However, the breadth-first search processes the vertices in a different order than the depth-first search. The breadth-first search first processed vertex 0, then processed the neighbors of the start point (1 and 4), then processed *their* neighbors (vertex 3), and so on. This contrasts with the depth-first search, which processed the vertices 0, 1, 3, and 5 to start with (in that order).

the effects of breadth-first and depth-first searches are similar—only the order of processing vertices differs

You should now be able to carry out depth-first and breadth-first searches by hand on a directed graph. Next we will specify and implement the two searches as static methods that can print the labels of the vertices of a `Graph`.

Depth-First Search—Implementation

One way to print the labels of a graph is with a depth-first search as specified in this static method:

> ### ◆ depthFirstPrint
>
> ```
> public static <E> void depthFirstPrint(Graph<E> g, int start)
> ```
> Static method to print the labels of a graph with a depth-first search.
>
> **Parameters:**
> g – a non-null Graph
> start – a vertex number from the Graph g
>
> **Precondition:**
> start is non-negative and less than g.size( ).
>
> **Postcondition:**
> A depth-first search of g has been conducted, starting at the specified start vertex. Each vertex visited has its label printed using System.out.println. Note that vertices that are not connected to the start will not be visited.
>
> **Throws:** NullPointerException
> Indicates that g is null.
>
> **Throws:** ArrayIndexOutOfBoundsException
> Indicates that the start was not a valid vertex number.
>
> **Throws:** OutOfMemoryError
> Indicates that there is insufficient memory for an array of boolean values used by this method.

In this specification, the parameter g may be any `Graph` with labels that can be printed by `System.out.println`. During a search, each time a vertex v is reached, that vertex is "processed" by activating `System.out.println` with the label of v as the argument.

The implementation of `depthFirstPrint` uses an array of boolean values declared as a local variable of the method, shown here:

```
boolean[ ] marked = new boolean[g.size( )];
```

This array has one component for each possible vertex of the graph g, and its purpose is to keep track of which vertices have been marked as visited by the search. In general, for a vertex number v, the component `marked[v]` is `true` if v has already been visited by the search and is `false` otherwise. The complete pseudocode for `depthFirstPrint` is short, as shown next.

1. Allocate the marked array (which automatically has all of its components set to `false`).

2. Activate a separate static method to actually carry out the search.

pseudocode for depth-first search

You may be wondering, "Why use a separate method in Step 2? Why can't we just carry out the search in the body of the `depthFirstPrint` method itself?" Good question. The answer is that we plan to use recursion: The start vertex is processed, and then recursive calls are made to process each of the start vertex's neighbors. Further recursive calls are made to process the neighbors' neighbors, and so on. So, if the work were carried out in the body of the `depthFirstPrint` method, each time a recursive call is made, we would do Step 1—clearing the `marked` array—and ... oops! Clearing the `marked` array at every recursive call will definitely lead to trouble.

The new method, executed in Step 2, will be called `depthFirstRecurse` with this specification:

♦ **depthFirstRecurse**
```
public static <E> void depthFirstRecurse
  (Graph<E> g, int v, boolean[ ] marked)
```
Recursive method to carry out the work of `depthFirstPrint`.

Parameters:
`g` – a non-null `Graph`
`v` – a vertex number from the `Graph` `g`
`marked` – an array to indicate which vertices of `g` have already been visited

Precondition:
`v` is non-negative and less than `g.size( )`, and `marked.length` is equal to `g.size( )`; for each vertex `x` of `g`, `marked[x]` is true if `x` has already been visited by this search; otherwise, `marked[x]` is `false`. The vertex `v` is an unmarked vertex at which the search has just arrived.

Postcondition:
The depth-first search of `g` has been continued through vertex `v` and beyond to all vertices that can be reached from `v` via a path of unmarked vertices. Each vertex visited has its label printed using `System.out.println`.

Throws: `NullPointerException`
Indicates that `g` is null.

Throws: `ArrayIndexOutOfBoundsException`
Indicates that `v` was not valid or `marked` was the wrong size.

Now let's examine the implementation of the `depthFirstRecurse` method. The first task is to mark and process the vertex `v`. After this, we will examine each of `v`'s neighbors. Each time we find an unmarked neighbor, we will make a recursive call to continue the search through that neighbor and beyond. The phrase "and beyond" is important because if a neighbor has another unmarked neighbor, then there will be another recursive call at that level, and so on, until we reach a vertex with no unmarked neighbors. This description of depthFirstRecurse is implemented at the top of Figure 14.4, and the actual depthFirstPrint method is implemented at the bottom of the figure.

Breadth-First Search—Implementation

The breadth-first search is implemented with a queue of vertex numbers. The start vertex is processed, marked, and placed in the queue. Then the following steps are repeated until the queue is empty: (1) Remove a vertex, *v*, from the front of the queue, and (2) for each unmarked neighbor *u* of *v*: process *u*, mark *u*, and then place *u* in the queue (since *u* may have further unprocessed neighbors).

The implementation of this breadth-first search is left to you in Programming Project 1.

FIGURE 14.4   Depth-First Search

Implementations

```
public static <E> void depthFirstRecurse(Graph<E> g, int v, boolean[ ] marked)
{
   int[ ] connections = g.neighbors(v);
   int i;

   marked[v] = true;
   System.out.println(g.getLabel(v));

   // Traverse all the neighbors, looking for unmarked vertices:
   for (int nextNeighbor : connections)
   {
      if (!marked[nextNeighbor])
         depthFirstRecurse(g, nextNeighbor, marked);
   }
}

public static <E> void depthFirstPrint(Graph<E> g, int start)
{
   boolean[ ] marked = new boolean[g.size( )];

   depthFirstRecurse(g, start, marked);
}
```

Self-Test Exercises for Section 14.3

9. Do a depth-first search of the Crococile Airlines graph (Figure 14.2 on page 735), starting at Sydney. List the order in which the cities are processed. Do the same for a breadth-first search.

10. Suppose you are doing a breadth-first search of a graph with *n* vertices. How large can the queue get?

11. What kind of search occurs if you replace a breadth-first search's queue with a stack?

14.4 PATH ALGORITHMS

Determining Whether a Path Exists

Frequently, a problem is represented by a graph, and the answer to the problem can be found by answering some question about paths in the graph. For example, a network of computers can be represented by a graph, with each vertex representing one of the machines in the network and each edge representing a communication wire between two machines. The question of whether one machine can send a message to another machine boils down to whether the corresponding vertices are connected by a path.

Either a breadth-first search or a depth-first search can be used to determine whether a path exists between two vertices, *u* and *v*. The idea is to use *u* as the start vertex of the search and proceed with a breadth-first or depth-first search. If the vertex *v* is ever visited, then the search can stop and announce that there is a path from *u* to *v*. On the other hand, if *v* is never visited, then there is no path from *u* to *v*.

Graphs with Weighted Edges

Often we need to know more than just *"Does a path exist?"* In the network example, each edge represents a communication wire between machines. Such a wire might have a "cost" associated with using it. The cost could be the amount of energy required to use the path, or perhaps the amount of time required for the wire to transmit a message, or even a dollars-and-cents cost required to use the wire to send one message. In any case, there could be many paths from one vertex to another, and we might want to find the path with the lowest total cost (that is, the path with the lowest possible sum of its edge costs).

This kind of question can be solved by using a graph in which each edge has a non-negative integer value attached to it, called the **weight** or **cost** of the edge.

Here's an example of a graph with edge weights:

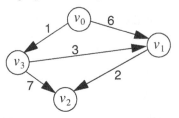

the shortest path between two vertices is the path with lowest total cost

In this example, there are several paths from vertex v_0 to vertex v_2. The path with the lowest total cost traverses the edge from v_0 to v_3 (with a cost of 1), and then from v_3 to v_1 (with a cost of 3), and finally from v_1 to v_2 (with a cost of 2). The total cost of this path is $1 + 3 + 2$, which is 6. There is a path with fewer edges (such as the path from v_0 to v_1 to v_2), but no other path has a lower total cost. The path with the lowest total cost is called the **shortest path**. (If you think of the weights as distances, then the term *shortest path* will sound like a sensible term.) The problem of finding the shortest path between two vertices of a graph occurs often in computer science (such as the network example) and in applications (such as finding the shortest driving distance between two points on a road map).

Here is a summary of the concepts we have introduced:

Weighted Edges and Shortest Paths

A **weighted edge** is an edge together with a non-negative integer called the edge's **weight**.

The **weight of a path** is the total sum of the weights of all the edges in the path. (Note: The weight of the empty path, with no edges, is always zero.)

If two vertices are connected by at least one path, then we can define the **shortest path** between two vertices. This is the path that has the smallest weight. (There may be several paths with equally small weights, in which case each of the paths is called "smallest.")

Shortest-Distance Algorithm

In this section, we will present an efficient algorithm called *Dijkstra's algorithm* (named for computer scientist Edsger Dijkstra, who proposed the algorithm) for finding the shortest path between two vertices. Throughout the section, we will use graphs with weighted edges where each weight is a non-negative integer. We will use pseudocode rather than a particular language, such as Java.

We start with a problem that's simpler than actually finding the shortest path from one vertex to another. We'll concentrate on simply finding the *weight* of the shortest path—in other words, the smallest possible sum of edge weights along a path from one vertex to another. This weight is called the *shortest distance*.

Dijkstra's algorithm actually provides more information than just the shortest distance from one vertex to another. In fact, the algorithm provides the shortest distance from a starting vertex (which we call `start`) to *every* vertex in the graph. The algorithm uses an integer array called `distance` with one component for each vertex in the graph. Here is the algorithm's goal:

we'll actually find shortest distances rather than shortest paths

---

Goal of the Shortest-Distance Algorithm

The goal is to completely fill the distance array so that for each vertex v, the value of `distance[v]` is the weight of the shortest path from `start` to v.

We'll illustrate how the algorithm works with this small graph:

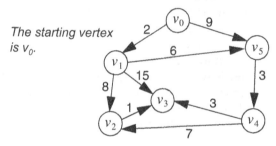

The starting vertex is v_0.

The algorithm begins by filling in one value in the distance array. We fill in zero for the component that is indexed by the `start` vertex itself, indicating that the weight of the shortest path from the `start` vertex to the `start` vertex itself is zero. This is correct since the empty path exists from the `start` vertex to itself. At this point, the distance array has one known value:

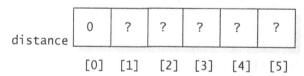

distance

$[0]$ $[1]$ $[2]$ $[3]$ $[4]$ $[5]$

At this point, we have one correct value, `distance[0]`. In the other locations we will write a value based on what we know so far. Because we don't know too much, our initial values won't be too accurate, but that's okay. In fact, the values we fill in will all be *infinity*, represented by the symbol ∞. The distance array with mostly ∞ is shown at the top of the next page.

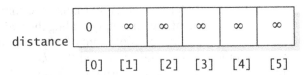

In an actual implementation, we would use some special integer value for ∞. For example, we could use −1 and make sure all the rest of our programming always treats an occurrence of −1 as if it were infinity.

Now we are ready to do some processing that will steadily improve the values in the distance array. We begin with an observation about the initial values that we've placed in the distance array: These initial values are actually correct, *if we are permitting only the empty path and ignoring all other paths*. In other words, if the empty path is the only path we are permitting, then there is a path from the start vertex to itself (namely the empty path with weight zero). But there is no way to get from the start vertex to any other vertex, and the fact that there is no path is represented by ∞ in the distance array.

the algorithm gradually improves the values in the distance array

Of course, permitting *only* the empty path is an overwhelming restriction. The key to the algorithm is in gradually relaxing this restriction, allowing more vertices to appear in permitted paths. As more and more vertices are allowed, we will continually revise the distance array so its values are correct *for paths that pass through only allowed vertices*. By the end of the algorithm, all vertices are allowed and the distance array has entirely correct values.

The idea we have described needs some refinement. How are newly allowed vertices selected? How do we keep track of which vertices are currently allowed? How is the distance array revised to permit the newly allowed vertices to appear in a path? These questions are addressed in the following list of three steps for the complete algorithm.

Step 1. Fill in the distance array with ∞ at every location, with the exception of distance[Start], which is assigned the value zero.

Step 2. Initialize a *set* of vertices, called allowedVertices, to be the empty set. Throughout the algorithm, a *permitted path* is a path that starts at the start vertex and in which each vertex on the path (except perhaps the final vertex) is in the set of allowed vertices. The final vertex on a permitted path does not need to be in the allowedVertices set. At this point, allowedVertices is the empty set, so the only permitted path is the empty path without any edges. (This empty path does contain one vertex, the start vertex. But since this vertex is the *final* vertex on the path, the vertex is not required to be in the allowed vertices set.)

Step 3. The third step is a loop. Each time through the loop we will add one more vertex to allowedVertices and then update the distance array so all the allowed vertices may appear on paths. Here's a brief summary of the loop:

```
// Loop in Step 3 of the shortest distance algorithm:
// n is the number of vertices in the graph.

for (allowedSize = 1; allowedSize <= n; allowedSize++)
{
    // At this point, allowedVertices contains allowedSize - 1 vertices,
    // which are the allowedSize - 1 closest vertices to the start vertex.
    // Also, for each vertex v, distance[v] is the shortest distance from
    // the start vertex to vertex v, provided we are
    // considering only permitted paths (i.e., paths where
    // each vertex except the final vertex must be in
    // allowedVertices).
```

Step 3a. Let next be the closest vertex to the start vertex that is not yet in the set of allowed vertices. (If several vertices are equally close, then you may choose next to be any of them.)

Step 3b. Add the vertex next to the set allowedVertices.

Step 3c. Revise the distance array so the new vertex (next) may appear on permitted paths.

```
}
```

The loop's computation hinges on the condition written just before Step 3a. The condition indicates that the allowedVertices set actually contains the allowedSize-1 vertices that are *closest* to the start vertex. The condition also indicates that distance[v] is always the shortest distance from the start vertex to vertex v, provided we are considering only permitted paths (that is, paths where all vertices except the final vertex must be in the set of allowed vertices). This condition is true the first time the loop is entered, and it is also true at the start of each subsequent iteration. The responsibility of the three steps—3a, 3b, and 3c—is to ensure the condition remains valid at the start of each iteration. Let's examine the three steps in some detail.

Step 3a. This step must determine which of the *unallowed* vertices is closest to the start vertex. There is a simple rule for choosing this vertex:

How to Choose the Next Vertex in Step 3a

In Step 3a, we will always choose the unallowed vertex that has the *smallest* current value in the distance array. (If several vertices have equally small distances, then we may choose any of them.)

For example, suppose we reach Step 3a and have this situation:

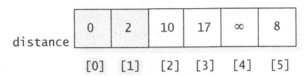

distance

0	2	10	17	∞	8
[0]	[1]	[2]	[3]	[4]	[5]

*In this example, the two shaded vertices, 0 and 1,
are already in the set of allowed vertices.*

Because vertices 0 and 1 are already in the allowed set, we cannot choose them as the next vertex. Among the other vertices, vertex 5 has the smallest current value in the distance array (the value is 8). So we would choose vertex 5 as the next vertex. In the answer to Self-Test Exercise 12, we will explain precisely *why* this rule works, but for now it is sufficient to know this is the correct way to select the next vertex.

Step 3b. In this step, we "add the vertex `next` to the set `allowedVertices`." The implementation of this step depends on how the set of allowed vertices is represented. One possibility is to implement `allowedVertices` as a set of vertex numbers, using an ADT for a set of integers. In this case, Step 3b merely inserts `next` into the set.

Step 3c. Finally, we must revise the distance array so the newly allowed vertex, `next`, is permitted on a path from the start vertex to another vertex. An example will explain the necessary revisions. Suppose vertices 0, 1, and 5 are already in the `allowedVertices` set, and we have just added vertex 2 as our next vertex, as shown here:

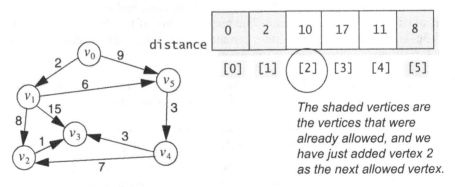

distance

0	2	10	17	11	8
[0]	[1]	[2]	[3]	[4]	[5]

*The shaded vertices are
the vertices that were
already allowed, and we
have just added vertex 2
as the next allowed vertex.*

Because we have just added vertex 2 as a newly allowed vertex, we must now update the distance array to reflect the fact that vertex 2 may now appear on paths.

For example, `distance[3]` is currently 17. This means that there is a path from the start vertex to vertex 3 that uses only vertices 0, 1, and 5 and that has a length of 17. Here's the key question: *If we also allow vertex 2 to appear on a path from the start vertex to vertex 3, can we obtain a distance that is smaller than 17?* A smaller distance might be possible by taking a two-part path, shown here:

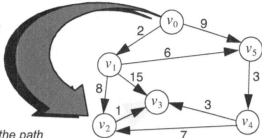

The first part of the path goes from the start vertex v_0 to the newly allowed vertex v_2 ...

... and the second part of the path consists of one more edge from the newly allowed vertex v_2 to vertex v_3.

This path has two parts: the part from the start vertex to vertex 2 and the part that has the single edge from vertex 2 to vertex 3. The total weight of this path is:

`distance[2]` + (weight of the edge from vertex 2 to vertex 3)

In our example, this sum is 11, which is smaller than the current "best distance to vertex 3." Therefore, we should replace `distance[3]` with this smaller sum. We must also create similar two-part paths for each of the other unallowed vertices, and if the two-part path is smaller than the current distance, then we modify the distance array. This provides the following refined pseudocode for Step 3c:

Step 3c (revised).   Revise the distance array so that the new vertex (`next`) may appear on permitted paths. The integer `n` is the number of vertices, and `v` and `sum` are local integer variables, as shown in this code:

```
for (v = 0; v < n; v++)
    if ((v is not an allowed vertex) and (there is an edge from next to v))
    {
        sum = distance[next] + (weight of the edge from next to v);
        if (sum < distance[v])
            distance[v] = sum;
    }
```

Notice that we do not consider a possible new, smaller distance to vertices that are already allowed vertices. That is because these vertices are all closer to the start vertex than `next` is, so `distance[next]` is going to be larger than the shortest distance to any of these vertices.

Also, when we are creating the new two-part paths, we consider only the case in which the second part of the path is a *single edge* from next to the end vertex. The reason for this is that a longer path from next to the end vertex would have to pass through other allowed vertices, meaning that we have a path that goes from the start vertex, through next, through *another* allowed vertex, and finally to the end vertex. But such a path will always be shorter by avoiding the next vertex altogether; just go from the start vertex to that other allowed vertex (using the shortest path) and then to the end vertex. Such a path, which does not go through the next vertex, is already permitted. We don't need to consider such a path again; we need only consider new paths that pass through the next newly allowed vertex.

The complete pseudocode for the algorithm is shown in Figure 14.5. The main loop actually stops at the number of vertices minus 1 because at that point, there is only one unallowed vertex, and this must be the farthest vertex from the start vertex so that no shortest paths can go through this farthest vertex.

We'll execute the algorithm on our example graph. Here's the situation after initializing the distance array:

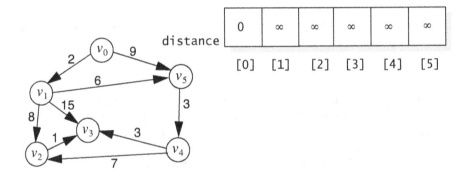

At this point, the set of allowed vertices is empty, and we will enter the main loop for the first time. In Step 3a, the value of next is set to vertex 0 (since distance[0] is the smallest value in the distance array). We then look at each unallowed vertex v with an edge from vertex 0 to vertex v. These are vertices 1 and 5, so we check to see whether we need to revise distance[1] and distance[5]:

- distance[0] + (the weight of the edge from 0 to 1) is 2. Because this is smaller than the current value of distance[1], we replace distance[1] with 2.

- distance[0] + (the weight of the edge from 0 to 5) is 9. Because this is smaller than the current value of distance[5], we replace distance[5] with 9.

FIGURE 14.5   Dijkstra's Shortest Distance Algorithm

Pseudocode

Input: A directed graph with positive-integer edge weights and n vertices. One of the vertices, called start, is specified as the start vertex.

Output: A list of the shortest distances from the start vertex to every other vertex in the graph.

The algorithm uses an array of n integers (called distance) and a set of vertices (called allowedVertices). The variables v, allowedSize, and sum are local integer variables. There is some special value (∞) that we can place in the distance array to indicate an infinite distance (which means there is no path).

Step 1. Initialize the distance array to contain all ∞ except distance[start], which is set to zero.

Step 2. Initialize the set of allowed vertices to be the empty set.

Step 3. Compute the complete distance array:
```
for (allowedSize = 1; allowedSize < n; allowedSize++)
{
```
    // At this point, allowedVertices contains allowedSize – 1 vertices, which are the
    // allowedSize – 1 closest vertices to the start vertex. Also, for each vertex v, distance[v]
    // is the shortest distance from the start vertex to vertex v, provided that we are
    // considering only permitted paths (i.e., paths where each vertex except the final vertex
    // must be in allowedVertices).

Step 3a. Let next be the closest vertex to the start vertex, which is not yet in the set of allowed vertices. (If several vertices are equally close, then you may choose next to be any of them.)

Step 3b. Add the vertex next to the set allowedVertices.

Step 3c. Revise the distance array so that the new vertex (next) may appear on permitted paths:
```
for (v = 0; v < n; v++)
    if ((v is not an allowed vertex) and (there is an edge from next to v))
    {
        sum = distance[next] + (weight of the edge from next to v);
        if (sum < distance[v])
            distance[v] = sum;
    }
}
```

Step 4. Output the values in the distance array. (Each distance[v] is the shortest distance from the start vertex to vertex v.)

At this point, the distance array is as shown below (with the allowed vertices shaded):

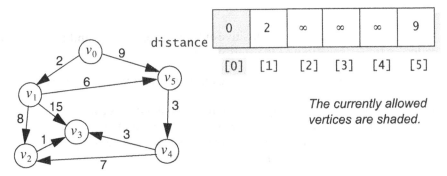

distance

0	2	∞	∞	∞	9
[0]	[1]	[2]	[3]	[4]	[5]

The currently allowed vertices are shaded.

The second time we enter the main loop, the value of `next` is set to vertex 1 (since `distance[1]` is the smallest value of the unallowed vertices). We then look at each unallowed vertex v with an edge from vertex 1 to vertex v. These are vertices 2, 3, and 5, so we check to see whether we need to revise `distance[2]`, `distance[3]`, and `distance[5]`:

- `distance[1]` + (the weight of the edge from 1 to 2) is 10. Because this is smaller than the current value of `distance[2]`, we replace `distance[2]` with 10.

- `distance[1]` + (the weight of the edge from 1 to 3) is 17. Because this is smaller than the current value of `distance[3]`, we replace `distance[3]` with 17.

- `distance[1]` + (the weight of the edge from 0 to 5) is 8. Because this is smaller than the current value of `distance[5]`, we replace `distance[5]` with 8.

At this point, the distance array is:

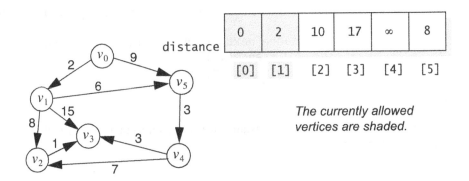

distance

0	2	10	17	∞	8
[0]	[1]	[2]	[3]	[4]	[5]

The currently allowed vertices are shaded.

The third time we enter the main loop, the value of next will be set to vertex 5 (since distance[5] is the smallest value of the unallowed vertices). We then look at each unallowed vertex v with an edge from vertex 5 to vertex v. Vertex 4 is the only vertex that is the target of an edge from vertex 5, so we check to see whether we need to revise distance[4]:

- distance[5] + (the weight of the edge from 5 to 4) is 11. Because this is smaller than the current value of distance[4], we replace distance[4] with 11.

At this point, we have this situation:

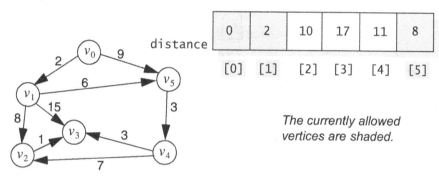

The currently allowed vertices are shaded.

The fourth time we enter the main loop, the value of next will be set to vertex 2 (since distance[2] is the smallest value of the unallowed vertices). We then look at each unallowed vertex v with an edge from vertex 2 to vertex v. Vertex 3 is the only such vertex, so we check to see whether we need to revise distance[3]:

- distance[2] + (the weight of the edge from 2 to 3) is 11. Because this is smaller than the current value of distance[3], we replace distance[3] with 11.

At this point, the situation is:

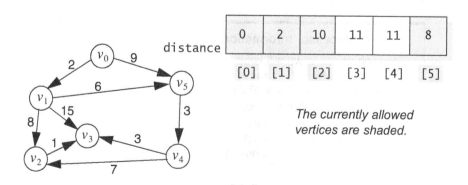

The currently allowed vertices are shaded.

The fifth time we enter the main loop, the value of next will be set to either vertex 3 or vertex 4 (since both distance[3] and distance[4] are 11). It doesn't matter which one we choose, so let's choose vertex 4. We then look at each unallowed vertex v with an edge from vertex 4 to vertex v. This is only vertex 3, so we check to see whether we need to revise distance[4]:

- distance[4] + (the weight of the edge from 4 to 3) is 14. Because this is *larger* than the current value of distance[3], we do not replace distance[3].

At this point, we are nearly done:

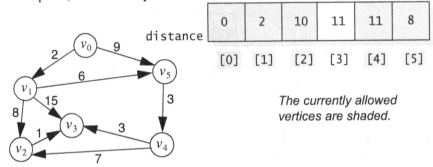

0	2	10	11	11	8
[0]	[1]	[2]	[3]	[4]	[5]

*The currently allowed
vertices are shaded.*

The main loop of the algorithm now stops. We don't need to process that last unallowed vertex (3), because it is the farthest vertex from the start vertex. For each vertex v, the value of distance[v] is the shortest distance from the start vertex (vertex 0) to v.

Shortest-Path Algorithm

We have shown how to compute the *weight* of the shortest path from a start vertex to each other vertex in a graph. But how can we compute the actual sequence of vertices that occurs along the shortest path? It turns out that Dijkstra's shortest-distance algorithm contains enough information to actually print the shortest path from the start vertex to any other vertex, provided that we keep track of one extra piece of information:

Predecessor Information for Shortest Paths

For each vertex v, we will keep track of which vertex was the next vertex when distance[v] was given a new, smaller value. We will keep track of these values in an array called predecessor so that for each vertex v, predecessor[v] is the value of next at the time when distance[v] was given a new, smaller value. (Note: predecessor[start] does not need to have a value, since distance[start] is never updated.)

The predecessor information is easy to keep track of. Each time we update distance[v] with the assignment distance[v] = sum , we must also update predecessor[v] with this assignment:

```
predecessor[v] = next;
```

When the algorithm finishes, the value of distance[v] is the weight of the shortest path from the start vertex to vertex v. Or distance[v] might be infinity, indicating that there is no path from the start vertex to vertex v. But when distance[v] is not infinity, we can actually print out the vertices on the shortest path from the start vertex to vertex v, using the following code:

```
// Printing the vertices on the shortest path from the start vertex to v:
// Vertices are printed in reverse order, starting at v, and going to start.
vertexOnPath = v; // The last vertex on the path.
System.out.println(vertexOnPath); // Print the final vertex.
while (vertexOnPath != start)
{
    vertexOnPath = predecessor[vertexOnPath];
    System.out.println(vertexOnPath);
}
```

In other words, the last vertex on the path to v is vertex v itself. The next-to-last vertex is predecessor[v], and the vertex before that is obtained by applying predecessor to the next-to-last vertex—and so on, right back to the start vertex. As indicated, this algorithm manages to print the vertices in reverse order, from vertex v back to the start vertex.

Self-Test Exercises for Section 14.4

12. When we select the next vertex in the shortest-distance algorithm, we need to select the unallowed vertex that is closest to the start vertex. How is this selection done?

13. Consider the graph we have been using throughout this section, except change the weight of the edge that goes from 0 to 5. Its new weight is 4. Go through the entire algorithm to compute the new distance array.

14. Compute the complete predecessor array for the previous exercise and use it to find the actual shortest path from vertex 0 to vertex 3.

CHAPTER SUMMARY

- Graphs are a flexible data structure with many occurrences in computer science and in applications. Many problems can be solved by asking an appropriate question about paths in a graph.

- There are several different kinds of graphs: undirected graphs (in which edges have no particular orientation), directed graphs (in which each edge goes from a source vertex to a target vertex), graphs with loops (i.e., an edge connecting a vertex to itself), graphs with multiple edges (i.e., more than one edge can connect the same pair of vertices), labeled graphs (in which each vertex has an associated label), and graphs with weighted edges (in which each edge has an associated number, called its weight).

- There are two common ways to implement a graph: an adjacency matrix or edge lists. The different implementations have different time performance for common operations such as determining whether two vertices are connected.
- There are two common ways to traverse a graph: depth-first search and breadth-first search.
- Dijkstra's algorithm provides an efficient way to determine the shortest path from a given start vertex to every other vertex in a graph with weighted edges.

? Solutions to Self-Test Exercises

1. The airline route graph has nine vertices, 14 edges, and no loops. A loop would be an excursion flight that takes off and lands at the same city.

2. It is simple (no loops, no multiple edges).

3. Your state graph should have 16 vertices and 48 directed edges. (There are 32 edges from Rule 1, and 8 edges each from Rules 2 and 3.) It is possible to go from the start state to the goal state in four moves.

4. For the removal method, suppose that k is the number of vertices that are being removed and that this will leave m vertices in the new, smaller graph. The method should allocate new, smaller arrays for the edges and labels (and these new arrays can be referred to by local variables of the method). Then copy the information for the first m vertices into these smaller arrays.

   The method that adds new vertices must allocate new, larger arrays and copy all the information from the old arrays to the new arrays.

In both methods, the final step is to make the instance variables (edges and labels) refer to the new arrays.

5. Suppose the vertex numbers of the two vertices are i and j. The method must interchange their labels and also interchange the rows and columns of the edges matrix. If you aren't careful, you might accidentally interchange edges[i][i] with edges[j][j] two times (once when you are interchanging the rows and once when you are interchanging the columns).

6. The adjacency matrix, a, could be a two-dimensional array of integers with a[i][j] storing the number of edges from vertex i to vertex j.

7. This is an open-ended question, but your answer should consider space requirements for each representation and time requirements for common operations.

8. Here is one solution:
```
public static <E> int maxEdges
(Graph<E> g)
{
    int i;
    int answer;
    int manyEdges;
    int maxEdges = 0;
    int[ ] ni;

    if (g.size( ) == 0)
        throw new
        IllegalArgumentException
        ("Graph is empty");

    for (i = 0; i < g.size( ); i++)
    {
        ni = g.neighbors(i);
        manyEdges = ni.length;
        if (manyEdges >= maxEdges)
        {
            answer = i;
            maxEdges = manyEdges;
        }
    }

    return answer;
}
```

9. Traversals sometimes make choices about which vertex to visit next. When we have such a choice, we will visit the vertex that is alphabetically first, giving these two orders: *Depth-first:* Sydney, Canberra, Adelaide, Melbourne, Hobart, Perth, Black Stump, Darwin, Brisbane. *Breadth-first:* Sydney, Canberra, Melbourne, Adelaide, Brisbane, Hobart, Perth, Black Stump, Darwin.

10. If *n* is 1, then the queue needs room for only one vertex. If *n* is more than 1, then the queue will never have more than *n*–1 entries. Here is why: The start vertex is in the queue only once (by itself), and then we remove the start vertex from the queue. Each other vertex is placed in the queue at most once, so the largest queue needed would occur if all *n*–1 vertices are neighbors of the start vertex.

11. A depth-first search.

12. From among the unallowed vertices, we select the vertex with the smallest current value in the distance array. This works because the current distance array contains the correct distance values if we are permitting only allowed vertices, and the currently allowed vertices are the n–1 closest vertices. Therefore, the shortest path to the nth closest vertex must pass through only currently allowed vertices, and therefore the distance array contains the correct value for that n^{th} closest vertex.

13. The new final distance array: (0, 2, 10, 10, 7, 4).

14. The new shortest path to vertex 3: vertex 0 to vertex 5, vertex 5 to vertex 4, vertex 4 to vertex 3.

PROGRAMMING PROJECTS

1. Rewrite the depthFirstPrint method from Figure 14.4 on page 758 so that it carries out a breadth-first search instead.

2. Use edge *lists* to reimplement the Graph class from Figure 14.3 on page 744. There should be no limit to the number of vertices. Also provide a new method that returns the edge list of a specified vertex.

3 Use edge *sets* to reimplement the Graph class from Figure 14.3 on page 744. There should be no limit to the number of vertices. Also provide a new method that returns the edge set of a specified vertex.

4 Implement a new class that is derived from the Graph. The new class should permit both edges and vertices to have labels.

5 Implement a method with three arguments: a graph, a starting vertex number, and an ending vertex number. The method determines whether there is a directed path from the starting vertex to the ending vertex.

6 Implement a new class for graphs with weighted edges. Use the ordinary Graph class as a superclass for your implementation. After implementing the new class, provide two extra methods to implement Dijkstra's shortest-distance and shortest-path algorithms.

7 Write a program to help a traveler plan the shortest traveling path from one city to another. The program should read a file of data containing a list of cities and a list of roads connecting the cities. Each road has a distance attached to it. Allow the user to enter queries of the form "City1, City2" and have the program print the shortest sequence of roads to travel from City1 to City2.

8 Write a program to help you make better social connections. The program should read a file of data containing a list of people in your community and a list of who knows whom. Allow the user to enter various queries about which people know each other, such as "How many people does Harry know?" or "Is there anyone whom both Harry and Cathy know?"

9 Choose some graph implementation and implement a graph member function to delete a vertex from the graph. The function should remove not only the vertex, but also all edges that have the vertex as the source or target.

10 Implement an undirected graph class by modifying any of the graph implementations discussed in this chapter.

11 Rewrite the maze program in Chapter 8 (page 429) using a graph class to represent the maze. A path should be generated with the entrance and exit as endpoints. Use a depth-first search to travel through the maze.

12 A *connected graph* is a graph that has a path from every node to every other node. For this project, you are given a connected, undirected, weighted graph in which every edge has a non-negative number called its *weight*. You must create a new graph with the same vertices as the original graph, but possibly fewer edges. Such a graph is called a *subgraph*, and we are looking for a particular subgraph called the *minimal spanning tree*, which has these properties:

1. It is a subgraph of the original graph.
2. It is still connected.
3. Among all possible connected subgraphs, it has a minimal total weight of its edges.

The algorithm you'll use was first devised by the Czech mathematician Vojtech Jarnik in 1930 and later rediscovered by Robert Prim (1957) and Edsger Dijkstra (1959). The algorithm starts by picking any vertex and creating a set V that contains only this vertex. We also create a set of edges, E, that initially begins as the empty set. The remainder of the algorithm adds edges to E one at a time. Each new edge that you add must be the lowest-weight edge that connects a vertex from V to a vertex that is not in V—and after the edge is added, the vertex that was not in V is added to V. The process continues until V contains all vertices.

Appendix A
Java's Primitive Types and Arithmetic Overflow

Java has eight primitive data types for storing numerical and other basic values. This appendix lists the eight types and some of their properties, such as the arithmetic overflow that can occur with the integer types.

```
byte
char
short
int
long
```

- These are Java's five integer types. Notice that the char type is included as one of the integer types, though it does have some special properties discussed below. Any value of these types is a whole number in the following limited ranges:

	Storage Requirement	Minimum Value	Maximum Value
byte	1 byte	−128	127
char	2 bytes	0	65,535
short	2 bytes	−32,768	32,767
int	4 bytes	−2,147,483,648	2,147,483,647
long	8 bytes	−9,223,372,036,854,775,808	9,223,372,036,854,775,807

- Constant integer values are written as a sequence of digits with no commas and sometimes a negative sign at the front, such as 4200 or −3942. Fixed long values include the letter L after the digits, such as 923672159321877L.

- When an integer expression is evaluated, the operands are examined to see whether there is any long data. If so, all the operands are converted to the long type, and the answer is also long. If there is no long data, then any byte, char, or short operands are converted to int, and the answer is also int.

  The fact that byte, char, and short operands are converted to int has consequences in the arithmetic of these values. For example, suppose that s, s1, and s2 are short variables, with s1 containing 1 and s2 containing 2. Then the assignment s = s1 + s2 causes a compilation error because s1 and s2 are converted to int values, and even though s1 + s2 is only 3, it is considered an int value. Java's compiler does not permit an assignment of one integer data type to a variable of a shorter type. The solution is a typecast that informs the compiler that the computed value is intended to be the short data type. In this example, we can correctly write the assignment:

  ```
  s = (short)(s1 + s2);
  ```

- When an integer value is too large for its data type, the result is called **arithmetic overflow**. In Java, an integer arithmetic overflow results in a wrong answer. For example, adding 1 to the largest int gives the smallest negative number as the answer. Arithmetic overflow can occur during an assignment to a variable, or it can occur in an intermediate value that is part of a larger arithmetic expression. Some examples are shown here:

```
// Compute an addition that causes arithmetic overflow because the answer is
// larger than the largest int value.
int i;
int i1 = 1000000000;
int i2 = 2000000000;
i = i1 + i2;
System.out.println(i);  // Prints wrong answer of -1294967296

// Compute approximately 2/3 of an integer value in a way that can cause overflow.
// The overflow occurs because the intermediate value k*2 could be more than
// the largest int, and therefore the final result is wrong.
int j;
int k = 2000000000;
j = k * 2 / 3;
System.out.println(j);  // Prints wrong answer of -98322432

// Compute 2/3 of an integer value in a better way. By doing the division first
// there is no possibility of an overflow.
j = 2 * (k / 3);
System.out.println(j);  // Prints right answer of 1333333332
```

Special Properties of the char Type:

- char values are non-negative integers used to represent printable characters. Each printable character is assigned one of these numbers, called the Unicode value of the character. For example, the Unicode value of 'A' is 65. The values from 0 to 127 match the ASCII character codes that you may have used in other programming languages. The complete list of Unicode characters is available at http://unicode.org/charts.

- When a char value is printed, the printable character is displayed rather than the integer value.

- A char constant can be written in four ways:

   — A single character within quote marks, such as 'A'.

   — One of the special character escape sequences, which are: '\n' (new line), '\r' (carriage return), '\b' (backspace), '\f' (form feed), '\t' (tab), '\'' (single quote), '\"' (double quote), and '\\' (backslash).

   — A sequence of up to three octal digits of the form '\nnn'. The number nnn is a base 8 (octal) number from 0 to 377 (which corresponds to a base 10 number from 0 to 255). For example, an alternative representation of 'A' is '\101' since 101 (base 8) is the same as 65 (base 10).

— A Unicode escape sequence of the form '\unnnn', where nnnn is a base 16 (hexadecimal) number with exactly four hex digits. For example, '\u0041' is 'A' since 41 (base 16) is the same as 65 (base 10).

float
double

These are Java's two data types for numbers that have decimal places. Double values follow an 8-byte format called the IEEE 754 standard for 64-bit floating point numbers. This standard has these properties:

- Double values range from about -1.7×10^{308} to 1.7×10^{308}. Numbers can be defined close to zero, down to about 4.9×10^{-324} on the positive side of zero or to about -4.9×10^{-324} on the negative size of zero.

- Double constant values with base 10 exponents can be written by placing the letter "e"or "E" before the exponent. For example, 4.2E19 is 4.2×10^{19}.

- Double values have about 14 to 15 significant digits. This means that the actual number stored in the computer can have inaccuracies beginning around the 15th digit. Because of these inaccuracies, you should avoid testing double numbers for exact equality (using the == operator).

- Special values: Computations that result in a value greater than about 1.7×10^{308} will result in a constant called Double.POSITIVE_INFINITY. Values smaller than about -1.7×10^{308} will result in Double.NEGATIVE_INFINITY. Values that are too close to zero will result in 0.0 (on the positive side) or –0.0 (on the negative side). Any undefined computation (such as division by zero) results in a constant called Double.NaN. Because of these special constants, computations with double numbers never cause an exception or crash. Instead, arithmetic overflow or illegal computations simply provide the appropriate constant value as a result.

The float type is similar to double but with only 4 bytes of storage (the IEEE 754 standard for 32-bit floating point numbers). Therefore, float values have a smaller range (about -3.4×10^{38} to 3.4×10^{38}), the values cannot get so close to zero, and the accuracy is only six or seven digits.

If an arithmetic computation involves float values but no double variables or constants, then the arithmetic is carried out using 4-byte float values with the corresponding limitations on ranges and accuracy. There are separate constants for Float.NaN, Float.POSITIVE_INFINITY, and Float.NEGATIVE_INFINITY.

boolean

A boolean value is one of two constants: true or false.

Appendix B
Java Input and Output

Earlier versions of Java had no classes to support input and output in a straightforward way. The result was a multitude of homegrown input/output classes, such as our own EasyReader and FormatWriter (which are still available at www.cs.colorado.edu/~main/edu/colorado/io).

Java 5.0 introduced a new class, Scanner, to support input of a variety of values, and a new printf method to provide formatted output. This appendix shows how to use the basic features of these new input/output items.

The Scanner Class

A Scanner is designed to be attached to an input file, the keyboard, or some other sequence of characters. Here are three examples:

```
// Create a Scanner called stdin that is attached to the System.in keyboard:
Scanner stdin = new Scanner(System.in);

// Create a second Scanner called datafile that is attached to a file "data.txt":
Scanner datafile = new Scanner(new FileReader("data.txt"));

// Create a third Scanner called s that gets its input from a String:
String expr = new String("   1234 Hello! ");
Scanner datafile = new Scanner(expr);
```

Once a Scanner is set up, numbers, strings, and other items can be read with easy-to-use methods. For example, after stdin is set up, the next line of input is read into a variable s with the statement:

```
String s = stdin.nextLine( );
```

Most of the other methods for the Scanner depend on the idea of dividing the input into pieces called tokens. Each token is a contiguous portion of the input sequence. Normally, the next token provided by a Scanner is obtained in two steps:

1. First, any delimiters are read and discarded. These are usually space characters, tabs, and the characters that mark the end of a line.

2. The next token then consists of as many characters as possible until the next occurrence of a delimiter (or the end of the input). The delimiter character is not part of the token.

For example, if the next few characters in the Scanner are "   1234 Hello! ", then the first token will be the characters 1234 and the second token will be Hello!.

The Scanner provides the methods shown on the next page to determine information about the next token.

Class Scanner

❖ **public class Scanner from the package java.util**
A Scanner object has methods for reading some primitive data values.

Specification (partial)

♦ **Constructors for the Scanner**
```
public Scanner(InputStream in) (such as new Scanner(System.in))
public EasyReader(File name) (such as new Scanner(new FileReader("data.txt"))
public EasyReader(String s)
```
Initialize this Scanner to read from an InputStream, a File, or a String.

Parameters:
in – the InputStream from which this Scanner will read
name – the name of a file from which this Scanner will read
s – the String from which this Scanner will get a sequence of characters

Postcondition:
This Scanner has been initialized so that its subsequent input comes from the specified location.

♦ **hasNext**
```
public boolean hasNext( )
```
Tests whether this Scanner has another token available.

Return Value:
The return value is true if this Scanner has at least one more token available; otherwise, the return value is false. Note that if the Scanner is attached to a keyboard, this method will wait until more input is provided before returning true.

♦ **hasNextDouble—hasNextInt**
```
public boolean hasNextDouble( )
public boolean hasNextInt( )
```
These are two of the methods that a Scanner provides to determine whether the next token can be read as a certain data type. There are a variety of other has... methods for other data types.

Returns:
The return value is true if this Scanner has another token, and that next token can be read as a value of a particular data type (double or int for these two methods); otherwise, the return value is false.

♦ **nextDouble—nextInt**
```
public double nextDouble( )
public int nextInt( )
```
These are two of the methods that a Scanner provides to read a token of a particular kind. There are a variety of other next ... methods for other data types.

Returns:
The next token in this Scanner has been read and converted to a particular data type, which the method returns.

Detecting and Reading Part of a Token with Patterns

The Scanner class has no methods to directly read part of a token. For example, if the next few characters of input are 42abc, there is no simple way to read the integer 42 and leave the abc for the subsequent token. However, by using Java's Pattern class, we can carry out some of these operations. We won't discuss the Pattern class in detail, but here is some code that you might find useful:

```
import java.util.regex.Pattern;

// This pattern will match just the first character of the next token:
public static final Pattern CHARACTER = Pattern.compile("\\S.*?");

// These patterns match numbers at the start of the next token. The UNSIGNED versions
// must not have a plus or minus sign at the front:
public static final Pattern DOUBLE =
    Pattern.compile("([+-]?((\\d+\\.?\\d*)|(\\.\\d+))([Ee][-+]?\\d+)?.*?");
public static final Pattern INT = Pattern.compile("[+-]?\\d+.*?");
public static final Pattern UNSIGNED_DOUBLE =
    Pattern.compile("((\\d+\\.?\\d*)|(\\.\\d+))([Ee][-+]?\\d+)?.*?");
public static final Pattern UNSIGNED_INT = Pattern.compile("\\d+.*?");
```

Here are some examples of how the patterns are used with a Scanner s to examine the start of the next token:

```
s.hasNext(DOUBLE)           // True if the start of the next token is a double number
s.hasNext(INT)              // True if the start of the next token is an integer
s.hasNext(UNSIGNED_DOUBLE)  // True if the start of the next token is an unsigned double
s.hasNext(UNSIGNED_INT)     // True if the start of the next token is an unsigned integer
```

If you know that the start of the next token matches a particular pattern, then you can use the following to read just that part of the token (leaving the rest of the token for a subsequent read operation). Be careful with these, though, because if the next token does not start with the required pattern, then the Scanner will skip ahead until it finds a token that does start with the pattern.

```
char c;
c = s.findInLine(CHARACTER).charAt(0);      // Gets first character of next token

// These examples read the start of the next token and convert it to a double or integer.
// In order for these to work, you must first use hasNext to ensure that the start of the
// next token matches the required pattern.
double d;
integer i;
d = new Double(s.findInLine(DOUBLE));
d = new Double(s.findInLine(UNSIGNED_DOUBLE));
i = new Integer(s.findInLine(INT));
i = new Integer(s.findInLine(UNSIGNED_INT));
```

The System.out.printf Method

In Chapter 1 (page 14), we introduced the System.out.printf method to print formatted output. Here is a complete list of the special characters and format specifiers that can be used in a printf format string:

Special character	In a format string, this will print...
\%	...a percent sign
\\	...a backslash
\n (or %n for better cross-platform support)	...a new line (moves down to next line)
\r	...a carriage return
\f	...a formfeed character
\b	...a backspace character
\t	...a tab
\"	...a double quote sign
\'	...a quote sign

Format specifier	Causes the next item to be printed as...
%b	...a boolean value (true or false)
%c	...a single character
%d	...a decimal (base 10) whole number.
%f	...a floating point number with six digits after the decimal point
%g	...a floating point number using scientific notation for large exponents
%s	...a string
%x	...a base 16 (hexadecimal) integer

Each of the format specifiers may have a sequence of optional extra information immediately after the percent sign. These appear in the following order, and each is optional:

- **The Argument Index:** This is a single positive integer followed by a dollar sign. If it appears, then it specifies which of the subsequent arguments to printf to use for the value of this printed item. For example, printf("%1$f %1$g", 42.3) will print the first argument (42.3) using both the f and g formats.

- **Flags:** These are one or more single characters. The character ∧ converts the output to upper case. The character – left-justifies the output. The character + will make sure that any number output is printed with a + or – sign at the front. The character (will print negative numbers in parentheses. For example, printf("%(d", -42) prints –42 in parentheses.

- **Width:** This integer specifies the minimum number of output spaces to use in printing the output. If extra spaces are needed, those spaces are inserted at the front of the output (unless the - flag is used). For example, `printf("%10d", 42)` prints 42 with eight spaces in front of the two digits.

- **Precison:** This is a decimal point followed by a number. The number indicates the number of digits to print after the decimal point for a floating point number. For example, `printf("%10.2d", 42.12345)` prints the fives spaces followed by the number 42.12 (rounding to two decimal digits). The total output has 10 characters (the five spaces, followed by the five characters of the output number).

Appendix C
Throwing and Catching Java Exceptions

An **exception** is a Java `Object` that is used to indicate abnormal conditions. When a method detects an abnormal condition, it can create an exception object and pass this object upward to the place where the method was activated. This whole process is called **throwing an exception**.

When an exception is thrown, the problem can sometimes be corrected—a technique called **catching the exception**. Other times, the problem is too serious to correct, and it will remain uncaught, eventually causing the Java runtime system to print an error message and halt the program.

How to Throw an Exception

Some Java statements automatically throw an exception when they are incorrectly used. For example, the evaluation of the expression (42/0) will throw an `ArithmeticException` because an integer division by zero is illegal. At other times, a method may detect a problem itself and throw an exception to indicate this problem. For example, Chapter 1 has a method with a specification that begins like this:

◆ **celsiusToFahrenheit**
    `public static double celsiusToFahrenheit(double c)`
    Convert a temperature from Celsius degrees to Fahrenheit degrees.

    Parameter:
    c – a temperature in Celsius degrees

    Precondition:
    c >= -273.15.

It is a programming error to call `celsiusToFahrenheit` with an argument that is below −273.15. In such a case, the `celsiusToFahrenheit` method will detect that the precondition has been violated and will throw an `IllegalArgumentException`, with statements such as these:

```
if (c < -273.15)
    throw new IllegalArgumentException("Temperature too small.");
```

The general form for throwing an exception uses the keyword throw, following this pattern:

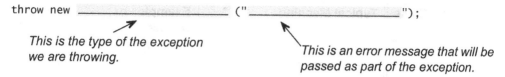

throw new _____ ("_____");

This is the type of the exception we are throwing.

This is an error message that will be passed as part of the exception.

Figure C.1 shows a list of common exceptions that a programmer may use to indicate problems. In Java terminology, these are actually called Throwable objects, and the list also indicates a further classification for each kind of Throwable object. We'll look at the meaning of that further classification next.

The RuntimeException and Error Classes

Most of the exceptions listed in Figure C.1 have a "further classification" of RuntimeException or Error. These are two particular kinds of Throwable objects with conventional meanings for programmers:

- RuntimeException: These tend to be exceptions that are caused by programming mistakes, such as the violation of a precondition.
- Error: These are problems with resources and the Java Virtual Machine. For example, running out of memory is a resource problem. Not having a needed class is an example of a problem with the Java Virtual Machine.

Catching an Exception

Sometimes an exception occurs, but the programmer has some way to handle the problem. In this situation, the programmer can use try/catch blocks of the following form:

```
try
{
    ||  Statements that might cause an exception to be thrown.
}
catch ( Type of the possible exception  e)
{
    |  These are statements to handle the problem. Within these
    |  statements, the name e refers to the exception object. For example,
    |  e.toString( ) is a message that's attached to the exception.
}
```

In this example, the variable name e was used for the name of the exception, but you can choose whatever name you like. The "type of the possible exception" is one of the exception data types, such as CloneNotSupportedException.

FIGURE C.1   Partial List of Java's `Throwable` Objects

Name of the Class	Typical Meaning	Examples or Discussion	Further Classification
`ClassCast Exception`	Attempting to use a reference as if it referred to an object of some class—but it doesn't.	Page 80	`Runtime Exception`
`CloneNotSupported Exception`	The `clone` method was activated in a class that forgot to implement `Cloneable`.	Page 83	`Exception (not Runtime)`
`EmptyStack Exception*`	Tried to pop or peek from an empty Stack.	Page 319	`Runtime Exception`
`IllegalArgument Exception`	An argument to a method violates the precondition.	Page 9	`Runtime Exception`
`IllegalState Exception`	A method was activated when the object was in a state that violates the method's precondition.	Page 150	`Runtime Exception`

`IndexOutOfBounds Exception`	An array index was used beyond the array's capacity.	`int[ ] a;`
		`a = new int[40];`
		`a[42] = 0;`
			`Runtime Exception`

`IOException`	An input or output error.	Trying to read after the end of a file.	`Exception (not Runtime)`

`NegativeArraySize Exception`	Allocating an array with a negative number of components.	`int[ ] a;`
		`int s = -1;`
		`a = new int[s];`
			`Runtime Exception`

`NoSuchElement Exception*`	Attempting to get another element out of an `Iterator` or other collection class when there are no more elements.	Page 291 or Page 362	`Runtime Exception`
`NullPointer Exception`	Attempting to access a method or instance variable of the null reference.	Page 55	`Runtime Exception`
`OutOfMemory Error`	The heap has no more memory.	Page 118	`Error`
`StackOverflow Error`	The execution stack has no more memory.	Page 419	`Error`
`UnsupportedOperation Exception`	A method of a class is not being provided by the class's programmer.	Page 291	`Runtime Exception`

*`EmptyStackException` and `NoSuchElementException` are part of `java.util`.

See `http://www.cs.colorado.edu/~main/java.html` for a listing of all Java `Throwable` objects.

As a specific example, consider the following code that tries to fill an array with clones of a given object. However, if the object is not cloneable, then the code fills the array with references to the actual object (rather than clones of the object):

```java
// In this code, obj is a non-null reference to a Java Object and copies is an array of objects.
// The variable i is an int.
try
{
    for (i = 0; i < copies.length; i++)
        copies[i] = obj.clone( );
}
catch (CloneNotSupportedException e)
{   // Fill the array with references to the actual object instead of clones.
    for (i = 0; i < copies.length; i++)
        copies[i] = obj;
}
```

If a section of code has the possibility of throwing several different types of exceptions, then the try block may be followed by several different catch blocks. After the final catch block, there can be one more block that starts with the keyword finally. The finally block is executed at the end, whether or not the exception is caught. For example, the following format has two catch blocks and a finally block:

```
try
{
    ‖  Statements that might cause an exception to be thrown.
}
catch ( Type of the first possible exception   e1)
{
```

These are statements to handle the problem. Within these statements, the name e1 refers to the exception object. For example, e1.toString( ) is a message that's attached to the exception.

```
}
catch ( Type of the second possible exception   e2)
{
```

These are statements to handle the problem. Within these statements, the name e2 refers to the exception object.

```
}
finally
{
```

These are statements that will always be executed after the above try and catch blocks. Note that this code is executed in all cases: when no exception occurs, when an exception is thrown and caught, or when an uncaught exception is thrown.

```
}
```

The throws Clause

Java has some exceptions that are neither a RuntimeException nor an Error. The examples in our list are CloneNotSupportedException and IOException, but there are several dozen more, and programmers can even create new classes of exceptions. You must follow a special rule when you write a statement that might throw one of these exceptions:

> When a method includes a statement that might throw an exception that is neither a RuntimeException nor an Error, there are two possibilities: (1) Catch the exception, or (2) include the name of the exception in a throws clause after the heading of the method.

The format of a throws clause is the keyword throws followed by the type of the possible exception. If there are several possible exceptions, then their types may be written separated by commas in a single throws clause. For example, the following main method has a throws clause indicating that it may throw a CloneNotSupportedException or an IOException:

```
public static main(String[ ] args)
throws CloneNotSupportedException, IOException
{

    These are statements that might throw an uncaught
    CloneNotSupportedException or an uncaught IOException.

}
```

Further Information

For a complete list of Java exceptions, follow the "Throwable Objects" link at http://www.cs.colorado.edu/~main/java.html.

Appendix D
ArrayList, Vector, Hashtable, and HashMap Classes

The Java Class Libraries in Java Version 1.2 included many collection classes that were updated to generic classes with Java 5.0. This appendix summarizes two of those classes, `Vector` and `Hashtable`, with additional material on `ArrayList` and `HashMap`. For complete documentation of the other JCL collection classes, go to `http://download.oracle.com/javase/1.5.0/docs/guide/collections/`or see the Collections link at `http://www.cs.colorado.edu/~main/java.html`.

The java.util.Vector and java.util.ArrayList Classes

Both the `Vector<E>` and `ArrayList<E>` generic classes implement the Java `List<E>` interface, which provides a collection class for a sequence of objects. Both the `Vector` and `ArrayList` implementations are similar to an array of objects, except that when the specified capacity is exceeded, they automatically grow. For efficiency, a programmer can also set an explicit capacity. In this case, the add operations will work efficiently (without allocating more memory) until the specified capacity is exceeded.

The `ArrayList` implementation is newer than `Vector` and is more efficient in many situations. However, some Java programs have more than one thread (separate computations that occur simultaneously or are interwoven with one another), and an `ArrayList` is safe for only one thread at a time (whereas a `Vector` is safe for access by multiple threads). The two classes also differ in how they test for equality of an object: `Vector` uses the `equals` method, whereas `ArrayList` uses the `==` operator.

The most important `Vector` and `ArrayList` methods are summarized here.

Constructor, clone, and toString Methods
`Vector<E>( )` or `ArrayList<E>( )`
>Create an empty `list` with an initial capacity of 10 and an increment amount of zero.

`Vector<E>(int initialCapacity)` or `ArrayList(int initialCapacity)`
>Create an empty `list` with the specified initial capacity and an increment amount of zero.

`public Vector<E> clone( )` or `public ArrayList<E> clone( )`
>Return a clone of this `Vector` or `ArrayList`. The items within this `Vector` or `ArrayList` are not cloned.

`public String toString( )`
>Return a printable `String` representation of this list.

Accessor Methods
`public boolean contains(Object obj)`
>Return `true` if `obj` occurs anywhere in this list. For `Vector`, the test makes use of `obj.equals( )` to determine whether any equal object occurs in the list. For `ArrayList`, the exact `obj` must appear in the list (using the `==` operator).

```
public E get(int index)
```
Return a reference to the element at the given index of this list (starting with index zero).

```
public int indexOf(Object obj)
```
Search for the first occurrence of obj in this list (using obj.equals for Vector but using the == operator for ArrayList). Return the index of this occurrence (or –1 if obj does not occur). Another version of indexOf has a second parameter to tell what index to start the search at.

```
public boolean isEmpty( )
```
Test whether this list is empty.

```
public Iterator<E> iterator( )
```
This method (added for Java 1.2) returns an Iterator for the elements of this list.

```
public int lastIndexOf(Object obj)
```
Search for the final occurrence of obj in this list, using obj.equals to test for equality. Return the index of this occurrence (or –1 if obj does not occur).

```
public int size( )
```
Return the number of elements currently in this Vector or ArrayList.

```
public E[ ] toArray( )
```
All elements of this list are copied into a new array that this method returns.

Modification Methods

```
public void add(E obj)
```
Add the specified element to this list at the next available index.

```
public void ensureCapacity(int minimumCapacity)
```
// This method is not part of the List interface, but it is part of Vector and ArrayList.
Reset the current capacity of this Vector or ArrayList to at least minimumCapacity. The add operations work efficiently (without allocating new memory) until this capacity is exceeded.

```
public void insertElementAt(E obj, int index)
```
// This is an extra method available for the Vector but not for other Lists.
Add the specified element to this Vector at the given index (which may be no bigger than the current size). Other elements that were at or after this index have been shifted upward to make room for the new element.

```
public boolean remove(Object obj)
```
// This is an optional List operation, implemented by both Vector and ArrayList.
Remove the first occurrence of the specified element from this list. The obj.equals method is used to find this occurrence, and the return value indicates whether or not such a value was found and removed.

```
public E remove(int index)
```
// This is an optional List operation, implemented by both Vector and ArrayList.
Remove the element of this list from the specified index (which must be less than the current size). Other elements that were after this index are shifted downward one spot. The return value is the removed object.

```
public void set(int index, E obj)
```
Changes an element of this list at the given index (which must be less than the current size). The new value for this element is obj, and the old value is no longer present at the index.

```
public void trimToSize( )
    // This is an extra method available for the Vector and ArrayList, but not other Lists.
```
Set the current capacity of this Vector or ArrayList equal to the number of elements it contains.

The Hashtable<K,V> and HashMap<K,V> Classes

Both Hashtable<K,V> and HashMap<K,V> are generic hash table classes that depend on the data types of keys (K) and the values (V) that are attached to the keys. Both classes implement Java's Map<K,V> generic interface, and the Hashtable is also an extension of Java's Dictionary class. The HashMap is unsafe for simultaneous access by more than one Java thread. The two classes also differ in how they test for a key: Hashtable uses the equals method, whereas HashMap uses the == operator. One other difference is that HashMap permits an inserted object to be null, but null is forbidden for Hashtable.

Both Hashtable and HashMap are implemented as open-address hash tables similar to the class in Section 11.2 of this book, with a specified capacity and a maximum load factor. When the maximum load factor is exceeded, the table automatically grows, and all entries are reentered into the larger table. The most important Hashtable and HashMap methods are summarized here:

Constructor, clone, and toString Methods
```
Hashtable<K,V>( ) or HashMap<K,V>( )
```
Create an empty hash table with a default initial capacity and a maximum load factor of 0.75. The keys are from class K, and the values are from class V.

```
Hashtable<K,V>(int initialCapacity) or HashMap<K,V>(int initialCapacity)
```
Create an empty hash table with a specified initial capacity and a maximum load factor of 0.75. The keys are from class K, and the values are from class V.

```
Hashtable<K,V>(int initialCapacity, float loadFactor) or
HashMap<K,V>(int initialCapacity, float loadFactor)
```
Create an empty hash table with a default initial capacity and a specified maximum load factor. The keys are from class K, and the values are from class V.

```
public Hashtable<K,V> clone( ) or public HashMap<K,V> clone( )
```
Return a clone of this hash table. The elements within this table are not cloned.

```
public String toString( )
```
Return a printable String representation of this hash table.

Accessor Methods
```
public boolean containsKey(Object key)
```
Determine whether key is the key of some object in this hash table. (Hashtable uses key.equals to test for equality of a key, whereas HashMap uses the == operator.)

```
public V get(Object key)
```
Search this hash table for an element that has the specified key. (`Hashtable` uses `key.equals` to test for equality, but `Hashmap` uses the `==` operator.) If such an element is found, then the return value is a reference to that element; otherwise, the return value is null. Note that the key is expected to be of type K, but may actually be any Java `Object`.

```
public boolean isEmpty( )
```
Test whether this hash table is empty.

```
public int size( )
```
Return the number of key/element pairs currently in this hash table.

Modification Methods

```
public V put(K key, V element)
```
Add the specified key/element pair to this hash table. If there was already an element with the specified key, then the return value is a reference to that old element (which is no longer in the table); otherwise, the return value is null. Note: `Hashtable` does not permit the inserted element to be `null`, but `HashMap` does.

```
public V remove(Object key)
```
If the specified key appears in this hash table, then that key and its associated element are removed, and the return value is a reference to the removed element; otherwise, the return value is null. To find the key, `Hashtable` uses the `equals` method, whereas `HashMap` uses the `==` operator.

Appendix E
A Class for Nodes in a Linked List

This appendix gives a generic class for nodes in a linked list, where each node contains data that is from the type of the generic type parameter. The class was originally developed in Chapter 4 using integer data; the modification to contain Java Object data was described in Chapter 5. The source code of this class is available at www.cs.colorado.edu/~main/edu/colorado/nodes/Node.java.

Generic Class Node

❖ **public class Node<E> from the package edu.colorado.nodes**
   A Node<E> provides a node for a linked list. Each node contains a piece of data (which is a reference to an E object) and a link (which is a reference to the next node of the list). The reference stored in a node can be null. Lists can be of any length, limited only by the amount of free memory on the heap. But beyond Integer.MAX_VALUE, the answer from listLength is incorrect because of arithmetic overflow.

Specification

♦ **Constructor for the Node<E>**
   public Node(E initialData, Node initialLink)
   Initialize a node with specified initial data and link to the next node. Note that the initialLink may be the null reference, which indicates that the new node has nothing after it.
   Parameters:
      initialData – the initial data of this new node
      initialLink – a reference to the node after this new node (this reference may be null to indicate that there is no node after this new node)
   Postcondition:
      This new node contains the specified data and link to the next node.

♦ **addNodeAfter**
   public void addNodeAfter(E element)
   Modification method to add a new node after this node.
   Parameter:
      element – the data to be placed in the new node
   Postcondition:
      A new node has been created and placed after this node. The data for the new node is element. Any other nodes that used to be after this node are now after the new node.
   Throws: OutOfMemoryError
      Indicates that there is insufficient memory for a new Node.

♦ **getData**
   public E getData( )
   Accessor method to get the data from this node.

> **Returns:**
> the data from this node

♦ **getLink**

```
public Node<E> getLink( )
```
Accessor method to get a reference to the next node after this node.

> **Returns:**
> a reference to the node after this node (or the null reference if there is nothing after this node)

♦ **listCopy**

```
public static <E> Node<E> listCopy(Node<E> source)
```
Copy a list.

> **Parameter:**
> `source` – the head reference for a linked list that will be copied (which may be an empty list where `source` is null)

> **Returns:**
> The method has made a copy of the linked list starting at `source`. The return value is the head reference for the copy.

> **Throws:** `OutOfMemoryError`
> Indicates that there is insufficient memory for the new list.

♦ **listCopyWithTail**

```
public static <E> Node<E>[ ] listCopyWithTail(Node<E> source)
```
Copy a list, returning both a head and tail reference for the copy.

> **Parameter:**
> `source` – the head reference for a linked list that will be copied (which may be an empty list where `source` is null)

> **Returns:**
> The method has made a copy of the linked list starting at `source`. The return value is an array where the `[0]` element is a head reference for the copy and the `[1]` element is a tail reference for the copy.

> **Throws:** `OutOfMemoryError`
> Indicates that there is insufficient memory for the new list.

♦ **listLength**

```
public static <E> int listLength(Node<E> head)
```
Compute the number of nodes in a linked list.

> **Parameter:**
> `head` – the head reference for a linked list (which may be an empty list with a null head)

> **Returns:**
> the number of nodes in the list with the given head

> **Note:**
> A wrong answer occurs for lists longer than `Int.MAX_VALUE` because of arithmetic overflow.

♦ **listPart**

```
public static <E> Node<E>[ ] listPart(Node<E> start, Node<E> end)
```
Copy part of a list, providing a head and tail reference for the new copy.

Parameters:

start and end – references to two nodes of a linked list

Precondition:

start and end are non-null references to nodes on the same linked list, with the start node at or before the end node.

Returns:

The method has made a copy of part of a linked list, from the specified start node to the specified end node. The return value is an array where the [0] component is a head reference for the copy and the [1] component is a tail reference for the copy.

Throws: IllegalArgumentException

Indicates that start and end do not satisfy the precondition.

Throws: OutOfMemoryError

Indicates that there is insufficient memory for the new list.

♦ **listPosition**

```
public static <E> Node<E> listPosition(Node<E> head, int position)
```
Find a node at a specified position in a linked list.

Parameters:

head – the head reference for a linked list (which may be an empty list with a null head)
position – a node number

Precondition:

position > 0

Returns:

The return value is a reference to the node at the specified position in the list. (The head node is position 1, the next node is position 2, and so on.) If there is no such position (because the list is too short), then the null reference is returned.

Throws: IllegalArgumentException

Indicates that position is zero.

♦ **listSearch**

```
public static <E> Node<E> listSearch(Node<E> head, E target)
```
Search for a particular piece of data in a linked list.

Parameters:

head – the head reference for a linked list (which may be an empty list with a null head)
target – a piece of data to search for

Returns:

The return value is a reference to the first node that contains the specified target. If the target is non-null, then the target.equals method is used to find such a node. The target may also be null, in which case the return value is a reference to the first node that contains a null reference for its data. If there is no node that contains the target, then the null reference is returned.

◆ removeNodeAfter

```
public void removeNodeAfter( )
```
Modification method to remove the new node after this node.

Precondition:
This node must not be the tail node of the list.

Postcondition:
The node after this node has been removed from the linked list. If there were further nodes after that one, they are still present on the list.

Throws: `NullPointerException`
Indicates that this was the tail node of the list, so there is nothing after it to remove.

◆ setData

```
public void setData(E newdata)
```
Modification method to set the data in this node.

Parameter:
`newData` – the new data to place in this node

Postcondition:
The data of this node has been set to `newData`. This data is allowed to be null.

◆ setLink

```
public void setLink(Node<E> newLink)
```
Modification method to set a reference to the next node after this node.

Parameter:
`newLink` – a reference to the node that should appear after this node in the linked list (or the null reference if there should be no node after this node)

Postcondition:
The link to the node after this node has been set to `newLink`. Any other node (that used to be in this link) is no longer connected to this node.

Implementation

```
// File: Node.java from the package edu.colorado.nodes
// Documentation is available from pages 791-794 or from the Node link at
// http://www.cs.colorado.edu/~main/docs/.

package edu.colorado.nodes;

public class Node<E>
{
    // Invariant of the Node<E> class:
    //    1. Each node has one reference to an E Object, stored in the instance variable data.
    //    2. For the final node of a list, the link part is null. Otherwise, the link part is a
    //       reference to the next node of the list.
    private E data;
    private Node<E> link;
```

```java
public Node(E initialData, Node<E> initialLink)
{
   data = initialData;
   link = initialLink;
}


public void addNodeAfter(E element)
{
   link = new Node<E>(element, link);
}


public E getData( )
{
   return data;
}


public Node<E> getLink( )
{
   return link;
}


public static <E> Node<E> listCopy(Node<E> source)
{
   Node<E> copyHead;
   Node<E> copyTail;

   // Handle the special case of the empty list.
   if (source == null)
      return null;

   // Make the first node for the newly created list.
   copyHead = new Node<E>(source.data, null);
   copyTail = copyHead;

   // Make the rest of the nodes for the newly created list.
   while (source.link != null)
   {
      source = source.link;
      copyTail.addNodeAfter(source.data);
      copyTail = copyTail.link;
   }

   // Return the head reference for the new list.
   return copyHead;
}
```

```java
public static <E> Object[ ] listCopyWithTail(Node<E> source)
{
    Node<E> copyHead;
    Node<E> copyTail;
    Object[ ] answer = new Object[2];

    // Handle the special case of the empty list.
    if (source == null)
        return answer; // The answer has two null references.

    // Make the first node for the newly created list.
    copyHead = new Node<E>(source.data, null);
    copyTail = copyHead;

    // Make the rest of the nodes for the newly created list.
    while (source.link != null)
    {
        source = source.link;
        copyTail.addNodeAfter(source.data);
        copyTail = copyTail.link;
    }

    // Return the head and tail references in a small array of two Java objects.
    answer[0] = copyHead;
    answer[1] = copyTail;
    return answer;
}


public static <E> int listLength(Node<E> head)
{
    Node<E> cursor;
    int answer;

    answer = 0;
    for (cursor = head; cursor != null; cursor = cursor.link)
        answer++;

    return answer;
}
```

```java
public static <E> Object[ ] listPart(Node<E> start, Node<E> end)
{
    Node<E> copyHead;
    Node<E> copyTail;
    Node<E> cursor;
    Object[ ] answer = new Object[2];

    // Check for illegal null at start or end.
    if (start == null)
        throw new IllegalArgumentException("start is null");
    if (end == null)
        throw new IllegalArgumentException("end is null");

    // Make the first node for the newly created list.
    copyHead = new Node<E>(start.data, null);
    copyTail = copyHead;
    cursor = start;

    // Make the rest of the nodes for the newly created list.
    while (cursor != end)
    {
        cursor = cursor.link;
        if (cursor == null)
            throw new IllegalArgumentException
            ("end node was not found on the list");
        copyTail.addNodeAfter(cursor.data);
        copyTail = copyTail.link;
    }

    // Return the head and tail references in a small array of two Java objects.
    answer[0] = copyHead;
    answer[1] = copyTail;
    return answer;
}

public static <E> Node<E> listPosition(Node<E> head, int position)
{
    Node<E> cursor;
    int i;

    if (position == 0)
        throw new IllegalArgumentException("position is zero");

    cursor = head;
    for (i = 1; (i < position) && (cursor != null); i++)
        cursor = cursor.link;

    return cursor;
}
```

```java
public static <E> Node<E> listSearch(Node<E> head, E target)
{
   Node<E> cursor;

   if (target == null)
   {  // Search for a node in which the data is the null reference.
      for (cursor = head; cursor != null; cursor = cursor.link)
         if (cursor.data == null)
            return cursor;
   }
   else
   {  // Search for a node that contains the non-null target.
      for (cursor = head; cursor != null; cursor = cursor.link)
         if (target.equals(cursor.data))
            return cursor;
   }

   return null;
}

public void removeNodeAfter( )
{
   link = link.link;
}

public void setData(E newData)
{
   data = newData;
}

public void setLink(Node<E> newLink)
{
   link = newLink;
}
}   // END OF Node CLASS
```

Note: See Section 5.5 on page 286 for the Lister class, which can provide an iterator for any linked list of nodes.

Appendix F
A Class for a Bag of Objects

This appendix gives a class for nodes in a linked list, where each node contains data that is a Java Object. The class was originally developed in Chapter 4 using integer data; the modification to contain Java Object data was described in Chapter 5. The implementation of this class is available at http://www.cs.colorado.edu/~main/edu/colorado/collections/LinkedBag.java.

This implementation makes use of the Node class (from Appendix E) and the Lister class (from Section 5.5).

Generic Class LinkedBag

❖ **public class LinkedBag<E> from the package edu.colorado.collections**
A LinkedBag<E> is a collection of references to E objects. The objects in the bag are allowed to be null.

Limitations:
(1) Beyond Int.MAX_VALUE elements, the methods countOccurrences, size, and grab are wrong.

(2) Because of the slow linear algorithms of this class, large bags will have poor performance.

Specification

◆ **Constructor for the LinkedBag<E>**
```
public LinkedBag( )
```
Initialize an empty bag.
Postcondition:
This bag is empty.

◆ **add**
```
public void add(E element)
```
Put a reference to an object into this bag. The new element may be the null reference.
Parameter:
element – the element to be added to this bag
Postcondition:
A reference to the specified object has been added to this bag.
Throws: OutOfMemoryError
Indicates insufficient memory for a new node.

♦ **addAll**
```
public void addAll(LinkedBag<E> addend)
```
Add the contents of another bag to this bag.

Parameter:
addend – a bag whose contents will be added to this bag

Precondition:
The parameter, addend, is not null.

Postcondition:
The elements from addend have been added to this bag.

Throws: `NullPointerException`
Indicates that addend is null.

Throws: `OutOfMemoryError`
Indicates insufficient memory to increase the size of this bag.

♦ **clone**
```
public LinkedBag<E> clone( )
```
Generate a copy of this bag.

Returns:
The return value is a copy of this bag. Subsequent changes to the copy will not affect the
original, nor vice versa. The return value must be typecast to a `LinkedBag` before it is used.

Throws: `OutOfMemoryError`
Indicates insufficient memory for creating the clone.

♦ **countOccurrences**
```
public int countOccurrences(E target)
```
Accessor method to count the number of occurrences of a particular element in this bag.

Parameter:
target – the reference to an `Object` to be counted

Returns:
The return value is the number of times that `target` occurs in this bag. If `target` is non-null,
then the occurrences are found using the `target.equals` method.

♦ **grab**
```
public E grab( )
```
Accessor method to retrieve a random element from this bag.

Precondition:
This bag is not empty.

Returns:
a randomly selected element from this bag

Throws: `IllegalStateException`
Indicates that the bag is empty.

♦ **iterator**

```
public Lister<E> iterator( )
```

Accessor method to generate and return a `Lister` that contains all the elements currently in this bag.

Returns:
a `Lister` containing the elements of this bag

Throws: `OutOfMemoryError`
Indicates insufficient memory for a new `Lister`.

Notes:
A `Lister` is a simple kind of `Iterator` implemented in `edu.colorado.nodes.Lister` (see Figure 5.4 on page 289). If changes are made to this bag before the `Lister` returns all of its elements, then the subsequent behavior of the `Lister` is unspecified.

♦ **remove**

```
public boolean remove(E target)
```

Remove one copy of a specified element from this bag.

Parameter:
`target` – an element to remove from this bag

Postcondition:
If `target` was found in the bag, then one copy of `target` has been removed and the method returns `true`. Otherwise, the bag remains unchanged and the method returns `false`. Note that if `target` is non-null, then `target.equals` is used to find `target` in the bag.

♦ **size**

```
public int size( )
```

Accessor method to determine the number of elements in this bag.

Returns:
the number of elements in this bag

♦ **union**

```
public static <E> LinkedBag<E> union(LinkedBag<E> b1, LinkedBag<E> b2)
```

Create a new bag that contains all the elements from two other bags.

Parameters:
`b1` – the first of two bags
`b2` – the second of two bags

Precondition:
Neither `b1` nor `b2` is null.

Returns:
a new bag that is the union of `b1` and `b2`

Throws: `NullPointerException`
Indicates that one of the arguments is null.

Throws: `OutOfMemoryError`
Indicates insufficient memory for the new bag.

Implementation

```
// File: LinkedBag.java from the package edu.colorado.collections
// Complete documentation is on pages 799-801 or from the LinkedBag link at
// http://www.cs.colorado.edu/~main/docs/.

package edu.colorado.collections;
import edu.colorado.nodes.Node;
import edu.colorado.nodes.Lister;

public class LinkedBag<E> implements Cloneable
{
    // Invariant of the LinkedBag<E> class:
    //    1. The elements in the bag are stored in a linked list.
    //    2. The head reference of the list is in the instance variable head.
    //    3. The total number of elements in the list is in the instance variable manyNodes.
    private Node<E> head;
    private int manyNodes;

    public Linkedbag( )
    {
        head = null;
        manyNodes = 0;
    }

    public void add(E element)
    {
        head = new Node<E>(element, head);
        manyNodes++;
    }

    @SuppressWarnings("unchecked")     // See the warnings discussion on page 265
    public void addAll(LinkedBag<E> addend)
    {
        Object[ ] copyInfo;

        // The precondition indicates that addend is not null. If it is null,
        // then a NullPointerException is thrown here.
        if (addend.manyNodes > 0)
        {
            copyInfo = Node.listCopyWithTail(addend.head);
            ((Node<E>)copyInfo[1]).setLink(head); // Link the tail of copy to my own head...
            head = (Node<E>)copyInfo[0]; // and set my own head to the head of the copy.
            manyNodes += addend.manyNodes;
        }
    }
```

```java
@SuppressWarnings("unchecked")    // See the warnings discussion on page 265.
public LinkedBag<E> clone( )
{  // Clone a LinkedBag object.
   LinkedBag<E> answer;

   try
   {
      answer = (LinkedBag<E>) super.clone( );
   }
   catch (CloneNotSupportedException e)
   {  // This exception should not occur. But if it does, it would probably indicate a
      // programming error that made super.clone unavailable. The most common error
      // would be forgetting the "implements Cloneable" clause at the start of this class.
      throw new RuntimeException
         ("This class does not implement Cloneable");
   }

   answer.head = Node.listCopy(head);
   return answer;
}

public int countOccurrences(E target)
{
   int answer;
   Node<E> cursor;

   // Implementation note: listSearch will use == when target is null.
   // listSearch will use target.equals(...) when target is not null.
   answer = 0;
   cursor = Node.listSearch(head, target);
   while (cursor != null)
   {  // Each time that cursor is not null, we have another occurrence of target, so we
      // add 1 to answer and then move cursor to the next occurrence of the target.
      answer++;
      cursor = cursor.getLink( );
      cursor = Node.listSearch(cursor, target);
   }
   return answer;
}

public E grab( )
{
   int i;
   Node<E> cursor;
```

```
      if (manyNodes == 0)
         throw new IllegalStateException("Bag size is zero");

      i =  (int)(Math.random( ) * manyNodes) + 1;
      cursor = Node.listPosition(head, i);
      return cursor.getData( );
   }

   public Lister<E> iterator( )
   {
      return new Lister<E>(head);
   }

   public boolean remove(E target)
   {
      Node<E> targetNode; // The node that contains the target

      // Implementation note: listSearch will use == when target is null.
      // listSearch will use target.equals(...) when target is not null.
      targetNode = Node.listSearch(head, target);
      if (targetNode == null)
         // The target was not found, so nothing is removed.
         return false;
      else
      {  // The target was found at targetNode. So copy the head data to targetNode
         // and then remove the extra copy of the head data.
         targetNode.setData(head.getData( ));
         head = head.getLink( );
         manyNodes--;
         return true;
      }
   }

   public int size( )
   {
      return manyNodes;
   }

   public static <E> LinkedBag<E> union(LinkedBag<E> b1, LinkedBag<E> b2)
   {
      // The precondition requires that neither b1 nor b2 is null.
      // If one of them is null, then addAll will throw a NullPointerException.
      LinkedBag<E> answer = new LinkedBag<E>( );

      answer.addAll(b1);
      answer.addAll(b2);
      return answer;
   }

}   // END OF LinkedBag CLASS
```

Appendix G
Further Big-*O* Notation

Formal Definition of Big-*O*

Throughout the text, we analyze the running times of algorithms in terms of the size of an algorithm's input. For example, in Section 11.1, we developed a binary search algorithm to search an array of n elements, looking for a specified target. On page 578, we saw that the maximum number of operations for the binary search is given by the following formula:

$T(n)$ = the maximum number of operations to search an n-element array
   = $18(\lfloor \log_2 n \rfloor + 1) + 2$

Big-*O* notation is a way of analyzing a function such as $T(n)$. The analysis throws away some information about the function but keeps other information that is most relevant to determining algorithm performance. In an informal way, you know enough to examine the function $T(n)$ for the binary search; you can "throw out the constants" and conclude that $T(n)$ is an $O(\log n)$ function.

In general, when we examine a function such as $T(n)$, the big-*O* analysis results in some simpler expression, such as $\log n$. The simpler expression is also a function of n. If we call this $F(n)$, then a typical big-*O* analysis provides a result of the form "$T(n)$ is an $O(F(n))$ function." In mathematical terms, this kind of result has a precise definition, as follows:

Formal Definition of Big-*O*

When we say that "$T(n)$ is an $O(F(n))$ function," we mean that there is some fixed number that we call the *threshold* and some constant multiplier that we call *c*, such that:

Whenever $n \geq threshold$, then $T(n) \geq F(n)$.

For example, consider the function $T(n) = 3n^2 + 9n$. Some arithmetic shows that whenever $n \geq 5$, then $3n^2 + 9n \geq 4n^2$. Therefore, using a threshold of 5 and a constant multiplier of 4, we can see that:

$3n^2 + 9n$ is an $O(n^2)$ function.

The graph at the top of the next page illustrates the meaning of a big-*O* expression. Notice that before the *threshold*, either of the two functions can be larger; anything can happen before this threshold value. But once n exceeds the threshold, the function $cF(n)$ is always greater than $T(n)$. Also notice that it is *c* multiplied by $F(n)$, and not simply $F(n)$, that we are comparing to $T(n)$.

So the graph illustrates the fact that "$T(n)$ is an $O(F(n))$ function."

If not used with some care, big-*O* expressions can grossly misrepresent the true running time of an algorithm. For example, if an algorithm runs in $O(n)$ time, then we could also say that it runs in $O(n^2)$ time (since any function that is below a constant times *n* will also be below the same constant times n^2). But, of course, it would be silly to say that an algorithm runs in $O(n^2)$ time when we know that it runs in $O(n)$ time. When a programmer gives a big-*O* time, he or she usually means that it is a "good" big-*O* expression.

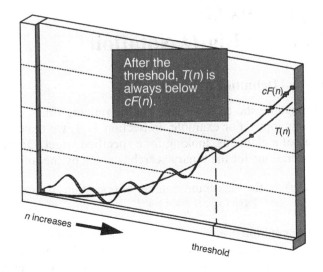

What Big-*O* Expressions Indicate

Big-*O* expressions are admittedly crude, but they do contain some information. A big-*O* analysis will not distinguish between a running time of $4n + 3$ and a running time of $100n + 50$, but it will let us distinguish between some running times and determine that some algorithms are faster than others. Look at the graphs of the four functions to the right. Notice that all three $O(n)$ functions eventually fall below the $O(n^2)$ function. This leads us to the following important big-*O* principle:

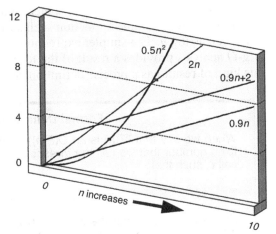

Big-*O* Comparison of Algorithms

Suppose two different algorithms perform the same task with different big-*O* times. With a sufficiently large input, the algorithm with the better big-*O* analysis will perform faster.

What exactly does it mean when we say "with a sufficiently large input"? Does this mean that an input size of $n = 100$ will result in a faster time from the algorithm with the better big-*O*? Or does it require $n = 1000$, or maybe even $n = 1,000,000$? Unfortunately, a big-*O* analysis does not tell us *how big* the input needs to be for the better big-*O* time to result in a faster algorithm. All that's known is that larger and larger inputs will *eventually* result in a faster time for the algorithm with the better big-*O* time.

Appendix H
Javadoc

Throughout the book, we have used nicely formatted comments to provide the specifications for Java classes. For example, the following specification for `celsiusToFahrenheit` appears just before its implementation in Figure 1.1 on page 11:

♦ **celsiusToFahrenheit**

    `public static double celsiusToFahrenheit(double c)`
    Convert a temperature from Celsius degrees to Fahrenheit degrees.
    Parameter:
    c – a temperature in Celsius degrees
    Precondition:
    `c >= -273.15.`
    Returns:
    the temperature c converted to Fahrenheit degrees
    Throws: `IllegalArgumentException`
    Indicates that c is less than the smallest Celsius temperature (–273.15).

How are pretty comments such as this generated? The answer is a special documentation comment that appears in a `.java` file, such as this:

```
/**
 * Convert a temperature from Celsius degrees to Fahrenheit.
 * @param c
 *   a temperature in Celsius degrees
 * @precondition
 *   c >= -273.15.
 * @return
 *   the temperature c converted to Fahrenheit
 * @throws IllegalArgumentException
 *   Indicates that c is less than the smallest Celsius temperature (-273.15).
 **/
```

This **documentation comment** is arranged to interact with a documentation tool called **Javadoc**, which is freely distributed with Sun Microsystems' Java Development Kit. Javadoc reads the documentation comments from a `.java` file and produces a collection of documentation pages in a format called **html** (hypertext markup language). As you may know, html pages are read and displayed by web browsers such as Mozilla Firefox, Microsoft Internet Explorer, or Google's Chrome Browser. For example, Javadoc can be applied to the preceding `celsiusToFahrenheit` documentation comment, and the resulting html page will contain the nicely formatted comment shown at the top of the page. The exact format may look different in your web browser, but the result will be roughly as shown. The html page created by Javadoc contains only documentation and no actual Java code. As you might guess, the motivation for this kind of documentation is *information hiding*.

The documentation allows other programmers to use the items you implement without knowing how you implemented those items. Let's look at the precise steps you carry out when you want to make your programming available to other programmers but still retain information hiding.

How to Use Javadoc to Provide Your Work to Other Programmers

1. **Documentation comments appear in your `.java` files.** Write your `.java` files in the usual way, but include documentation comments such as the one shown earlier. We'll discuss the general format for these documentation comments in a moment.

2. **Other programmers need access to your `.class` files.** Compile each `.java` file in the usual way. Each `.java` file that you compile creates a corresponding `.class` file. For example, when you compile `TemperatureConversion.java`, you get `Temperature-Conversion.class`. You can move your `.class` files to a location where other programmers can access them.

3. **Run the Javadoc tool on each of your `.java` files.** From the command line, Javadoc is executed by typing the command `javadoc` and the name of the `.java` file. For example:

   ```
   javadoc TemperatureConversion.java
   ```

   Javadoc creates an html file. In this example, it is a file called `TemperatureConver-sion.html`. Later, we'll look at some additional options that can be put on the command line.

4. **Move all your Javadoc `html` files to a public place where a web browser can read them.** For example, I have moved all my Javadoc `html` files to the directory:

   ```
   http://www.cs.colorado.edu/~main/docs/
   ```

   If you point your web browser to this directory, you will see all of my public documentation. You may need to talk with your computer system administrator to find out how to create a public place for your own documentation to reside.

5. **Put the JDK graphics files in an `images` subdirectory.** Below your `javadocs` directory, you should create a subdirectory called `images`. The Java Development Kit provides a collection of graphics images, and you can copy these to your own `images` subdirectory. Javadoc will use the graphics in the html pages that it creates. (The latest JDK release places these images in a subdirectory `java\docs\api\images` for Windows or `java/docs/api/images` for Unix.)

Now you need to know how to write those Javadoc documentation comments. (They're not as cryptic as they look.)

How to Write Javadoc Documentation Comments

We will put Javadoc comments in two places: before each class definition (such as `public class TemperatureConversion`) and before most public methods (such as `public static void print-Number`).

Documentation comments begin with /** (two stars rather than just one). A documentation comment ends with */, but for consistency, you can use **/ instead. Many programmers place a single asterisk (*) at the start of each line in the comment. The single asterisk is not required, but it does make it easy to see the entire extent of the documentation (and Javadoc ignores the asterisks).

Javadoc Documentation for a Description of the Whole Class

The top of each documentation comment contains a description of the class or method. Javadoc uses the first sentence of the description as part of an index, so aim for a concise account of the most important behavior in the first sentence. If needed, subsequent sentences can provide details.

After the description, the rest of the documentation consists of a series of **Javadoc tags**. Each tag alerts the Javadoc tool about certain information. For example, one of my classes, called TemperatureConversion, has the Javadoc comment shown here, just before the class declaration:

```
/**
* The TemperatureConversion Java application prints a table
* converting Celsius to Fahrenheit degrees.
* @author
*    Michael Main (main@colorado.edu)
**/
public class TemperatureConversion...
```

The Javadoc tag @author indicates that the name of the class's author will appear next (perhaps with extra information, such as an e-mail address). In the html page produced by Javadoc, a large heading is provided for the whole class, and each individual tag is made into a boldface heading, so within a web browser, the html page contains a section similar to this:

❖ **public class TemperatureConversion**
  The TemperatureConversion Java application prints a table converting Celsius to Fahrenheit degrees.
  Author:
  Michael Main (main@colorado.edu)

The documentation for a class will usually contain a description and an author tag.

Javadoc Documentation for Individual Public Methods

Each public method of a class may also have a Javadoc comment preceding its implementation. My documentation for a method generally includes these items:

1. **A description of the method.** For example, celsiusToFahrenheit has this description at the top of the documentation comment:

   ```
   /**
   * Convert a temperature from Celsius degrees to Fahrenheit.
   ```

2. **Parameters.** Each parameter of the method is documented by using the tag @param, followed by the parameter name and a description of the parameter. For example, part of our first Javadoc comment is:

   ```
   * @param c
   *    a temperature in Celsius degrees
   ```

Warning: Some of the other tags shown below won't work unless you put at least one @param tag first. If there are no parameters, I suggest an @param tag that looks like this:

```
* @param - none
```

3. **Precondition.** The most recent Javadoc tool does not have a tag for preconditions. However, you can create and use new tags of your own. So our Javadoc comment lists the precondition as shown here:

```
* @precondition
*   c >= -273.15.
```

For this new tag to work correctly, we will need to include an option on the Javadoc command line. In particular, to use the precondition tag on Node.java, we will run Javadoc like this:

```
javadoc -tag precondition:a:"Precondition:" Node.java
```

This option tells Javadoc that we are going to use a new tag that will be indicated by @precondition in our Javadoc comments. The :a: stands for "all" and means that all occurrences of the @precondition tag should be put in the documentation along with a heading, which in this case is "Precondition:". The heading will always appear in boldface in the documentation that Javadoc creates.

4. **The returns condition or postcondition.** You can list a returns condition after the Javadoc tag @return. For example, we wrote:

```
* @return
*   the temperature c converted to Fahrenheit
```

A returns condition is appropriate when the method's behavior is entirely described by its return value. More complex methods need a complete postcondition instead of a returns condition. A complete postcondition describes other effects of the method, such as printing output. There is no Javadoc postcondition tag, but you can use @postcondition as a new tag so long as you put the -tag postcondition:a:"Postcondition:" option on the command line when you run Javadoc. For example, suppose our method converted the parameter c to Fahrenheit degrees and printed the result instead of returning the value. Then the documentation could look like this:

```
* @postcondition
*   The Fahrenheit temperature equivalent to c has been
*   printed to System.out.
```

5. **Exceptions.** Each exception that a method can throw should be listed in the documentation comment. Start with the tag @throws and then write the name of the exception type (such as IllegalArgumentException) followed by a description of what the exception indicates. For example, our exception was documented like this:

```
* @throws IllegalArgumentException
*   Indicates that c is less than the smallest Celsius
*   temperature (-273.15).
```

Controlling html Links and Fonts

The Javadoc tags that have been described are sufficient to clearly document the code you'll write throughout this text. There are two other features you might want to add. Under the @author tag, you list your name and e-mail address. It would be nice if a reader could simply click on that address in a web browser to send e-mail to you. This is possible by using some simple html to revise the author section as shown in the shaded portion here:

```
/**
 * The <CODE>TemperatureConversion</CODE> Java application prints a table
 * converting Celsius to Fahrenheit degrees.
 * @author
 *   Michael Main
 *   <A HREF="mailto:main@colorado.edu"> (main@colorado.edu) </A>
 **/
```

The first part of the shaded line, `<A HREF="mailto:main@colorado.edu">`, is an html command that will put a **mailto link** on the documentation page. Within a web browser, the link appears as the text (`main@colorado.edu`). To send e-mail to the address, a user clicks on the link. The characters `</A>` at the end of the line are an html command to indicate the end of the link. Within a browser, the new documenation appears like this:

❖ **public class TemperatureConversion**

  The `TemperatureConversion` Java application prints a table converting Celsius to Fahrenheit degrees.

  Author:
  Michael Main (main@colorado.edu)

The difference between this and the original version is that the link (main@colorado.edu) is underlined and probably in a bright color to indicate that it is a link.

You may have noticed a second difference: In this version, the name `TemperatureConversion` appears in a special "code" font that looks like code from a program. This font was controlled by putting the html tag `<CODE>` to turn on the special font and the tag `</CODE>` to turn off the special font.

Running Javadoc

Once you have Javadoc comments in your code, you can run the Javadoc program to produce the html files. For example:

```
javadoc  Names of one or more .java files to process
```

These are the complete options that I usually use:

```
javadoc -author -source 1.4 -public -tag param -tag
  -tag precondition:a:"Precondition:"
  -tag postcondition:a:"Postcondition:"
  -tag return
  -tag throws
  -tag example:a:"Example:"
  Names of one or more .java files to process
```

The -author option allows us to put @author in the Javadoc comments, followed by the author's name. The -source 1.4 allows us to use certain features of Java Version 1.4. The -public option indicates that we want to generate documentation for only the public members of a class. The other options (all starting with -tag) indicate the order in which we want the documentation to appear: precondition first, then postcondition, then the return specification, then the throws specification, and finally an example tag (to let me give an example of how the method is used). Two of these options (return and throws) are built into the Javadoc system, so for these we need to write only -tag return and -tag throws. The precondition, postcondition, and example tags are not built into Javadoc, so the extra information at the end (such as :a:"Precondition:") tells Javadoc how we want these tags to appear in the documentation.

The rest of this appendix lists the complete TemperatureConversion implementation, including all Javadoc comments, which are printed in bold.

Java Application Program

```
// File: TemperatureConversion.java
// A Java application to print a temperature conversion table.
// Additional Javadoc information is available in Figure 1.1 on page 11 or at
// http://www.cs.colorado.edu/~main/docs/TemperatureConversion.html.

/*******************************************************************************
 * The <CODE>TemperatureConversion</CODE> Java application prints a table
 * converting Celsius to Fahrenheit degrees.
 *
 * @author Michael Main
 *    <A HREF="mailto:main@colorado.edu"> (main@colorado.edu) </A>
 ******************************************************************************/
public class TemperatureConversion
{
    /**
     * The main method prints a Celsius to Fahrenheit conversion table.
     * The String arguments (args) are not used in this implementation.
     * The bounds of the table range from -50C to +50C in 10 degree increments.
     **/
    public static void main(String[ ] args)
    {
        final double TABLE_BEGIN = -50.0; // The table's first Celsius temperature
        final double TABLE_END   =  50.0; // The table's final Celsius temperature
```

```
        final double TABLE_STEP  =  10.0; // Increment between temperatures in table

        double celsius;                    // A Celsius temperature
        double fahrenheit;                 // The equivalent Fahrenheit temperature

        System.out.println("TEMPERATURE CONVERSION");
        System.out.println("----------------------");
        System.out.println("Celsius      Fahrenheit");

        for (celsius = TABLE_BEGIN; celsius <= TABLE_END; celsius += TABLE_STEP)
        { // Each iteration prints one line of the conversion table.
            fahrenheit = celsiusToFahrenheit(celsius);
            System.out.printf("%6.2fC", celsius);
            System.out.printf("%14.2fF\n", fahrenheit);
        }
        System.out.println("----------------------");
    }


    /**
    * Convert a temperature from Celsius degrees to Fahrenheit degrees.
    * @param c
    *   a temperature in Celsius degrees
    * @precondition:
    *   c >= -273.15.
    * @return
    *   the temperature c converted to Fahrenheit
    * @throws IllegalArgumentException
    *   Indicates that c is less than the smallest Celsius temperature (-273.15).
    **/
    public static double celsiusToFahrenheit(double c)
    {
        final double MINIMUM_CELSIUS = -273.15;
        if (c < MINIMUM_CELSIUS)
            throw new IllegalArgumentException("Argument " + c + " is too small.");
        return (9.0/5.0) * c + 32;
    }

}
```

Appendix I
Applets for Interactive Testing

It's useful to have a small interactive test program to help you test class methods. Such a program can be written as a Java **applet**, which is a Java program written in a special format to have a graphical user interface. The graphical user interface is also called a GUI (pronounced "gooey"), and it allows a user to interact with a program by clicking the mouse, typing information into boxes, and performing other familiar actions. With a Java applet, GUIs are easy to create, even if you've never run into such goo before.

This appendix, which shows one simple pattern for developing such applets, is online at: `http://www.cs.colorado.edu/~main/javasupp/applets.pdf`.